STRATHCLYDE UNIVERSITY LIBRARY
30125 0036
D0421430

ANDERSONIAN LIBRARY
WITHDRAWN
FROM
LIBRARY
STOCK
STRATHCLYDE

Cases and Readings for Marketing for Nonprofit Organizations

PHILIP KOTLER
Northwestern University

O. C. FERRELL
Texas A&M University

CHARLES LAMB
Texas Christian University

Prentice-Hall, Inc., Englewood Cliffs, New Jersey 07632

Library of Congress Cataloging in Publication Data

Main entry under title:

Cases and readings for marketing for nonprofit
organizations.

Includes bibliographical references.

1. Marketing. 2. Corporations, Nonprofit.
3. Marketing—Case studies. I. Kotler, Philip.
II. Ferrell, O. C. III. Lamb, Charles W.

HF5415.C2854 658.8 82-7616

ISBN 0-13-119081-4 AACR2

Printed in the United States of America

10 9 8 7 6 5 4 3 2 1

ISBN 0-13-119081-4

Prentice-Hall International, Inc., *London*
Prentice-Hall of Australia Pty. Limited, *Sydney*
Prentice-Hall Canada Inc., *Toronto*
Prentice-Hall of India Private Limited, *New Delhi*
Prentice-Hall of Japan, Inc., *Tokyo*
Prentice-Hall of Southeast Asia Pte. Ltd., *Singapore*
Whitehall Books Limited, *Wellington, New Zealand*

To

Nancy (Kotler)
Mary (Ferrell)
Sharon (Lamb)

Contents

Preface

Marketing is relevant not only to businesses but to every organization that provides "something of value" to clients or the public. Colleges, hospitals, museums, charities, politicians, and just about any organization attempts to provide "something of value" to individuals or groups that represent a broadly defined market. Today, many private and public nonprofit organizations recognize that the use of marketing offers a new way to serve the public or client and that marketing can help the organization to achieve its own goals too.

Many nonprofit organizations are creating marketing positions, and nonprofit organization managers desire college courses, professional development programs, and other educational materials on the topic. Managers in nonprofit organizations are interested in the feasibility and desirability of using marketing concepts in dealing with their publics. Therefore, this book focuses on the topics and issues in marketing of use to the nonprofit organization manager. Those individuals who make decisions in governmental agencies, social cause organizations, and similar organizations can use this book to help them improve the efficiency and effectiveness of their exchanges with clients. Also, students of marketing with limited or no experience in nonprofit organizations can utilize this book to learn more about marketing and the application of marketing in nonprofit organizations.

Cases and Readings for Marketing for Nonprofit Organizations represents a joint effort by the editors to provide articles and cases to broaden and apply the concepts of marketing to nonprofit organizations. The selected articles describe specific applications of marketing for nonprofit organizations as well as discuss the adaptation of marketing concepts and theory to nonprofit organizations. The cases illustrate specific real-world applications of marketing in nonprofit organizations. All the cases are based on real situations, and most of the cases identify the actual organization.

The articles and cases selected for this book utilize the same organization as *Marketing for Nonprofit Organizations*, second edition, by Philip Kotler. Both books are divided into six parts. Part I (Understanding Marketing) explains the nature, role, and relevance of marketing to nonprofit organizations. Part II (Organizing Marketing) shows how marketing can be organized in nonprofit organizations to carry out marketing analysis, planning, and control. Part III (Analyzing Marketing Opportunities) describes the major concepts and tools available to the organization to help it understand its markets and potential strategies. Part IV (Planning the Marketing Mix) discusses the four major instruments—product, price, place, and promotion—that constitute the organization's strategic and tactical means for relating to its markets. Part V (Attracting Resources) deals with attracting three major marketing resources—people, funds, and votes. Finally, Part VI (Adopting Marketing) examines how marketing principles and techniques can be adapted to the marketing of anything—services, persons, places, and ideas.

Since the learning should be an active process, the cases provide an opportunity for students to make decisions or evaluate the marketing activities of nonprofit organizations. Each case should illustrate marketing decisions or problems and encourage discussion about the salient issues. These cases provide an integrative focus for conceptual marketing material found in the readings and in *Marketing for Nonprofit Organizations*, second edition by Philip Kotler. Variety in case length and complexity allows instructors to match cases to the course and level of students.

The articles were selected to be practical and useful in making marketing decisions for nonprofit organizations. Marketing's evolving role in nonprofit marketing is traced over the last 15 years, but most of the articles focus on how marketing concepts can be applied to specific nonprofit marketing problems. Most marketing texts and articles deal with institutions and practices found in the private-for-profit sector. This makes it difficult for nonprofit organization managers—public administrators, educators, museum directors, hospital administrators, family planners, religious leaders, foundation directors, social activists, urban planners, and others—to gain a direct and comprehensive idea of marketing that is relevant to their types of organizations. The articles selected provide an introduction to marketing for these administrators.

The editors would like to express their sincere appreciation to all participants in the development of this book. First, we would like to thank the authors and the case writers who were willing to share their ideas and experiences with us. Their contribution made this project possible and their cooperation in allowing us to publish or reprint their work is appreciated. All contributors' authorship is indicated on each case and article. We would also like to acknowledge the technical assistance of Linda Nafziger, Sandy Henderson, and Paula Talbot at Illinois State University.

Finally, we want to thank our students for their comments and insight on the cases and readings included in this book.

P. KOTLER
O.C. FERRELL
CHARLES LAMB

Cases and Readings for Marketing for Nonprofit Organizations

I: UNDERSTANDING MARKETING

Most people associate marketing with the business sector of the economy. Marketing theory and practice began and has attained its highest level of development in this sector. Today, many public and private nonprofit organizations recognize that they have publics or clients to work with from a marketing point of view. The private nonprofit sector accounts for more than one-fourth of the American economy. Although there are unique characteristics of the nonprofit sector, application of marketing principles used in the business sector provides the opportunity for improved management of public and private nonprofit organizations.

In Part I we examine how managers in the nonprofit sector can apply marketing to problems of their organizations. Marketing's evolving role in the nonprofit organization is traced over the last 15 years and factors influencing marketing's ability to assist nonprofit organizations are covered in detail. Examples of applying marketing principles to the profit service sector (the Disney philosophy) and the nonprofit sector (higher education) provide an opportunity for the reader to view marketing theory and practice in operation.

The first article is "Broadening the Concept of Marketing" by Philip Kotler and Sidney J. Levy. They view marketing as a pervasive societal activity that goes beyond the selling of toothpaste, soap, and steel. The authors interpret the meaning of marketing for nonbusiness organizations and the nature of marketing functions such as product improvement, pricing, distribution, and communication in such organizations. Kotler and Levy consider whether traditional marketing principles are transferable to the marketing of organizations, persons, and ideas.

The second article is "Factors Influencing Marketing's Ability to Assist Non-profit Organizations" by Philip D. Cooper and George E. McIlvain. Increased demand for marketing in the nonprofit sector has fostered a need for better methods of assessing the environment for marketing in specific nonprofit settings. This article presents a method for assessing the current environment for marketing in specific nonprofit "industries" which calls for an analysis of three influencing factors. These factors are: (1) the social, legal, and political forces regulating the industry; (2) the level of sophistication of data available from the industry; and (3) the level of potential application for the tools of marketing in the industry.

The third and fourth articles, "Mickey Mouse Marketing" and "More Mickey Mouse Marketing" by N. W. (Red) Pope, contend that the financial industry would do well to emulate the marketing effectiveness of Mickey Mouse. Although this article was written for financial managers, we believe that the ingredients of success used by Disney and useful considerations for nonprofit organizations. One of the world's most famous characters has become a respected and envied symbol of the very best there is in target marketing, sales techniques, and customer relations. The leader which sets the standards that others in the theme park industry seek to match is the Disney organization. Many nonprofit organizations could utilize some aspects of the Disney consumer-oriented philosophy.

The final article is "Product Portfolio Diagnosis for U.S. Universities" by Gerald D. Newbould. Product portfolio diagnosis is a classification system for the products, either goods or services, of a corporation. As early as 1972, it was being employed by more than 100 U.S. corporations to assist in top-management decisions. Its now widespread use among a variety of corporations suggests that it could be a valid generalization of organizational effectiveness, and hence may be applicable to nonprofit organization such as higher education. This article develops a variant of product portfolio diagnosis for U.S. universities and colleges and, by way of example, it is illustrated empirically for the midwestern university market.

Finally, an introductory case entitled "SIOP—A Poison Prevention Program" is provided as an example of a successful nonprofit organization utilization of marketing principles. This case serves as a warm-up case before handling the longer and more detailed cases that follow.

Broadening the Concept of Marketing

PHILIP KOTLER

SIDNEY J. LEVY

The term "marketing" connotes to most people a function peculiar to business firms. Marketing is seen as the task of finding and stimulating buyers for the firm's output. It involves product development, pricing, distribution, and communications; and in the more progressive firms, continuous attention to the changing needs of customers and the development of new products, with product modifications and services to meet these needs. But whether marketing is viewed in the old sense of "pushing" products or in the new sense of "customer satisfaction engineering," it is almost always viewed and discussed as a business activity.

It is the authors' contention that marketing is a pervasive societal activity that goes considerably beyond the selling of toothpaste, soap, and steel. Political contests remind us that candidates are marketed as well as soap; student recruitment by colleges reminds us that higher education is marketed; and fund raising reminds us that "causes" are marketed. Yet these areas of marketing are typically ignored by the student of marketing. Or they are treated cursorily as public relations or publicity activities. No attempt is made to incorporate these phenomena in the body proper of marketing thought and theory. No attempt is made to redefine the meaning of product development, pricing, distribution, and communication in these newer contexts to see if they have a useful meaning. No attempt is made to examine whether the principles of "good" marketing in traditional product areas are transferable to the marketing of services, persons, and ideas.

The authors see a great opportunity for marketing people to expand their thinking and to apply their skills to an increasingly interesting range of social activity. The challenge depends on the attention given to its marketing will either take on a broader social meaning or remain a narrowly defined business activity.

THE RISE OF ORGANIZATIONAL MARKETING

One of the most striking trends in the United States is the increasing amount of society's work being performed by organizations other than business firms. As a society moves beyond the stage where shortages of food, clothing, and shelter are the major problems, it begins to organize to meet other social needs that formerly had been put aside. Business enterprises remain a dominant type of organization, but other types of organizations gain in conspicuousness and in influence. Many of these organizations become enormous and require the same rarefied management skills as traditional business organizations. Managing the United Auto Workers, Defense Department, Ford Foundation, World Bank, Catholic Church, University of California has become every bit as challenging as managing Procter and Gamble, General Motors, General Electric. These nonbusiness organizations have an increasing range of influence, affects as many livelihoods, and occupy as much media prominence as major business firms.

All of these organizations perform the classic

Reprinted with permission from *Journal of Marketing*, January 1969, pp. 10–15; published by the American Marketing Association.

business functions. Every organization must perform a financial function insofar as money must be raised, managed and budgeted according to sound business principles. Every organization must perform a production function in that it must conceive of the best way of arranging inputs to produce the outputs of the organization. Every organization must perform a personnel function in that people must be hired, trained, assigned, and promoted in the course of the organization's work. Every organization must perform a purchasing function in that it must acquire materials in an efficient way through comparing and selecting sources of supply.

When we come to the marketing function, it is also clear that every organization performs marketing-like activities whether or not they are recognized as such. Several examples can be given.

The police department of a major U.S. city, concerned with the poor image it has among an important segment of its population, developed a campaign to "win friends and influence people." One highlight of this campaign is a "visit your police station" day in which tours are conducted to show citizens the daily operations of the police department, including the crime laboratories, police lineups, and cells. The police department also sends officers to speak at public schools and carries out a number of other activities to improve its community relations.

Most museum directors interpret their primary responsibility as "the proper preservation of an artistic heritage for posterity."[1] As a result, for many people museums are cold marble mausoleums that house miles of relics that soon give way to yawns and tired feet. Although museum attendance in the United States advances each year, a large number of citizens are uninterested in museums. Is this indifference due to failure in the manner of presenting what museums have to offer? This nagging question led the new director of the Metropolitan Museum of Art to broaden the museum's appeal through sponsoring contemporary art shows and "happenings." His marketing philosophy of museum management led to substantial increases in the Met's attendance.

The public school system in Oklahoma City sorely needed more public support and funds to prevent a deterioration of facilities and exodus of teachers. It recently resorted to television programming to dramatize the work the public schools were doing to fight the high school dropout problem, to develop new teaching techniques, and to enrich the children. Although an expensive medium, television quickly reached large numbers of parents whose response and interest were tremendous.

Nations also resort to international marketing campaigns to get across important points about themselves to the citizens of other countries. The junta of Greek colonels who seized power in Greece in 1967 found the international publicity surrounding their cause to be extremely unfavorable and potentially disruptive of international recognition. They hired a major New York public relations firm and soon full-page newspaper ads appeared carrying the headline "Greece Was Saved From Communism," detailing in small print why the takeover was necessary for the stability of Greece and the world.[2]

An anti-cigarette group in Canada is trying to press the Canadian Parliament to ban cigarettes on the grounds that they are harmful to health. There is widespread support for this cause but the organization's funds are limited, particularly measured against the huge advertising resources of the cigarette industry. The group's problem is to find effective ways to make a little money go a long way in persuading influential legislators of the need for discouraging cigarette consumption. This group has come up with several ideas for marketing anti-smoking to Canadians, including television spots, a paperback book featuring pictures of cancer and heart disease patients, and legal research on company liability for the smoker's loss of health.

What concepts are common to these and many other possible illustrations of organizational marketing? All of these organizations are concerned about their "product" in the eyes of certain "consumers" and are seeking to find "tools" for furthering their acceptance. Let us consider each of these concepts in general organizational terms.

Products. Every organization produces a "product" of at least one of the following types:

Physical products: "Product" first brings to mind everyday items like soap, clothes, and food, and extends to cover millions of *tangible* items that have a market value and are available for purchases.

Services: Services are *intangible* goods that are subject to market transaction such as tours, insurance, consultation, hairdos, and banking.

Persons: Personal marketing is an endemic *human* activity, from the employee trying to impress his boss to the statesman trying to win the support of the public. With the advent of mass communications, the marketing of persons has been turned over to professionals. Hollywood stars have their press agents, political candidates their advertising agencies, and so on.

Organizations: Many organizations spend a great deal of time marketing themselves. The Republican Party has invested considerable thought and resources in trying to develop a modern look. The American Medical Association decided recently that it needed to launch a campaign to improve the image of the American doctor.[3] Many charitable organizations and universities see selling their *organization* as their primary responsibility.

Ideas: Many organizations are mainly in the business of selling *ideas* to the larger society. Population organizations are trying to sell the idea of birth control, and the Women's Christian Temperance Union is still trying to sell the idea of prohibition.

Thus the "product" can take many forms, and this is the first crucial point in the case for broadening the concept of marketing.

Consumers. The second crucial point is that organizations must deal with many groups that are interested in their products and can make a difference in its success. It is vitally important to the organization's success that it be sensitive to, serve, and satisfy these groups. One set of groups can be called the *suppliers*. *Suppliers* are those who provide the management group with the inputs necessary to perform its work and develop its product effectively. Suppliers include employees, vendors of the materials, banks, advertising agencies, and consultants.

The other set of groups are the *consumers* of the organization's product, of which four sub-groups can be distinguished. The *clients* are those who are the immediate consumers of the organization's product. The clients of a business firm are its buyers and potential buyers; of a service organization those receiving the services, such as the needy (from the Salvation Army) or the sick (from County Hospital); and of a protective or a primary organization, the members themselves. The second group is the *trustees* or *directors,* those who are vested with the legal authority and responsibility for the organization, oversee the management, and enjoy a variety of benefits form the "product." The third group is the active *publics* that take a specific interest in the organization. For a business firm, the active publics include consumer rating groups, governmental agencies, and pressure groups of various kinds. For a university, the active publics include alumni and friends of the university, foundations, and city fathers. Finally, the fourth consumer group is the *general public*. These are all the people who might develop attitudes toward the organization that might affect its conduct in some way. Organizational marketing concerns the programs designed by management to create satisfactions and favorable attitudes in the organization's four consuming groups; clients, trustees, active publics, and general public.

Marketing Tools. Students of business firms spend much time studying acceptance: product improvement, pricing, distribution, and communication. All of these tools have counterpart applications to nonbusiness organizational activity.

Nonbusiness organizations to various degrees engage in product improvement, especially when they recognize the competition they face from other organizations. Thus, over the years churches have added a host of nonreligious activities to their basic religious activities to satisfy members seeking other bases of human fellowship. Universities keep updating their curricula and adding new student services in an attempt to make the educational experience relevant to the students. Where they have failed to do this, students have sometimes organized their own courses and publications, or have expressed their dissatisfaction in organized protest. Government agencies such as license bureaus, police forces, and taxing bodies are often not responsive to the public because of monopoly status; but even here citizens have shown an increasing readiness to protest mediocre services, and more alert bureaucracies have shown a growing interest in reading the user's needs and developing the required product services.

All organizations face the problem of pricing their products and services so that they cover costs. Churches charge dues, universities charge tuition, governmental agencies charge fees, fund-raising organizations send out bills. Very often specific product charges are not sufficient to meet the organization's budget, and it must rely on gifts and surcharges to make up the difference. Opinions vary as to how much the users should be charged for the individual services and how much should be made up through general collection. If the university increases its tuition, it will have to face losing some students and putting more students on scholarship. If the hospital raises its charges to cover rising costs and additional services, it may provoke a reaction from the community. All organizations face complex pricing issues although not all of them understand good pricing practice.

Distribution is a central concern to the manufacturer seeking to make his goods conveniently accessible to buyers. Distribution also can be an important marketing decision area for nonbusiness organizations. A city's public library has to consider the best means of making its books available to the public. Should it establish one large library with an extensive collection of books, or several neighborhood branch libraries with duplication of books? Should it use bookmobiles that bring the books to the customers instead of relying exclusively on the customers coming to the books? Should it distribute through school libraries? Similarly the police department of a city must think through the problem of distributing its protective services efficiently through the community. It has to determine how much protective service to allocate to different neighborhoods; the respective merits of squad cars, motorcycles, and foot patrolmen; and the positioning of emergency phones,

Customer communication is an essential activity of all organizations although many nonmarketing organizations often fail to accord it the importance it deserves. Managements of many organizations think they have fully met their communication responsibilities by setting up advertising and/or public relations departments. They fail to realize that *everything about an organization talks*. Customers form impressions of an organization from its physical facilities, employees, officers, stationery, and a hundred other company surrogates. Only when this is appreciated do the members of the organization recognize that they all are in marketing, whatever else they do. With this understanding they can assess realistically the impact of their activities on the consumers.

CONCEPTS FOR EFFECTIVE MARKETING MANAGEMENT IN NONBUSINESS ORGANIZATIONS

Although all organizations have products, markets, and marketing tools, the art and science of effective marketing management have reached their highest state of development in the business type of organization. Business organizations depend on customer goodwill for survival and have generally learned how to sense and cater to their needs effectively. As other types of organizations recognize their marketing roles, they will turn increasingly to the body of marketing principles worked out by business organizations and adapt them to their own situations.

What are the main principles of effective marketing management as they appear in most forward looking business organizations? Nine concepts stand out as crucial in guiding the marketing effort of a business organization.

Generic Product Definition. Business organizations have increasingly recognized the value of placing a broad definition on their products, one that emphasizes the basic customer need(s) being served. A modern soap company recognizes that its basic product is cleaning, not soap; a cosmetics company sees its basic product as beauty or hope, not lipsticks and makeup; a publishing company sees its basic product as information, not books.

The same need for a broader definition of its business is incumbent upon nonbusiness organizations if they are to survive and grow. Churches at one time tended to define their product narrowly as that of producing religious services for members. Recently, most churchmen have decided that their basic product is human fellowship. There was a time when educators said that their product was the three R's. Now most of them define their product as education for the whole man. They try to serve the social, emotional, and political needs of young people in addition to intellectual needs.

Target Groups Definition. A generic product definition usually results in defining a very wide market, and it is then necessary for the organization, because of limited resources, to limit its product offering to certain clearly defined groups within the market. Although the generic product of an automobile company is transportation, the company typically sticks to cars, trucks, and buses, and stays away from bicycles, airplanes, and steamships. Furthermore, the manufacturer does not produce every size and shape of car but concentrates on producing a few major types to satisfy certain substantial and specific parts of the market.

In the same way, nonbusiness organizations have to define their target groups carefully. For example, in Chicago the YMCA defines its target groups as men, women and children who want recreational opportunities and are willing to pay $20 or more a year for them. The Chicago Boys Club, on the other hand, defines its target group as poorer boys within the city boundaries who are in want of recreational facilities and can pay $1 a year.

Differentiated Marketing. When a business organization sets out to serve more than one target group, it will be maximally effective by differentiating its product offerings and communications. This is also true for nonbusiness organizations. Fund-raising organizations have recognized the advantage of treating clients, trustees, and various publics in different ways. These groups require differentiated appeals and frequency of solicitation. Labor unions find that they must address different messages to different parties rather than one message to all parties. To the company they may seem unyielding, to the conciliator they may appear willing to compromise, and to the public they seek to appear economically exploited.

Customer Behavior Analysis. Business organizations are increasingly recognizing that customer needs and behavior are not obvious without formal research and analysis; they cannot rely on impressionistic evidence. Soap companies spend hundreds of thousands of dollars each year researching how Mrs. Housewife feels about her laundry, how, when, and where she does her laundry, and what she desires of a detergent.

Fund raising illustrates how an industry has benefited by replacing stereotypes of donors with studies of why people contribute to causes. Fund raisers have learned that people give because they are getting something. Many give to community chests to relieve a sense of guilt because of their elevated state compared to the needy. Many give to medical charities to relieve a sense of fear that they may be struck by a disease whose cure has not yet been found. Some give to feel pride. Fund raisers have stressed the importance of identifying the motives operating in the marketplace of givers as a basis for planning drives.

Differential Advantages. In considering different ways of reaching target groups, an organization is advised to think in terms of seeking a differential advantage. It should consider what elements in its reputation or resources can be exploited to create a special value in the minds of its potential customers. In the same way Zenith has built a reputation for quality and International Harvester a reputation for service, a nonbusiness organization should base its case on some dramatic values that competitive organizations lack. The small island of Nassau can compete against Miami for the tourist trade by advertising the greater dependability of its weather; the Heart Association can compete for funds against the Cancer Society by advertising the amazing strides made in heart research.

Multiple Marketing Tools. The modern business firm relies on a multitude of tools to sell its product, including product improvement, consumer and dealer advertising, salesman incentive programs, sales promotions, contests, multiple-size offerings, and so forth. Likewise nonbusiness organizations also can reach their audiences in a variety of ways. A church can sustain the interest of its members through discussion groups, newsletters, news releases, campaign drives, annual reports, and retreats. Its "salesmen" include the religious head, the board members, and the present members in terms of attracting potential members. Its advertising includes announcements of weddings, births and deaths, religious pronouncements, and newsworthy developments.

Integrated Marketing Planning. The multiplicity of available marketing tools suggests the desirability of overall coordination so that these tools do not work at cross purposes. Over time, business firms have placed under a marketing vice-president activities that were previously managed in a semi-autonomous fashion, such as sales, advertising, and marketing research. Nonbusiness organizations typically have not integrated their marketing activities. Thus, no single officer in the typical university is given total responsibility for studying the needs and attitudes of clients, trustees, and publics, and undertaking the necessary product development and communication programs to serve these groups. The university administration instead includes a variety of "marketing" positions such as dean of students, director of alumni affairs, director of public relations, and director of development; coordination is often poor.

Continuous Marketing Feedback. Business organizations gather continuous information about changes in the environment and about their own performance. They use their salesmen, research department, specialized research services, and other means to check on the movement of goods, actions of competitors, and feelings of customers to make sure they are progressing along satisfactory lines. Nonbusiness organizations typically are more casual about collecting vital information on how they are doing and what is happening in the marketplace. Universities have been caught off guard by underestimating the magnitude of student grievance and unrest, and so have major cities underestimated the degree to which they were failing to meet the needs of important minority constituencies.

Marketing Audit. Change is a fact of life, although it may proceed along invisibly on a day-to-day basis. Over a long stretch of time it might be so fundamental as to threaten organizations that have not provided for periodic reexaminations of their purposes. Organizations can grow set in their ways and unresponsive to new opportunities or problems. Some great American companies are no longer with us because they did not change definitions of their businesses, and their products lost relevance in a changing world. Political parties become unresponsive after they enjoy power for a while and every so often experience a major upset. Many union leaders grow insensitive to new needs and problems until one day they find themselves out of office. For an organization to remain viable, its management must provide for periodic audits of its objectives, resources, and opportunities. It must reexamine its basic business, target groups, differential advantage, communication channels, and messages in the light of current trends and needs. It might recognize when change is needed and make it before it is too late.

IS ORGANIZATIONAL MARKETING A SOCIALLY USEFUL ACTIVITY?

Modern marketing has two different meanings in the minds of people who use the term. One meaning of marketing conjures up the terms selling, influencing, persuading. Marketing is seen as a huge and increasingly dangerous technology, making it possible to sell persons on buying things, propositions, and causes they either do not want or which are bad for them. This was the indictment in Vance Packard's *Hidden Persuaders* and numerous other social criticisms, with the net effect that a large number of persons think of marketing as immoral or entirely self-seeking in its fundamental premises. They can be counted on to resist the idea of organizational marketing as so much "Madison Avenue."

The other meaning of marketing unfortunately is weaker in the public mind; it is the concept of sensitively *serving and satisfying human needs.* This was the great contribution of the marketing concept that was promulgated in the 1950s, and that concept now counts many business firms as its practitioners. The marketing concept holds that the problem of all business firms in an age of abundance is to develop customer loyalties and satisfaction, and the key to this problem is to focus on the customer's needs.[4] Perhaps the short-run problem of business firms is to sell people on buying the existing products, but the long-run problem is clearly to create the products that people need. By this recognition that effective marketing requires a consumer orientation instead of a product orientation, marketing has taken a new lease on life and tied its economic activity to a higher social purpose.

It is this second side of marketing that provides a useful concept for all organizations. All organizations are formed to serve the interest of particular groups; hospitals serve the sick, schools serve the students, governments serve the citizens, and labor unions serve the members. In the course of evolving, many organizations lose sight of their original mandate, grow hard, and become self-serving. The bureaucritic mentality begins to dominate the original service mentality. Hospitals may become perfunctory in their handling of patients, schools treat their students as nuisances, city bureaucrats behave like petty tyrants toward the citizens, and labor unions try to run instead of serve their members. All of these actions tend to build frustration in the consuming groups. As a result some withdraw meekly from these organizations, accept frustration as part of their condition, and find their satisfactions elsewhere. This used to be the common reaction of ghetto Negroes and college students in the face of indifferent city and university bureaucracies. But new possibilities have arisen, and now the same consumers refuse to withdraw so readily. Organized dissent and protest are seen to be an answer, and many organizations thinking of themselves as responsible have been stunned into recognizing that they have lost touch with their constituencies. They had grown unresponsive.

Where does marketing fit into this picture? Marketing is that function of the organization that can keep in constant touch with the organization's consumers, read their needs, develop "products" that meet these needs, and build a program of communications to express the organization's purposes. Certainly selling and influencing will be large parts of organizational marketing; but, properly seen, selling follows rather than precedes the organization's drive to create products to satisfy its consumers.

CONCLUSION

It has been argued here that the modern marketing concept serves very naturally to describe an important facet of all organizational activity. All organizations must develop appropriate products to serve their sundry consuming groups and must use modern tools of communication to reach their consuming publics. The business heritage of marketing provides a useful set of concepts for guiding all organizations.

The choice facing those who manage nonbusiness organizations is not whether to market or not to market, for no organization can avoid marketing. The choice is whether to do it well or poorly, and on this necessity the case for organizational marketing is basically founded.

NOTES

1. This is the view of Sherman Lee, Director of the Cleveland Museum, quoted in *Newsweek,* April 1, 1968, p. 55.
2. "PR for the Colonels," *Newsweek,* March 18, 1968, p. 70.
3. "Doctors Try an Image Transplant," *Business Week,* June 22, 1968, p. 64.
4. Theodore Levitt, "Marketing Myopia," *Harvard Business Review,* July–August, 1960, pp. 45–56.

Factors Influencing Marketing's Ability to Assist Non-profit Organizations

PHILIP D. COOPER
GEORGE E. McILVAIN

During the last decade marketing practitioners have become increasingly interested in applying their skills to marketing problems in the non-profit sector. Concurrently, the positive response of non-profit organizations in the 70's to marketing indicates the inevitability of the diffusion of the tools and concepts of marketing into the non-profit sector. The market for marketing techniques in the

Reprinted with permission from *Proceedings of the Southern Marketing Association,* Fall 1980, pp. 314–318.

non-profit sector is quickly moving from its introductory state in the 70's to a growth stage in the 80's. The task marketing faces as the 80's begin is to formally recognize the non-profit sector as a new customer of marketing and develop specially designed packages of marketing tools to assist these new users of marketing.

The diffusion of this sometimes controversial business concept into sensitive non-profit settings must be implemented with caution. Looking back at the 70's it is readily apparent that this process of diffusion has been pursued rather haphazardly. The marketing discipline received a few black eyes due to the fact that marketing tools were hastily applied in non-profit settings by practitioners before a full assessment of the users needs was completed. If the marketing discipline is to avoid further embarrassment in the 80's, a method must be devised to assist marketing practitioners assess the environment for practical applications of marketing in this new area. Marketing practitioners already working for non-profit operations and marketing consultants wishing to service these organizations could then use this methodology to develop a frame of reference that would be of use when conducting a marketing needs analysis for various non-profit "industries." [1]

This manuscript proposes a method for assessing the current environment for marketing in specific non-profit situations. Following this method, marketing practitioners can accurately assess any organization's current environment and quickly determine key areas where marketing tools can be most efficiently applied to help the organization accomplish its goals and objectives.

This method of assessment calls for an analysis of three factors that are seen as directly influencing the final outcome of any attempt to apply marketing tools to nonprofit organizations. The first of these influencing factors is the degree of regulation experienced by the industry from social and political/legal forces. The second factor influencing the efficient application of marketing tools is the level of sophistication of the data available from the industry. The final influencing factor is the level of potential application of various marketing tools to the industry.

REGULATORY PARAMETERS

The first factor marketing practitioners need to analyze in assessing the potential for marketing applications in a non-profit setting is the regulatory environment. This environment consists of the organization's various publics that restrict or regulate the operational options open to the organization. These restrictions and regulations come in the form of social pressures from various groups and governmental regulation through laws and regulatory agencies.

Social Regulations. When the marketing discipline moved into the non-profit sector it took on broadened social responsibilities. The fact that many non-profit organizations deal in socially sensitive issues such as the right to life (family planning clinics) has led many people to feel that some marketing techniques are too manipulative to be used in these areas. Hence, it is critically important that marketing practitioners remain keenly aware of the potential power and profound influence that marketing tools may have over an organization's consuming publics. A study conducted by Laczniak, Lusch and Murphy concerning marketing and ethics revealed the following:

1. Social marketing is a two-edged sword perceived to have major beneficial elements, but also containing the potential to cause significant ethical controversies.
2. The accountability of social marketers will be a major societal concern.
3. When judging social marketing from an ethical standpoint, it appears to be difficult to separate the ethics of applying marketing techniques to social ideas and the programs from the ethics of the ideas themselves. [2]

Hence, the potential social impact of using certain marketing tools may well serve to severely limit the practical application of those tools in the non-profit sector. For example, aggressive marketing of family planning clinics may be perceived by many to have adverse social effects of first increasing the awareness of the availability of abortions and consequently increasing the teenage pregnancy rates in the community.

Governmental Regulations. Rather than restricting the use of marketing in the non-profit sector, government regulations legislation and agencies have actually facilitated its use. For example, the FTC in numerous regulatory moves has allowed many professions such as law and medicine to use promotion to disseminate information of use to the consumer which previously was unable to be freely disseminated. This was accomplished by major professional associations such as the American Medical Association building into their "codes of ethics" such restrictions. The results of the FTC moves will hopefully bring competition into the professions.

Regulatory bodies are just one facilitator. Another has been governmental legislation. Perhaps the most notable has been Public Law 93-641. This law basically set up what is known as the Health System Agencies. It worked to introduce marketing into the health profession by forcing the health delivery systems to acknowledge the single most important element in marketing—the consumer. The consumer (defined as a person not involved in the delivery of health care) had to comprise more than half of the board which voted on requests to obtain new equipment, bricks and mortar and other requests by community health providers.

AVAILABILITY AND SOPHISTICATION OF DATA

The second factor that must be assessed when determining how effectively marketing tools can be applied to specific non-profit industries is the level of sophistication of the data available from the industry. In many non-profit industries data is often difficult to obtain and tends to lack the level of sophistication of data available in the private (profit) sector of the economy.

One reason that information is difficult to obtain is the fact that many non-profit organizations are not required to report the vital statistics of their operations to any one central agency (such as the Federal Government). Most non-profit organizations account for their activities only to their sources of funding. Further, many operations have several sources of funding and account for the funds devoted only to the source that donated the funds. Therefore, each funding source gets only a partial picture of the organization's total operations. Additionally, many of these non-profit operations are apparently reluctant to divulge their full financial picture to every provider of funds since funds may be cut back by one source if it knows the organization is receiving a healthy grant from another source and may be able to survive with a smaller contribution.

Information on non-profit operations then must often come from several data sources. Some of the possible sources are normally used by market researchers such as the census bureau and chamber of commerce. Others may appear quite unorthodox (United Fund Organizations, local arts councils and local human services departments). The important point here is that the search for information on these non-profit operations must not be limited to conventional research sources. To do so will severely limit the amount and quality of data gathered.

Perfect Information. Most market analysts realize and accept the fact that inferences must often be made using data that are something less than "perfect information." Given the problems cited in the above discussion about data sources, one can readily assume that perfect information on non-profit organizations will be even further out of reach than it is for the analysis of private for-profit operations. Parameters must still be set for data collection purposes if any order is to come of the information sourcing process. The following are summary statistics on any given non-profit industry that may prove helpful as a focus in data gathering:

1. Service mix offerings
   a. Types of services
   b. Number of organizations offering the service
2. Financial resources mix
   a. Types of funding used
      (1) Local grants
      (2) State grants
      (3) Federal grants
      (4) Foundations
      (5) Public solicitation
      (6) Fees charged
   b. Number using each type of funding
   c. Number using combinations of funding sources
3. Size
   a. Budget (cash flows)
   b. Number of employees
      (1) By organization
      (2) Total industry-wide
   c. Number of volunteers
      (1) By organization
      (2) Total industry-wide
   d. Number of customers serviced
      (1) By type of service
      (2) By organization
      (3) Total industry-wide
4. Facilities
   a. Number and type
      (1) By organization
      (2) Total industry-wide
   b. Location
      (1) By address
      (2) Zip code
      (3) Census tract

Data collection. Once the data needs are set, data collection can begin. This phase of the analysis will probably prove to be the most frustrating given the current general level of business sophistication in the non-profit sector. Generally speaking, it is most likely that the marketing practitioner will be able to find all of the aforesaid statistics from one or even a number of sources. This problem arises for several reasons.

First, most non-profit operations are not required to account for their activities in the same detail and frequency as profit-making operations. Thus, records required for reporting purposes are usually all the market analyst will have unless special studies have been conducted recently at the local level. This situation is partly due to the fact that many of these organizations are run by professionals such as doctors, artists, musicians or others who relate to the cause of the organization but have no business background.

Another reason that data collection is difficult in the non-profit sector is that no comprehensive reporting systems exist. For example, even if data are collected on the number of senior citizens who have requested transportation services in the past year by zip code, it is unlikely that these figures would ever become part of a summary report since no central agency exists to compile the statistics. Thus, the marketing practitioner must not only be a market analyst, he must also become a data collection agency.

A third factor that compounds the data collection problem is the sheer number of the organizations that provide services in this sector. For example, one large mid-western city has over a thousand organizations that fall into the category of human services organizations. Some organizations service very specific needs of a small clientele (the Gay Switchboard) and others provide a large array of services to a very diverse clientele (The United Way). This coupled with the fact that the human services area is lacking in data sophistication and reporting systems makes this one of the most difficult areas to analyze.

At times it seems that what the research analyst needs to know about non-profit organizations and what is being reported cross paths at random points. However, in general there seems to be a declining order of sophistication in data collection and reporting systems development within the non-profit sector. The eight classes of non-profit organizations referred to earlier [3] are arranged in Table 1 in descending order of data sophistication and systems development.

TABLE 1: ***Industry classes arranged by level of data sophistication and availability***

1. Health care organizations	5. Public service agencies
2. Educational facilities	6. Professional organizations
3. Political organizations	7. Religious organizations
4. Cultural organizations	8. Human services

Examples. A few examples will serve to posit the range of sophistication between classes 1 and 8 in Table 1. First, a view of the best information available can be depicted by a short example of the actual statistics available on the mental health care segment of the health care industry in a large city. The following information was available pertaining to mental health care facilities:

1. Census tract maps showing coverage of mental health centers and satellites by census tracts
2. Matrix of services provided by mental health centers
3. Matrix of diagnoses by mental health centers
4. Statistical re-cap of services by facility
5. Shared services matrix for mental health centers
6. Demographic information on mental health care clients (sex, race, weekly income and age)

Data of this level of sophistication are clearly useful to the market analyst. With these data the analyst can develop customer profiles, study the various market segments, analyze the current service mix and suggest changes if needed.

At the other extreme is the human services industry. This industry consists of many small specialized organizations and has a poorly developed (almost nonexistent) reporting system. Unless a recent survey has been conducted by the city or regional planning commission, the market analyst will more than likely be able to obtain only a physical accounting by zip code of these organizations. Summary statistics are almost nonexistent. Chances are the analyst will need to conduct a survey of all members in the human services industry to obtain any usable information. Thus, an analyst interested in this industry must first develop a data base capable of supplying summary statistics.

LEVEL OF APPLICATION

After the marketing practitioner/consultant has investigated the regulatory parameters and has a feel for the quality of the data that may be obtained from the industry, he can analyze the marketing mix options and determine which marketing tools have the best potential for application. This analysis should include a clear definition of the market parameters and a market segmentation analysis. Following these analyses, the practitioner can pursue strategy designed to fill the needs of one or more of the non-profit industries.

The marketing practitioner will meet with mixed success in attempting to complete a market structure analysis in a non-profit setting. This problem relates to problems discussed earlier under the data collection section. As the analyst gets further down the list in Table 1, he will experience increased difficulty in defining the parameters of the industry in question. Market segmentation analysis may well be impossible to perform in any great detail in less sophisticated industries. Thus, a general feel for the size and potential of the market may be all that is gained from a market structure analysis in some industries. Industries such as those at the top of the list in Table 1, however, should have statistics that are sophisticated enough to produce a very useful market structure analysis.

Implementation Tools—The 4 P's. Once the market structure analysis is completed, the practitioner is ready to develop a product or service line capable of satisfying the marketing needs of selected non-profit industries. It is important at this point to reiterate the fact that the tools of marketing may vary in range of application from one non-profit industry to another. Thus, the marketing tools developed may vary widely from one industry to the next. On the other hand, however, the product mix should always contain at least some element from each of the four basic tools of marketing—price, place, promotion and product.

The Need to Re-tool. Some interesting things begin to happen to the four P's of marketing when they are applied in the non-profit sector. Price, place, promotion and product all take on new roles and identities as they move from the product-dominated profit sector to the services-dominated non-profit sector. This transition was first formally recognized by health care marketers. Cooper (1979) has suggested that problems may occur if the four P's of marketing are directly transferred to non-profit organizations without acknowledging the difference in the environments. If the health care environment is considered, he proposes the use of C.A.P.S. to replace the four P's. [4] The C.A.P.S. of health care marketing are as follows:

C: Costs/Considerations (price)
A: Availability/Access (place)
P: Promotion with emphasis on Public relations/ Atmospherics rather than on advertising
S: Service development (product) [5]

Hence, the marketing practitioner must develop four reshaped tools of marketing for use in specific non-profit situations. Instead of the traditional dollars and cents approach to pricing, the market analyst must study more intangible things such as the costs of time and convenience to a potential customer. The primary place considerations become much more oriented to convenience and accessibility rather than channels of distribution. Promotional considerations are more weighted to public relations, publicity and atmospherics due to the high cost of mass media exposure. Finally, product decisions in the non-profit sector become predominately services/service line decisions.

Opportunity Assessment Matrix. To assist the marketing practitioner in assessing the opportunities for applying marketing tools to the non-profit sector, an opportunity assessment matrix has been developed. This matrix appears in Table 2. The level of application for any given tool of marketing may range from low to high depending on the needs of each individual non-profit industry. The comments in each cell in Table 2 are based on an assessment of the potential for marketing applications as determined from a survey of one large midwestern city. A few examples will serve to exemplify the range of difference in potential these organizations have for marketing.

Health Care. As indicated by the "higher" assessments in the matrix (Table 2), the market structure analysis should be slanted more toward product/service line analysis and facilities location/design analysis than on pricing or promotion.

Market segmentation analysis can be linked to customer profiles for each of the services (product lines) being offered by the health care operation. Each service offered can then be analyzed to determine market share and potential for growth given the location and strength of competition. New service ideas can be studied for possible addition to the existing line of services to better utilize existing facilities.

The existing services mix should also be studied to determine which services are in the various life cycle stages. Some may even need to be eliminated. Other product/service considerations important in the health care industry include service quality level considerations, service package design and product differentiation.

Conversely, ethical limitations tend to reduce the use of promotional tools in the health care industry. HMO's are allowed to use personal selling techniques in order to get their alternative offer across to prospective customers. Television advertising and sales incentive, however, have been severely limited by the American Medical

TABLE 2: ***Opportunity assessment matrix example***[a]

Nonprofit Industry	*Level of application*			
	Product	*Place*	*Price*	*Promotion*
Health care organizations	High	Medium–high	Low–medium	Low–medium
Educational facilities	High	Medium	Low–medium	High
Political organizations	High	Medium	Low–medium	High
Cultural organizations	Medium	Low–medium	High	Medium–high
Public service agencies	Medium–high	High	Low	Low–medium
Professional organizations	High	Low	Medium	Low–medium
Religious organizations	High	Medium	Low–medium	Low
Human services organizations	High	Low–medium	Low	Medium–high

[a]The contents of each cell represent an assessment of one major mid-western city as an example only.

Association. Public relations and atmospherics have been and will probably continue to be the most useful tools in this industry.

Many large hospitals have for years had a public relations person on the staff. Publicity is a very useful and inexpensive form of advertising for these operations. A problem with many health care operations is making the erroneous assumption that public relations is all there is to marketing. The marketing analyst must know enough about the local media to be able to recognize when the media are being utilized well or poorly.

Atmospherics is the other marketing promotion tool that has strong application in the health care industry. Atmospherics may be defined as the designing of buying and consuming environments in a manner calculated to produce specific cognitive and/or emotional effects on the target market. [6] Atmospherics can be analyzed qualitatively to determine their effect on the consumers' senses of smell, sight, hearing and touch. For example, the Center for Reproductive Health in a major city tried to create an atmosphere that encouraged group interaction so that young women having an abortion would not feel alone with their problems. Group discussion during the abortion process and recovery period was introduced as a means to avert apprehension and potential depression.

Cultural Organizations. Cultural organizations operate in quite a different environment than health care operations. In fact, the opportunity for the application of marketing tools is just about the reverse of the levels of application in the health care industry. Product and place considerations are medium to low in their level of application, while promotion and pricing tools have a high or medium level of application (see Table 2).

Pricing tools have a wide range of application in the cultural industry. The tools most applicable include cost/benefit analysis, price elasticity, variable price pricing, credit terms and price promotion.

Cost/benefit analysis is useful in studying the donations market. The analyst should pay particular attention here to the seemingly imbalanced exchange process where the donor of funds seems to give but not receive. The intangible benefits of prestige and community improvement must be highlighted in the donations exchange process to dispel the donor's feelings that the transaction is totally one-sided.

Price elasticity becomes an important marketing concept to cultural operations when they are analyzing the effects of proposed increases in ticket prices. Price elasticity is very difficult to measure. The important factors to consider regarding price elasticity are the current price levels, the magnitude of the change and psychological effect of the price change. For example, a ticket price change of $.50 from $4.50 to $5.00 is not of great magnitude; however, the psychological impact of a $5.00 ticket may be great enough to effectively price the organization out of certain markets.

Variable price pricing has proved to be a very useful tool for cultural organizations. By varying the prices of seats at theatre performances, symphonies, operas, etc., cultural operations can skim the market with "best seat" prices and penetrate the market with lower priced tickets.

Credit terms and price promotion are also very effective pricing tools for cultural organizations. Package discounts for season tickets have been used quite extensively for a number of years. Credit terms, however, have been used with less frequency. This option can be used in non-profit areas just as effectively as it has been in the profit sector.

Place considerations take on a much lower profile in cultural organizations when compared to their relative importance in the health care industry. As indicated in Table 2, place considerations tend to have a low to medium level of application in cultural organizations. Facilities are few in number and relocation is too expensive to consider due to the size of the facilities and budgetary constraints. Site selection, can, however, be of some use to the cultural industry in the event that new facilities are being planned. Site location studies can be used to strategically locate a new facility near the cultural operation's target markets.

Place considerations can also be applied in areas where it is possible to physically move the product (concert, play or exhibit) to another location. Good examples of this are outdoor concerts like Arts in the Parks programs or Arts in Prisons programs.

Another important place consideration for cultural organizations is timing. Cultural operations must apply a generic approach to defining and analyzing their competition before time schedules are set for cultural events. The marketing consultant must be especially creative in thinking through a listing of all possible forms of entertainment that may compete with cultural events. Once the competitive structure has been analyzed, the scheduling of events can be strategically plotted using dates and times that can have a positive effect on attendance.

SUMMARY

Examples of successful applications of marketing tools in the non-profit sector are numerous today. Non-profit organizations are beginning to realize the fact that all businesses carry on certain functions even though there may be no department or specific person charged with performing that function. Hence, the marketing function has been one of the most overlooked in the non-profit sector.

The concept of marketing for non-profit organizations has been theoretically justified. Operational parameters have been defined. Yet to date, no orderly method of assessing the environment for marketing in the non-profit sector has existed. Thus, there has existed an obvious gap between theory and practice.

The method of analysis proposed in this article is designed to help fill that gap. By analyzing the three influencing factors discussed in this article, marketers can intelligently assess the potential for marketing applications in specific non-profit industries. In addition, an estimate of the probability of achieving favorable results can be made given the organization's current regulatory environment, the availability and quality of data and the potential need for each of the marketing tools.

The non-profit sector of the economy offers marketing practitioners a whole new set of opportunities to which marketing tools can be applied. Following the method of analysis presented in this article, the marketing practitioner can gain a much clearer picture of the structure of the local non-profit business environment and more effectively assess the marketing needs of any given industry. Once the marketing needs are assessed, the market analyst can develop a package of marketing services that contains the necessary marketing tools adjusted to fit the needs of the specific industry being analyzed.

REFERENCES

[1] Philip Cooper and George McIlvain, "Opportunities for Marketing in the Non-Profit Sector," Working Paper Series 79-1, Memphis State University.

[2] Gene R. Laczniak, Robert F. Lusch and Patrick E. Murphy, Social Marketing: Its Ethical Dimensions," *Journal of Marketing,* 43 (April, 1979), p. 30.

[3] Cooper and McIlvain, op.cit.

[4] Philip D. Cooper, "Health Care Marketing CAPS: Specific Areas for Marketing's Contribution," in Philip D. Cooper, *Health Care Marketing:* Issues and Trends (Germantown, Maryland: Aspen Systems, 1979), pp. 97–98.

[5] Ibid.

[6] Philip Kotler, *Marketing for Non-Profit Organizations* (Englewood Cliffs: Prentice-Hall, Inc., 1975), p. 219.

Mickey Mouse Marketing

N. W. (RED) POPE

The financial industry would do well to emulate the marketing acumen of Mickey Mouse.

The world's most famous character has become a respected and envied symbol of the very best there is in target marketing, salesmanship and customer relations. The leader which sets the standards that others in the attraction industry seek to match is the Disney Organization.

And in that marketing magic initially concocted by Walter Elias Disney over 50 years ago there are some very valuable lessons for the financial industry. For while the business of entertainment and the business of finance appear as far apart as an X-rated movie and a Disney G release, there is one obvious and necessary common denominator both share.

People.

People inside, and people outside. Customers and employees.

How Disney looks upon people, internally and externally, handles them, communicates with them, rewards them is, in my view, the basic

Reprinted with permission from *American Banker,* July 25, 1979.

foundation upon which its five decades of success stands. The banking and thrift industry, conversely, has appeared to put more emphasis on results, solutions, growth and problems than on the basic method for achieving results or growth or solving problems with solutions—i.e., people.

People. Inside and outside. Customers and employees.

Sitting as I do everyday in the shadow of Cinderella's Castle (East), and exposed to the Pixie Dust which permeates the atmosphere hereabouts. I have come to observe closely and with reverence the theory and practice of selling satisfaction and serving millions of people on a daily basis successfully. It is what Disney does best. It is one of the things banking needs to improve on most.

If anyone better understood the direct relationship between employees and customers I haven't heard about him or her. If ever there was an organization built on people interfacing with people, it is Disney.

For two articles I will relate to the financial industry some of the personnel policies and customer relations theories of the late Walt Disney and his successors in the theme park business, with the obvious hope that our customers will someday be able to say what almost every person who has been to Disneyland or Walt Disney World has said: "It was everything I expected, it was worth every penny, and I was served to my satisfaction by people who were enthusiastic, knowledgeable and pleasant."

The articles will dwell on the internal side—the people on the theme park payroll—and the customers, those who pay. But to Disney the two are so intertwined it may be difficult to separate one from the other. As you follow the piece, always keep your bank's policies, theories, philosophies and methods in mind in relation to how Disney does it. Compare your way with the Disney way.

Put aside the fact the Disney organization has been at the entertainment business for more than 50 years and in the theme park business for almost 20 years.

And don't consider the fact Walt Disney Productions has an ample supply of cash and financial support to do some rather remarkable things now and again. In the early days the exact opposite was true. So the Disney strength of today grew out of some rather lean times of yesterday. My point has more to do with attitude, philosophy, direction and execution than cash or credit.

The beauty of it all is that the "Disney Way" has been in effect since Steamboat Willie changed his name to Mickey Mouse. Success did not prompt Walter Elias Disney to establish specific consumer and staff procedures and approaches. Rather, his innovative usual methods of people management brought about Disney's overall success as an organization.

There's little question about the fact that Disney is in the entertainment business. So it is natural that show business terms are employed. Instead of Personnel, there is Casting. That alone gets the average young man or woman in the right frame of mind when he or she goes in for a job. And that's important at Disney. The frame of mind is the difference between being an employee, or being a Cast Member. Show biz, if you will.

At Disney if your job has you interfacing with the public in any way whatsoever, you're "onstage" when you do your thing. If your work is not public-interfacing, you're "backstage." One is not better than the other. That is emphasized. It takes both to "put on the show," as the Disney people say it, and they mean just that.

No little, insignificant jobs at all. That is emphasized. It takes many people, doing many types of jobs, to put on the show every day. No job is without its importance to the show. The first time a new Disney cast member goes to his or her job there is a feeling of being a part of the overall success.

The most obvious element at Casting is the professionalism. Those who interview and hire and place are pros in the personnel business. They know what they are doing, and how to do it. An interview at Disney is impressive to the thousands of people, most of them young, who apply for jobs. And there are up to 14,000 jobs at Walt Disney World in season. Be aware that first impressions on the potential employee are as important as those on the employer.

What kind of people are interviewing job applicants at your bank? Do they give the proper impression to applicants? Is your personnel function really professional?

The new Cast Member, once hired, is given written instructions as to the steps he/she will go through in preparation-to-work stages. Written information, not verbal. He is told when to report, where to report, what to wear to report, how long he will be in each training phase. He is provided a booklet that tells him, or her, what is expected in appearance, hair style and length, from makeup to jewelry, from clean fingernails to acceptable shoes. Regardless of age or sex or job to be performed, there is conformity to the code. Everything is in writing. No chance for misinformation, misinterpretation. Attention to detail.

Everyone must attend Disney University and 'pass' Traditions 1 before going on to specialized or technical training. That's right, Disney U.—a multilevel educational institution run on Disney property by a full-time staff. In addition to several basic Disney philosophy courses there are evening classes in Spanish or accounting or drama or disco dancing. All Cast Members are eligible to attend and college credits are given for many courses.

Traditions 1 is an all-day experience wherein the new hire gets a constant offering of Disney philosophy and operational methodology. Every audio-visual and static presentation method is used. And no one is exempt from the course, from VP to entry-level part-timer. All must matriculate at Disney U. before any time is spent on a job, backstage or onstage.

Here is where banks so often fail to take advantage of a marvelous opportunity. We don't have our policies in writing. We tell the new people to "report on Monday." That's it. When they show up, we so often hand them benefits booklets that are out of date and expect them to decipher the material. If a briefing is given, it is boring, ill-produced, lacks imagination and is usually way over the heads of those forced to sit through it. Our principal method of indoctrinating a new hire resembles handing a new recruit a gun and showing him which end to hold, and then walking off, leaving the person to load, aim and fire the best he can.

Disney expects the new CM to know something about the company, its history and success, its management style before he actually goes to work. Every person is shown, during Traditions 1, how each division relates to other divisions, and how each division—Operations, Resorts, Food and Beverage, Marketing, Finance, Merchandising, Entertainment, etc.—relates to "the show." In other words, here's how all of us work together to make things happen. Here's your part in the big picture.

Are you listening?

The new CM shows up his first day at Disney U. He is ushered into a room with round tables, four to the table. Coffee and juice and a Danish are offered. It is 8:30 a.m. A name tag is given each person, but we'll get into that later. The "instructor" is with that group for the next eight hours.

Everyone is introduced—not by the instructor, or by himself. The four people at the table are asked to get to know each other and then all of them will introduce each other. Immediately you know three other people by name, face, where they came from and their future jobs. You are a part of a group now, not alone—one of the crowd.

All of you gather for a picture. You smile. When your Traditions 1 day is over at 4:30 p.m., you are given a copy of the weekly Disney newspaper for the theme park and there on the front page is your group photo, with your name in the caption! Impressed? Certainly.

For about half of your eight hours you're in a classroom setting, watching films or slides or listening to an enthusiastic young lady use magnetic elements to show how the company operates. The other four hours are spent on a guided tour of the park. Onstage, backstage—you are exposed to it all. And at lunchtime you are taken to one of the many company cafeterias and treated to as much lunch as you desire. Free. Impressed? You begin getting the idea this company wants you to be happy on the job, and knowledgeable.

How many banks take their new hires throughout the facility, explaining each department's function and how all relate to the business of the bank? Do we treat our new hires to a lunch? Take their picture, give them the company newspaper, explain the benefits properly?

Sure, your bank isn't Walt Disney World and you don't have the people, the money to do all that. Are you sure you don't? Have you tried?

Remember those name tags? Everyone at a Disney theme park wears one; every person who works for any Disney enterprise wears one. Everybody. From the chairman of the board of Walt Disney Productions to that guy sweeping cigarette butts off Main Street after the parade. The dishwasher few people see, the ticket taker at the entrance, the secretaries, security people—everyone wears a name tag.

With only the first name on it. That's it. President of Disney Productions, director of marketing, popcorn vendor, cook, first name only.

And the rule is that when addressing each other, only first names will be used. No Mr. or Mrs. or Miss or Ms. First names, please. It is part of the "family feeling" Disney advocates. It is part of the oneness, the unity, the "no one is better than anyone else" policy.

Can you imagine the average teller addressing the chairman of the board as "Charlie." Or the janitor calling the VP/commercial loans by his first name? Perhaps banks need to be more formal than entertainment entities. It is probably expected that banks not be too familiar, too folksy, for money and credit is perceived as a more serious business than the attractions business.

Or is it? Have we structured ourselves so stiffly; are we so status-level-position conscious that communication doesn't properly occur? Do we have the feeling that sometimes it is "Them" and "Us"? Do we demand formality, aloofness?

After a day to learn what's what, get the Pixie Dust, the name tag and the photo, the new CM is dispatched to his/her job-training assignment. Very little OJT occurs at WDW—Walt Disney World. On-the-job observing, perhaps, but little training.

Example. My two kids, ages 18 and 16, average intelligence, reasonably quick, are accepted to be Casual Temporarys—summer, Christmas, Easter, etc., employment.

They are to take tickets, either at the main entrance or the Magic Kingdom entrance. Take tickets. That's it. How tough can that be?

Four eight-hour days of instruction are required before they can go "onstage"! They are paid to learn, but before a Disney CM interfaces with a Guest—Disney has no customers at theme parks, only Guests—the management must be absolutely certain that the CM can, and will, perform properly. After all, we are dealing with Guest Satisfaction, they say. Nothing is spared to assure Guest Satisfaction.

"Why," I inquired, "does it take four days to learn how to take tickets?" Waste of time, I thought.

My two Traditions 1 graduates, with his new haircut and her "a-little-lipstick-only" makeup, jump to the defense of 32 hours of education in the fine art of taking tickets.

I was informed there are x varieties of tickets, each having special meaning. What happens if someone wants to know where the restrooms are, when the parade starts, what bus to get back to the campgrounds, what the park's hours are, where do we eat inside, what happens if I lose my child, how many bricks in the castle? Questions ad infinitum.

"We need to know the answers or where to get the correct answers quickly," I am advised. "After all, Dad, we're onstage and help produce the show for our Guests. Our job, every minute, is to help the Guest enjoy the park.'

Wow! Can you imagine one of our bookkeepers, a proof operator, a secretary, a collector rising to the defense of four days of intensive prejob training so they could better serve our customers? Well, why not?

After four days, they went on the line. First to observe, then to try it under careful supervision. After a few hours, they were put to the task. It is this way in every job throughout the park where some specific training is required and general knowledge demanded. Regardless of the time it takes or the instructional costs, no one interfaces with a Guest until he or she is proved ready to properly serve that Guest.

Stop and examine the average bank's teller training programs. The New Accounts person. Baptism under fire.

And so I said to my minimum-wage-to-start-with tycoons after the first day, "How does it feel to be ticket takers?"

Again I was berated.

"Ticket takers? Dad, we're WDW Hosts."

I had forgotten. Everyone onstage and backstage in the theme park area itself has a title with the word "host" in it. There is no Policeman. There is a Security Host. There is no monorail driver; there is a Transportation Host. There are no street cleaners, there are Custodial Hosts. No french fries server, but a Food and Beverage Host. Guests have hosts, don't they? Certainly, so everyone at Disney is a Host or Hostess.

And everyone who interfaces with a Guest in the park is "themed"—costumed to fit the job. The world's largest laundry does all those costumes and uniforms every day, or all night, as the case may be. Come to work in the morning and after clocking in go to Wardrobe. Show biz again.

Mike Mescon, the incredibly provocative Georgia State professor/lecturer, says if he headed a bank he would drop almost all bank titles and use instead the term, Salesperson. For, Mr. Mescon emphasizes, that's what it is all about. Selling. Low-key or hard-sell, salesmanship and customer service are two elements that separate banks from one another. The bank that can train its people properly, motivate its people, reward its people and has its people enthusiastically representing that bank on and off the job will win.

Walt Disney was a marketing magician, no doubt. But his keen insight into personnel and customer relations, separately and collectively, enabled him to create the world's most successful entertainment conglomerate by starting with a mouse he drew and named Steamboat Willie in 1928.

The next article, also keying on The Disney Way, will highlight Customer Relations and feature several marketing approaches banks might use to sell to their target groups.

More Mickey Mouse Marketing

N. W. (RED) POPE

Nothing I've had published in 30 years prompted more mail or phone calls than "Mickey Mouse Marketing," the first of two articles concentrating on customer and staff relations as practiced by the Walt Disney organizations.

While this could mean all my previous stuff was pretty bad, it might also mean this piece was particularly good. I don't think it was either. What

Reprinted with permission from *American Banker,* September 12, 1979.

I think prompted the cards and calls was that the gist of the article touched some of banking's exposed nerves.

A banker in New York wrote he had known for years how good Disney was at customer relations, and how bad his bank was at it, but he hadn't been able to get money to do much about the latter. The Denver banker said he knew his bank's training was horrible, but management hadn't given that priority billing. The Pennsylvania banker remarked that until bankers cared as much about how well the customer was served as how well the bank was served, banking would never change its customer relations.

An Ohio banker wrote me stating that odds were pretty long on bankers looking upon their personnel as high priorities. His way of stating that was "human resources inside our banks are yet to be ranked as important as computers, branch offices or, for that matter, the board of directors' annual retreat. In the main, staff morale is not all that big a need to too many bank managers."

The good part about the letters was that people apparently were moved to critical introspection upon reading the piece. The bad part was that almost without exception everyone admitted management apathy or lack of commitment.

Incidentally, Disney does not make its programs or methods or manuals or personnel available, as a rule, to outsiders on a "for sale" or consulting basis.

Now, back to Part Two in the continuing saga of how Walt Disney World, and other Disney entities, look upon their bread (staff) and butter (guests). Remember, please, as you read on, compare how your bank does things with the way Mickey Mouse and his associates do them.

Of the 100 million people who have passed through Walt Disney World's turnstiles since October, 1971, a great many ask seemingly stupid questions about the place. Stupid to us, perhaps, but not to Disney. Like how many bricks are in the Castle, how many lights are there in the theme park, how many boats do you have here, how long did it take to build this place, how much did it cost, how many telephones are there in the whole place, how often do you have to paint the submarines, how many hot dogs do you sell here each year? Ad infinitum.

To many businesses this sort of barrage of trivia inquiry would lead to an abrupt, "How should I know, kid!" To Disney it is the sort of stuff dreams (and attendance) are built on. And if any employee (Host or Hostess) cannot give the answer to any question . . . that's right . . . any question, then there is a telephone exchange to call. Immediately. The minute the question is asked and the Disney staffer can't answer it, call that number and ask!

Twenty-four hours a day a cadre of switchboard operators with factbooks to rival the largest phone books in America are standing by to answer those "very stupid" questions, on the spot. Like, the most meals served in a single day was 220,500 (12/31/75). And 13 million ketchup packets are given out annually and 24 tons of french fries are sold every week, and 3½ million pounds of hot dogs were sold to the guests last year.

And if you add up all the boats and rafts and submarines and ferrys and canoes and other floating materiel throughout the 27,400 acres, you'd have the seventh largest navy in the World, and that's a fact.

The bottom line is: serve the guest. If someone cares about hot dogs, tell 'em the answer. Whatever the guests wants to know, get 'em the facts, now!

Sometime, stand in you lobby and watch your personnel attempt to answer basic, not stupid, questions. How much are your safe deposit boxes? What are your CD rates? How much can I get for a Canadian dollar? Does your bank have a branch office in the south part of town? What's your best rate on an auto loan? What hours are your driveins open?

Maybe the person asked doesn't have the answers, or perhaps shouldn't try to give out rates, but how does she, or he, respond? How does he, or she, serve the customer?

One fast rule at Disney theme parks is that no

employee will be served before a guest. In fact, Disney provides cafeterias, breakrooms, snack bars and other facilities for its people "backstage." This includes special live and automated teller operations our Sun Bank runs for Disney employees so they can do their banking conveniently.

If you want a soft drink and you work at Disney, go backstage. If you want to buy a Minnie Mouse blouse, do it at the company store. Need a check cashed? Backstage. From toilets to parking, Disney makes sure its guests' needs are not slowed by staff use. While we in banks don't run theme parks, I'll have to admit I've seen our bank employees in teller lines ahead of customers.

Every week Walt Disney World's cast communications division of Disney University produces an eight-page 8½ × 11 newspaper called Eyes and Ears. One glance at its contents and you know it was prepared for Disney people. It is a people publication, featuring all sorts of activities, improved employment opportunities, special benefits, educational offerings and even a complete classified section. The stories are very short, newsy, punchy. Lots of pictures of cast members. A brief feature perhaps. And I've never, never seen a single photo in that newspaper in seven years that showed anyone not smiling. Contrived? Maybe, but it got to me, didn't it?

Banks produce some of the worst employee publications possible. Poor writing, inadequate story selection, not enough photos, and often those published are poor quality, and too much about the brass or the home office. And the reason is, I think, that we expect people in marketing or personnel or some other division to take on the paper as an additional job. We don't hire newspaper people to produce newspapers. We hire loan officers to make loans, and auditors to audit, and managers to manage, but we feel some obligation to assign the internal communications to someone as an afterthought, an extra job, assuming it is a simple, quick thing.

"Give it to the boss' nephew . . . he used to write for the high school newspaper."

One evening during a BMA conference when some of us were "learning from one another," the subject of company publications, house organs, arose. Most of us agreed poor quality was a standard. One member of the group admitted, blushingly, that his personnel director had decreed the bank would have some sort of newspaper to appease all the EEOC types, and to show some union that his bank "talked" with its people, regardless of content or quality. He said the bank president wanted to prove, if the need arose, that his bank had an ongoing communications vehicle, content notwithstanding.

Disney feels, on the other hand, that informed people are happier, less confused, more aware of benefits and opportunities, and more cognizant that management genuinely wants and strives to communicate. In addition to the weekly newspaper, Disney produces on a regular basis single-page bulletins for management, two-page "hot news" bulletins with promotions and transfers on a regular basis and, less frequently, an eight-page standard-size newspaper for all cast members.

The written word is most important to employees of any company. But it must be professionally done to properly communicate. A cheap, shoddy and poorly-constructed publication will be obvious to the intended readers. Perhaps they will take that to mean management isn't all that interested in doing any better. And that publication is an extension of the bank. How we are perceived by those that see it, inside or out, is cause for concern.

Disney also cares what its staff members think about the theme park as a place to work. When your reputation and continuation in business depends upon how well employees serve paying customers, then perhaps some attention should be given to the "care and feeding" of the employees. (Hear that, banks?)

There are several types of employees at a Disney theme park, from the permanent year-'round types, to what Mickey terms "the casual temporary cast member." This means summers and holidays and maybe weekends, when the attendance is greatest and staff needs are highest. Like my two kids taking tickets during peak seasons. Disney is a master at being able to use parttimers, keeping the higher paid group at a minimum, a trick many banks are beginning to pick up, especially in the teller area.

As the summer ends some 3,000 casual temporaries are returning to school, Disney asks each to complete a simple questionnaire, anonymously. My job was, my division or department was, my age is, my formal education is, I live miles from the park, etc. I am a: man-woman-. Notice it didn't say male, female. They find out some basics first.

Then they ask the respondent to check one of five applicable answers, from very good to poor, to these:

- I think the reputation Walt Disney World has with the public is . . .
- Looking at Walt Disney World compares with other companies, I would say it is managed . . .
- How did you feel when you told people what company you worked for?
- How did you feel your wage (salary) compared with wages (salaries) paid for similar jobs outside Walt Disney World?
- Inside Walt Disney World?

There there are questions about hiring practices and procedures, the orientation program, the initial training given. Did you feel satisfied with your job? How important did you feel it was? Was it interesting?

For eight pages and eighty-four questions the Disney management wants to know, from those in the less glamour jobs all the way to the more outstanding positions, if its people are happy, treated fairly, trained properly and communicated with. Why? Because the basis for operating a theme park dedicated to the happiness of all sorts of people must be . . . happy people. Inside. People with pride, respect for the employer. And to get those kids back next summer, Disney knows it has to offer the best surroundings, training and opportunities.

Banks are beginning to pay some heed to what its employees think about working conditions and opportunities, too. Next to interest paid on time deposits, salaries and wages are the second highest cost in most banks. The cost of turnover is exorbitant. Our training has been inadequate. We have not been competitive in the personnel marketplace. And, like Disney, a bank is a service business which requires people to interface with the customer in so many transactions.

When the energy business hit Florida, and California, and gasoline became as precious as glass slippers, Disney realized its large contingent of people, working literally around the clock, might be hardpressed to get gas to come to work. Mobilization occured. First, in all publications car pools were encouraged and, via computer, actually designed for everyone on the payroll. Large buses were contracted to run regular schedules from the largest neighborhood areas to the park, for 90 cents. And if eight or more cast members arranged a car pool and would agree to pay for gas, oil and maintenance, Disney would provide a van! Free! Finally, to assure some gas for work-oriented travel, Disney put in its own cast gas station!

Many banks have opted to reduce the lighting, raise the thermostat, or permit removal of jackets. But Disney, keying to employee needs, went further. It did the analysis, it made the decisions to lease vans, work out car pool schedules and set up bus routes, before it asked for employee cooperation. Many banks I'm aware of asked every employee interested in a car pool to contact personnel.

The obvious happened. Both people contacted personnel. Perhaps had the banks leased vans, set up the routes, put the thing into service and said: "Okay, we've committed and set it up, now you take advantage of it," more people would have done just that. Waiting for enough volunteers to come forth will seldom provide sufficient personnel to fight the battle, much less win the war.

I hope all bank vice presidents (and above) are sitting down to read these next two items.

Annually all the "white collar" types at Walt Disney World, the management if you will, undertake a week-long program called cross-utilization. In essence it means giving up the desk, the secretary and the white collar and donning a themed costume or an apron and heading for the frontline action. For a week the "bosses" sell tickets or popcorn, dish out ice cream or hot dogs, load and unload rides, park cars, drive the monorail or trains, or take on any of the 100 "onstage" jobs that make the park come alive to guests.

According to my sources at Disney, the cross utilization concept is designed to give management a better "hands on" view of how the guests need to be served and, at the same time, management gets a better understanding of what the cast member must go through to properly serve the guests. And assignments are made for Cross U, not selections offered. You take the job given you and head for wardrobe, and a long eight hours on your feet with a smile on your face, ready or not.

Now, all the time you've been reading this you have been envisioning the VP, instalment credit in a drive-in teller cubicle, the VP/trust holding down a collector's job, perhaps the VP/marketing working in the proof department, the president of the bank handling the new accounts desk and all those dumb questions. There's the commercial loan VP operating the mailroom, and somehow our operations VP is in marketing trying to handle a newspaper reporter's persistent questions about why the "little man" is being charged so much interest while, at the same time, attempting to compute market share for 15 branch offices manually.

Kind of makes you smile, doesn't it?

Secondly, and I quote from a recent Eyes and Ears: "As many of you are aware, our vice presidents and directors (Note: a director at Disney is a level below a VP, in a management function such as director of marketing, director of finance, director of food and beverage, etc.) have been scheduling themselves to visit the Magic Kingdom to increase their awareness of both the guest experience and the work experience of our cast members. So don't be surprised if you're stopped during your workday to chat with one of our VPs or directors. He's genuinely anxious to see your operation and what you do each day!"

Following that statement to the troops there is a schedule showing what day which VP or director will be in the park. Both day and night shifts are covered. And wouldn't you know . . . those VPs and directors are supposed to write a report on their findings!

What is all this mingling about? What is this orchestrated entry into the trenches with the folks doing the dirty jobs going to achieve? Well, for my money it is going to tell one heck'uva lot of hardworking people that "somebody up there cares."

How can you spend eight hours shoving out those fries, alongside a couple of sweatin' and smilin' kids making $3.20 an hour, and not be learning something positive about personnel relations, and management?

How can you stand there for eight hours, smiling and saying "Howdy" to 60,000 people, trying to answer their questions in Spanish, direct them to the nearest rest rooms, look at their faces of anticipation, and not learn something about the consumer public?

Perhaps periodically it would be most revealing, and educational, if the bank's brass, and some of our board members for that matter, came down to the lobby on a Monday morning. Or meandered out into the drive-in lanes on a Friday afternoon. Talked to the people in line. Or took the place of that person in the teller window. Chances are it wouldn't take many such trips for improved communications to come about, for some improved benefits to be put in, for some staff morale to improve and for productivity on both ends to get even better.

Mutual understanding for each other's needs and problems. Mutual respect for each other, as people, and as fellow bankers.

To all those who say they are too busy, whose schedules won't permit them to idle away a couple of hours doing such things, I'd suggest the demands upon senior executives at Walt Disney World at peak season are at least as compelling as those of most bankers. It is, I submit, a matter of priorities. He who sees the need, who wants to fill it, will. Case closed.

Disney has a private recreating area with lake, rec hall, picnic areas, boating and fishing and volleyball and family-outing opportunities ad infinitum for its cast members' exclusive use—professionally staffed.

There is a library, staffed, with everything from "How To Do It" books to the latest fiction best sellers, for the benefit of the cast members.

There is a division of Disney University called cast activities. Its sole purpose is to provide educational, recreational, entertainment and cost-saving opportunities to the employees.

Several women from casting make the rounds of all work areas; offices, backstage and onstage, daily to check cast members' hair lengths, makeup, general appearance. Disney has rules about how to dress. You understand them when you report to work. You get one warning. The public sees fresh-faced, neatly-attired people serving them, but that didn't happen by accident.

There is no question that much of Disney's success with people, inside and out, stems from quite a bit of regimentation. Some say it is militaristic in fact. And, in spite of all those smiling faces out there in Fantasyland, there are more than a few sour attitudes behind the braces.

But in spite of the rules, the regulations, the demand that everyone do everything The Disney way, there is no question the people who work there have a special feeling for that 50-year-old mouse. They know the management overtly works at employee relations. They are cognizant that if they want a lifetime career, or a summer's employment, there is a cornucopia of possibilities within the organization. They know all this because the company management puts employee relations just under guest relations as a top priority, and not far under.

And that is, of course, the real answer.

When a company's customers are happy with the service and the product, and find enthusiastic and knowledgeable personnel who are anxious to help, chances are that company will continue to enjoy the lucrative patronage of those customers for a long, long time.

When a company's employees know, and are continually reminded, that their employer is genuinely concerned with and has interest in their personal well-being, and undertakes meaningful programs to manifest that interest, chances are things are alive and well inside the shop.

Hark! Could that be your bank's employees whistling as they arrive for the day's toil? Listen . . .

"Hi ho, hi ho, it's off to work we go. . . ."

Product Portfolio Diagnosis for U.S. Universities

GERALD D. NEWBOULD

Product portfolio diagnosis is a classification system for the products, either goods or services, of a corporation. As early as 1972, it was being employed by over 100 U.S. corporations[1] to assist in top management decisions. Its now widespread use[2] among a variety of corporations suggest that it could be a valid generalization of organizational effectiveness, and hence, may be applicable to higher education. This article develops a variant of product portfolio diagnosis for U.S universities and colleges and, by way of example, it is illustrated empirically for a mid-western university market.

THE PRODUCT PORTFOLIO MATRIX IN BUSINESS

Observation in business led to the development of some independent hypotheses: that market share is strongly and positively correlated with profitability, that profitability varies over the product life cycle, and, that the stage of the product life cycle has implications for the ease of gaining, the cost of gaining, and the cost of holding market share. These were repeatedly confirmed empirically. The earliest recognition that these independent hypotheses could be combined is usually asscribed to the Boston Consulting Group.[3] Table 1 is a typical representation of their work. The particular form shown relates to the Group's choice of a performance indicator, which is cash throw-off. In the *N.W. quadrant* are the products labeled "stars." A product here is one for which demand is growing quickly and for which the corporation has a high share of the market. The products are profitable but will need cash, in addition to that which they generate, to finance further growth. In the *S.E. quadrant* are the "dogs"—any product which has low opportunity for growth and the corporation's share of the

TABLE 1: ***Product portfolio to matrix (day)***

		Market share dominance (ratio of company share to share of largest competitor) Hi	Lo
Market growth rate (annual rate in constant dollars relative to GNP growth)	*Hi*	*Stars*	*Problem Children*
	Lo	*Cash Cows*	*Dogs*

Source: G. D. Day, "Diagnosing the Product Portfolio," *Journal of Marketing,* April 1977, p. 32.

Reprinted with permission from *Akron Business and Economic Review,* Spring 1980, pp. 39–45.

market is low. Maintaining the existing hold is usually expensive; in business, product lines in this quadrant are regarded as the candidates for termination or sale. The *N.E. quadrant* (low market share, high market growth) typified as the "problem children," represents products which have a high demand for cash; by investing heavily (to gain market share) it would be possible to turn a problem child into a star, or, if the growth rate lapses or the investment does not result in increased market share, the problem child becomes a dog. The *S.W. quadrant* represents profitable products in dominant market positions but with little or no prospect of growth and these generate cash for use on growth products and for the development of new products. The main danger in this quadrant is in overestimating the size of the market and thereby continuing to reinvest in this quadrant rather than using the resources for the stars or problem children.

The product portfolio has various uses. First, it is a diagnostic device, since the information of the location of products in the matrix is useful in reviewing total product mix strategies: second, as with any portfolio (whether the members of the portfolio are securities, properties, medics on a surgical team, or managers in a management team), so too with a product portfolio—a decision on an individual member of the portfolio is not made in isolation but only after the impact on the whole portfolio is assessed: third, there are strategic (or flexibility) advantages in having a mixture of products, particularly of cash cows and stars; and fourth, there are broad-based strategies appropriate to each quadrant which management can choose (examples: expand, maintain, invest, divest). The next section translates this model into the higher education environment.

THE PRODUCT PORTFOLIO MATRIX IN HIGHER EDUCATION

Management techniques and models developed in business are finding increasing acceptance in higher education. One report in 1973 concluded "that the two fields (business and higher education) are so different as to preclude any useful exchange of management skills,"[4] but this is not the case. The reports of applications and proposed applications of business methods into higher education are frequent[5] and for marketing (where the product portfolios were developed), the commonalities between business and higher education are extensive[6] particularly now that higher education is entering a period of excess capacity and increased competition for dwindling market segments.

Table 2 shows a product portfolio matrix adapted to the higher education environment. The parallel rests on the argument that a product is the output of an organization designed to meet the needs of consumers, and, in higher education, educational programs meet this definition.[7] In addition, the concept of market share is equally valid for a corporation or a university, and, for both, the

TABLE 2: ***Product portfolio matrix in higher education***

		Market share dominance (ratio of F.T.E. students of largest competing university to F.T.E. students of university X)	
		Hi	*Lo*
Market growth rate (growth in F.T.E. students over past 5 years)	*Hi*	*Stars* Program 1	*Problem Children* Program 2
	Lo	*Cash Cows* Program 3	*Dogs* Program 4

market needs to be defined carefully (local, regional, national; intermediate, end-use, etc.). Finally, the actual measure for market growth rate may change, but both corporations and universities can talk about market growth with equal meaning.

There may be a difference in the objective function. In business, the function in a product portfolio matrix may be corporate profitability or (as in the Boston Consulting Group matrix) cash throw-off. In higher education, the objective function could vary from one institution to another, exactly as in business, but, for example, could be a variation of the Group's cash throw-off. It would be valid, following this example to consider as a "cash cow" some large program with no growth prospects generating state subsidy funds in excess of the cost of the program; or a relatively new program, with good growth prospects, which absorbs more resources than it is generating could be considered a "problem child." Alternatively, the objective function for education may be more complex—it could be defined in terms of academic prestige, intellectual growth or intellectual challenge. In actual use the objective function is a management decision tailored to the purposes to which the matrix is to be used, of which the fundamental one is to pursue the stated objectives of that institution. As will be emphasized later, a product portfolio matrix is only as useful as the care used in its construction; the choice of objective function is one critical decision in construction. Here, purely for illustrative purposes, the objective function is resources—it is assumed that the university in question is in a position of having to make serious decisions about the disposition of its limited resources; it has to decide from where resources are to be released and to where resources can be best put.

The real problem in translating the product portfolio matrix from business to higher education is that of validation. In business, it is commonly accepted that profitability, and cash throw-off, are related to market share and to the stage of the product life cycle; this is based upon experience for many products in many corporations. One way to translate the portfolio matrix into higher education would be to repeat the way it was developed in business: extensive empirical studies and repeated observations of the relationships that formed the basis of the matrix approach. The repetition would be ideal and would lay carefully the foundation for using product portfolio diagnosis in universities. However one purpose of this article is to check whether there is value in the extensive validation studies by looking at the product portfolio matrices themselves in universities. Thus if the matrices do not appear translatable into higher education, or do not appear relevant, then there is no point in going through the long validation preamble. Hence, one purpose is to show that for a mid-western market a matrix can be constructed and, from it, implications arise which may be meaningful and useful to the senior managements of the universities in that market.

THE CHOSEN MARKET

Definition of "market" has long occupied economists and marketers and there is no universally accepted procedure. The market chosen for illustration relates to masters degrees offered by the three state universities in a major mid-western conurbation. Master's degrees were chosen because at this level, more than the undergraduate level, students have exercised a careful choice of program and university—this arises simply from the learning experiences at the undergraduate level about programs and subsequent careers, programs and personal objectives and the quality of various universities offering the desired program. The exercise of careful choice makes management decisions easier since the "market" is less fluid and capricious. State universities were chosen so that fees were approximately equal and the students were purchasing programs in their own effective price range. A conurbation was chosen to allow overlap of the universities geographic catchment areas. Some evidence of the overlap is shown in Table 3. The universities are approximately equal in enrollment; the smallest is 75% the size of the largest. University A and University C are very closely matched on the criteria in Table 3; University B is a less close match to the other two since it does pull from a wider area, including out-of-state. Nevertheless, it is a definite competitor of the other two universities.

Enrollment data on a full-time equivalent basis were collected for the academic period Fall, 1974 to Fall, 1978, using state board documents. A forecast of the Fall, 1981 enrollment was made using an extrapolation model chosen to maximize predictive power (i.e., the co-efficient of determination). The model and the forecast for each program are shown in the appendix table. The prediction of the Fall, 1981 enrollment has been used to classify the program's growth. However, when R^2 is 33% or less, the program carries an asterisk in the matrices. This is to signify the program as "high risk"—in other words enrollment is so variable (with respect to time) that a decision on these programs, either expansion or contraction, must be taken with even more than usual care. In fact, the appropriate way to approach these high risk programs is to regard them as such, that is, the university is concerned with a portfolio of products and a balanced portfolio can afford a reasonable proportion of high risk members but not a large proportion of high risk ones. For state universities, this would probably adversely affect the funding from the state, or at the very least make the university's plans subject to higher-than-normal levels of scrutiny by the state. Regardless of R^2 (which suggests riskiness rather than trend), the programs have been classified with the breakpoint between "high" and "low" growth set at a Fall, 1981 enrollment of 5% greater than Fall, 1978. The breakpoint of 5% was chosen on the basis that growth of more than 5% would require additional faculty and other expensive resources by Fall, 1981, whereas growth of less than 5% could be accommodated, at least up to 1981, by stretching faculty–student ratios and other resources. An alternative breakpoint would have been to split programs by positive growth and negative growth. Accepting that the university has stated its objectives and chosen the appropriate objective function for the matrices, this split would indicate programs requiring additional resources (positive market growth) and those capable of releasing resources (negative market growth). It is, as indicated, essential that objectives be known. If for example an objective is that no faculty member is ever to be fired, or that one program is essential to the achievement of university's objectives, these must be incorporated in the decision. The danger with any management technique is persons being unable to use the technique properly in the proper context—here for example, the danger is regarding the label that emerges for a program from the matrices as being the decision, rather than being a label that a decision process should commence. Clearly, given the peculiar sensitivity of faculty to misinterpretation, choice of a breakpoint is a critical one since it determines whether a particular program becomes labeled inside the university as a "star" or a "cash cow," or, as a "problem child" or a "dog," and, obviously, certain psychological and organizational effects can be anticipated once the labels are

TABLE 3: ***Overlap of enrollment, universities A, B, and C***

	University A	*University B*	*University C*
Enrollment from own county and county of other two universities	70%	56%	89%
Enrollment from own county and all bordering counties	92%	78%	97%
Enrollment out of state	3%	7%	2%
Computer enrollment	93%	77%	100%

assigned. There is no *a priori* breakpoint, nor one that can be offered for use in all universities; one part of the proper use of the matrix will be the intelligent selection and usage of the breakpoint between "high" and "low" growth.

The enrollment data for 1978 were used to measure market share. In business it is accepted that the strategic implications differ whether market share is measured simply (e.g., one university's enrollment/all universities'' enrollment) or relatively (e.g., enrollment for the largest university/next largest enrollment for a university). It is further accepted[8] that the relative measure leads to a better understanding of the competitive situation. For example, knowing the market share is, say, 28% conveys less strategic information than knowing that the largest competitor's share is twice your share and your share is twice that of the remaining competitor. In line with this belief, a high market share is defined in this paper only when the enrollment of one university is 125% or more of that of the next largest university. It follows that it is possible—as in History in Table 5 and Biology in Table 6—for no university to have a high market share, but in the other 17 masters programs, one university does have a "high" share. Again the choice of 125% rather than some other breakpoint, is critical to the labeling of individual programs and there is no theoretical or empirical guidance available. Senior college management would have to behave as their counterparts in business do and exercise their judgement and accumulated experience to select breakpoints.

Using these measures, four groups of product portfolio matrices were constructed for the three competing universities. The three universities are not identified. The data used are publicly available but since this is an illustrative article there is no value in identifying the universities. Before the illustration is put into practice and used for decision-making the following are necessary:

1. The breakpoint between "high" and "low" growth needs to be justified to determine at what breakpoint resources might possibly be required, or released, in each university;
2. The growth rate itself needs extensive analysis; here extrapolation is used as a working device but in reality demographic factors, demand analyses, and other considerations need to be incorporated into the forecast; and,
3. The breakpoint between "high" and "low" market share needs discussion to determine how much market power conveys advantage to the market leader.

Clearly, without these analyses carried out by each university, based on participation by the deans, chairpersons, and faculty concerned, it would be potentially counterproductive and unfair to label programs according to the mnemonics of the product portfolio matrix.

PROFESSIONAL MASTER'S DEGREES

Table 4 shows a product portfolio matrix for each of the three competing universities for the professional master's degrees offered by all three: Business, Education, Engineering, Music, and Physical Education.

Of the three universities, the matrices suggest that University A, the largest of the three, has the most difficult future ahead of it in this professional area. University A has neither stars (the hope for the future) nor cash cows (to finance growth in other programs). It has three problem children (Business, Music, Physical Education); for each problem child, a decision will be necessary as to whether additional resources are going to be injected in order to "buy" market share and thereby gain the stability and viability that goes with increased market share. Further, University A has two dogs (Education, Engineering) which is one more than either University B or University C. For these two programs, some difficult decisions may have to be made as to whether these programs are to be phased out.

Table 4 further suggests that Universities B and C have some balance and, hence, the senior

TABLE 4: *Product portfolios: professional master's degrees*

Market share

University A

Market growth	*Hi*	*Lo*
Hi	*Stars*	*Problem children* Business Music Physical Education
Lo	*Cash Cows*	*Dogs* Education Engineering*

University B

Market growth	*Hi*	*Lo*
Hi	*Stars* Music Physical Education	*Problem Children* Business
Lo	*Cash Cows* Education	*Dogs* Engineering*

University C

Market growth	*Hi*	*Lo*
Hi	*Stars* Business	*Problem Children* Music Physical Education
Lo	*Cash Cows* Engineering*	*Dogs* Education

managements face less difficult problems. Each has at least one star. For University C it is Business and while University B has two stars (Music and Physical Education), they combine in aggregate to fewer students than the single star of University C. Each university has a cash cow (Education for B, Engineering for C), both substantial in size, which could be used as a source of resources to finance the growth of their stars. University B has one problem child (Business), which is a large one and about which a decision ought to be made as to whether a substantial additional commitment to it should be made, whether it be merely maintained, or whether it be trimmed. University C has two problem children (Music, Physical Education) both relatively small and for which probably modest additional resources may result in increased market shares.

The senior management of each university could build its own product portfolio matrix and work toward decisions based upon it. For example, University A might decide to select one of its problem children and invest resources in the chosen program in order to turn it into a star, thus putting more balance into its portfolio. It may further decide to use resources from outside of the professional masters programs as a source of resources. (Table 6 suggests Physics or Mathematics could be used in this way.) The alternative approach is better but more difficult. It is for each senior management to construct, as here, matrices for its own university and for the competing universities, and then make decisions based not only upon its own matrix but also upon those of the competitors. With this alternative University A might be better able to select which problem child to build on. It might even make sense for each university to consult the others to avoid more than one university plunging for the same masters program—in business this would of course be a violation of antitrust law!

Overall, Table 4 (excepting University A which is imbalanced) shows the diversity that is found in business—some products in each quadrant, which enables major strategic decisions to be made about which programs should be expanded, which maintained and which trimmed. However, these balanced portfolios of highs and lows in market growth and market share are not found in the humanities and social sciences.

HUMANITIES AND SOCIAL SCIENCES MASTER'S DEGREES

Table 5 shows the product portfolio matrices for the three universities for all master's degrees in the humanities and social sciences common to the three universities. The imbalance in the portfolio is clear. There are no stars that are not "high risk" programs. The "low risk" programs are cash cows and dogs.

University A is again the one with the real difficulties. It has only "high risk" problem children and dogs in the humanities and social science; all of its nine programs are where it has a low share of each market. Universities B and C are better positioned, and B is in a better position than C since it does have two stars, although "high risk" ones. History is a dog for all three universities (since none has a dominant market share).

The overall impression from the matrices in Table 5, apart from imbalance, is that the humanities and social sciences have the characteristics of resources potentially available for other areas, and, an area where there may have to be many difficult decisions about the future of programs.

SCIENCES MASTER'S DEGREES

Table 6 shows the matrices constructed for common science master's programs. Biology is a "high risk" dog in all three universities. Unlike in the professional and the humanities/social science areas, University A is now the best positioned University. It has one star and two cash cows which could be used to finance the star. Universities B and C have only problem children and dogs, suggesting that, for Universities B and C, these science programs could become net releasers of resources for use elsewhere.

NON-COMMON MASTER'S PROGRAMS

So far, analyses have been confined to masters programs offered by all three universities. There is no reason to limit product portfolio matrices in this way (but it does make initial description more easy). Table 7 shows master's programs which are not common to all three.

University C is the easiest to interpret. It has one

TABLE 5: ***Product portfolios: humanities and social science master's degrees***

Market share

University A

Market growth	*Hi*	*Lo*
Hi	*Stars*	*Problem Children* Speech & Audio* Languages*
Lo	*Cash Cows*	*Dogs* English, Philosophy, History, Economics, Psychology, Sociology, Political Science*

University B

Market growth	*Hi*	*Lo*
Hi	*Stars* Speech & Audio* Languages*	*Problem Children*
Lo	*Cash Cows* English Philosophy Sociology	*Dogs* History Economics Political Science* Psychology

University C

Market growth	*Hi*	*Lo*
Hi	*Stars*	*Problem Children* Speech & Audio* Language*
Lo	*Cash Cows* Economics Political Science* Psychology	*Dogs* English Philosophy History Sociology

star (Computer Science), and Universities A and B are not competing with it—clearly, a program for expansion. University A has one star also, but a "high risk" one. It has three problem children. University B has no dogs and it has four stars (Geology, Architecture, Art, Geography), two (Architecture, Art) without competition and three cash cows which could be the source of resources to finance the stars, or, to push for market leadership with its problem child (Home Economics).

TABLE 6: *Product portfolios: science master's degrees*

Market share (columns: Hi, Lo); *Market growth* (rows: Hi, Lo)

University A

Market growth	Market share: Hi	Market share: Lo
Hi	*Stars* Chemistry	*Problem Children*
Lo	*Cash Cows* Physics* Mathematics	*Dogs* Biology*

University B

Market growth	Market share: Hi	Market share: Lo
Hi	*Stars*	*Problem Children* Chemistry
Lo	*Cash Cows*	*Dogs* Biology* Physics* Mathematics

University C

Market growth	Market share: Hi	Market share: Lo
Hi	*Stars*	*Problem Children* Chemistry
Lo	*Cash Cows*	*Dogs* Biology* Physics* Mathematics

ALL MASTER'S PROGRAMS

Table 8 is a composite of Tables 4, 5, 6 and 7 and thus covers the whole field of master's programs. Looking over the whole field, the matrices do have the balance and diversity that is common in business (though University A is still the imbalanced one). Each now has stars, representing growth and excellence in the future; cash cows which could assist in the growth of the stars; dogs, which could be trimmed or phased out to release resources; and problem children, for which decisions on expansion, maintenance or trimming will be called for.

SUMMARY

Product portfolio matrices have proved useful and meaningful in business for corporations providing a wide variety of products and services. Their value has been proved by the better concen-

TABLE 7: ***Non-common master's programs***

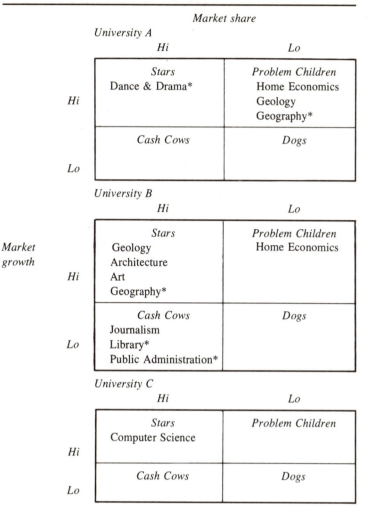

Market share

Market growth

University A

	Hi	*Lo*
Hi	*Stars* Dance & Drama*	*Problem Children* Home Economics Geology Geography*
Lo	*Cash Cows*	*Dogs*

University B

	Hi	*Lo*
Hi	*Stars* Geology Architecture Art Geography*	*Problem Children* Home Economics
Lo	*Cash Cows* Journalism Library* Public Administration*	*Dogs*

University C

	Hi	*Lo*
Hi	*Stars* Computer Science	*Problem Children*
Lo	*Cash Cows*	*Dogs*

tration of senior managerial time and the better use of scarce resources that results when the matrix highlights the problems and the opportunities. This article has attempted to show the potential application of product portfolio ideas to higher education. The steps outlined are to delineate the market, to define and estimate future market growth, to define and measure market share, and, to allocate programs to one of the four quadrants. Each of the steps is critical and needs care in definition and measurement, and, in universities the tasks should involve, wherever possible, the deans, chairpersons, and faculty of the programs. No step should become mechanical since this would oversimplify the problems and prevent discussion of the problems. The final, and most difficult step is to use the resulting matrices to initiate the decision making process. Again, the dangers of mechanization and oversimplification need to be stressed. The matrices do not provide automatic

TABLE 8: ***All master's programs***

Market share

University A

Market growth	*Hi*	*Lo*
Hi	*Stars* Chemistry Dance & Drama*	*Problem Children* Music Physical Education Home Economics Geology Business Speech & Audio* Geography* Languages*
Lo	*Cash Cows* Physics* Mathematics	*Dogs* Education Engineering* English Philosophy Political Science* History Economics Psychology Sociology Biology*

University B

Market growth	*Hi*	*Lo*
Hi	*Stars* Art Music Geology Architecture Physical Education Speech & Audio* Languages* Geography*	*Problem Children* Business Chemistry Home Economics
Lo	*Cash Cows* Education English Philosophy Sociology Public Administration* Journalism Library*	*Dogs* Engineering* History Political Science* Psychology Biology* Physics* Economics Mathematics

University C

Market growth	*Hi*	*Lo*
Hi	*Stars* Business Computer Science	*Problem Children* Music Physical Education Chemistry Speech & Audio* Languages*
Lo	*Cash Cows* Engineering* Economics Political Science* Psychology	*Dogs* Education English Philosophy Mathematics Biology* Physics* History Sociology

APPENDIX: Projected enrollments—master's programs

Program	*Extrapolation*[a]	*Coefficient of determination*[b] *(%)*	*Enrollment Fall 1981 (Fall 1978=100)*
Music	Exponential	89	150
Business	Power	86	109
Physical education	Linear	45	105
Education	Log	41	100
Engineering[c]	Power	33	101
Economics	Linear	94	95
English	Linear	94	58
Sociology	Exponential	91	70
History	Power	89	95
Philosophy	Linear	84	63
Psychology	Linear	71	104
Political science[c]	Log	23	91
Speech and audiology[c]	Power	22	106
Languages[c]	Log	1	109
Chemistry	Power	67	115
Mathematics	Log	56	79
Physics[c]	Log	28	100
Biology[c]	Exponential	8	101
Home economics	Power	92	129
Architecture	Linear	91	147
Computer science	Power	87	132
Geology	Power	86	139
Journalism	Exponential	75	85
Art	Power	51	109
Drama and dance[c]	Linear	32	150
Geography	Power	18	118
Library	Linear	9	95
Public administration[c]	Log	4	100
Nursing[d]	—	—	—

[a]Curve used to forecast enrollment.

[b]"Goodness of fit" between enrollments 1974–1978 and time.

[c]Coefficient of Determination so low that these programs are treated as "high-risk."

[d]Insufficient observations.

strategies. Each program has to be discussed in terms of the alternatives broadly outlined for it by its position in the matrix—alternative solutions are not ruled out. The discussions should center upon the costs (in terms of enrollments and consequent funds) of either expansion (in the case of cash cows and occasionally problem children), or, retrenchment (in the case of dogs and problem children). Only when the limitations of the data are understood and all the alternatives have been explored should decisions based on product portfolio matrices be made. In this respect the matrices do not really differ from any other managerial technique, but they may offer a sound, and particularly relevant, framework for the difficult decision making that lies before the senior managers of U.S. universities and colleges.

NOTES

1. "Meads Technique to Sort out the Losers," *Business Week,* March 11, 1972, pp. 124–130.
2. P. Kotler, "Strategies for Introducing Marketing into Non-profit Organizations," *Journal of Marketing,* Vol. 32, 1979, pp. 37–44.
3. B. D. Henderson, "The Product Portfolio," 1970, "Cash Traps," 1972, and "The Experience Curve Reviewed: The Growth-Share Matrix on the Product Portfolio," 1973. *Perspective Series,* Boston Consulting Group.
4. J. D. Millet, "Higher Education Management versus Business Management," *Educational Record,* Fall, 1975, p. 221.
5. See P. Kotler, "Strategies for Introducing Marketing into Non-profit Organizations," *Journal of Marketing,* Vol. 43, 1979, pp. 37–44, W. F. Massy, "A Dynamic Equilibrium Model for University Budget Planning," *Management Science,* Vol. 23, No. 3, 1976, pp. 248–256; D. S. P. Hopkins and W. F. Massy, "A Model for Planning the Transition to Equilibrium of a University Budget," *Management Science,* Vol 23, No. 11, 1977, pp. 1161–1168; R. Zemsky, R. Porter, and L. P. Oedel, "Decentralized Planning: To Share Responsibility," *Educational Record,* Summer 1978, pp. 229–253.
6. P. Doyle and G. D. Newbould, "A Strategic Approach to Marketing a University," *Journal of Educational Administration,* forthcoming, October, 1980.
7. P. Kotler, P. Doyle and G. D. Newbould.
8. G. S. Day, "Diagnosing the Product Portfolio," *Journal of Marketing,* April 1977, pp. 29–38.

SIOP—A POISON PREVENTION PROGRAM

It is a sad fact that in the United States over 1,500,000 children each year are the victims of accidental poisoning. Although the number of poisonings has not changed appreciably, the severity has certainly decreased. In 1968, for example, 22% of the recorded poisonings were due to salicylates (a crystalline compound, as in aspirin for relieving pain). In 1981, only 3% of poisonings were caused by these agents. The decrease is due to child safety containers and the effectiveness of poison prevention efforts. The most tragic aspect of the accidental poisoning is that 95% of the children poisoned are under adult supervision at the time, so most incidents could be averted if the parents of the victims took ordinary safety precautions.

These statistics have prompted the development of poison control centers based in hospitals throughout the country. Brokaw Hospital's Poison Control Center in Bloomington–Normal, Illinois, is typical of many of these facilities; it is coordinated through the hospital's pharmacy department. Brokaw Hospital's pharmacy staff decided that they had an obligation to do more than merely be efficient in treating poisonings as they occurred. They felt that active attempts had to be made to lower the number of accidental poisonings within the community. This resolution among the pharmacy staff initiated a movement to investigate the basic problem and implement an effective marketing strategy to prevent poisonings.

Through marketing research, it became appar-

Most of the material in this case was developed by Terry Trudeau, College of Pharmacy, Howard University, Washington, D.C.

ent to the staff members that children will eat or drink just about anything. It found that most poisoning agents are located in and around the house. The most commonly ingested substances were plants, household cleaning products, aspirin, vitamins, and cold medicines—in that order.

The principal poisoning substance is plants (12% of reported poisonings). Plants are rarely toxic (depending on species encountered), but they are a real challenge to the manner in which poison prevention and identification efforts are developed.

Four basic factors have been identified as leading to childhood poisonings: (1) accessibility of toxic agents, (2) the inquisitive nature of children, (3) the limited environment of a small house or apartment, which causes children to play near poisonous products (as in the kitchen or basement), and (4) the problems of communicating with children who are too young to understand the dangers of toxic products. The communications aspect was seen as the most crucial factor in establishing an effective poison prevention program.

DEVELOPMENT OF THE SIOP PROGRAM IN BLOOMINGTON–NORMAL, ILLINOIS

Presented with these facts, Terry Trudeau, director of the Poison Control Center, set about the task of developing an educational program that would teach children to avoid poisons and would instruct teachers and parents in the basics of poison prevention. This year-round program drew on existing ideas concerning poison prevention, and innovation was provided by staff members and professionals within the community.

A key aspect of poison prevention is the use of an easily recognized symbol. The traditional symbol for poison has been the skull and crossbones, but research shows that children often are attracted to this symbol because it suggests "playing pirate for fun," rather than danger and death. Symbols developed by other poison control centers in the United States also were ruled out, since none had sufficient impact to inspire a year-round poison prevention effort. It was decided to develop a new poison symbol that would be easily recognized, yet repellent to all age groups.

Designed with the help of the Illinois State University art staff, the symbol shown in Figure 1 has proved effective in tests with preschool and kindergarten children. Named "SIOP," the symbol is a stylized green snake against a bright orange, circular background. The symbol is effective both because of its colors (green has proved to be repellent, and orange is among the hues that are first recognized) and because of its shape (the circle is the first shape children recognize and remember). The SIOP symbol comes with an adhesive band that is long enough to fit around most household products. The band is also orange, a color not frequently used in commercial packaging, thus increasing the visibility of the symbol from all angles.

SIOP was designed to be as frightening to children as possible. This improves the chances that children will stay away from the symbol, even though they might not know what it stands for.

FIGURE 1: ***SIOP symbol***

Source: Terry Trudeau, Howard University, and Frank Braden, Lifemark Corporation, Houston, Texas.

However, the key to making the SIOP symbol an effective deterrent to all children was the creation of an educational program that conditions children to stay away from SIOP. Whenever and wherever children see the fanged green snake, they are taught to say, "No! SIOP!" (which is *poison* spelled backward). In addition, "Happy," the Poison Prevention Dog, was developed to serve as a foil to SIOP and teach children to avoid poisons. Happy barks whenever SIOP is near. This theme of good versus bad is carried throughout the program.

Locally, some programs have recruited a clown to add visibility to the program when displaying materials at such places as malls, children's fairs, and parties. Her name is Eppy Kak (Ipecac) and she is billed as the Poison Prevention Clown. Ipecac, by the way, is the drug used by parents to promote vomiting of ingested poison. Eppy Kak entertains by juggling, making balloon animals, telling jokes (bad ones), and playing kid games. A babysitter's guide to poison prevention has proven to be the most popular promotional piece to date.

The launching to the SIOP program coincided with the beginning of the National Poison Prevention Week. Much publicity was used in the area, including newspaper, television, and radio coverage of the new poison symbol. Distribution of the first SIOP symbols was accomplished by using the telephone company's mailing list to send SIOP stickers and a guide to poison prevention to each family in the county. Educational materials were delivered to all kindergartens, nursery schools, and day care centers. Teachers received a packet of materials containing instructions for using the program year-round. Each child received an activity book, a story pamphlet, a poison prevention guide, and a button. Additional materials were supplied on request.

Today, when new residents arrive in the community, they are sent SIOP stickers and pamphlets. The materials are also distributed in the school system. Natural childbirth classes, the public health department, and Brokaw's pediatrics ward help perpetuate the program by distributing SIOP materials. Grants from such organizations as the Jaycees and the Brokaw Hospital Service League have enabled free distribution of the materials. Many pharmacists serve on a speaker's bureau to present educational programs to schools and PTA groups.

Development of the program involved a joint effort among the Bloomington–Normal Jaycees, area universities, and the hospital.

Project Chairman and Brokaw Hospital Poison Control Director Terry Trudeau described the "Siop Program":

> The educational materials teach children to stay away and say "No! Siop!" (Poison spelled backward) whenever they see the symbol. What makes Siop different from other poison sticker programs is that Siop is also a comprehensive educational program geared at doing two things: teaching children to stay away from poisonous products and teaching poison prevention rules to children and adults. The "Siop Program" does not rely on a simple symbol scaring children away from poison, but rather educates through a coordinated total program.

EXPANSION OF SIOP BEYOND BLOOMINGTON–NORMAL, ILLINOIS

The program has spread worldwide with the help of strategically placed publicity. The SIOP program at Brokaw Hospital continues to receive inquiries each day from various locations. Each program participant is encouraged to use and expand upon the materials developed to make these effective for their geographic area. Materials have been translated into Spanish and German; some materials, such as a poison prevention plant brochure, have been expanded to include plants found in the specific region where the program will be implemented.

Terry Trudeau and others involved in developing the SIOP program feel greatly rewarded since the program's inception eight years ago. Among the many awards received is a federal grant from the Consumer Product Safety Commission for continued service in poison prevention. Several research studies indicate that the SIOP program creates intellectual awareness of poisons and an ability to discriminate poisonous from non-poisonous products. Also, SIOP warning labels have a greater effect on visual discrimination than any other symbol available for testing. Most important has been the decrease in the number of calls made to the center. And the severity of reported poisonings has diminished to an appreciable extent. But as the program has gained national and international acceptance there has been some criticism.

ANALYSIS OF EFFECTIVENESS

Dr. Morris K. Jackson, Department of Anatomy, Louisiana State University Medical Center, Shreveport, offered the following opinion concerning the use of a stylized snake as the central focus of the SIOP program:

> Most ophiologists become quite ired at the use of a snake, symbol or not, which is designed to create an adverse and negative reaction about snakes. The reinforcement of negative thoughts and false conceptualizations about snakes, we fear, might create animosity towards an already overhated creature. We argue that SIOP might establish a new generation of hardened snake-phobes in the future and likewise stir the "dragons of Eden" within adults today. Most of us would like for the American public to think of the snake as the two entwined serpents on the staff of the caduceus—the symbol of healing and the physician, instead of SIOP the poison bearer. Can we afford to overlook another onslaught (however subtle) against the snake, even though SIOP was never intended to be a snake? Conversely, SIOP is very effective in his role and many parents are grateful. Can we afford not to have a SIOP?

In 1981 an attitudinal study was conducted in Springfield, Illinois, to test whether the SIOP program negatively influenced childhood conception of snakes. The sample for this study was made up of 90 three- and four-year-old children from four different nursery school classrooms. Two of the classrooms were used as an experimental group and two as the control, with 45 children in each group. The results were published in *Hepatological Review*.

The results from the analysis of data suggested that there was no significant difference between the groups tested. The data collected in the study indicated that the SIOP program has no significant effect on a child's attitudes toward snakes. Neither does the program have a significant effect on their conception of good and bad snakes.

The SIOP Poison Prevention Research and Education Program believes that it is based on thorough research and creates no negative childhood attitudes toward snakes. The program has been proven effective due to the dramatic reduction of accidental poisonings in those communities where the program has been implemented. Therefore, according to the SIOP supporters, the answer to Dr. Jackson's final questions is readily evident. Where the health and welfare of our children is involved, we can ill afford not to have a SIOP.

Also, a study has been published in the *American Journal of Public Health* to evaluate the effectiveness of the SIOP Poison Prevention Program, which included an educational program and the use of warning labels, on improving verbal and visual discrimination of poisonous and non-poisonous products for preschool children. The study sample consisted of 156 day care and nursery school children randomly assigned to one of four treatment groups: (1) education program with SIOP warning labels, (2) educational program, (3) SIOP warning labels, and (4) control.

A combination of the educational program with the use of SIOP warning labels proved to be the most effective approach in both verbal and visual discrimination. The educational program proved more effective for verbal discrimination and the SIOP warning labels proved more effective in improving visual discrimination. The results suggest two components for an effective poison prevention program: an intellectual awareness of poisons and an ability to visually discriminate poisonous from nonpoisonous products. The educational program tended to facilitate intellectual awareness while SIOP warning labels had a greater effect on visual discrimination.

FUTURE DIRECTIONS

New ways are constantly sought to improve and spread the SIOP program and materials. The program is now becoming a national effort; Texas and Louisiana have adopted it, and other areas are in the process of doing so. Worldwide recognition is extending the program, with inquiries coming from as far as Australia and France. New ideas about distribution and target markets (such as industrial chemicals) are being explored in an effort to develop a single, comprehensive poison prevention program for the country. Although accidental poisonings will always be a problem, the SIOP program is taking positive steps to prevent them.

Overall, the SIOP program remains one of the most scientifically based and validated prevention programs of any type in existence. Terry Trudeau provides the following summary of the current challenge.

Our main problem is that of coordination. The program has become so large that it is no longer a part-time effort. Orders roll in for materials that must be handled by our printer as he has time. I feel that if an educational publisher could be recruited to handle the program its continued success would be assured. However, to date we have had no serious inquiries. Personally, I'm happy that SIOP has done so well, yet because we are involved in a number of other things, the developers of SIOP are hesitant to make the program our life's work. The questions we are asking are whether we should be content with the success we have had (and the research we have added to the field) or should we reach for new levels and markets? Time and geographic considerations will have the major impact on our decisions.

Summing up my thoughts, we have certainly achieved our local goals of decreasing the number and severity of childhood poisonings in our area. The Brokaw Poison Center has become a visible entity within the community. Due to lack of full time personnel connected with the SIOP program, the program will spread mainly by diffusion of materials and information. If an educational publisher is recruited to spear-head the program, it will be actively promoted. This would represent a new phase in program development.

II: ORGANIZING MARKETING

Creating a market-oriented organization requires the support of top management and an effective organization design. The nonprofit organization must assess the need for using marketing and developing the marketing function. Marketing research and marketing planning are important considerations when developing a marketing function for a nonprofit organization.

For Part II we have selected articles and cases that focus on issues in the effective administration of marketing effort. Procedures for carrying out the marketing plan and an effective marketing information system to aid in marketing control are important in organizing marketing in a nonprofit organization. Throughout this section we focus on questions and issues that relate to necessary involvement for the nonprofit sector to develop a marketing organization.

The first article is "Why Data Systems in Nonprofit Organizations Fail" by Regina Herzlinger. She points out that nonprofit institutions have as much need for efficient information and control systems as for-profit organizations do; after all, top management in the "nonprofits" are similarly burdened with acute budgeting problems and policy issues whose resolution depends on the availability and sensible exploitation of accurate, current data. But the unbusinesslike accounting practices that characterize many government agencies and the seat-of-the-pants managerial style of many private agency executives result in neglect and poor handling of the in-house information systems. This article examines this phenomenon and offers guidelines—as well as some hope—for improvement.

The second article is "Marketing: One YMCA Attacks the Problems" by Jacqueline Janders. This selection examines how a nonprofit organization such as the YMCA can use marketing technology. The Milwaukee YMCA developed and implemented some marketing plans and found the experience very rewarding. This article explores these experiences.

The third article, by Seymour H. Fine, is entitled "Strategic Planning in the Marketing of a Government Program." Many CETA administrators believe that they are dealing in jobs for the economically disadvantaged. Fine suggests not only jobs, but also alternative products for CETA. A marketing plan is built around these new-product opportunities. The government-sponsored worker training program is thus added to the list of societal problems that could utilize marketing principles.

The fourth article is "The Marketing Audit: A Tool for Health Services Organizations" by Eric N. Berkowitz and William A. Flexner. These authors highlight the important concerns in the "hands-on" development and implementation of a marketing plan for health care services.

Cases in this section include "Planned Parenthood of Atlanta" and "District of Columbia Summer Youth Program."

Why Data Systems in Nonprofit Organizations Fail

REGINA HERZLINGER

The director of a large social service agency in a New England state was told at fiscal midyear that unexpectedly lower tax revenues had forced a 5 percent reduction in his budget (or about $100 million). The distribution of the cut among the different programs was left to his judgment, but he couldn't respond to the order in a reasonable manner because he lacked the resources that would have given him the needed information. The state's use of a line-item, object-of-expense budgeting and accounting system frustrated his efforts to learn how much money had been committed to different programs; the statistical system that was supposed to tell him how many people were served and how many services were delivered wasn't working; and, to boot, the most recent cost data were four months out of date.

Lacking relevant information, he had to make a judgment solely on the basis of political considerations. He chose to cut the budgets of those programs affecting people with the least political influence—abandoned children and the mentally retarded.

The state of control and information systems in most nonprofit organizations is dismal. Despite billions of dollars spent to provide relevant, accurate, and timely data, few nonprofit organizations possess systems whose quality equals those found in large, profit-oriented corporations. Nonprofit organizations do not lack data; if anything, they enjoy an overabundance of numbers and statistics. Rather, they lack *systematically* provided information to help management do its job. Without good information, it is obviously difficult for managers to make reasoned and informed decisions, evaluate performance, motivate their employees, and protect the institution against fraud.

This problem is by no means confined to public agencies; it also crops up in private, nonprofit organizations.

Consider the case of one voluntary agency that delivered services ranging from medical care to adult education classes. Once boasting a healthy endowment and a substantial yield on its endowment, the agency had suffered through three consecutive years of increasing deficits and was suspended on the brink of bankruptcy.

Its director was a controversial person who had converted it from a stodgy, upper-class "charity" to a vital, existing organization. Or so her supporters said. Her detractors, convinced that she was responsible for the precarious financial position, accused her of wasting money on frivolous, faddish activities that benefited neither their participants nor the organization's reputation.

Was she a superlative manager or an incompetent? The answer to that question was vital to the organization's future. But it couldn't be answered objectively; the agency's board simply had too little information with which to evaluate the quality of her management. The agency had no budget, no output data, and such a poor system of internal controls that even the number of members was in doubt.

Many nonprofit organizations are deficient in the routinized internal control that ensures the integrity of the accounting for expenditures and

---

Reprinted by permission of the *Harvard Business Review*. "Why data systems in nonprofit organizations fail" by Regina Herzlinger (January–February 1977), pp. 81–86.

services. The welfare error rate is a familiar subject of newspaper stores. Often as high as 40 percent, the error rate consists of seemingly random underpayments and overpayments to welfare recipients. It is vivid evidence of a poor system of internal control.

A similar case is the Guaranteed Student Loan Program, administered by the Office of Education of HEW. Every one of the program's annual financial statements has received an "adverse" opinion from the General Accounting Office. This opinion is rendered, in part, because the program's managers do not know the magnitude of the loans they have insured and therefore can accurately account for neither the contingent reserves account on their balance sheet nor the loss expense account on their income statement. The loan volume outstanding is estimated at $7 billion to $8 billion—with an unknown amount in the range of $1 billion for which there are no proper accounting records. The possibilities for fraud in these cases are staggering.

The presence of a management information system does not guarantee its proper use, of course. Many hospitals, for example, identify their outpatient departments as "money losers," while in fact the outpatient department frequently substantially offsets the total operating costs of the hospital and may even contribute to covering the direct costs of its inpatient side.

The losing position of the outpatient department is merely an artifact of some states' medical aid systems, in which a ceiling is placed on the reimbursement a hospital receives per inpatient day, while reimbursement for the outpatient department is handled on a "cost or charges, whichever is lower" basis. To maximize reimbursement, a hospital will allocate as many "joint costs" as possible to the outpatient department and thereby create an accounting "loser." This system of cost accounting is perfectly sensible for purposes of reimbursement, but it creates an unfair basis for the evaluation of the manager of an outpatient department.

More serious are situations in which the data network leads to a totally inappropriate course of action. In the mid-1960s, the U.S. Department of Labor designed an elaborate information system for programs to train the hard-core unemployed and place them in useful employment. While the system measured many aspects of cost and output, one measure was of paramount importance: number of people placed in jobs. When Labor Department supervisors visited a local manpower office, they particularly wanted to know the number of placements the director had generated.

The directors of the local programs got the message. Soon they were ensuring a high placement rate through a practice known as "creaming"—that is, they skimmed the cream of the unemployed and accepted only persons who were temporarily unemployed and who had a high probability of appropriate placement. This strategy was obviously antithetical to the purpose of the national program.

In some far-removed location in a public agency or a private nonprofit organization, computing equipment frequently stands idle, away from prying eyes—another symptom of the problem. It is idle because the computer has not "worked out" for its intended purpose. Its intended purpose may have been based on a totally unrealistic notion of what an information system can do. When the inevitable failure occurs, the computer gets the blame, anthropomorphically, and ignominiously disappears.

Computer graveyards are most often found in large hospitals and welfare departments. They have mammoth data-processing requirements that supposedly can be met by buying large computers and "integrated" management information system packages. The systems will somehow solve all the organizations' information needs, from record keeping to planning and control reports. Since the human mechanisms for obtaining and "inputting" the data are weak, however, an integrated system never quite succeeds. Moreover, the technical problems of programming and operating such a system are sometimes beyond the capability of the organization and its system contractor.

AT THE ROOT OF THE PROBLEM

A major cause of the problem is the method of financing such organizations. Funding in block grants, which vary with neither volume nor quality of service and which are made before the work is done, does not reward effective and efficient performance and gives managers little incentive to encumber themselves with tighter controls.

The best way to change this attitude is to make the form of funding more like the financing mechanism used in the private sector. Financing the *consumers* of services—rather than the *suppliers* of services—would impose the discipline of the marketplace on the organizations. Consumers, armed with purchasing power, could pick and choose among them.

Such a policy change, however, is unlikely to occur. Proposals for it have been aired since early in the twentieth century; the most recent one is Milton Friedman's plan for the use of vouchers in education. Although the federal government has experimented with vouchers in education and housing, it shows little sense of urgency about adopting these mechanisms. Even the laudable negative income tax idea—a voucher-like device which, among other benefits, would eliminate much of the paper pushing in welfare departments—is now languishing in academic journals.

Admittedly, nonprofit organizations are beset by demands for data from financial supporters and other parties. A typical hospital files financial and statistical reports with a number of insurance companies, the state in which it is located, the federal government, the planning agencies in its area, the licensing authorities, the certificate-of-need agency personnel, and the quality and utilization review administration—not to mention the financial statement it prepares, on a fund-accounting basis, for its own board of trustees. None of these statements duplicates another in content or format. School systems use an accounting system recommended by the U.S. Office of Education that has more than one million possible entries!

Obviously, many factors inhibiting improved information handling are beyond the control of a nonprofit organization. Yet the one factor accounting for most failures of information systems lies directly within the control of the organization: the characteristics and attitudes of top management.

Rarely does one hear the executives of a nonprofit organization described as being "good with numbers." More frequently, the accolades are "creative," "innovative," "caring," or "great scholars." Being good with numbers may actually do the managerial image a disservice, for it implies the absence of such qualitative skills as creativity, courage, and humanitarianism. Indeed, some managers of nonprofits view their lack of quantitative skills as a rather endearing imperfection—like having freckles.

Many of these managers were initially professionals who carry with them the culture and attitudes of the professional, including strong resistance to quantitative measures of their organizations' activities. They argue, sometimes persuasively, that professional work is too complex and diffuse in its impact to be easily accounted for and that naive attempts to account for its outcome might undermine the credibility and integrity of the work itself.

A case in point is the experience of the state of Michigan, which in 1969 began a program to collect data on the resources and achievements of its school systems. The purpose of the assessment was to link expenditures with results and presumably to hold school personnel responsible for their performance.

The project was greeted with such hostility that the department of education retreated from its original goals. The report on the third year of the project stressed that the assessment "is not to be viewed as an evaluation of Michigan schools. Instead it is to provide information on . . . student needs." The next year the department expanded its cautionary position, explaining that the program "does not indicate which schools or districts are most effective or efficient."[1]

Many professionals-turned-managers do not command the technical skills required for the design and implementation of a good information system. When I have taught accounting to top executives of large nonprofit organizations, they have often told me that until then they had never been able to understand their own financial statements.

A lack of technical skills and an institutionalized aversion to measurement, when combined with the traditional definition of the role of manager in these organizations, lead many managers of nonprofit institutions to abdicate the task of designing and implementing a sound information system to their staffs, particularly to their accountants. A manager will say, "I don't know much about these numbers, but my accountant is a genius." It is doubtful that the manager has the capability to judge an accountant's genius.

SOME SOLUTIONS

The problem of the multiplicity of external demand for data could be partly reduced through coordination of the agencies that fund a particular organizational entity in the design of the data system for monitoring the program. The many federal agencies that finance community health centers could, for example, design a single system that would meet not only their data needs but also those of the insurance companies and the state welfare departments involved.

We should not, however, be overly sanguine about the likelihood of this solution. Under the present structure of federal and most other government units, the different groups have no reason to coordinate. Moreover, organizations and benefactors fund programs for different reasons, and they are unlikely to agree on a common data set that meets all their needs. Finally, even if federal and state agencies could cooperate on information system design, their actions would still be subject to legislative review, which is not always intelligent or objective.

An approach different from most has been taken by the National Centers for health Statistics and for health Services Research and Development. They have designed a data system for planning and evaluating purposes. The network, now in its early stages of implementation, involves these steps:

- The federal level specifies a very small amount of information for each program to generate.
- State and local programs receive funding for experimentation with the installation of systems that meet their internal needs.
- The federal government reimburses the state and local bodies for providing the required data.

This approach has several admirable aspects: (1) the requirements for external data are kept to a minimum; (b) the operational programs are given the opportunity, and funding, to integrate the external data into a system that meets their needs; and (c) the users must pay for the data. The user payment feature is important and unusual because the payment is direct and thus tends to make agencies asking for the data more sensitive to the financial impact of their requests.

Until the necessity and feasibility of approaches like that of the National Centers are recognized, nonprofit organizations must limp along individually as best they can. Much depends on the quality of their managers, who, as I pointed out earlier, are often long on professional training and experience but short on administrative skills and experience. The management component of most professional training is usually completely absent, limited to office practices such as billing, or covered through a quick survey course of administrative techniques—a week on accounting, a week on interpersonal behavior, and so on. This level of education is unlikely to develop people with the skills and attitudes of professional managers. Many professional schools, however, are beginning to offer their students appropriate managerial training courses.

GUIDELINES FOR MANAGERS

Of course, the impact of that trend will not be felt for a while, so the main thrust of the improvement of information systems must lie with present managers. Here are some suggestions for improvement of the design, installation, and operation of information systems:

System Design. The top manager who remains uninvolved in the design of the content of the system negates the reason for its existence. Participation in the system design process ensures that the system is relevant and responsive to management's needs.

It is also important to recognize that information systems must meet different needs (also, some questions can be answered on a totally ad hoc basis). The framework developed by Robert N. Anthony is very useful for classifying different types of information systems.[2] He distinguishes three managerial functions and delineates the characteristics of the different kinds of information systems needed to support these functions.

Measurement of output and efficiency in most nonprofit institutions is a big problem. The output is usually a service, with a host of measurable attributes. Furthermore, since the output is generally not sold, it is impossible to measure it in financial terms by assigning it a market value. Some system designers go overboard in an attempt to solve the problem. A small nursing agency, for example, drew up a list of 103 finely grained output measures and 21 efficiency measures per nurse. To get an overall measure of effectiveness, the agency then adjusted and weighted these criteria in some arcane manner. Such efforts result in data of dubious validity. A balanced solution sets a standard of measurement without excessive elaboration.

An important component of the design phase is the stipulation of the means for implementing the system, including estimates of time required, cost involved, and milestones to be achieved. This step is frequently omitted or neglected because managers justify information systems on a "cost-saving" basis and fear that documentation of the costs of installing the system will belie their initial estimates.

Since most nonprofit organizations seriously underfund their information system activities, it is unrealistic and unnecessary to justify installation of a new design on a cost-saving basis. Rather, they should be justified on benefit/cost reasoning—that is, that the benefits of the system will exceed its cost. And the design phase should include meticulous documentation of these costs.

The design phase should also include designation of the organizational unit that will install and/or operate the system. Otherwise, such responsibility is diffused along the breadth of the organization. This leads to difficulties in assigning responsibility and authority.

Installation. An important and frequently neglected pre-condition to success is adequate pretesting of the form and content of the system. The organization should not stint in the planning and financing of the pretesting phase.

Extensive training of those who will use and operate the system is a worthwhile investment. Because of the high rate of turnover at the top level of most nonprofit organizations, it is important to "institutionalize" the system through training.

Thorough documentation of all aspects of the form and content of the system is an essential part of the installation process, especially the preparation of manuals explaining how every item of input or output is to be measured. At a minimum, the organization should draw up a chart of the accounts used for reporting purposes and give a detailed explanation of how and when they are to be recognized. This is a tedious job, often neglected. Furthermore some designers gain power from the absence of documentation, making them the only ones who know how to run the system.

Operation. An information system used regularly by top management for making such key decisions as budget allocation will eventually overcome any initial flaws of design and installation. At the same time, it is important to designate an appropriate organizational unit for the routinized production of the information. If this unit is different from the one that designed the system, the people in the former unit will be less reluctant to modify the system. This policy of separation, however, may cost the organization much more money than having one unit responsible for the operation of the system as well as its design.

Most of the issues in the design and implementation of these information systems in nonprofit institutions are similar to those in profit-oriented organizations. If the condition of such systems in these two types of organizations were also the same, we would enjoy a much more efficient economic environment.

NOTES

1. Jerome T. Murphy and David K. Cohen, "Accountability in Education—the Michigan Experience," *The Public Interest,* Summer 1974, p. 62.
2. See Robert N. Anthony, *Planning and Control Systems: A Framework for Analysis* (Boston: division of Research, Harvard Business School, 1965), particularly the first three chapters.

Marketing: One YMCA Attacks the Problems

JACQUELINE JANDERS

One of the earliest examples of marketing in the YMCA took place in New York City right after the Civil War. The original concept of the YMCA was a simple Association of young men united in Christ. Men used to meet regularly in religious reading rooms usually located above shops and stores.

The city was teeming with saloons and theatres and dance halls from which the Association wanted to attract the young men. One evening, as a group of YMCA members sat discussing how they could get more young men to join the association, one of their number, businessman J. Pierpont Morgan, said, "If you want to attract the young men of today, you'll have to bring the YMCA down out of these upper rooms." That is just what they did and the first YMCA building was constructed in 1869.

Ever since the YMCA came down out of the upper rooms and began providing services for which dues and fees are charged, the YMCA has been in the "marketplace."

At its most elementary level a market exists whenever a buyer and a seller come together for a mutually beneficial exchange of a product, a service, an idea. Usually it is an exchange involving money. Now, the YMCA has not thought in terms of buying and selling, but we do provide programs

---

Reprinted with permission from *Perspective Magazine*/Journal of Professional YMCA Directors in the United States.

and services for which people pay dues and fees. Therefore in a sense there is a buyer and a seller and we have created a market.

As in the story above there is much more to marketing than that which takes place at the point of exchange. This article is about the value and the process of marketing in today's multi-service YMCA.

If we are indeed concerned with "being about our Father's business" and enriching the lives of people, we should use every management skill available to us. The most successful YMCA's are those which have truly thought they were in the "People Business" and have focused on satisfying the needs of people. Modern marketing can facilitate this process.

MORE THAN SEMANTIC

The problem with most discussions of marketing is that what gets emphasized is *promotion and selling,* not marketing. The difference is more than semantic. Selling focuses on the needs of the seller; the YMCA's need to enroll members and sign up participants. While selling is a part of marketing, marketing moves far back from the point of sale and focuses on the needs of the buyer; the potential member, the customer.

Marketing asks the questions: Who is the customer? Where is the customer? What are the customer's needs and wants? . . . And what value-satisfying programs and services can we provide that the customer will want to buy? I do not mean to imply that selling is unimportant. It is very important and I shall have more to say about selling later. But because marketing is a more complex and sophisticated management process, it often gets ignored.

Marketing is concerned with the identification of the needs and wants of potential members and the whole series of activities associated with the creation and delivery of programs and services which satisfy these needs. It is a concept which starts with top management and must become a way of thinking in every nook and cranny of the organization. YMCA directors are very program and operations oriented. Sometimes we think and act as if we were in the program business instead of the people business. Marketing is a management approach which is customer-oriented. The program or product is the consequence of the marketing effort not the starting point.

The Milwaukee YMCA initiated an in-depth Marketing Training Project in Fall, 1973 for all professional management staff. President M. Brutus Baker; Dick Protzmann, Vice President for Branch Operations; Larry Smith, Director of Manpower Development; and I were the Marketing Training Project Team for planning and implementation of the program. Professor Dick Berry, Management Specialist in Marketing from the School of Business and Management of the University of Wisconsin, was our co-planner, consultant and trainer.

The Marketing Training Project had two objectives:

- A professional staff trained in the application of marketing principles and techniques to the end that these will be applied to the planning, development, packaging and promotion of YMCA programs . . . And because we are a results-oriented organization we established a measurable objective. . . .
- Six useful marketing proposals for new or improved programs and creation of new markets to help achieve our corporate operating goals.

Briefly, the design of the training project was:

- Selected readings, prepared by Berry to introduce us to the study of marketing as a modern management discipline
- A series of seminars and workshops for additional input, exploration and training in the many aspects of the marketing function
- Establishment of task teams to help internalize and put into practice learnings about marketing

The content of the several workshops and seminars included:

- Marketing strategy and the marketing-mix concept
- Marketing planning
- Customer orientation at contact point of front desk and telephone inquiry
- The role of the public relations program in marketing
- The application of counsellor selling techniques
- Telephone contact and sales
- Corporate planning and setting Branch unit objectives

There were so many components to the Marketing Training Project that time and space here will not permit me to adequately report on all of them. Perhaps the concept of marketing and its dynamic implications for the YMCA can best be demonstrated by sharing with you the work of the marketing planning task forces and some of the results of their work.

ESTABLISHING THE MARKETING PLANNING TASK FORCES

As I have already suggested in the statement of objectives and the design of the training project the task forces had two purposes:

1. Training: to be a vehicle for practicing and internalizing marketing principles and techniques
2. Results: preparation of 6 useful marketing proposals that could be made operational in the Milwaukee YMCA

The function of the task forces was Marketing Planning. The project team selected six program areas which we believed would best lend themselves to the experience; either because they were operated Association-wide and would be familiar to most staff, or because they were recognized problem areas, or because they were considered to be key market areas. It was decided to establish a marketing task force to develop a marketing plan for each of the following:

- Health Clubs
- Tot Time preschool education program
- Y-Indian Guides—parent–child program
- Family Program and Membership
- Camping
- Food Service

Six professional marketing directors, laymen from business and industry, were recruited to serve as marketing consultants to the task teams. Each of these people agreed to meet with one of the task forces. Their function was to bring marketing expertise to the planning and an objective point of view to the program area. A Staff Chairman for each group was appointed to work with the various consultants and trainers, and to present the final marketing proposal.

Each of the 43 professional staff people in the Milwaukee YMCA was assigned to one of these task forces. Ideally, members of a marketing planning group should be selected for their creative ability, expertise in the program area, commitment to the task and influence in carrying out the resulting marketing program.

However, in this case because the primary purpose was training, *all staff were assigned,* across organizational lines, selected only partly for their interest, commitment or expertise in the particular program area.

After the task forces had met several times I was assigned to work with them. Obviously the success of each group depended upon the degree to which full group interaction could be generated and sustained. My job was to help them pull together as a single creative unit building on each other's ideas and working toward a common goal.

At the same time I needed to keep before the groups all of the marketing concepts and methods Berry had given us in the initial 2 day seminar.

MARKETING MIX

One of the most helpful tools provided during the first workshop was the concept of the "Marketing Mix." The marketing mix is the idea that there is a pattern of important elements or ingredients in every marketing plan. These elements are the 4-p's . . . product, place, price and promotion.

The mixing of these factors, which management controls, with external forces bearing upon the market, results in the formula for success which becomes the marketing plan. The external forces with which the 4-p's must be considered are consumer buying behavior, life styles, competition, the law, etc., which management does not control, but about which it must be thoroughly knowledgeable.

In order for the planning groups to properly mix all of the ingredients, Berry had stressed the importance of situation analysis and focusing on objectives. Roughly, the thought process and discussion from which ideas will flow and plans will evolve looks something like this:

Focus on objectives:

- What segments of the market are we dealing with?
- What are the needs of the customer?
- How can we satisfy these needs?
- What do we really want to do?
- Program or service objectives.

Situation analysis:

- Consider broad strategies.
- Consider corporate operating goals.
- Consider the customer viewpoint.
- Analyze strengths and weaknesses.
- What are the problems and opportunities?
- Consider the product.
- Consider the organization's resources.
- Consider competition.

Mix all of the above . . . explore the resulting ideas . . . build on the best ideas . . . assess the minimum requirements to meet customer needs . . . identify features and benefits that will have the greatest customer impact . . . apply resources of time, money, staff and facilities. If workable, develop the idea and document the plan. If *not* workable, keep mixing alternative ideas.

The examples I will use to reveal the marketing planning process are taken from the experiences of the task forces. We were a-borning something new for the YMCA and there is no shame in suffering birth pains.

OVERCOMING ROAD BLOCKS

One of the problems all of the task forces initially encountered was the shift from marketing theory to practice. For example, the matter of setting objectives.

It was at first difficult for the groups to distinguish between identifying the objectives of the task team itself and the objectives of the program area they were assigned. In other words: What was indeed the task of the group and what was expected of them? And what were the objectives of the program category they were assigned? And again, what were the objectives of the marketing plan they would develop?

As you may imagine, some task force members wanted to set dollar and enrollment objectives similar to those they had already identified in the Branch budgets. These were the operators. Others who thought marketing means promotion leaped immediately to set promotion and advertising objectives. Others dealt with the ideal philosophical purposes of the YMCA and still others with the individual curriculum, program or fitness objectives.

The truth of the matter is that all of these are legitimate considerations in the marketing mix, but the group had another obstacle to overcome first. It was that of understanding and believing in their mission. A marketing planning group is essentially an invention or idea group. Our purpose was to identify new market segments, create a new program or improve an old one based on the needs of the market segment and to devise ways and means, including new promotion techniques, to deliver the program. Considerable time was spent in each group clarifying the above.

As each group began to analyze its marketing opportunities and group members were beginning to build on each other's ideas the following road blocks would also appear:

"We're already doing all we can." "We can't attract any more people until we get a new building." "It's really the price that's too high," "We tried that in my former Association and it didn't work." "No YMCA program should be self-sustaining." "People don't really want what they need." "That's P.R.'s job!"

Participatory management, in the involvement of line managers in corporate planning and decision making, always sounds like a grand idea. However, the additional effort and responsibility it demands requires a lot of extra hard work. And who needs that?

If the work of the task forces was ever to get off the ground and become productive we had to clarify our mission and find a positive focus. It occurred to me that if the groups could picture the total corporate planning process and realize that they had been given the opportunity to participate in strategic planning for the Association it would clarify what we were doing.

They would see that this was a serious assignment, the results of which would greatly influence the future of the Milwaukee YMCA. A brief blackboard outline helped the groups see how strategic marketing planning fits into the total planning processes of the Association.

Further, they began to see that the kind of planning now required of them could serve their own interests later in the establishment and achievement of Branch unit objectives. These insights helped the groups gain confidence in their function as planners and we were able to move on.

IDENTIFYING THE PROGRAM AND MARKET AREA OF EXPLORATION

The next step was to define and agree upon the program and market area in which the task force was to work. This may seem like a simple step in view of the assignments given. It really was not so obvious. For example, my first meeting with the family program and membership task force went something like this:

Minutes of three previous meetings were distributed which revealed that the group had done some homework. They had researched and discussed the philosophy of family program in the Milwaukee YMCA. They had compiled a list of physical and educational program offerings and membership statistics on the two family serving Branches in operation at the time. They had also identified membership enrollment objectives for these two Branches for the coming year.

I asked the group which specific market they were interested in programming for. "Well, what do you mean? We're interested in selling memberships. We need to program for men, women, boys and girls . . . all of them, of course!"

This response demonstrated that we needed to get a better focus on the work of the task force if we were going to create any new markets or develop any new programs (the real work of the task force). We needed to narrow the perimeters of our work or time limitations and frustration would immobilize the team.

I rephrased the question, this time with a program emphasis. "What are the programs that you believe are most needed or wanted by families?" This resulted in some narrowing identification, mostly of physical programs, youth activities and health club services. Then one group member said, "Look, it's a package. Only Family Memberships are available, so when you buy a membership you get it all for the whole family—Mom, Dad and all the kids."

We were getting nearer to answering the original question so I asked, "Can we identify a YMCA family? Is it just any old combination of men, women, boys and girls?" There followed some discussion about how the young couple in the high-rise could be considered a "family," and that the teenager whose parents buy him a membership is certainly "part" of a family. Well, after several more hours and the aid of a "life cycle" chart and a close look at the characteristics of the families already enrolled, the group identified that the specific market segment we were most interested in was "young families, fathers and mothers with children between the ages of 6 and 12, living together."

At subsequent meetings we further defined the

program and market by looking in depth at the needs, desires, problems and capabilities of the target families. We zeroed in on the developmental tasks of children in this age category. We discussed the predominant life style and family income and educational level of the families in the prescribed Branch service areas. We looked at the number and the concentration by neighborhoods of the target families.

We brainstormed about the real needs of families in this life cycle. Many of us personally recalled how we felt as children or parents at these ages. What were our desires, our needs, the normal problems of family life? How did or how could the Y have helped? We looked at how existing programs could help strengthen family life. In short, we conducted a total situation analysis of what we really wanted to do in relation to the needs of the families who were the target market segment we had identified.

By defining the program area in consumer terms and by focusing on the real needs of families the task force became more innovative. We began to deal more with family communications, values and relationships.

These, even more than physical fitness and leisure time activities, were seen as the real needs to be satisfied through family programming. New ways of appealing to couples and involving whole families were explored. New program ideas emerged. Women, with their changing roles, attitudes, self image and aspirations were identified as a whole new market on which to concentrate.

Outside marketing consultants were helpful. "You have to realize that people do not need the YMCA to exist," one said. "However, as their basic needs are provided for, people begin to realize that man does not live by bread alone. The satisfactions the Y is concerned with are the intangible, though very real needs of most people. We have to first identify and then find ways of helping people recognize these needs; then we can satisfy them."

On another occasion during a heated discussion one of the outside marketing consultants said:

> Look, you people act as if you're ashamed to charge a legitimate fee for your programs. If you believe in your basic service you know its value, and you want to make it available to as many folks as possible.
>
> To keep the price of the basic service as reasonable as possible, you have to charge the full cost on the extra services that people want. It's a different market. In our company we know what our basic service is. It has to do with our purpose. Anything extra we offer we charge what we need to . . . so we can continue to provide our basic service to more and more people at a reasonable rate.

Bravo!

COMPILING AND APPLYING BACKGROUND MATERIAL

Adequate preparation of information relative to the program and market subject area is absolutely essential to successful marketing planning.

A narrative description of each program category and some statistical data on existing programs had been prepared for each of the task forces at the time of assignment in order to get them started. To enable us to do a thorough situation analysis, considerably more research and documentation of facts had to be compiled as questions came up.

Most of this data was assembled by the task forces from existing information readily available in our own or other YMCA records or from published sources such as census tracts, etc. Generally no new market studies were undertaken by the task forces. The Health Club task force conducted one small survey to test "felt-needs" of potential members.

The information needed for each of the program areas we were considering included:

- *Market size and trends:* Number of people in the market segment, the number and size of families, were they increasing, decreasing or relocating in the service area? . . . mobility, income, life style, purchasing preferences, etc.
- *Competition:* Who and what is our competi-

tion? . . . visit it, collect samples of advertising and literature, compare prices and benefits, observe sales techniques, etc.

- *Technical program information:* Program resources available within the Y or in the field. Research or development already underway. Example: Havighurst's "Developmental Tasks and Education" was used by the Camping task force; Milwaukee Area Technical College tested Tot Time teachers' curriculum; National YMCA and other research in the field of family life education was reviewed.
- *YMCA policy or legal controls:* The Tot Time task force considered State of Wisconsin standards for preschool programs. The Camping task force considered YMCA and American Camping Association standards.

Here are other examples of how the above information was secured and its usefulness to the task forces.

Market-Size and Trends. The Tot Time task force compiled statistical population data on children under five years of age for each branch service area.

This information helped us identify that in some instances we were operating preschool programs in locations determined by where the facilities or teachers were available and primarily counting on these outside sources to provide enrollment. An examination of the statistics, by neighborhoods, revealed that the concentrations of very young families with children of this age were actually located elsewhere in the service area. These facts were certainly important in our "Place" considerations.

The statistics also revealed that the population under 5 years of age in the Greater Milwaukee area is approximately 100,000. Further, that of this number only 4,400 were enrolled in any kind of nursery program.

From the compiled information the Tot Time task force was able to identify and locate its target market segment and conclude that the growth potential for Tot Time programs was extensive for the next two to five years, based on the size and trend of the market.

On Competition. The Health Club task force members individually visited and filed reports on seven private and commercial competitive health clubs in the Greater Milwaukee area, and three successful YMCA health clubs in other cities. The most valuable learnings from these visits were:

- The importance of quality: clean, comfortable, attractive, even posh facilities commensurate with the tastes of the market segment most likely to pay for these services.
- Complete customer-orientation . . . use of counsellor selling. In every instance the potential customer was asked, "What do you want to accomplish?" Then the sales counsellor concentrated on showing how the health club membership could help the member achieve his personal goals.

The strength in the commercial clubs was the emphasis on sales.

Research indicated that their weakness is that there is only the most superficial attention to health and fitness programs and almost no expertise in this area. Whereas the YMCA has the expertise and the programs, our greatest weakness was in not having any kind of focus on sales.

An example of this fact came out in one of our counsellor selling workshops. During a role-playing exercise the professional YMCA director, upon meeting the prospect, conducted a tour of the facilities. The overwhelming tendency was to talk only about the facilities. "This is our beautiful pool." "Here's our exercise room." "We have massage available, too."

Obviously, most of these facilities when they are seen speak for themselves as to what they are. We must translate our knowledge of the facilities into customer needs. An illustration:

> With an electric drill in one hand and a block of wood with a hole in it in the other hand our trainer said, "Nobody has a need for this electric drill." Holding up the block of wood with the hole in it, he

said, "What there is a tremendous need for is holes! We market the drill because it satisfies the customer's need for holes."

We market gyms and pools and exercise rooms to satisfy the customer's need for health, fitness, fun, fellowship, weight control, relaxation, etc.

Far more important in a tour of facilities is the communication with the prospect about who he/she is . . . how they happened to come to the Y . . . what it is they would like to accomplish . . . where they live . . . the family's interests . . . what kind of work they do.

All of these give us clues as to how a health club or Y membership can help satisfy the prospect's needs . . . but only if we do more listening than talking. When we talk about our program and facilities it must be in terms of benefits to the prospect.

If we have designed our program to meet customer needs instead of our own ego needs for a marvelous and highly technical program, and if we relate to the potential member in terms of his needs, it will become clear what he wants to hear about and what benefits and features to talk about.

IMPLEMENTING THE MARKETING PLANS

One of my favorite pragmatic friends holds a theory that "idea people" are great but ideas are a dime a dozen. "It's the implementors of the world who count," he says. "They get the job done." The Marketing Task Force approach is a way of getting the new ideas originated by the people who will be responsible for implementing them. Obviously, follow-through is essential.

RESULTS

There is no doubt that the first objective for the formation of the task forces was achieved—that of training. The learnings which took place during the Marketing Training Project are evidenced in attitudinal changes that have influenced management decisions up and down the organization. The conscious application of marketing principles has affected manpower planning, training, program development and allocation of resources.

Customer-orientation and a focus on satisfying the needs of people has influenced volunteer involvement and support as well as enrollments. The marketing approach has subtly influenced day to day judgements. The staff have become better planners.

There is less resistance to charging appropriate fees. Better pricing and improved promotion efforts have resulted in increased earned income in 1974. Tot Time enrollments increased from 585 students in the fall of '73 to 704 today. Health Club membership has increased from 689 to 1228. The number of families enrolled in family-serving Branches has increased from 2,199 to 2,960.

There is a growing awareness of what happens in the non-profit market. For instance: You have designed a program and you have budgeted it with all the overhead to break even with an enrollment of 20 people. If, because you have overestimated the need, or inadequately promoted it, only ten participants are enrolled you not only have a no profit situation, you have a deficit . . . to which you must apply donor subsidy. This is poor management, not philanthropy.

Now on the other hand if we deliberately plan to subsidize a program, it is a different matter. Suppose we provide a program to meet a specific need and it is purposely planned, with a maximum enrollment, to be a deficit operation.

To increase the number of these programs is of course to increase the overall deficit . . . a point not often thought about outside of non-profit management. If the reasons for operating this program at a deficit are sound, then this is where contributed dollars belong.

The YMCA is a non-profit organization. It should be non-profit by intent and good management not by accident and poor management!

The second objective for the formation of the task forces was substantially achieved with the completion and acceptance of four of the six marketing proposals. Each of the four completed proposals received a "go" decision from top management.

Within the framework of the organizational structure and the corporate planning system of the Milwaukee YMCA, the marketing plans are largely being implemented in the branches. This means that branch staff and boards of managers set branch unit objectives in the program area and develop action plans from the recommendations of the marketing proposals. Action plans include designation of staff responsibility, time schedules and budget requirements.

Several of the marketing proposals called for increased corporate staff and general office support in the form of more centralized direction or coordination of the program. Additional resources have been mustered to help implement the marketing plans. Examples:

- Maintenance Reserve funds have been allocated to renovate the Central Branch Health Club entrance as recommended
- A highly skilled professional Health Club Director has been employed for this unit. Fifty percent of his responsibilities include conducting a training school for health club personnel for all branches with emphasis on massage and sales.
- The Public Relations staff of the General Offices has been increased with the employment of a Director of Communications to aid in the development of interpretive materials and promotion of programs.
- Increased coordination of the Tot Time program and the addition of YMCA Movement Education to the program were recommended by the Tot Time Task Force. One Branch Executive has taken the responsibility to get all Tot Time teachers, from across the Association, together on a regular basis for review of objectives, study, discussion and coordination of the recommended curriculum. Training in YMCA Movement Education has been added to the program under the direction of the Assistant Vice President for Physical Education. Standards for teacher credentials and salary ranges have been established.
- Recruitment of a professional staff person to coordinate Y-Indian Guide programs for 3 or 4 Branches in a geographic district is underway. The revving up of an Association-wide Y-Indian Guide lay organization is being considered. The possibility of the Milwaukee Association hosting the 1979 National Longhouse Convention, 20 years after its last convention in Milwaukee in 1959, is under consideration.
- A market study and analysis of population data for the Greater Milwaukee area, segmented by Branch service areas and neighborhoods was conducted. This information reinforced the decision to merge two Branches and helped gain acceptance of the merger. This information is also available to staff for planning in the Branches.

Because marketing is a management approach that grew out of the profit motivation of a free enterprise system many people have not seen what it has to do with the YMCA, a non-profit organization. I believe that marketing is a way of thinking and a management discipline that is as applicable to the YMCA as other management tools adopted from business and industry . . . from business office practices to Management by Objectives.

In business, the motivation for marketing planning is to satisfy customers and to make a profit. In the Milwaukee YMCA the motivation is to attract people to the Association to have an influence for good upon their lives . . . and to break even.

I believe that a marketing approach can help us achieve YMCA purposes. It is a new way of thinking about how to manage the People Business.

Strategic Planning in the Marketing of a Government Program

SEYMOUR H. FINE

Among the reasons for the failure of some government programs is the inadequate dissemination of relevant information to appropriate target audiences. Because "man despises that which he does not know," involvement and participation by these publics is often not obtained. In the past, an underlying philosophy has pervaded the government sector that its function was just to provide, that the responsibility for obtaining information about what is being provided rests with the potential user. Many agency administrators perceived their role to be that of supplying services and programs that will be adopted by some automatic process. Perhaps administrators believed that just as ignorance of the law is no excuse for breaking the law, ignorance about government programs is similarly a poor excuse for nonutilization.

There is a growing awareness among policymakers that it is not sufficient for a new program to be well conceived and expertly designed. Program planning must include an important marketing component whose objective is to educate those for whom the program is intended as well as other publics. Increasingly, marketing's role in the public sector has been demonstrated as a number of programs, considered as "products," have been disseminated through the application of marketing philosophy and methods. Examples are energy conservation, reduced speed limits, "buckle up for safety," and so forth. These applications have come to be called *social marketing*.

One may anticipate the danger that the growing trend toward such new uses of marketing could lead to indiscriminate applications in the spirit of: "Give a boy a hammer and he's sure to find things that need pounding." This could occur as it becomes fashionable to "name drop" various marketing concepts or to employ marketing methods in isolation, that is, without an overall marketing plan. A common example is the tendency to embark on an advertising campaign without first carefully examining product design, pricing, or distribution aspects of the marketing process. An analogy would be the act of applying a coat of wax to an automobile whose body dents are about to be repaired and must yet be repainted. By contrast, undertaking a marketing activity that is part of an overall framework increases the likelihood of orderly and efficient resource allocation. The plan serves as a basis for monitoring results and reshaping policy where necessary.

Strategic Planning in Social Marketing. The supplier of any product offering, whether a tangible object, a service, or an ideational product such as "employ the handicapped," derives significant benefits from the preparation of a comprehensive marketing plan, which is a road map charting the strategies to be employed in attaining the organization's objectives. Standard fare in the private sector, marketing plans are useful too in social marketing, as this paper attempts to demonstrate. This paper is a synopsis of a strategic plan drawn up for an agency sponsoring a worker training program for the economically disadvantaged. It thus illustrates the use of marketing planning in a social marketing context (Fine, 1981).

BACKGROUND

Late in the 1970s, a fork had been reached in the road to government-sponsored worker programming. One branch continued the philosophy of the past—that of maximizing the quantity of

---

From a marketing plan prepared by Seymour H. Fine for the Employment and Training Administration, and Professor Fine's book, *The Marketing of Ideas and Social Issues* (New York: Praeger, 1981).

structurally unemployed individuals placed into jobs. That approach served the objective of immediate reduction of unemployment figures and thus provided attractive statistics. Moreover, many saw the chief purpose of government-funded programs as simply to fill entry-level jobs with workers unqualified for little else—on the surface a not unreasonable goal.

The drawback here was that such programs did not ameliorate, but instead perpetuated the hard-to-employ situation, while not going far enough to upgrade the marketability of these individuals. Still worse, employers had been left with a poor taste for virtually all government-sponsored training programs (Carlson et al., 1978, p. 1): "The publicly financed employment and training system has become so expensive, so complicated, and so ingrained in and out of society, that past business attitudes and institutions must be substantially altered . . . (Special Report No. 31, 1978, p. 11).

Branching sharply from the road to immediate placement is an approach that seeks to provide an improved supply of labor by enhancing the long-term quality of the economically disadvantaged. Instead of instant gratification of employment needs, this approach addresses the problem with a more enduring philsophy, saying in effect not "Let us employ the hard-to-employ," but rather, "Let's help the hard-to-employ become easier to employ."

Faced with growing disenchantment on the part of business, in January 1978 the government inaugurated a new program under the Comprehensive Employment and Training Act (CETA), Title VII, called the Private Sector Initiative Program (PSIP), under which businesspeople were given wide latitude to run the CETA show. This was to be accomplished by establishing regional Private Industry Councils (PICs) dominated by the private sector rather than by government. One of these PICs ordered that a marketing plan be drawn up because it viewed itself not as a group of individuals who were to devise programs dealing with unemployment and training activities, but as businesspeople starting up a firm to sell a product at a profit.

It was an innovative idea. Using a zero-based approach, the PIC set out to treat the employment situation very much the way a marketer attempts to solve a human problem (fill a need, satisfy a want, etc.) by designing and marketing a product. The first step was to state the objective of the PIC.

The *objective* in any marketing endeavor is to satisfy one or more target markets by supplying products so designed as to be acceptable to those markets. This objective provides the mission, or product, of the firm. It answers the question "What business are we in?" In conventional marketing, attainment of that objective is usually measured in terms of financial profit. But in social marketing, usually what is sought is widespread adoption or utilization of the idea being propounded in a manner that most benefits the target markets.

In the present case, the Private Industry Council first stated its objective as providing jobs. However, after discussion among Council members, it became apparent that their objective was to increase productivity in industry through improving the quality of that portion of the labor supply consisting of the economically disadvantaged.

Two Markets—Two Products. However, as marketers, the PIC served not one, but two distinct target markets and they had to design a unique product offering for each one. One market consisted of participating firms, and for this market the product designated was *productivity*. The PIC's task was to "sell" client firms on the idea that the PSIP was aimed at increasing productivity—something that all businesses are eager to buy. Economic systems throughout history have set improved productivity as an important industrial objective, and productivity depends, at least somewhat, on conscientious and efficient workers. So it was fitting that a plan for marketing an employment program should consider the idea of improved productivity as its product offering.

The other market served by the PIC was made up of potential applicants for job training programs. These recruits typically have a history of poverty, low educational attainment, weak vocational skills, social problems, and inability to hold a job. They are likely to have antisocial habits, be unsure of themselves, and often take time out from work to resolve family problems. In general, they desire immediate gratification and may have difficulty waiting for payday. Many possess innate talent that is wasted because they lack self-esteem by which to sell themselves. Some are convinced of their worthlessness and are afraid to say otherwise. Perhaps their greatest need is to acquire the ability to earn regular income.

The role of the social marketer is to translate the satisfaction of consumer needs into the design of a specific offering. In this case, the social product to be marketed to the job recruits was designated as *earnability*—the capacity to earn a regular income.

Thus two objectives were specified for the PSIP, corresponding to the needs of its two markets. Each objective identified a product to be marketed—productivity for the market of participating employers, and earnability for potential applicants. They are the two "product lines" within the "product mix" of the PSIP, and the foci of the marketing plan discussed in the remainder of this paper.

The plan appears in five parts, each part representing a strategic marketing factor: market segmentation, product design, distribution, pricing, and promotion. Strategies are discussed for each of the two focus products/markets.

MARKET SEGMENTATION

The Markets of Participating Firms. Different industries have differing seasonal labor needs, and strategy was suggested to time the promotional effort for the PIC to conform to these requirements—what could be called segmentation by seasonal demand. Given the constraints on such resources as the amount of time available to job development staffers, mailing facilities, and so on, it makes sense to contact firms at the time of the year when they are likely to be most r[illegible] An analogy is seen in the manner in which s[illegible] and loan associations usually time their adv[illegible]tising programs to conform to quarterly interest-payment periods. For example, construction contractors seek extra workers in March, the apparel and needle trades in April, and the leather industry in June. Some industries show no apparent particular seasonality, but those that do are listed in Table 1, which indicates periods of the year in which promotion to each industry should be directed.

The Recruit Market. A second segmentation strategy was proposed, this time for the recruit market, based on the readiness of the recruit for employment. It is explained by a two-dimensional model, containing four cells (Table 2). The first dimension considers achievement in vocational skills, and the second considers the degree of personal and/or family stress affecting the recruit. The model offers a basis for planning the placement of recruits into appropriate programs.

Recruits belonging in cell 1 possess sufficient vocational skills and at the same time are relatively free of personal and/or family stress. Cell 2 recruits enjoy some freedom from stress but are in need of vocational training. Cell 3 recruits do not lack vocational skills but suffer from personal and family problems. Recruits in cell 4 are doubly disadvantaged, exhibiting both types of problems.

Having proposed segmentation of the private-sector market according to seasonal demand, and the recruit market according to employment readiness, the actual products for these respective markets are discussed in the next section.

PRODUCT STRATEGY

Within the two specified product lines, the PSIP spawned several programs, which in marketing parlance may be viewed as product forms:

1. On-the-job-training (OJT), under which the employer may be subsidized at a rate upward of 50% of starting wage.

TABLE 1: *Fiscal-year media plan*[a]

	Oct.	*Nov.*	*Dec.*	*Jan.*	*Feb.*	*Mar.*	*Apr.*	*May*	*June*	*July*	*Aug.*	*Sept.*
Medium												
Local newspaper (250-line insertion)	RRR	R	B	R	RRR	FR	FR	R	FR	R	R	FR
Flyer mailings, all F (%)	5	3	10	2	5	25	15	10	10	5		5
"Out-of-home" posters, all R (%)	3	10	2	5	25	15	10	10	5		5	5
PSAs on local radio	RRR	R	R	R	RRR	FR	FR	R	FR	R	R	FR
Industry Concentrations												
Lumber and wood products												
Retail trade												×
Transportation						×						
Finance, insurance and Real Estate								×				
Construction contracting						×						
Mining, agriculture						×						
Textile mill products										×		
Apparel and needle products							×					
Furniture and fixtures					×							
Chemical and allied products						×						
Petroleum and coal products									×			
Rubber and miscellaneous plastics							×					
Leather industry									×			
Stone, glass, and ceramics							×					
Machinery (excluding electrical)						×						
Electrical goods and machinery												
Automobile industry								×				
Aircraft industry			×									
Instruments and clocks			×									

[a]F, promotion to the audience of participating firms; R, promotion to the recruit audience.

TABLE 2: ***Segmentation of recruits by employment readiness***

		Recruit's vocational skills	
		Good	*Poor*
Personal/family stress	Mild	Cell 1	Cell 2
	Serious	Cell 3	Cell 4

2. Classroom training (CT) in both clerical and vocational skills.
3. The Targeted Job Tax Credit (TJTC) program, permitting private for-profit employers to be eligible for tax credits upon hiring disadvantaged individuals from among specific target groups, including welfare recipients, handicapped, poor youth, poor Vietnam veterans, cooperative-education participants, and ex-convicts (Special Report No. 31, p. 14). An employer may obtain the training subsidy as well as the tax credit by both hiring and training the disadvantaged.
4. Work experience programs encouraging recruits to gain practical exposure to job settings on a part-time basis (e.g., while still in school).

Productivity, according to economists, may be increased by improving the quality of the labor force, investing in more efficient capital equipment, or automation (Lovelock and Young, 1979, p. 168). This study is obviously concerned with only the first of these alternatives, and product strategy for productivity then amounts to the design of programs for optimally equipping PSIP recruits to become productive workers. This means not only vocational training for recruits but also enhancing their capacity to report to work on time and consistently.

Strategy for product improvement must consider the following areas of disillusionment with government training programs experienced in the past by industry:

1. Red tape and overregulation
2. Adverse publicity
3. Bias against business participation on the part of some government officials
4. Unreliability of employees
5. Termination after training
6. Lost productivity of trainers
7. Poor returns on training investments
8. Employees taking unfair advantage of unemployment and compensation privileges

An agenda of steps ameliorating product deficiencies is an integral part of a marketing plan. In the present case, one would include (numbers correspond to the items listed above) the following:

1. An official to be designated as an ombudsman or "red-tape cutter" for participating firms, with a "hot-line" phone number for the purpose.
2. The theme to be emphasized that the PIC represents a new brand of CETA. Indeed, PIC should be made a brand name, which will be promoted with the goal of making it well known, respected, and hopefully rendered generic. The producer of a branded item tolerates nothing but quality output for long-term welfare of the firm.
3. Private-sector participation is now mandated by law. At least 50% of the PIC membership must now be drawn from the business community and there is every reason to believe that businesspersons are answering the call with the intention of becoming actively involved.

4–8. Expansion of programs designed to improve the quality of the PIC recruit. Before "selling" the recruit to employers, care must be taken that he or she is indeed "salable."

Earnability. The social product, earnability, is the capacity of an individual to earn money in steady employment. A recruit acquires earnability by attaining at least some of the following:

1. A feeling of investment in the commitment to a job preparation program
2. Basic and vocational skills
3. Employment habits such as promptness and

regularity of attendance, getting along with others, proper dress and hygiene, and so on

4. Self-confidence
5. Assurance that personal problems need not hamper job performance and that sources of help are readily available
6. Understanding and utilization of his/her capabilities
7. Regular income

Earnability is secured by most people through education or from work habits developed early in life, but for many who were deprived of these privileges, CETA programs can fill a serious void. However, earnability is not the same thing to all target individuals. As with many products, its design must be differentiated into forms that suit the needs of different market segments. Earlier, a model was proposed for segmenting the recruit market into four groups according to employment readiness. If that segmentation strategy is to be useful, a package of earnability, or product form, should be defined to suit each of the four submarkets. Referring to the model in Table 2, the following product forms were suggested:

Cell 1: These recruits are ready to be assigned to available positions under Title VII, except that some may require orientation in world-of-work habits.

Cell 2: Here, too, applicants may be placed into job slots, but they will also be enrolled in some form of training. Their employers are thus eligible for a combination of Title VII and TJTC support.

Cell 3: The product form for these recruits includes job placement together with counseling or referral to an appropriate agency for social services. The employer should be made aware that, although he is obtaining a trained worker, some patience will be necessary to deal with the stress factor.

Cell 4: Earnability in this cell is made up of job training placement, together with personal/family help, as in cell 3.

Earnability: A Psychosocial Component. A key feature of this study is the advocacy of a program for counseling and referral of recruits on individual problems and for family services, what might be termed the "psychosocial component" of the strategic plan. Recruits not only have vocational and educational deficiencies, but also bring to the job situation family and personal problems which are amenable to support services. It is extremely difficult for enrollees who are beset with personal problems to apply themselves to vocational training. If product strategy for earnability could include help with child care and other family support services, the likelihood of regular job attendance would be increased.

Preliminary investigation in connection with the present study revealed enthusiastic support for a psychosocial program within the PSIP. One survey of business found that general orientation counseling could be the "most useful of all government-financed programs for providing stable employment for disadvantaged youth" (Carlson et al., 1978, pp. 18, 19). Reporting on a 15-year study, Shore and Massimo (1979) assert:

> Comprehensive vocationally-oriented psychotherapy continues to show promise as a technique for reaching so called "hard-to-reach" adolescents, influencing their adjustment positively even into mid-life (p. 245).

The PIC is in an enviable and timely position to consider arranging for such help as an integral component of its product mix. The concepts of caring and sharing enter into what might otherwise be considered cold and inhumane aspects of industrialization.

This part of the plan has discussed design and improvement of the product offerings to the PIC's consumers. The first section focused on productivity to industry and the second earnability to recruits. But the distinction between the two products was drawn only for expository purposes; the two are closely intertwined. A more productive worker enjoys greater earnability, which in turn, improves productivity. Many large firms, IBM for example, maintain on-site staff to help employees with personal problems. But most businesses comprising the PIC's primary market cannot afford to offer this service to their personnel. It seems reasonable that the PIC, in dealing with a constituency of small firms, can and should consider such programming to be within its scope and thereby fill an important need of its consumers. The idea should be of great interest to employers, who in the past have suffered because of poor work habits of CETA recruits and other employees.

DISTRIBUTION—PARTIES TO THE PROCESS

In the same way that a distribution system for a tangible product is made up of series of firms—producer, wholesaler, retailer, and so on, the channel of distribution—social marketers are aware of a set of institutions involved in one way or another with the delivery of a social product such as the PSIP. The concept points up the reality that the social marketer operates not in a vacuum, but within a network of other community-based organizations (CBOs).

The channel structure (Figure 1) for the distribution of the PSIP begins with the "prime sponsor," the regional CETA organization. Next, the PIC serves in an advisory capacity on PSIP matters. In terms of channel concepts the PIC is the "producer" or marketer of PSIP. Because the PIC has two sets or consumers, the private sector and the disadvantaged unemployed, the channel presented in Figure 3 forks into two branches, one for each of the products/markets, although several channel members interact with both. The chart is self-explanatory and is not elaborated upon here. The crux of this brief section is this: as with middlemen in conventional marketing, if each member of the channel contributes to the marketing process by performing its implicitly designed functions, effective delivery of the product to the consumer is facilitated.

PRICING STRATEGY FOR THE PSIP

Social Price. In addition to monetary prices, individuals give up or "pay" other resources in exchange for product offerings which they buy. These social prices include time, effort, psyche, and changes in life-style, and should be taken into account in the design and promotion of any product, but especially in the case of social products such as productivity and earnability. Adam Smith put it this way: "The real price of everything, what everything really costs to the man who wants to acquire it, is the toil and trouble of acquiring it" (in Kotler, 1975, p. 176).

A commercial marketer sets a price sufficiently high to ensure a profit and low enough to attract a sale. Somewhat similarly, the social marketer seeks to extract sufficient involvement or sacrifice from the adoption to create respect for the social product while keeping the extent of the commitment that the consumer must make low enough so as not to drive him or her away. If the price is too high, PSIP will not sell, but if the price is too low, it might be perceived as lacking credibility or importance.

The Price of the PIC Brand of Productivity. Client firms have become disenchanted with high prices they have paid for taking part in government-sponsored training programs. These high prices are just another way of viewing their complaints listed earlier, and correcting these ills may be seen as a price-reduction campaign. The marketing approach thus provides a double-barreled implement for planning promotion strategy. The goodwill of participating firms must be regained by not only offering a high-quality brand of productivity, but at a reasonable social price. For example, not only must PSIP be associated with a better prepared recruit, but in addition, the amount of red tape expected of employees is to be demonstrably reduced and similarly for other points of contention. At the same time, the "contract" must not characterize Title VII or TJTC provisions as "giveways," lest the program become suspect. The two-way nature

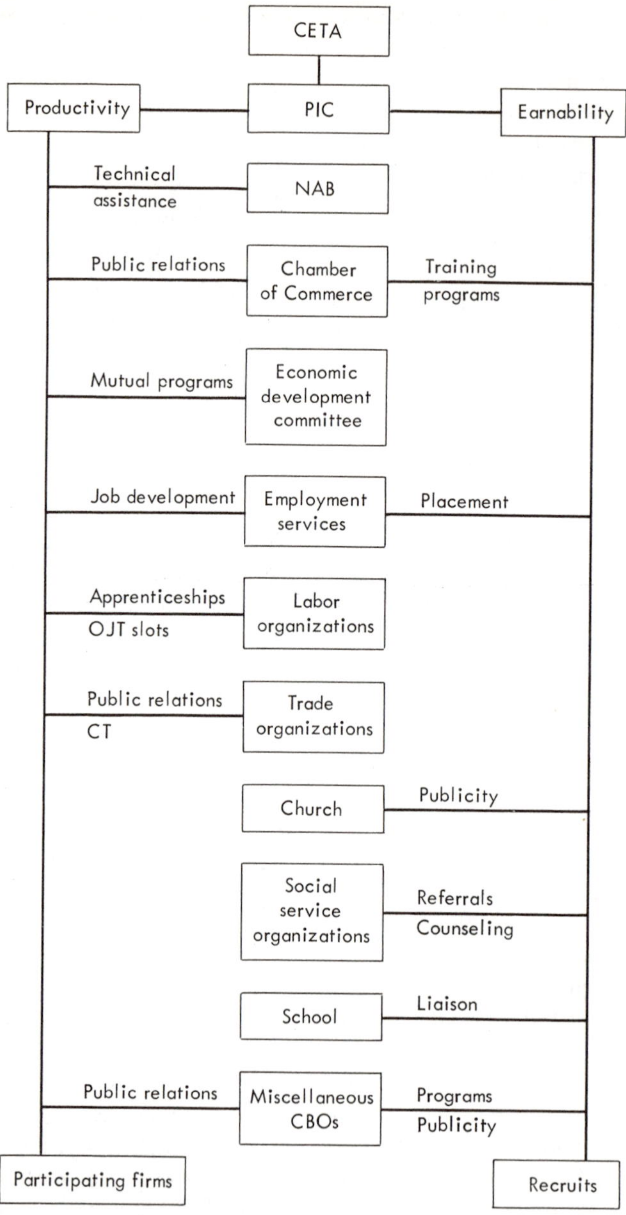

FIGURE 1: ***A channel of distribution for two CETA products***

of the exchange transaction must be upheld. Thus the tax credit is a product form offered in exchange for the price of training time, and Title VII subsidies are exchanged for time (and patience) required to break in a new recruit, and so on.

The very name assigned to the primary market for the PSIP (i.e., the participating firms) connotes a social price paid by these customers when they purchase the PIC brand of productivity. They participate by making training slots available and by interacting with job development staff. Moreover, the PSIP invites participation of private-sector input into the planning process, the essence of the PSIP idea.

Social Price Paid by Recruits. These concepts also apply to recruits who purchase earnability. A commitment to the program must be elicited from all enrollees so that they too will have a sense of investment through participation, in exchange for the benefits which they derive. Recruits sacrifice all of the social prices listed above, in exchange for the PIC brand of earnability—time, effort, psyche, and life-style change. Pricing strategy dictates that the program be so devised as to systematically set these prices at levels not too high nor too low. Thus, complicated intake procedures might discourage enrollment. But if entry is made too simple, the program could appear superficial. The price must be "right."

One of the first tasks asked of new employees is to fill out forms, which they often find difficult to do (frankly, I know a Ph.D. who finds most forms enigmatic). PIC could sponsor classes in the art of filling out employment applications, attendance being free but mandatory for all recruits. (The time and effort of attendance are social prices to be paid in exchange for the product, earnability.)

Summarizing, "price tags" bearing social prices such as the few alluded to in this brief section, and "fastened" to PSIP products, have neither numbers nor dollar signs printed on them. Instead, they signify certain nonmonetary sacrifices expected of consumers in exchange for productivity and earnability. These prices are part of the exchange process, and to the extent that they constitute fair payment in that exchange, they need to be considered in marketing planning.

PROMOTION

The promotion component of a marketing plan is sometimes known as the "advertising plan," and is often erroneously considered to be the *only* part of a marketing plan. However, by first examining the markets, products, and distribution and price factors, a broader background is obtained for campaign planning.

Promoting Productivity to Industry. An important communications objective is to instill in the private-sector market the impression of a totally new and important source of workers, reversing the poor image that firms have about workers supplied through government support. The objective of the promotion program is therefore to create awareness of a new product, create favorable association, and encourage "switching" from other brands of labor sources. Copy strategy is to emphasize freedom from government interference, less competition from PSE, and quality in favor of subsidy. If the PIC's workers will now have access to new forms of counseling which may result in more diligent attendance on the job, that fact serves as food for ad message design. By broadcasting such aspects of the program, one hopes to restore employers' shattered confidence in CETA. The CETA brand having been disappointing, the PIC will now offer a new, improved brand of productivity to the private sector and will advertise it as such. Message themes could include:

CETA Goes Private Sector

The New CETA

The Private-Sector CETA

The product being innovative, it is necessary to build awareness through repeated exposure of the message. That is, strategy will emphasize frequency of ad placement rather than broad reach across a wide market. Productivity messages will be carried in both print and broadcast vehicles and fullest advantage should be taken of opportunities for public service announcement (PSA) spot broadcasts. In addition, direct mail is a highly efficient medium for promoting the PSIP program. Direct mail permits pinpointing specific industries that can be reached at strategic points in time, that is, when their hiring needs are greatest (see Figure 1). Such practice also reduces the possibility of a sudden heavy demand for workers, which is likely to result from a large general mailing. Brochures, booklets, Western Union Mailgrams, and flyers may be used as vehicles in direct-mail campaigns.

While mass media create awareness, industry involvement in PSIP will require interpersonal promotion as well. The new PIC brand of productivity will need one-to-one selling to stress such innovative aspects as the new procedures under which recruits will be processed. Employers will probably be pleased to hear that their preferences for quality and long-term worker commitment are to underlie the PIC program. It will be refreshing news to them, that they, and not politicians, will now have first call upon well-prepared recruits. Personal selling of "Productivity through PIC" could also be affected through the medium of guest speakers at industrial organization meetings. Staff members and others well informed about the program may arrange to be invited to functions by various industrial groups, where they can speak and answer questions about the advantages of the PIC as a source of workers.

Other promotional and public relations techniques have been invoked by PICs around the country, including press announcements, luncheons and dinners with potentially concerned leaders, well-publicized colloquia on structural employment, and coordination of manpower programs (Summary Report, October 1978, p. 41).

Promoting Earnability to Recruits. Although there is general agreement that PSIP must be sold to industry, promotion aimed at the recruit market appears to have been overlooked in PIC programs. The prevalent feeling is that recruits obtain employment information automatically, and are always ready to go to work, and that PSIP does not have to be sold to them. Such an approach may adequately serve programs seeking to do nothing but place applicants into entry-level jobs, but it is inconsistent with the concept of earnability. The market for earnability consists of those who not only want jobs, but who are willing to invest in self-betterment. If PSIP is to be an improvement over its predecessors, it must appeal to applicants interested in enhancing their capacity to earn money, and not just to obtain jobs, a premise that guides copy strategy proposed in this section.

As an audience, recruits should be quite receptive to such message appeals. For they have *had jobs,* but still *have little money*. They have repeatedly experienced the pain of quickly losing jobs. Earnability is to be billed as more important than a job. Copy strategy is to convince recruits that while they are now job *seekers,* they must become job *keepers,* and that PSIP will show them the way.

Another message theme in the campaign to attract recruits concerns the status of manual work. Because society attaches greater dignity to white-collar jobs, schools herd youngsters into academic programs, and some vocationally oriented individuals develop low opinions of themselves. But not everyone is interested or equipped to become a so-called professional. Promotion messages should be structured about such values as the work ethic, and should build feelings in workers that they are valuable and needed. Respect for manual dexterity in technology should be emphasized, and the "lowly trades" elevated: "It was soiled hands that built this country," and so on.

The hard-to-employ are not readers of newspapers, so that print ads for this market have a high "cost per thousand" (CPM), the yardstick of efficiency with which a medium reaches its audience. The aim of print campaigns is thus mainly to reach a "referring audience" of such individuals and institutions as welfare workers, schools, churches, and so on, from which earnability messages can be relayed to target recruits.

Similarly, CPM is extremely high for reaching this market via radio stations serving wider areas. Even where a geographic match can be found between vehicle and audience, programming compatibility must be achieved, as with rock music, for example. On the other hand, classical music is frequently "piped in" to waiting rooms in doctors' offices, where messages could reach recruits either directly, or as a "pass-along" audience.

"Out-of-home" media such as billboards and bus cards should be considered. Some movie theatres show spot announcements, and one wonders why the PIC should not advertise in the phone directory yellow pages under the heading "Employment." Earnability may also be promoted by circulating handbills, brochures, and flyers at church and social functions, timing the distributions to coincide with the need for increasing recruit enrollment.

As observed in discussing the campaign to promote productivity, mass media are useful principally to create awareness; personal modes of communication are needed to bring recruits closer to actual adoption of earnability (enrollment). Posters placed in neighborhood shop windows serve this purpose and are quite inexpensive. Their cost effectiveness is extended still further as the very process of introducing them into the shops provides the opportunity for personal interaction between a PIC representative and a "middleman," the shopkeeper. They may, of course, also be placed on bulletin boards in schools, community centers, and so on. An effective forum for personal selling of earnability is the neighborhood sectarian church. The PIC could build relationships with key religious leaders in the community, who are generally quite receptive to the cause of improving the lot of the economically disadvantaged.

Scheduling. Promotion strategy (Table 1) was planned for a fiscal year which, for the PIC, runs from October 1 to September 30. The schedule provides for a "continuity program" of 20 newspaper ads during the year, four aimed at firms and 16 at recruits, although this proportion can be readily modified to suit seasonal requirements. With both products, newspaper ad scheduling is pulsed for increased frequency at the start of the fiscal year and in advance of peak anticipated demand from firms. Trimonthly 250-line ads could gradually change to monthly appearances. Flyers are to be mailed according to the percentages indicated—about two to six per firm during the year. Extra mailings should go out to firms having a concentration of hiring patterns during the months listed in Figure 1. The pace of distribution of posters is such that promotion to recruits precedes promotion to industry. The point here is that ideally, if a job slot opens up, a recruit should be on hand to fill it. Fullest advantage should be taken of free local radio spots (PSAs). The 7:00 p.m. to midnight periods are suitable for earnability spots to the recruit audience, but the employer market may be reached during the more popular (and difficult to obtain) "drive times," 6:00 to 10:00 a.m. and 3:00 to 7:00 p.m.

DISCUSSION

For too long some policymakers have held the elitist view that their responsibility is just to provide programs, without concerning themselves about the dissemination of information and delivery of those programs to the various relevant publics. A few planners have jumped aboard the advertising bandwagon in the belief that they were thereby completing the marketing function.

But product design and promotion are only two of the four components of the marketing mix. This paper has advocated a holistic approach to the application of the marketing model, in contrast to a tendency to consider only the product offering or only advertising. By integrating all four marketing factors—product, promotion, price, and place—the overall framework guides the effort and unearths facets of the program otherwise overlooked.

As a case in point, vocational training of the economically disadvantaged was treated as a product to be marketed. A synopsis was presented of a strategic plan for a marketing program, illustrating the use of marketing theory and practice in what is called social marketing—the application of marketing concepts to the dissemination of societally beneficial programs, with special emphasis on those sponsored by public and nonprofit institutions.

In a postscript to the Special Report Number 31 (1978), Chairman Eli Ginsberg synthesized the thrust of the situation with respect to the structurally unemployed by observing: "The unemployed youth must become part of the job system or else we must accept the fact that they would become part of the crime system, or the welfare system." This is the awesome responsibility facing employment planners, and similarly for many other program sponsors. Strategic marketing planning is an extremely useful device to be employed in dealing with these problems.

REFERENCES

Carlson, Jack, et al. (1978), "A Survey of Federal Employment and Training Programs." Washington, D.C.: Chamber of Commerce of the U.S., September.

Fine, Seymour H. (1981), *The Marketing of Ideas and Social Issues*. New York: Holt, Rinehart and Winston (Praeger Division), August.

Kotler, Philip (1975), *Marketing for Nonprofit Organizations*. Englewood Cliffs, N.J.: Prentice-Hall, Inc.

Lovelock, C., and R. H. Young (1979), "Look to Consumers to Increase Productivity," *Harvard Business Review,* May–June, 168–178.

Shore, Milton F., and Joseph L. Massimo (1979), "Fifteen Years After Treatment: A Follow-up Study of Comprehensive Vocationally-Oriented Psychotherapy," *American Journal of Orthopsychiatry,* 49(2) (April), 245.

Special Report No. 31 (1978), The National Commission for Manpower Policy, Washington, D.C., November.

Summary Report (1978), Private Industry Council Development, Corporation for Public/Private Ventures, October.

The Marketing Audit: A Tool for Health Service Organizations[1]

ERIC N. BERKOWITZ

WILLIAM A. FLEXNER

Marketing is increasingly recognized as an effective tool in the management of health services. Some potential benefits recently cited in the literature include: improved capacity to respond to the needs and wants of consumers, personnel and the community in general; clarification in the development of long-range strategies and objectives; and more effective allocation of resources within the organization [1–3].

Marketing of health services involves analyzing organizational interactions (transactions) with donors, patients, employees and regulators of the organization [4]. However, before undertaking any marketing program, the factors that affect the organization's internal operations and its relations with the environment must be assessed. As Ireland notes [5]:

> Ideally, a hospital that is developing a marketing program should begin by conducting a series of research studies to gather information that will help

Reprinted from *HCM Review,* Fall 1978, pp. 51–57, by Eric N. Berkowitz and William A. Flexner, by permission of Aspen Systems Corporation,

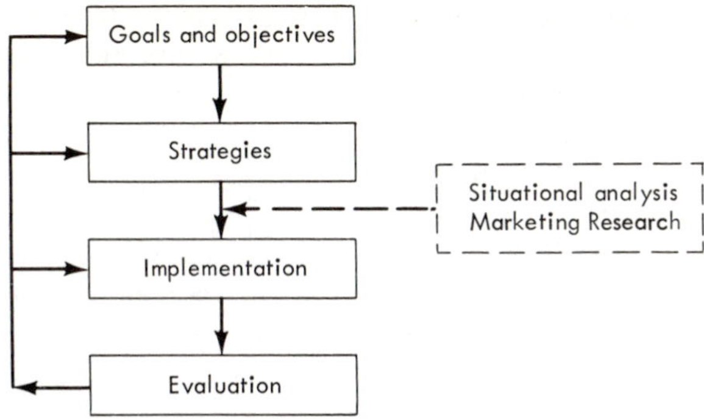

FIGURE 1: ***A typical health planning model***

> define the characteristics, needs, and wants of its market and marketing segments, so that it can develop or revise its services and accommodations accordingly.

Unfortunately, assessments such as Ireland proposes are often done late in the planning process of health organizations. However, an early marketing inquiry—the marketing audit—may be more beneficial.

TWO APPROACHES TO PLANNING

Typically, the planning sequence in health organizations includes the specification of goals, translation of these into operational objectives, development of strategies to achieve the goals and objectives, implementation of the strategies, and finally feedback or evaluation to modify or adjust current strategies and implementation procedures [6]. Figure 1 shows this sequential process.

In this planning approach, understanding the organization's environment and particularly its marketplace usually occurs after the product and service strategies have been defined. While this information may aid in "selling" the product or services being offered, the timing is too late to determine whether the products or services being produced are those that are wanted or needed.

Marketing literature and practice provide another planning sequence. (See Figure 2.) In this model, the consumer of health services (whether viewed as the physician, the patient, the government or some other purchaser) is recognized as the focal point for making the key choices that dictate the organization's success. With a marketing approach, the consumer is considered at the beginning of the planning process [7]. Consumers may be grouped into segments based on behavior or needs. Included in this initial analysis are a consideration of both the internal capabilities of the organization, and the preferences and needs of the organization's current and potential consumers. This examination of the organization's internal aspects identifies the range of activities that can be

FIGURE 2: ***A marketing planning model***

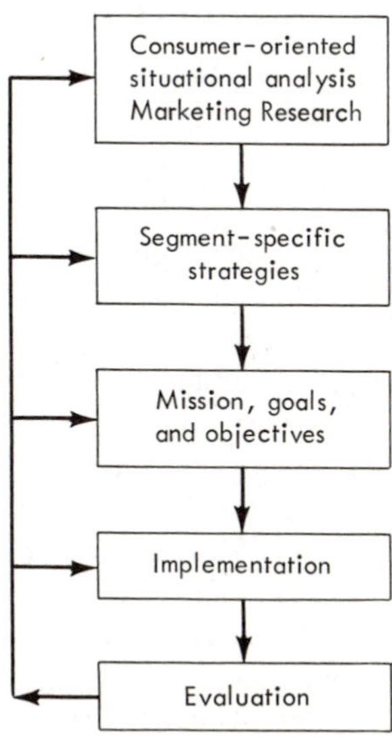

performed, as well as the strong and weak points among these activities.

Once this situational or segmentation analysis is completed, the second step in the process associates various strategies with particular segments of consumers. Forecasts of the potential demand from each segment are then often attempted. Only after this step has been completed does the organization consider specific goals and objectives, and the means for implementing the chosen strategies.

As can be seen, the two approaches differ only in terms of the process flow. This difference, however, is critical in terms of structuring consumer-responsive strategies and plans. Traditionally, health service organizations have planned from the inside to the consumer. Yet regulatory, resource and competition trends are requiring the change from a traditional to a marketing planning strategy. A marketing approach starts the process with the consumer, letting the consumer's needs and wants guide the strategy of the organization. Here the consumer is at the beginning of the planning process, around which selective strategies, objectives and goals are constructed. For any organization changing to a marketing orientation, the process should begin with a marketing audit.

THE MARKETING AUDIT

Audits have typically been a procedure used in accounting for internal control. Because marketing can be a critical activity contributing to the efficient and effective operation of any organization, the need for marketing audits in non-traditional businesses is increasing. As many health organizations begin to recognize the marketing function and to formulate marketing objectives, an early marketing audit is essential. This process provides a foundation on which to develop programs and standards for evaluation.

The Meaning of a Marketing Audit. In its most basic sense, an audit is an evaluation of a firm's activities. Bell has suggested that "a marketing audit is a systematic and thorough examination of a company's marketing position" [8]. Shuchman more precisely outlines this practice as [9]:

> a systematic, critical, and impartial review and appraisal of the total marketing operation: of the basic objectives and policies and the assumptions which underlie them as well as the methods, procedures, personnel, and organization employed to implement the policies and achieve the objectives.

A variety of reasons for conducting a marketing audit exists. The dynamic nature of society and the health care industry, in particular, requires up-to-date information for the organization to operate effectively. One must periodically monitor the organization's position and activities to assess their responsiveness to market needs and preferences.

In this dynamic environment, a marketing audit has many purposes [10]:

- It appraises the total marketing operation.
- It centers on the evaluation of objectives and policies and the assumptions that underlie them.
- It aims for prognosis as well as diagnosis.
- It searches for opportunities and means for exploiting them as well as for weaknesses and means for their elimination.
- It practices preventive as well as curative marketing practices.

The Nature of an Audit. Conducting an audit can be an extremely complex task. In essence, it involves examining the entire scope of the organization's activities. Through a broad-based approach, certain cogent issues within each area of marketing operations (product and service design, promotion, price, location) can be identified for analysis in greater depth. Figure 3 shows the scope of the marketing audit procedure.

The audit process is represented as a series of circles expanding outward from the consumer. One begins by looking at the size of the consumer market and the various ways that it can be divided or segmented. To this information must be added information concerning one's own health service

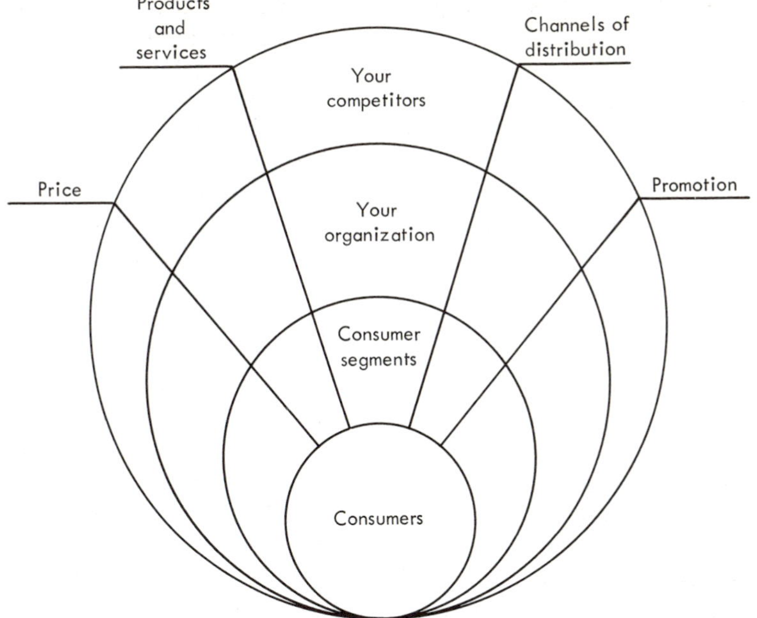

FIGURE 3: ***The scope of the marketing audit***

organization. Often there are internal constraints that must be determined before devising marketing strategies. Beyond the organization, an assessment needs to be made of the competition, its strengths and weaknesses.

Cutting across each of these circles are the organizing or controllable variables that ultimately come together to define the marketing strategy. These marketing mix variables include the product or service offered, the price at which it is offered, the way in which it is promoted and the channels through which the product or service is distributed [11]. At each stage of the marketing audit, these variables must be considered.

Areas of Inquiry in the Marketing Audit Procedure. For any organization, some factors may appear more relevant than others. The more important and common areas of inquiry for each circle represented in Figure 3 will be listed here in the form of questions to serve as a guide in the marketing audit process. These questions indicate that an audit is an information gathering process. Analysis will then depend on the audit team's foresight and management skill.

The market and market segments

1. How large is the territory covered by your market? How have you determined this?
2. How is your market grouped?
   a. Is it scattered?
   b. How many important segments are there?
   c. How are these segments determined (demographics, service usage, attitudinally)?
3. Is the market entirely urban, or is a fair proportion of it rural?
4. What percentage of your market uses third party payment?
   a. What are the attitudes and operations of third parties?
   b. Are they all equally profitable?
5. What are the effects of the following factors on your market?
   a. Age

b. Income
c. Occupation
d. Increasing population
e. demographic shifting
f. Decreasing birthrate

6. What proportion of potential customers are familiar with your organization, services, programs?
   a. What is your image in the marketplace?
   b. What are the important components of your image?

The organization

1. Short history of your organization:
   a. When and how was it organized?
   b. What has been the nature of its growth?
   c. How fast and far have its markets expanded? Where do your patients come from geographically?
   d. What is the basic policy of the organization? Is it on "health care," "profit"?
   e. What has been the financial history of the organization?
      (1) How has it been capitalized?
      (2) Have there been any account receivable problems?
      (3) What is inventory investment?
   f. What has been the organization's success with the various services promoted?
2. How does your organization compare with the industry?
   a. Is the total volume (gross revenue, utilization) increasing, decreasing?
   b. Have there been any fluctuations in revenue? If so, what were they due to?
3. What are the objectives and goals of the organization? How can they be expressed beyond the provision of "good health care"?
4. What are the organization's present strengths and weaknesses in:
   a. Medical facilities
   b. Management capabilities
   c. Medical staff
   d. Technical facilities
   e. Reputation
   f. Financial capabilities
   g. Image
5. What is the labor environment for your organization?
   a. For medical staff (nurses, physicians, etc.)?
   b. For support personnel?
6. How dependent is your organization upon conditions of other industries (third party payers)?
7. Are weaknesses being compensated for and strengths being used? How?
8. How are the following areas of your marketing function organized?
   a. Structure
   b. Manpower
   c. Reporting relationships
   d. Decision-making power
9. What kinds of external controls affect your organization?
   a. Local?
   b. State?
   c. Federal?
   d. Self-regulatory?
10. What are the trends in recent regulatory rulings?

Competitors

1. How many competitors are in your industry?
   a. How do you define your competitors?
   b. Has this number increased or decreased in the last four years?
2. Is competition on a price or nonprice basis?
3. What are the choices afforded patients?
   a. In services?
   b. In payment?
4. What is your position in the market—size and strength—relative to competitors?

Products and Services

1. Complete a list of your organization's products and services, both present and proposed.

2. What are the general outstanding characteristics of each product or service?
3. What superiority or distinctiveness of products or services do you have, as compared with competing organizations?
4. What is the total cost per service (in-use)? Is service over/under utilized?
5. What services are most heavily used? Why?
   a. What is the profile of patients/physicians who use the services?
   b. Are there distinct groups of users?
6. What are your organization's policies regarding:
   a. Number and types of services to offer?
   b. Assessing needs for service addition/deletion?
7. History of products and services (complete for major products and services):
   a. How many did the organization originally have?
   b. How many have been added or dropped?
   c. What important changes have taken place in services during the last ten years?
   d. Has demand for the services increased or decreased?
   e. What are the most common complaints against the service?
   f. What services could be added to your organization that would make it more attractive to patients, medical staff, nonmedical personnel?
   g. What are the strongest points of your services to patients, medical staff, nonmedical personnel?
   h. Have you any other features that individualize your service or give you an advantage over competitors?

Price

1. What is the pricing strategy of the organization?
   a. Cost-plus
   b. Return on investment
   c. Stabilization
2. How are prices for services determined?
   a. How often are prices reviewed?
   b. What factors contribute to price increase/decrease?
3. What have been the price trends for the past five years?
4. How are your pricing policies viewed by:
   a. Patients
   b. Physicians
   c. Third party payers
   d. Competitors
   e. Regulators

Promotion

1. What is the purpose of the organization's present promotional activities (including advertising)?
   a. Protective
   b. Educational
   c. Search out new markets
   d. Develop all markets
   e. Establish a new service
2. Has this purpose undergone any change in recent years?
3. To whom has advertising appeal been largely directed?
   a. Donors
   b. Patients
      (1) Former or current
      (2) Prospective
   c. Physicians
      (1) On staff
      (2) Potential
4. What media have been used?
5. Are the media still effective in reaching the intended audience?
6. What copy appeals have been notable in terms of response?
7. What methods have been used for measuring advertising effectiveness?
8. What is the role of public relations?
   a. Is it a separate function/department?
   b. What is the scope of responsibilities?

Channels of distribution

1. What are the trends in distribution in the industry?
   a. What services are being performed on an outpatient basis?
   b. What services are being provided on an at-home basis?
   c. Are satellite facilities being used?
2. What factors are considered in location decisions? When did you last evaluate present location?
3. What distributors do you deal with? (e.g., medical supply houses, etc.)
4. How large an inventory must you carry?

The marketing audit is the starting point. Examining the issues raised in these questions will allow a more viable, effective marketing strategy to be developed. For the health organization beginning its marketing plan, the audit process will establish parameters for the program and goals to be accomplished.

Many of the questions raised within the marketing audit already are being considered in some form by health planners. In this sense, marketing planning may seem no different from methods presently used. Yet the key difference is *when* these questions are examined. A marketing orientation begins with the consumers of the service. The audit process then continues internally after information is gained from the market place. This approach follows an external sequence, while traditional health planning methods proceed in the opposite direction.

Because the health care organization operates in a dynamic environment, the audit should become a part of the regular planning sequence. Each question should be reevaluated to highlight changes that may have important strategic implications for the organization in fulfilling its goals.

The marketing audit provides guidance for improving the organization's profitability, competitive position and overall performance. This is accomplished by clarifying the setting in which strategies, goals and objectives related to future action can be intelligently generated.

NOTE

1. The authors thank Steven R. Orr, Vice President, Corporate Planning, Fairview Community Hospitals, Minneapolis, Minnesota, for his assistance in the preparation of this article.

REFERENCES

[1] Ireland, R. C. "Using Marketing Strategies to Put Hospitals on Target." *Hospitals* 51 (June 1, 1977) p. 54–58.

[2] O'Halloran, R. D., Staples, J. and Chiampa, P. "Marketing Your Hospital." *Hospital Progress* 57 (1976) p. 68–71.

[3] Clarke, R. N. "Marketing Health Care: Problems in Implementation." *Health Care Management Review* 3:1 (Winter 1978) p. 21–27.

[4] Shapiro, B. P. "Marketing for Nonprofit Organizations." *Harvard Business Review* (September–October 1973) p. 123–132.

[5] Ireland. "Using Marketing Strategies." p. 55.

[6] Hyman, H. *Health Planning* (Germantown, Md.: Aspen Systems Corporation 1975) Ch. 3.

[7] Keith, R. J. "The Marketing Revolution." *Journal of Marketing* (January 1960) p. 35–38.

[8] Bell, M. L. *Marketing: Concepts and Strategies* 2nd ed. (Boston: Houghton Mifflin Co. 1972) p. 428.

[9] Shuchman, A. "The Marketing Audit: Its Nature, Purposes, and Problems," in *Analyzing and Improving Marketing Performance, Report No. 32* (New York: American Management Association, 1959) p. 13.

[10] Shuchman. "The Marketing Audit." p. 15.

[11] McCarthy, E. J. *Basic Marketing: A Managerial Approach* 5th ed. (Homewood, Ill.: Richard D. Irwin, Inc. 1975).

PLANNED PARENTHOOD OF ATLANTA

In early May 1974, Ms. Julie Dallas, a summer intern of Planned Parenthood of Atlanta, was trying to determine what actions to take with regard to the increasing problem of unwanted pregnancies among teenagers and the growth of venereal disease for this group. She felt that greater usage of condoms (also called rubbers or prophylactics) by teenagers would help both these problems somewhat and wanted to develop a case to present to condom manufacturers to convince them to initiate a marketing campaign oriented toward teenagers. Several summer interns would be joining the staff in the next two weeks and would be available to help conduct any research that would be beneficial to this effort. Ms. Dallas had to design a program to make use of these interns when they arrived.

BACKGROUND ON THE PLANNED PARENTHOOD OF ATLANTA

The Planned Parenthood of Atlanta (PPA) is one of 190 local affiliates of the Planned Parenthood Federation of America. The first birth control clinic in the United States was opened in 1914 by Margaret Sanger, who later formed the National Birth Control League. Sanger was a nurse by profession, working mainly with underprivileged persons in New York City. Her work stimulated her to become an activist in the early women's rights movement, with emphasis on the right of women to control conception. Although her early concern was with individual rights, the scope of the movement has broadened to include the issue of population control on national and international levels.

In 1939, the League evolved into the Planned Parenthood Federation of America, sometimes also known as Planned Parenthood/World Population. The stated purposes of the federation are:

1. To provide leadership in
   a. Making effective means of voluntary fertility control, including contraception, abortion, and sterilization available and fully accessible to all.
   b. Achieving a U.S. population of stable size in an optimum environment.
   c. Developing appropriate information, education, and training programs.
2. To support the efforts of others to achieve similar goals in the United States and throughout the world.

Planned Parenthood of Atlanta was formed in 1964 by a group of concerned citizens organized by Mrs. Herbert Taylor. After a period of provisional affiliation, the Atlanta association became a full affiliate of the Federation in 1967. The original intention of PPA was to provide education in the area of birth control for the Metropolitan Atlanta community and to stimulate public health agencies to provide various birth control services. Reducing the number of unwanted pregnancies (among both married and unmarried women) is one of the primary goals of PPA, and they have been using a summer intern program for the past few years to conduct programs in this area oriented toward teenagers.

Early in its existence, Planned Parenthood of Atlanta realized that existing agencies for birth control were handling maximum loads and needs for services were not being met. When federal funds were made available, PPA opened its own clinic in January 1966 at the Bethlehem Community Center. By 1973, seven Planned Parenthood clinics were providing service to approximately 9,000 persons annually. In addition to operating these clinics, they distribute literature and provide speakers throughout the area, mostly directed toward the problem of unwanted pregnancies.

Prepared by Kenneth L. Bernhardt and Danny N. Bellenger, Associate Professors of Marketing, Georgia State University.

Originally, the PPA operating funds came entirely from membership dues and private donations. By 1974, funding was received from United Way and federal and state government family planning programs.

BACKGROUND ON POPULATION PLANNING

As shown in Exhibit 1, the fertility rate (number of children/woman) in the United States has been on the decline since the late 1950s, and had reached 2.4 by 1970. In 1974, the rate was approximately 2.1 children per woman, considered the theoretical rate whereby zero population growth can be achieved.

The annual birthrate (percent of women of childbearing age who have a child in that year) was declining as shown in Exhibit 2. The rate dropped between 1961 and 1971 in every age category for both whites and nonwhites. Among nonwhite teenagers, however, the rate dropped by only 16% during that period, and dropped by only 3% between 1968 and 1971. The greatest disparity between the birthrates of the two racial groups also occurs among teenagers, with the birthrate of nonwhites almost 2½ times that of whites.

Exhibit 3 presents data concerning unwanted

EXHIBIT 1: ***Total fertility rate for the United States, 1800–1970*** [a]

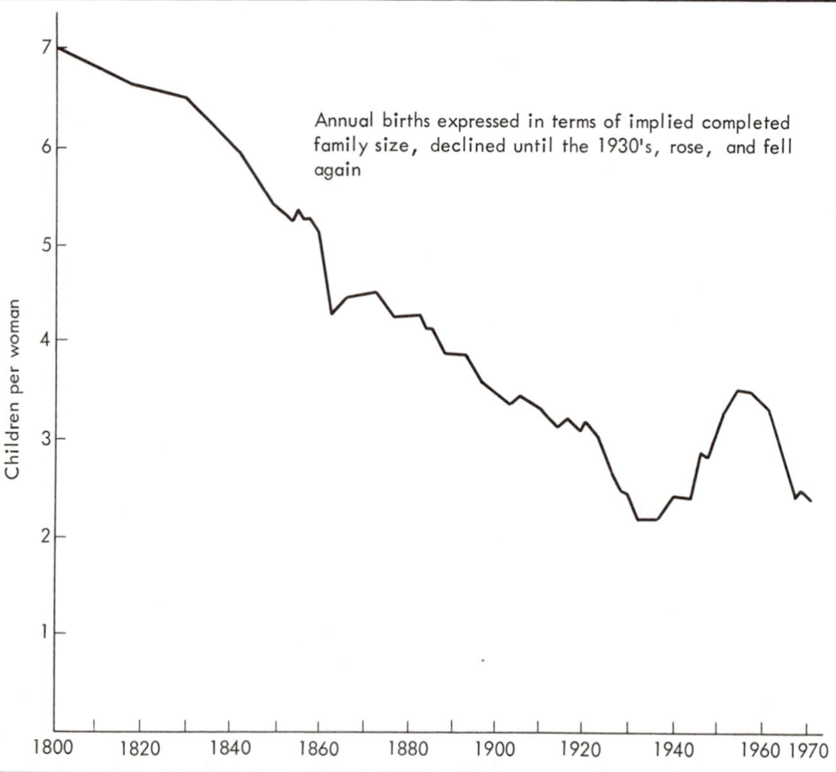

[a]Prior to 1917, data available only for white population; after 1917, for total population.

Source: Prior to 1917—Ansley Coale and Melvin Zelnik, *New Estimates of Fertility and Population in the United States* (Princeton, N.J.: Princeton University Press, 1963). 1917 to 1968—U.S. National Center for Health Statistics, *Natality Statistics Analysis,* Series 21, Number 19, 1970. 1969 to 1971—U.S. Bureau of the Census. *Current Population Reports,* Series P-23, No. 36, ''Fertility Indicators: 1970,'' 1971. The figure for 1971 is based on an unpublished Census staff estimate.

EXHIBIT 2: ***Birth rates by age of mother and color in the United States, 1961–1971***

	White					Nonwhite				
Age	*1961*	*1965*	*1968*	*1971*	*Percent change 1961–1971*	*1961*	*1965*	*1968*	*1971*	*Percent change 1961–1971*
15–19	7.9[a]	6.1	5.5	5.4	−32	15.3	13.6	13.3	12.9	−16
20–24	24.8	18.0	16.3	14.5	−42	29.3	24.7	20.1	18.5	−37
25–29	19.4	15.9	14.0	13.5	−30	22.2	18.8	14.5	13.6	−39
30–34	11.0	9.2	7.3	6.6	−45	13.6	11.8	9.1	8.0	−41
35–39	5.3	4.4	3.4	2.7	−49	7.5	6.4	4.9	4.0	−47
40–44	1.5	1.2	0.9	0.6	−60	2.2	1.9	1.5	1.2	−45

[a]Table is read as follows: in 1961, of all white women between 15 and 19 years of age, 7.9% gave birth.

EXHIBIT 3: ***Unwanted fertility in the United States, 1970*** [a]

Race and Education	*Most likely number of births per woman*	*Percent of births 1966–70 unwanted*	*Theoretical births per woman without unwanted births*
All women	3.0	15	2.7
College 4+	2.5	7	2.4
College 1–3	2.8	11	2.6
High school 4	2.8	14	2.6
High school 1–3	3.4	20	2.9
Less	3.9	31	3.0
White women	2.9	13	2.6
College 4+	2.5	7	2.4
College 1–3	2.8	10	2.6
High school 4	2.8	13	2.6
High school 1–3	3.2	18	2.8
Less	3.5	25	2.9
Black women	3.7	27	2.9
College 4+	2.3	3	2.2
College 1–3	2.6	21	2.3
High school 4	3.3	19	2.8
High school 1–3	4.2	31	3.2
Less	5.2	55	3.1

[a]Based on data from the 1970 National Fertility Study for currently married women under 45 years of age.

fertility in the United States broken down by education and race. The table shows that the overall expected number of births per each woman is 3.0, with the figure being 2.9 for white women and 3.7 for black women. The figure ranges from a low of 2.3 children for a black woman who is a college graduate to a high of 5.2 children for a black woman who never went to high school. The same relationship between education and number of births is very similar for college-educated blacks and whites, but black women with a low level of education have a much greater number of children than white women of comparable education. The largest portion of this difference can be attributed to the difference in the percent of births that were unwanted for the two groups.

Column 2 in Exhibit 3 presents data concerning the percent of births that were unwanted. Of children born in 1966–1970 to black college graduates, only 3% were unwanted, while over half of those born to black women who never went to high school were unwanted. Column 3 in the table presents data concerning the theoretical births per woman eliminating unwanted births. It shows that if unwanted births were eliminated, black women who never went to high school would only have 41% more children than black married college graduates (instead of the actual figure of 126% more children). Thus it appears that the problem is not so much one of motivation differences among the groups as it is a lack of education about and/or availability of contraceptive methods.

Although the birthrates for teenagers have been decreasing as shown in Exhibit 2, the rates of illegitimacy have been drastically increasing. In 1960, 15% of births to teenage mothers were illegitimate, while in 1968, this figure was 27%. For white teenagers, the percentage in 1968 was 16% and for nonwhite it was 55%.

Exhibit 4 presents details on illegitimate birthrates by race and age. Illegitimate children are usually unwanted. In 1971, among unmarried teenagers who were pregnant, 83% of the white girls and 72% of the black girls reported their pregnancies as unwanted. In 1973, 75% of the abortions in Georgia were for teenagers, another indicator of the large number of unwanted pregnancies in this age group.

EXHIBIT 4: ***Illegitimate live births expressed as percentage of live births, by age of mother and color, in the United States, 1961–1968***

	White			*Nonwhite*		
Age	*1961*	*1965*	*1968*	*1961*	*1965*	*1968*
Under 15	49.9[a]	57.3	61.0	81.7	86.4	90.8
15–17	12.4	17.3	23.4	56.2	62.5	68.8
18–19	5.9	9.1	12.8	35.6	38.9	44.3
20–24	2.4	3.8	5.1	20.9	23.0	26.4
25–29	1.3	1.9	2.0	14.4	16.3	16.8
30–34	1.1	1.6	2.0	13.2	14.9	15.5
35–39	1.4	1.9	2.5	13.0	14.9	15.7
Over 40	1.7	2.2	2.8	12.7	14.0	15.7

[a]Table is read as follows: in 1961, of all live births to white women under 15 years of age, 49.9% were illegitimate.

In addition to the problems resulting from unwanted pregnancies, the sexually active person faces the possibility of venereal disease. Over the last decade, the incidence rates of gonorrhea have increased drastically as can be seen from Exhibit 5, particularly for persons under 25. Currently, gonorrhea ranks first among reportable communicable diseases in the United States. During fiscal year 1973, 809,681 cases were reported, while estimates of actual occurrence were around 2,500,000 cases.

While venereal disease is not in the specific domain of Planned Parenthood of Atlanta, it is of concern since one of its prime targets—the sexually active teenager—is particularly susceptible. Also, Planned Parenthood of Atlanta is interested in this problem because Atlanta has the highest reported rate of gonorrhea in the United States with incidence rates approximately three times as high as the national figures presented in Exhibit 5.

A major study concerning unwanted fertility among teenagers was conducted in 1971 by the Institute for Survey Research at Temple Univer-

EXHIBIT 5: ***Gonorrhea ratio per 100,000 population by age group, in the United States, 1960–1972***

Age	*1960*	*1970*	*1972*	*Percent change, 1960–1972*
15–19	412.7[a]	782.2	1,035.4	151
20–24	859.2	1,541.5	1,813.5	111
25–29	485.5	827.8	921.6	90
30–39	192.1	312.9	347.2	81
40–49	52.1	80.4	84.6	62

[a]Table is read as follows: In 1960, for every 100,000 persons between 15 and 19 years old, 412.7 persons contracted gonorrhea.

sity as part of the Commission on Population Growth and the American Future which was established by President Nixon in July 1969. Appendix A presents some data from this study concerning sexuality, contraception, and pregnancy among unwed female teenagers which is based on a national study of 4,611 teenagers.

APPENDIX A: Sexuality, Contraception, and Pregnancy among Young Unwed Females in the United States*

The Data. Interviews were completed with females selected in such a way as to represent a national probability sample of the female population, aged 15 to 19, living in households in the United States. In addition to the sample of respondents in housing units, another probability sample was taken of university students living in dormitories. The two samples provided a total of 4,611 interviews, of which 1,479 were with black females and 3,132 were with whites and other races. (Throughout the study, "white" refers to nonblack respondents.) The large proportion of black interviews was the result of a sampling scheme stratified by race.

The sole criterion for eligibility in this study was age, with the provision that only one eligible female could be selected (randomly) from any one household (or any one room in a college dormitory). Women of any marital status were accepted. About 10% of the respondents have even been married; the concern of this paper is with the other 90%, those who have never been married.

The Never Married. For data on prevalence of intercourse, see Table 1.

TABLE 1: ***Never-married females who have had intercourse, by age and race (%)***

	Percent[a]		
Age	*Black*	*White*	*Total*
15	32.3	10.8	13.8
16	46.4	17.5	21.2
17	57.0	21.7	26.6
18	60.4	33.5	37.1
19	80.8	40.4	46.1
Total	53.6	23.4	27.6

[a]Percentages computed omitting those who have always used contraception, those who gave no answer to the several questions on contraceptive use, and those whose answer to this question was coded other.

CURRENT SITUATION

Each summer for the past few years, one or more interns had joined the PPA staff for the summer. The interns were typically undergraduate and graduate students interested in some aspect of public health. The interns during the summers of 1972 and 1973 had concentrated on a program of distributing free condoms to male teenagers in various recreation centers in low-income areas of Atlanta. One purpose of these efforts was to determine how receptive these teens were to this method of contraception.

In May 1974, Ms. Julie Dallas joined the staff of PPA as part of a field internship for her graduate

*From "Sexuality, Contraception and Pregnancy among Young Unwed Females in the United States," by Melvin Zelnik and John F. Kantner, in Commission on Population Growth and the American Future, *Research Reports, Volume I, Demographic and Social Aspects of Population Growth,* edited by Charles F. Westoff and Robert Parke, Jr., 1972.

work in Public Health at the University of Michigan. She decided that she wanted to do more with her summer project than had been done in the past. After consultations with top PPA officials, she decided to concentrate on a project that would provide research results useful in convincing condom manufacturers to undertake a marketing education and distribution program oriented toward teenagers.

The immediate problem Ms. Dallas faced concerned what type of research to do to obtain information useful for this objective. She felt that she could obtain the cooperation of the city of Atlanta Recreation Department, and could conduct interviews with teenagers at various parks during the summer. The summer interns, two black students and one white student, would be available to help gather data for the study.

In addition to providing information useful to their campaign to convince condom manufacturers to promote to this target group, PPA wanted to develop information from the study which would help them develop a strategy to increase their services to best meet the needs of the teenagers. For example, they wondered whether they should open more clinics, distribute more free samples, offer more counseling services, create and distribute more brochures (an example of a PPA information sheet is included in Appendix B), or what else they could do to help reduce the large number of unwanted pregnancies among this age group.

Two professors at a leading local business school had agreed to help analyze the data they collected from their research and advise them on the study design. A meeting was scheduled for the following week. Among the questions which she needed to answer before that meeting were the following: (1) what the objectives of the research should be; (2) how she should define the sample population for the study; (3) what type of research to conduct—group interviews, a survey study, an experimental study, or some other type; and (4) what specific questions concerning attitudes and behavior should be asked in the research. As the interns would be arriving shortly, it was impera-

TABLE 2: ***Knowledge of onset of fecundity, by age and race, both intercourse statuses (%)***

	"When can a girl first become pregnant?"							
	When period begins		*Sometime later*		*Don't know or no answer*		*Total*	
Age	*Black*	*White*	*Black*	*White*	*Black*	*White*	*Black*	*White*
R has had intercourse								
15	45.6	46.2	49.7	51.3	4.7	2.5	100.0	100.0
16	52.4	55.3	45.9	40.2	1.7	4.5	100.0	100.0
17	50.6	64.4	47.7	32.8	1.7	2.8	100.0	100.0
18	55.2	71.2	42.3	27.6	2.5	1.2	100.0	100.0
19	71.6	63.1	27.8	33.5	0.6	3.4	100.0	100.0
Total	56.4	62.4	41.6	34.8	2.0	2.8	100.0	100.0
R has not had intercourse								
15	46.7	48.5	47.4	45.2	5.9	6.3	100.0	100.0
16	53.6	53.6	43.4	40.8	3.0	5.6	100.0	100.0
17	65.1	62.8	30.7	32.9	4.2	4.3	100.0	100.0
18	53.3	64.6	43.7	31.6	3.0	3.8	100.0	100.0
19	64.0	67.1	31.2	29.9	4.8	3.0	100.0	100.0
Total	54.1	57.6	41.5	37.5	4.4	4.9	100.0	100.0

tive that she be well prepared for the meeting so that any adjustments necessary could be made quickly.

For data on basic biological knowledge, see Tables 2 and 3.

The Sexually Active. For data on the sexually active, see Tables 4, 5, and 6.

Table 7 attempts to show what conjunction there is between first use of contraception and the beginning of sexuality. Although there is a looseness of the data since age in years is the only increment, the results do give a clear indication of what percentage do not begin using contraceptives immediately. The summary statistics show that 50% of the blacks and about 64% of the whites begin using contraceptives at the same age as they become sexually active.

Tables 8, 9, and 10 present additional data on contraception.

The relative unimportance of commercial sources other than drugstores may appear surprising in view of the importance of the condom. In cases where the condoms were obtained by the male, there is undoubtedly a considerable amount of doubt about the source.

APPENDIX B: PPA Information Sheet on Condoms*

It is wise to know about MORE THAN ONE METHOD OF BIRTH CONTROL in case you stop using the one you are using now.

The CONDOM, or rubber, is a method of birth control which many couples have used. It is a good method of birth control. It is also a good way to protect against the spread of infection (V.D.) from a man to a woman or from woman to a man.

How to Avoid Mistakes

1. The CONDOM will work if it is used EVERY TIME!

TABLE 3: ***Knowledge of pregnancy risk within menstrual cycle by age and race, both intercourse statuses (%)***

	When is a girl most likely to							
	Right before, during, or after period		*About two weeks after*		*Any time*		*Total*	
Age	*Black*	*White*	*Black*	*White*	*Black*	*White*	*Black*	*White*
R has had intercourse								
15	43.2	44.6	17.5	41.1	39.3	14.3	100.0	100.0
16	53.0	43.8	17.5	43.6	29.5	12.6	100.0	100.0
17	49.5	34.7	18.3	51.3	32.2	14.0	100.0	100.0
18	55.6	24.1	16.1	62.6	28.3	13.3	100.0	100.0
19	34.3	29.6	23.1	59.9	42.6	10.5	100.0	100.0
Total	46.7	33.0	18.8	54.4	34.5	12.6	100.0	100.0
R has not had intercourse								
15	51.0	48.8	17.7	30.6	31.3	20.6	100.0	100.0
16	46.9	47.0	16.7	36.6	36.4	16.4	100.0	100.0
17	44.2	48.2	17.6	40.3	38.2	11.5	100.0	100.0
18	49.4	37.0	17.9	49.9	32.7	13.1	100.0	100.0
19	47.9	33.1	20.0	55.3	32.1	11.6	100.0	100.0
Total	48.2	44.3	17.6	40.3	34.2	15.4	100.0	100.0

*Planned Parenthood Association, 118 Marietta Street, N.W., Atlanta, Georgia 30303.

2. To check for holes you can blow the condom up like a balloon,
3. When the man removes his penis from the woman's birth canal, he should hold the condom so that it does not slip off.
4. If a condom is used several times, be sure to check EACH TIME that it has no holes.

Some men do not like to use the condom because they have to stop the loveplay leading up to intercourse to put it on. If the woman puts the condom on for the man, it can become a part of the loveplay and may make the man more willing to use this method of birth control.

Couples should discuss a method of birth control TOGETHER before they use the method. Since we are giving you condoms which you may take home, you may want to show them to your teenagers. Its simple to explain to them how this important method of birth control works.

Condoms can be purchased at any drug store for nominal costs without a prescription or can be secured from the Planned Parenthood Clinics.

No method of birth control is guaranteed 100% effective. To increase protection foam may be used by the female partner when the man is using the condom.

A nurse is always available at the Downtown Clinic for supplies or telephone help. Daily from 2:00 p.m. until 8:00 p.m. and from 9:00 a.m. until 4:30 p.m. Saturdays. *Phone:* 688-9300

TABLE 4: ***Percent that had first intercourse at each age, by current age and race*** [a]

	Current age									
Age at first intercourse	*15*		*16*		*17*		*18*		*19*	
	Black	*White*	*Black*	*White*	*Black*	*White*	*Black*	*White*	*Black*	*White*
<12	17.3[a]	8.0	3.0	5.5	5.0	1.1	3.3	6.0	0.9	1.4
13	14.2	17.5	6.0	3.7	4.6	1.3	3.7	4.3	2.6	1.2
14	34.7	30.8	21.8	10.4	7.2	6.9	6.6	2.8	4.2	0.6
15	33.8	43.7	31.9	29.8	30.3	14.4	10.8	6.8	8.2	1.3
16	—	—	37.3	50.6	36.9	51.4	29.5	16.6	25.0	11.7
17	—	—	—	—	16.0	24.9	32.8	30.3	34.0	23.7
18	—	—	—	—	—	—	13.3	33.2	23.3	35.7
19	—	—	—	—	—	—	—	—	1.8	24.4
Total	100.0	100.0	100.0	100.0	100.0	100.0	100.0	100.0	100.0	100.0

[a]Table is read as follows: of black girls currently 15 years old who have had intercourse, 17.3% first had intercourse before age 13.

TABLE 5: ***Percent distribution of frequency of intercourse in "last month" by age and race*** [a]

	Frequency in last month									
	None		*1–2*		*3–5*		*6 or more*		*Total*	
Age	*Black*	*White*	*Black*	*White*	*Black*	*White*	*Black*	*White*	*Black*	*White*
15	45.3[a]	49.6	34.4	27.4	14.6	13.3	5.7	9.7	100.0	100.0
16	46.4	45.2	30.4	37.1	16.2	2.6	7.0	4.1	100.0	100.0
17	38.6	32.1	40.2	35.4	15.7	18.0	5.5	14.5	100.0	100.0
18	44.6	35.0	33.8	24.9	13.2	21.4	8.4	18.7	100.0	100.0
19	33.6	33.8	25.1	23.1	31.1	18.9	10.2	24.2	100.0	100.0
Total	41.0	37.3	32.6	28.6	18.8	18.0	7.6	16.1	100.0	100.0

[a]Table is read as follows: 45.3% of 15-year-old nonvirgins did not have intercourse in the last month.

TABLE 6: ***Percent distribution of contraceptive use status, by age and race*** [a]

	Contraceptive use status									
	Never		Sometimes		Always		No answer		Total	
Age	Black	White	Black	White	Black	White	Black	White	Black	White
15	27.3[a]	34.1	49.5	44.2	19.6	18.8	3.6	2.9	100.0	100.0
16	21.4	19.5	59.6	56.5	15.2	21.9	3.8	2.1	100.0	100.0
17	10.6	12.4	69.1	68.7	19.5	15.8	0.8	3.1	100.0	100.0
18	10.6	13.1	72.0	68.0	16.4	17.7	1.0	1.2	100.0	100.0
19	10.6	12.1	76.1	59.1	8.6	26.4	4.7	2.4	100.0	100.0
Total	14.9	16.0	67.0	61.3	15.4	20.5	2.7	2.2	100.0	100.0

[a]Table is read as follows: 27.3% of 15-year-old black nonvirgins never use any method of contraception.

TABLE 7: ***Age of first intercourse by age at first use of contraception, for blacks and whites(%)*** [a]

	Age at first intercourse									
Age at first use	<12	13	14	15	16	17	18	19	N.A.	Total
					Black					
<12	18.8[a]									0.9
13		33.6								2.3
14			39.9							5.0
15				44.1						12.5
16					54.1					20.1
17						63.8				18.3
18							71.2			9.1
19								52.0		1.4
N.A. (age)										13.3
N.A. (use)/never used										17.1
Total	4.8	5.3	12.3	20.7	26.2	18.3	7.3	0.4	3.2	100.0
					White					
<12	31.0									1.2
13		34.2								1.5
14			51.3							4.2
15				58.3						8.8
16					65.0					18.6
17						69.1				16.0
18							72.9			16.6
19								83.6		6.8
N.A. (age)										8.7
N.A. (use)/never used										17.6
Total	3.8	4.0	6.9	13.9	25.1	18.8	18.2	6.5	2.8	100.0

[a]Table is read as follows: 18.8% of black teenagers who had intercourse before age 13 began using contraceptives before age 13.

TABLE 8: ***Percent distribution of most recently used contraception method, by age and race***[a]

Method recently used	15		16		17		18		19		All ages	
	Black	*White*	*Black*	*White*	*Black*	*White*	*Black*	*White*	*Black*	*White*	*Black*	*White*
Pills	9.6[a]	2.3	29.4	8.8	21.0	21.4	31.6	25.9	33.4	41.9	26.5	25.0
Foam, jelly, or cream	3.6	2.0	1.8	1.6	3.0	2.7	3.6	4.8	5.0	1.6	3.5	2.7
IUD	3.0	0.0	0.7	0.0	3.4	0.0	4.7	1.3	4.8	0.9	3.6	0.6
Diaphragm	1.0	0.0	0.7	0.0	0.2	0.0	3.0	2.0	1.0	3.9	1.2	1.7
Condom	38.8	25.9	33.4	41.8	32.2	20.1	26.4	16.1	34.3	16.3	32.5	21.8
Douche	7.8	4.3	15.4	4.5	17.7	1.2	7.8	4.0	10.3	1.5	12.1	2.9
Withdrawal	18.5	48.2	5.4	25.3	10.5	41.2	8.6	34.3	4.0	26.2	8.5	33.0
Rhythm	0.0	0.0	0.0	6.2	0.0	2.8	2.2	1.3	0.0	2.5	0.5	2.6
Douche and withdrawal	1.7	7.8	0.7	2.0	3.6	1.9	2.6	2.5	2.4	0.7	2.3	2.2
Condom and other	16.0	9.5	12.5	9.8	8.4	8.7	9.5	7.8	4.8	4.5	9.3	7.5
Total	100.0	100.0	100.0	100.0	100.0	100.0	100.0	100.0	100.0	100.0	100.0	100.0

[a]Table is read as follows: 9.6% of black 15-year-olds who use contraceptives used the "pill" most recently.

TABLE 9: ***Percent giving specified reason for not using contraception, by race***[a]

Reason	*Black*		*White*	
Trying to have baby; didn't mind if pregnant	24.2[b]		12.1	
Too young; infrequent sex; didn't think could get pregnant	27.8	49.1	16.4	58.9
Time of month when couldn't get pregnant	21.4		42.5	
Hedonism—heedlessness[c]	7.2		9.6	
Knowledge—logistic[d]	12.7		14.2	
Partner objects; wrong to use	3.0		4.5	
Other[e]	3.8		0.7	
Total	100.0		100.0	

[a]Refers to first reason given. Percentages computed omitting those who have always used contraception, those who gave no answer to the several questions on contraceptive use, and those whose answer to this question was coded "other."

[b]Table is read as follows: 24.2% of the black teenagers who specified a reason for not using contraceptives said they were trying to have a baby or didn't mind if they got pregnant.

[c]"No fun to use"; too "inconvenient"; "didn't want to use"; "just didn't."

[d]Didn't have contraception available; didn't know where to obtain; didn't know about contraception.

[e]"Dangerous," medical reason for believing to be infecund; "too expensive."

TABLE 10: ***Percent distribution of sources of contraception, by age and race***[a]

	15		*16*		*17*		*18*		*19*		*Total*	
Source	*Black*	*White*	*Black*	*White*	*Black*	*White*	*Black*	*White*	*Black*	*White*	*Black*	*White*
Private physician	7.5	0.0	10.6	6.1	8.5	7.6	8.9	12.2	5.2	21.2	7.8	12.7
Drugstore[b]	60.3	78.1	57.2	67.8	64.0	67.4	61.5	64.6	66.1	58.5	62.8	64.3
Hospital clinic	22.7	0.0	24.6	0.0	17.3	4.2	20.3	5.4	18.5	9.7	19.8	5.5
Other type of clinic[c]	6.4	7.0	7.6	8.1	7.2	13.0	8.8	10.6	9.7	9.0	8.3	10.0
Other[d]	3.1	14.9	0.0	18.0	3.0	7.8	0.5	7.2	0.5	1.6	1.3	7.5
Total	100.0	100.0	100.0	100.0	100.0	100.0	100.0	100.0	100.0	100.0	100.0	100.0

[a]Excludes those who never used contraception, who did not answer the general question on use of contraception, who claimed never to have obtained contraception and those who provided no answer on source.

[b]Includes those who responded private physician and drugstore.

[c]Includes those who responded hospital clinic and other type of clinic.

[d]Includes "friends," "relatives," and "commercial establishments other than drugstores."

DISTRICT OF COLUMBIA SUMMER YOUTH PROGRAM

In the 1960s, the local political, economic, and social climate of Washington, D.C., was clearly undergoing change, as it was in other major cities with large minority populations. The youthful black power movement was growing increasingly militant. ''Colored'' became Negro, which became black as the preferred name for black Americans. And black was now beautiful, and proclaimed as such. Black Washingtonians also wanted their ''fair share'' of economic and social equality.

For the third consecutive year, the federal government provided funds to the District of Columbia for the purpose of conducting a summer program for the district's underprivileged youths. The funds were provided to the Youth Programs Unit of the D.C. government. In a city with a population of 750,000 people and a public school system enrollment of approximately 150,000, the 1968 D.C. Summer Youth Program was unique for three important reasons. First, the city, which had experienced racial street riots (officially termed ''civil disobedience''), had only three months before initiation of the summer program. Second, it was decided that in order to offer program activities which better satisfy the needs of the community, community members were to have a substantial role in the program planning and operations. This decision would not only allow the community to identify its own needs and develop programs to meet these needs but also to ensure greater community involvement in the summer program. Third, the federal government insisted that an independent evaluation be conducted to determine the effectiveness of the more than $2 million to be spent this summer. Accordingly, the D.C. government contracted with a consulting research organization to evaluate the 273 program activities funded by the Youth Programs Unit. (Figure 1 presents the 1976 D.C. organization, indicating a change in organizational name of the Youth Programs Unit.)

In June 1978, the consultants met with Joe James, Director of the Youth Programs Unit, and his staff of two professionals assigned to the planning and conduct of the summer program. Joe James, a young ambitious professional, came from a background in the District of Columbia's Recreation Department to head up the Youth Programs Unit. Although James did not have a plan with specific goals, objectives, subobjectives, activities, and so on, he was committed to the concept of community inputs in the design of program activities. He was under great pressures. It was late: a plan had not been developed ''because everybody spent the last three months trying to keep the city from burning.'' The Mayor's office was committed to a ''cool summer'' and ostensibly did not care what summer activities were funded as long as the District of Columbia did not emulate the April riots or those experienced by several other cities. ''I had good programs last year and I'll fund some of those again,'' said James. Also, some informal neighborhood street

---

This case was prepared by Edward J. Cherian as part of a joint project by the State University of New York at Albany and Rensselaer Polytechnic Institute to develop case materials on the delivery of service at the state and local government levels for use in graduate programs in public administration. The project has been made possible by an institutional grant from the United States Office of Education under Title IX, Parts A and C, of the Higher Education Act of 1965, as amended, and was directed by Professor Donald Axelrod, State University of New York at Albany, and Professor William Wallace, Rensselaer Polytechnic Institute.

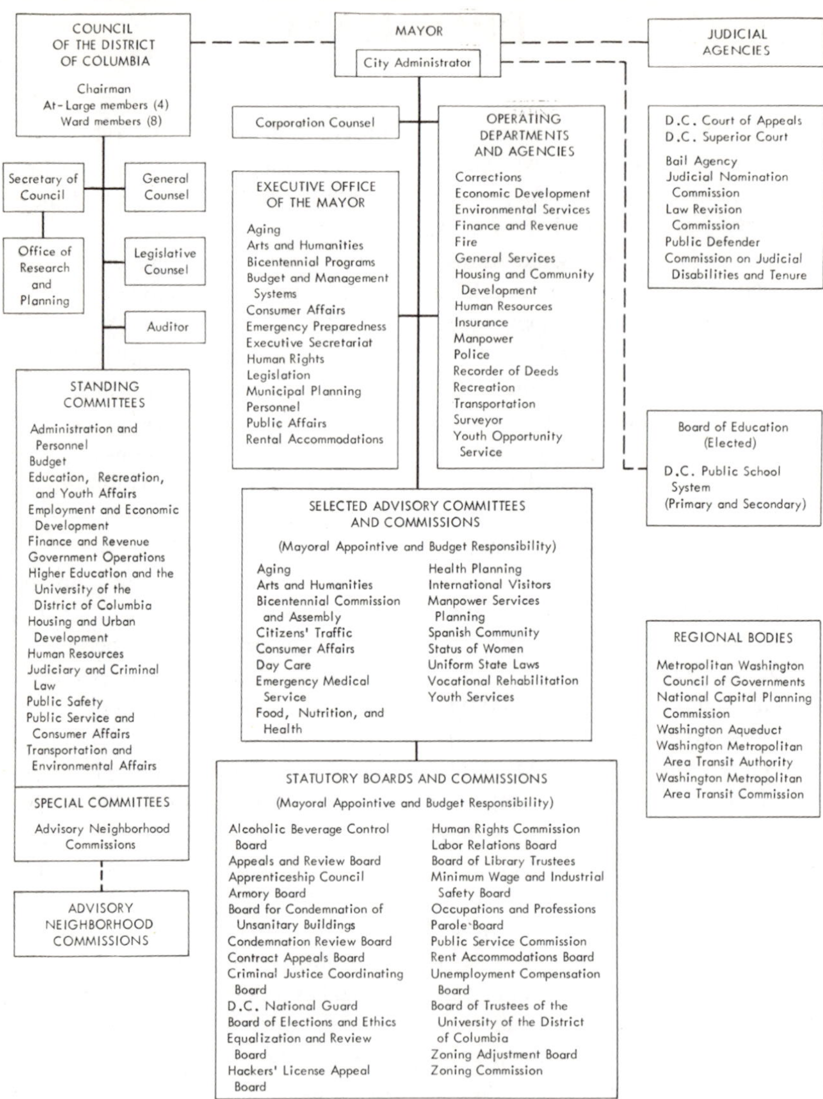

FIGURE 1: ***Organization of the District of Columbia government***

leaders, who had followings of youth, expected programs of their choosing to be funded this summer.

To facilitate community involvement, the District of Columbia was divided into four districts which contained a total of 20 neighborhood areas identified by population concentrations. Each neighborhood area was represented by a community group, called a Neighborhood Planning Council (NPC). The Councils consisted of members elected by the community, through whom it was hoped community participation would be enhanced. Funds were allocated to each area dependent upon the number of youths from low-income families[1] in that area. Within the limitation provided by the amount of funds available and with the requirement that programs provide "wholesome activities," NPCs were allowed full leeway to develop their own activities to meet the needs of their specific youth populations; 273 activity programs were funded within the 20 areas during the summer of 1968.

But the city was tense; small racial incidents seemed to be magnified in the news media. Black residents were fearful of their own neighbors and began tagging their cars with "soul brother" stickers in the hope that the identification would prevent damage. In a community that had ostensibly achieved racial peace years before, with low unemployment, with a large percentage of the labor force in white-collar and stable government jobs, a vocal and youthful black power movement was surfacing.

THE SUMMER EFFORT

All public service programs operate with constraints on time and money, and the Summer Youth Program was no exception: activities were late getting started, and center locations and staff were slow in coming together and making their existence known to the community.

Add to this the tense racial environment and the perception of hostility that many youths expressed toward the establishment (i.e., District of Columbia and federal governments), and the constraints appear quite formidable.

Table 1 represents the original fund allocation, the supplemental fund allocation,[2] and the number and percentage of participants and staff actually observed participating in summer youth activities.

Table 2 presents the fund allocation, staff, and participants as a function of program activity type. Since the NCPs were permitted to determine the nature of the program best suited to the needs of youth in their areas, this table may reflect the needs of the employment and mixed (multipurpose) programs. It may be noted from Table 3 that 68.9% of the total funds were allocated to recreation programs, 13.0% to education, 7.7% to employment, and 10.4% to mixed programs.

Because the Summer Youth Program was conceived and implemented in a highly decentralized style, no central publicity or announcement was utilized in initiating the program. Recruitment was most frequently accomplished by staffs spreading the word and/or canvassing individual neighborhoods door to door. The efficiency of decentralized recruitment did, of course, vary from program to program, but a more systematic recruitment effort may have excluded some youths indicating an interest in the program.

THE EVALUATION EFFORTS

The design and conduct of a meaningful evaluation was an equally difficult problem, greatly hampered by the lack of specific program objectives against which a traditional evaluation construct could be developed. To meet the problems inherent in examining programs *in vivo,* the consultants chose to carry out interviews with the various persons connected with the program activity and to compare their attitudes. The following populations were interviewed: program participants, the neighborhood participants, the Neighborhood Youth Corps,[3] program directors and senior aides (adult staff), nonparticipant youths, Neighborhood Planning Council chairmen and members, and the D.C. Youth Programs Unit staff.

Data collected from the summer programs were tabled and organized and 35 representative sample sites were selected. The sample of program activities was weighted to be representative of the total population of program activities under way. Field information[4] then visited each selected site for the purpose of aiding data collection. Subsequently field informants revisited all 273 sites to validate initial data collected and to ensure that data that were dependent on estimates were sufficiently reliable.

Seventy-four participants in the 1968 Summer Youth Program were interviewed at the 35 sample sites. Participants (45 males and 29 females) were chosen at random and interviewed at their centers.

TABLE 1: ***Total allocations, observed staff, and observed participants by neighborhood planning council area, summer 1968***

	Available funds		*Total allocation*		*Observed participants*		*Observed staff*	
Area	*Original allocation*	*Special allocation*	*Amount*	*Percent*	*Number*	*Percent*	*Number*	*Percent*
Total:	$2,036,263	$101,519	$2,137,782	100.0	21,861	100.0	3395	100.0
1	30,516	3,355	33,871	1.6	331	1.5	45	1.3
2	10,629	2,150	12,779	0.6	55	0.3	8	0.2
3	18,112	2,795	20,907	1.0	404	1.8	11	0.3
4	7,895	1,800	9,695	0.5	209	1.0	7	0.2
5	76,073	6,200	82,273	3.8	717	3.3	111	3.4
6	17,450	2,610	20,060	0.9	345	1.6	38	1.1
7	22,860	3,415	26,275	1.2	400	1.8	34	1.0
8	115,999	5,453	121,452	5.7	2,055	9.4	178	5.2
9	125,025	4,285	129,310	6.0	1,214	5.6	221	6.5
10	136,473	3,600	140,073	6.6	1,209	5.5	198	5.8
11	110,405	4,826	115,231	5.4	1,244	5.7	196	5.8
12	24,046	1,850	25,896	1.2	845	3.9	165	4.9
13	33,979	1,750	35,729	1.7	275	1.3	29	0.9
14	83,223	5,414	88,637	4.2	2,140	11.0	411	12.1
15	267,246	12,044	279,290	13.1	2,345	10.7	381	11.2
16	269,238	8,767	278,005	13.0	1,724	7.9	396	11.7
17	92,339	2,575	94,914	4.4	872	4.0	164	4.8
18	297,099	13,440	310,539	14.5	2,699	12.3	404	11.9
19	168,400	7,740	176,140	8.2	1,408	6.4	191	5.6
20	129,256	7,450	136,706	6.4	1,100	5.0	207	6.1

TABLE 2: *Total programs, fund allocation, staff, and participants by type of program activity, summer 1968*

Type of program	Program activities		Original allocation		Total staff		Participants	
	Number	Percent	Amount	Percent	Number	Percent	Number	Percent
Total:	273		$2,036,263		3,395		21,861	
Administration	3		11,359		23		—	
Total minus administration	270	100.0	2,024,904	100.0	3,372	100.0	21,861	100.0
Preschool	43	15.9	214,574	10.6	465	13.8	2,401	11.0
Youth center	81	30.0	823,561	40.7	1,360	40.3	8,359	38.2
Teen center	40	14.8	294,757	14.6	408	12.1	3,299	15.1
Multicenter[a]	10	3.7	163,204	8.1	249	7.4	1,671	7.6
Block and street camps	37	13.7	187,204	9.2	403	12.0	2,425	11.1
Work skills	14	5.2	95,836	4.7	108	3.2	517	2.4
Job development/ employment	7	2.6	58,405	2.9	61	1.8	298[b]	1.4
Beautification	4	1.5	14,675	0.7	51	1.5	205	0.9
Culture/science/ art center	12	4.4	69,169	3.4	85	2.5	588	2.7
General recreation and athletics	4	1.5	36,086	1.8	62	1.8	407	1.9
Other	18	6.7	67,433	3.3	120	3.6	1,691	7.7

[a]Includes 8 multipurpose centers and 2 preschool/youth center combinations.

[b]This figure is an estimate of the average number of weekly job referrals and is not the same as the number of participants in other programs.

TABLE 3: ***Fund allocation, number of program activities, number of participants, and observed staff be type of program, summer 1968***

	Amount	*Percent*
Allocation		
Total allocation	2,036,263	
Administration	11,359	
Total, minus administration	2,024,904	100.0
Education	262,373	13.0
Recreation	1,394,583	68.9
Employment	156,228	7.7
Mixed	211,720	10.4

	Number	*Percent*
Number of program activities		
Number of programs	273	
Administration	3	
Total, minus administration	270	100.0
Education	55	20.4
Recreation	175	64.8
Employment	21	7.8
Mixed	19	7.0
Number of participants		
Total participants	21,861	100.0
Education	2,876	13.1
Recreation	16,040	73.4
Employment	872	4.0
Mixed	2,073	9.5
Number of observed staff		
Total observed staff	3,395	
Administration	23	
Total, minus administration	3,372	100.0
Education	533	15.8
Recreation	2,312	68.6
Employment	207	6.1
Mixed	320	9.5

The ages of interviewees ranged from 7 through 18, with the greatest number being between 14 and 15. The average age is somewhat older than that of the total population due to the fact that preschool age children (for obvious reasons) were not interviewed. Despite this, the age distribution of the sample participant population does reflect the emphasis of the Summer Youth Program on youths 15 and under.

PROGRAM PARTICIPANTS IN 35 SAMPLE SITES: ***Sample interviewed***

Age	7–10	11	12	13	14	15	16	17–18
Number	6	7	11	9	11	13	10	7

Seventy-one youths who did not participate in the program were selected and interviewed at random from the neighborhoods surrounding the 35 sample sites. The sample included 53 males and 18 females, with ages ranging from 8 to 19 (average 15.4 years). The average age of the group is similar to that of the program participants' sample.

PROGRAM NONPARTICIPANTS: ***Sample interviewed***

Age	8–10	11	12	13	14	15	16	17–19	NR
Number	3	2	7	3	17	9	24	4	

With program operations, participants, and staff constantly changing, it was difficult to gather observations representative of ongoing events. This resulted in differences in sample populations and, hence, in determining numbers of participants and staff members. In the case of participants, many of the activities did not require attendance records, and therefore some evaluation results contain estimates based on the average number of youths being served at various sites. With respect to staff, the problems of recruitment and hiring as well as job maintenance resulted in the need for an estimate of on-board staff as opposed to any fixed number obtained either at the initiation or termination of a program activity.

Initially, field activities of the evaluation effort were directed by Barbara Jones, a senior research associate of the consultant's organization who by training and experience was well qualified for such an effort. Barbara, raised in a white middle-class family, had completed undergraduate and graduate degrees in psychology and had spent several years working for the State of California Juvenile Delinquency Program. She designed a project to examine each of the 273 summer program activities in terms of:

1. Fiscal allocations
2. Number of participants
3. Number of staff members
4. Types of activities
5. General observations

Based on this initial examination, 35 program activities representative of all types of summer programs were selected for in-depth examination in different geographic areas. In addition, NPC chairmen, co-chairmen, youth representatives, and staff members from the Youth Program Unit were interviewed to determine interactions between various organizations; in particular, community youths' attitude toward the existing D.C. government structure.

To collect information most efficiently from the population of participating youths, the evaluation consultants decided to recruit, train, and utilize resident youths as interviewers. Accordingly, 10 youths ranging in age from 15 to 20 years were selected and trained as field informants. To carry out the evaluation, a store-front field office, central to the target areas, was rented and equipped. After orientation and training, the field informants conducted initial site visits at all 273 programs, while themselves participating in program activities to maximize their relationship with program participants.

The first successful applicant informers were mostly from middle-class families, college-bound, dressed in coat and tie; 40% were white. With this team, Barbara found it difficult to initiate discussions with street youths and the virtually all black staff. [The District of Columbia's population is 72% minority (mostly black), as is 97% of the public-school population.]

Barbara was replaced by Boris Frank, a black psychiatric social worker and lifelong D.C. resident. "I'm not going to advertise for no kids with ties—I can find who I need by taking my coat off and hanging out at the right street corners." Frank retained two of the original group of field informants and recruited eight street-smart youths—"thugs," said Frank. Data collection forms and questionnaires were prepared covering various types of program participants to be interviewed:

1. The *site validation form* was used to gather data at each of the 273 programs.
2. The *program participant form* was used to gather in-depth information at 35 centers from youths who participated in programs.
3. The *NYC staff form* was used to gather in-depth information from youths working as staff members at the 35 programs examined in depth.
4. The *program directors and senior aides form* was used to gather in-depth information from adult staff members.
5. The *nonparticipant form* was used to interview nonparticipating youths for comparison purposes.

In addition to these structured interviews, senior staff from the consultant's organization interviewed NPC chairmen, co-chairmen, and youth representatives, as well as members of the Youth Program Unit staff. (Such interviews were more sophisticated, sometimes structured, sometimes unstructured.)

An in-depth analysis was performed at 35 sample centers. The centers chosen reflected the distribution of activities in the total Summer Youth Programs by geographic location and by type of program activity. Sample centers were chosen in all four NPC districts covering 16 NPC areas. In Table 4 a comparison of the distribution of sample centers with the total Summer Youth Program by activity type is presented. Interviews were held with program participants, NYCs, senior aides, adult staff, and center directors to determine attitudes toward the program.

The data from program participants, NYCs, and senior staff members indicate a strong identification between NYCs and program participants, rather than between NYCs and senior staff. To verify this finding, a comparison of future employment aspirations of NYCs and program participants was performed as a means of obtain-

TABLE 4: ***Comparison of sample programs and total programs by type of summer program***

	Total summer youth program		*Sample sites*	
Type of program activity	*Number*	*Percent*	*Number*	*Percent*
Total:	270	100.0	35	100.0
Preschool	43	15.9	6	17.0
Youth center	81	30.0	9	25.0
Teen center	40	14.8	4	11.0
Multicenter	10	3.7	1	2.8
Block and street camps	37	13.7	3	8.5
Work skills: skills workshop	14	5.2	2	5.7
Job development/employment: job centers, employment odd jobs	7	2.6	3	8.5
Beautification	4	1.5	1	2.8
Culture/science/art: youth adv. center, art skills, arts and crafts	12	4.4	3	8.5
General recreation and athletics	4	1.5	1	2.8
Other	18	6.7	2	7.4

ing an indication of similarities between these two populations. Program participant data were derived from site validation forms and NYC data from the NYC interview format. Responses were coded according to the nine *Dictionary of Occupational Titles* job classifications and indicate an extremely high degree of correlation between the future aspirations of youths in the NYC program and youths participating in summer activities. Staff members also frequently appeared to accept the NYCs as program participants rather than as younger and less experienced co-staff. Many cited NYCs as beneficiaries of the summer program activities together with program participants. Indeed, the NYCs frequently seemed to see themselves as program participants.

An attempt was made to identify attitudes on the part of the various population groups involved in summer activities, and to identify the impact of developing (or not developing) plans for summer programs. Table 5 presents these attitudes.

INTERVIEW RESPONSES

Perhaps the most interesting dimension of understanding the 1968 Summer Youth Program was the response of program participants (and some nonparticipants) to specific questionnaire items. Seventy-four program participants of the 1968 Summer Youth Program were interviewed at the 35 sample sites. Participants were chosen at random and interviewed at their centers. The sample population included 45 males and 29 females from the ages of 7 to 18—the greatest number being between 14 and 15.

What do you think about the activities in the program? ($N = 74$)

Very good program		*Program OK*		*Program poor*		*No response*	
No.	*%*	*No.*	*%*	*No.*	*%*	*No.*	*%*
24	34	43	58	3	4	3	4

TABLE 5: *Attitudes of four populations toward purpose of 1968 Summer Youth Program*[a]

Sample population	*Total*		*Positive*		*Neutral*		*Somewhat negative*		*Negative*		*To give teens work*		*Don't know or no response*	
	Number	*Percent*	*Number*	*Percent*	*Number*	*Percent*	*Number*	*Percent*	*Number*	*Percent*	*Number*	*Percent*	*Number*	*Percent*
Program participants	74	100	17	23	10	14	40	54	3	4			4	5
Neighborhood youth corps	59	100	13	23	8	14	29	46			6	11	3	5
Program directors and senior aides (adult staff)	49	100	25	51	22	45			1	2			1	2
Nonparticipant youths	43	100	11	24	13	31	13	31	6	14				

[a]Positive: To benefit youths.
Neutral: To give youths something to do and some place to go.
Somewhat negative: to keep youths off the streets (riot control)
Negative: Expresses hostility toward program (e.g., antiblack).

What don't you like about this program? (*N* = 74)

Nothing disliked		*Something disliked*	
No.	*%*	*No.*	*%*
55	74.3	19	25.7

What, in particular, don't you like about the program? [*N* = 20 (2 responses by one youth)]

Inappropriate:		*Insufficient or inadequate:*		
Schedule	*Staff*	*Facilities*	*Equipment*	*Activities*
2	4	2	2	2

Other	
Participants	*Other*
6	2

What activities would you like to see next year? (*N* = 74)

More of same		*Something not offered now*[a]		*More jobs*	
No.	*%*	*No.*	*%*	*No.*	*%*
66	89	6	8	2	3

[a]Activities specified: horseback riding, fishing, golf.

Have you learned from the program? (*N* = 74)

Learned something from program		*Learned nothing*		*No response*	
No.	*%*	*No.*	*%*	*No.*	*%*
63	84	6	8	5	7

What was learned from the program? (*N* = 63)

Specific skill		*Character improvement (e.g., get along with others, assume responsibility, etc.)*	
No.	*%*	*No.*	*%*
33	53	20	32

Other		*Not specified*	
No.	*%*	*No.*	*%*
7	11	6	10

Why are there summer programs? (*N* = 74)

Positive: to benefit youth		*Neutral: give kids some place to go, something to do*		*Somewhat negative: kids off streets, riot control*	
No.	*%*	*No.*	*%*	*No.*	*%*
17	23	10	14	40	54

Negative: hostile; take advantage of people; antiblack		*Don't know*		*No response*	
No.	*%*	*No*	*%*	*No.*	*%*
3	4	2	3	2	3

What problems have you had in administering the programs? (*N* = 49)

Problems	*No problems*
30	19

Specify: (*N* = 55, multiple responses)

Equipment	*Facilities*	*Staff*	*Activities*	*Planning*
15	4	6	3	2

Security	*Community with NPC*	*Money and red tape*	*Counseling and orientation for NYCs*
2	4	7	2

In-program discipline	*Community involvement*	*Other*
3	2	5

Why is there a summer program? (*N* = 49)

Positive: benefit youth	*Somewhat negative: keep youths off street*
25	22

Negative: free babysitting	*No response*
1	1

In reference to goal orientation, a more revealing response was obtained which required the respondent to specify the goals of his or her particular program.

Does your program have specific goals, and if so, what are they? ($N = 49$)

Yes	*No*	*No response*
46	5	0

Goals stated in specific terms:	*Goals stated in general non-action-oriented terms:*
e.g., expose youths to various team sports; teach them graphic arts; teach children to do one thing for themselves	e.g., help children; keep youths off street

Over 70% of the respondents felt that the purpose of the program was to "keep us busy and out of the way for the summer"; 58% that the program was set up as a riot-control measure. It should be noted that despite the youths' feeling that the program was not set up to benefit them directly, they were eager participants and felt they had benefited from their summer's experience. This response, then, by the youths may not reflect negative attitudes toward the program itself but may instead be directed to the youths' perception of the general purposes of the program.

In light of the fact that the NYCs were closest in age to the program participants, they usually communicated with them more successfully than with any other staff members, and thus they were able to influence their perceptions substantially. Had the NYCs understood the purpose of the program more clearly, the participants may also have gained a greater understanding, enabling both groups to derive more benefit from the program.

Forty-nine senior staff members were chosen at random at the sample sites and interviewed. The sample population consisted of 21 males and 28 females ranging in age from 18 to 43. Of the 49 adult staff members, 36 were residents of the neighborhoods surrounding the centers.

Over half of the staff were able to enunicate program goals in such a way as to direct the course of program activities, but *none* of the staff interviewed could verbalize specific goals for the Summer Youth Program as a whole.

Seventy-one youths who did not participate in the Summer Youth Programs were selected at random from neighborhoods surrounding the 35 sample sites and interviewed. The sample nonparticipant youth population included 53 males and 18 females. Ages of interviewees ranged from 8 to 19 and averaged 15.4 years. The average age of the group is similar to that of the program participants sample.

Do you know about summer programs? ($N = 71$)

Yes		*No*		*Misinformation*		*No response*	
No.	*%*	*No.*	*%*	*No.*	*%*	*No.*	*%*
43	61	20	28	8	11	0	

Do you know about summer youth programs? If so, what do they provide? ($N = 43$, multiple responses)

Recreation programs	*Employment placement and training*	*Education and preschool*
40	5	4

Cultural enrichment	*Art and home economic skills*	*Type of information not specified*
4	5	2

If known, why not interested? ($N = 37$)

Hostile: won't participate in antiblack or baby programs		*Working, going to school, family responsibilities*	
No.	*%*	*No.*	*%*
5	13.5	14	38

Has to find job or job training		*Interested*		*Nothing there of interest*	
No.	*%*	*No.*	*%*	*No.*	*%*
10	27	1	2.7	7	19

What program activities, jobs, etc, would you have participated in?

Activities available		*Activities not available*		*Don't know*	
No.	*%*	*No.*	*%*	*No.*	*%*
49	70	5	7	4	5.7

Won't participate in whitey or baby programs		*None; no time*		*No response*	
No.	*%*	*No.*	*%*	*No.*	*%*
4	5.7	6	6.7	3	3.3

Activities desired: 2, post office jobs; 2, "pride"; 1, U.S. Army.

Why are there summer youth programs? (N = 43)

Positive: beneficial		*Neutral: gives youths something to do and some place to go*	
No.	*%*	*No.*	*%*
11	24	13	31

Somewhat negative: riot prevention, keep youths off streets		*Negative: antiblack; take advantage of people*	
No.	*%*	*No.*	*%*
13	31	6	14

Despite the fact that both participating and non-participating youths indicated that what they wanted was what was offered, hostility to the Summer Youth Program in general was evidenced. Many of the same youths who stated that the program activities offered what they wanted also felt that the Summer Youth Program was a *buy-out,* a kind of riot control. Summer programs have long been sought after and provided in middle-class neighborhoods without the onus of riot control or copping out. Clearly, the youth in D.C. wanted the same kinds of services. A frequent suggestion to alleviate this attitude was that the programs be extended to a year-round effort.

In October 1968, Joe James conducted a review of the summer's activities after reading the consultant's final report. He was displeased. "OK, consultants, tell me what I should do next year." "Specifically, develop a plan for the 1969 Summer Youth Program. As I see it, that plan should include the following discrete components: an overall goal statement, two to six objectives, subobjectives, and activities necessary to advise me as to the "what, how, when, who, and how much of the next year's program.' I also need your specific advice as to how the program should be evaluated next year. Let's make every effort to reach agreement on the criteria for evaluation *now.*"

NOTES

1. The federal government's property index was utilized: that is, a family of four whose annual income is $3,600 or less is considered low-income, with a scale of increasing family size to increasing income.
2. Additional funds were provided late in the summer to the D.C. Youth Program Unit from the Office of Economic Opportunity.
3. Originally an OEO-funded program for low-income youths, now funded by the U.S. Department of Labor. Both in-school youths 14 to 21 years old and out-of-school youths 16 to 22 years old may participate for full-time or part-time employment.
4. The term *informant* is used here in an anthropological sense: that is, an individual able to serve as a bridge between two dissimilar populations.

III: ANALYZING MARKETING OPPORTUNITIES

To apply marketing techniques to use in nonprofit organizations, markets must be defined and measured. Estimating market demand and future market demand are very important steps in planning marketing activities. Selecting a market to serve and targeting the marketing strategy to that selected market should guide marketing efforts.

Consumer or client analysis is helpful to pinpoint individual buyer behavior or organizational buyer behavior. This helps to understand consumer's needs and wants. Information and decision evaluation and post decision assessment must be analyzed to design a marketing strategy to achieve desired objectives. Marketing opportunities or circumstances favorable to marketing success must be understood so that consumer oriention is possible.

The first article, by F. Kelly Shuptrine and Ellen M. Moore, is entitled "The Public's Perceptions of the American Heart Association." The authors maintain that there is inadequate published information on the public's perceptions and attitudes toward voluntary service, nonprofit health organizations. Furthermore, little is known about how these attitudes/perceptions are related to actual donor behavior. The purpose of their study is to determine general perceptions, knowledge, and attitudes of the public toward the American Heart Association and likes/dislikes of charities in general. Research in this area can have important implications in providing insight and suggestions for corrective actions by voluntary health organizations.

The second article is "Marketing Research in Health Services Planning: A Model" by William A. Flexner and Eric N. Berkowitz. The authors point out that decisions about the design and delivery of services by private clinics, hospitals, neighborhood health centers, and health maintenance organizations (HMOs) are made primarily by professionals. Yet consumer input into these decisions is increasingly being sought, even demanded. Generally, this input has been obtained by four methods: (1) consumer representation on boards, (2) consumer advocacy (e.g., Ralph Nader's Health Research Group), (3) a diagnosis of the community (the community being regarded as the patient) and assessment of the community's needs, and (4) behavioral and social science research.

The third article in this section is "A Marketing Segmentation Approach to Transit Planning, Modeling, and Management," by Christopher H. Lovelock. Services that are developed, priced, distributed, and promoted to appeal to a mass market may fall short of their potential because people's needs and behavior patterns often differ sharply. By segmenting the market into different groups, based on such factors as individual characteristics, attitudes, behavior, and location, important insights can often be obtained into market dynamics. This makes it possible to develop services which are closely tailored to the needs of specific segments. This article examines alternative ways of segmenting the market for public transportation services and considers the implications for marketing strategy.

Cases in this section include "Massachusetts State Lottery" and "United Way of Penobscot Valley."

The Public's Perceptions of the American Heart Association: Awareness, Image and Opinions

F. KELLY SHUPTRINE
ELLEN M. MOORE

There is little published information on the public's perceptions and attitudes toward voluntary service, non-profit organizations or on how these attitudes/perceptions are related to actual donor behavior. Limited image/perception studies of voluntary health organizations have been reported [5, 13]. A couple of confidential studies examined by the authors concerning awareness, image and attitudes of voluntary health organizations were rather limited and provided little useful information for organizational change. Some recent research studies have focused on variables that affect a person's willingness to give or comply with a request [3, 7–10]. These compliance techniques are designed to ultimately benefit the charitable cause by increased giving. Other reports [6, 11, 12] have touched on the issues of declining contributions, the beginnings of real competition (especially, most activist charities versus the United Way), and the attacks of sharp critics who want to abolish charities and turn their duties over to government. Beik and Smith [2] also did a geographic segmentation study on American Heart Association contributors in Pennsylvania. However, there again is no input on how the public perceives the roles of charitable institutions.

Charitable organizations want to cultivate the support of a public or some segments of the public to produce resources such as money, time, and encouragement [4]. Once this is accomplished, the benefits that are generated can be returned to the public through the organization's sponsored activities. Therefore, the purpose of this study is to determine general perceptions, knowledge, images, and attitudes of the public toward a specific voluntary health agency, the American Heart Association. Research in this area can have important implications in providing insight and suggestions for corrective actions by voluntary health organizations.

METHOD

Personal interviews were conducted in the fall of 1979 with 130 households in a southeastern metropolitan area. The interviews were the first conducted in a three-phase process to obtain information about three voluntary health organizations.

The questionnaire was developed by consulting with persons knowledgeable in the voluntary health service field, reviewing American Heart Association pamphlets, and through two pretests, each with approximately 100 households in the proposed, study area. An area survey sampling plan of tracts was used. Streets, blocks, and households were randomly selected with alternatives within each area to obtain a minimum of 125 interviews for each phase of the survey.

The survey was administered by selected senior marketing research students. Each interviewer was trained in the art of the interviewing process

Reprinted with permission from *Proceedings of the Southern Marketing Association,* Fall 1980, pp. 281–284.

to alleviate response errors in the data. Two practice/pretest sessions aided the refinement of the questionnaire and provided experience for the interviewers.

The voluntary health organization used in the study, the American Heart Association (AHA), was one of the three top-ranked receivers of philanthropic support in 1978 as listed in the American Association of Fund-Rasing Counsel publication [1]. The other two organizations (American Cancer Society and March of Dimes) are being used in the second and third phase of the research.

The questionnaire included:

- A list of respondent demographics.
- A list of goals and activities of the AHA plus some activities of other organizations to determine awareness and knowledge.
- A list of adjectives and descriptive phases to be scaled to profile the AHA. There was an original list of 45 items that were reduced to 18 items after two pretests.
- Overall like/dislike scale of charities in general, how good a job the AHA is doing, and how much money out of $100 respondents would give to the AHA.
- A question that asked if the respondent had donated time and/or money to the AHA (this breakdown was used in the analysis to discuss most of the other questions).
- An open-end question for additional views on the AHA and charities in general.

FINDINGS

The demographic profile of respondents is upscale as a whole in terms of education, job type, and income when compared to available Bureau of the Census averages. The greatest proportion of respondents were married, white, female, and are employed full time. The family incomes range between $15,000 to $30,000 3–4 individuals are in the household, and most have some college education or are college graduates. The greatest proportion of respondents have lived over twenty years in the city.

Some demographic characteristics of those respondents that contribute money to the American Heart Association differ in some part from those respondents that do not contribute money. A substantially *greater* percentage of respondents that have *not* donated money within the last year are younger, have more than 5 individuals in the household, have lived less than five years in the area, and have moderate household incomes ($10,000–$29,999). Those who have been *most likely* to donate money within the last year are older, have either low (less than $10,000) or high household income ($30,000 or more), have fewer individuals in the household (4 or less), and have lived more than 20 years in the area (see Table 1). Thus, demographic profiles of money contributors versus non-contributors differ, and provide useful possibilities for market targeting.

Attitude Toward Giving. Respondents were asked about giving money to charitable organizations in general. Those subjects that have donated money to AHA or served as a volunteer for AHA within the last year responded most often that giving to charitable organizations is something that they "find very rewarding" (54%, respectively). Basically, there were no major differences between those who gave money and those who were volunteers (see Table 2). Overall, the greatest majority of respondents' attitudes toward giving money to charitable organizations in general is something that they find very rewarding or like to do.

Opinions. Subjects were given the opportunity to express opinions in their own words to an open-end question on charitable organizations. The greatest proportion of respondents (45%) had no comments or no opinions. Thirteen percent of the respondents expressed positive, supportive views of charities in general. Negative opinions were expressed concerning inefficiency or misuse of funds (8%), annoying solicitation methods (4%), and bad experiences with a specific charity

TABLE 1: *Selected demographic characteristics of respondents who donated money to the American Heart Association*

Demographic characteristic	*Donated money* Yes (%)	No (%)	*n*	*Demographic characteristic*	*Donated money* Yes (%)	No (%)	*n*
Age				Individuals in household			
< 30	11	89	28				
30–39	59	41	27	1–2	54	46	50
40–49	29	71	21	3–4	48	52	60
50–59	60	40	30	⩾ 5	25	75	20
⩾ 60	75	25	24				
Household income				Years in city			
< $10,000	62	38	13				
10,000–14,999	15	85	13	⩽ 5	20	80	20
15,000–19,999	41	59	29	6–10	35	65	26
20,000–29,999	38	62	29	11–15	46	54	11
30,000–39,999	56	44	16	16–20	46	54	11
⩾ $40,000	58	42	12	>20	61	39	62

TABLE 2: *Attitude toward giving to any charitable organization*

Statement	*Total Sample (%) (n = 130)*	*Donated money (%)* Yes (n = 61)	*No (n = 69)*	*Served as volunteer (%)* Yes (n = 13)	*No (n = 116)*
Find very rewarding	45	54	36	54	44
Like to do	36	32	38	38	34
Don't care about one way or the other	12	10	14	8	13
Don't like to do	5	2	9	0	6
Dislike greatly	2	2	3	0	3

(2%). Five percent of the respondents stated a preference for having all charitable organizations consolidated, such as fund raising by the United Way (see Table 3).

How Good a Job. Subjects were asked: "Overall, how good a job do you think the American Heart Association is doing?" Overall, the greatest percentage of respondents felt AHA was doing a "good job" (50%). Those subjects that had donated money to AHA reported most often an excellent job (38%) or a good job (39%). As one might expect, a substantially greater proportion of respondents (62%) that had served as volunteers for AHA reported most often that AHA was doing an excellent job (see Table 4).

Knowledge/Awareness of Activities. Subjects were given a checklist of activities, slogans, programs, etc. to indicate whether the AHA or some other organization conducted or sponsored each item. Subjects were given a "don't know/does not apply" response and were also allowed to mark as many organizations that they felt may apply. The specific items and responses for the AHA are provided in Table 5. For the first four

TABLE 3: ***Expressed opinions to open-ended question about any charitable organization***

Categories of opinions expressed most often	*Percent respondents (n = 130)*
No opinion about charities/no strong feelings/no comments	45
Positive image/do good work/are needed/valuable	13
Misuse of funds/accountability/ bureaucratic/inefficient	8
Prefer to have all organizations under one (United Way mentioned most often)	5
Solicitation methods are bothersome/ annoying	4
Other charities (bad experience with a specific charity)	2
Other opinions	23

programs, approximately 70% or more of the total sample was able to correctly identify these programs as AHA sponsored. The most surprising result was the small proportion of total respondents (25%) that were able to identify a major campaign slogan of AHA "We're Fighting for Your Life." A small, but notable proportion of respondents incorrectly identified the advertising slogans or activities of the American Cancer Society (12%), Muscular Dystrophy (12%), American Lung Association (Christmas Seals) (6%), and the United Way (8%) as that of the AHA. Interestingly, the Christmas Seal campaign was most often incorrectly identified by AHA *volunteer* workers than by money contributors.

Donation of Funds. Respondents were told to assume they were given $100 to donate to charitable organizations. Interviewers asked the subjects to divide up the $100 in any way they wanted or give it all to one charity. Four categories were provided: the three top-ranked receivers of philanthropic support in 1978, which included AHA, and their "Favorite charity" (see Table 6). The greatest proportion of all respondents giving to AHA, would give between $26 and $40 dollars (25% of total sample). However, 35% of the total sample would not give anything. Respondents who have donated to AHA within the last year indicated $26 to $40 most often (38%), yet twenty percent indicated they would *not* donate any money. Of value to the AHA for future efforts, it is seen that of those who did not give in the last year, 39% would be willing to give $16 – $40 to the AHA. They may simply need to be reached by more effective communication and solicitors.

Image of AHA. This section of the questionnaire was designed to discover the respondents' image of the AHA. Subjects were given 18 terms to mark along one of five responses: 1, extremely; 2 moderately; 3, slightly; 4, not at all; 5, don't know. Table 7 shows the terms provided and the responses of the total sample. Looking at the average scale values, the AHA is seen as being highly professional, effective, prestigious, responsible,

TABLE 4: ***Job performance of the American Heart Association***

Category	*Total sample (%) (n = 130)*	*Donated money (%)*		*Served as volunteer (%)*	
		Yes (n = 61)	*No (n = 69)*	*Yes (n = 13)*	*No (n = 116)*
Excellent job	24	38	12	62	19
Good job	50	39	59	23	53
Fair job	14	15	13	0	15
Poor job	2	2	3	0	3
Very poor job	1	0	1	0	1
Don't know	9	6	12	15	9

TABLE 5: ***Knowledge/awareness of respondents of activities conducted by the American Heart Association***

Activities	Total sample (%)	Percent identified as AHA: Donated money		Served as volunteer	
		Yes	No	Yes	No
	(n = 130)	(n = 61)	(n = 69)	(n = 13)	(n = 116)
AHA related activities					
Hypertension screening	68	72	64	69	67
To reduce premature death and disability from cardiovascular diseases	81	82	80	77	81
Nationwide stroke programs	71	82	63	92	69
Diet; fat-modified eating patterns	74	74	74	85	72
We're Fighting for Your Life	25	25	27	15	27
Activities of other charities					
Programs for mass immunization against rubella (March of Dimes)	5	5	5	0	5
We Care (American Cancer Society)	12	12	12	8	12
Thanks To You It Works (United Way)	8	7	9	0	9
Jerry Lewis Labor Day Telethon (Muscular Dystrophy)	1	2	0	0	1
Christmas Seal Campaign (American Lung Association)	6	10	3	17	5
Combats Neuromuscular disease (Muscular Dystrophy)	12	12	12	8	12

TABLE 6: ***Proportion of hypothetical funds ($100) given to the American Heart Association***

Dollar amount would give to American Heart Association	Total sample (%)	Respondents who have donated to AHA within the last year (%)	Respondents who have not donated to AHA within the last year (%)
	(n = 130)	(n = 61)	(n = 69)
0	35	20	48
$1–15	5	5	4
16–25	21	16	25
26–40	25	38	14
41–75	13	20	7
76–100	3	3	1

TABLE 7: ***Overall image of the American Heart Association*** [a]

Category	*Average scale value*	*1 Extremely (%)*	*2 Moderately (%)*	*3 Slightly (%)*	*4 Not at all (%)*	*5 Don't know (%)*
Professional	1.6	44	41	5	1	10
Effective	1.8	31	32	5	2	8
Prestigious	1.9	31	42	12	5	10
Dependent on government support	2.9	9	19	14	25	32
Responsible	1.7	23	39	11	1	11
Persuasive	2.1	26	37	23	5	8
Progressive	1.8	35	40	12	2	10
Research oriented	1.5	51	24	9		17
Annoying	3.7	2	2	17	67	10
Efficient	2.0	21	49	11	3	15
Beneficial	1.6	63	46	9	1	7
Over-rated	3.3	8	9	21	49	14
Honest	1.6	40	32	5	1	22
Educational	1.6	45	35	10		10
Modern	1.7	38	35	9	2	17
Gimmick oriented to raise funds	3.1	10	12	22	38	19
Prevention oriented	1.7	42	32	7	4	15
Dependent on donations	1.4	58	25	6	1	11

[a]Don't know category was not included in calculating average scale value. Sample size = 130. Percentages don't equal 100 due to rounding.

progressive, honest, educational, modern, prevention oriented and dependent on donations. In addition, the AHA was perceived as not at all annoying and only slightly over-rated and gimmick oriented to raise funds. The category, dependent on government support, had the greatest proportion of respondents to indicate don't know. In general, respondents' overall image is very positive and favorable.

The average image profiles of respondents categorized as donors or nondonors of time or money were also compared. Again, the images are highly positive. Surprisingly, little differentiation was noted among any of the sub-groupings (because of the small differences, the figure showing these images is omitted).

DISCUSSION AND CONCLUSIONS

The results of this empirical survey indicate that contributors to the American Heart Association (AHA) are more likely to be older, with low income (less than $10,000) or high income ($30,000 or more), have four or fewer individuals in the household, and have lived more than 20 years in the area. Targeting-wise, this part of the population is easily identifiable and one the AHA could concentrate more of its efforts.

In awareness of AHA activities, most of the respondents were able to identify four of them. However, *only* 25% of the sample recognized a major slogan of the AHA—"We're Fighting for Your Life." If AHA wants to continue with this slogan, it needs to improve its communication efforts. In addition, there were other activities performed by other organizations that were incorrectly identified as AHA sponsored [up to 12% for We Care (AC) and Combats Neuromuscular Disease (Muscular Dystrophy)]. If these activities are regarded as positive, they may marginally help AHA efforts; but if they are regarded negatively, they would hurt AHA solicitation efforts.

Overall, the AHA was regarded as doing a good to excellent job (74%). However, 62% of those who have served as volunteers versus 38% of money contributors feel the AHA is doing an excellent job. Volunteers are likely to be better informed/more motivated and thus have a more positive view. In considering how they might divide up a hypothesized $100 to charities, 35% of the total sample would not give the AHA anything. *Twenty percent* of those who donated money within the last year would not give anything to the AHA (hard to explain, perhaps some recent negative experience/publicity concerning AHA). However, 47% of those who did not give anything in the last year would give from $16–$100. This result suggests that the AHA should seek out these people and ask for their support.

The scale used to profile the image of AHA showed it to have a very positive image and this finding held up when profiles were made comparing contributors to non-contributors and volunteers to those who do not volunteer time. This positive image and the result from how people would give money if they had $100 to give suggests that perhaps many people are not motivated to give. It is suggested that these people (especially those who did not give within the last year) would be likely to contribute if they were contacted and asked for their support.

In conclusion, it was found that our respondents' basic attitude toward giving was very positive (81% like to do and find it very rewarding). Most of our respondents had no additional comments or strong opinions about the AHA or charities in general. However, 14% of the respondents felt that charities (including AHA) need to show accountability, may misuse funds, use some annoying solicitation methods, and are often bureaucratically inefficient. A good communication program that fully disclosed what the organization is set up to do, how it does it (including how funds are used—fund raising and activity allocated) would likely be effective in answering these people's doubts and perhaps switching them to active supporters of your organization. Such a communication program also would be likely to be beneficial in increasing support from those who are currently neutral or positive in their opinions toward your organization.

REFERENCES

[1] American Association of Fund-Raising Counsel (1979), *Giving USA*, (500 Fifth Avenue, New York, New York).

[2] Beik, L. L. and Scott M. Smith, (1979), "Geographic Segmentation: A Fund Raising Example," Neil Beckwith, *et al. 1979 Educators' Conference Proceedings*, American Marketing Association, 485–488.

[3] Cialdini, R. B., J. T. Cacioppo, R. Basset, and J. A. Miller, (1978), "The Low-Ball Procedure for Producing Compliance: Commitment Then Cost," *Journal of Personality and Social Psychology*, 36, 463–476.

[4] Kotler, Philip, (1975), Marketing for Non-profit Organizations, Englewood Cliffs, N.J.: Prentice-Hall, Inc.

[5] Mindak, W. A. and H. M. Bybee (1977), "Marketing's Application to Fund Raising," in R. M. Gaedeke, *Marketing in Private and Public Nonprofit Organizations*, Santa Monica; California: Goodyear Publishing Company, Inc., 347–355.

[6] Newsweek, (1979) "The Charity Battle," May 7, 33–36.

[7] Reingen, P. H. (1978), "On Inducing Compliance with Request," *Journal of Consumer Research,* 5, 96–102.

[8] Reingen, P. H. and J. P. Kernam, (1977) "Compliance with an Interview Request: A Foot-in-the-Door, Self-Perception Interpretation," *Journal of Marketing,* 14, 365–69.

[9] Scott, C. A. (1977), "Modifying Socially-Conscious Behavior: The Foot-in-the-Door Technique," *Journal of Consumer Research,* 4, 156–164.

[10] Scott, C. A. (1976), "The Effects of Trial and Incentives on Repeat Purchase Behavior," *Journal of Marketing,* 13, 263–268.

[11] *The State* (1979), "Carl Bakal: An End to Charity," Columbia, S.C., November 25.

[12] *U.S. News and World Report* (1979), "Why Charities Tighten Their Belts," February 26, 76–79.

[13] Wood, L. A. (1977), "How the Public Views Voluntary Health Welfare Organizations," *Public Relations Journal,* March, 24–25.

Marketing Research in Health Services Planning: A Model

WILLIAM A. FLEXNER

ERIC N. BERKOWITZ

Health services have been defined as "all personal and public services performed by individuals or institutions for the purpose of maintaining or restoring health" [1]1. Decisions about the design and delivery of services by private clinics, hospitals, neighborhood health centers, and health maintenance organizations (HMOs) are made primarily by professionals. Yet consumer input into these decisions is increasingly being sought, even demanded. Generally this input has been obtained by four methods: (a) consumer representation on boards, (b) consumer advocacy (for example, Ralph Nader's Health Research Group), (c) a diagnosis of the community (the community being regarded as the patient) and assessment of the community's needs, and (d) behavioral and social science research [2].

These four methods provide for firsthand contact between health professionals and the lay public and a medically objective review of health care requirements. Yet, in application, weaknesses in the methods may be revealed, such as presumed representation of the whole consumer population, a tendency toward professional domination of decisions, and ineffective integration of consumer input into the organization's planning. These weaknesses often preclude the creation of programs and services that are sensitive and responsive to all sectors of the population [3].

The strengths of the four methods must be integrated into a managerial structure in order to produce programs and services that are satisfactory to health care consumers. To accomplish such integration, a framework is needed, and marketing research can provide it.

Marketing research is the organizational ac-

Reprinted with permission from *Public Health Reports,* Department of Health, Education, and Welfare, Vol. 94, November–December 1979, pp. 503–513.

tivity of systematically gathering, recording, and analyzing the information needed to make planning and implementation decisions that affect the quality or intensity of an organization's interactions with consumers [4, 5]. We propose that a marketing research model and marketing research methods be incorporated into the health services planning process at the institutional level.

MARKETING: RESPONSIVENESS TO CONSUMERS

In business, marketing is the matching of a company's capabilities and resources with consumers' needs and wants [6, 7]. Needs and wants are the things that are important to consumers and that underlie their behavior. Because consumers' preferences and expectations vary, companies provide many different products or services. Through marketing, management can foster mutually beneficial exchanges between the company and specified segments of consumers. Exchanges occur when something of value is given up for something of value received—goods, services, money, attention, devotion, ideas, and so forth [8].

Defined in this way, marketing encompasses far more than the narrow activities of advertising or promotion in a traditional business setting. To be successful a business or any other organization must satisfy various consumer segments by providing appropriately designed products or services. Simultaneously, it must also achieve its internal goals and objectives, whether these be defined as profit, market share, health outcomes, or patient compliance. To reach these goals, a business or an organization has to offer the right product or service at the right price and deliver it at the right time and place. When planning is oriented toward the marketplace, effective and efficient exchanges are more likely to take place between the business or organization and its consumers. Such an orientation, however, requires an understanding on the part of management as to how and why consumers choose specific products or services in the marketplace.

MARKETING IN THE HEALTH SECTOR

In the health sector, consumers' needs are traditionally viewed as equivalent to their health or medical care requirements [9–11]. Health providers create "products" to respond to these requirements. These products (usually specific services) include the technical knowledge and skills of the provider, the technological capacity of the institution in which the provider functions, and the specific tests, surgical procedures, and regimens that are prescribed.

Health professionals primarily consider health services in technical terms [12]. Consumers, on the other hand, often use very different criteria when considering health services [13, 14], placing greater emphasis on the nontechnical components of service delivery from which they expect to derive values or benefits. These benefits become, in turn, surrogates in the consumers' minds for the technical components of the health service. Among the nontechnical benefits that consumers desire or expect in a medical facility are a pleasing appearance, physical comfort, an opportunity for effective communication with the staff, and ease in obtaining services [15]. Priority in program planning should be given to identifying the benefits that most influence consumers in deciding whether or not to use health services and where to obtain them. Consumers' choices of sources of health care are becoming increasingly important to health care management because consumers are beginning to shop around for care [16]. If services are to be responsive to consumers' preferences and expectations, the benefits that consumers seek have to be identified. Information on consumers' preferences and expectations also has to be made available to managers in a usable form before decisions are made about the service design.

TWO PLANNING APPROACHES

Collection of information from consumers should be a primary concern of any organization. The time of collection in terms of the planning sequence is also of great importance. Managers of

FIGURE 1: ***Models for planning health programs***

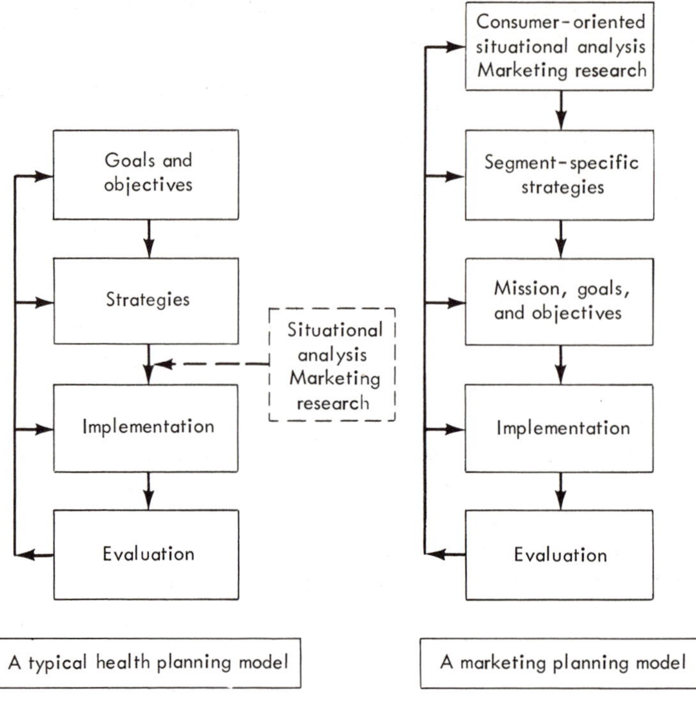

Source: Adapted from reference 18.

clinics, hospitals, neighborhood health centers, and HMOs typically consider information about consumers' preferences and behavior only after they have set goals and objectives and decided on service strategy [17]. That is, they turn to consumers only after having already decided what they are going to do for them. And although the information about consumers collected at this stage may aid in selling the services being offered, it comes too late to be of value in helping managers determine whether the consumers actually want or need the services.

In a marketing approach, the planning sequence is different. Consumers are the focal point for the key decisions that determine the organization's success or failure (Fig. 1). Therefore consumers are considered at the beginning of the planning process [18]. Information gathered from and about them provides the foundation for defining the organization's goals and objectives. Consumers are viewed in terms of subgroupings, or segments, based on similar behavior or preferences. Each segment is profiled according to identifiable characteristics. In the initial analysis, both the organization's internal capabilities and the preferences of its current constituency are taken into account.

Once the initial analysis is completed, a strategy is devised for each segment of consumers. Only after consumers have been segmented, does the organization specify its operational goals and objectives and the means that will be used to achieve them through control of the design, location, price, and promotion of services.

A marketing approach and traditional approaches in the health sector differ only in the timing of the steps in the planning process. This difference, however, is critical to the design of strategies that are sensitive to consumers' preferences. Traditionally, the planning of health services organizations has been done from inside the organization out to the consumer. That is, the organization determines what the health professionals' needs are, what consumers should have, and how consumers' needs are to be filled. Current trends and pressures, however, such as those causing consumers to shop around for service alternatives, dictate a change from the traditional approach to one more responsive to the marketplace. Because planning begins with the consumer in a marketing approach, consumers' preferences and needs, particularly those not directly related to medical techniques, guide the organization's strategy. Consumer segments then form the basis on which appropriate and selective strategies, objectives, and goals can be constructed. Because information is available from consumers, programs and services can be made more responsive to them. Consequently, the levels of their satisfaction can be expected to be higher because of the greater congruence between their expectations and the actual service features.

INTEGRATING RESEARCH ON CONSUMERS

As the conceptual framework for market-oriented health services planning in Figure 2 shows, the essential link in such planning is between research on consumers and planning and control by management. To respond appropriately to consumers' preferences, an organization needs to have an information gathering or research program that is well integrated into the management process. There are three phases in this process. The first two involve the research program. In the first phase, the extent of the problem is determined in qualitative terms. Management seeks to learn what factors affect relationships between the organization and its consumers. In the second place,

FIGURE 2: ***A framework for integrating consumer research and management planning and control***

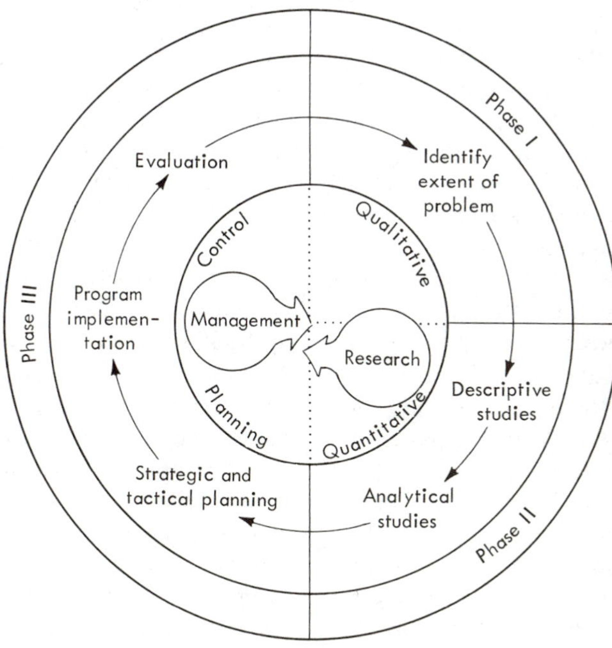

quantitative studies are conducted to identify the various consumer segments in the health care marketplace so that their future behavior can be forecast.

Upon completion of the research, the information must be disseminated, so that the results can be translated into programs that are sensitive to consumers' preferences and needs. This translation is done in the third phase. This management phase involves the formulation of plans incorporating the results of the research, implementation of these plans, and the evaluation of their results. As program outputs are observed and measured against the plans, new problems may surface, creating a need for additional information. Thus, for an organization to be effective, research has to be a dynamic process and an integral part of planning.

APPLYING THE MARKETING MODEL

Many hospitals are currently trying to broaden their target markets from primarily inpatient care to a wide range of non-inpatient services. In one plan under consideration in a major midwestern metropolitan area, for example, hospitals would provide acute care through ambulatory (outpatient) services. (We use this plan throughout this paper to illustrate the actual application of a marketing model to health services planning.) The outpatient market in this metropolitan area already includes large fee-for-service multispecialty group practices, HMOs, and neighborhood health centers. Consumers also are served in part by hospital emergency rooms. As with traditional business services, successful expansion of hospitals into a new market—the outpatient market—requires an understanding on the part of the managers about consumers' perceptions of the hospital, as well as the identification of the potential segments of the market that would use hospital-based ambulatory care services. A marketing approach can aid in such an exploration.

Phase 1: Qualitative Studies. In the first phase of the investigation, the components of the problem or problems relevant to planning decisions are delineated. Often health care providers assume that they understand these components. However, because consumers may have different perceptions, an opportunity should be taken at the outset of planning to verify or challenge providers' conventional assumptions [13].

Several qualitative research techniques are used in this phase of investigation. The first, focus group discussion, is used frequently in business to elicit consumer perceptions about a given subject [19, 20]. After a representative group of actual or potential consumers is brought together, a general subject for discussion is introduced by a moderator, who generates discussion by a few carefully selected "focusing" questions. In a focus group discussion, the aim is to elicit emotional and subjective statements revealing the participants' preferences in respect to the issues under discussion. The participants' statements are subsequently analyzed to identify the components of the research problem that seem worthy of more exact assessment. As opposed to other methods of qualitative group research, such a discussion is supposed to be as expansive as possible, so that the full range of participants' opinions are revealed. Group consensus is not a goal.

In our study in the midwestern metropolitan area, focus group discussions helped clarify key elements in consumers' perceptions of hospitals. In these discussions, four focusing questions were posed to determine what consumers—when new in a city—considered important about hospitals, what in a hospital indicated that the place was all right, or on the other hand, that they should never go back, and what influenced them in determining a hospital's reputation for quality. The discussions were held in the evening in the community rooms of a public library and a commercial bank. Participants were selected by telephone solicitation of households in the appropriate geographic area. Criteria for the participants' selection included having no exposure to a hospital in the previous 6 months and having no family member working in the health field.

In our analysis of the focus group discussions, we identified nine attributes related to consumers' perceptions of hospitals. Six have some face validity, since they have been cited in earlier studies as important dimensions in consumers' perceptions and choices of hospitals [21–24]; namely, attitude of the staff, the quality, cost, location, and range of services, and the appearance of the facility. Interestingly, however, the focus group discussions elicited three other organizational attributes not mentioned in the literature; namely, the hospital's reputation, the hospital's cleanliness, and the hospital affiliation of the respondent's personal physician. All nine attributes were included in the quantitative phase of our analysis. Transcripts of the focus group discussions were of help in preparing attitude statements for the survey instrument that we used in the second phase of the research.

A second qualitative research technique, the individual depth interview, is often used to clarify issues that have been raised in focus group discussions, but in a form too vague for useful pursuit in quantitative research [25]. In individual depth interviews, the decision-making processes or reasoning of the participants is probed on a one-to-one basis through structured questionnaires, comprised primarily of open-ended questions. Although the responses to such questions are subjective, analysis of the responses can further clarify the problem under consideration.

A third kind of qualitative research, nominal group and delphi processes, is used when group consensus is desired [26]. In these processes, a highly structured format is used to minimize group interaction and, consequently, to help the group reach creative or judgmental decisions. By working within a group, the managers or planners can reach agreement on the critical issues related to future planning decisions.

Phase 2: Quantitative Studies. Once the components of the problem are defined, the second phase of research begins. The conditions that affect the relationship between the organization and its consumers are identified through descriptive studies [4]. The behavior and the demographic profiles of both the consumers and the providers are then assessed. The demographic profiles show who comprises the market and who provides services to the segments within it. Much of the data needed for descriptive studies can be found in secondary sources, both inside and outside the organization: patient origin studies, previous research studies, clinic or hospital discharge or case-mix records, county records, census data, and so forth. Secondary sources are used whenever possible since they speed data collection and reduce costs.

Figure 3 shows some of the data that a hospital might want to have available in its information system to improve the efficiency and effectiveness of a descriptive market analysis. The solid-line boxes indicate how data should be stored; namely, by patient, by physician, and by service. The two-way classifications that the manager should have available are also shown (broken-line boxes). In a case-mix analysis, for example, the number of patients by diagnosis and by physician, as well as by average length of stay, would be valuable information for managers to have to plan the organization's strategies.

Other sources of data for descriptive studies vary in terms of ease of access and the complexity of the data collection methods. In some cases, the data must be collected through survey instruments. Care in planning the questionnaire's design, selecting the sample, and administering the survey will prevent the introduction of systematic error through the data collection method. Distinct tradeoffs exist with each type of data-gathering approach—mail questionnaire, telephone interview, and personal interview—and therefore the kind of information required must figure in the selection of the correct alternative. The criteria for this selection include the cost, timeliness, and sensitivity of the information that the method can be expected to provide. After collection, the data are compiled to address the research hypotheses and are analyzed by appropriate techniques so that the patterns of association

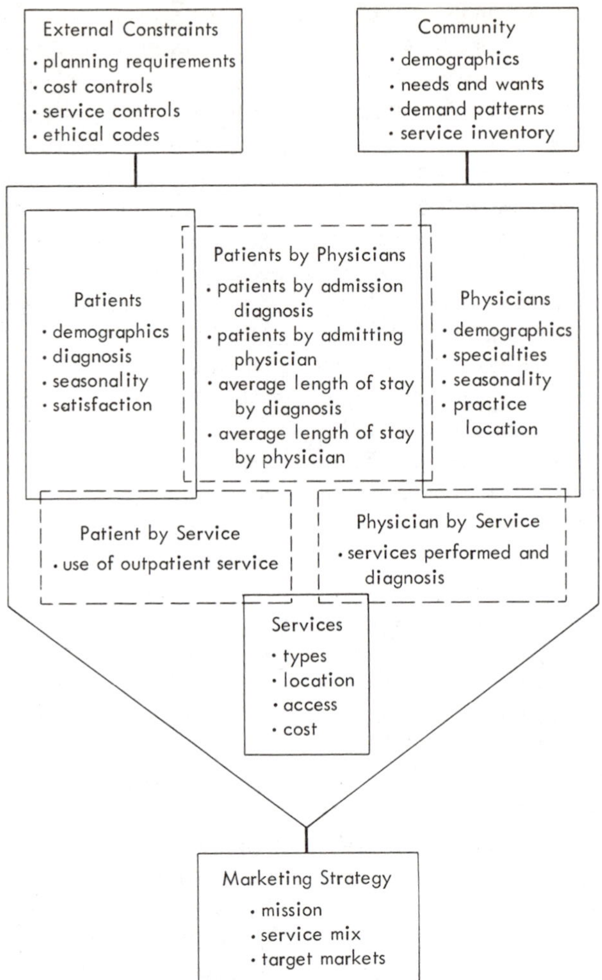

FIGURE 3: ***Information needed to formulate a marketing strategy in the hospital setting***

or relationship among the variables can be determined.

Planners and administrators need to know how to group consumers in segments based on their demographic characteristics as these relate to consumers' service preferences or service utilization patterns. Planners and administrators also need to know how changes in the service design might affect utilization. Forecasting the future behavior of the various consumer segments requires careful study and analysis, a requirement that analytical studies can meet. By such studies, (a) information about the relationships between the variables that identify the consumer segments can be determined, (b) the research environment can be monitored so that before and after relationships can be specified, and (c) any other factors that might have been responsible for the phenomenon under investigation can be identified. Although a discussion of analytical approaches is not within the scope of this paper, it is appropriate to note that recent advances in multivariate statistics permit data to be examined in an operationally useful way [27–29]. For example, differences between several segments can be identified by discriminant analysis, and underlying attitudes can be structured by factor analysis.

Whenever possible, both the descriptive and analytical studies are conducted with the same survey instrument. But, when they are necessary and appropriate, quasi-experimental before and after studies are done. Before and after studies are particularly helpful if new services or new service features are available for testing before full implementation.

In our study in the midwestern metropolitan area, data for assessing consumers' perceptions of hospitals, as well as for identifying consumer profiles and market segments, were gathered by a mail questionnaire. The questions in this instrument were designed to elicit the importance to the respondents of various hospital attributes, the respondents' attitudes toward hospitals and health care, and the respondents' demographic characteristics. The content of the eight-page survey instrument was based on analysis of the content of the focus group discussions. The survey instrument was sent to 4,844 randomly selected households in the area, along with a post card which, when returned with the completed form, made the respondent eligible to win a television set. There were 1,465 usable responses (response rate 30.2 percent). There were 1,446 respondents who answered the question, "Do you have a personal physician?" Of these, 1,213 (83.9 percent) responded affirmatively and 233 (16.1 percent) negatively. These results are similar to those in other studies in which the size of the segment of the consumer population with no physician has been estimated [30, 31].

In the study, our overriding concern was what the potential was for expansion of outpatient services by the hospitals in the area. People in the area with no personal physician were viewed as the potential users of these services. Thus, the research problem was first to determine what attributes of hospitals were important to this group in choosing a hospital and then to profile this segment relative to consumers who had a personal physician. Table 1 shows how each of nine attributes (which had been identified as being important in phase 1, the qualitative portion of the research) were rated in importance by the two groups. Although both groups rated all nine attributes as rather important, significant differences were observed for seven attributes. For example, the range of services and the reputation of the hospital were more important to consumers with a physician. Yet it is interesting that even this group of consumers rated the attribute of having one's physician affiliated with the hospital as only the sixth most important hospital attribute.

Once the existence of different needs is determined, each consumer segment is profiled. Hospital management can then determine whether potential or actual consumers who match the profile are present in the hospital's current service area in sufficient numbers to justify the establishment of appropriate outpatient services.

In our example, consumers with and without a physician differed significantly in respect to a variety of demographic and social characteristics (Table 2). Two distinct profiles emerged. The consumers with no physician tended to be younger, to be single, and to include more males than the other group. The respondents without a physician were more likely to rent than own their own homes, and unlike the group with a physician, almost half had lived at their present address less than 3 years. Consumers without a physician were also more likely to have their medical expenses paid primarily through a prepaid health plan or through a mixture of Medicaid, self-pay, and other means. Analysis of the racial differences between the two groups suggested that minority respondents were less likely to have a personal physician. The small number of minority respondents in the study sample precluded more detailed analysis of this variable. However, even though the number was small, it reflected the proportion of minorities in the population in the survey area.

A third area of investigation focused upon the

TABLE 1: ***Importance of various hospital attributes to consumers with and without a personal physician***

Hospital attributes	*Values for consumers with a physician,*[a] $\overline{X}$	*Values for consumers without a physician,*[a] $\overline{X}$	*Pooled "t" significance level of difference*
Location	2.30	2.43	Not significant
Cost of services	1.94	2.04	Not significant
Quality of care	1.09	1.17	<0.005
Range of specialized services	1.76	2.03	<0.001
Attitude of staff	1.41	1.69	<0.001
Reputation	1.69	1.96	<0.001
Cleaniness of facilities	1.27	1.49	<0.001
Appearance and decor	2.73	3.00	0.001
Hospital affiliation of consumer's physician	1.80	2.59	<0.001

[a]Values are mean responses on a 5-point scale on which "very important" = 1 and "not very important at all" = 5.

attitudes of the two consumer segments toward hospitals and health care. A profile of consumers' attitudes is often helpful, because an understanding of them may provide direction for explaining plans and encouraging acceptance of new services. Table 3 shows that the differences between the consumers with no physician and those with a physician extended beyond demographic characteristics to attitudes. For ease of discussion, the attitude statements from the survey instrument have been arranged by topical areas. The first set of statements relates to hospital systems in general. The consumers with a physician appeared to be more discriminating with regard to hospital systems. Some significant differences were observed between the two consumer segments in respect to four statements (No. 2, 3, 5, and 6). The responses of the consumers with a physician indicated that they did not believe that all hospitals were alike. They also apparently believed that better hospitals offered a wide range of services and were associated with medical schools.

Although no significant differences were observed in respect to the statements on the questionnaire relating to time, the two segments clearly differed as to whether they had an opportunity for personal choice. As expected, the consumers with no physician appeared to be more skeptical about allowing a physician to control hospital choice. They indicated that they would prefer a consumer rating service for hospitals. Also, this segment expressed the belief that it helps to find out about a hospital from someone who has been there and that advertising would provide an appropriate source of information about hospital services and rates. For six of the seven statements related to choice, differences between the two groups were significant at the 0.01 level or better.

On the price dimension, both segments agreed that if hospitals were run like a business, costs would decrease. Yet significant differences were observed between the two consumer groups as to

TABLE 2: *Comparison of demographic profiles of consumers with and without a physician*[a]

Demographic characteristic	Percent of consumers with a physician	Percent of consumers without a physician
Age group		
20–29	20	37
30–39	24	29
40–49	18	12
50–59	17	14
60 and over	21	8
	χ^2 = 49.4, df = 4, P <0.001	
Marital status		
Single	12	36
Married	74	55
Other	14	9
	χ^2 = 86.2, df = 2, P <0.001	
Sex		
Male	31	53
Female	69	47
	χ^2 = 39.3, df = 1, P <0.001	
Children		
0	51	59
1	16	15
2	20	14
3	9	8
4 or more	4	4
	χ^2 = 6.4, df = 4, P = N.S	
Home ownership		
Own home	82	65
Rent home	18	35
	χ^2 = 35.0, df = 1, P <0.001	
Years at present address		
Less than 1	6	12
1–3	16	31
3–5	15	16
5–10	19	21
10–25	31	15
More than 25	13	5
	χ^2 = 61.2, df = 5, P <0.001	
Occupation		
Managerial	12	11
Skilled trade	6	10
Laborer	4	5
Officer worker	14	13
Technical	4	5
Professional	24	30
Homemaker	22	10
Student	1	8
Retired	13	7
	χ^2 = 66.0, df = 8, P <0.001	
Education		
Less than 12 years	8	6
High school graduate	28	16
Technical-vocational school	12	11
Some college	19	22
College graduate	21	28
Graduate or professional degree	12	17
	χ^2 = 17.7, df = 6, P <0.007	
Annual income		
Under $8,000	11	18
$8,000–$11,999	10	10
$12,000–$15,999	12	20
$16,000–$19,999	15	15
$20,000–$24,999	18	13
$25,000 or more	34	24
	χ^2 = 28.2, df = 5, P <0.001	
How medical expenses paid		
Self-paid	23	21
Mostly insurance	57	38
Mostly Medicare	7	3
Mostly Medicaid	1	1
Prepaid plan	8	27
Other	5	10
	χ^2 = 92.0, df = 5, P <0.001	
Race		
Caucasian	97	94
Other	3	6
	χ^2 = 6.93, df = 1, P <0.001	

[a]df = degrees of freedom, N.S. = not significant. Percentages add vertically to 100 percent except when rounded.

TABLE 3: ***Attitudes of consumers with and without a personal physician about hospitals and their services***

Statements used to elicit consumers' attitudes	Values for consumers with physician,[a] $\overline{X}$	Values for consumers without physician,[a] $\overline{X}$	Pooled "t" significance level of difference[b]
Hospital systems			
1. Some hospitals are better than others	1.63	1.64	0.907
2. I prefer a hospital with my same religious affiliation	3.40	3.72	*<0.001*
3. The best hospitals have a wide range of services	2.45	2.67	*<0.001*
4. New teaching hospitals usually have all the services you need	2.83	2.87	0.512
5. Most hospitals are all alike	3.58	3.41	*0.016*
6. Hospitals associated with medical schools and universities are usually better	2.67	2.48	*0.008*
7. There are not enough hospitals to care for the people who need them	3.79	3.83	0.570
8. People's faith in hospitals has gone down dramatically in the last 2 years	2.86	2.78	0.229
9. All hospitals should offer special services like diet workshops, stop smoking programs	3.02	3.13	0.216
10. It is important for all hospitals to have plans for low-income consumers	2.03	2.05	0.767
Time			
11. It usually takes forever to check in for emergencies	2.89	2.80	0.289
12. Hospitals should find some way to help pass the time while you wait	3.02	2.92	0.203
13. It often takes days to learn of test results from hospitals	2.73	2.70	0.625
14. In an emergency it's best just to go to the closest hospital	2.35	2.31	0.627
15. I always choose the hospital that is closest to where I live for my medical needs	3.36	3.33	0.723
Having choices			
16. I don't choose my hospital, my doctor does	2.31	2.67	*<0.001*
17. It's easier to go to the hospital when I have a problem than to get an appointment with a doctor	3.57	3.24	*<0.001*
18. I trust my doctor's opinion about hospitals	1.90	2.32	*<0.001*
19. It would be nice to have a consumer rating service	2.13	1.94	*<0.001*
20. It's important to ask around to learn a hospital's reputation	2.70	2.59	0.108
21. Hospitals should advertise their services and rates	2.98	2.69	*<0.001*
22. Before choosing a hospital, it's best to find someone who's been there	3.27	3.09	*0.010*
Hospital ambience			
23. Most hospitals have a sterile, cold atmosphere	3.34	3.27	0.319

[a]Values are mean responses on a 5-point scale on which "strongly agree" 1 and "strongly disagree" 5.
[b]Italicized numbers are significant at <0.05.

TABLE 3: ***continued***

Statements used to ellicit consumers' attitudes	*Values for consumers with physician,*[a] $\overline{X}$	*Values for consumers without physician,*[a] $\overline{X}$	*Pooled "t" significance level of difference*[b]
24. Cleanliness is one of the first things I check when entering a hospital	2.22	2.48	*<0.001*
25. The hospital building tells a lot about how people are cared for	3.36	3.39	0.647
26. When I enter a hospital, the first thing I do is look at how it is decorated	3.96	3.96	0.928
27. Hospitals should make their waiting rooms nicer places to sit	3.00	2.93	0.276
Price			
28. If hospitals were run like a business, costs would go down	2.72	2.81	0.225
29. Hospitals don't really try to keep costs down	2.50	2.54	0.603
30. If hospitals start to advertise, costs will go up	2.83	3.01	*0.014*
31. If hospitals were to share services, costs would be lower	2.18	2.04	*0.016*
32. Hospital costs seem to be rising for no real reason	2.74	2.85	0.172
33. Governments should be more active in lowering hospital charges	2.60	2.52	0.349
34. The best way to lower hospital costs would be to close some hospitals	3.32	3.21	0.104
35. The saying "you get what you pay for" is definitely true in medicine	3.64	3.68	0.593
Interpersonal relations			
36. I often feel intimidated in hospitals	3.36	3.15	*0.008*
37. The attitude of the hospital staff is one of the best ways to tell what the hospital is like	2.23	2.29	0.364
38. Nurses should show more respect for patients	2.55	2.69	0.051
39. Most people who work in hospitals forget patients are human	3.52	3.35	*0.019*
40. It's hard to get a straight answer when you ask a question in a hospital	2.83	2.84	0.888
41. I've had good feelings about the hospitals I have been in	2.10	2.43	*<0.001*
Hospital management and operations			
42. Hospital billing procedures are too complicated	2.64	2.54	0.248
43. I often wonder who is in charge when I enter the hospital	2.94	2.90	0.590
44. Hospitals should survey patients to see what their feelings are	2.08	1.99	0.154
45. It is very rare that hospitals make mistakes in billing people	3.52	3.67	*0.028*
46. Health care is big business	1.63	1.55	0.114
47. I feel that most hospitals have high ethical standards	2.25	2.33	0.179
48. It is irritating to be given medicine without being told the purpose	1.70	1.62	0.179

the strategies for lowering costs. Although neither segment appeared to believe that advertising would raise costs, the consumers with a physician were not so sure. Both segments agreed that sharing services would lower costs, but the consumers without a physician were more positive about this strategy. The respondents with no physician seemed to have had more negative experiences in interpersonal relationships. For example, they were more likely to report that they felt intimidated by hospitals and did not have good feelings about them.

In the final area of investigation, hospital management and operations, there were significant differences between the segments on only one statement (No. 45). Both groups indicated that they felt billing mistakes were not unusual, but again this opinion was more strongly held by the segment without a physician.

The two groups had rather interesting differences in attitudes. The segment with no physician appeared to be far more critical and negative about hospitals and health care. Yet the commonalities between the two groups cannot be overlooked. Both segments expressed the belief that the current number of hospitals is sufficient. And as their ranking of hospital attributes revealed, neither group paid much attention to hospital ambience. Both groups expressed general agreement that hospitals do little to keep costs down and that government intervention in this area would help. Both segments indicated that they would prefer more surveys of patients and agreed that health care is big business.

Phase 3: Planning, Implementation, and Evaluation. In the final phase of the marketing research approach, the results of data collection are translated into feasible programs. At this point the concepts illustrated in figures 1 and 2 can be integrated into the planning process. Following an outside-in approach, consumer-based research is conducted and specific segments profiled. Next, strategies and tactics must be devised. The information gathered in the qualitative and quantitative phases of the research is then used in conjunction with organizational expertise to devise program strategies and tactics. Such information can validate or challenge the subjective knowledge of the organization's managers. When different subgroups have different preferences and profiles, programs may have to be set up for each of them. Criteria for evaluating program implementation are outlined, as is done in the present planning process. Program effectiveness, for example, is measured by analyses of service utilization, revenues and costs, consumers' compliance and satisfaction, and health outcomes. A program is more likely to be successful with a marketing research approach than with traditional health planning, because with a marketing approach, a monitoring system is designed specifically for each segment of consumers before implementation begins.

In our study, consumers with no physician differed from consumers with a physician in many respects. Particularly interesting were the results showing the importance that each consumer segment attached to various attributes in selecting a hospital. Consumers with no physician placed less importance on all nine hospital attributes on which they were queried than did consumers with a physician. Of particular note were the significant differences between the two groups in their rating of the importance to them of a hospital's range of services, reputation, and appearance.

Demographically, also, the two segments differed. The consumers with no physician tended to be young, single males with relatively high levels of education. These consumers were more critical of hospitals and less concerned with a hospital's size or reputation. Their attitudes implied that the traditional association with a physician was not essential, indeed, was possibly not even desirable. The responses of these consumers showed that they preferred to maintain control and decide for themselves which health resources to use and when. Therefore, a hospital or other health care system seeking to respond to these values would need to provide access for these consumers to an organized, integrated system of health services that they could use as needed on a periodic basis. This conclusion does not imply that members of this segment might not align themselves with a specific physician if a long-term problem were to occur. Given their current health status, however, they consider a personal physician to be less essential than a comprehensive system to which they can have relatively immediate access. Managers of hospitals and other organized systems of health care should consider creating programs and services for this market segment. Following are some guidelines for making some of the necessary strategic decisions:

- Services should focus primarily on short-term acute care, not on emergency and nonacute chronic conditions. (The segment with no physician views an appropriate set of services more favorably than a wide range of them.)
- Services should be designed so as to provide consumers with alternatives in terms of the type of health manpower that they see, the times and places that services are offered, and the basis on which they are offered—walk-in visits or appointments. (The desire to have a choice and be in control of decisions seems to be a key characteristic of consumers with no personal physician.)
- Information about services should be made available in carefully targeted ways, such as by advertising and stimulation of word-of-mouth referrals. A consumerrating service might also be appropriate for reaching the target market. (Consumers with no physician seem to put a high value on having information about their available options.)
- Finally, management might want to survey actual and potential consumers to determine their feelings about the specific mix of services that should be offered and the best way to present them.

CONCLUSIONS

In a marketing approach to planning, problems are defined and studies are designed in the sequence that we have shown. First, the extent of the problem is determined by qualitative research. Second, the characteristics and current behavior patterns of the participants in the health care marketplace are described. Third, trends and relationships are analyzed in order to identify the various segments of consumers and to forecast their future behavior and future utilization of health care services.

Already widely used in business, the marketing approach is beginning to be applied successfully in the health care field. In a family practice clinic in the Southwest, for example, the results of personal interviews with clinic patients, as well as information from an adjacent hospital, helped to identify a segment of consumers who preferred to have access to nonemergency, acute-care medical services outside of the hospital on a 24-hour walk-in basis. Because of the estimated size of this segment, planning has begun at the clinic to add a 24-hour walk-in medical service to its existing appointment-based services. This new program will provide the clinic an opportunity for growth as well as remove a considerable portion of the current inappropriate demands on the hospital's emergency room.

In a 170-bed community hospital in a major mid-western city, individual depth interviews with private practice physicians were used to identify ways to increase the number of physicians affiliated with the hospital. This investigation revealed that physicians newly entering practice in the area had a need for help in setting up their offices. The hospital therefore appointed a management staff to assist private practice physicians who affiliated with the hospital to apply modern management methods in their offices.

The approach to planning presented here may seem in many respects obvious to health care providers. Yet the differences between it and the traditional approach, which are highlighted in figure 1, are distinct. In a marketing planning model, phases 1 and 2 of marketing research (Fig. 2) take place before any strategies or tactics are decided upon. Marketing research is just that, an examination of the market, that is, of an organization's present and potential customers or users. Information about these groups (their attitudes, perceptions, needs, and wants) dictates the organization's strategic decisions.

Planning and research are not separate activities, each producing a distinct outcome. Rather, they are both part of a sequence of actions, beginning with consumer research and ending with the service mix appropriate to the organization's various publics.

Upon implementation of plans and feedback from evaluation or control procedures, this total sequence of activities becomes a dynamic process and enables the organization to adjust effectively and rapidly to the factors that determine the success or failure of its programs.

REFERENCES

[1] Levey, S., and Loomba, M. P.: Health care administration: a managerial perspective. J. B. Lippincott Company, Philadelphia, Pa., 1973, p. 4.

[2] Scutchfield, F. D.: Alternate methods for health priority assessment. J Community Health 1:29–38, fall 1975.

[3] Flexner, W. A., and Littlefield, J. E.: Comment on alternate methods of health priority assessment. J Community Health 2: 245–246 (Letters to the editors), spring 1977.

[4] Green, P. E., and Tull, D. S.: Research for marketing decisions. Ed. 3. Prentice-Hall, Inc., Englewood Cliffs, N.J., 1976.

[5] Schoner, B., and Uhl, K. P.: Marketing research: information systems and decision making. Ed. 2. John Wiley & Sons, Inc., New York, 1975.

[6] McCarthy, E. J.: Basic marketing: a managerial approach. Ed. 5. Richard D. Irwin, Inc., Homewood, Ill., 1975.

[7] Hughes, G. D.: Marketing management: a planning approach. Addison-Wesley, Reading, Mass., 1978.

[8] Kotler, P.: Marketing for nonprofit organizations. Prentice-Hall, Inc., Englewood Cliffs, N.J., 1975.

[9] Fuchs, V.: The growing demand for medical care. N Engl J Med 279: 190–195, July 25, 1968.

[10] Jeffers, J. R., Bognanno, M. F., and Bartlett, J. C.: On the demand versus need for medical services and the concept of 'shortage.' Am J Public Health 61: 46–63, January 1971.

[11] Donabedian, A.: Aspects of medical care administration. Harvard University Press, Cambridge, Mass., 1973.

[12] Egdahl, R. H., and Gertman, P. M.: Technology and the quality of health care. Aspen Systems Corporation, Germantown, Md., 1978.

[13] Flexner, W. A., McLaughlin, C. P., and Littlefield, J. E.: Discovering what the health consumer really wants. Health Care Management Rev. 2: 43–69, fall 1977.

[14] Stratmann, W. C.: A study of consumer attitudes about health care: the delivery of ambulatory services. Med Care 8: 537–548, July 1975.

[15] Kasteler, J., et al.: Issues underlying prevalence of "doctor-shopping" behavior. J Health Soc Behav 17: 328–339, December 1976.

[16] Brooks, E. F., and Madison, D. L.: Primary care practice: forms of organization. *In* Primary care and the practice of medicine, edited by J. Noble. Little, Brown and Company, Boston, Mass., 1976, pp. 67–89.

[17] Hyman, H.: Health planning. Aspen Systems Corporation, Germantown, Md., 1975.

[18] Berkowitz, E. N., and Flexner, W. A.: The marketing audit: a tool for health service organizations. Health Care Management Rev 3: 51–57, fall 1978.

[19] Reynolds, F. D., and Johnson, D. K.: Validity of focus group findings. J Advertising Res 18: 21–24, June 1978.

[20] Calder, B. J.: Focus groups and the nature of qualitative research. J Marketing Res 14: 353–364, August 1977.

[21] Parker, B., and Srinivason, V. A.: Consumer preference approach to the planning of rural primary health care facilities. Operations Res 24: 991–1025, September–October 1976.

[22] Ware, J.: Consumer perceptions of health care services: implications for academic research. J Med Educ 50: 839–849, September 1975.

[23] Ware, J., and Snyder, M.: Dimensions of patient attitudes regarding doctors and medical care services. Med Care 13: 669–682, August 1975.

[24] Wind, Y., and Spitz, L.: Analytical approach to marketing decisions in health care organizations. Operations Res 24: 973–990, September–October 1976.

[25] Kerlinger, R. N.: Foundations of behavioral research. Ed. 2. Holt, Rinehart and Winston, New York, 1973.

[26] Delbecq, A. L., Van de Ven, A. H., and Gustafson, D. H.: Group techniques for program planning: a guide to nominal group and delphi processes. Scott, Foresman and Company, Glenview, Ill., 1975.

[27] Kerlinger, F. N., and Pedhazur, E. J.: Multiple regression in behavioral research. Holt, Rinehart, and Winston, Inc., New York, 1973.

[28] Sheth, J. N.: Multivariate methods for market and survey research. American Marketing Association, Chicago, Ill., 1977.

[29] Frank, R. E., Massy, W. F., and Wind, Y.: Market segmentation. Prentice-Hall, Inc., Englewood Cliffs, N.J., 1972.

[30] Andersen, R., Lion, J., and Anderson, O. W.: Two decades of health services: social survey trends in use and expenditures. Ballinger Publishing Co., Cambridge, Mass., 1976.

[31] America's health care system: a comprehensive portrait. *In* Special report. Robert Wood Johnson Foundation, Princeton, N.J., 1978, pp. 4–15.

A Market Segmentation Approach to Transit Planning, Modeling, and Management

CHRISTOPHER H. LOVELOCK

The importance of marketing for public transportation has received increasing attention in the ten years since Schneider's seminal work on this issue was first published [23]. Recently, it has provided the topic of an entire Transit Marketing Conference, co-sponsored by the Urban Mass Transportation Administration and the American Public Transit Association.

There is a risk that marketing may be seen simply as a managerial activity designed to maximize transit ridership, and as having little relevance for transportation planners and researchers. As emphasized by Kotler, marketing involves analysis, planning, implementation, and control, manifesting itself in carefully formulated programs designed to achieve specific objectives [14]. In most instances, it involves the careful selection of a limited number of target markets, rather than a quixotic attempt to win every market and be all things to all people. As part of this process, marketing requires understanding the needs of each different target market and developing products or services which attempt to meet these needs.

This article will focus on a key marketing concept, market segmentation, and discuss its relevance for planning and modeling as well as for management. First, it looks at what is implied by the concept of market segmentation, at the potential value of dividing a mass market into smaller

Reprinted from *Proceedings of the Sixteenth Annual Meeting of the Transportation Research Forum,* 1975, pp. 247–258. By permission of The Richard B. Cross Company, Oxford, Indiana 47971.

groups, and at the criteria which must be satisfied if meaningful segments are to be developed for use in a specific operational context.

Alternative methods of segmenting the transit market are then evaluated in the context of relating modal choice behavior to both the characteristics of individual travelers and the types of trip that they make.

Finally, findings are presented from a survey of a specific sub-segment, namely, adults in middle-income, suburban, car-owning households, located within a short distance of local transit routes. This study showed that nontransit users perceived public transportation very differently from regular users and were also less well informed about the specifics of local services.

SEGMENTING THE MARKET FOR "MASS TRANSIT"

It is sometimes observed that the term "mass transit" is an unfortunate one, since it implies a mass market with undifferentiated needs and characteristics [24]. In practice, as will be shown, the demand for public transportation is made up of many submarkets (or market segments) representing people of different ages, sexes, occupations, and income levels, traveling for various purposes, with varying degrees of frequency, at different times of day, and between different locations. Certain segments may be much more important than others from the standpoint of defining and achieving transit objectives.

Although every transit operation is likely to have somewhat different priorities, the objectives for transit tend to fall into two broad categories. The first concerns the diversion of travelers from private automobiles, with a view to achieving such goals as reducing traffic congestion, noise and air pollution, energy consumption, and traffic accidents, as well as avoiding the need for new highways and parking facilities. The second is concerned with improving mobility for those who presently lack access to adequate transportation, either because they do not own a car or lack access to one on a regular basis, or else are unable to drive.

If these goals are to be achieved, it is immediately apparent that planners must set objectives for managers of planned or existing transit systems in terms of encouraging ridership among specific segments of the population, rather than in vague terms of "maximizing ridership" for the overall system.

Various researchers, including Smerk, Lovelock, Reed, and Watson and Stopher, have emphasized the importance of developing transit services which are responsible to the needs of different market segments [16, 22, 25, 30]. This is especially necessary when attempting to encourage a modal shift from autos to transit. Failure to take these varying needs into account and failure to adopt communications and pricing strategies which are tailored to the characteristics of specific segments can only weaken transit's prospects for competing successfully against private automobiles.

Transportation models, too, need to reflect the structure of the market. If transportation objectives focus on specific segments of the travel market, then it is important that models be developed which can predict (and perhaps explain) the behavior of these segments.

Pointing to the limited explanatory power of highly aggregative models based upon economic analysis, a number of transportation researchers have stressed the need to develop a better understanding of the ways in which consumers arrive at model choice decisions. [12, 15, 26]. Particular interest has been shown in learning more about how behavioral variables such as attitudes relate to modal choice [1, 11].

DEFINING MARKET SEGMENTATION

In the context of the private firm, market segmentation may be defined as the two-stage process of, first dividing the consumer market into meaningful buyer groups, and then creating specific marketing programs for each group such that financial profits will be maximized. In the case of urban public transportation (which has largely ceased to be profitable financially), the objective function theoretically centers, on attaining specified social goals (e.g., helping achieve new air pollution standards) which can justify a defined level of deficit spending on transit. Unfortunately, transit's success or failure is all too often measured simply in terms of gross ridership statistics.

In evaluating a market and developing appropriate programs, one of three broad alternative strategies can be followed. The first is *market aggregation,* treating all consumers as similar and offering a standard product for everyone. Historically, "mass transit" has tended to fall into this category.

At the opposite end of the scale is *total market disaggregation,* where each consumer is treated uniquely. In the last analysis, each individual may be thought of as a separate market segment, on the grounds that each person is slightly different from everybody else in personal characteristics, behavior patterns, needs, values, and attitudes [29]. Total disaggregation of the population has particular appeal for the modeler, in as much as it can be argued that the best way to develop an understanding of how travel decisions are made and how they may be influenced is to study individual consumers.

Recognizing the dangers inherent in taking an undifferentiated, mass market approach to transportation planning and management, interest has been shown in developing disaggregative behavioral models of modal choice [28]. I believe that understanding the behavior of individual travelers can yield valuable insights for model builders, and also assist transit managers in developing strategies for influencing modal choice decisions. However, there are limits as to how far disaggregation can be carried. Planners have to develop transportation systems for populations which may run into the millions, total disaggregation can quickly become a complex and expensive procedure when running large simulation models, and there are limits to the ability of transit managers to provide personalized service in buses designed to seat fifty people and trains which may carry as many as fifteen hundred at a time.

Obviously, there has to be a happy medium between complete aggregation of the population on the one hand and total disaggregation on the other. This is where the third strategy, that of *market segmentation,* promises to be of value. It calls for grouping consumers into segments on the basis of intra-group similarities and inter-group differences. Wilkie notes that market segmentation may be viewed as a descriptive process, in that it recognizes both individual differences and group similarities [31]. Segments can be developed either by dividing a large, amorphous group into smaller groups with certain characteristics in common, or "built from the ground up" by assigning individuals to one of several groups according to certain specific characteristics which each person possesses.

The concept of market segmentation is based upon the propositions that (1) consumers are different, (2) differences in consumers are related to differences in market behavior, and (3) segments of consumers can be isolated within the overall market. Engel, Fiorillo and Cayley summarize a number of benefits which may be expected to result from a segmentation approach [8], including:

1. A more precise definition of the market in terms of the needs of specific groups, why they behave as they do, and possible ways of influencing behavior
2. A better ability to identify competitive strengths and weaknesses, and opportunities for winning specific segments from the competition
3. More efficient allocation of limited resources to the development of programs that will satisfy the needs of target segments
4. Clarification of objectives and definition of performance standards

The basic problem is to select segmentation

variables which are likely to prove useful in a specific operational context. Kotler proposes three criteria [13], each of which must be satisfied if meaningful market segments are to be developed:

Measurability: It must be possible to obtain information on the specific characteristics of interest.

Accessibility: Management must be able to identify chosen segments within the overall market and effectively focus marketing efforts on these segments.

Substantiality: The segments must be large enough (and/or sufficiently important) to merit the time and cost of separate attention.

Wilkie stresses the importance of choosing segmentation variables which are useful as correlates of behavior and can be related to strategic considerations [31]. He also argues that the best segments are those which display "homogeneity within and heterogeneity between groups", in other words, there should be minimal within-group variation and maximal between-group variation.

SELECTION OF SEGMENTATION VARIABLES

How can the transportation market be segmented, and which variables are likely to yield *useful* segmenting descriptors? In order to see how segmentation variables relate to modal choice decisions (and, perhaps, influence the outcome of such decisions), a flowchart of the decision process is shown in Exhibit 1. This illustrates the stages through which an individual traveler is posited to go in selecting a mode for a specific trip and is based upon an earlier, more complex model to which explicit segmentation variables have been added [16, 17].

This diagram helps us categorize *who* is traveling, and also *why, when, where,* and *how* they are making a trip. It serves to indicate some of the many ways in which the travel market can be segmented, as well as providing insights into modal choice behavior patterns and how they may be influenced. The traveler is seen as specifying the modal attributes desired for a particular trip, then evaluating alternative modes to see which is perceived as providing the best "match" for this trip, choosing that which is perceived as the optimal mode, and then making the trip.

Two broad categories of potential segmentation variables are represented here: (1) traveler-related variables and (2) trip-related variables.

As shown in Exhibit 1, travelers can be described according to demographic characteristics, such as age, income, sex, etc., which, in turn, may be related to certain lifestyle characteristics such as car ownership and ability to drive. They can also be segmented by locational variables, such as where they live, work, shop, and so forth; by their actual travel behavior patterns; and, finally, by various psychological variables, which may be linked to such behavior as attitudes and values, or perceptions and knowledge of alternative modes.

Trip-related variables are shown as being categorized in four basic ways: the purpose for which they are made; the size of the party making a particular trip; the length and nature of the route linking origins, destinations and any intermediary points; and the time of day, week, month, or season at which the trip is made.

It is immediately evident that many of these variables are inter-related. Thus, car ownership and ability to drive are in large measure a function of age and income characteristics. Other demographic characteristics may be related to home and work locations, as well as to trip making behavior.

Certain personal characteristics are obviously linked to the type of trips made. People in most full-time jobs have to commute to and from work each weekday, while students have to go to school or college each day during the school year. With a few exceptions (such as traveling salespeople) these journeys are repetitive in nature, being made at approximately the same time each day and between the same two points. In short, they are "committed" trips. Other types of trips, such as

EXHIBIT 1: ***Relationship of segmentation variables to model choice decisions***

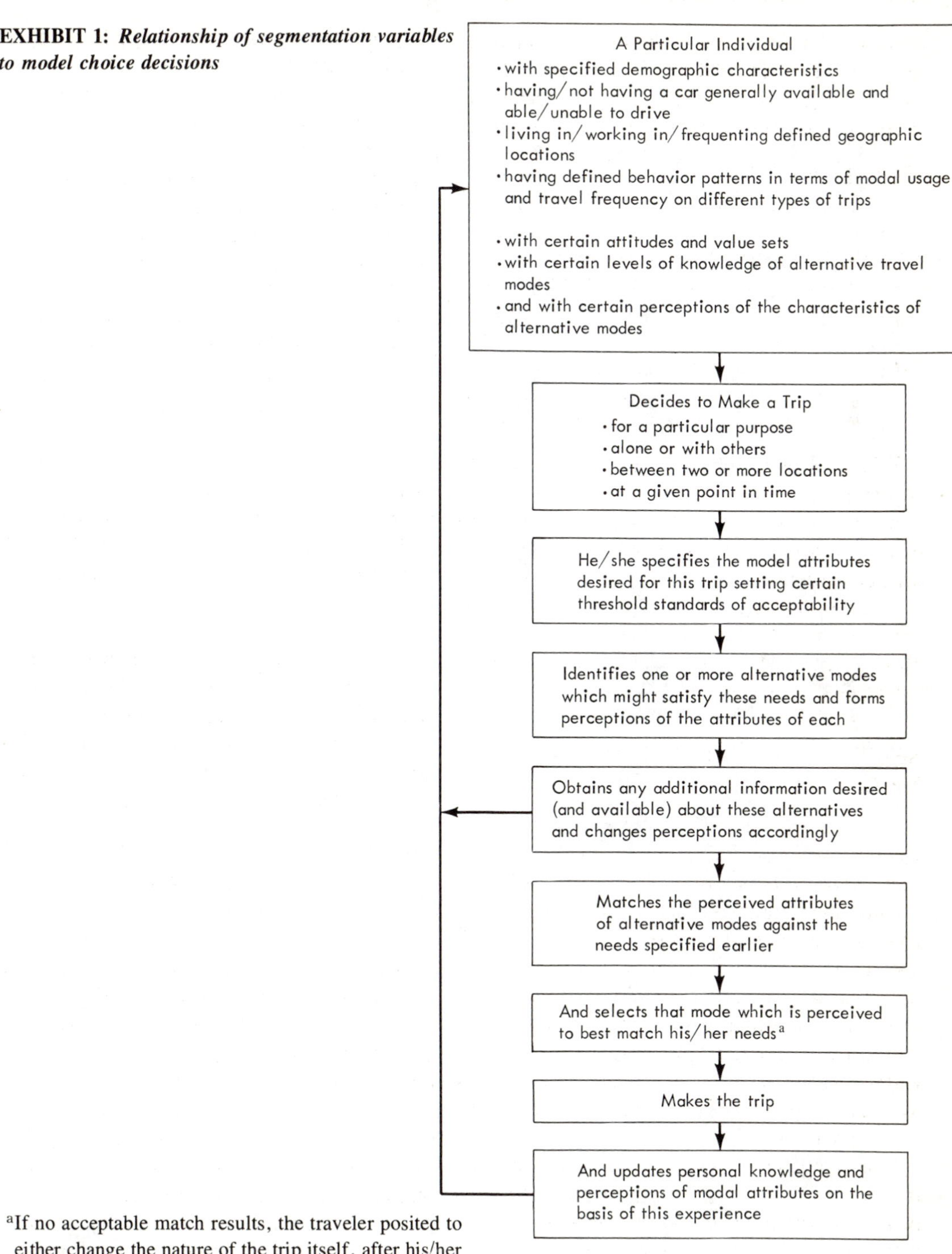

A Particular Individual
•with specified demographic characteristics
•having/not having a car generally available and able/unable to drive
•living in/working in/frequenting defined geographic locations
•having defined behavior patterns in terms of modal usage and travel frequency on different types of trips
•with certain attitudes and value sets
•with certain levels of knowledge of alternative travel modes
•and with certain perceptions of the characteristics of alternative modes
Decides to Make a Trip
•for a particular purpose
•alone or with others
•between two or more locations
•at a given point in time
He/she specifies the model attributes desired for this trip setting certain threshold standards of acceptability
Identifies one or more alternative modes which might satisfy these needs and forms perceptions of the attributes of each
Obtains any additional information desired (and available) about these alternatives and changes perceptions accordingly
Matches the perceived attributes of alternative modes against the needs specified earlier
And selects that mode which is perceived to best match his/her needs[a]
Makes the trip
And updates personal knowledge and perceptions of modal attributes on the basis of this experience

[a]If no acceptable match results, the traveler posited to either change the nature of the trip itself, after his/her requirements or else not make the trip at all.

shopping or recreational, may be said to be "discretionary" in nature, in that there is usually some flexibility in timing and/or the locations visited.

Exhibit 2 shows the distribution of trip purposes by time of day and week experienced by the GO Transit rail service in Toronto, highlighting variations in the nature and timing of travel demands among existing transit users. The study found that travelers at off-peak and weekend periods were less frequent users of the system and that the proportion of the two sexes varied by time of day and week.

Which of all these numerous segmentation variables is likely to prove useful to planners, modelers, and managers? Let's first evaluate them from the standpoint of defining objectives for public transportation.

RELATING TRANSIT OBJECTIVES TO SEGMENTATION VARIABLES

Improving Mobility. It is immediately apparent that objectives relating to improvement of personal mobility tend to be keyed to the needs of specific demographic segments who do not own a car or may not be able to drive one. These groups usually include the elderly, young people, handicapped persons, and low-income groups.

Frequently, transit-related legislation specifically singles out these segments for special attention. Even though some of these segments may be relatively very small (the handicapped, for example), transit planners and managers must still cater to their needs. Ideally, this requires identifying the home origins of as many as possible, the destinations they most need to visit, evaluating their ability to pay, and assessing the extent to which it is necessary and/or feasible to modify vehicle characteristics, promotional strategies and operating policies to meet their special needs. For example see [4].

Modal Shift. Objectives relating to modal shift are concerned with getting people out of their cars and into public transportation. Here the target may at first appear to be simply the four-fifths of all American households which own automobiles. However, when looking at specific objectives, it becomes apparent that priorities need to be set. For instance, if our concern is with reducing energy consumption, then we might usefully attempt to group consumers according to quantity of gasoline they consume annually (presumably a function of

EXHIBIT 2: ***Trip purpose of peak, off-peak Saturday and Sunday riders*** [a]

Trip Purpose	*Weekdays*			
	Peak	*Off-peak*	*Saturdays*	*Sundays*
Work	• • • • ● ● ● ● ● ● ● ● ● ●	• • • • • • • ●	• • • • ●	• •
Business	. • •	• • •	. •	.
Shopping	. • •	• • • • •	• • • • • ●	
School	• • • • • • •	. • • • • • •	.	.
Entertainment	•	. • • •	• • • • •	• •
Social	•	. • •	. • ●	• • • • ●
Personal		. •	•	
Recreation			. •	• • •
Other		.	. • • • •	. • •

[a] ● Represents 1,000 trips; • represents 100 trips; represents fewer than 100 trips.

Source: [20].

miles driven, frequency of trips, and ownership of cars yielding poor gas mileage). If relieving congestion is our concern, then it makes sense to focus on people driving along specific routes during defined periods of the day or week.

Planners and researchers can play an important role here in seeking to identify key groups. However, identification is not enough; it is also important to evaluate the factors motivating the choice of automobiles over other modes for individuals within these groups, as well as to discover how susceptible various subcategories of individuals are to switching to public transportation. This is where the consumer research and the model builder may be able to develop useful insights for transit management.

INSIGHTS FROM PAST RESEARCH

Location. Many studies highlight the importance of location as a segmentation variable, indicating that transit's share of the travel market is a function of the accessibility of origins and destinations from stopping points on the transit route.[1] For interurban rail or bus transit, accessibility is perhaps best measured in terms of travel time. A study of the GO Transit rail service in Toronto showed that GO's market share of all "in scope" trips declined from a high of 41.2 percent, when both origin and destination were within ten minutes' walk of the station, to a mere 1.8 percent of trips originating ten to fifteen minutes' drive from the suburban station and terminating fifteen to twenty minutes' transit ride-plus-walk from the downtown station (Exhibit 3). On the basis of other transit research in Toronto, Bonsall has suggested that the effective catchment area (or "transit envelope") for local bus service is about one thousand feet [2].

EXHIBIT 3: ***GO transit market share by origin/destination zones***

Origin[a] *(suburbs)*	*Destination zones*[b] *(central Toronto)*	*GO transit market share (%)*
XX2	002	41.2
XX4	002	39.8
XX2	004	22.4
XX4	004	15.8
XX2	005	12.7
XX2	006	9.2
XX6	002	10.5
XX4	005	6.7
XX4	006	5.3
XX6	004	6.5
XX6	005	2.6
XX6	006	1.8
		14.5

[a]*Origin zones* in the two suburban corridors were defined as follows:

XX2: Less than 10 minutes walk from the station (innermost zone)

XX4: 5–10 minutes drive from the station (excluding 10 min. walk area)

XX6: 10–15 minutes drive from the station

[b]*Destination zones* within the Central Toronto area were defined as:

002: Less than 10 minutes walk from Union Station (innermost zone)

004: Up to 10 minutes transit ride plus walk (excluding innermost zone)

005: 10–15 minutes transit ride plus walk

006: 15–20 minutes ride plus walk.

Source: [18].

The implications of location as a segmentation variable are twofold. First, if planners want people living or working in a particular geographic location to use transit, they must ensure that transit service provides acceptable access levels to both their origin and principal destination locations. Second, transit marketers are wasting time and money if they try to market their service for trips whose origins and/or destinations lie outside the transit envelope. For this reason, geographically specific media such as direct mail or billboards may be a more cost-effective means of communicating with potential riders than wide-area media such as TV and radio. Another advantage of direct mail is that it can tailor information on routes, fares, and schedules to the needs of a specific location (residents of a local area or employees at a specific plant, for example).

Demographics. How useful are demographic variables (other than geographical location) as a means of segmenting that great bulk of the American population which travels by car? It is known that demographic variables may influence the modal attributes desired by consumers and the relative importance they attach to them. Golob *et al.*, Stopher and Lavender, Dobson and Nicolaidis, and Watson and Stopher have all conducted research which indicates that groups with different socioeconomic variables display different preferences for transportation mode attributes [6, 9, 27, 30]. Often the group which stands out most prominently from the others is the elderly.

However, it is worth noting that business marketers consider demographics as only one of several possible methods of segmentation and not necessarily the most useful at that. Haley cites a number of studies which suggest that demographic variables are, in general, poor predictors of behavior and less than optimum bases for segmentation strategies [10].

Trip Characteristics. A number of researchers have found that people's needs differ according to the type of trip they are making. For instance, Paine, Nash, Hille and Brunner identified the relative importance given to various modal attributes for both work and non-work trips [21]. Their study showed that speed, punctuality, and timing considerations were significantly more important for work trips than for non-work trips. However, for non-work journeys, travelers were noticeably more price sensitive and more concerned about weather protection while waiting and having to walk more than one block; they also placed greater emphasis on clean, comfortable vehicles, on availability of package and baggage space, and on the ability to take along family and friends. Domencich and Kraft, too, have found that demand for shopping trips is much more price elastic than that for work trips [7].

MULTIDIMENSIONAL SEGMENTATION

Thus far, segmentation has been discussed primarily from a unidimensional standpoint. In practice, classification may be more useful if it is undertaken along two or more dimensions simultaneously, to yield a variety of subsegments.

It is my belief that transportation researchers and modelers should be taking a matrix approach to segmentation, with meaningful traveler characteristics along one axis and trip characteristics along the other. In such an approach, each cell would represent a separate sub-segment. It might be hypothesized that each sub-segment would have somewhat different modal attribute preferences and might therefore be expected to show variations in modal choice behavior from other cells. Moreover, such an analysis could well yield insights into preference and behavior differences that are presently obscured by segmentation along a single dimension.

Little research is known to have been conducted along such lines, although Bucklin found marked differences in modal choice behavior among shoppers according to (1) the size and composition of the shopping party, (2) the shopper's marital status and stage in life-cycle, and (3) the time of day and/or week at which the shopping was done [3, pp. 59–61].

Whether or not a sub-segment merits separate analysis will depend primarily on its size. Some cells will contain insufficient travelers. However, by use of multidimensional scaling and cluster analysis, it should then be possible to group modal attribute requirements for different cells according to their similarities to one another, thus collapsing many small cells into a limited number of larger groups, which will satisfy Wilkie's criterion of minimizing differences within groups and maximizing them between groups.

In a number of urban areas, large-scale transportation censuses have been conducted which correlate travel behavior (including modal choice) with data on personal characteristics. Such censuses can provide the basis for an understanding of the size of different traveler/trip cells as outlined above, and the nature of the data available may in itself help determine which bases of segmentation should be employed.

Transportation and population censuses are also valuable in yielding demographic data by geographic area, enabling transportation researchers and managers to identify both the size and geographic location of the segments. Information may be available for population units as small as a city block. This approach has particular value for marketing urban transit services in that these provide transportation along predefined routes which can be related to the characteristics of populations within the surrounding transit envelope.

AN EXAMPLE OF SEGMENTATION IN TRANSIT RESEARCH

Although transportation censuses may describe modal choice behavior, they cannot necessarily *explain* it. By breaking the market down into a series of progressively smaller groupings, it may be possible for researchers to develop new hypotheses into the behavior of specific subsegments.

Such an approach may be particularly useful when seeking to explain differences in model choice behavior among individuals who are realistically in a position to choose between either car or transit for specific journeys, and who appear to have similar demographic characteristics. As suggested in Exhibit 1, personal values, attitudes, perceptions, and knowledge of alternatives may all contribute to determining the outcome of modal choice decisions.

To improve our understanding of the different cells in the segmentation matrix described earlier, therefore, it may be necessary to conduct additional research into (1) the modal requirements of specific subsegments, (2) their perceptions of the various attributes of different modes, and (3) the extent of their knowledge of alternative modes. In this way, it may be possible to relate "soft" characteristics like personal preferences to more readily identifiable personal characteristics such as demographics and behavior patterns.

San Francisco Area Study. With a view to determining the relationship between modal choice behavior and travel perceptions and knowledge, a large scale consumer survey was made in the San Francisco Area of a carefully defined subsegment of the population [16]. The sample was confined to adults aged 18 to 65 years in middle income, car-owning households situated in suburban cities 20–30 miles from San Francisco and located within a quarter-mile of a local transit route and one mile of a trunk-line interurban transit route. Various controls were used to exclude any respondents who might be captive transit users, due to inability to drive or lack of access to an automobile.

Using several measures of reported behavior, the 1,328 remaining respondents could be assigned to one of four categories of transit user behavior:

1. Non user—had never used transit (13.6%)
2. Non-user—but had used transit in the past (49.5%)
3. Occasional transit user (30.1%)
4. Regular transit user by choice (6.9%)

To find out how respondents perceived the characteristics of car, bus, and commuter train travel, they were asked to rate the three modes separately on each of twelve attributes, using a seven-point semantic differential scale keyed to polar opposite descriptors. For instance, on the characteristic of punctuality, the favorable pole was labeled "on-time arrivals" and the unfavorable pole "late arrivals." The results are shown in Exhibit 4 and indicate distinctly different profiles for each of the three modes.

EXHIBIT 4: ***Mean ratings for car, bus and train travel***[a]

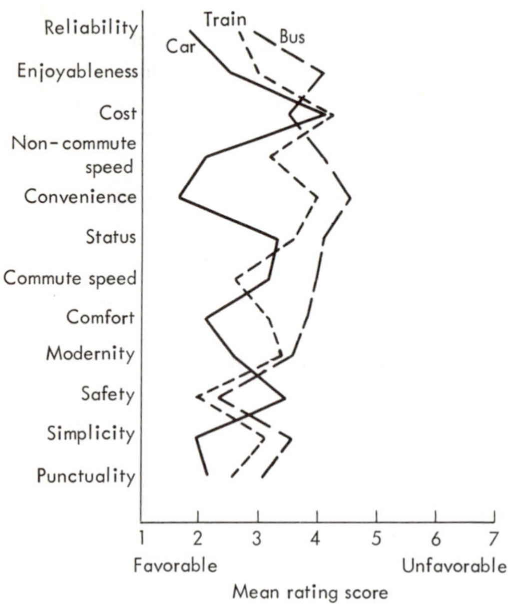

[a]All differences between each of the three possible modal pairs were statistically significant at the $p < 0.01$ level except for the Bus-Train difference on "Modernity."

When respondents were segmentated according to their transit usage category, there was often a significant difference in their perceptions of the characteristics of the three modes (Exhibit 5). As a broad generalization, the more often people used public transportation, the more favorable their ratings of bus and train travel; by contrast, regular transit users tended to rate car travel somewhat less favorably on most characteristics (despite the fact that they were car owners and drivers themselves).

The findings for bus travel are highlighted graphically in Exhibit 6, showing the difference in ratings for non-users and regular users (for clarity, the two non-user groups have been combined and occasional users excluded). As can be seen, the differences are largest for convenience, simplicity ("simple to use"—"complicated to use"), enjoyableness, and comfort. With the exception of cost, non-commute speed, safety and punctuality, all differences in ratings between users and non-users are statistically significant at the $p > .05$ level or better. How should we interpret these findings? Can we infer that one explanation for non-users' failure to ride transit lies in the fact that they perceive transit service as much less competitive with the automobile on many attributes than do regular transit users?

Essentially, this begs the question of whether attitudes cause behavior or vice-versa. Behavioral scientists are divided on this point. A majority hold the view that attitudes (of which perceptions are a subset) are intervening variables which account for behavioral differences. Others, however, argue that attitudes often represent a rationalization for behavior.[2]

I incline towards the view that perceptions are both a cause and an effect of modal choice behavior, with the former the more significant. It is noteworthy that when respondents were asked how confident they were about the ratings they had made of bus travel, non-users showed significantly less confidence in their judgments than users (Exhibit 7).

One of the problems in encouraging car travelers to make use of transit is that many of them are basically unfamiliar with this mode. In the survey, respondents were asked a series of questions designed to test their knowledge of bus services from their community to San Francisco (these questions were phrased in terms of providing information to a new neighbor who had asked for assistance). As can be seen in Exhibit 8, the less respondents used transit, the more ignorant they were about the specifics of the service.

It is entirely possible that two individuals may have the same modal attribute requirements for a given trip, but perceive competing modes in different ways. Essentially, then, it is not the "real" or engineering attributes of a mode which may determine success or failure in attracting travelers, but the *perceived* attributes. An obvious corollary is that a person cannot be expected to use a mode

EXHIBIT 5: ***Consumer ratings of car, bus and train travel, by transit usage class*** [a]

	Never used	*Past user (not now)*	*Occasional user*	*Regular user (by choice)*
N:	*181*	*656*	*399*	*92*
Car travel				
Reliability	1.70	1.76	1.86	1.92*
Cost	4.04	4.02	4.19	4.51
Enjoyableness	2.51	2.54	2.69	2.57
Non-commute speed	2.29	2.10	2.10	2.02
Convenience	1.49	1.52	1.66	1.77*
Status	3.12	3.33	3.36	3.14*
Commute speed	3.12	3.03	3.23	3.49*
Comfort	2.08	2.11	2.27	2.25
Modernity	2.57	2.52	2.75	2.76
Safety	3.30	3.51	3.79	3.69
Simplicity	1.95	1.95	2.16	2.12
Punctuality	2.14	2.01	2.24	2.44*
Bus travel				
Reliability	2.92	2.81	2.73	2.25
Cost	3.65	3.65	3.68	3.35
Enjoyableness	4.37	4.28	4.05	3.41*
Non-commute speed	4.26	4.17	4.15	3.75
Convenience	4.74	4.70	4.39	3.17*
Status	4.13	4.10	4.12	3.79*
Commute speed	4.17	4.00	3.81	3.51
Comfort	3.96	3.98	3.86	3.20*
Modernity	3.60	3.64	3.49	3.07*
Safety	2.35	2.35	2.33	2.02
Simplicity	3.79	3.64	3.55	2.58*
Punctuality	3.31	3.11	3.02	2.72
Train travel				
Reliability	2.82	2.55	2.55	2.15
Cost	4.04	4.19	4.30	4.33
Enjoyability	3.40	3.12	2.99	2.63
Non-commute speed	3.33	3.26	3.09	3.09
Convenience	4.31	3.86	3.86	2.91*
Status	3.59	3.54	3.50	3.13*
Commute speed	2.95	2.74	2.78	2.34*
Comfort	3.37	3.33	3.30	2.81*
Modernity	3.71	3.55	3.60	2.81*
Safety	2.12	2.08	2.04	1.97*
Simplicity	3.59	3.07	3.06	2.57*
Punctuality	2.84	2.63	2.64	2.12*

[a]Ratings could range from 1 to 7, with a low number constituting a very favorable rating and a high number a very unfavorable one.

*Differences are statistically significant at $p < .05$ level.

EXHIBIT 6: ***Ratings of bus travel by non-transit users and regular transit users***

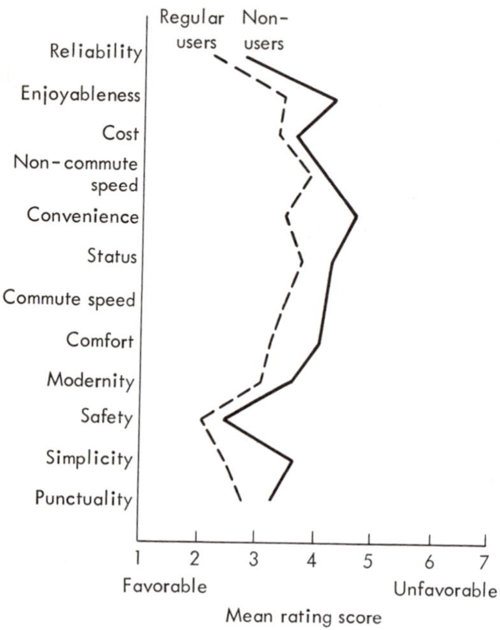

[a]Includes both past and "never used" groups.

of which he or she is largely ignorant. For these reasons, perceptions of specific attributes and the extent of overall knowledge may constitute important variables in modal choice decision-making.

The findings presented from the San Francisco area study suggest a strong link between perceptions of modal attributes and modal choice behavior, but longitudinal studies are needed to test the hypothesis that perceptions and knowledge levels explain behavior, rather than the other way around. If it can be shown that they do, then an attempt should be made to incorporate these variables in future modal choice models, especially when focusing on subsegments of the population which are prime candidates for switching from auto to transit.

Managerial Implications. Clear evidence that perceptions and knowledge levels do influence modal choice behavior among defined segments of the population would have important implications for transit management. If non-users located in transit service areas are deterred from using public transportation because they are either ignorant of the availability and specifics of service or else perceive transit attributes in an unfavorable

EXHIBIT 7: ***Confidence in judgements of bus travel by transit usage class***

	Usage class				
Degree of confidence	*(A) Never used*	*(B) Used in past, but not now*	*(C) Occasional user*	*(D) Regular user*	*Total*
Extremely	3.7%	6.7%	3.9%	30.5%	7.1%
Very	16.7	30.2	39.4	43.9	32.1
Somewhat	49.4	40.9	45.2	23.2	42.1
Only slightly	22.2	19.8	11.0	2.4	16.3
Not at all	8.0	2.5	0.6	0.0	2.5
	100.0	100.0	100.0	100.0	100.0

Measure of association	γ	*Significance*
All usage classes	–.322	<.001
(A) + (B) and (D) only	–.677	<.001

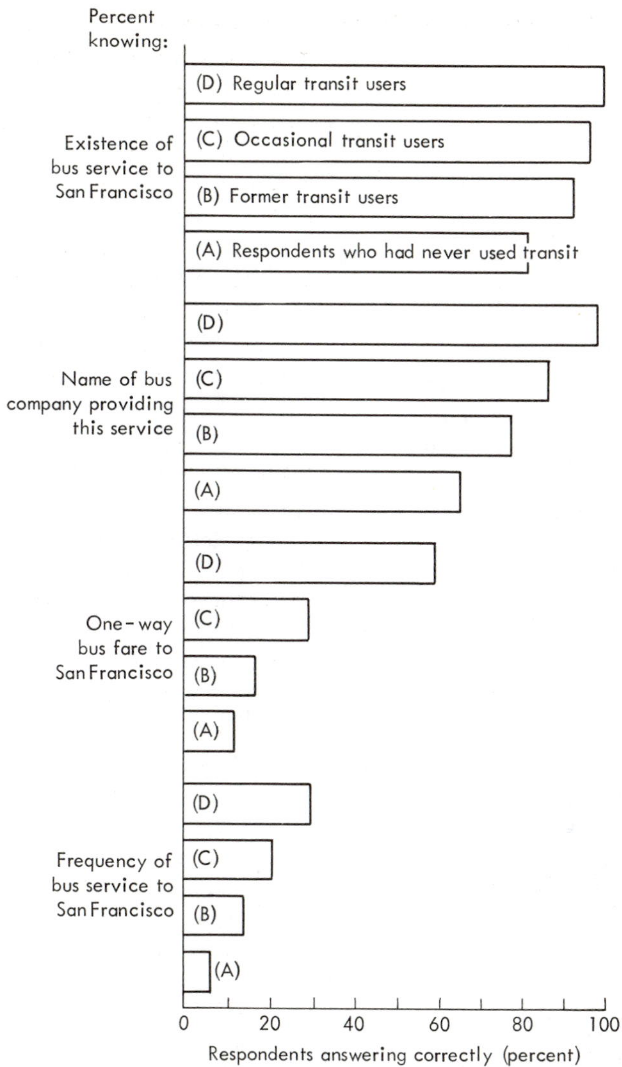

EXHIBIT 8: ***Knowledge of interurban bus service (to San Francisco) by transit usage class***

light, then marketing communications programs designed to correct misperceptions and provide needed information may be able to influence modal choice behavior in many instances.

However, for such an approach to prove effective, it would be most important to tailor the content of the communications to those target segments whom research had shown to be the most likely to change their behavior as a result of (a) obtaining specific needed information and (b) changing their perceptions of specific attributes. A broad based campaign along the lines of "Ride the Bus, It's Nicer than You Think" is unlikely to achieve much.

CONCLUSIONS

This paper has attempted to emphasize both the importance and the benefits of taking a segmentation approach to transportation planning, modeling, and management.

Various bases of segmentation were discussed, including geographic location, other demographic variables, and trip characteristics. It was argued that greater emphasis should be placed on multidimensional segmentation, as opposed to categorizing consumers along only one dimension at a time. By focusing on specific subsegments of the population, it may be possible to obtain new insights into the modal choice behavior of certain groups which have particular significance in terms of achieving transportation objectives.

Although the emphasis in this paper has been directed towards segmentation's application for public transportation, it should be stressed that it is also a potentially valuable concept for a broad range of urban transport services. Issues such as toll road pricing, ramp metering, preferential freeway lanes, parking supply management, and highway safety campaigns all have behavioral implications. Decisions in these areas may benefit from research and analysis which yield a better understanding of the needs and behavior patterns of different highway user segments.

NOTES

1. Summarized in [16], Appendix B.
2. For an overview of this controversy, see [5].

REFERENCES

[1] Allen, W. Bruce, and Isserman, Andrew. "Behavior Modal Split." *High Speed Ground Transportation Journal* (Summer 1972): 179–99.

[2] Bonsall, J. A. *Dial-A-Bus: The Bay Riders Experiment*. Toronto: Ontario Department of Transportation and Communications, August 1971.

[3] Bucklin, Louis P. *Shopping Patterns in an Urban Area*. Berkeley: Institute of Business and Economic Research, University of California, 1967.

[4] Cantelli, Edmund J. et al. *Transportation and Aging: Selected Issues,* Washington, DC: Supt. of Documents, Stock #1762-0042, 1970.

[5] Day, George S. "Theories of Attitude Structure and Change." In *Consumer Behavior: Theoretical Sources,* edited by S. Ward, and T. S. Robertson Englewood Cliffs, NJ: Prentice-Hall, 1973.

[6] Dobson, Richardo, and Nicolaidis, Gregory C. "Preferences for Transit Service by Homogeneous Groups of Individuals." *Proceedings,* Transportation Research Forum, 1974.

[7] Domencich, Thomas A., and Kraft, Gerald. *Free Transit*. Lexington, MA: Lexington Books, 1970.

[8] Engel, James F., Fiorillo, Henry F., and Cayley, Murray A. (eds.). *Market Segmentation: Concepts and Applications*. New York: Holt, Rinehart and Winston, 1972.

[9] Golob, Thomas F.; Canty, Eugene T.; Gustafson, Richard L., and Vitt, Joseph E. "An Analysis of Consumer Preferences for a Public Transportation System." *Transportation Research 6* (March 1972): 81–102.

[10] Haley, Russell I. "Benefit Segmentation." *Journal of Marketing* 32 (July 1968): 30–5.

[11] Hartgen, David T., and Tanner, George H. "Investigations of the Effect of Traveler Attitudes in a Model of Modal Choice Behavior." *Highway Research Record,* no. 396 1971, 1–14.

[12] Horton, Frank E. "Behavioral Models in Transportation Planning." *Transportation Engineering Journal,* Proceedings of the ASCE, May 1972, 411–20.

[13] Kotler, Philip. *Marketing Management*. Englewood Cliffs, NJ: Prentice-Hall, second ed., 1972 (See especially chapter 6).

[14] Kotler, Philip. *Marketing for Nonprofit Organizations*. Englewood Cliffs, NJ: Prentice-Hall, 1975.

[15] Le Boulanger, H. "Research Into the Urban Traveller's Behaviour." *Transportation Research 5* (1971): 113–25.

[16] Lovelock, Christopher H. *Consumer Oriented Approaches to Marketing Urban Transit*. Ph.D. dissertation, Stanford University. Springfield, VA: National Technical Information Service, #PB-220 781, 1973.

[17] Lovelock, Christopher H. "Modeling the Modal Choice Decision Process." *Transportation 4* (1975).

[18] Metropolitan Toronto and Region Transportation Survey (MTARTS). *GO Transit Commuter Rail Project*. Special Report No. 9 (Second Household Survey, 1968).

[19] Oi, Walter Y., and Shuldiner, Paul W. *An Analysis of Urban Travel Demands*. Evanston, IL: Northwestern University Press, 1962.

[20] Ontario, Government of, *People on the GO*. Report C4. Toronto, Ont.: Department of Highways, June 1969.

[21] Paine, Frank T., Nash, Allen N., Hille, Stanley J., and Brunner, G. Allen. "Consumer Attitudes Towards Auto vs. Public Transit Alternatives," *Journal of Applied Psychology*. November–December 1969, pp. 472–80.

[22] Reed, Richard R. *Market Segmentation Development for Public Transportation*. Stanford University, 1973. Springfield, VA: National Technical Information Service, #PB-227 178/AS.

[23] Schneider, Lewis M. *Marketing Urban Mass Transit—A Comparative Study of Management Strategies*. Boston, MA: Harvard Business School Division of Research, 1965.

[24] Schneider, Lewis M. "Marketing Urban Transit." Highway Research Record, No. 318, 1970, 16–19.

[25] Smerk, George M. "Mass Transit Management." *Business Horizons,* December 1971, 5–16.

[26] Sommers, Alexis J. "Towards a Theory of Traveler Mode Choice." *High Speed Ground Transportation Journal* (January 1970): 1–8.

[27] Stopher, Peter R., and Lavender, J. P. "Disaggregate Behavioral Travel Demand Models: Empirical Tests of Three Hypotheses." Transportation Research Forum *Proceedings,* 1972.

[28] Stopher, Peter R., Lisco, Thomas E. "Modelling Travel Demand: A Disaggregate Approach, Issues and Applications." Transportation Research Forum *Proceedings,* 1970.

[29] Twedt, Dik Warren, "The Concept of Market Segmentation." In *Handbook of Modern Marketing,* edited by V. P. Buell. New York: McGraw-Hill, 1970.

[30] Watson, Peter L., and Stopher, Peter R. "The Effects of Income on the Usage and Valuation of Transport Modes." Transportation Research Forum *Proceedings,* 1974.

[31] Wilkie, William L. *An Empirical Analysis of Alternative Bases of Market Segmentation*. Unpublished Ph.D. dissertation, Graduate School of Business, Stanford University, 1971.

MASSACHUSETTS STATE LOTTERY

In early February 1972, the Lottery's director, assistant director, and deputy directors met to consider further steps to implement the recently enacted state lottery. They were under considerable time pressure because the bill passed by the legislature on September 27, 1971, had been designated an "emergency law" to indicate that the lottery should be made operational as soon as possible. Accordingly, a tentative decision was made to instigate the lottery in April 1972. By the end of January, the main staff positions had been filled and a meeting was then called to decide what kind of marketing program should be followed. The Commission had already set up headquarters in a new building, purchased computer equipment, selected an advertising agency, and visited other states that had lotteries in order to gain background information. Three other states—New Hampshire, New York, and New Jersey—had already been operating lotteries.

Prepared by Dharmendra T. Verma and Fredrick Wiseman.

During the strategy formulation meeting various issues were raised, including whether the lottery administrators were ready to make specific marketing plans or whether they should try to generate some primary marketing data. Some of the administrators believed that they should go ahead and specify a marketing program. They pointed to the urgency of the situation as well as to the available data from the other state lotteries. Vern Fredericks, one of the deputy directors, strongly asserted: "We should copy the features of the other state lotteries, especially New Jersey, which has been so successful. What worked well in New Jersey will work in Massachusetts. We don't have time to go around doing marketing studies here. Besides, why should a ticket buyer in Boston be any different from someone buying a ticket in New York City or Newark?"

But others believed it was necessary to find out something about people's attitudes toward various aspects of a lottery. Donald Phillips, another deputy director, argued: "It is difficult to decide on specific aspects of a lottery, such as what price to charge and what kind of prize distribution to offer, unless we know how Massachusetts residents feel. The other states have made many changes or are considering changes in their initial programs. Also, how do we decide which features to copy when we're not sure what factors are responsible for a successful lottery? We should undertake a study to give us the kind of information we need to help design our marketing program."

FORMULATION AND ORGANIZATION OF THE STATE LOTTERY

The Massachusetts State Lottery was established by the State Lottery Law enacted by the Senate and the House of Representatives of the Commonwealth of Massachusetts on September 27, 1971.[1] The two major purposes of the lottery as stated by the majority whip of the Massachusetts House of Representatives, William Q. MacLean, Jr., were "to raise revenue for the cities and towns in Massachusetts and to decrease organized (illegal) gambling within the state."

The Massachusetts Lottery Law specified, among other things, that prizes should amount to no less than 45% of total revenues; that costs for operation and administration should not exceed 15%; and that a minimum of 40% should go to the state treasury for subsequent disbursement to the cities and towns. In addition, the legislative act designated the bill an "emergency law" which was to be implemented as soon as possible. The salient features of the legislation are reproduced in Exhibit 1.

EXHIBIT 1: ***The State Lottery Act—selected sections***

Section 23: There shall be, in the office of the state treasurer, a state lottery commission, hereinafter called the commission, consisting of the state treasurer, the secretary of public safety or his designee, the state comptroller or his designee, and two persons to be appointed by the governor for terms coterminous with that of the governor. No more than four members of the commission shall be of the same political party. The state treasurer shall be the chairman of the commission. . . .

Section 24: The commission is hereby authorized to conduct a state lottery and shall determine the type of lottery to be conducted, the price, or prices, of tickets or shares in the lottery, the numbers and sizes of the prizes on the winning tickets or shares, the manner of selecting the winning tickets or shares, the manner of payment of prizes to the holders of winning tickets or shares, the frequency of the drawings or selections of winning tickets or shares and the type or types of locations at which tickets or shares may be sold, the method to be used in selling tickets or shares, the licensing of agents to sell tickets or shares, provided that no person under the age of twenty-one shall be licensed as an agent, the manner and amount of compensation, if any, to be paid licensed sales agents, and such other matters necessary or desirable for the efficient and economical operation and administration of the lottery and for the convenience of the purchasers of tickets or shares and the holders of winning tickets or shares. . . .

The commission shall make a continuous study and investigation of the operation and administration of similar laws in other states or countries, of any literature on the subject which from time to time may be published or available, of any federal laws which may affect the operation of the lottery, and of the reaction of citizens of the commonwealth to existing and potential features of the lottery with a view to recommending or effecting changes that will tend to better serve and implement the purposes of the state lottery law. . . .

Section 25: The apportionment of the total revenues accruing from the sale of lottery tickets or shares and from all other sources shall be as follows: *(a)* the payment of prizes to the holders of winning tickets or shares which in any case shall be no less than forty-five per cent of the total revenues accruing from the sale of lottery tickets; *(b)* the payment of costs incurred in the operation and administration of the lottery, including the expenses of the commission and the costs resulting from any contract or contracts entered into for promotional, advertising or operational services or for the purchase or lease of lottery equipment and materials which in no case shall exceed fifteen per cent of the total revenues accruing from the sale of lottery tickets, subject to appropriation; and *(c)* the balance to be used for the purposes set forth in clause *(c)* of section thirty-five [. . . shall be credited to the Local Aid Fund . . . and shall be distributed to the several cities and towns in accordance with preestablished provisions.]

Section 27: No person shall be licensed as an agent to sell lottery tickets or shares if such person engages in business exclusively as a lottery sales agent. Before issuing such license the director shall consider the financial responsibility and security of each applicant for licenses, his business or activity, the accessibility of his place of business or activity to the public, the sufficiency of existing licenses to serve the public convenience, and the volume of expected sales. . . .

Section 29: No person shall sell a ticket or share at a price greater than that fixed by the commission. No person other than a licensed lottery sales agent shall sell lottery tickets or shares, except that nothing in this section shall be construed to prevent any person from giving lottery tickets or shares to another as a gift.

No ticket or share shall be sold to any person under age eighteen, provided that a person eighteen years of age or older may purchase a ticket or share for the purpose of making a gift to a person under age eighteen. . . .

Source: The Commonwealth of Massachusetts, Chapter 813, Act H 5925, 1971.

The Lottery Commission consisted of five members, with the State Treasurer serving as chairman. The other members were the Secretary of Public Safety, the State Comptroller, and two persons appointed by the governor for terms coterminous with that of the governor. The specific responsibilities of the Commission are also outlined in Exhibit 1.

In November 1971, Dr. William E. Perrault, Chairman of the Mathematics Department at Boston State College, was appointed director of the state lottery by the State Treasurer with the approval of the governor. The director was responsible for the supervision and administration of the lottery.

The next few weeks were spent in setting up the organization structure and filling the administrative positions necessary to start the lottery operation. Computer equipment was purchased and a Boston advertising firm was appointed. The first year advertising and promotional budget was approximately $1 million. By the end of January, most of the staff had been appointed and operating plans were being formulated. A partial organization chart is presented in Exhibit 2. Initial funding for the staffing requirements was provided by the state legislature with the stipulation that this money be returned to the state out of revenues from ticket sales.

The marketing staff consisted of Louis J. Totino, Deputy Director—Marketing, three district managers, and 18 field representatives. Each of the representatives was to service the various Massachusetts retail outlets which would be licensed to sell the lottery tickets. In addition, the commission entered into a $300,000 contract with a Cambridge-based major consulting firm, Arthur D. Little, Inc. The objective of the contract was to advise in the planning, design, and implementation of the lottery.

Other Forms of Gambling in Massachusetts. In addition to the lottery there were several other types of legal gambling in Massachusetts. These were parimutuel horse and dog racing and beano. Total receipts to the Commonwealth from horse and dog racing had increased from $19.4 million in 1968 to almost $29 million in 1971.[2] Beano was expected to return at least $1.0 million (10% of gross receipts) to the state in 1972.

EXHIBIT 2: ***Partial organizational chart***

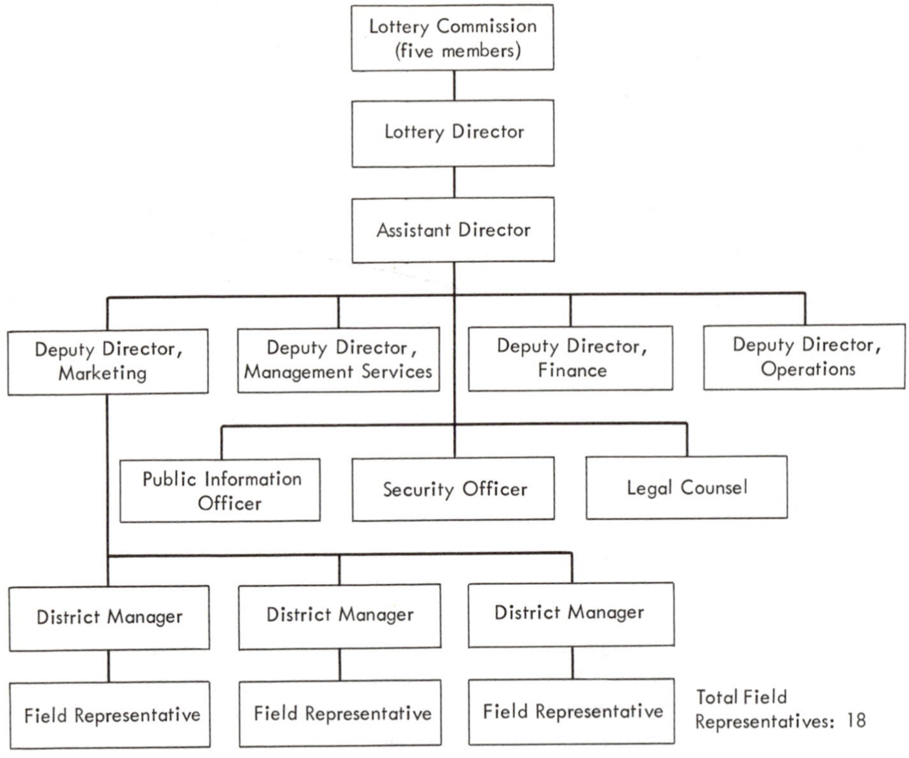

Source: Drawn from Massachusetts Lottery Commission records.

Recent changes had been made in the Massachusetts laws to allow Sunday horse racing and to increase the length of the racing season. Also, additional beano legislation was being considered which would increase the maximum allowable daily prize, from $50 to $200; to allow games on Sunday; and to allow each licensee to hold more than one game per week.

Illegal gambling also thrived within the state, with the most well-known varieties being off-track betting and the "numbers" game. Officials of the state legislature believed that sales of the lottery tickets and the fact that no more local newspapers published the "number" would cut down revenues in the "numbers" by about 20 to 25%.

BACKGROUND ON OTHER STATE LOTTERIES

New Hampshire Sweepstakes. In 1963, the state legislature of New Hampshire passed the New Hampshire Sweepstakes Law. This law set up a sweepstakes commission with responsibility to "conduct public drawings at such intervals and in such places within the state as it may determine."[3] The stated purpose of the sweepstakes, the first of modern times in the United States, was to provide New Hampshire's cities and towns with additional revenue to aid in defraying educational costs.

The state law limited participation in the sweepstakes to individuals over 21 years of age.

The law also specified that tickets, priced at $3 by the sweepstakes commission, could be sold only at state-owned liquor stores and at state-regulated horse racetracks. Further, as part of the act creating the sweepstakes, the legislature included a provision that made it possible for any city or town, by referendum, to elect not to have tickets sold within its boundaries.

Only one sweepstakes drawing was held during each of the first two years of operation, 1964 and 1965. The exact prize distribution, which totaled approximately 35 to 40% of gross revenue, was a direct function of tickets sold. Top prize was $50,000 and additional major prizes were set at $25,000, $12,500, and $10,000. In all, there were approximately 400 prizes awarded for each $500,000 worth of tickets sold, over 95% of these being consolation prizes between $100 and $500.

In 1964, gross revenue from the first sweepstakes drawing totaled $5.7 million. After accounting for operating expenses, the commission was able to return a total of $2.8 million to the cities and towns in which tickets were sold. Ticket sales for the following year declined almost 20% and there was approximately a $300,000 reduction in revenue returned by the state.

A consumer study conducted by a University of New Hampshire professor in 1965 revealed a number of insights into the characteristics of the typical purchaser. Among these were that (1) 88% of all buyers came from out of state and (2) among neither residents nor nonresidents was the number of tickets purchased significantly related to family income. A more complete discussion of the findings of the New Hampshire consumer study is given in Exhibit 3.

EXHIBIT 3: ***New Hampshire consumer study***

The characteristics of purchasers of New Hampshire tickets can be summarized as follows:

1. 88% come from out of state.
2. 67% are male.
3. 80% of the men and 60% of the women are married.
4. 82% support four persons or less.
5. 50% are between 40 and 60 years of age.
6. 75% purchased three tickets or less.
7. 50% obtained the ticket themselves.
8. 10% made a special trip to get the tickets.
9. 52% of the nonresidents are in New Hampshire for recreational purposes.
10. 65% completed high school and 11% have more than college training-levels of educational achievement which are significantly above the national average.
11. 31% have incomes of $10,000 or more, 75% have incomes over $5,000 and 10% have incomes below $3,000—the income pattern being significantly higher than the national average.
12. In terms of income and education levels, resident winners are not as different from the state population as nonresident winners are from the national population.
13. Residents tend to buy more tickets per purchase than nonresidents.
14. Resident and nonresident winners are comparable in the relationship which exists between family incomes and the number of persons supported.
15. Among neither residents nor nonresidents in the number of tickets purchased related significantly to family income.

These findings provide a picture of Sweepstakes participants which is quite different from that which might have been anticipated on the basis of historical precedent. If, as the analysis shows, the number of tickets purchased is unrelated to income, why are the poor not participating much more heavily in the Sweepstakes?

At least three intuitive explanations for these results can be offered. It is clear that the majority of the purchasers come from outside of New Hampshire. Federal statutes limiting the use of the mails for lottery purposes were enacted before the turn of this century and remain in full force. As a result, the buyer, or someone acting for him, must personally come to New Hampshire to obtain a ticket. For nonresidents to get a ticket, therefore, some travel will be required. However, travel is not something the poor or their friends can readily afford, particularly for recreational purposes.

A second factor, the price of the tickets, may also have an impact. At three dollars each, tickets are not easily obtained by those who prefer to do their gambling on the basis of a nickle, dime or quarter a day.

Finally, the Sweepstakes is essentially an "investment" form of gambling in that the results are not known until well after the money has been picked out. This lag has probably contributed to the noticeable lack of interest inveterate and professional gamblers have demonstrated in the Sweepstakes. Perhaps the poor who gamble do not like the deferred outcome this form of wager entails as much as they like gambling where results are known within 24 hours.

The "typical" Sweepstakes ticket purchaser appears from this study to be a middle-aged married man who has a good education and is earning a relatively high income with which he supports a small family. He has come to New Hampshire for the purpose of having a good time, which apparently includes buying a few Sweepstakes tickets.

As a means of raising public revenue, the New Hampshire Sweepstakes does not appear to be extracting a disproportionate amount of money from those in society who are least able to pay for government services.

Source: New Hampshire Sweepstakes Commission. Survey conducted by Professor S. Kenneth Howard, University of New Hampshire, 1965.

In an attempt to increase yearly gross revenue, the commission decided to have two drawings in 1966. The result of this change was unexpected, as gross revenue again fell significantly. The following year brought about the first major change in the running of the sweepstakes. The state legislature granted permission for tickets to be sold at sweepstakes commission offices, at toll booths along the state highway, and most important, at retail business establishments. It was expected that with the increased number of ticket outlets, sales and interest in the sweepstakes would also increase. In anticipation of this, the Commission decided to conduct three drawings in 1967. This marketing program remained in force through 1970. The result of this strategy was a substantial decline in sales during the first two years, followed by a leveling off at approximately $2.0 million during the next two years. The gross revenue, operating expenses, prizes paid, and educational aid contribution figures for the years 1964–1970 are given in Exhibit 4.

New York State Lottery. New York had considered having its own lottery for many years, but it was not until the initial success of the New Hampshire sweepstakes that the New York state legislature passed the New York State Lottery Law in 1965 and 1966.[4]

EXHIBIT 4: ***New Hampshire sweepstakes, operating results, 1964–1970***

Year	*Gross revenue*	*Operating expenses*	*Prizes paid*	*Net to education*
1964	$ 5,740,093	$1,172,010[a]	$1,799,995	$ 2,768,088
1965	4,566,044[b]	678,679	1,400,000	2,487,365
1966	3,889,056	633,447	1,414,993	1,840,616
1967	2,577,341	578,578	943,565	1,055,198
1968	2,054,434	364,162	800,150	890,122
1969	2,017,667	358,710	790,599	868,358
1970	2,019,367	391,208	791,596	836,563
	$22,864,002	$4,176,794[c]	$7,940,898	$10,746,310

[a]Includes $587,710 paid to the Internal Revenue Service for 10% wagering tax.

[b]Includes $664,448 refund from the Internal Revenue Service, including interest.

[c]Includes $580,876 paid to the State Liquor Commission for sale of tickets; therefore, total revenue paid to the state—$11,327,186.

Source: New Hampshire Sweepstakes Commission.

The New York law required that 45% of the gross receipts of lottery ticket sales be applied exclusively for the purpose of providing aid to primary, secondary, and higher education, and for providing scholarships. It also provided that no more than 40% of the proceeds be awarded as prizes and no more than 15% be used for all administrative expenses, including promotion and commissions to vendors.

New York's marketing program differed significantly from that of New Hampshire. Tickets were priced at $1 and drawings were scheduled monthly. The advertising campaign centered around the purpose of the lottery and used the theme: "Give a dollar to education." It was believed that people would not mind contributing to educational costs if they also had a chance of winning a large amount of money at the same time. This approach was also expected to minimize social criticism of the lottery.

Distribution, as in the New Hampshire plan, was very limited and tickets could be purchased only at about 4,000 banks and at government buildings. These outlets were chosen by the New York Lottery Commission to gain respectability for the lottery and to minimize the risk of underworld influence and other forms of corruption. The prize structure for the monthly lottery was established on the basis of each million tickets sold. A total of $400,000 was to be allocated among approximately 1,100 winners. The major prizes were $100,000, $50,000, $5,000, and $2,000. There were also ten $1,000 winners. The remainder of the prizes were for $500 and $100.

Ticket sales for the first 10 drawings (June 1967 through March 1968) averaged 5.3 million tickets per month. This level was below expectations based on the performance of the New Hampshire Sweepstakes.[5]

On April 1, 1968, a law passed by the U. S. Congress took effect which restricted banks from being used as outlets for selling lottery or sweepstakes tickets in any state. This required the New York Commission to adopt a new distribution policy. Foremost consideration was given to those outlets that were reputable and willing to provide the necessary push in the selling of tickets. Hotels, motels, drug, and variety stores were the types of stores that were sought. Licenses were granted to 13,000 business establishments and a 5% commission on ticket sales was to be paid to all vendors. (In New Hampshire, the sales commission was 4% for state stores and 8% for private vendors.) The immediate consequence of the required change in distribution policy was a reduction in ticket sales, as shown in Exhibit 5.

New York, as well as New Hampshire, also came under the provisions of a second federal law. This one prohibited information regarding any aspect of a lottery or sweepstakes from being communicated in a media vehicle that crossed over state lines. Hence no radio or television advertising of any sort was allowed. Even winners could not be identified or interviewed over radio or television networks. Further only those newspapers that were distributed within the state could be used for transmission of lottery information. With such restriction, point-of-purchase displays, billboards, and in-state newspapers became heavily used as the means by which the lottery or sweepstakes commission communicated with their potential purchasers.

During the fiscal years April 1968 through March 1969 and April 1969 through March 1970, New York ticket sales totaled nearly $4.9 million and $4.7 million, respectively. Both years' sales were considerably below the average $5.3 million in ticket sales of the first 10 months. During 1970–1971, bonus $2 and $3 lotteries were scheduled to be held on an alternating quarterly basis in an attempt to stimulate sales. Ticket sales increased during the fiscal year 1970–1971 to $70 million, with the $3 Summer Special lottery contributing a record $17 million to gross revenues. Also, the New York Commission held three special 50-cent weekly lotteries on a test basis in November, December, and January. Gross sales averaged approximately $900,000. The $2 lottery had not been started. Exhibit 6 shows the sales record, by month, for all drawings held between April 1970 and March 1971.

New Jersey State Lottery. In January 1971,

EXHIBIT 5: ***Gross receipts of New York State Lottery, by month (millions of dollars)***

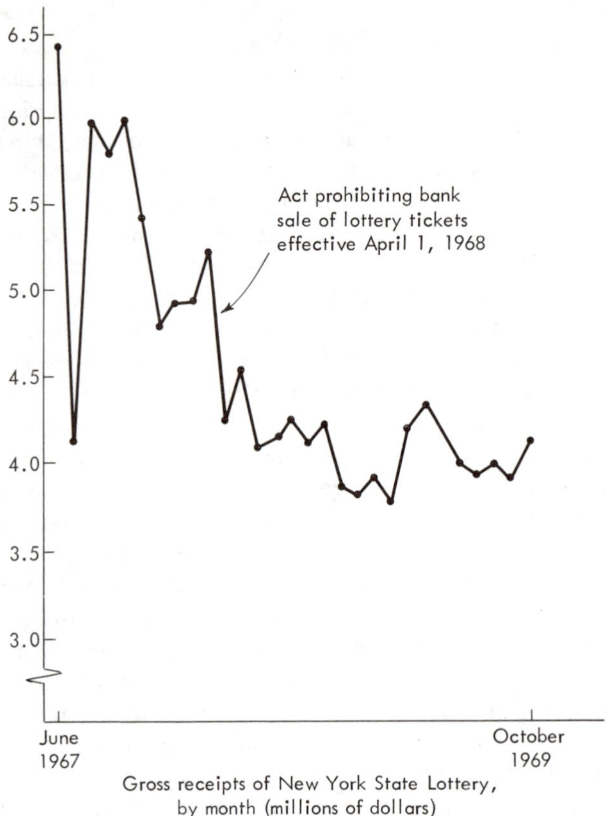

Source: New York State Lottery Commission records.

New Jersey became the third state to commence lottery operations.[6] The New Jersey lottery differed from the New Hampshire and New York lotteries in a number of ways: tickets were priced at 50 cents; drawings were held weekly; vending machines as well as sales personnel were used to sell tickets; supermarkets were emphasized heavily in the distribution network; and tickets could be purchased from vending machines up until the day of the drawing.

As in New York, New Jersey's prize distribution was based on the sale of one million tickets. For each million tickets there were 1,000 prizes, with the total prize money amounting to $158,000 to be distributed as follows:

Number of winners	*Prize*
1	$50,000
9	4,000
90	400
900	40

Since, by state law, a minimum of 45% of gross revenue had to be returned in the form of prize money, $67,000 was left undistributed. This

EXHIBIT 6: ***New York State Lottery operating results, 1970–1971***

Sales month[a]	*Gross sales*	*Commissions retained*	*Net revenues*
April 1970	$ 3,948,275.00	$ 225,076.05	$ 3,723,198.95
May	3,785,567.00	215,748.37	3,569,818.63
June	3,688,096.00	208,424.99	3,479,671.01
July	3,309,573.00	188,538.28	3,121,034.72
August	3,220,801.00	182,954.10	3,037,846.90
September	3,169,871.00	179,665.78	2,990,206.22
Summer Special ($3)	16,747,581.00	940,210.68	15,807,369.32
October	3,606,144.00	205,326.78	3,400,817.22
November 50-cent Special	765,752.00	55,861.20	709,890.80
November	3,384,900.00	193,798.70	3,191,101.30
December 50-cent Special	1,001,995.50	74,312.91	927,682.59
December	3,276,925.00	188,588.16	3,088,336.84
Holiday Special ($3)	8,667,298.00	489,182.02	8,178,115.98
January 50-cent Special1971	938,887.00	69,265.66	869,621.34
January	3,303,844.00	189,728.95	3,114,116.05
February	3,806,400.00	218,178.34	3,588,221.66
March	3,461,860.00	197,549.83	3,264,310.17
Total:	$70,083,768.50	$4,022,410.80	$66,061,357.70

[a]Net revenues are collected in the month following the sales month.

Source: New York State Lottery Commission.

money was used to finance a special "Millionair's" drawing in which the prize distribution was as follows:

Number of winners	*Prize*
1	$1,000,000
1	200,000
1	100,000
7	10,000
215	500
2,025	100

New Jersey promoted its lottery heavily with the use of newspaper, billboard, and point-of-purchase advertisements and promotional materials, such as placemats which were given to restaurant owners to be used on their tables.

Tickets were sold at approximately 6,000 retail establishments, with the heaviest concentration being at large supermarkets. Vending machines were also placed at high traffic locations, such as bus, train, and airport terminals. A 5% commission was paid to vendors for each ticket sold. In addition, bonus money totaling 1% of gross revenue was paid to outlets that sold prize-winning tickets. For example, the outlet selling the "Millionaire" winning ticket was given a $10,000 bonus.

In its initial year of operation, the New Jersey lottery sales totaled 282 million tickets (see Exhibit 7 for weekly sales data). The New Jersey State Lottery Planning Commission in 1970 had said: "Our estimate of gross revenues for the first full year of operation will be about $30 million, although there is a substantial amount of possible error in this figure. The potential revenues, of course, may be somewhat higher, but some mar-

EXHIBIT 7: ***New Jersey State Lottery operating results, 1971***

1971 drawing date		*Total number of tickets sold (millions)*	*1971 drawing date*		*Total number of tickets sold (millions)*
January	7	4.7	July	1	5.8
	14	2.5		8	5.6
	21	3.7		15	5.4
	28	3.9		22	5.4
				29	5.4
February	4	4.9			
	11	5.8	August	5	5.3
	18	5.8		12	5.2
	25	5.7		19	5.2
				26	5.3
March	4	5.9			
	11	6.1	September	2	5.3
	18	6.1		9	5.3
	25	6.0		16	5.2
				23	5.4
April	1	6.0		30	5.5
	8	5.9			
	15	5.9	October	7	5.5
	22	5.6		14	5.5
	29	5.8		21	5.4
				28	5.5
May	6	5.9			
	13	6.0	November	4	5.4
	20	5.9		11	5.5
	27	5.9		18	5.4
				24	5.3
June	3	5.9			
	10	5.8	December	2	5.4
	17	5.9		9	5.1
	24	5.9		16	5.3
				23	5.2
				30	5.0
			Total for 1971		282.2

Source: New Jersey State Lottery Commission.

gin must be allowed for errors and experimentation in the initial stages.'' Thus the first-year sales, totaling $141 million, far exceeded the Planning Commission's estimate.

Recent Developments

Both New Hampshire and New York reacted to the New Jersey success by changing many of the basic characteristics of their own lotteries.

New Hampshire. New Hampshire, which had expanded its number of retail outlets to 850 in 1971, decided to institute a weekly 50-cent drawing in addition to its now quarterly $3 sweepstakes drawing. Drawings were held each Friday and tickets could be purchased as late as Tuesday. On Wednesday, tickets for the following week's drawing were put on sale. Also, a bonus drawing was scheduled in October of each year, with the top prize being $100,000. A June 25, 1971, news release by the sweepstakes Commission concerning this new lottery is shown as Exhibit 8. During the first week of the 50-cent ticket, 207,957 tickets were sold, and for 1971, gross lottery revenue (which included the 13 sweepstakes and the 50-cent drawings beginning July 23) amounted to $4.3 million.

EXHIBIT 8: ***New Hampshire Sweepstakes Commission news release***

50/50 N.H. Sweeps Poised for Takeoff

The Sweepstakes Commission announced today that tickets for the new 50/50 N.H. Sweeps will go on sale at all outlets on July 14. The ticket price has been set at 50¢ and provides a chance at a top prize of $50,000, as well as hundreds of other prizes.

Public drawings will be held every Friday morning beginning July 23. The first drawing will take place on the State House Plaza in Concord. Prizes will be determined by a randomly selected 5-digit number. Each ticket has a 5-digit Sweeps number. If a ticket matches the winning 5-digit Sweeps number for that drawing date, the holder of that ticket wins at least $5,000 and qualifies for a super drawing with a chance to win $50,000 or $10,000. It is estimated that super drawings will be held every 2 or 3 weeks, depending on ticket sales. A variety of additional prizes of varying amounts will be awarded. The prize schedule is best explained by example.

Selected winning Sweeps number	*Your Sweeps number*	*Prize*
12345	12345	$5,000 Minimum. Chance at $10,000 or $50,000
12345	x2345	$500
12345	xx345	$50
12345	xxx45	Weekly Bonus Chance at $500 next week
12345	xxxx5	Hold for special BONANZA drawing to be held at least quarterly with minimum prize pool of $50,000.

Flyers will be distributed within the next several days explaining the prizes and drawings in greater detail. All existing sales outlets will be selling the 50/50 Sweeps tickets along with the regular $3.00 Sweeps tickets. It is anticipated about 200 additional private outlets will be authorized by the Commission.

The Commission explained that the new 50/50 N.H. Sweeps is patterned after the successful New Jersey Lottery; however, the Commission believes that the N.H. program provides a more exciting prize structure. In the New Jersey program there is an 8-day delay between the end of sales and the weekly drawing. This has been eliminated in the N.H. program since the drawing will take place during the same week. This improves the action. This is in harmony with one of the slogans for the new 50/50 N.H. Sweeps program, "Where The Action Is!".

Source: New Hampshire Sweepstakes Commission.

New Hampshire also added a new dimension to the purchase of lottery tickets which was called the Uniticket. This permitted any resident or visitor to the state to buy a 50-cent lottery ticket for a 12-, 24-, or 52- week period at a cost of $6, $12, or $25, respectively. Further, subscribers could select their own number and were also guaranteed renewal rights on this number. Advertisements suggested that residents and tourists purchase Unitickets for themselves, or as gifts for friends, relatives, or associates.

Three further changes in this marketing program were made in 1971 to increase the number of winners. The first was that buyers of the 50-cent ticket were given ten $3 sweepstakes tickets if their weekly ticket number was one more or one less than the winning number. The second change established a "Scramble Bonus," in which a ticket holder won $25 if his ticket contained the five digits of the winning ticket number in any order. The third change was to increase the number of prize winners for the $3 sweepstakes ticket. The new prize distribution for each 100,000 tickets sold was as follows:

Number of winners	Prize
1	$50,000
1	10,000
1	5,000
5	2,000
20	500
100	100
300	50

New York. New York, like New Hampshire, also changed its lottery substantially. The $1 monthly ticket was discontinued and replaced by a weekly 50-cent ticket, the prize structure was changed, and the distribution network was streamlined by dropping a number of outlets. A news release issued by the New York State Lottery Commission in January 1972 described the new 50-cent lottery:

> New York State's 50-cent Lottery offers the advantages of fast action and fast payoff. Drawings are held weekly on Thursday at various locations within New York State. Tickets may be purchased from any of approximately 7,200 licensed vendors. A new Lottery begins each Wednesday. . . . For each series of one million 50-cent tickets sold, 10,000 prizes are offered weekly.
>
> The prizes, for each million tickets sold, are:
>
> | | | |
> |---|---|---|
> | 1 first prize | $50,000 | all six digits of winning number (in exact order) |
> | 9 second prizes | 5,000 | last five digits |
> | 90 third prizes | 500 | last four digits |
> | 900 fourth prizes | 50 | last three digits |
>
> Those holding the last two digits (9,000 per million tickets sold) will participate in the next bonus drawing and should retain their tickets to await the results of that drawing. . . . Of the more than 7,200 vendors licensed to sell lottery tickets, virtually every line of business is represented, including supermarkets, department stores, hotels and motels, restaurants, drugstores, variety stores, specialty shops, bars, liquor stores and others.

The New York Commission decided against the policy of awarding large major prizes in its bonus drawing. Instead, they selected a prize distribution which featured a relatively large number of smaller prizes. For example, if $150,000 was available in the bonus pool,[7] the prize distribution would be:

Number of winners	Prize
1	$22,500
1	7,500
6	1,500
79	379
945	85

The first 50-cent drawing took place on January 20, 1972, and sales of 3.2 million tickets were recorded. During the subsequent four weeks, sales of 3.6 million, 4.0 million, 4.2 million, and 4.8 million tickets, respectively, were achieved.

New Jersey. As New Jersey entered into its second year of operation, two changes were announced by the New Jersey Lottery Commission. The first was to offer a subscription ticket which was identical to New Hampshire's Uniticket except for the fact that an individual was assigned a number rather than being able to select his own. The second was to double the total number of ways that buyers could qualify for the millionaire drawing. This was done by making all those with tickets whose first two numbers matched the winning number eligible for the drawing. A new prize distribution was also established, creating 2,000 more cash prizes in the "Millionaire" drawing which was held once every five or six weeks:

Number of winners	Prize
1	$1,000,000
1	200,000
1	100,000
27	10,000
443	500
4,252	100

EXHIBIT 9: ***Comparative data for various state lotteries***

	First-year lottery revenues[a]		*1971 Lottery revenues*		*1971 estimates*		
State	*Total (millions)*	*Per capita*	*Total (millions)*	*Per capita*	*Population (thousands)*	*Number of households (thousands)*	*Per capita income*
New Hampshire	$ 5.7	$ 7.70	$ 4.3	$ 5.81	738	225	$3,608
New York	61.7	3.39	70.1	3.85	18,237	5,893	4,797
New Jersey	141.1	19.60	141.1	19.60	7,168	2,218	4,539
Massachusetts	—	—	—	—	5,689	1,760	4,294

[a]The first year of operation for the various state lotteries was as follows: New Hampshire, 1964; New York, 1967–1968; and New Jersey, 1971.

Source: Various State Lottery Commissions and the *Statistical Abstract of the United States: 1971.*

Present situation. In preparation for the February meeting, staff members of the Massachusetts Lottery Commission had prepared two summary tables showing comparative data on the other three states and their lottery operations. These are presented in Exhibits 9 and 10. At this same time, two other states—Connecticut and Pennsylvania—had decided to start lotteries and were in the process of preparing plans. Also, New Hampshire, fearing lost sales from the soon to start Massachusetts Lottery, had under consideration further changes in their sweepstakes. One such plan involved daily drawings with a 25-cent ticket price. It was in this general context of uncertainty and time pressure that the Director of the Massachusetts Lottery had called the February staff meeting.

EXHIBIT 10: ***Summary: structure of state lotteries, January 1972***

			Prize distribution[a]		
State	*Price*	*Frequency of drawing*	*Number*	*Amount*	*Number of outlets*
New Hampshire	50 cents	Weekly	1	$5,000 minimum—chance at $50,000 or $10,000	850
			9	500	
			90	50	
			900	Bonus chance of $500 in the next drawing	
			119[b]	25 (Scramble Bonus)	
	$3	Quarterly	1	$50,000	
			1	10,000	
			1	5,000	
			5	2,000	
			20	500	
			100	100	
			300	50	

(table continues)

EXHIBIT 10: ***continued***

New York	50 cents	Weekly	1	$50,000	7,200
			9	5,000	
			90	500	
			900	50	
	$3	Infrequent intervals	1	$50,000 a year for 20 years	
			1	100,000	
			1	50,000	
			1	25,000	
			10	10,000	
			10	5,000	
			10	4,000	
			10	3,000	
			10	2,000	
			100	1,000	
			Plus an unspecified amount of $500 prizes depending on the number of tickets sold		
New Jersey	50 cents	Weekly	1	$50,000	6,000
			9	4,000	
			90	400	
			900	40	

[a]Prize distribution is based on sales of 100,000 tickets for New Hampshire and 1,000,000 tickets for New York and New Jersey.

[b]Maximum number. The actual number of $25 prizes depends on the number of different digits in the week's winning number.

Source: Various state lottery commissions.

NOTES

1. The bill was passed by a two-thirds majority overriding the veto of the governor: by a 171 to 53 vote in the state House of Representatives and a 26 to 13 vote in the State Senate. No public referendum was required in Massachusetts.
2. Total parimutuel handle from horse and dog racing was $308.9 million; total attendance was 4.4 million during the 439 racing days.
3. New Hampshire Sweepstakes Law, Chapter 284:21:h.
4. State law required passage by two successive sessions of the legislature in addition to a public referendum. The referendum, held at the general election in November 1966, passed by a 2 to 1 margin.
5. See Exhibit 11 for comparative data on the three states with lotteries.
6. The act creating the lottery was approved by residents at the general election on November 11, 1969, by a 4.5 to 1 margin.
7. The $150,000 would come from prize money that was undistributed in the 50-cent weekly prize distribution.

UNITED WAY OF PENOBSCOT VALLEY

Mr. Gurney "Bud" Clancy, Director of the United Way of Penobscot Valley, sat in his Hammond Street office and thought about the task of determining the United Way Campaign Goal for 1977.

The 1976 drive, which would be "kicked off" during the coming month, sought to raise $528,988 from the Maine communities of Bangor, Brewer, Orono, Old Town, Eddington, Glenburn, Hampden, Hermon, and Milford. The sum of the projected operating budgets submitted by the 26 area agencies that received financial support from the United Fund was the source of this target figure. (See Exhibit 1 for an account of fund-raising goals and actual contributions from previous years.)

Mr. Clancy anticipated that the addition of budget requests from two or three new agencies who sought United Way assistance beginning in 1977 would push that year's campaign goal up to about $658,988.

Despite this probable increase in the 1977 quota over the 1976 amount, Mr. Clancy believed that the Penobscot Valley area offered sufficient fund-raising potential to yield that amount. In fact, with the addition of two new communities (Bucksport and Millinocket) in 1977 to the United Way of Penobscot Valley, he strongly suspected that his organization sat in the midst of a community that could afford to give $1,000,000 during 1977.

However, Mr. Clancy felt that he should explore in detail the fund-raising potential within the area before he settled upon a specific target figure for 1977. In particular, he was concerned about where the potential lay and how it might be tapped.

UNITED WAY OF AMERICA FUND-RAISING OPERATIONS

The 39 local campaigns that comprised the first United Way drive in 1919 (known at that time as the Community Chest) yielded a total of $19,651,000. Today, the United Fund of America raises more than $1,000,000,000 in an operation that relies heavily upon the participation of more

EXHIBIT 1: ***United Way of Penobscot Valley, campaign goals and amounts raised, 1969–1975***

Year	*Total amount requested*	*Campaign goal*	*Total amount raised*	*Percent of goal realized*
1975	$580,595	$534,781	$465,000	86.95
1974	530,219	463,115	436,000	94.1
1973	471,910	412,350	366,992	89.0
1972	444,345	396,466	366,836	92.5
1971	412,100	366,135	351,500	96.0
1970	401,343	351,327	326,291	92.9
1969	381,288	336,958	312,148	92.6

Source: United Way of Penobscot Valley.

This case was prepared by Karl A. Boedecker, University of San Francisco. It is designed to serve as the basis for class discussion rather than to illustrate either effective or ineffective handling of an administrative situation.

than 20,000,000 volunteers. Approximately 88% of the 1975 total campaigns raised $750,000 or less, a fact that underscored the role of medium-sized and smaller communities in the overall effort.

Contributions from employees (both labor and management) provided 60% of total funds raised. Corporate gifts in the names of the donor companies accounted for 29% of all support, and the remainder came from residents, foundations, and special gifts.

The national office has provided an outline of how to assess community potential for fund raising in a systematic manner. The process was based upon a consideration of demographic, geographic, and economic characteristics of an area, along with an estimate of community needs. (See Exhibit 2 for an outline of the variables included.)

EXHIBIT 2: ***Assessment of community campaign potential***

Population

1. Size of community—Population growth or loss, a factor in assessing giving market.
2. Demographic and age complexion—the number of male and female workers; number of female heads of households; number of females as second-wage earners; number of blue- and white-collar workers; marital status; educational status; school enrollment; and racial and ethnic makeup.
3. Urban, suburban, and rural areas of community.
4. Commutation patterns—Indicator of where people live, work, shop, and seek services.

Geography

1. United Way boundaries—Uncovered areas and potential for area-wide efforts.
2. Population clusters—Nonagricultural employment versus agricultural employment.
3. Concentration of industries—Are they within United Way's boundaries?

Economic Factors

1. Comparison of employment and unemployment levels over two- or three-year period (overall and by specific trade group).
2. Inflation—The rate of inflation and its effect on the economy. The campaign case should deal with increased needs and the shrinking dollar as a result of inflation.
3. Study of campaign fund-raising results (five- to ten-year analysis) as compared to an assessment of the community's fair-share giving potential will show whether actual campaign performance is gaining or losing ground toward achieving full potential.
4. Corporate profits—A look at selected national firms that have local branches and their rate of profit. *(Source: U.S. News and World Report, Fortune, Forbes, Business Week, Wall Street Journal,* and United Way of America's publication *National Corporations Corporate and Employee Giving to United Way Campaigns.)* The projection of industry profit is also available by trade group.
5. Two- to three-year comparison of bank deposits—A substantial increase may mean that more spendable income is available.
6. E.B.I. (Effective Buying Income)—Comparison of percent of E.B.I. contributed to United Way in the previous year with current year can show change in buying power and also how much of the potential United Way is able to generate. *(Source:* United Way of America's publication *Measurements of Campaign Performance.)*
7. Retail sales index—Two-year comparison.
8. An analysis of selected major corporations, governmental units, and educational institutions, with their projected estimates of employment at campaign time.
9. Any recently established firms in the community that can create new corporate as well as employee contributions.
10. Consumer Price Index—Expresses the cost of living increases in percentage points.
11. Stockmarket trends.
12. Tax levels in a community.
13. Cost of living.
14. Median family income.
15. Wage and salary levels for various industrial groups for supervisory and nonsupervisory personnel. (*Source:* U.S. Department of Commerce, Bureau of the Census.)

Source: United Way of America.

EMPLOYEE GROUP GOALS

The national office suggested several alternative methods for establishing employee group goals. (See Exhibit 3 for a detailed illustration.) However, all were set in specific dollar terms which were derived from the multiplication of the number of employees times a dollars-per-capita figure. The latter was determined according to an average figure which took into account prevailing wage levels, the total community potential for fund raising, and trade-group categories of industries. (See Exhibits 4 through 6 for national data related to employee contributions.)

The United Way of Penobscot Valley utilized a figure of $2.30/hour (the minimum wage) in its calculations of employee contribution potential. (See Exhibits 7 through 10 for information about the responses to the 1975 fund-raising efforts in the Penobscot Valley area.)

Mr. Clancy fully recognized the crucial role of employee contributions and was quite concerned about his local campaign's performance in this category. He felt that access to employees through company cooperation was critical, especially in the establishment of payroll deduction plans. In particular, he worried about what he perceived as a reluctance on the part of area employers to allow United Way people to make appeals to employees of area firms at the plants or stores. He was also concerned about the apparent reluctance of

EXHIBIT 3: ***Methods for calculating employee campaign goals***

Separate Goal for Management and Employees: Acme Company

Employees

Number of employees (excluding executives)	900
Times 12 hours average pay: $4.00 × 12 (1 hour's pay per month)	$48.00
Employee group goal (excluding executives) (900 × $48.00)	$43,200.00

Executives

Number of Executives	100

Salary range	*Number of executives*	*Suggested guide fair share*	*Total*
$10,000–15,000	60	1% annual income	$ 7,500
$15,000–30,000	35	1½% annual income	11,812
$30,000–50,000	5	2% annual income	4,000
Executive group goal			$23,312
Add: employee group goal			$43,200
Total employee group goal			$66,512

Single Goal for Management and Employees: Acme Company

Total number of employees	1,000
Times 12 hours average pay: $4.00 × 12	$48.00
Employee/executive group goal (1,000 × $48.00)	$48,000.00

As mentioned earlier, detailed data on salary ranges or payroll information may not be readily available on a company-by-company basis. An alternative method in this situation is to use the average hourly earnings within specific trade groups to set employee group goals.

Trade Group Averages

Trade group	(1) Average hourly earnings[a]	(2) Fair share per employee	(3) Company employment [col. (1) × 12]	(4) Employee group goals [col. (2) × col. (3)]
Contract construction	$7.06	$84.72	1,300	$110,136
Paper and allied products	4.75	57.00	800	46,000
Printing and publishing	5.19	62.28	275	17,127
Transportation equipment	5.80	69.60	500	34,800
Petroleum and coal	6.06	72.72	1,300	94,536

[a]*Source:* "Employment and Earnings," U.S. Department of Labor, Bureau of Labor Statistics; and United Way of America's publication *Trade Group Giving 1975*.

The figures above are national averages for the trade groups listed and are used only to illustrate this method of computing employee group goals. A community, if it does not wish to use national average earnings, can adjust the hourly earnings figure (column 1) to reflect local variations. (*Source:* Local State Employment Office statistics or *Employment and Earnings*, a monthly publication, U.S. Department of Labor, Bureau of Labor Statistics.)

Source: United Way of America.

EXHIBIT 4: ***Average contributions of firms and employees by trade group, all U.S. communities, 1975***

Industry	*Average contribution of the firm ($/employee)*	*Average contribution of an employee*
Contract construction	$ 6.10	$12.41
Textile mill products	6.61	12.08
Paper and allied products	11.56	18.29
Chemicals and allied products	16.43	30.91
Miscellaneous fabricated metal products	9.26	16.80
Electrical equipment and supplies	8.87	23.58
Railroad transportation	7.79	13.72
Transportation services	13.58	12.64
Electric companies and systems	27.22	38.61
Petroleum	24.38	24.87
Department stores	13.41	16.80
New and used car dealers	1.99	2.80
Commercial and savings banks	39.40	31.21
Life insurance	23.77	26.95
Hotels and motels	4.56	5.96
Leather and leather products	11.99	14.98

Source: United Way of America.

EXHIBIT 5: ***Average contributions of firms and employees by trade group, communities raising $500,000 to $749,999, 1975***

Industry	*Average contribution of the firm ($/employee)*	*Average contribution of an employee*
Contract construction	$10.12	$10.14
Textile mill products	6.45	11.68
Paper and allied products	10.38	14.99
Chemicals and allied products	8.59	31.30
Miscellaneous fabricated metal products	6.45	12.87
Electrical equipment and supplies	7.52	19.07
Railroad transportation	6.05	13.07
Transportation services	17.05	19.63
Electrical companies and systems	15.08	29.04
Petroleum	5.90	6.00
Department stores	9.14	10.35
New and used car dealers	8.35	11.75
Commercial and savings banks	30.67	23.77
Life insurance	12.53	17.99
Hotels and motels	4.63	3.92
Leather and leather products	14.48	13.02

Source: United Way of America.

EXHIBIT 6: ***Average contributions of firms and employees by trade groups, communities raising $1,000,000 to $1,999,999, 1975***

Industry	*Average contribution of the firm ($/employee)*	*Average contribution of an employee*
Contract construction	$ 9.63	$12.74
Textile mill products	5.19	13.20
Paper and allied products	10.98	22.88
Chemicals and allied products	16.91	30.03
Miscellaneous fabricated metal products	5.99	11.59
Electrical equipment and supplies	6.51	24.84
Railroad transportation	6.48	20.69
Transportation services	9.36	19.96
Electrical companies and systems	18.86	36.17
Petroleum	19.79	8.84
Department stores	9.33	11.09
New and used car dealers	.48	.55
Commercial and savings banks	40.43	30.57
Life insurance	19.60	26.04
Hotels and motels	4.00	4.38
Leather and leather products	4.92	6.05

Source: United Way of America.

EXHIBIT 7: ***Company and employee response by industry (numbers), Bangor area, 1975***

Industry	*Number of firms*	*Average number of employees per firm*	*Number of firms that made company contributions*	*Number of firms with executives who made contributions*	*Number of firms with employees who made contributions*
Banking and insurance	13	52	10	13	11
Electrical/ chemical/oil	11	49	8	10	8
Shoe	8	200	8	5	7
Manufacturing	11	521	10	73	8
Contractors/ distributors	24	31	14	19	19
Utilities	10	14	8	6	8
Transportation	11	87	5	8	8
Auto dealers/ suppliers	20	35	20	13	13
Restaurants/ hotels/motels	26	34	11	5	4
Department stores	25	43	9	12	18
Paper	7	206	3	4	7
Textiles	2	172	1	1	2

Source: United Way of Penobscot Valley.

EXHIBIT 8: ***Company and employee response by industry (percentages), Bangor area, 1975***

Industry	*Number of firms*	*Percent of companies that made company contributions*	*Percent of companies with executives who made contributions*	*Percent of companies with employees who made contributions*
Banking/insurance	13	77	100	85
Electrical/ chemical/oil	11	73	91	73
Shoe	8	100	63	88
Manufacturing	11	77	64	73
Contractors/ distributors	24	58	79	79
Utilities	10	80	60	80
Transportation	11	45	73	73
Auto dealers/ suppliers	20	100	65	65
Restaurants/ hotels/motels	26	42	19	15
Department stores	25	36	48	72
Paper	7	43	57	100
Textiles	2	50	50	100

Source: United Way of Penobscot Valley.

EXHIBIT 9: ***Average contributions of employees and companies by industry, Bangor area, 1975***

Industry	*Number of firms*	*Average gift per employee*	*Average gift per executive*	*Average gift per company*
Banking and insurance	13	$ 6.56	$ 72.91	$1,771.15
Electrical/chemical/oil	11	7.35	112.90	784.64
Shoe	8	1	17.33	425
Industrial manufacturing	11	1.45	36	881.18
Contractors/distributors	24	6.78	42.05	380.21
Utilities	10	22.52	120.83	1,495.90
Transportation	11	4.34	65.42	283.75
Auto dealers/suppliers	20	5.45	54.04	413.25
Restaurants/hotels/motels	26	0.70	6.47	57.69
Department stores	25	3.15	17.06	301
Paper	7	1.69	38.51	906.29
Textiles	2	0.60	31.25	650

Source: United Way of Penobscot Valley.

EXHIBIT 10: ***Actual and potential employee contributions by industry, Bangor area, 1975***

Industry	*Calculated potential contributions (employees)* [a]	*Actual contributions*	*Gap*	
			Dollars	*Percent*
Banking and insurance	$ 18,795.60	$ 4,468	$ 14,327.60	76.2
Electrical/ chemical/oil	14.986.80	3,992	10,994.80	73.4
Shoe	44,104.80	1,602	42,502.80	96.4
Industrial manufacturing	158,037.60	8,316	149,721.60	94.7
Contractors/ distributors	20,644.80	5,074	15,570.80	75.4
Utilities	37,756.80	30,809	6,947.80	18.4
Transportation	26,523.60	4,167	22,356.60	84.3
Auto dealers/ suppliers	19,402.80	3,831	15,571.80	80.3
Restaurants/ hotels/motels	24,619.20	625	23,994.20	97.5
Department stores	30,001.20	3,426	26,575.20	88.6
Paper	39,882	2,448	37,434	93.9
Textiles	9,494	208	9,286	97.8

[a]$2.30 (minimum wage) × 12 (hours) (= $27.60) × number of employees.

Source: United Way of Penobscot Valley.

employers to cooperate in the establishment of payroll deduction plans. He could only speculate as to whether this resulted from area executives' attitudes toward fund-raising drives, toward the United Way, toward employee participation at job sites, toward payroll deduction schemes, or from other factors which he had not considered.

COMPANY-GIVING GOALS

The determination of a yardstick for company giving proved to be even more difficult than the assessment of the potential for employee giving.

The majority of firms have tended to rely most heavily on their numbers of employees as the central consideration in their decisions about how much to give. This has sometimes been inappropriate since, due to varying degrees of labor intensity from one firm to the next, the number of employees in a business may not furnish a meaningful guide to its ability to give. An operation with a high labor content in the sales dollar may have shown a low dollar-per-employee figure relative to a more automated business, even when the total contribution of the former, taken as a percentage of pretax profits, was higher. Thus contributions-per-employee comparisons will be misleading unless profits per employee are also considered.

In the past, companies have considered the following factors in their decisions about how much to give:

1. The company's previous contributions.
2. Earnings.
3. Its relative position in the community.
4. The size of its installation and level of employee contributions.
5. The level of giving by others.
6. The effectiveness of the local United Way, including the caliber of volunteers and staff leadership.
7. The contributions of competitors.
8. Programs and services geared toward prevention.
9. Fiscal and program accountability.
10. New or innovative programming.
11. The scope of the agency package.
12. Goal increase.
13. The proportion of company employment to total nonagricultural work force.

In addition to the items listed above, a few companies have gone so far as to include assessments of:

1. The number of employees residing in the United Way service area.
2. The documented needs of the community and how they relate to present levels of support.
3. The influence of top community leaders.
4. The involvement of corporate executives in the campaign.
5. The extent of services to "our" employees (beneficiary studies).
6. The extent of corporate involvement in the creation and/or solution of the problems.
7. The inclusiveness of United Way "package."
8. What new and innovative efforts are being made by the United Way and participating agencies to become more efficient and more effective.
9. Whether or not ineffective services have been eliminated or redirected to meet unmet or priority needs.
10. The extent of effective cooperation between governmental and United Way service delivery systems at the local level.

The United Way staff worried that the heavy reliance by companies upon a "past-giving" standard worked against their goal of fair-share participation by individual firms. Under the past-giving approach, businesses determined current contributions by taking the previous years' sum and adding a small to moderate amount. This focus upon "bulk dollars" has diverted attention from the ability to contribute based upon pretax profits and, in a period of rapidly rising business earnings, has meant that relative contributions (as measured according to profits per employee) have declined accordingly. (See Exhibit 11 for the figures that document this decline.)

The tendency to rely solely upon trade-group averages as a yardstick for company giving has also created some problems. In some instances, the gifts of large firms have distorted category averages, and the collective averages for certain trade groups have been below reasonable giving standards as measured by an ability-to-contribute technique. Furthermore, recent trends toward mergers and conglomerates have blurred the distinctions between trade groups and rendered impossible any meaningful classification of some firms.

Thus the United Way continued to prefer the use of pretax earnings as a basis for calculating a contribution standard. (See Exhibit 12 for an illustration of how they suggest that this might be done.)

The United Way's attitude toward the existence of a significant unrealized potential for company giving was best summed up in the following quote, which ran under the heading "Upsetting the Status Quo":

> The need for a unified and more positive approach to corporations is obvious. United Ways have received relatively little in increased giving from corporations during a period in which individual giving has grown immensely and corporate earnings have risen dramatically. Corporate growth generally has outstripped corporate giving by so much that today the giving of even the most generous corporations appears relatively static and barely meets the increased costs of maintaining service levels.

EXHIBIT 11: ***Corporate gifts to United Way campaigns and corporate profits before taxes***

Year[a]	*Total corporate gifts to United Way campaigns (in millions)*	*Total corporate profits before taxes (in billions)*	*Gifts as a percent of profits*
1960	$172.2	$ 49.7	0.35
1961	176.0	50.3	0.35
1962	181.3	55.4	0.33
1963	188.3	58.9	0.32
1964	196.8	66.3	0.30
1965	202.3	76.1	0.27
1966	213.0	82.4	0.26
1967	218.2	78.7	0.28
1968	231.6	84.3	0.27
1969	251.5	78.6	0.32
1970	249.5	70.8	0.35
1971	259.6	81.0	0.32
1972	270.7	93.0	0.29
1973	280.7	105.1	0.28
1974	287.8	106.2	0.27

[a]Campaign conducted in indicated year for allocations the succeeding year.

Source: United Way of America.

EXHIBIT 12: ***Calculation of campaign quotes by the use of pretax profits as a guide***

Assuming that the statistics that best reflect size and income are local employment and local pretax profits, United Ways could develop and incorporate campaign quotas with the built-in ability factor as follows:

A. Firm X (an example)

Method I

Corporate profits before taxes	$1,200,000
Number of employees	1,000
Profitability per employee	$1,200
Local employment—Firm X	500
Local profits before taxes ($1,200 × 500)	$600,000
1% of local profits	$6,000

Method II

Where Profitability Per Employee is known

Local employment × Profitability Per Employee × .01
500 × 1200 × .01 = $6,000

B. Trade Group X (an example)

Corporate profits before taxes	$2000,000,000[a]
Number of employees	100,000[a]
Profitability per employee	$2,000[b]
Local employment—Trade Group X	13,000
Local trade group profits before taxes ($2,000 × 13,000)	$26,000,000
1% of local trade group profits	$260,000

[a]*Source:* U.S. Department of Commerce.
[b]This may be known locally by the trade group members or by comparison with other firms within the trade.

When actual corporate pretax earnings are not known, they can be estimated as illustrated above.

Source: United Way of America.

INDIVIDUAL GIVING GOALS

The development of individual fair-share standards began during the 1940s. In 1942, the American Federation of Labor and the Congress of Industrial Organizations endorsed donations to the War Chest and advocated that their members contribute one hour's pay per month. The Community Chest drives of that era (forerunners of the United Way) adopted a similar approach in the setting of guides for employee gifts.

In 1944, the Cleveland campaign devised a guide for giving that was intended to serve as a standard against which individual contributors could assess their "fair-share" contributions.

The United Way has continued to promulgate fair-share giving standards, although they have preferred to label them as "suggested guides for giving" or "suggested giving guides." The ones employed in the past have been slightly graduated, ranging from 0.6% of earnings to 3% of earnings.

THE ST. PAUL, MINNESOTA, EXPERIENCE

As a result of what the local chapter perceived as dramatic declines in the potential for community support of their United Way effort, the St. Paul Chapter undertook a market research project in 1975. A declining economy coupled with rising price levels led them to launch an investigation for which there were two objectives: (1) to explore attitudes toward the United Way and its agencies, and (2) to help assess the potential for raising money during the forthcoming fall campaign.

The resulting effort solicited the opinions of 340,000 employees from nine area firms, 30% of whom responded.

The attitudinal measures indicated that people held generally favorable attitudes toward the United Way, but were unaware of the organization's low administrative costs. Furthermore, the study suggested that area residents did not seem to realize that many of the agencies that received funds provided direct benefits to donors.

Based on additional data analysis, the St. Paul organization also reported the following conclusions:

1. Support of the United Way was far below "fair-share" standards for all income levels.

2. Giving performance was related positively to income. Annual salary was a major determinant of employee giving.
3. The person least likely to donate was a young female in a clerical job who earned less than $10,000 a year.
4. Age was a factor that related positively to giving levels for male donors.
5. The donor who gave the least was a male, blue-collar worker under 35 who earned less than $15,000 per year.

IV: PLANNING THE MARKETING MIX

We now examine the planning and blending of specific marketing instruments or variables into a program of action to reach marketing objectives. The nonprofit organization must find the best combination for its marketing decision variables. Marketing programming and budgeting are necessary to coordinate product decisions, price decisions, distribution systems, sales force decisions, advertising, sales promotion, and public relations decisions. These marketing-mix decision variables must be selected to use an optimal level of expenditures to maximize the attainment of objectives.

The first article in Part IV is "An Empirical Investigation of the Appropriateness of the Product Life Cycle to Municipal Library Services" by John L. Crompton and Sharon Bonk. The authors point out that the core concept of marketing is the transaction, which is an exchange of values between two parties, and suggest that transactions occur with all organizations that have publics. This paper represents an attempt to assess the validity and utility of the product life cycle as it applies to the field of municipal libraries. In this context, a transaction occurs when an individual gives his or her time, money, or support in exchange for the library service offered. The usefulness of the product life cycle is suggested for other nonprofit organization.

The second article is "Marketing Communications in Nonbusiness Situations or Why It's So Hard to Sell Brotherhood like Soap" by Michael L. Rothschild. In order to use marketing communications techniques effectively for public- and nonprofit-sector problems, one must consider the extreme differences between these and private-sector problems. Major differences may include the presence of very high or very low involvement, issues offering few perceivable benefits to individuals, and high monetary prices. A framework for considering cases of very high and very low involvement is considered and options for marketers are presented.

The third article is "Public Services—To Charge or Not to Charge" by John L. Crompton. Crompton points out that there is increased interest in the potential of imposing or raising prices for public services. Using leisure services as an illustration, this article discusses the many facets to be considered in public-sector decisions.

The fourth article is "A Hungry Problem for Zoos: In Search of New Prey" by Carol Kovach. An extreme case, the zoo, is used to illustrate the potential of nonprofit sectors for generating a research base to be used in planning the marketing mix. The topic of new "product" development is explored from the perspective of the zoo.

The fifth article is "Distributing Public Services: A Strategic Approach" by Charles W. Lamb, Jr., and John L. Crompton. Distribution decisions are concerned with how an agency makes its services available to a clientele. Distribution adds value to services by making them available at convenient times and places. The authors note that in the past, public administrators frequently have not given high priority to ensuring that distribution of specific services between areas in the same political jurisdiction was equitable. However, in recent years trends have emerged that have caused administrators to be more concerned with equitable service distribution.

Cases in this section include ''Tuesday Evening Concert Series''; ''Simon's Rock College''; ''Alaska Native Arts and Crafts Cooperative, Inc.''; ''The Threat of Rumor to the Nonprofit Organization''; and ''Kent State University: Copying with an Image Crisis.''

An Empirical Investigation of the Appropriateness of the Product Life Cycle to Municipal Library Services

JOHN L. CROMPTON

SHARON BONK

In recent years there has been an increased acceptance that marketing concepts and techniques are applicable to non-profit activities as well as to business activities. This movement has been spearheaded by the writings of Philip Kotler (for example, Kotler and Levy 1969, Kotler 1972, Kotler 1975). He points out that the core concept of marketing is the transaction, which is an exchange of values between two parties. Kotler (1972) suggests that transactions occur with all organizations which have publics and he has termed this viewpoint a generic concept of marketing. He states that the robustness of the generic conception of marketing "will be known in time through testing the ideas in various situations" (Kotler: 1972, p. 52). This paper represents an attempt to assess the validity and utility of the product life cycle as it applies to the field of municipal libraries. In this context, a transaction occurs when an individual gives his time, money or support in exchange for the library service offered.

STRUCTURE OF THE LIBRARY INDUSTRY

A market may be defined at a variety of different levels of aggregation. In utilizing the product life cycle concept it is important to specify and define the "product," that is, which market levels are being considered. Figure 1 suggests that six market levels can be meaningfully distinguished: industry, product categories, firms, product lines, products and brands. These are briefly defined in the following paragraphs.

The library services *industry* is that group of service enterprises whose primary aim is to serve consumers' library needs.

Product categories are public and non-public provision, which when aggregated together comprise the market structure of the library services industry. Public refers to the summation of government supplied library provision. Non-public refers to libraries in commerce, institutions, private research organizations or homes. Both categories provide opportunities for meeting information needs. They have sufficiently distinctive characteristics to meaningfully differentiate them from each other. They are differentiated by the nature of the restrictions on their use and the nature of their individual service collections.

Firms are the individual agencies which provide public library services at four levels of government.

Product lines are clusters of items which compete more intensively with each other than with other clusters of items because they are direct substitutes.

Products are individual resource items within a product line representing specific components of each product line, e.g., books, films, projection equipment, works of art, records, tapes.

Brands are distinctive units of a product identified through specific library programs and ser-

Reprinted with permission from *Journal of the Academy of Marketing Science*, Spring 1978, pp. 77–90.

FIGURE 1: ***Structure of the library industry***

Industry	LIBRARY SERVICES INDUSTRY
Product Categories	Public sector; Non-public sector
Firms	(Public sector:) Federal; State; Regional; Local (city and county)
Product Lines	(Local:) Information; Education; Recreational/ entertainment
Products	(Education:) Multi-media resources; Books; Art
Brands	(Books:) Specific A; B; Library C; Programs D

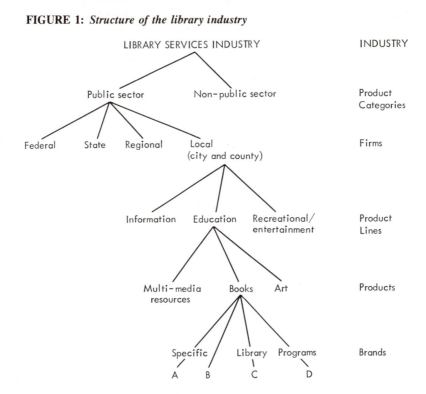

vices, e.g. library X's history book collection may be very different from that of library Y or library Z.

For the illustrative purposes of this article all components of the Library Services Industry have been identified, but for simplicity of exposition only one component at each level of the industry has been developed. The other components can be similarly extrapolated within this framework.

The time scale of product life cycles will lengthen at higher levels of the hierarchy shown in Figure 1. Life cycles of particular local library programs (brands) for example, writers' workshops or story hours, may be less than one year duration while those for city library systems may already have endured for many decades. Level of aggregation is an important distinction since at each level of the hierarchy, the product life cycle concept has a different degree of applicability and utility. Specification of the level under discussion clearly influences interpretation of the concept. This paper focuses on life cycles for individual cities (firms) and their aggregated pattern.

UTILITY OF THE CONCEPT

Conceptually, the product life cycle should be applicable to municipal library services. Library services are discretionary consumer product purchases, characterized by high substitutability. Thus they are subject to replacement by newer, superior products. Their evolutionary process is conceptually no different from that of products in the supermarket. The library services offered by municipal agencies should change constantly in response to consumer demand and hence exhibit distinctive life cycles. Similarly, agencies themselves, as organizations, are substitutable if superior alternatives emerge to replace them. This point was endorsed by Gardner (1965, p. 20):

> Like people and plants, organizations have a life cycle. They have a green and supple youth, a time

> of flourishing strength, and a gnarled old age. We have all seen organizations that are still going through the diseases of childhood, and others so far gone in the ridigities of age that they ought to be pensioned off and sent to Florida to live out their days . . . An organization may go from youth to old age in two or three decades or it may last for centuries.

The rate at which a product moves towards the end of its life cycle is determined by the degree of competition from potential substitute products. The sources of competition to which city library services are exposed can be identified from the taxonomy developed in Figure 1. First, competition comes from other industries which are also primarily supported by government funds, such as police, parks, sanitation, etc. Competition from other city services for market share of tax dollars has always been present, but in recent years proliferation of government services has intensified this competition. Non-tax supported industries which offer potential substitute products also offer competition. For example, the private and commercial offerings of information gathering and recreational material provided by television, radio, films, newsstand magazines, and a new but growing field of private information service firms.

At the product category level, intra-industry competition from the non-public sector has not been a major contributing source of competition to city public libraries because this sector tends to provide its services to relatively small, exclusive and specialized clientele market segments. For example, universities generally restrict their services to registered students, faculty and staff. Corporate libraries serve the specialized wants of corporate employees, and medical libraries serve health professionals.

Competition from other firms offering similar services, such as the county or the next city's library, is the main form of inter-firm competition, especially since the trend is towards reducing restrictions on use and honoring library cards from other local communities. The creation or expansion of metropolitan and regional library systems, which have emerged in recent years, is a particularly prominent source of competition. State, and federal libraries generally serve a complementary rather than a competitive role. State libraries are available to all citizens in the state but they usually offer support or coordination services channeled through regional or local libraries. Only when this distribution channel is not available, for example in the State of Vermont where there are rural areas without easy access to public libraries, are books mailed direct to citizens from the State library. Similarly, at the federal level, the Library of Congress and the libraries of federal agencies are available to all citizens. However, these sources generally serve as support services acting through local libraries.

A longitudinal analysis of municipal library services enables the present situation to be viewed in the perspective of the long term context. The life cycle concept, if its validity is demonstrated, offers a framework to those concerned with providing library services. It enables not only the present status of the field to be evaluated, but also its likely future status. The principal values of the product life cycle model are its utility as a predictive or forecasting tool and its use as an aid in planning and policy formulation. If municipal library services can be shown to have passed distinctive stages of the life cycle, then it seems reasonable to assume that this pattern will continue in future years. Given this framework, strategic and tactical decisions concerning future service policy can be made with more confidence.

METHODOLOGY

In order to identify a true life cycle pattern data, have to be adjusted to allow for population changes; changes in the level of personal consumption; and price changes, including the impact of inflation. In this study, the criterion measure adopted to trace product life was market share. Market share refers to the share of the total municipal city budget allocated for library services. Using this measure ensures that the data reflect the level of market acceptance, rather than actual ''raw'' data which may be misleading. Market share effectively adjusts for these concerns.

Calibration of the life cycle was in annual increments along the horizontal axis of the graph. The annual market share of total city expenditures held by municipal libraries from 1909 to 1974 for each of 25 cities was graphed. The data represented a complete longitudinal set with the exception of 1913, 1914, 1920, and 1921 which were unavailable. Data were interpolated for those years. The longitudinal data were extracted from the U.S. Bureau of Census publication *City Government Finances* for 25 major American cities which constitute 13 percent of the U.S. population. City expenditures for capital and operating purposes on libraries were expressed as a percentage ratio of total city expenditures. This served to illustrate the market share of libraries vis-à-vis all other services provided by the city. The Bureau of the Census (1975, p. 109) defined Library Services as: Public Libraries operated by the city (except those operated as part of a school system primarily for the benefit of students and teachers, and law libraries) and support of privately operated libraries.

The underlying premise, implied by the use of the financial market share measure adopted, is that if municipal library services were perceived as meeting community needs, then their share of the city budget would remain unchanged or increase. If they were not meeting those needs, their market share would decrease. This assumes that priority status for city expenditure allocations accurately reflects citizen support and preferences for the various services provided.

ANALYSIS AND INTERPRETATION

Figure 2 shows the aggregated life cycle for the 25 cities in the sample. It illustrates the level of market penetration achieved by library services in the major municipal markets examined. [Figure 3 shows the life cycle for Detroit and Denver alone.]

Municipal public library services have been available for over a century. The *introductory* stage of the municipal public library product life cycle began in 1833 with the first truly public library. However, it was not until after the Civil War that communities began to provide library services for all citizens. Growth was slow during this period. Massachusetts, the first state to pass an enabling act in 1851, reported in 1890 that approximately 70 percent of its communities had some provision for public library services (Massachusetts Free Public library Commission 1891). Further west, development was slower. For example, towns in Texas did not begin to appropriate monies for public libraries until well into the 20th century (Davis, 1976).

However, by 1909, most major cities had public library services operating independently of the social libraries and philanthropic funding that played an important role in the beginnings of many public libraries. In World War I., libraries were provided for the use of servicemen in camps, on ships, and overseas at over 2,500 supply points (Johnson 1970). These services were well used and many persons who were introduced to library services during their military careers returned home with an increased interest in reading and libraries. During this period, libraries played a prominent role in the efforts of educators and social workers to ''Americanize'' the new imigrant populations. Attention to these new ''publics'' is reflected in the substantial growth in market share achieved between 1916 and 1923.

The onset of the Depression stimulated the beginning of the *take-off* stage (1929–1946). The Depression intensified demand for library services. The demand came from the unemployed, who desired to enhance their literary skills or depth of knowledge in order to improve their chances of securing a job; to seek free recreation and entertainment to pass the time; or simply to keep warm during their enforced leisure. Proportionate city budget allocations for libraries rose in response to these demands as a part of public payroll programs which employed workers

FIGURE 2: ***Library expenditures as percentage of total city budget***

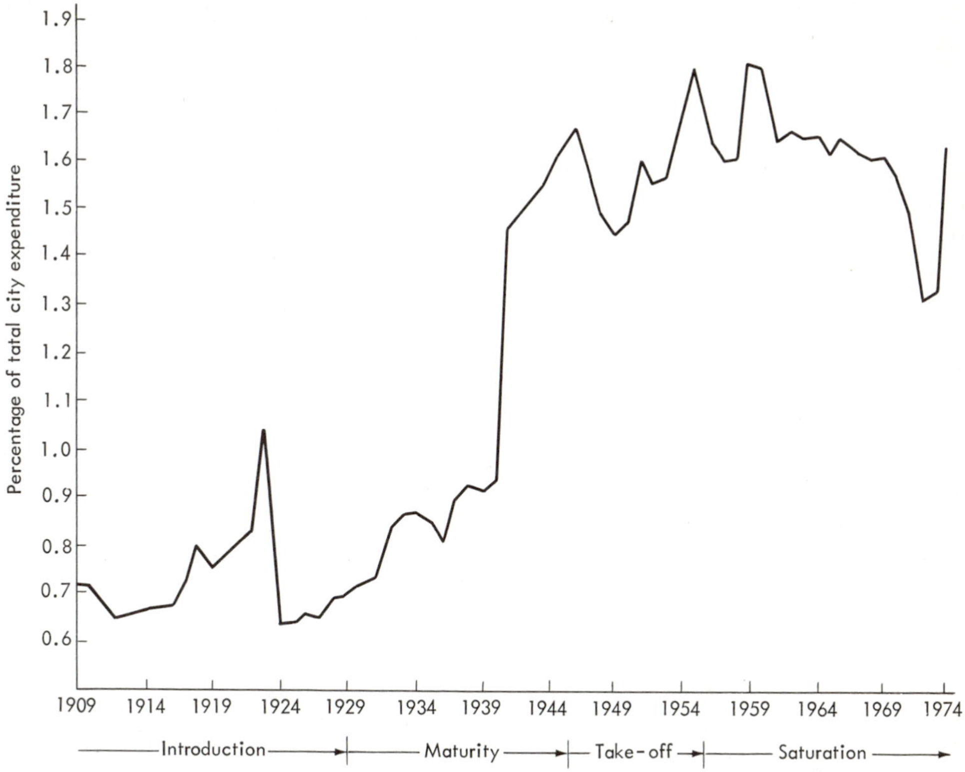

in public libraries and in some cases provided construction funds for library buildings. The most dramatic increase in this *take-off* stage occurred with the advent of World War II. During this period, public libraries expanded their services far beyond their accustomed role of supplying educational recreational reading material. Johnson (1970, p. 372) states: "In maintaining public morale, in serving business and industry, and in the broad fields of adult education and public information, the wartime services of libraries can hardly be overestimated."

The early years of the *maturity* stage (1946–1955) were characterized by a retrenchment as some of the expanded services offered during the war were reduced and libraries reverted back to their more traditional role. In the early fifties the steady growth characteristic of this stage continued, peaking in 1955, despite the chill of the McCarthy era with its lists of banned books.

In the *saturation* stage (1955–1969) the libraries' market share remained remarkably stable. More money flowed into libraries than ever before, but it was state and federal money. As the libraries had relied on philanthropy in the earlier years, they now began a period of reliance on money above and beyond the local appropriations which had been, and will likely continue to be, an important source of support for public libraries. The local committment was not enough to sustain the requirements of new buildings, expanded services, and larger and better trained staffs.

During this stage state contributions going directly to public library budgets increased almost 800 percent from $7 million in 1955 to $54 million in 1969–1970. Federal programs commenced with

FIGURE 3: ***Detroit and Denver library expenditures as a percentage of total city budget***

the passage of the Library Services and Construction Act in 1956. In 1972, the LSCA Title II appropriations peaked at over $46 million with a total federal expenditure that year for libraries of $58 million. The high annual $100 million contribution by federal and state governments to public libraries represented a 30 percent increase in funding beyond the total municipal contributions of $346 million in 1970–1971. (Wellish *et al*. 1974)

During these peak years of federal library spending the market share of city budget allocated to the public library dropped, so that, ironically, as more innovation in programming and increases in resources and personnel were introduced, local support for the urban public libraries declined. However, the trend towards what appeared to be the onset of *decline,* was arrested in 1975. In that year federal spending was reduced and in order to avoid reduction in level of service, cities had to increase the market share of city expenditures allocated to library services (Urban Libraries Council 1977). This increase appears to have been stimulated by an upturn in demand and adverse public reaction to cuts in services which were implemented as the result of reduced market share in the preceding years.

In general, it is probably true that the present low level of libraries' fiscal priority (around 1.5 percent of total city budget) would appear to protect them from substantial demise. The amount of money allocated to libraries is sufficiently small relative to total city budgets that cuts in the library budget are not likely to lead to substantial savings in the city budget. Further erosion of their already minimal budget may effectively lead to the destruction of the service (Janoslovsky, 1975). It is at this point, in considering the ultimate destiny of the product, that an important difference is apparent between the application of the product life cycle concept to the public sector and to the commercial sector. In the public sector elimination of a service is unlikely. Even if its "collective good" or "superior merit" values could be measured and a cost benefit analysis undertaken demonstrating that costs exceed benefits, political realities are likely to prevent elimination. It has been suggested that the morally symbolic and educational functions of the public library which were responsible for its beginning and rise, will sustain it. Robert Salisbury called this moral function part of our "civic mythology" (Conant and Molz 1972). Survival at a *petrification* level for a minimum, appears assured. By definition, the commercial sector is unable to perpetuate a product irrespective of costs and benefits. Such a policy would lead to bankruptcy and removal from the market place.

ALTERNATIVE OUTCOMES

The product life cycle concept recognizes that libraries, like all other products, ultimately will enter a decline stage within which four outcomes are possible. The first possible outcome is Death. In this situation they will be forced out of existence and their functions and programs be discontinued. This is unlikely to occur since libraries have been accepted as a legitimate civic responsibility for over a hundred years in the major cities and as such would appear to be endemic at least for the forseeable future. It is politically inconceivable that basic municipal facilities such as libraries would be totally abandoned and legislated out of existence in any city. However, Harris (1976) has suggested that the "democratic dogmas" that once enveloped the leaders, reformers, and general populace has diminished in importance. This may lead to a decline in public library services. The data suggest some cities are experiencing such a decline. For the reasons cited earlier, libraries' market share can probably only be reduced to a minimum threshold level which must be adequate to retain the city's moral and cultural self image. Hence, the second possible outcome, which at this time appears the most probable, is Petrification. Petrification suggests libraries will remain available indefinitely as a city service. However, their market share is likely to resemble their share in the Introduction stage, since they will be reduced to providing only the core services which provided the initial rationale for being a civic responsibility.

The third possible outcome is to extend or stretch out the life of the product by developing new markets, new programs and alternative sources of finance other than the traditional tax base. For example, increased sharing of resources by different types of libraries or greater use of fees for services. If libraries define their business in a narrow sense, that is, in terms of providing leisure reading and printed reference material they may indeed fall to a level of *petrification*. However, if they define their mission in a more generic sense and introduce new products to satisfy the demands of their target markets, they may gain a greater share of the municipal budget and experience a growth surpassing the saturation stage. Essentially this involves Levitt's (1965) notion of market stretching. If market stretching of library services can be achieved by adopting these strategies, the implication is that greater public support for libraries could be secured which, in turn, would be reflected in a large share of the city budget.

The fourth possible outcome is Merger. In this situation library services would no longer be considered a viable service alone. A more generic approach would be thrust upon the department by a mandated merger with other departments with complementary functions. Examples would be merger with school districts, with leisure services departments, or human resource departments. Within this new larger department, market share of city resources for libraries may either continue to decline or, because they are part of a larger department, be maintained or increased through more secure political support. A move towards sharing physical facilities and materials is likely to gain support as budgets and programs are threatened.

SUMMARY AND IMPLICATIONS

Reference has been made in the paper to important differences between the political forces which shape market share in the public sector and the market forces which shape market share in the commercial sector. However, the democratic process suggests that political forces are representative of market forces because political votes accurately reflect consumer wishes in assessing priorities for budget allocations. If this relationship is in fact valid, the product life cycle concept would appear to be equally as appropriate for use in the public sector. This paper has empirically evaluated the appropriateness of the product life cycle concept to library services in major cities and found it to be a reasonably accurate description of the historical evolution of those services.

Recognition of the product life cycle concept in the library service industry has implications for managerial strategy and the management skills required for maximum effectiveness. For example, as a department (or program or facility within a department) moves from one stage to another, changes in the managerial role occur (Crompton and Hensarling 1977). Some managers may be better equipped and more successful at initiating a new department or program while others may be more effective at developing an existing department and still others at rescuing an ailing agency. The manager who is good at setting short-range objectives and taking risks at the birth of an organization may be much less useful in shaping long term plans and laying the ground work for growth in the take-off phase of the organization's life cycle. In functional terms, the early stages require skills predominantly related to the library technology, that is, expertise in such areas as selection and purchase of new resources, cataloguing and processing, display materials, and development of library programs. As the department grows in size and reaches *maturity,* administrative skills become of paramount importance. However, at this stage the manager's preoccupation with administrative tasks may preclude concern for innovation and change. As the department begins to *decline* there is often renewed awareness of the importance of continual program innovation and renewed emphasis on technology. At each stage, different types and levels of management capabilities, styles, philosophies and methods are required if the department is to prosper. If the requisite functions are not performed, at least to a minimum level of competency, the life cycle curve of the department will accelerate prematurely towards *decline,* failing to achieve its optimum potential.

The product life cycle concept requires library managers to recognize that municipal library departments exist in a competitive environment even though they are in the public sector. Since library services appear to have passed through fairly distinctive life cycle stages to this point, it seems reasonable to assume that this pattern will continue in future years. Nevertheless, the response of library managers to the various sources of competition will enable the curve to be modified. The present life cycles stage suggest various possible outcomes for the future of library services. Their ultimate destiny will depend upon the managerial modifications effected.

Recognition of the concept provides a long term framework which assists in interpreting the present status of libraries and understanding the forces acting upon them. As Levitt (1974) pointed out, it is important to know where the present is in the continuum of competitive time and events. The product life cycle permits current events to be interpreted within a proper perspective and enables the manager to see beyond the exhaustive detail of short term crises. A short term "brush-fire fighting" crisis orientation, enables libraries only to react to situations. Recognition of the life cycle and adoption of appropriate planning and management strategies provides a longer term framework which should enable library services to retain intiative by active preplanning rather than each effort being a stopgap response to an immediate situation.

Considerable amounts of judgement must still be used in application of the concept. This restricts its precision, but it remains a powerful tool. Perhaps its usefulness is best summarized by Wasson (1971): "The product life cycle alone does not furnish an easily-read road map of an automatically unfolding highway to successful strategy. Rather it provides a framework of expectations—a set of patterns of the kinds of developments to which we need to be on the alert and for which we need to plan in advance."

REFERENCES

Conant, Ralph and Molz, Kathleen. 1972. *The Metropolitan Library*. Cambridge, Mass., MIT Press.

Crompton, John L., and Hensarling, David. 1978. "Some Suggested Implications of the Product Life Cycle for Public Recreation and Park Agency Managers." *Leisure Sciences* Vol. 1, No. 3, 295–304.

Davis, Donald G., Jr., 1976. "Rise of the Public Library in America-Texas." Paper presented at the Library History Seminar V, Philadelphia.

Gardner, John W. 1965, "How to Prevent Organizational Dry Rot." *Harper's Magazine* (October) 20–26.

Harris, Michael. 1976. "Public Libraries and the Decline of Democratic Dogmas." *Library Journal,* 101 (November): 2225–2230.

Janoslovsky, Rich. 1975. "Public Libraries Hit By Money Troubles Deteriorate Rapidly." *Wall Street Journal* (October 14) page 1.

Johnson, Elmer, D., 1970. *History of Libraries in the Western World.* Metuchen, New Jersey: Scarecrow Press.

Kotler, Philip and Levy, Sidney, 1969. "Broadening the Concept of Marketing." *Journal of Marketing,* Vol. 33 (January): 10–15.

Kotler, Philip, 1972. "A Generic Concept of Marketing," *Journal of Marketing,* Vol. 35 (April): 46–54.

Kotler, Philip, 1975. *Marketing for Non-Profit Organizations.* Englewood Cliffs, New Jersey: Prentice-Hall.

Levitt, Theodore, 1965, "Exploit the Product Life Cycle." *Harvard Business Review* (November–December): 81–94.

Levitt, Theodore, 1974. *Marketing for Business Growth,* New York: McGraw-Hill.

Massachusetts Free Public Library Commission. 1891. *Report.* Boston, Wright and Potter.

U.S. Bureau of the Census, 1975, *City Government Finances.* Series G.F. 74-No. 4. Washington, D.C.: U.S. Government Printing Office.

Urban Libraries Council and Government Studies and Systems Inc., 1977, *Improving State Aid to Public Libraries,* Washington, D.C.: National Commission on Libraries and Informational Services.

Wasson, Chester R., 1971. *Product Management: Product Life Cycles and Competitive Marketing Strategy.* St. Charles, Illinois: Challenge Books.

Wellisch, Jean B. *et al.* 1974. *The Public Library and Federal Policy.* Wesport, Conn.: Greenwood Press.

Marketing Communications in Nonbusiness Situations or Why It's So Hard to Sell Brotherhood like Soap

MICHAEL L. ROTHSCHILD

The use of marketing techniques outside the private sector has increased dramatically in the past few years. Marketing is now utilized by government, education, health and social services, charity and many other types of nonbusiness (public and nonprofit) organizations desiring to communicate a point of view or elicit a particular behavior. One unfortunate similarity in both business and nonbusiness applications of marketing has been a high failure rate due to reasons ranging from poor needs assessment to poor delivery.

Problems more prevalent in nonbusiness cases include the intangibility of nonbusiness products, the nonmonetary price of purchase, the extreme lack of frequency of purchase, the lack of behavioral reinforcers, the need to market to an entire but heterogeneous society/market, and the extreme levels of involvement varying from very low to very high. Because of these factors, the transference of marketing principles from the business to the nonbusiness sector is far more complex than originally had been thought.

The extreme divergence of nonbusiness situations must also be taken into account. One thinks of business as dealing primarily with products and nonbusiness as dealing primarily with services, yet the nonbusiness sector also markets products. One thinks of monetary prices in the private sector and nonmonetary prices in the nonbusiness sectors, yet businesses are very concerned with minimizing time and inconvenience costs for their customers while many nonbusiness organizations charge monetary prices (e.g., the Post Office, universities, charities). This paper deals with emerging tendencies in nonbusiness marketing communications and offers direction to those developing strategy or research. The cases discussed tend to be those which differ from private sector cases; those which are similar to private sector cases can avail themselves of existing work.

By not considering differences associated with nonbusiness products, marketers are neglecting the concept of a systematic situation analysis. This neglect often is coupled with the inexperience of the nonbusiness manager who may think of communications as the essence of marketing. As Weibe (1951) noted, the nonbusiness manager who sees the private sector's use of marketing communications tools asks, "Why can't you sell brotherhood like soap?" The answer, this paper suggests, is that it is very difficult for marketing communications to have an impact outside the private sector because of the key issues mentioned above. These issues, a framework to present the problems facing nonbusiness marketers, and some options for nonbusiness managers and researchers also are discussed.

COMMUNICATIONS EFFECTIVENESS: ISSUES AND HYPOTHESES

Marketing communications is generally used in conjunction with product, price, and distribution; its potential can be most fully realized when its development follows the other marketing tools. In

Reprinted with permission from *Journal of Marketing*, Spring 1979, pp. 11–20; published by the American Marketing Association.

such a framework, one should consider non-communications aspects to develop insights into communications issues. There are four major issues which impact on potential communications effectiveness outside of the private sector and lead to several hypotheses:

- Product differences
- Pricing differences
- Involvement differences
- Segmentation differences

Product and Price

Product: The product must first be considered for its benefits so that appropriate behavior can be appropriately reinforced. In nonbusiness situations, traditional communications strategies may be inadequate due to difficulties in communicating a potential benefit to the consumer. Communicators seek out the Unique Selling Proposition to show consumer benefits of appropriate behavior. In the nonprofit area, often only weak personal benefits can be found which do not reinforce or maintain long-term behaviors. In order to establish or maintain a behavior, there must be a positive reinforcer (Rachlin 1970). In many nonbusiness cases, neither positive nor negative reinforcers are readily perceivable.

Secondly, one must consider the recipients of the product benefits. In the private sector, the purchaser of the product is generally also the consumer or a member of the consuming unit (e.g., the family). In nonbusiness cases, the product often provides little direct measurable benefit to the purchaser. For example, a person who considers purchasing the concept of driving more slowly pays (in time lost) for a product which primarily benefits society (with greater energy reserves). Since the purchaser may not immediately perceive the personal benefit, it must be pointed out more clearly. Many social issue promoters and charities experience this difficulty.

Another product difference between profit and nonprofit markets is that most nonbusiness products, services, or issues are intangible and cannot be shown in advertising. It is considerably more difficult to describe this product to the public/market. Where an object can be shown, it is generally not the product itself, but rather the producer of the product (e.g., an orchestra or university) or some mechanism involved with the product (the potential purchaser of a military experience is shown, for example, a tank).

Finally, one must consider whether there is at least some minimal level of latent demand for the product or issue at hand. In the private sector, a large percentage of new products fail because they do not meet a need or fill a void. Often in nonbusiness cases, there is no latent demand or interest in the product, service, or issue. When there is no voluntarily sought after exchange, it is difficult to elicit behavior.

Price: The underlying theme of price has traditionally been related to monetary issues; price is generally a function of cost and profit or of elasticity of demand constraints. In nonbusiness cases, often there is no monetary cost. Since marketing deals with exchanges of value, one must consider the nonmonetary costs of the product.

One difficulty lies in the diverse nature of nonmonetary costs which include time cost (driving more slowly, joining the military), inconvenience cost (appropriately depositing litter) and psychic cost (the fear of giving blood). Each of these costs may be perceived as greater than monetary costs which dominate the price of consumer products.

The difficulties of nonmonetary pricing also are reflected in the potential perception of the nonmonetary issues as either cost or benefit. For example, the military experience product has attributes of potential danger and separation from family. For some these attributes are seen as costs; for others these are benefits. Monetary costs, in comparison, are rarely perceived as benefits.

While it is generally accepted in the private sector that communications strategies differ as a function of the cost of the product, there are few if any data which report success at overcoming some of the very high nonmonetary prices of nonbusiness products. When nonmonetary (and difficult to measure) prices are combined with intangible (and difficult to measure) product benefits the results may be a staggering communications problem which may not be solvable via traditional strategies. These points lead to the following hypotheses:

H_1: The lower the perceived personal value (positive reinforcement, quid pro quo) to the individual, relative to the cost (monetary and/or nonmonetary), the more difficult the behavior change task, and the lower the likelihood of success of marketing communications.

H_2: The lower the latent or preexisting demand for the object, the more difficult the behavior change task, and the lower the likelihood of success of marketing communications.

Involvement. In the past several years, involvement has emerged as a popular construct which is hypothesized as acting as a mediating variable in learning, information processing, attitude change, and behavior development. While most of the recent involvement work has examined private sector marketing, the major contribution of this construct may lie in its value in nonbusiness situations; here it seems that the range of involvement becomes more extreme in both the very high and very low ranges and therefore information processing, decision making, and communications effects may differ dramatically.

In a recent explication (Houston and Rothschild 1978), involvement is felt to consist of three component parts:

- Situational Involvement [SI]: the level of concern generated by an object across a set of individuals at a particular point in time (Hupfer and Gardner 1971; Rhine and Severence 1970; Apsler and Sears 1968).
- Enduring Involvement [EI]: the preexisting relationship between an individual and the object of concern (Sherif, Sherif, and Nebergall 1965; Sherif and Sherif 1967; Rhine and Polowniak 1971).
- Response Involvement [RI]: the complexity of cognitive, affective, and conative development at several points along a sequence of information gathering and decision making activities (Bowen and Chaffee 1974; Rothschild and Houston 1977; Park 1976; Payne 1976).

SI and EI are felt to interact and impact upon RI so that SI determines the mean level of RI, and EI determines the variance about the mean. Most of the existing involvement research has considered the impact of communications stimuli on response involvement (Krugman 1965; Ray, et al. 1973; Johnson and Scileppi 1969).

In Rothschild (1978), two models of affective development are proposed. In the high involvement case, attitude precedes behavior; the main impact of advertising is on the development of awareness and knowledge while additional personal selling is necessary to generate behavior. In the low involvement case, advertising directly affects behavior (at least in the short run) due to the absence of a well-informed attitude structure.

The construct of involvement is a key to understanding the differences, difficulties, and constraints encountered in using marketing communications techniques in the nonbusiness sectors; involvement gives insight into how individuals receive and use information in different situations. These differences need to be considered in developing a communications plan.

The product and price differences discussed above lead to varying levels of SI, and, therefore, ultimately to varying styles of information processing, learning, and decision making. In addition, one's past experience with the issue (EI) will also affect these dependent variables. One can speculate that levels of RI will be distributed as shown in Figure 1. That is, nonbusiness will, in many cases, generate more extreme levels of involvement than typically found in private sector cases. What has been thought of as high and low involvement in the private sector may only cover the mid-range of possible societal involvement levels. While private sector goods and services seem to be distributed over the middle of the

FIGURE 1: ***A hypothetical continuum of response involvement levels***

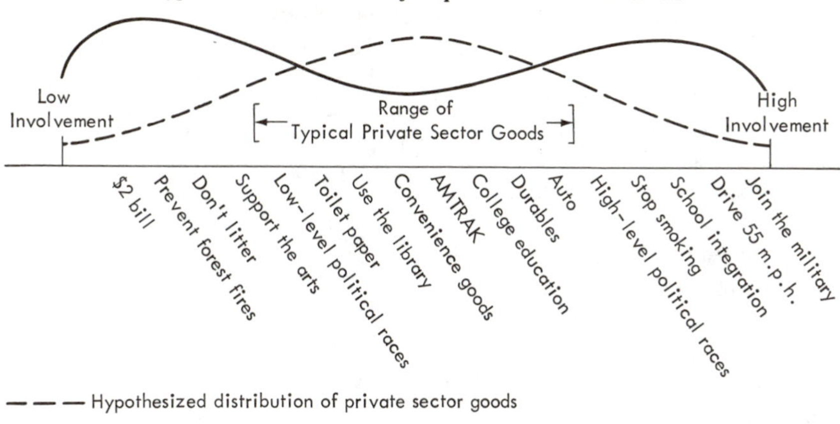

continuum, nonbusiness issues may be slightly bimodal, favoring both extremes.

The marketing issues can be considered from the perspective of intuitively low or high involvement cases. In the low involvement case, the behavior has so little positive value to the individual that any price (in terms of the cost of inconvenience, information processing, or behavior change) will be too high for the value received. Because of the low value placed on any one form of behavior by the individual, only a short-run impact can be made. The change will be at best short-run because there is no reason to integrate the behavior into the belief structure; there is no positive reinforcing stimulus.

This scenario differs from the private sector case in that long-run behavior is established as a result of positive reinforcers. In a stimulus-response sense, one can envision the following:

$$S_1 \rightarrow R_1 \rightarrow S_2 \rightarrow R_2 \ldots n$$

where S_1 = the communications stimulus
R_1 = initial behavior
S_2 = the reinforcer
$R_2 \ldots n$ = repeat behavior

In the typical business sector model, S_1 (advertising) leads to R (purchase) which in turn leads to S_2 (a product or service which is perceived to have a favorable or equitable cost/benefit relationship). S_2 is necessary for long-run behavior; S_1 can only lead to short-run behavior.

In the nonbusiness case, issues of low individual involvement are often brought to the person's attention because there is some value to either society as a whole or some segment of society which is advocating a change in behavior. Often, there is cost to the individual and benefit to a larger group. In such a case, the individual would not consciously choose to be deflected from his/her inertial and apathetic path of least effort. There often is not a sufficiently strong S_2 to maintain behavior.

The issues discussed for low involvement will also hold in high involvement cases. In addition, present behavior may be so strongly related to the individual's central belief structure that most cost/benefit ratios will fall short of giving the individual a reasonable benefit in return for the cost associated with the desired behavior. Past individual behavior will overwhelm a current marketing communications effort.

For the very high involvement case, communications will fail if there is not a perceived benefit of high centrality. There must be a benefit which is both communicable and central to a large segment of the target market. Again, the discussion leads to these hypotheses:

H_3: The greater the involvement level of the object, situation, or issue (due primarily to complexity or price), the more difficult the behavior change task, and the lower the likelihood of success of marketing communications.

H_4: The greater the past involvement level of the individual (due primarily to past experience or the strength of social or cultural values), the more difficult the behavior change task, and the lower the likelihood of success of marketing communications.

Segmentation. Segmentation remains a cornerstone in applying the marketing concept to the practice of private sector marketing. In order to meet needs, one develops products to satisfy one or more distinct market segments and/or communicates the virtues of divergent benefits to divergent segments. Additionally, if a particular segment is felt to be unresponsive or unprofitable, it can be ignored.

In many nonbusiness cases, these options remain feasible and segmentation strategies will be called for, but in many others, all members of society must behave in a certain way and all must purchase the same product. Similarly, if the organization's mandate is to serve all of society, then unappealing segments must also be considered.

Furthermore, there are nonbusiness problems where all members of society must comply for the best interests of society (and themselves). An example occurred when Sweden shifted from driving on the left to driving on the right side of the street. All members of society needed to change behavior simultaneously. Other examples include the decimalization of currency in Great Britain and the metrification of measurement in the United States. All three cases allow segmentation in communications strategies, but do not allow for segmentation in the sense that some members of society can be neglected due to the difficulty in changing behavior.

It has been shown that cumulative response to messages occurs as a function similar to a modified exponential function and approaches an asymptote well below 100% of the potential audience (Kotler 1971). If nonbusiness communication is charged with gaining a response from all members of society, the cost of raising the asymptotic level of the response function may be quite high. A final hypothesis is offered:

H_5: The greater the level of participation needed within the society, the more difficult the behavior change, and the lower the likelihood of success of marketing communications.

SEVERAL EXEMPLARS

In the absence of a well-developed data set, several historical cases are examined to see the extent to which they fit the hypotheses. Each case should be considered not just for itself, but also as a representative of a class of objects or issues with similar values on the variables discussed above.

Military Enlistment. A review of situational involvement suggests the following difficulties. The product is a complex bundle of intangible attributes which combine as one family of brands in the generic product class of "multiyear experiences." The benefits are intangibles such as personal growth, education, skill training, excitement, adventure, travel, and opportunity to help one's country. The price is also complex, but predominantly is several years of one's life. Additionally, it includes giving up the right to make many independent decisions, changing life style, losing privacy, and the psychic cost related to the uncertainty of such a decision. The complexity of the product and its high cost make it intuitively very high in situational involvement.

Enduring involvement (the sum of past experiences) suggests further difficulties. For most individuals, there will be no prior usage experience from which to draw insights. There also will be limited experience in major issue decision making, since most prospective purchasers are 17- to 21-years of age. Finally, the decision concerning military enlistment has impact from peer, social class, and cultural values. Little prior experience plus great outside pressure suggest high enduring involvement.

On a more positive note, there seems to be a fair level of preexisting or latent demand, since some 400,000 units of product are purchased each year. In addition, the market for this product is highly segmentable; this also helps to ease the task of marketing communications.

Considering the above, response involvement would be extremely high and complex. Marketing theory would suggest here that the potential impact of advertising would be limited and that personal selling would be key to closing sales, as has been the case. The Army has found that advertising aids in attracting walk-in traffic, requests for information, and increasing knowledge, but has little to do with direct impact on behavior. While recruiters are more important than advertising, research has shown that without advertising, the efficiency of recruiters is diminished (Martin 1978). One should also note that numerous product changes since the inception of the all-volunteer military force have made the product more competitive in its class, thus enabling communications tools to be more effective in discussing potential reinforcers.

55 Mile-per-Hour Speed Limit. The generic issues of fuel consumption and speed of driving have generally had low situational involvement for most people. Even an "energy crisis" and several years of government messages have left many people apathetic regarding a behavior change in these areas. Therefore, the product being marketed can be seen as having little perceived value to many individuals although there is value to society in energy savings and a reduction in fatal accidents. Since most individuals cannot perceive a value, they will consider the costs of time and ego associated with driving at slower speeds.

Enduring involvement is much higher, though, for it is difficult to unlearn a lifetime of behavior, socialization (i.e., large cars with large engines are meant to be driven at high speeds), and values (i.e., time is a scarce commodity to be put to productive use) (Bem 1970; Rokeach 1968).

This shows the futility of marketing products with little preexisting or latent demand and no positively reinforcing attributes. There is little that marketing communications, per se, can do in such a case. The burden must fall on developing a more favorable cost/benefit relationship. The marketers of the 55 mile-per-hour speed limit have so far been unable to do this.

The 55-mile-per-hour speed limit case also highlights the difficulty of marketing to an entire society. In addition to the above problems, the behavior of those who comply with the limit is not reinforced when they see the energy conserved at the expense of their time wasted by fellow citizens. It is difficult to accomplish meaningful change when the majority has no incentive to comply.

Anti-litter. The issue of littering has low situational involvement for most people. Marketing theory would postulate that for low involvement, private sector products, advertising, and promotion could have a strong, short-run impact (Ray, et al. 1973; Rothschild 1979). This paper makes a similar prediction for low involvement, public sector issues. That is, promotion can elicit short-run behavior with regard to nonbusiness issues as well.

Marketing has been successful in the long run for low involvement, consumer products when the products have a perceived advantage (or at least no disadvantage) for the consumer. In these cases, communications tools can lead to initial behavior and product benefits can lead to repeat behavior. Again, there is little perceived value to the individual in acceding to exhortations to stop littering. Only if one's behavior change led to some reinforcement would one continue with the new behavior. In most cases, an end to one's littering will lead to no perceivable diminution of over-all levels of litter and, generally, one's past experiences will have led to such a prior belief. There probably is some latent demand for a clean environment, but without greater societal cooperation, unrewarded efforts will lapse back to old patterns. In isolated, unlittered areas the preserved clean environment does provide a reward.

A cessation of littering behavior offers benefits to society and costs to the individual because it is less convenient than the old behavior. In order for the new behavior to continue (assuming communications can have a short-run impact), there must be a benefit or reinforcement for the individual.

Voting: A Special Case of Short-Run Behavior. This is an area which covers a wide range of involvement with offerings as diverse as presidential races, county clerk races, and referenda. A recent review of voting behavior shows a wide variety of involvement levels and a correspondingly wide range of potential communications impact (Rothschild 1978).

Over the past 30 years, political science data have consistently shown that political communications have very little impact on voting behavior (Lazarsfeld, Berelson, and Gaudet 1948; Campbell 1966; Campbell, Gurin, and Miller 1954; Key 1966; Blumler and McQuail 1969). In retrospect, one can see that virtually all reported cases have dealt with a race having high situational involvement (generally presidential). This strong pool of data supports the high involvement model.

In the past few years, a new set of studies has shown a significant impact of communication on voting behavior (Palda 1975; Kline 1972; Patterson and McClure 1976; Rothschild and Ray 1974). These studies have concentrated on lower level, or low situational involvement, races, and the findings are consistent with the low involvement model. Since there are fewer strong beliefs concerning issues in low level races, communications can more easily impact; since there is a strong belief that voting is a desirable behavior, it will take place; since the desired behavior is very short-run (one may vote on election day and then return to apathy), there is no need to develop the types of reinforcement which lead to long-run behavior. Indeed, the mere act of voting is reinforcing; one has been a good citizen, performed one's duty, and met society's expectations.

The impact of both marketing and societal variables in the voting cases can be seen. In all elections, there is a societal pressure to behave. In high level races, there are inputs from more credible news media and peers along with strong enduring involvement based on past voting behavior which outweigh the impact of marketing communications. In low level races, there is less enduring involvement, less interest, less news media, and less peer influence to dissipate the marketing communications influence. In this low involvement case, the above scenario, coupled with no need for long-run behavior, leads to the potential for a strong marketing communications impact.

A summary of the four cases is presented in Table 1.

OPTIONS FOR THE MARKETER

Given a predominance of unfavorable communications situations in the nonbusiness sectors, what options are available to the marketer?

In a study of nonbusiness communications, the point has been made that nonadvertising promotional tools can be very valuable (Mendelsohn 1973). In the private sector, firms generally rely quite heavily on advertising; in the nonbusiness arena, there is much more likely to be a reliance on public relations, sales force, or other nonadvertising tools since:

- Advertising is often frowned upon as an unethical and manipulative tool;
- the organizations often have very limited financial resources to use on communications; and
- when resources are available, they often are controlled by law or charter and cannot be used for advertising.

TABLE 1: ***Summary of the four cases***

Case	Situation involvement	Enduring involvement	Benefits/ reinforcers	Costs	Cost/ benefit	Preexisting demand	Segmentation	Conclusion
Military enlistment	Very complex High cost	Little past experience Cultural values	Personal intangibles	Several years of one's life Personal rights	Very good for some segments	Fairly high	Very specific and limited	Marketing communications can impact
55-mph speed limit	Low Little interest	Central beliefs	Few personal benefits Weak societal benefits	Time Ego/macho	Poor	Virtually none	All drivers	Low likelihood of marketing communications impact
Antilitter	Low Little interest	Past non-reinforcing experiences	Few personal benefits Moderate societal benefits	Inconvenience	Poor	Low	All members of community	Short-run impact possible Long-run impact difficult
Voting	High to low—depends on race	Central beliefs Pressure to behave	Good citizenship	Time inconvenient Infrequent/ low	Favorable for voting Less favorable for analyzing issues	Moderate	All citizens $\geq$18 years of age	Short-run impact likely Long-run impact not necessary

There are, though, communications tools which circumvent the above constraints and offer the potential of greater credibility and, as a result, more strength as an influencing agent. Mendelsohn (1973) has discussed several of his own studies where nontraditional (to marketing) tools were successfully used. These include:

A television program. "The CBS National Drivers Test" gave drivers a chance to test their knowledge and skills in their home. The program overcame driver indifference to hazards, made them cognizant of their driving problems, and directed them to a mechanism to remedy problems. The program overcame low involvement and generated appropriate behavior (35,000 drivers enrolled in driver education programs as a result).

A short film. "A Snort History," a cartoon about alcohol and traffic safety, was shown as a short subject in movie theatres. It served to overcome the apathy of low involvement and educate thousands of viewers on a subject of generally low interest.

A television series. "Cancion de la Raza," a soap opera series in Los Angeles, served to provide information to the Chicano community about a number of day-to-day legal and social problems encountered by members of the community. By presenting information in a familiar manner, reach was high and learning took place (although no data were presented to support this reported result).

The three examples are presented to suggest that in nonbusiness areas, marketers need to consider tools which go beyond those traditionally employed in the private sector. In many areas of extreme high and low involvement, the tools to be employed must be even more diverse than those suggested above. For many issues, behavior change or development can only occur as a result of an educational process conducted through the schools or the home. If brotherhood is an issue to be marketed, perhaps it must be done through the schools, the home, or legal channels.

If use of the product has no perceived positive reinforcement associated with it which would make long-run behavior desirable, then the product can be changed so that there is negative reinforcement associated with improper (or lack of) behavior. Bem (1970) discussed this issue in relation to self-perception theory and attitude behavior relationships. He felt that stateways (the law) can change folkways (norms and values). By being forced to behave, people will see that their behavior is not harmful or costly; their attitudes then change to become consistent with their new behavior and long-run behavior results.

Ray et al. (1973) make a similar suggestion in presenting the dissonance-attribution hierarchy of effects model. They posit that a forced initial behavior may be necessary in order to get proper long-run attitudes and behavior in very high involvement cases where there is no individual incentive to behave in a certain way.

Enzensberger (1974) put this legal strategy in proper perspective by suggesting that behavior change acquired through communications is stronger than that which results from any manner of external force. Attribution theory would concur that if the individual could attribute his/her own behavior to an acquiescence to force, it would not be internalized as strongly as if the behavior were attributed to a voluntary judgment. Whenever possible, then, marketing communications would be preferable to legal sanction.

Finally, the role and purpose of marketing communications vis a vis the remainder of the marketing mix should be kept in mind. A very high percentage of business sector products and services fail because they do not meet a need or offer a perceivable benefit to the consumer. This should be kept in mind in nonbusiness cases as well. Communications cannot carry a poor product offering; in too many nonbusiness cases, the offering has little appeal or little benefit to the individual. While this is certainly a *caveat* for marketing in any sector, it is especially noteworthy in the nonbusiness sectors, given the other obstacles to success which exist.

SUMMARY AND CONCLUSIONS

This paper has presented a number of issues which need to be considered in a situation analysis sense before objectives or strategies can be developed in a marketing communications campaign. The tools, techniques, and theories developed in the private sector can be valuable in the public and nonprofit sectors, but their limitations must be recognized.

Before developing a nonbusiness communications campaign, one must consider:

The involvedness of the situation and the relevant segments. Due to the potentially very high and very low levels, traditional promotion tools may be inadequate. Given the current state of the art of marketing communications, one must conclude that what can work reasonably well in private sector consumer goods cases may not work at all for nonbusiness cases. While most consumer goods exist within a broad range of middle level involvement, many nonbusiness issues exist in either very high or very low involvement environments. These environments may call for an enlarged set of communications tools and strategies.

The available positive and negative reinforcers. Since the benefits of nonbusiness issues may be less apparent to the message recipient, it is incumbent upon the sender to consider all possible behavior reinforcers. This especially would be the case where the more apparent benefits are societal rather than individual.

The nonmonetary costs. The costs associated with behavior towards nonbusiness issues may include several nonmonetary costs which raise the cost of behaving beyond the level of the perceived benefit. In such a case, communications tools will be hard pressed to present a convincing case for elicitation of the desired behavior.

The level of latent demand. Many nonbusiness marketing campaigns exist as a result of the efforts of a small group of individuals. When little latent demand exists, then little desired behavior will follow.

The relevant segments. For virtually all issues, there will be at least a small segment of society for whom the issue will have positive value, another segment for whom compliance with the law will be sufficient motivation, and another segment for whom engaging in the socially beneficial act will be sufficient motivation. For many issues, there will remain a large segment for whom a direct personal benefit must be shown if appropriate behavior is to result. This paper has considered issues relating to this last segment. The manager must, of course, consider the trade-offs of using segmentation strategies and whether or not segmentation is a permissible strategy.

The wide range of communications alternatives. Given the limitations of traditional marketing communications tools, one also must consider alternatives such as movies and television programs, or even broader alternatives such as in-school or in-home educational communications. It is generally felt that public service spots are not very effective. Perhaps the money spent on their production could be used more efficiently in one of the nontraditional media suggested above.

As has been noted several times in this paper, nonbusiness marketing problems are generally very different from and often more complex than traditional marketing issues. To improve managers' abilities to deal with these differences, several areas of research which deal with the major issues of the paper should be considered:

- Several researchers are currently considering the measurement of involvement as it pertains to private sector goods. This work should be extended to the nonbusiness arena where potential involvement differences are great.
- The work in behavioral learning theory has had very limited marketing application in both business and nonbusiness areas (Carey, et al. 1976; Deslauriers and Everett 1977; Everett,

Hayward, and Meyers 1974; Kohlenberg and Philips 1973; Powers, Osborne, and Anderson 1973). Research in the use of positive and negative reinforcers, reinforcement schedules, and shaping procedures could be insightful. Given the nature of nonbusiness issues, they may lend themselves to behavioral learning work; transferences could then be made to the private sector.

- Communications alternatives are needed. Testing to be done here could follow established private sector methods used on traditional media.

These areas of research can be further divided into two classes:

- Research to establish the relevant consumer perception with respect to the various dimensions of the model presented above.
- Research to generate and test the effectiveness of various marketing strategies armed at overcoming some of the inherent characteristics which suggest low likelihood of success.

One benefit of examining nonbusiness issues is that the limits of existing private sector techniques are tested. This paper has examined the limits of marketing communications with respect to three variables: (1) extreme levels of involvement, (2) the absence of reinforcers, and (3) the need for highly centralized attributes. By determining limits for existing theories and techniques, the discipline of marketing communications will grow and the potential for strategic success will increase.

REFERENCES

Apsler, R., and D. Sears (1968), "Warning, Personal Involvement and Attitude Change," *Journal of Personality and Social Psychology,* 9 (June), 162–166.

Bem, D. J. (1970), *Beliefs, Attitudes and Human Affairs,* Belmont, CA: Brooks/Cole.

Blumler, J. G., and D. McQuail (1969), *Television and Politics: Its Uses and Influences,* Chicago: University of Chicago Press.

Bowen, L., and S. Chaffee (1974), "Product Involvement and Pertinent Advertising Appeals," *Journalism Quarterly,* 51 (Winter), 613–621.

Campbell, A. (1966), *Elections and the Political Order,* New York: John Wiley and Sons.

———, G. Gurin, and W. E. Miller (1954), *The Voters Decide,* Evanston, IL: Row, Peterson.

Carey, R. J., S. H. Clicque, B. A. Leighton, and F. Milton (1976), "A Test of Positive Reinforcement of Customers," *Journal of Marketing,* 40 (October), 98–100.

Deslauriers, B. C., and P. B. Everett (1977), "The Effects of Intermittent and Continuous Token Reinforcement on Bus Ridership," *Journal of Applied Psychology,* 62 (August), 369–375.

Enzensberger, A. M. (1974), *The Consciousness Industry: On Literature, Politics, and Media,* New York: Seabury.

Everett, P. B., S. C. Hayward, and A. W. Meyers (1974), "The Effects of a Token Reinforcement Procedure on Bus Ridership," *Journal of Applied Behavior Analysis.* 7 (Spring), 1–9.

Houston, M. J., and M. L. Rothschild (1978), "A Paradigm for Research on Consumer Involvement," working paper, 12–77–46, Madison: University of Wisconsin.

Hupfer, N., and D. Gardner (1971), "Differential Involvement with Products and Issues: An Exploratory Study," Proceedings of the Association for Consumer Research.

Johnson, H., and J. Scileppi (1969), "Effects of Ego-Involvement Conditions on Attitude Change to High and Low Credibility Communication," *Journal of Personality and Social Psychology,* 13 (September), 31–36.

Key, V. O. (1966), *The Responsible Electorate,* Cambridge, MA: Harvard University Press.

Kline, F. G. (1972), "Mass Media and the General Election Process: Evidence and Speculation," paper presented at the Syracuse University Conference on Mass Media and American Politics, Syracuse, New York.

Kohlenberg, R., and T. Phillips (1973), "Reinforcement and Rate of Litter Depositing," *Journal of Applied Behavior Analysis,* 6 (Fall), 391–396.

Kotler, P. (1971), *Marketing Decision Making: A*

Model Building Approach, New York: Holt, Rinehart and Winston.

Krugman, H. (1965), "The Impact of Television Advertising: Learning Without Involvement," *Public Opinion Quarterly,* 29 (Fall), 349–356.

Lazarsfeld, P. F., B. R. Berelson, and H. Gaudet (1948), *The People's Choice,* New York: Columbia University Press.

Martin, A. J. (1978), Personal Communications.

Mendelsohn, H. (1973), "Some Reasons Why Information Campaigns Can Succeed," *Public Opinion Quarterly,* 37 (Spring), 50–61.

Palda, K. S. (1975), "The Effect of Expenditure on Political Success," *Journal of Law and Economics,* 18 (December), 745–771.

Park, C. (1976), "The Effect of Individual and Situation-Related Factors on Consumer Selection of Judgment Models," *Journal of Marketing Research.* 13 (May), 144–151.

Patterson, T. W., and R. D. McClure (1976), "Television and the Less Interested Voter: The Costs of an Informed Electorate," *The Annals of the American Academy of Political and Social Science,* 425 (May), 88–97.

Payne, J. (1976), "Task Complexity and Contingent Processing in Decision Making: An Information Search and Protocol Analysis," *Organizational Behavior and Human Performance,* 16 (May), 366–387.

Powers, R. B., J. G. Osborne, and E. G. Anderson (1973), "Positive Reinforcement of Litter Removal in the Natural Environment," *Journal of Applied Behavior Analysis,* 6 (Winter), 579–586.

Rachlin, H. (1970), *Introduction to Modern Behaviorism,* San Francisco: W. H. Freeman.

Ray, M. L., A. G. Sawyer, M. L. Rothschild, R. M. Heeler, E. C. Strong, and J. B. Reed (1973), "Marketing Communications and the Hierarchy of Effects," in *New Models for Mass Communications Research, Volume II, Sage Annual Reviews of Communication Research,* P. Clarke, ed., Beverly Hills: Sage.

Rhine, R., and L. Severence (1970), "Ego Involvement, Discrepancy, Source Credibility and Attitude Change," *Journal of Personality and Social Psychology,* 16 (October), 175–190.

———, and W. Polowniak (1971), "Attitude Change, Commitment, and Ego Involvement," *Journal of Personality and Social Psychology,* 19 (February), 247–250.

Rokeach, M. (1968), *Beliefs, Attitudes and Values,* San Francisco: Jossey-Bass.

Rothschild, M. (1978), "Political Advertising: A Neglected Policy Issue in Marketing," *Journal of Marketing Research,* 15 (February), 58–71.

——— (1979, in press), "Advertising Strategies for High and Low Involvement Situations," in *Attitude Research Plays for High Stakes,* J. Maloney, ed., Chicago: American Marketing Association.

———, and M. Houston (1977), "The Consumer Involvement Matrix: Some Preliminary Findings," in *Contemporary Marketing Thought,* B. Greenberg and D. Bellenger, eds., Chicago: American Marketing Association.

———, and M. L. Ray (1974), "Involvement and Political Advertising Effect: An Exploratory Experiment," *Communication Research,* 1 (July), 264–285.

Sherif, M. and C. Sherif (1967), *Attitude, Ego-Involvement and Change,* New York: John Wiley and Sons.

———, ———, and R. Nebergall (1965), *Attitude and Attitude Change,* Philadelphia: Saunders.

Wiebe, G. D. (1951), "Merchandising Commodities and Citizenship on Television," *Public Opinion Quarterly,* 15 (Winter), 679–691.

Public Services—To Charge or Not to Charge?

JOHN L. CROMPTON

Since Proposition 13 was passed in California, it has become symbolic of a broad cross-section of national public opinion on taxation at federal, state, and local levels.[1] At the time of the Proposition 13 victory, a lead editorial in *The Wall Street Journal* commented, "sentiment is suddenly crystallizing that taxes are too high and that the services government delivers are a poor bargain."[2]

Awareness of this growing sentiment has spurred government agencies at all levels to seek sources of revenue other than tax funds. In particular, public agencies have been reexamining the potential for imposing or substantially increasing prices for their services.[3] The extent to which users should pay directly for public services has long been a controversial issue. This article explores the opportunities and problems associated with user pricing of public leisure services.

Leisure services are a particularly interesting example of public-sector pricing because the diversity of recreation programs requires a variety of objectives and prices. The opportunities and problems confronting a public recreational-services agency in its pricing decisions are related to its pricing objectives—the results an agency expects for the prices it charges.

In some cases, the price adopted for a particular program may reflect several conflicting objectives. For example, if the major goal is to ensure maximum opportunity for participation in a particular program, a relatively low user price should probably be charged. However, this policy may also discourage the commercial sector from developing a similar service. Hence, in the long run, a low user price may serve to reduce leisure opportunities available in the community. The price finally adopted will probably depend on the agency's priorities and will represent the best compromise between objectives.

This article discusses and evaluates seven pricing objectives frequently used by leisure-service delivery agencies: economic equity, social equity, maximum opportunity for participation, maximizing revenue, rationing, positive user attitudes, and commercial-sector encouragement.

ECONOMIC EQUITY

Economic equity seeks to price each service at a level that is economically fair and equitable to both participants and nonparticipants. Much of the debate about equitable pricing revolves around whether a particular program exhibits the characteristics of private, merit, or public services. The differences between these categories are summarized in Exhibit 1.

If a program exhibits the characteristics of a *private* service, its benefits are received exclusively by participating individuals rather than by the rest of society. It is technically possible to exclude persons who are not willing to pay for the programs or services provided. Golf courses, marinas, tennis courts, or recreation centers are examples of facilities that may exhibit private-service characteristics. The case for financing services through direct charges to users is clear-cut when they are perceived to be private. If benefits from the services are not likely to spill over to other citizens, it is reasonable to expect an agency to adopt a price that requires users of the facilities to pay for their full costs.

Reprinted by permission from *Business* Magazine, March–April 1980, pp. 31–38.

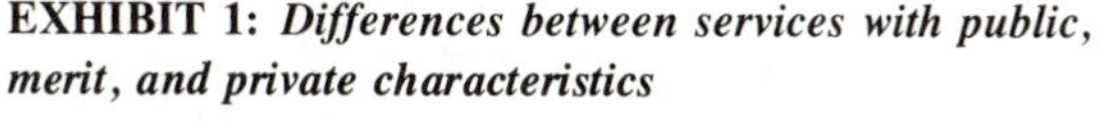

EXHIBIT 1: ***Differences between services with public, merit, and private characteristics***

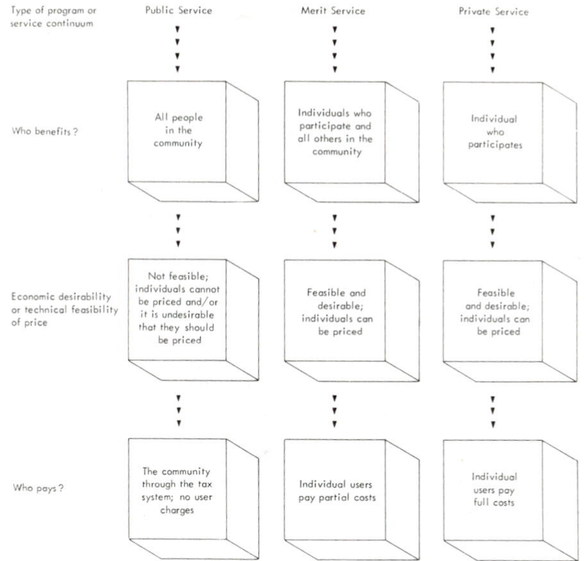

In contrast, and at the other end of the continuum (Exhibit 1), a *public* service in its pure form is equally available to all. Often this is because there are no feasible ways of excluding any individuals from enjoying benefits of the service. In these cases, a pricing system is not practical. Public parks are examples of leisure facilities that usually exhibit public-service characteristics.

Alternatively, activities such as tennis or golf, for which it is feasible to levy a user price, may on occasions be offered as public services if these activities are perceived by society to contribute to the physical health, mental health, cultural knowledge, or welfare of citizens—an investment in human capital from which everyone in society benefits. This may be particularly applicable to citizens with lower incomes who do not have the private means for satisfying particular recreational wants. Hence, it is sometimes argued that imposing user prices may not be desirable, even when technically possible, if less affluent people will be excluded from participating. For example, the National Park Service charges an admission price to most of its facilities, but it does not charge for admission to the Gateway Recreation Areas in New York City or San Francisco because these facilities are intended to be easily accessible to low-income urban populations. Similarly, it may be argued that certain leisure amenities such as parks improve the physical quality of a townscape or make it a more desirable place to live. Charging a price for the use of such amenities may be considered unreasonable because they increase the value of everybody's property.

Merit services are a less clear-cut category; they lie somewhere on the continuum between public and private services. They are considered meritorious because, although part of the benefit accrues to the individual (as it also does in private services), there are spill-over benefits that accrue to the whole community. Consequently, although user prices may be charged for merit services, it is not reasonable to expect that the revenue from such pricing should cover all costs. Participants should be subsidized to the extent to which benefits are perceived to accrue to the whole of society.

Most leisure services in the public sector for which user prices are charged are not totally self-supporting; most are also supported by tax funds. This suggests that such services are perceived as merit rather than private services. Tax subsidy can *only* be justified if collective benefits accrue to the whole community subsidizing the program. In some communities there is support for this philosophy. For example:

> In Oakland there appears to be a basic belief that recreational activities are wholesome, worthwhile, and character building, and consequently should be (partially) subsidized from the general revenue sources of the city.[4]

There is considerable sympathy for the contention that a price should not be charged for the opportunity to view and enjoy the natural beauty of the nation's national parks, or that to charge for visits to historical sites, such as the Statue of Liberty, would be in poor taste. Consequently, the U.S. Congress, in some of the legislation enacted to establish federal recreation and park areas, has mandated that no prices should be charged for using those areas. It has been suggested that benefits to society, as well as to the individual, may accrue from activities such as visits to various kinds of historical sites, major scenic or scientific areas, or from participation in interpretive programs offered by some recreational agencies.[5] At the same time, it appears to be more difficult to classify picnic areas, campgrounds, and beaches as merit services. The extent to which leisure services contribute to an intellectually and emotionally healthy population is not firmly and clearly established. For example, one study states:

> We suspect there are as many emotionally ill-adjusted wandering through the woods or lying on the beaches as there are cooped up in apartments before T.V. sets. Conversely, there may well be as many well adjusted who never go near (a public recreation program or facility) as who do.[6]

An important point in understanding this classification is that the particular location of a program on the public/merit/private continuum shown in Exhibit 1 is dependent on whom the agency and its publics perceive as benefiting from that program. For example, the classification of any given activity may vary between geographical areas. In a high-income neighborhood, a golf facility may be perceived as a private service from which only the participant accrues benefits. Hence, all costs incurred should be covered by user prices. In a low-income neighborhood, an identical golf-course facility may be considered the "poor man's country club," a pure public facility charging no user price. In this case, the whole community may be perceived to gain from opportunities for the wholesome activity for all citizens; through improvement of the living environment, which increases the value of everybody's property; or from the psychological satisfaction of knowing that the less wealthy have recreational opportunities that they could not otherwise afford.

Exhibit 2 indicates that *users* of a community service typically seek to shift perceptions of their

EXHIBIT 2: ***Conflicting thrusts of different publics that seek to influence pricing decisions***

activity as far as possible away from the private end of the continuum toward the pubic end, in order to persuade the agency and the community that more of the costs should be paid from tax revenues, with user prices kept to a minimum. On the other hand, the *general public* increasingly seeks to shift community services away from the public and toward the private end of the continuum, to make participants pay more for the benefits they receive.

The role of the commercial operator in this conflict is likely to vary. Those entrepreneurs who regard themselves as competing with the public-agency service will likely support the general tax-payer who is seeking to make users pay a higher price. For example, private campground operators continually lobby for increases of the much lower fees charged at campgrounds operated by public agencies. Higher prices provide more opportunities for entrepreneurs to compete successfully. However, in situations where the service offered is complementary rather than competitive, entrepreneurial support is likely to be with user interest groups. Lower prices may mean more participants, who may then require a particular commercial service. For example, concessionaires operating in public facilities seek to increase the amount of traffic passing through their concession. The actual point on the continuum at which a particular activity is located will probably depend on the relative size and political strength of the various groups.

One other dimension of economic equity that needs to be addressed is the inequity occurring when people from outside a community use facilities that are subsidized in part by community members. User pricing is the only way to make people who live and pay taxes outside of the community contribute toward the cost of the services they use. For example, some states such as Idaho, Maine, New Hampshire, and Vermont charge higher prices to nonresidents for camping in state parks. This policy is particularly appropriate in situations where a broader range of services are offered, or larger facilities are developed than are required to meet the wants of a resident population.

SOCIAL EQUITY

Public agencies frequently contend that pricing imposes a hardship on poor people. This position was demonstrated in a statement made by the executive director of the California Park and Recreation Society in response to Proposition 13, which sharply reduced property taxes in the state:

> The poor and the minorities will suffer the most as a result of Proposition 13. They are the ones who rely most heavily on California's recreation facilities and programs. The rich and the upper middle-class can afford to go to Lake Tahoe, to Carmel by the Sea and to San Francisco for their recreation. The poor cannot. They need our parks, our swimming pools and our programs.[7]

There are at least three responses to this line of argument.[8]

First, property taxes, the primary source of tax revenues for most local community services, tend to bear much more heavily on low-income groups than on higher income groups. This is because property taxes generally represent a larger proportion of a poor family's total income than of a wealthier family's total income. It has been suggested that the burden on low-income groups would be less if user prices were charged for public services because poor families may now pay more in rent as a consequence of general property taxation than they would under some alternative pricing arrangement.[9] It is argued that the poor may be better off if they are charged user prices and given the option of not participating in the service (therefore avoiding payment for it), rather than being mandated to pay for services they do not want through the property tax system. Support from disadvantaged groups for more user pricing of leisure services was reported in a nationwide pricing survey completed for the U.S. Heritage Conservation and Recreation Service. The study concluded:

> The greatest support for user fees came from the elderly, the low income, and rural residents. Often these characteristics corresponded to persons with low rates of participation (non-users). Lesser support for user fees (although supporters are still a majority in all cases) came from the young, high income, and college educated groups. Often, these characteristics corresponded to persons with high rates of participation (users).[10]

A second view holds that if a community does wish to subsidize low-income individuals' use of public services, then it may be better to provided reduced or zero-priced charges to them, rather than to offer subsidized services to all regardless of income. The administrative method commonly used to implement this policy is to give the less affluent a card that must be presented when a particular service is used. Prerequisites for successful implementation of differential pricing are that such pricing should not cause resentment from the majority of client groups and should avoid placing a stigma on persons receiving the low-price privileges.

Finally, there is some evidence and opinion that recreational services offered by public agencies do not serve the low-income population very well. Indeed, some argue that it is *subsidized* leisure services that impose hardships on poor people, not those for which reasonably high user prices are charged. The essence of this argument is:

> By and large, the supply of free public parks in the United States is less adequate in crowded city areas where people are poor, than it is in suburban and higher income residential areas, where the people concerned are more nearly able to pay for their own outdoor recreation. On a state or national basis, the discrepancy is even worse: the really poor people do not own the private automobiles which are necessary to get to most state parks and to all national parks and national forests, nor can they in most areas afford travel costs of such visits. The argument that free public parks help the poor is almost wholly myth.[11]

Services supported by taxes are not free; they represent a subsidy from nonusers to users. This subsidy may well be operating in a way contrary to that which might normally be expected. It has been observed that:

> Recreation and park services appear to be an excellent example of a 'distorted price system.' This is a system in which the richer elements in society are subsidized by workers at the lower end of the income scale. Such a system results, therefore, in a perverse income or benefit distribution.[12]

For example, people who visit museums, zoos, or aquariums, or who use boat marinas, may have above-average incomes. Yet they may receive a subsidy from the relatively poor if the cost of these facilities is partially met out of tax revenues. Even if some of the visitors are poor, the relatively wealthy receive the same dollar subsidy at a free facility as do the poor.[13] Further, it has been suggested that because much of the price paid to participate in recreation is in the form of travel cost and time cost, public funds allocated to leisure services constitute subsidies for the wealthier people who can afford the travel to the site and the time required to enjoy the experience.[14]

Often, subsidized services may be justified because they are targeted directly at low-income groups. However, it has also been pointed out that if the objective is to make opportunities more equal, that could be accomplished better by making direct cash payments to low-income groups rather than by providing services that many may not want.[15] Recipients could then use the cash in accordance with their own preferences and pay for whatever services they prefer to purchase. Too often it appears that the decision to provide public or merit services can be interpreted as an imposition of the preferences of elected or appointed decision makers on an inarticulate clientele. In such cases, a product orientation rather than a marketing orientation is being adopted, since decision makers provide services they think a clientele needs, rather than services that the client group indicates it wants.

Financing leisure services from revenues received from user pricing releases those citizens who do not wish to participate or use a service from having to pay its cost. A substantial proportion of low-income people do not use certain kinds of services. Hence, it is socially inequitable that they should be required to pay for those services through the tax system.

MAXIMUM OPPORTUNITY

The objective of maximum opportunity for participation is concerned with adopting a price that will encourage relatively large numbers of potential clients to participate. To achieve this, the monetary price is likely to be very small or zero. If adopted when a new service is being offered, it may help make the program "visible" quickly and provide it with initial momentum. However, the initial price probably will become the reference point for future pricing of the service. Establishing a low price initially is likely to limit the size of subsequent price increases.

Price may also be a communicator of a service's quality. For example, an attractive indoor swimming pool in a metropolitan area was frequently overcrowded on weekends. The manager decided to use pricing as a rationing measure to reduce congestion. Accordingly, the price for weekend admission to the pool was substantially increased. This led to more people traveling to the pool from much farther distances than before and to *increased* use. Apparently the clientele rationalized that because the price was so much higher at this pool than any other in the area, and higher during weekends than on weekdays, then the experience available at this pool on weekends must be superior.[16]

The rationale for low or zero pricing of leisure services frequently includes a suggestion that these services meet a need felt by all citizens in the community. For this reason, it is argued that such services should be regarded as pure public services and their cost should be fully met from tax revenues. But the suggestions that all people "need" recreation and that it should be provided free often has been challenged. For example, one authority states:

> For some reason recreation professionals seem to implicitly assume that the population's need for recreation must be fully satisfied. This would seem to be a very heroic assumption and completely inconsistent with the way we view other goods and services in our economy—even food.[17]

He goes on to ask, "Why should the public sector subsidize recreation facilities?" He argues that participants should be required to pay reasonable user prices for leisure services, just as they do for most other goods and services, even if it means that some of this need goes unsatisfied.

Traditionally, many public leisure-service agencies have adopted a maximum-opportunity pricing objective, since it has been assumed that if many participate, then the agency is best serving society. However, because the majority of people probably do not participate in the agency's programs, such an assumption does appear to be challengeable.

MAXIMIZING REVENUE

Many leisure-service agencies have experienced a reduction in tax-revenue support in recent years. User pricing offers an alternate source of funds that may help compensate. Restrictions on a new program stemming from financial constraints may be removed if the new offering is self-financed out of user-price revenues. The key to maximizing these revenues is in estimating price elasticity of demand. If the purpose of the price increase is to increase total revenue, then prices can only be raised in those recreational programs or services for which demand is relatively inelastic.

A small amount of research work has been reported on the price elasticity of demand for public leisure services. This research provides some insights into the impact of price on participation. Results from an analysis of the 1972 nationwide outdoor-recreation survey suggest that the demand for these activities is inelastic:

> Overall roughly a 5 percent increase in price would result in a 1 percent decrease in the quantity demanded. In other words, a 5 percent increase in the sum of the monetary travel costs plus the admission charges would result in only 1 percent decrease in the total number of activity days consumed at a given recreation site.[18]

These findings were supported by a study completed for the U.S. Heritage Conservation and Recreation Service. This study showed that participants would be willing to pay substantially higher user prices at public outdoor-recreation areas for all of the activities considered in the study. Many managers surveyed reported that there was often initial resistance to new or increased prices, manifested by a reduction in the number of participants; however, most managers commented that this effect disappeared within two or three years.[19] This was also the experience of private campground operators who reported that reduced activity levels after a price increase were temporary in many cases.[20]

Inelastic demand at state and national recreation and park areas results because an increased entrance price usually represents only a small percentage of the total cost of visiting such areas. Once the monetary and time costs of traveling to and from the site have been included, relatively large percentage increases in price are likely to have relatively little effect on attendance:

> A $1 increase to a recreationist must surely seem less than monumental after having already purchased thousands of dollars worth of equipment and spent perhaps over a hundred dollars in traveling enroute and return.[21]

In contrast, a relatively small increase in price may result in a substantial decrease in participation at facilities located close to population areas because the user price represents a relatively large percentage of the total cost of the visit to such a facility. A decrease in participants is particularly likely to occur if other programs are available that could serve as a subsitute, or if children or disadvantaged groups formed a substantial proportion of the clientele. For example, a study of price elasticity at selected swimming pools in England concluded that "juveniles react much more—by staying away—to price increases than adults. The optimum admission price for juveniles (that is, the one which generates most total revenue) is approximately half that of adults."[22] In contrast, Brunswick Corporation (which operates ten-pin bowling centers in urban areas) reported, "it has been our experience that increasing prices does not adversely affect usage."[23] This may be accounted for by ten-pin bowling being perceived by users as an activity for which there is no obvious substitute.

Two studies of museums offer some clues into the impact of price changes on demand for leisure services. Researchers found little change in the composition of the visitor population to the Royal Museum in Toronto after the institution of a modest $.25 fee. The only significant change was a relative increase in the proportion of first-time visitors.[24] The experience of the Natural History Museum in San Diego suggests that it may be important to distinguish short- and long-term effects of charging a price for the first time. After institution of a $.50 entry fee, attendance dropped by 50% in the first year; but after two years of "education," attendance had risen to the level achieved before the user price was charged.[25]

RATIONING

User pricing as a rationing device may serve two different functions. First, it may indicate which services are most desired by client groups. Second, it may be used to reduce overcrowding. User pricing performs a rationing function by excluding those potential users of a service who are not willing to pay as much as other potential users. It thereby allocates the service to those willing to make greater sacrifices.[26] This is important because providing services at no cost often leads to very heavy use. If a service provided free or at an unrealistically low price triggers excess demand, "cries of alarm" often suggest that more provision is needed. Yet there may be little information about the value of the service and the relative legitimacy of its claims on resources.[27]

Heavy use does not necessarily indicate satisfaction with a leisure experience. For example, if a low admission is charged to a municipal swimming pool, it may become a free baby-sitter service. Attendance does not measure satisfaction or clients' evaluation of the service; it merely records individuals' use of the amenity. Higher prices provide decision makers with valuable information about the extent of satisfaction or benefit that users perceive a service to provide. Prices offer some basis for comparison between programs and a rare opportunity to force the public to reveal preferences.

User pricing may be used to reduce crowding at particular times in particular areas. The resources required for some leisure services may not be expanded easily to meet additional demand. For example, a tennis court, boat marina, or softball diamond can only accommodate a fixed number of participants at any one time. Hence, some mechanism is needed to determine who should have priority. Price is one way of resolving the problem.

Typically, a leisure facility is used intensively during a relatively brief period of time, moderately at other times, and is wholly unused for much greater periods of time.[28] Charging different prices could ration use at peak times. Prices could be charged on days or in seasons of heaviest use, but not at other times, as one inducement to a more nearly uniform pattern of use. For example, prices could be charged in heavily used, but not in lightly used, camping areas as a means of spreading use geographically. Alternatively, several price levels could be employed to influence users to choose certain times, areas, and/or activities. Such charges could not be effective unless they were high enough to be a real burden to the users who paid them and a real savings to those who avoided them.[29]

Price is usually thought of as the amount of money that must be sacrificed to acquire a service. However, price should be conceived more broadly than this, for money is only one way that people pay for services. Sometimes, time costs are more influential than monetary costs in determining whether or not an individual will participate in a program. Time costs may involve more personal sacrifice than money for some client groups, and they may arise in a variety of ways. For example, a golfer may have an exhaustive effort to find out about available golf courses and their operating policies. When a course has been selected, time is required to travel to and from the facility. Finally, time loss may occur through waiting in line at peak times to play a game, or through having to contend with overcrowding and congestion that slows down play on the course. Hence, waiting time may be an alternative to monetary price for reducing overcrowding. This may make is possible for a manager to offer client groups a choice of rationing devices.

Time involves very different costs for various groups in the population.[30] The value of time is related to its opportunity cost in terms of the value of the earnings or alternative experiences that would have been gained during the time of the wait. For example, for the young and the retired, waiting time frequently has a lower cost than it does for the busy executive. The relatively poor and the wealthy also value time and money differently. Consequently, each type of client group could be permitted to pay in that coin least expensive to its members:

> Some consumers will prefer faster service and higher money prices; others slower service and lower money prices; still others, moderate prices and moderate time costs. Those constituents who prefer paying in money to buy time can do so, but those who do not prefer to pay in money will be able to avoid doing so.[31]

If this principle were applied to a racquetball complex, it would mean that those prepared to pay a high monetary price would be permitted to make reservations a month ahead. Those prepared to pay a moderate monetary price could make reservations one week ahead and risk either having to play at an off-peak time or being placed on a waiting list for a court at peak time. Finally, those prepared to visit the facility without a reservation in the hope that courts may become available might pay a relatively low monetary price, but would risk paying a substantial time price.

POSITIVE USER ATTITUDES

Some have suggested that abuses such as graffiti, littering, and vandalism occur because participants pay little or nothing for the privilege of using facilities. One author says:

> It is argued by some that provision of *anything* at zero price tends to diminish its psychological, as well as economic, value. Some sense of personal contribution or support may enhance the visitor's feelings of responsibility towards, and esteem of, the facility. The impact of such psychological value on possible acts of vandalism is obvious.[32]

However, others believe that when a price is charged, users may feel they have more right to "tear up" a facility. U.S. Forest Service data indicate that costs for vandalism and littering in the national forests were greater per user in areas where prices were charged.[33] However, reasons other than the fee itself may explain this difference. Indeed, the U.S. Forest Service also reported that less vandalism and better security in campgrounds that charge users a price have led to greater use of these campgrounds by the elderly and families with children.[34]

COMMERCIAL ENCOURAGEMENT

If leisure services are heavily subsidized, then, in effect, the public agency is following a policy of excluding the commercial sector from offering a similar service. It has been said that "we cannot give away bread and expect people to rush into the bakery business at the same time."[35] Pricing that offers incentives for private investment would relieve crowding pressures by increasing the supply.

A study completed for the U.S. Heritage Conservation and Recreation Service found that average user prices for camping at federal recreation areas where prices were charged were $1.94, with a range from $1.42 to $2.40.[36] In comparison, average private campsite charges were reported by the National Campground Owners Association at $5.83, with a range from $4.00 to $7.75. Clearly, this discrepancy is likely to discourage commercial campground development near federal areas.

A lead editorial in *The Wall Street Journal* discussed this problem: Gore Mountain Ski Center, a public facility operated by New York State, received an annual tax subsidy of $50,000 a year and was constructed with tax-free bonds. It applied for $264,000 in federal grants to help fund a $2.87 million capital extension that involved installing snow-making machinery and other equipment. The balance of the capital was raised by issuing tax-free bonds. With these advantages, Gore Mountain charged $400 for a family season pass. Commercial resorts in the area charged an average of $1,125 because they had to pay commercial prices for investment capital, without any assistance from federal grants, and needed to show a return on their investment.[37] It appears that the publicly operated state project was gradually forcing the commercial operations out of business.

FACTORS INHIBITING USER PRICING

These are at least three situations in which user pricing of public recreation services may not be appropriate. First, there may be legal or legislative restrictions on charging a price. For instance, such restrictions are found on many of the more recently legislated areas administered by the National Park Service. Examples include Gateway East, Gateway West, Cape Cod, and Indiana Dunes. In contrast to those national parks designated before 1961, many of the newer parks were not established on federal lands. Consequently, the National Park Service had to buy these lands.

Despite arguments concerning social equity discussed earlier, it seemed incongruous to the Congress that when large sums of taxpayers' money were appropriated to purchase the parks, taxpayers should have to pay to use them. For this reason, no admission prices are permitted at these parks.

In other parks, the express wish of the donors of the park preclude user prices. For example, at the Lyndon B. Johnson National Historic Site, President and Mrs. Johnson expressed the firm view that admission to the park should always be free. President Johnson justified this by stating, "What wasn't given is coming out of their pockets as tax monies."[38]

Second, the technical difficulty of imposing a charge for use of an area, such as a public park to which access is not controlled, may preclude pricing. Presumably, access could be controlled by building a fence around the park and charging admission; however, this may lead to a third factor, namely, that the costs incurred to facilitate charging admission may exceed the revenues collected. In this case, it is uneconomical to collect the charges.

Often, in remote park facilities or at off-peak times in local facilities, the level of use may be so low that revenues from pricing do not cover the costs of collection. A decision to charge a price may entail high personnel and set-up costs. Constructing gatehouses at each entrance to a park and manning these gates involve initial capital outlays and significant payroll cost increases.[39] A variety of devices have been tried to overcome this problem, and some have been successful. Examples include using a permit system; paying for a ticket from an automatic vending machine and displaying it prominently (so it can be subjected to occasional spot checks); and using coin-operated gates.

Finally, in some cases there has been a reluctance to increase user prices because any increase in revenues caused decision makers to reduce the agency's support from taxes by an equivalent amount. This may be an appropriate strategy by decision makers if they perceive it as benefitting the taxpayer. However, it serves as a disincentive to an agency that finds that instead of having additional revenues to improve the delivery of its services, its only reward is the equivalent loss of a source of financial support—a source that might be difficult to regain in the future. In addition, the agency may lose political support from user groups angered by the new pricing policy.

NOTES AND REFERENCES

1. "The June 6 Revolt," *The Wall Street Journal,* June 8, 1978, p. 18.
2. Ibid.
3. James Ring Adams, "Coping With Proposition 13," *The Wall Street Journal,* October 10, 1978, p. 14.
4. Robert M. Odell, "Use of Recreation Service Charges," *Governmental Finance,* February 1972, p. 19.
5. Marion Clawson and Jack L. Knetsch, *Economics of Outdoor Recreation* (Washington, D.C., Resources for the Future, 1966), p. 267.
6. Ibid., p. 270.
7. "Proposition 13 Will Slash Park and Recreation Funds," *Dateline,* Summer 1978, p. 11.
8. Calvin A. Kent, "Users' Fees for Municipalities," *Governmental Finance,* February 1972, p. 3.
9. Selma J. Mushkin, "An Agenda for Research," in Selma J. Mushkin, ed., *Public Prices for Public Products* (Washington, D.C., Urban Institute, 1972), p. 441.
10. U.S. Heritage Conservation and Recreation Service, *Evaluation of Public Willingness to Pay User Charges for Use of Outdoor Recreation Areas and Facilities* (Washington, D.C., U.S. Government Printing Office, 1976), p. 10).
11. Clawson and Knetsch, *Economics of Outdoor Recreation.*
12. David E. Chappelle, "The 'Need' for Outdoor Recreation: An Economic Conundrum," *Journal of Leisure Research,* Fall 1973, p. 51.
13. Borris W. Becker, "The Pricing of Educational-Recreational Facilities: An Administrative Dilemma," *Journal of Leisure Research,* 1975, no. 2, p. 88.
14. Chappelle, "The 'Need' for Outdoor Recreation."

15. Richard A. Musgrave and Peggy B. Musgrave, *Public Finance in Theory and Practice* (New York, McGraw-Hill, 1976), p. 65.
16. Personal conversation with Mr. Jack Black, general manager of the Commonwealth Swimming Pool, Edinburgh, Scotland.
17. Chappelle, "The 'Need' for Outdoor Recreation."
18. Robert C. Lewis, "Policy Formation and Planning for Outdoor Recreational Facilities," in *Outdoor Recreation: Advances in Application of Economics* (Washington, D.C., U.S. Department of Agriculture, Forest Service, 1977), p. 64.
19. U.S. Heritage Conservation and Recreation Service, *Public Willingness to Pay User Charges*, p. 17.
20. Ibid, p. 30.
21. Kenneth Gibbs, "Economics and Administrative Regulations of Outdoor Recreation Use," in *Outdoor Recreation: Advances in Application of Economics* (Washington, D.C., U.S. Department of Agriculture, Forest Service, 1977), p. 103.
22. Local Government Operational Research Unit, *Planning and Management of Indoor Swimming Pools* (Reading, England, Royal Institute of Public Administration, 1974).
23. Brunswick Corporation, *Annual Report*, 1974.
24. Duncan Cameron and David S. Abbey, "Museum Audience Research: The Effect of an Admission Fee," *Museum News*, November 1962, pp. 25–28.
25. William A. Burns, cited in Becker, "Pricing of Educational-Recreational Facilities."
26. Werner Z. Hirsch, *The Economics of State and Local Government* (New York, McGraw-Hill, 1970), p. 31.
27. Jerome W. Milliman, "Beneficiary Charges—Toward a Unified Theory," in Selma J. Mushkin, ed., *Public Prices for Public Products* (Washington, D.C., Urban Institute, 1972), p. 29.
28. Clawson and Knetsch, *Economics of Outdoor Recreation*, p. 274.
29. Ibid., p. 274.
30. Odell, "Use of Recreation Service Charges," p. 18.
31. Eugene Smolensky, Nicolaus T. Tideman, and Donald Nichols, "Waiting Time as a Congestion Charge," in Selma J. Mushkin, ed., *Public Prices for Public Products* (Washington, D.C., Urban Institute, 1972), p. 96.
32. Becker, "Pricing of Educational-Recreational Facilities."
33. Roger N. Clark, *Control of Vandalism in Recreation Areas—Fact, Fiction, or Folklore?* Washington, D.C., U.S. Department of Agriculture, Forest Service, 1976).
34. U.S. Heritage Conservation and Recreation Service, *Public Willingness to Pay User Charges*, p. 45.
35. H. L. Diamond, "The Private Role in the Provision of Large-Scale Outdoor Recreation," in B. L. Driver, ed., *Elements of Outdoor Recreation Planning* (Ann Arbor, University Microfilms, 1970), p. 172.
36. U.S. Heritage Conservation and Recreation Service, *Public Willingness to Pay User Charges*, p. 44.
37. "Mike Brandt's Competitors," *The Wall Street Journal*, September 12, 1975, p. 4.
38. Southwest Region, National Park Service, *Resources Management Plan, Lyndon B. Johnson National Historic Site* (Washington, D.C., National Park Service, 1977).
39. U.S. Heritage Conservation and Recreation Service, *Public Willingness to Pay User Charges*, p. 39.

A Hungry Problem for Zoos: In Search of New Prey

CAROL KOVACH

Marketing research generated from and about organizations and problems associated with the public and not-for-profit (NFP) sectors is still relatively rare compared with that focusing on business-oriented concerns, reflecting the newly-broadened concept of marketing into these non-business sectors. But the problems lie deeper than mere newness; not only is this domain of research in its infancy, but it is in danger of never reaching childhood, let alone the heights of adulthood and old-age. This situation arises in part because of a lack of attention and nourishment given to both of these ''new'' sectors, as well as the theoretical assumptions which are being used as the launching pads of inquiry.

Most of the theories and concepts which are used as starting points for research are derived from the business sector, but are used indiscriminately for applications in the non-business sectors. These theories are rarely carefully examined for their ''goodness of fit,'' but rather assumed to be correct. The major research activities focus on making those parts of existing theories which fit most easily illustrate how appropriate marketing is to these new sectors, and neglecting to point out those parts which don't fit, or which need major (or minor) adjustments to do so. This approach ignores what might be extremely valuable information for theory development in a generic sense. It also leads to an ''all lose'' situation, with neither business gaining insight from the broadened scope of marketing, nor the non-business sectors having their needs met by the promises made by marketing.

The potential of the public and NFP sectors for interesting, fascinating, and conceptually rewarding research is as yet untapped, not only in terms of the diversity of organizations to be found within their boundaries, but also for the ramifications for theory development, verification, or even contradiction.

PURPOSE OF THE PAPER

The purpose of this paper is to suggest a different approach to broadening the concept of marketing than that which has been employed. To date, the broadening process has been accomplished by an incremental strategy, taking a particular marketing theory and trying it out for fit on a few public or NFP organizations randomly. While this may have been a logical starting place for the broadening process, it also suggests drawbacks, not so much in its basic logic, but in its application. The theories and organizations which have tended to be selected as targets for inquiry have represented the more straightforward, ''easy'' ones, in that they have usually been those which had some clear, easily definable attributes which had distinct similarities to those found in many business organizations. From a marketing perspective, the theories which were chosen for transplanting appeared to have been selected with an intuitive, perhaps even unconscious bias toward those which were more obvious, and which *could* intrinsically fit those organizations better.

While this may have been an appropriate strategy in the initial excursions and explorations into the P/NFP sectors, this paper suggests that the time may have come for a more daring, radical set

Reprinted with permission from *Proceedings of the American Marketing Association Educators' Conference,* 1978, pp. 350–354; published by the American Marketing Association.

of strategies to be invoked. This is illustrated by the use of an "extreme" organization from the public and/or NFP sectors—the zoo. While incremental strategies nibble away at the new sectors with old tools, avoiding the necessity of seriously revising or reconceptualizing them, or even the standard ways of understanding and researching organizations, it is hoped that the zoo example offers a fresh view of these sectors. An underlying rationale is that there is a need for organizations which fall within the domain of the public, and more especially, the NFP sector, for societal or other reasons, must be understood for what they are, what they stand for, and what they need from marketing. With this in mind, the zoo is used as a *catalyst,* and not as an all-encompassing example of the totality of the diverse set of organizations in the NFP sector.

The divergent approach that the zoo example offers has two advantages. Firstly, it allows for a more vivid understanding of the sector and its attendant needs. Secondly, it allows for a more creative way to open up the boundaries and assumptions so rigidly held by many marketers about the "generic concepts," building on the problem-solving approach suggested by Gordon [1] in the use of synectics. In this approach, problem-solving is approached by the use of metaphorical situations totally unlike the original problem context as a way of generating a broader range of ideas than that which occurs when only the mind-blocking problem looms large and formidable. Seemingly absurd ideas are not summarily discarded at the expense of other, more sensible ones; it is often found that such absurd ideas form the basis of new, exciting, and creative solutions. In a similar fashion, the utilization of an extreme NFP organization allows for the creation of new ideas, which may not be generated for many years using the incremental, safe approach to broadening the concepts of marketing.

New "product" development is taken as the theoretical framework for examining in more detail business-generated theories and their implications for the NFP sector. Ideas which are addressed are the product mix/portfolio, life-cycle, and packaging. These have significance for the meaning of new product development within different contexts, and suggest their importance for understanding marketing in some organizations found in the NFP sector.

The zoo is characterized as being extreme in part because it conjures up images of an odd, weird, silly, etc., place. It is extreme in many of its structural and functional aspects, but more importantly, for marketing it represents another dimension of the NFP sector.

ZOOS AND THEIR PRODUCTS

The definition of the product of a zoo requires a little discussion. Kotler [3] suggests three basic concepts of product: formal, core and augmented, while the traditional characterization of product attributes (item, line and mix) is based on the more tangible types of products most commonly associated with the business sector. This leads to both semantic and practical problems when attempting to define a zoo's product, because there is a good deal of confusion surrounding the central purpose of a zoo to start with. The following brief discussion helps to illustrate the dilemma.

When an organization is asked the perennial question: "what business are you in" what is really being asked is a series of provoking questions to establish both its formal product (physical object or service offered) and core product definition (the essential utility or benefit being offered). The augmented product comprises some totality of benefits, often greater than the sum of the formal and core products. In taking this approach toward the business of the zoo, and the concomitant definition of its product, a more helpful question might be: "when is a zoo *not* a zoo?" One very primitive, yet realistic answer, would be "when it has no animals," which suggests that animals are indeed an essential ingredient of any zoo. But how do they relate to the concept of product? They are definitely not the formal product, in that they are not *per se* offered for sale, or given in exchange for anything, nor are they much to do with core product in Kotler's sense, since this represents a "one-step removed" concept of the formal product. And yet without animals the zoo ceases to exist.

Looking at this question from the zoo's perspective they would clearly indicate that their major concern is with and about animals and their housing. If the zoo was asked what it spent most of its time "developing," they would overwhelmingly indicate "animal exhibits" and "new animals." While this may or may not meet with the approval of all concerned with zoos, it is nevertheless a very real priority. Thus, from the perspective of the zoo, its "product" from an internal management orientation is "Animals + exhibits (housing)." However, as this "new product" does not neatly fit into Kotler's three concepts, any more than a film fits into the definition of the product of a movie theatre, some reconceptualization of the relationship between product and "new product development" theories need to be considered.

For the purpose of this paper, the formal product of the zoo is defined as "a view of the animals," the core product "enjoyment and education;" the augmented product would be a combination of the core and the formal, plus the sale of whatever toys, film and food might seem appropriate, as well as rental of cameras, strollers, etc.—the total "gestalt" which a zoo suggests—atmosphere, beauty, tranquility, park-like setting, etc. The "generator" of the product(s) or mechanism for allowing them to exist, however, remains an important element, which shall be dubbed "generative product" for the sake of nomenclature.

These "generative products" consist mainly of the animals which are available to the zoo, and the showcases used for exhibiting them. A sub-set of the "showcasing" might be the ways in which the total exhibit is communicated to the viewing public. This may take the form of signing pictures, etc., to help the public to appreciate and understand both the animal *per se,* and the rationale behind the particular exhibit, or any special feature thereof. The zoo, however, must work primarily with its collection of animals, because it is the *collection* which is the most important attribute of the quasi-product.

THE PRODUCT MIX: A LIVELY CHOICE

The theoretical assumptions underlying the product-mix concept are that an organization is at liberty to choose both its product width and depth parameters. It can opt for a full-line, all-market strategy; a market-specialist approach, or a product-line specialization. Alternatively it may wish to offer limited product lines; specific products; or be a special-situation specialist. The organization, not the environment, is the locus of control, as it is responsible for the decision regarding the product-mix.

If we examine the case of the zoo, this choice is clearly not an internal decision. The product-mix is constrained by a variety of externally-imposed factors. Firstly, zoos operate within very limited budgets, with most publicly-owned zoos only being given sufficient monies for the feeding of the animals and the salaries of employees. Funds for new exhibits, renovations, etc., must be raised separately by the zoo, or its counterpart, the zoo association, from other sources. Similarly, zoos are rarely given money for new animal acquisition; this is carried out either on the basis of exchanging animals between zoos, or purchasing them outright. (This latter mode is often avoided because of the red tape involved in obtaining permits resulting from prohibitions on inter-state and inter-national transportation of animals).

Zoos also have physical constraints. They are special-purpose built facilities. A monkey cannot be put in an elephant's home; a giraffe cannot be placed in a bear's enclosure. Unlike a museum, which has far more flexibility for displaying its paintings or sculptures, allowing it to "change its face" relatively easily, the zoo generally can only replace existing types of animals with similar ones, not only for spatial and safety reasons, but disease. Another aspect of the physical constraint is that zoos cannot often expand their collection because of the limitation of space of the zoo's grounds. Each animal exhibit requires considerable display and maintenance areas, as well as special handling requirements. Zoos have prescribed boundaries, beyond which the noise, smell and physical presence of the animal must not stray. If a zoo is over-crowded, the disease problems, and potential for death, become disastrous. Additionally, zoos have a difficult time asking for new space. The residents in the immediate locality conjure up all kinds of scenarios of possible escapes. In Chester, England, each time the zoo wanted to expand, the neighboring publics envisioned the elephant going on a rampage in their back-yard cabbage patches, or inviting and encouraging "the wrong type of person" to visit the zoo.

The zoo's main "selling point" is its collection of animals; this represents the fundamental reason why visitors visit it. If this is characterized as a "product line" then each species of animal represents a different "line," although there may be some particular animals, like giraffes or elephants, which are generically included in the "mammal" line, but constitute a special line of their own for zoo visitor purposes. The product-portfolio is traditionally characterized as having depth and breadth, but little attention is paid to what constitutes a *base-line* for an organization's product needs in terms of the public image. Theoretically, the six strategies referred to earlier are all possible; for a zoo to be a zoo, it must have certain animals in its collection, e.g., elephant, giraffe, lion, tiger, bear, snake, monkey, leopard. This norm has been created through the traditionally-generated concept of a zoo on the part of the public. A few "zoos" have chosen to adopt a product-line specialization approach (the Arizona-Sonora Desert Museum), a limited product-line strategy (the Santa Barbara Zoo), or special-situation (Seaworld),[1] but these cases are relatively rare compared with the number of zoos which have opted for some type of full-line, all-market strategy, either deliberately or through default. Thus, for most zoos, the product portfolio must include certain types of animals as the base-line for claiming zoo status (and, more recently, for accreditation as a particular class of zoo).

This "obvious" example suggests a different theoretical concept of the product-mix paradigm than that commonly associated with business-generated models. It highlights the constraints both normative and physical which operate to influence the product-mix decision. Additionally, a further constraint which is only marginally applicable to most business situations is very important for a zoo; while it may theoretically select its portfolio mix according to the values of having certain animals, it must also take into consideration the *situational* context of its location. Koalas can only be kept in climates where there is ready access to the right amount and type of eucalyptus leaves; dolphins cannot be kept alive unless there is adequate provision for salt-water (Brookfield Zoo has to ship its dolphins to Florida once a year in order to clean out the pool). Other constraints may be the cost of feeding (e.g., when the price of herrings went up in Europe, the Chester Zoo made an immediate policy decision that no more penguins were to be acquired); of displaying (safety, expense, aesthetics); heating and cooling (tropical fish die if they do not have constant temperatures; at the now-defunct Manchester Zoo, many died in the winter when the heating system broke down).

Once these types of constraints have been fully understood then the zoo must make further decisions on how many of each type of animal it wishes to include in its portfolio/collection. Is it sufficient to have one or two buffalo, or are buffalo best seen as a herd? (The Denver zoo sold off most of its herd of buffalo some years ago, and by so doing destroyed one of their key features.) At what point is the exhibit/generative product "new" when measured by the number of animals?

Figure 1 suggests a different representation of the product-mix decision parameters than is traditionally portrayed. Rather than the conventional 2-dimensional array of breadth (number of

FIGURE 1: ***A reconceptualization of the product-mix***

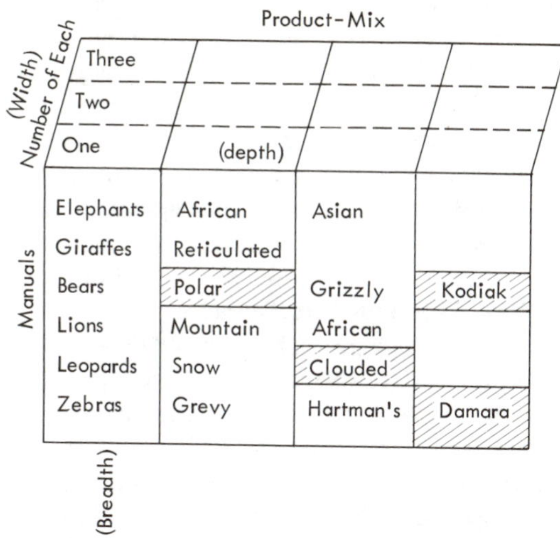

different product lines) and depth (average number of items in each line), this 3-dimensional matrix includes width—defined as "the number of each type of animal," or, more generically, "the number of item x variety". This may be more applicable, in the business sector, to organizations such as retail outlets, where the manager must decide not only on the product lines to be stocked and the range within each, but also how many of each in order to meet the potential needs of customer demand. This then becomes a demand-generated statistic, whereas in the case of the zoo, it is more naturally or reproductively generated (i.e., the number of monkeys will depend on their sex, age, ability to reproduce, desirability of reproduction from the zoo's perspective, as well as the optimal number to have in an exhibit for educational, conservation, and aesthetic purposes).

Kotler [3] also suggests a third dimension—consistency—which he characterizes as being related to end use or production-oriented requirements; for the zoo, this could be stretched to fit conceptually, but the width definition seems to have more generalizability. In Figure 1, some cells are shaded to indicate that they are "null" cells for any given zoo, being precluded for reasons of cost, climate, food availability, etc. A zoo must recognize its environmental (physical and other) constraints in order to fully and realistically determine its possible and optimal portfolio selection.

THE PRODUCT LIFE CYCLE: A LIFE AND DEATH BATTLE

The concept of product life cycle in business is based upon the notions associated with competition from others in the same or similar industry, and the environmental influences and acceptance patterns. When a company introduces a new product into the market, it hopes to make a killing by beating everyone to the consumer, or keeping ahead of its competition by offering a sufficient number of innovations or quality differentiation attributes; occasionally a company may fall flat on its face. Typically, the costs associated with the development of a new product are high, with the originating company only recouping them if it is successful in selling a sufficient quantity in the first "wave" of enthusiasm prior to others entering the market and benefiting by the pioneering company's research and development work. The zoo situation is similar, but with a few marked differences. The zoo is not faced with the same type of competition from the same industry, in that zoos are scattered over the entire country, with each zoo serving a particular city. But in the country as a whole, the zoos are competing, but more on a peer level, or among the avid zoo going population. The type of competition that is relevant is other entertainment or educational facilities within a zoo's ambit. While the Los Angeles zoo does not face direct competition in Los Angeles, the San Diego Zoo a couple of hundred miles away represents a formidable competitor. On its own turf, the other cultural and recreational attractions, most notably Disneyland, are also serious contenders for the public's attention. Thus, new product development at the zoo must take these environmental considerations into account.

The range of ''new'' products consists of (a) completely new, e.g., computers prior to the computing age, and (b) a new twist to an old product, e.g., digital watches. The zoo manifests a different range of ways of defining new products, or variations on these two:

Completely New

1. *Births:* One perennial new product at the zoo is a new baby animal. Everyone loves a cuddly, harmless (mostly) baby. They are always newsmakers, with the media giving priority to this aspect of the zoo over most others. Zoos have learned to take advantage of this ''new'' product, and have partitioned off part of their zoos to accommodate the animals (the Children's Zoo), so that they can be enjoyed in a particular manner by an especially susceptible segment of their visiting public—children.

Births are an obvious way of acquiring a new product, but the costs are not entirely predictable. When the Chester Zoo found that it had a pregnant elephant, it was elated; the cost was eventually found to be the life of the father, who went beserk and had to be shot before its rampage through the zoo destroyed man, animals and exhibits. Also, births may be seen as a replacement mechanism, either long or short run, although zoos must engage in this type of new product development as a group in order to supply their own needs and those of conservation. Natural sources can no longer supply both the needs of zoos and the natural replenishment of animals in the wild.

2. *Acquisitions:* New products/animals may also be acquired by exchanges with other zoos, purchases, or even by safaris into the wild of foreign or domestic countries. The costs of this latter method are extremely high, and transportation mortality rates increase the possibility of failure.

3. *Rare or exotic animals as gifts:* Occasionally a foreign government may wish to present a particularly rare or exotic animal to a country to show its diplomatic warmth or good intentions. The panda is an example; it made significant impact on the visitor numbers at the National and London zoos; the Koala, which was given by Australia to the San Diego Zoo, represented an unexpected bonanza. But this type of new product has its problems. Costs of feeding and care, etc., may have to be ignored in favor of political expediency. And the choice in accepting the animal may be based on political considerations rather than the needs of the zoo.

New Twists on Old Products

4. *New groupings:* These constitute a form of new product; a few animals may have been exhibited in individual cages, but a grouping of a number of them of the same type, or of different types, may give a different understanding to the visitor. The cost of this type of development may be unexpected. Two monkey-eating eagles of different sexes were displayed in the same cage at the Los Angeles Zoo with the intention of having them mate. The practical result was the death of the male at the vicious claws of the female.

5. *The exhibit:* While the animals represent an important aspect of a new product, an equally, and perhaps even more important aspect is the packaging of the animals—the exhibit itself. Zoos face problems in this area in that because animals are kept in captivity, considerable care must be taken in constructing their habitats. If the wrong material is used on the floor, the giraffe may not be able to grip the ground, and may split itself apart as was the case with Victor in England in 1977. Similarly, an animal may eat the substance out of which its new exhibit is made, and die from toxic or other poisoning. Monkeys are notorious for being capable of unscrewing any available screw fastening by their unflagging efforts; elephants are uncanny at undoing their shackles by constantly knocking them until they hit the right point for them to come free. Thus, while the concept of a different way of exhibiting animals is an attractive proposition, in practice it is fraught with danger. Not only might the total concept be a disaster, but the animals could die, or the public might react in unexpected ways. At one zoo, the exhibit simulat-

ing a jungle environment was so "natural" that the public was in constant fear of falling or of having their belongings snatched by other members of homo sapiens in the darkened entrance.

Creating new exhibits is also extremely costly. Each exhibit is a one-of-a-kind proposition; while technology is exchanged between zoos, many times the materials being used are completely new, or have never been tried out in that context or with that animal. Each new exhibit is an adventure into the unknown, and while the rewards may be very high, the costs may also be high, not only in terms of money, but also effort and safety.

6. *Communication:* A further method of introducing a new product is embodied in the concept of communication. While animals and their packaging (exhibits) constitute important elements of the total generative product, without adequate communication there is no way for the visitor to be able to relate to the animals, their setting, why the exhibit is unique, etc. Traditionally, this has been done via the written media: signs. Signs of varying quality and quantity are displayed somewhere in the vicinity of the animals, but often with little regard for the needs of the viewer. For educational trips, a docent (guide) is provided for the groups of schoolchildren, and they typically select a particular type of animal (e.g., mammals or reptiles) to focus on for that day's visit. Traditionally this is done with a lecture-format, with the children being expected to listen and absorb the new knowledge much as in a classroom setting. Other ways of communicating information about animals constitutes a new twist on the product. This may take the form of some audio system, a visual aid exhibit, or some other method of helping the visitor to appreciate what they are seeing. Along the non-technological dimension, the type of information conveyed may also represent a form of new product.

Revival of Interest

7. *Pathological/morbid fascination:* A strange, yet human-oriented way of "introducing" a new product refers to reviving interest in an already existing member of a zoo's collection. If some bizarre attrocity or accidental death occurs, it gains significant publicity. When the giraffe in England made front-page news for over a week because of its unfortunate mating accident, the zoo gained many new visitors. The hippo, Bubbles, made what was otherwise a rather unattractive animal into an enormously popular one. But this type of publicity is usually gained by some unplanned event. And the event can turn out to be a disadvantage for a zoo. It has no control over the type of publicity and the emotions it wishes to evoke. But while the cost of obtaining new visitors this way may not always be welcome, it is tantamount to introducing a new product.

These ideas on types of products must be accompanied by an analysis of the product lifecycle. For the zoo, the concept of product life cycle incorporates two important dimensions, in that it has both a literal and conceptual meaning. Each animal has its own biological life-cycle, which must be integrated into any decision on acquisitions, etc. Each animal or exhibit also has its analogous life-cycle (introduction, growth, maturity and decline), which must also be taken into consideration. For the zoo's portfolio optimization, both of these aspects must be meshed together carefully.

In terms of an animal's conceptual life-cycle, Drucker's [2] categories appear to be particularly useful, especially when linked to the idea that zoo visitors possess different degrees of "liking" for animals and exhibits. A visitor's attitude and receptiveness toward each animal needs to be assessed in order to determine whether it is worth packaging that animal in a new, perhaps costly, exhibit; is the animal intrinsically attractive enough to warrant this type of investment, or would new packaging make it more attractive? For example, a monkey and a hippo arouse different feelings in humans, leading to a distinct partialness on the part of some zoo visitors. The new packaging of the monkey may be far more cost-effective than a new enclosure for the hippos. Drucker's pragmatic approach to understanding the types of products and how they are viewed by the consuming public (zoo goers in this case) is particularly helpful (Figure 2):

1. *Tomorrow's breadwinners* (new or improved products): exhibits are particularly important if the range of animals is already sufficient.
2. *Today's breadwinners* (yesterday's innovations; current contributers): what is attractive today may not be sufficient to entice the public to visit the zoo often.
3. *Repairables* (product capable of becoming breadwinners if revamped): for the zoo this may mean renovating an exhibit, or adding more animals to the exhibit for group effects.
4. *Yesterday's breadwinners* (popular before; now rather "has been"): this may be influenced by the trends and environmental influences; e.g., the King Tut exhibit may thrust some animals associated with Egypt into the lime-light in 1978 in Los Angeles, but they may fade from significance in 1979 or 1980.
5. *The "also-rans"* (yesterday's "high hopes" which failed to capture the attention expected; they will never realistically be winners): a new gorilla exhibit may have been touted as "the thing" to see, but the public's superficial interest in gorillas may make it marginally interesting to them, although biologically rewarding to the zoo's staff.

FIGURE 2: ***Three-dimensional diagram of product life-cycle***

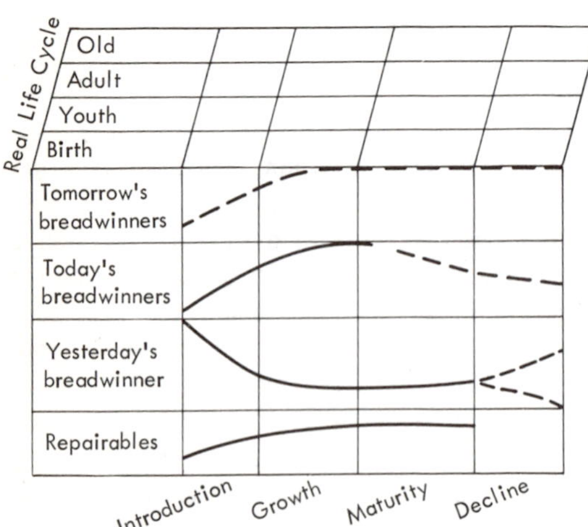

For the zoo as a total entity, the concept of product life-cycle raises some interesting dilemmas. In the business-derived theories the concept of *saturation* is used to describe the situation where the market as a whole has so many competitors that it cannot absorb any more. While this concept is useful in a limited sense to zoos, it is marginal; most cities have already made the intuitive decision that one zoo is sufficient for its residents' needs.

A more useful concept is *satiation,* which addresses the problem of the number of times a visitor will visit the zoo, as well as at what point the visit becomes boring, unexciting, or just plain tedious—the point at which the tiredness factor sets in. The entertainment industry has had to face these problems. Disneyland makes its facilities sufficiently attractive to the Southwest that most visitors to the region are brought there by residents; children are often taken one or two times a year, as the number of attractions is sufficiently large that one visit will not be capable of incorporating them all. Sea World in San Diego faced the problem that when it put in extra exhibits it stretched its visitor-stay to more than 3–4 hours (half a day), thus extending its visit duration to the point where it could only get in one shift of visitors comfortably. It was faced with the decision of whether to limit its attractions to fit in with a half-day visit, or expand them (and its price) to a full day.

This aspect of the product life cycle can be analyzed in terms of Kotler's [3] characterization of (a) one-timers (b) infrequently purchased products and (c) frequently purchased. The zoo hopes to fall in the third category; however, little research has been done into what makes many potential zoo goers view the zoo a one-time or infrequently/frequently purchased experience.

The importance of the satiation concept to new product development is most evident. If the zoo can understand the philosophy and motivation behind the decision to go to the zoo and the length of time spent in the zoo, it can begin to design its new products (both in terms of animals and exhibits) to meet these needs. But most of this is not entirely controllable.

CONCLUSIONS

From this brief analysis of a zoo a fresh perspective on product development strategies suggests several points which need to be addressed, not only by other types of organizations in the public and NFP sectors, but perhaps also by business organizations:

1. The definition of the product of some organizations may not be sufficient as currently allowed for in the theory; there needs to be some way of identifying what the "generative product" is, and its role in marketing theory.
2. The product-mix is more constrained in some organizations by external forces.
3. The concepts of "generative product" and "new product development" need to be related in a more generic manner, and reconceptualized in terms of non-business needs.
4. The base-line concept of an organization's product-portfolio might be a useful concept for business and non-business organizations.
5. The addition of depth to the 2-dimensional conceptualization of the product-mix diagram allows for greater understanding of the intricacies of some situations.
6. The life-cycles of each type of Drucker's "products," suggests a segmented approach to planning.

By using the zoo as a catalytic type of example of one class of organizations to be found in the public and NFP sectors (recognizing that the zoo may be either public or NFP, or some hybrid), suggests some additional factors which need to be incorporated into the concepts associated with products and their development. This "leaping" from the usual to the unusual type of organization presents an opportunity for rethinking old theories, perhaps strengthening them in places, or high-lighting aspects which do not seem to be adequately developed in the business-derived models.

By merely replicating studies using these business-derived theories and placing them in the non-business sectors without sufficient forethought limits both the growth of marketing theory as a whole and the usefulness of marketing to the public and NFP sectors. In order to accomplish this a symbiotic relationship needs to be developed between marketing researchers and public/NFP sector organizations so that each can aid the other in meaningful ways.

NOTE

1. Seaworld is classified as an "aquatic zoo" and is an important contributor to zoo/marine animal research.

REFERENCES

[1] Gordon, William J. *Synectics: The Development of Creative Capacity*. New York: Harper and Row, 1961.

[2] Drucker, Peter F. *Managing for Results: Economic Tasks and Risk-Taking Decisions*. New York: Harper and Row, 1964.

[3] Kotler, Philip. *Marketing Management: Analysis, Planning and Control*. Englewood Cliffs, New Jersey: Prentice-Hall, 1976.

Distributing Public Services: A Strategic Approach

CHARLES W. LAMB, JR.

JOHN L. CROMPTON

DISTRIBUTING PUBLIC SERVICES: A STRATEGIC APPROACH

It has been said that "virtually all of the rawest nerves of urban political life are touched by the distribution of urban service burdens and benefits."[1] Special-interest groups, influentials, and voters in general often evaluate public agencies and officials based upon their perceptions of the extent to which existing service delivery systems satisfy their desires.

Distribution decisions are concerned with how an agency makes its services available to a clientele. Distribution adds value to services by making them available at convenient times and places. A library located in Chicago is of little use to a student living in a small community in Alabama who needs information for a term paper that is due in a week. However, the students' school or municipal library can provide the information when and where it is needed.

In the past, public administrators frequently have not given high priority to ensuring that distribution of specific services between areas in the same political jurisdiction was equitable. However, in recent years two major trends have emerged which have caused administrators to be more concerned with equitable service distribution.

First, retrenchment is taking place in the 1980s after the rapid expansion of government services which characterized the 1960s and early 1970s.[2] When services are static or declining in quantity and quality, citizen interest in the fairness of their distribution is likely to be more prominent than when there is a service surplus with which to satisfy new demands.

Second, "because of judicial decisions, the call for an equitable distribution of public services is no longer merely a political slogan: it ranks as a legitimate, constitutionally based assertion that local officials must address."[3] The potential interventionist role of the courts is added incentive for public agency managers to give greater attention to service distribution decisions. In recent years civil rights lawyers have had some success in filing suits against various local governments challenging alleged intracommunity disparities in the provision of a variety of public services. Challenges to the legality of urban service distribution patterns are brought primarily on three legal foundations:[4]

1. The equal protection clause of the 14th Amendment to the U.S. Constitution, which provides that: "No state shall make or enforce any laws which shall abridge the privileges or immunities of citizens in the United States . . . nor deny to any person within its jurisdiction the equal protection of the laws."
2. The Voting Rights Act of 1965.
3. Revenue-sharing legislation—principally the State and Local Assistance Act of 1972 but also the Housing and Community Development Act of 1974.

These three legal foundations make every community potentially vulnerable to having its service distribution patterns scrutinized by the

Prepared by Professors John L. Compton and Charles W. Lamb.

federal courts. Cases have shown that the courts can mandate specific distribution performance where inequities are demonstrated, down to dictating the number and location of street lights and the size and location of sewers.

A STRATEGIC APPROACH TO DISTRIBUTION

The strategic approach presented here is intended to assist public administrators in systematically identifying and resolving disparities in distribution. Distribution outcomes are the result of a series of separate yet related decisions. These decisions, which are illustrated in Figure 1, may be viewed as comprising parts of a system. This article focuses on the components, and interrelationships between components, of this system.

The strategic distribution decision process begins with an analysis of existing distribution patterns. The purpose of this is to identify who is getting how much of what and where. When this is revealed, objectives are set that seek to amend or perpetuate existing distribution patterns. When objectives are established, the optimum pattern of distribution for meeting those objectives is designed. This involves determining whether (1) distribution should be relatively intensive, selective or exclusive; (2) services should be delivered either directly or indirectly; and (3) single or multiple approaches should be adopted to reach targeted client groups.

After the desired pattern of distribution has been determined, appropriate specific facility locations are identified. Locations should be selected on the basis of their ability to contribute to these desired patterns of distribution.

When these interrelated distribution decisions have been made, the service is delivered and its results and impacts are monitored. These are evaluated against the established distribution objectives so that appropriate adjustments can be made to the system. Thus distribution decisions are interrelated rather than independent, and dynamic rather than static.

ESTABLISHING DISTRIBUTION OBJECTIVES

Objectives are the end results that an agency wants to obtain, so establishing or revising existing distribution objectives is an essential first step. These objectives guide all subsequent distribution decisions and actions of the agency. In addition, they provide a basis for measuring objectively what progress has been made toward their accomplishment.

The selection of specific distribution objectives will vary among agencies, services, and perhaps geographic areas, based on a variety of factors. Police and fire department distribution objectives may be based on response times. These objectives may specify the desired lapsed time from the time the service is requested until it is delivered. In the private sector this is referred to as order cycle time. A library's distribution objective may state

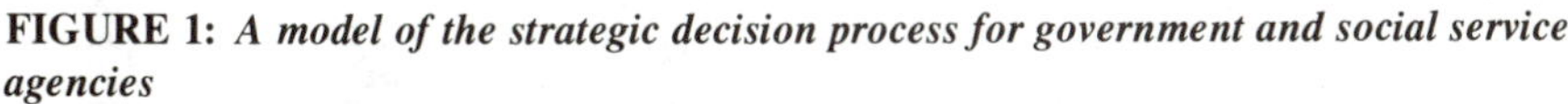

FIGURE 1: ***A model of the strategic decision process for government and social service agencies***

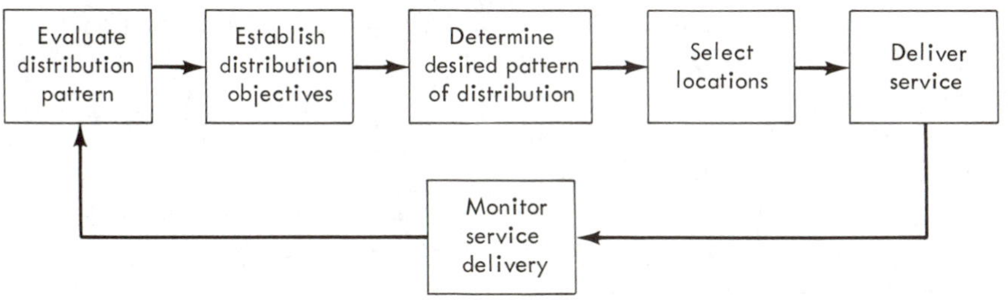

the number of units that it hopes to circulate during a specified period of time. Other types of specific distribution objectives may include:

- A municipal park department which states a distribution objective as "ensuring that there is a playground facility within a quarter of a mile of every household in the city by May 1985"
- A family counseling department which has a distribution objective of "visiting each client family in their home every month"

When distribution objectives are being established, other marketing-mix decisions, such as prices to be charged, programs to be offered, and promotional communications, also need to be considered. Therefore, the role of distribution should be carefully integrated into the overall marketing plan to achieve an integrated, cohesive strategy. Distribution decisions cannot be made in a vacuum. They affect, and are affected by, other organizational and marketing-mix decisions.

REVISING DISTRIBUTION OBJECTIVES

Revision of distribution objectives may be provoked by a variety of stimulants. Periodic reviews and evaluations undertaken by the agency will identify the extent to which existing distribution networks are comparable with the needs and desires of target clienteles. Distribution objectives and strategies should be revised as changes occur in the distribution of target markets or in consumer preferences.

An example of such changes is the recent move in some cities to take police officers out of patrol cars and put them back on neighborhood foot patrols. Surveys of merchants and residents have revealed a desire for visible law enforcement efforts in the neighborhoods. Some surveys have also indicated a preference for officers to be assigned specific territories as opposed to city-wide patrols. These people feel that if officers get to know specific neighborhoods, and if merchants and residents become personally acquainted with the policemen assigned to their areas, crime rates may be reduced.

Major environmental changes such as new laws and regulations, factory closings, or urban renewal projects may also require that existing objectives and strategies of distribution be revised to accommodate the needs of persons residing in the areas affected by these environmental changes.

Amendments to distribution objectives may be necessary when a new service is introduced. When new services are similar to existing programs, any amendments may be relatively minor. In other instances, new distribution objectives and the design of an entirely new distribution system may be required.

New objectives must also be developed when an agency decides to offer an existing service to a new target market or new geographical area since the distributional needs and preferences of these new markets may be different. Factors such as financial resources and the availability of mass transportation facilities often dictate that programs for inner-city residents be offered either in their neighborhoods or near transit lines. These factors may not be as important in suburban communities. Therefore, distribution objectives and strategies appropriate in one target market may be inappropriate when offering the program to another target market.

Distribution objectives may be adjusted when a new department of an agency is established or when two or more departments are merged. Mergers often result from budget cuts, recognition that economies of scale can be achieved by combining two or more departments or agencies, or from efforts to make a variety of services more accessible and convenient to clientele. The multiservice centers are analogous to department stores or shopping centers when customers can satisfy a variety of needs at one location.

DETERMINING THE PATTERN OF DISTRIBUTION

When objectives have been established, the optimum pattern of distribution outlets for meeting those objectives should be designed. The pattern of distribution is determined by three types of decisions. The first concern is with the level of intensity, or number of outlets for the service in a given area. The second decision is whether to distribute services directly or indirectly. The third decision is whether to adopt either single or multiple approaches to reaching target client groups.

INTENSITY OF DISTRIBUTION

Generally, the intensity of distribution of a service should meet the needs and preferences of target markets but not exceed them. Too few locations may fail to provide the needed level of service and too many locations may incur unnecessary costs. Although the marketing concept directs that client wants should be satisfied, this has to be achieved within some constraints; otherwise, it can be carried to illogical extremes. The term "marketing mania" has been used to describe organizations that become obsessively responsive to the fleeting whims of a clientele without adequate concern for cost considerations.[5] The decision regarding intensity of distribution should be guided by the distribution objectives, but will also be influenced by such factors as the financial condition of the agency, its available resources, the volume of demand expected, and the availability and extent of complementary or similar services offered by other agencies.

A basic factor influencing intensity decisions is the trade-off between costs and accessibility. Intensity of distribution, accessibility, and costs are directly related. The greater the intensity of distribution, the greater the accessibility of the program and the higher the cost. Unfortunately, there are no standard means for assessing the trade-off between cost and accessibility.[6] The decision therefore remains somewhat subjective.

As Figure 2 shows, intensity of distribution can be viewed in terms of both facilities and services. The intensity of distribution of *facilities* refers to the relative number of physical facilities that an agency operates. The intensity of distribution of *services* refers to the relative number of locations where a person can receive the service. This distinction between facilities and services is important because some services are "deliverable." That is, the service can be separated from the facility.

The fact that services are separable from an agency's physical facilities often allows personnel to overcome constraints by delivering services to clienteles at locations that are convenient to them. Counseling, for example, need not take place in agency offices. It may take place at any location where counselors and clients can meet. Probation services, outreach youth programs, and educational courses taught on commuter trains are other examples of deliverable services. In other instances, the facility is very much a part of the service and the two are not generally separable. Swimming pools and parks provide services that are directly linked to physical facilities. In these instances, people must travel to the facility to receive the service.

In Figure 2, intensity of distribution is characterized as three points along two continua that range from intensive through selective to exclusive. *Intensive* distribution of facilities entails having many physical facilities to service the target market clientele. At the extreme, intensive dis-

FIGURE 2: ***Intensity of distribution continua***

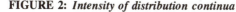

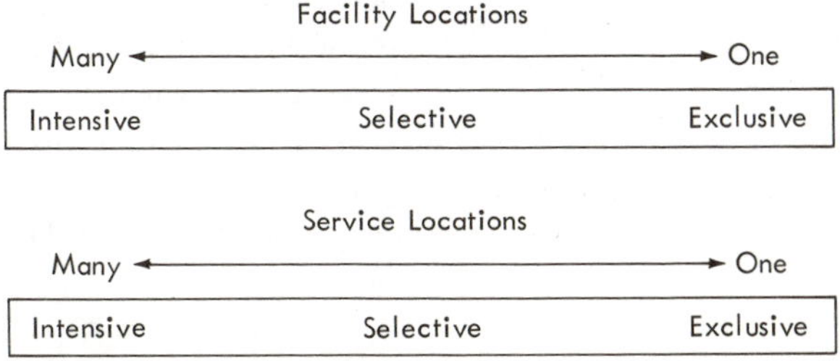

tribution of *facilities* would entail facilities adjacent to each potential user's residence. A more likely situation would be to have facilities available in most neighborhoods. Frequently, tot lots are distributed intensively so that the facilities are within walking distance for all children. Accessibility is maximized. Intensive distribution of *service* entails providing the service directly to clients in their homes or having it readily available and within easy access.

Intensive distribution appears to be ideally compatible with the marketing concept since distance is a major determinant of facility and service use. However, this is not necessarily the case; as we have seen, there is generally a direct relationship between intensity of distribution and costs. Since nonusers of services are also taxpayers, the marketing concept requires that attention be paid to their wants as well as to those of users. Frequently, nonusers, or their political representatives, desire that reasonable economies of distribution be achieved at the expense of client convenience.

Selective distribution entails having *facilities* and/or *services* available at several locations. Selective distribution presumes that members of target markets are willing and able to travel some distance to use the facility or receive the service. It also recognizes the inability of agencies to provide some services directly to all users. Selective distribution is a compromise between the economies of scale associated with exclusive distribution and the preference of clients for personalized delivery of service. Community centers are typically selectively distributed. Other examples include branch campuses for universities, schools, and parks within a community, branch libraries, satellite welfare offices, and family planning clinics. If a selective distribution strategy is adopted, locations should be selected which are most convenient for the target clientele. For example:[7]

- Young adults' pregnancy counseling clinics should be where young adults live and work.
- Welfare offices should be where clients live.
- Social security and legal services should be near senior citizens' homes
- Playgrounds should be where families with young children live.

Exclusive distribution is the provision of *facilities* and/or *services* in only one location within a community or target market area. Immobile facilities offering specialized services such as hospitals often use exclusive distribution. Exclusive distribution has the advantage of minimized costs and maximized control. The disadvantage, of course, is inconvenience to a large portion of the target market.

By having one large library in a major city, duplication of books, staff, and building costs can be avoided. The citizen gains to the extent that he or she uses an extensive collection of books. Restricting the number of locations forces the client to travel, costing him or her more in terms of time, transportation, convenience, and personal "energy."

A state university may be an example of exclusive distribution. The cost of running the university is minimized by operating only one campus, but the travel costs to clients of attending classes at that institution are likely to be high. If the university decides to distribute its educational product more intensively throughout the state, it will face all the classic distribution questions faced by large business firms: how many branch locations should be established, how large should they be, where should they be located, and what specialization should take place at each branch.[8]

Hypothetically, then, an agency may have nine intensity-of-distribution alternatives from which to choose. However, only seven of the nine possibilities appear to be realistic options. Figure 3 illustrates these alternative intensities of distribution available to the agency and suggests possible services that might most appropriately fit into seven of the nine cells.

What are the strategic implications of Figure 3 and the alternatives that it offers? Basically, the model recognizes that it is not appropriate to con-

FIGURE 3: ***Intensity of distribution alternatives***

Facilities \ Services	Intensive	Selective	Exclusive
Intensive	Neighborhood playgrounds	Supervised play at neighborhood play-grounds	
Selective	Police, fire	Parks, schools, libraries	
Exclusive	Garbage collection	Bookmobiles	Hospitals, universities, swimming pools

sider facilities and service delivery as synonymous. They can often be treated as separate components. Clearly, the separability of facilities and services provides tremendous opportunities for agencies to reach into the community to service their target markets.

Consider the case of educational programs offered through the mail and/or on television. These programs illustrate the use of exclusive facilities and intensive service distribution. The use of roving leaders by recreation agencies is another example of intensive distribution of services without any physical facilities.

Traditionally, many public agencies have administered. They have developed worthy passive facilities to serve the public that showed up and used them. Although their facilities suggested that they were constrained to using a selective or exclusive pattern of distribution, some recognized that their services could still be intensively distributed through outreach program. Hence an increasing number of agencies have been reaching out into the community to make services available to those who would otherwise be unable to experience them.

TRENDS IN DISTRIBUTION INTENSITY

In the 1960s and 1970s social service delivery moved increasingly from exclusive distribution toward decentralization and diffusion of services which represent more selective or intensive distribution patterns.

For example, there was a movement to close problem-ridden and ineffective state prisons and correctional centers in favor of community-oriented places where the number of clients may be smaller and the administrative problems more manageable. Similarly, some state and county licensing services began locating branch offices in neighborhood shopping centers for consumer convenience.[9] Agencies have tried to make services more accessible to local residents by providing local service centers which are open extended hours and weekends and by coordinating the delivery of a variety of local services at a single location.

This movement away from exclusive distribution suggests that social service agencies are becoming increasingly responsive to the marketing concept. These agencies received substantial increase in funding to enable them to bear the cost of these increased service levels. For example, between 1949 and 1959 public expenditures for health, education, and welfare services increased approximately 100%, from \$13.6 to \$27 billion, and between 1959 and 1969 expenditures increased 310%, from \$27 to \$83.8 billion.[10]

The trend toward tax reductions which gained momentum in the late 1970s may be accompanied by a reversal of the decentralization movement, back toward more exclusive distribution patterns. By closing local facilities and centralizing services, costs to the agency can be reduced. However, these costs are transferred to the potential consumer in terms of time, transportation, and convenience.

DIRECT AND INDIRECT DISTRIBUTION

The decision as to whether to distribute services directly or indirectly is somewhat analogous to a manufacturer's decision to sell either directly to customers or indirectly through retailers or wholesalers. In the public sector indirect distribution takes place when two or more agencies are involved in the delivery of a service.

Figure 4 illustrates three alternative distribution options that the federal government might use to distribute funds to needy citizens. The first option, direct distribution, entails providing funds directly to those citizens who qualify under the requirements of the program. Social security payments are an example of this alternative. Alternatively, the federal government might use one or more indirect distribution alternatives. It might distribute funds to state agencies, for example, and require the state agencies either to allocate the funds to qualified jurisdictions in the state or to distribute the funds or services directly to qualified citizens or projects. The Land and Water Conservation Fund, which provides matching grants for acquiring or developing outdoor park and recreation facilities, is an example of this alternative.

Indirect distribution alternatives may be selected by state, regional, and local governments as well as by the federal government. The Austin, Texas, Parks and Recreation Department, for example, distributes some services indirectly by financing selected community education programs operated by school districts within the city. Their rationale is that these services can be distributed more efficiently by using this indirect approach since the school systems have conveniently located facilities and qualified staff available. Indirect distribution networks may include private- as well as public-sector organizations. For example, an indirect distribution system for providing food for the needy includes retail grocers, who accept food stamps in lieu of cash. Medicare and medicaid are also examples of public/private-sector collaboration in the distribution of social services.

SINGLE- OR MULTIPLE-OUTLET DECISIONS

There is often a tendency to develop standardized uniform distribution systems designed to accommodate common needs shared by all clients. Unfortunately, attempting to accommodate the common needs shared by all often results in the failure to respond adequately to the particular needs of any market segment. The recognition that different segments of a market have different

FIGURE 4: ***Examples of direct and indirect distribution***

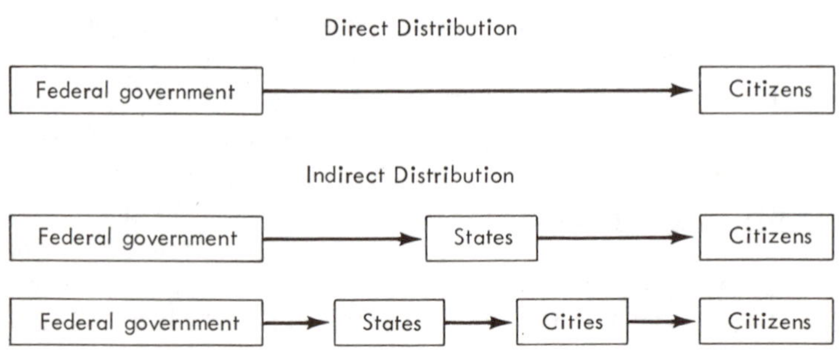

facility and service delivery needs is essential for the implementation of the marketing concept.

Figure 5 provides a simple example of how a library might use multiple distribution patterns to reach various market segments effectively. The main library appeals to researchers and others who desire an extensive collection of resources at one location and persons who seek specialized sorts of information and/or services. Branch libraries appeal to people who live close to each branch and do not require extensive collections or specialized information or services. Most people who use these libraries seek either leisure reading materials or limited research information. The main appeal of the bookmobile is its convenience to users. Outreach programs have improved library services through offering them in association with senior citizen centers, day care centers, or headstart programs.

Each of the four market segments has different needs and different distribution preferences. By providing multiple-distribution types of outlets, the library is able to reach a larger portion of its total market and to provide services consistent with their needs. All markets that are appropriate for segmentation should also be considered candidates for multiple types of distribution outlets.

SELECTING LOCATIONS

Location of facilities is a critical part of any distribution system, and selecting location is an integral part of the strategic distribution decision process. When the desired pattern of distribution has been determined, appropriate facility locations have to be identified. If the location and size of a facility are not optimum, then no matter how good its subsequent service offerings, management, promotion, or pricing strategies, the facility is unlikely to achieve its full potential. Conversely, a well-located facility may be successful in spite of inadequacies in operating management. The success of management and marketing techniques in upgrading an agency's operating efficiency and effectiveness may be less than the upgrading that may be forthcoming from improved initial locational decisions.

Location is likely to have a considerable impact on the probability of successful exchange relationships being fostered with target groups since it will largely determine client access, level of utilization, and cost of services. The geographic proximity of services to potential consumers in itself produces increased rates of use. The general conclusion about location and utilization is that use varies directly with distance from the facility. Many studies have illustrated this point. For example:

- A study of the Roxbury Multi-Service Center in Boston revealed that almost half of its users lived within a half mile of the Center and two-thirds of them lived on either side of a main traffic artery on which the center was located.[11]
- The clientele of a community psychiatric service in the Bronx in New York came almost ex-

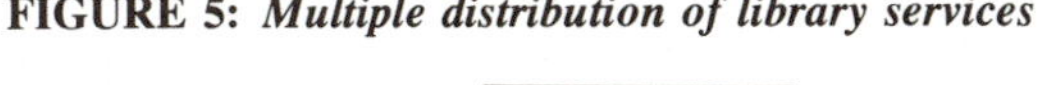
FIGURE 5: ***Multiple distribution of library services***

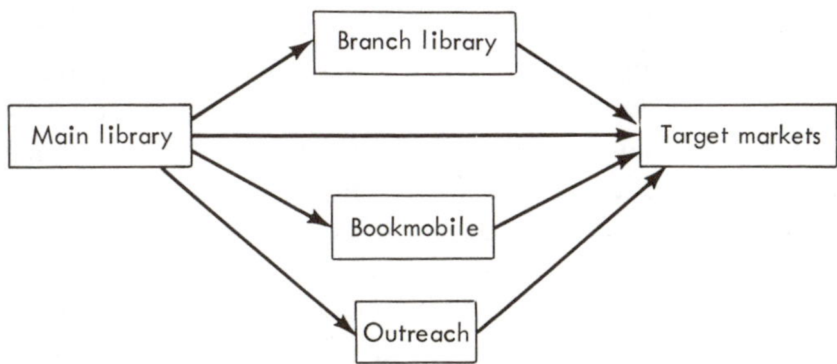

clusively from "within a five-block radius of the center . . . within walking distance, and the existence of major means of transportation near to the centers had a negligible effect."[12]

- It is well known that as health care becomes relatively optional, the probability of seeking such care is likely to vary inversely with the distance to sources of care. This "Jarvis' Law" effect has been analyzed for both inpatient psychiatric and ambulatory medical services. Jarvis's Law states the utilization varies inversely with the square of the distance to the source of care.[13]

The thinning out of users with distance strongly suggests that consumers do look upon travel with its accompaniments of time, transport fare, and so forth as a cost to be paid for obtaining services. Beyond a certain point they are unwilling to pay the cost.[14]

REASONS FOR INAPPROPRIATE FACILITY LOCATION

It has been said that Conrad Hilton was once asked to identify the most important factor in determining the success or failure of a hotel. He responded that there are three important determinants of a hotel's success: location, location, and location. Similarly, leading retail stores will generally not locate in a city unless they are able to secure a site that provides a high degree of visibility and convenient access to their target market(s). They are willing to pay a substantial premium in order to acquire a preferred location.

Public agencies frequently have failed to recognize the crucial importance of location. Many facilities are currently located in inappropriate places. "The development of our existing pattern of hospitals has been due rather to social attitudes, administrative convenience and economic expediency, than to the medical needs of the community."[15] Although the writer was referring to hospitals in England, the statement is even more appropriate in the United States[16] and may be generalized beyond hospitals to embrace most other types of public facilities. Why are public facilities located inappropriately? Five main factors appear to have contributed to this anomaly.

First, some social service delivery agencies have inherited facilities that were located on the basis of decisions made long ago. These facilities may reflect an orientation toward a distribution of population and target markets that has changed considerably since the time they were built. For example, the distribution of firehouses over time is likely to become inappropriate. Neighborhoods once filled with old wooden buildings may have been replaced by high-rise office buildings, or a district of once-fine apartment buildings may have become overcrowded and run down. Travel and response times to fire calls may now be beyond acceptable limits. However, the cost of abandoning an existing facility for a new one in a superior location may be prohibitive.

Second, the land and/or building may have been donated. This is a particularly dominant factor in explaining the distribution of parks since many cities have acquired over half their parkland from donations. In such cases, the site of a park is dictated by the donor, not by the desires of the consuming public.

Third, local, county, state, or federal offices are often centralized in one building or complex because it is administratively convenient for the agencies to be located in close juxtaposition. This expedites bureaucratic procedures, but they may not be in the most desirable location from the consumers' perspective.

Fourth, facilities are located in a particular place because a site was available. There are, for example, many areas where parks should be located, and where decision makers would like to site them, but there is no space available. This problem is particularly acute in central urban areas.

Finally, locations are selected because the land is relatively inexpensive. This is perhaps the most popular criterion currently in use for site selection in the public sector. This criterion frequently fails to consider the potentially increased benefits of revenues and/or greater utilization that may accrue to the agency if the facility were located on a more expensive, but more visible and accessible site. Proper site selection entails an analysis not only of cost considerations, but also of revenue and benefit considerations, including accessibility of the location for the target markets it is intended to serve.

Frequently, public jurisdictions rationalize that they cannot afford to purchase prime locations because the cost of acquisition is too high or because the opportunity cost of removing valuable property from the tax roles would adversely affect the jurisdiction's tax base. For these reasons, public facilities are often sited at less visible and less accessible locations that are not sought by commercial interests. Decision makers often fail to recognize that a short-run decrease in costs may increase long-run costs to the potential consumers and inhibit the agency from achieving its marketing goals.

ADOPTING A MARKETING APPROACH TO FACILITY LOCATION

Recently, there appears to have been a more conscientious effort to adopt a marketing approach to location. The trend toward decentralization of government and social services and the establishment of neighborhood service centers was motivated by the assumption that such facilities are better able to reach and help the unserved. This is achieved by such facilities being more accessible in terms of their location, their open atmosphere, and their style of intake and operation.[17] Without decentralization it is argued that certain services are not available where people live and experience most of their problems. Some services are located too far away for people who lack the transportation fare or the energy to get "downtown."

The movement toward greater consumer orientation in location decisions is illustrated by the decision rules adopted by several cities for prioritizing new branch library locations. Some combination of the following four decision rules appear to be frequently used by major cities:[18]

1. Priority is given to a maximum distance rule. Libraries are located so that a significant number of residents do not live further than an acceptable minimum distance from a branch library. In Rochester, New York, for example, this acceptable distance is two and a half miles. However, in some cities, for example Richmond, Virginia, this acceptable maximum distance to the nearest library is adjusted to take account of the race and wealth of each neighborhood. Because low-income residents have limited mobility, libraries are located so that residents of poor neighborhoods have to travel a shorter distance to reach the nearest branch library. It is felt that greater accessibility will increase use on the part of low-income citizens.
2. The size of existing branches is related to the density of neighborhoods. Standards are used for the number of square feet of library space needed per 1,000 residents. If a neighborhood is deficient in branch library space based on this density standard, it is given extra consideration when the location of a new branch is decided.
3. In Charlotte, North Carolina, in addition to the foregoing two decision rules, circulating levels and citizen requests are also considered. Neighborhoods that use available library services heavily and neighborhoods that have been particularly outspoken in seeking additional library service are given extra consideration when locational choices are made.
4. Some adjustment and compromise to the optimum location derived by adopting these decision rules may be required because no land is available at the optimum location.

The specific location decision rules for particular services are likely to vary, but a consumer orientation should be the focus for all distribution decisions. Marketing-oriented public managers should first analyze the characteristics of the target market and then locate facilities to provide the desired services at acceptable costs. The starting point should be to identify the location that would provide most appropriate access to the target clientele and then to compromise from that optimum location as little as possible in selecting a specific site for the facility. The site selection process should not start by identifying a convenient or inexpensive site and then trying to justify its appropriateness for meeting the needs of the target population.

EVALUATING DISTRIBUTION PATTERNS

Evaluation is critical to successful initiation and adjustment of strategic distribution decisions because it measures the extent to which distribution objectives have been achieved. If the desired objectives are not being fulfilled, information provided by evaluation will suggest what type or levels of adjustment should be made to the distribution system or its objectives.

Three types of indicators may be used for assessing the adequacy of distribution patterns in meeting objectives.[19] They are indicators based on resources, activities, or results.

- *Resources* are inputs to the service distribution system which may include money, personnel, facilities, and equipment.
- *Activities* are the way in which the resources are used: for example, the speed with which firemen respond to fire alarms and suppress fires, the number or frequency of policemen who patrol streets and the number of arrests they make, or the frequency with which sanitation workers collect refuse.
- *Results* are the outputs that measure what happens as a direct consequence of the service delivered. How much stolen property has been recovered? How much refuse has been collected? What is the water pressure at the tap?

The differences between these three types of indicators can be illustrated with police services. One might analyze police distribution in terms of (1) the number of police patrolmen per 1,000 neighborhood residents (a resource indicator); (b) the average response time for each neighborhood, that is, the time from receipt of a call for service until a police officer's arrival at the scene (an activity indicator); or (c) the clearance rate for each neighborhood, that is, the percentage of crimes cleared by the arrest of someone suspected of committing crimes (a results indicator).

There is a fourth type of indicator, which is perhaps the most meaningful of all, but it is probably the most difficult to use. This indicator is impact:

- Impact of a service can be defined as the difference between results given the existence of the service and conditions that would exist in the absence of a service.

This difference is very difficult to identify. In absolute terms impact measures are of little practical value. Since whole services are unlikely to be eliminated, it seems fruitless to ask such questions as: "What would be the crime rate if there were no police?" or "What health hazards would exist in neighborhoods if there were no refuse collection?" However, in relative terms impact measures would appear to be most valuable: "What is the impact on the crime rate in a particular neighborhood of a 5% increase in the police force?" "How many people will move to a school district because of a 10% increase in educational expenditures per pupil?" The best way to measure these impacts is by experimentation. Measurements are taken of relevant indicators before the experiment, preferably several times over a substantial period, and after the introduction of the new procedure, again preferably several times.

Data for specific indicators of resources, activities, results, and impacts may be obtained by gathering field data about services and facilities and/or by conducting surveys of citizens. In selecting units of analysis, priority should be given to choosing units that are most relevant to making decisions for each service. This basis for decisions usually will lead to selecting service districts as the unit of analysis. Because service district boundaries for various services often will differ, one from another, (for example, each firehouse is intended to serve a particular area, which is likely to be different form the public schools' service area, and different from refuse collection routes), systematic comparison of parts of the jurisdiction that are well or poorly served cumulatively will be difficult to make.[20] However, by mapping the findings for each service, and by developing transparent overlays for them, visual identification of relatively deprived and relatively well-off areas, in terms of the quantity and quality of services, can be identified. This information also can be computerized, using a code for each street and block. In this way comparisons among services for each block in the jurisdiction would be possible.

CONCLUSIONS

In this article a systematic approach to formulating public section distribution decisions has been suggested. Too often ad hoc decisions are made about locating a facility or delivering a service without the full implications of that decision being recognized. Each element in the distribution system affects the others. The adoption of objectives to direct the pattern of facility and service distribution will facilitate the most appropriate location selections. Periodic evaluations will assess effectiveness of implementation, given the objectives agreed on.

Decisions about the distribution of services touch the lives of all citizens. A citizen's perception of public officials or an agency is often based upon a fairly small number of experiences which have been satisfactory or unsatisfactory. In an era of declining public agency budgets, and accompanying service cuts, the high visibility to citizens of public service delivery systems is likely to make their distribution subject to an increasing amount to critical evaluation.

REFERENCES

[1] Robert L. Lineberry, *Equity and Urban Policy* (Beverly Hills, Calif.: Sage Publications, 1977), p. 13.

[2] William H. Lucy, and Kenneth R. Mladenka, *Equity and Urban Service Distribution* (Washington, D.C.: Department of Housing and Urban Development, National Technical Information Service, 1977).

[3] Astrid E. Merget and William M. Wolff, Jr., "The Law and Municipal Services: Implementing Equity," *Public Management* 58 (August 1976), pp. 2–8.

[4] Lucy and Mladenka, op. cit., p. 98.

[5] Theodore Leavitt, "Retrospective Commentary on Marketing Myopia," *Harvard Business Review* (September/October 1975), p. 180.

[6] Donald M. McAllister, "Equity and Efficiency in Public Facility Location," *Geographical Analysis* 8 (January 1976), p. 61.

[7] Douglas B. Herron, *Marketing Management for Social Service Agencies* (Columbus, Ohio: The Association of Professional YMCA Directors, 1978).

[8] Philip Kotler, *Marketing For Nonprofit Organizations* (Englewood Cliffs, N.J.: Prentice-Hall, Inc., 1975), p. 165.

[9] Herron, op. cit., p. 20.

[10] Neil Gilbert and Harry Specht, *Dimensions of Social Welfare Policy* (Englewood Cliffs, N.J.: Prentice-Hall, Inc., 1974), p. 109.

[11] Robert Perlman, *Consumers and Social Services* (New York: John Wiley, 1975), p. 55.

[12] *Ibid.*, p. 57.

[13] Robin E. McStravic, *Marketing Health Care* (Germantown, Md.: Aspen Systems Corporation, 1977), p. 167.

[14] Perlman, op. cit., p. 57.

[15] P. Cowan, "Hospitals in Towns: Location and Siting," *Architectural Review* vol. 137 (1965), pp. 417–421.

[16] J. P. Rigby, *Access to Hospitals: A Literature Review* (Crawthorne, England: Transport and Road Research Lab., 1978), p. 32.

[17] Perlman, op. cit., p. 5.

[18] Lucy and Mladenka, op. cit., p. 40.

[19] Lucy and Mladenka, op. cit., p. 58.

[20] Lucy and Mladenka, op. cit., p. 89.

TUESDAY EVENING CONCERT SERIES

Because of the rapid increase in artists' fees, the Board of Directors of the Tuesday Evening Concert Series (TECS) was considering, in the fall of 1973, increasing the price of season memberships for the 1974–1975 season. Besides three pricing proposals before the board, there were also three policy decisions under consideration:

1. What caliber of artist should TECS contract?
2. How can the series best be promoted?
3. How often should ticket prices be raised?

BACKGROUND INFORMATION

TECS was a nonprofit organization founded in 1948 and affiliated with the University of Virginia. According to the constitution: "The purpose of the Tuesday Evening Concert Series is to make available to the general public, including students, faculty, and local residents, a nonprofit series of musical events designed to enrich the cultural life of the community." The operating philosophy of the TECS was to provide a variety of chamber music (music for soloists or small ensembles), excellently performed, at relatively inexpensive prices.

The series itself consisted of eight concerts performed on Tuesday evenings in the period from October to April. The university provided the use of Cabell Hall (seating capacity 1,000) for the concerts at no charge. Admission to the concerts was, for the most part, restricted to season ticket holders of the TECS. Season memberships in the 1973–1974 series were priced at $9 for students and $12 for regular members and entitled the holders to a nonreserved seat in Cabell Hall.

The TECS was run by a volunteer board of directors consisting of 10 student members and 16 nonstudent members (mostly faculty and wives of faculty). Ernest Mead, Chairman of the Music Department, and Vincent Shea, the connoisseur Financial Vice President of the University, were ex-officio members of the Board. According to the bylaws, the president of the series must be a student. Although the board had the final say in the selection of performers, Mrs. John Forbes had handled all the actual booking of the artists for the last 12 years, with the support of the program committee. The programs were presented to the TECS Executive Committee and Messrs. Mead and Shea. Before the final program decision was made, the board of directors' approval was sought.

COST INFORMATION

The major operating expense of the series was the cost of the artists who performed at the eight concerts. Historically, artists' fees accounted for approximately 87% of the series' expenses; programs, advertising, printing, and receptions comprised most of the remainder.

The artists were usually contracted for a year or more in advance through their booking agencies, which handled the transportation and negotiated the performance fees. The great majority of artists gave their agency an "asking price" which was then subject to negotiation with interested parties. The amount of flexibility in the asking price varied from artist to artist. In general, the greater the reputation of the performer, the firmer the asking price was likely to be.

As Exhibit 1 illustrates, artists' fees for the eight concerts increased considerably in recent years. The overall increase from the 1966–1967 season to the 1973–1974 season was 54%. For the last

---

four years, artists' fees increased at slightly less than 10% per year.

In the past seven years, nine artists or groups of artists appeared more than once. The prices for which they appeared are outlined in Exhibit 2. Since several of these performers continued to appear at considerably reduced fees, Exhibit 2 probably understates the degree to which artists' fees increased in recent years. For comparison purposes, Exhibit 3 provides some additional measures of general price trends in the 1966–1973 period.

EXHIBIT 1: ***Total artists' fees for eight programs***

Season	*Artists' fees*	*Percent change over previous season*
1966–1967	$ 8,200	+30.2
1967–1968	7,980	−2.7
1968–1969	8,175	+2.4
1969–1970	8,954	+9.5
1970–1971	9,800	+9.4
1971–1972	10,700	+9.2
1972–1973	11,600	+8.4
1973–1974	12,600	+8.6

EXHIBIT 2: ***Fees paid to TECS performers who appeared more than one time***

	1966	*1967*	*1968*	*1969*	*1970*	*1971*	*1972*	*1973*
Rampal and Veyron-Lacroix[a]		$700		$700				$1,500
Peter Frankel			$1,500	$1,500				
Janos Starker		$1,100				$2,000		
The Marlboro Trio					$800		$900	
Festival Winds[b]				$1,400				$1,350[b]
The Early Music Quartet			$750			$1,100		
The New Cleveland Quartet[b]						$950		$1,250
The Juilliard String Quartet	$1,000		$1,700		$2,000			
The Hungarian String Quartet[b]					$1,100		$1,300	$1,250[c]

[a] Appeared in the 1972–1973 season.
[b] Booked to appear in the 1973–1974 season.
[c] Part of a four-concert "package" from one agency.

EXHIBIT 3: ***Selected price trends, 1966–1973***

	1966	*1967*	*1968*	*1969*	*1970*	*1971*	*1972*	*1973*	*Percent increase (1966–1973)*
Consumer Price Index									
All items	97.2	100.0	104.2	109.8	116.3	121.3	125.3	132.7[a]	36.5
All services	95.8	100.0	105.2	112.5	121.6	128.4	133.3	138.4[a]	44.5
Out-of-state undergraduate tuition at UVA	$1,037	$1,037	$1,042	$1,057	$1,214	$1,217	$1,374	$1,447	39.5
Regular membership (TECS)	$10	$10	$10	$10	$10	$12	$12	$12	20.0
Student membership (TECS)	$7.50	$7.50	$7.50	$7.50	$7.50	$9	$9	$9	20.0

[a] July.

A number of factors influenced the final price at which an artist or group of artists appeared for the TECS. The Tuesday restriction on performance dates tended to limit the negotiating position of the TECS vis-à-vis a booking agent who was trying to fit his client into a crowded schedule of concerts. Similarly, the proximity of Charlottesville to the artists' adjoining concerts had a bearing on the price charged. A pianist who was performing in Washington or Richmond on Wednesday would normally come at a lesser fee than if he or she were playing in St. Louis the next day.

Another factor that operated to reduce costs for the TECS was the booking of performers in a "package" from one agency. In past years the series has dealt with two or three major New York agencies for the majority of its concerts. Thus in the 1973–1974 season, for example, a package of four performers was bought for $7,000, a considerable saving over the sum of the artists' individual prices.

The nature of the series itself enabled it to attract performers of outstanding ability within its limited budget. Because of the reputation of the TECS as a discerning and discriminating series, various artists had performed at reduced rates. Furthermore, many outstanding performers were so impressed by the hall's excellent acoustics, the audience, and the university in general that they were willing to appear again at reduced fees. These good relations between agents, artists, and TECS were largely due to the efforts of Mrs. Forbes as chairman of the program committee, and of the committee itself.

REVENUE INFORMATION

Historically, season memberships accounted for about 83% of total revenue. Exhibit 4 illustrates the change in season memberships from 1966 to 1973, and Exhibit 5 provides total revenue figures over the same period. Although both the regular and student memberships fluctuated, the number of student memberships sold had been particularly volatile in recent years. Of the last five seasons, four were sellouts. A particularly successful season was often due—at least in part—to an active membership chairman.

In addition to the revenue derived from the sale of season memberships, the TECS also generated revenue from a number of other sources. In 1972–1973, eighteen sponsor memberships were sold at $36 each. These memberships consisted of two season tickets for the sponsor and a third which went into a pool of tickets available free to local high school students. Sponsor memberships were sold largely to local businesses.

A total of $598 was generated through the sale of memberships to the second half of the 1972–1973 series. Other sources of revenue included ticket sales at the door (only when season tickets were sold out: $94 in 1972–1973), interest on

EXHIBIT 4: ***Season memberships*** [a]

Season	*Regular*	*Percent change over previous season*	*Student*	*Percent change over previous season*	*Total*	*Percent change over previous season*
1966–1967	634	−1.1	328	+2.8	962	+0.2
1967–1968	561	−11.5	230	−29.9	791	−17.8
1968–1969	687	+22.5	349	+51.7	1036	+31.0
1969–1970	725	+5.5	320	−8.3	1045	+0.9
1970–1971	628	−13.4	274	−14.4	902	+13.7
1971–1972	731	+16.4	335	+22.3	1066	+18.2
1972–1973	688	−5.9	349	+4.2	1037	−2.7

[a]The capacity of Cabell Hall is 1,000 persons.

EXHIBIT 5: ***Total ticket revenue***

Season	*Total ticket revenue* [a]	*Percent change over previous season*
1966–1967[b]	$ 9,916	+49.2
1967–1968	8,162	−17.7
1968–1969	11,072	+35.7
1969–1970	11,499	+3.9
1970–1971	9,782	−17.6
1971–1972[b]	13,562	+38.6
1972–1973	13,815[c]	+1.9

[a]Total income minus interest on savings deposits.
[b]Ticket prices increased.
[c]First year in which tickets were sold for the second half of the series and individual tickets at the door.

EXHIBIT 6: ***University population***

Year	*UVA student body*	*UVA faculty and staff*
1966	7,873	766
1967	8,597	867
1968	9,011	1,015
1969	9,735	1,155
1970	10,852	1,200
1971	12,351	1,260
1972	12,907	1,404
1973 estimate	13,500	1,524
Percent change, 1966–1973	+71.5	+96.4

Source: Office of Institutional Analysis.

savings deposits, and the McIntire Fund. After each season the McIntire Fund gave the TECS a subsidy according to the following formula: the difference between the regular membership price and student membership price ($3 in 1972–1973), multiplied by the number of student members, up to a maximum of $1,000.

TECS also received an indirect subsidy from Mrs. Forbes. The job of Program Committee Chairman was about half-time, and a person qualified to replace her could have expected anywhere from $5,000 to $7,500. She also spent (without reimbursement) about $100/year on long-distance phone calls and $250 for a once-a-year concert managers' convention in New York City. She had just been elected to another three-year term (1973–1976) as Program Committee Chairman. Assuming that she might be reelected in 1976, she would be unable, for personal reasons, to continue to serve in this capacity beyond 1979.

MARKET

Exhibit 6 gives some indication of the market for TECS members in recent years. Clearly, the potential demand for series tickets within the university community had increased very rapidly since 1966.

In addition to increasing ticket prices, the TECS took several other steps to increase total revenue. For instance, in recent years TECS oversold the concerts by about 100 seats. Because some members only attended a few of the eight concerts, there were always a certain number of empty seats at any given performance. A head count of empty seats conducted in the fall of 1972 revealed that, on the average, about 125 seats were unoccupied during the first four concerts. Consequently, the series now attempted to sell roughly 1,100 memberships and had increased the target to 1,200 for next year.

A second related course of action the TECS adopted in 1972–1973 was the sale of memberships for the second half of the Series. After counting the average number of empty seats at the first four concerts, the series then attempted to sell half-season memberships at $8 for regular members and $6 for students. In other words, the series was oversold twice: once at the beginning of the season and once midway through the season. In the event that more than 1,000 people appeared at Cabell Hall, approximately 40 folding chairs could be set up in the aisles to accommodate the overflow.

Finally, the board of directors recently passed a resolution allowing the solicitation of charitable contributions. Although the board did not wish to actively promote contributions, there would be a notice on the 1973–1974 ticket order form to the effect that tax-deductible contributions would be accepted.

POLICY AND PRICING DECISIONS

At recent board meetings a number of policies central to the ticket pricing problem were discussed. There was some disagreement as to which policies TECS should adopt, and it was recognized that, at the next board meeting, these differences would have to be settled before the pricing decision could be made.

First, there was the question of the caliber of artists that TECS should bring to Charlottesville. Although everyone agreed that the quality of the performances was good, some felt that it should be "great" ("it is great only one-fourth to one-half of the time now"). Those who advocated upgrading the quality of the series pointed out that the "masters" drew standing-room-only crowds, while other performers did not fill the hall. In the fall of 1973, the maximum fee for one artist or group was $2,000; one proposal was to raise this to $3,500 for two of the eight concerts. Another proposal was to abandon the fixed maximum fee altogether and adopt a total fixed budget of $20,000, allowing TECS occasionally to present those elite artists who charged upward of $5,000. Both proposals recognized that, since membership could not be increased significantly, a price increase would be necessary. Opponents of the proposals were skeptical that the Charlottesville audience would be willing to pay the price necessary to attract artists of substantially higher caliber than those presently available. They also argued that some members enjoyed the highly experimental nature of some of the programming, the ambience of the concerts, and that it was possible to enjoy an evening of fine music, competently—but not "greatly"—played, in an attractive setting.

Related to the issue of quality was the question of promotion. Some board members felt that low prices arouse suspicion about the quality of the product, whereas high prices increase the perceived value. In fact, when prices were raised in 1966 and again in 1971, season memberships also increased (Exhibit 4). It was further argued that increased prices would enable TECS to book "big names," and that this would be a promotional benefit. Opponents of this strategy pointed out that, with the present level of quality, the series had sold out four of the last five years.

An important consideration in directing promotional efforts efficiently was the ratio of student memberships to regular memberships. With the present price differential of $3, the first 333 student memberships actually brought in the full $12 because of the McIntire Fund subsidy. Each student membership over 333, however, generated $3 less in revenue than a regular membership. Furthermore, if the differential between regular and student prices increased, it would become financially desirable to have fewer student members.

A final recommendation for promoting TECS involved establishing better communications between the board and the members via meetings and/or newsletters. It was argued that increased communication would stimulate interest and involvement.

Many of these policy proposals entailed an increase in ticket prices, and the board members recognized the necessity of raising prices occasionally. However, there was disagreement on how often prices should be raised. Frequent price increases may antagonize the membership, even though inflation of artist fees may justify it. Long periods without increases could be damaging in two ways: revenue is lost while costs are rising, and a momentum is established, making it even more difficult to raise prices later. One proposal offered to the board advocated not increasing the price more frequently than every three years. Other members felt that prices should be raised whenever necessary to effect the board's plans and policies for the coming season.

After the board settled these matters of policy, a decision would have to be made concerning ticket prices for the 1974–1975 season (tickets for 1973–1974 were already on sale). There were three proposals before the board:

	Student membership	*Regular membership*
Present prices	$ 9	$12
Proposal I	13	16
Proposal II	9	24
Proposal III	15	20

The first (I) proposal was intended only to keep pace with inflation and would not permit upgrading the series.

The second (II) was suggested specifically to allow for two "special" concerts per year, at which artists presently out of TECS's price range would appear.

The third (III) was advocated as a means of financing a significant increase in the quality of the series.

Prices "comparable" to the TECS tickets are quoted below:

Present prices, regular membership	$1.50
Proposal I prices, regular membership[a]	2.00
Price of movie in Charlottesville	2.00
American Film Theater Series[b]	3.75
Carnegie Hall, cheapest ticket	3.00
Kennedy Center, cheapest ticket	3.00

[a]Same calculation can be made for proposals II and III.
[b]Eight Enchanted Evenings, series cost—$30. Available in Charlottesville.

The three proposals had unequal following among the board members. The board had to make a pricing decision in the early fall of 1973, as the program committee needed to know what the budget would be for the 1974–1975 season; artists were booked a year in advance.

SIMON'S ROCK COLLEGE

Simon's Rock College, Great Barrington, Massachusetts, called itself an "early college," a residential, four-year school offering a liberal college education to students too young to have finished high school. The ideal student whom Simon's Rock sought had, in fact, completed only the tenth grade.[1]

This novel educational philosophy caused substantial problems both in identifying prospective students and persuading them to apply. In autumn 1973, Dr. Baird Whitlock, the president, examined the situation. In the 1972/73 school year Simon's Rock had run a deficit equal to about 10 percent of its total operating revenues. The school could eliminate such deficits with increased enrollment. In addition, increasing the student body was part of a long-range goal to bring the school's size up to eight hundred students. "We believe the market is there," said Dr. Whitlock, "if only we can find it."

BACKGROUND

Two ideas underlay the founding of Simon's Rock. The first was the belief that late adolescents, aged sixteen to twenty, formed a relatively

This case was prepared by and used with permission of Professor David L. Rados. Reprinted with permission from David L. Rados, Owen Graduate School of Management, Vanderbilt University.

homogeneous segment of society. A report on late adolescents published by the College Entrance Examination Board noted "the marked similarities of young people in this age group in contrast to persons, say, two years younger or older," and it stated that adolescents were "in control of mature mental processes but not yet of organized egos and distinct life plans."[2]

There was evidence of their mental maturity. Throughout the country, large numbers of secondary school juniors and seniors took college-level courses under a program developed by the College Board. At Simon's Rock thirty-seven first-year students, ages sixteen and seventeen, were tested for "general educational development" in fall 1973, and their scores compared with those of high school seniors, typically a year or two older. The Simon's Rock students scored far above the national average for high school seniors, meaning that most colleges would consider them ready for college work.

While these adolescents were mentally and physically mature by age sixteen, many had not achieved emotional maturity. These were often years of turbulence and identity crisis, years in which the adolescent confronted the necessity to choose, without the help of tradition, his work, his social role, even his identity. These years were a period of intense emotional change, in which the adolescent established a sense of personal identity, achievement, and self-esteem.

The failure of traditional educational patterns to meet the needs of late adolescents formed the second line of thought. Passage by late adolescents through these "middle years" was ruptured by the abrupt transition from secondary school to college. Neither the last two years of secondary school nor the first two of college served late adolescents well. The unpredictability of college admissions disrupted the high school students' academic and emotional growth. For some it was a source of emotional disturbance. Those in college were taught by professors mostly interested in narrow scholarly pursuits, with little time for psychological needs of adolescents. Moreover students who did take college-level courses in high school were often required to duplicate the work in college, because few colleges had effective programs for granting exemptions.

It was from these ideas that Elizabeth B. Hall, the founder and first president, conceived of an early college that would deliberately blur the distinction between high school and college and offer a climate in which the late adolescent could develop and mature.

The school was founded in 1964 as a nonprofit educational organization in the Commonwealth of Massachusetts, and the first class entered in September 1966. Mrs. Hall financed the school with three million dollars from the estate of her father and a grant of seven hundred thousand dollars, along with the gift of the campus and fourteen-room residence from her mother. At that time the campus was one hundred and ninety acres and included three ponds, a swimming pool, and ski trails. The school's name derived from a glacial erratic on the site.

In 1970, when the first class graduated, Simon's Rock was given authority to grant the Associate in Arts Degree by the Board of Higher Education of the Commonwealth of Massachusetts. As of autumn 1973, this was still the only degree Simon's Rock could award. But it had applied for accreditation from the New England Association of Schools and Colleges. Once accredited it could expect prompt receipt of authority to grant a Bachelor of Arts degree from the Massachusetts Board of Higher Education. Administration officials were hopeful the school would be accredited by 1975 or possibly earlier.

THE STUDENTS

Simon's Rock did not use traditional terms for its classes. Instead the entering class was called Class I, the second year Class II and so on. Enrollment, somewhat over two hundred students, had shown little growth during the past four years (see Exhibit 1). Until 1970 no male students

EXHIBIT 1: ***Changes in student body size, 1969–1973***

Academic year	*Continuing students*	*Students entering in:* September	*Students entering in:* February	*Total enrollment*	*Graduated*	*Withdrew*
1969–70	111	48	1	160	24	48
1970–71	87	106	4	197	21	60
1971–72	112	117	8	237	51	65
1972–73	113	110	12	235	42	88
1973–74	105	102	?	207[a]	26	?
1974–75	115					

[a]Assuming 10 new students in February 1974, with 26 graduating and a 40 percent attrition.

Source: Director of Admissions, *Report,* September 21, 1973

were admitted but by 1973, about 35 percent of the students were male.

There were many ways a student could enter Simon's Rock and many ways he could leave. For example, depending on age and education, students could enter either in Class I, Class II, or Class III, and either in September at the beginning of the first semester or in Februrary at the beginning of the second. The two most common reasons for leaving Simon's Rock were graduation and transfer to other colleges, and each of these could take place in a number of ways, discussed in Exhibit 2. Exhibit 3 shows causes of turnover in the academic year 1972/73.

EXHIBIT 2: ***Ways students can graduate or transfer, by entering class***

1. **If the student enters in Class I,** age fifteen or sixteen, he may leave with:
   a. High school equivalency, after two years.
   b. Associate of arts degree, after four years.
   c. Bachelor of arts, after four years but only after Simon's Rock receives degree-granting authority.
   d. Transfer to a four-year college, after two years. The student who leaves after two years often receives advanced standing.

Class I students rarely leave after one year because without a high school equivalency they can not get into college and few wish to return to high school as seniors.

2. **If the student enters in Class II,** age sixteen or seventeen, he may leave with:
   a. High school equivalency, after one year. As Simon's Rock does not see itself as a prep for college this route is discouraged.
   b. Associate of arts, after three years.
   c. Bachelor of arts, after four years but only after Simon's Rock receives degree-granting authority.
3. **If the student enters in Class III,** age seventeen or eighteen, he may leave with:
   a. Associate of arts, after two years.

This student already has a high school diploma, and will not be allowed to study for the bachelor of arts, as this is the traditional college route that Simon's Rock does not wish to follow.

Source: School records.

EXHIBIT 3: ***Explanation for withdrawing***

		Number
Graduated		43
Academic reasons	10	
Disciplinary reasons	3	
Leave of absence (registered for 1974)	1	
Transferred to other colleges	41	
Plans unknown	33	88
Total student turnover		131

Source: School records.

EXHIBIT 4: ***Admissions figures, 1970–1973***

Academic year	*Inquiries*	*Applied %*	*Interviews*	*Applied*		*Accepted*		*Enrolled*	
1970–71	1505	13	322	202	63%	122	60%	106	86%
1971–72	1198	23	490	276	56%	150	55%	117	78%
1972–73	1360	14	387	200	51%	141	70%	110	78%
1973–74	1942[a]	9	374	170	45%	114	61%	102	89%

[a]Includes 432 inquiries from the Student Search Service, which arrived in June and July, 1973.
Source: Director of Admissions.

Exhibit 4 shows the admission figures for the years 1970 to 1973. Exhibit 5 shows the sources of information utilized by applicants. Exhibit 6 shows financial aid granted to students. Exhibit 7 gives some reasons for students coming to Simon's Rock.

ADMISSIONS PROCEDURES

The applicant normally went through several steps in applying to Simon's Rock. He first filed a preliminary application in the academic year preceding the one in which he hoped to enroll. A student planning to enter in September 1975 would file his application during the previous year, 1974/75. Then, except for unusual circumstances, he came to Simon's Rock for an interview and tour of the campus. He was permitted, if space was available, to stay overnight in the dormitories and was given three complimentary meals. After the interview he completed the full application form. The student's parents also completed a form, and two teacher recommendations were required.

Academic performance was judged on the basis of school grades and College Board test scores. Students in the tenth grade took the Secondary School Admissions Test. Students in eleventh or twelfth grade took either the Preliminary Scholastic Aptitude Test or the Scholastic Aptitude Test itself. This last test was the standard "College Board" test required by hundreds of colleges and

EXHIBIT 5: ***Students' sources of information about Simon's Rock, from completed application blanks***

Source	*Number*	*Percent*
Current or former students, or parents	50	30
Siblings	8	5
Friends at other schools	26	16
Principals, headmasters, teachers, counselors	41	24
Publications and publicity[a]	17	10
Professional consultants	9	5
Student Search Service	7	4
Acquainted with Mrs. Hall[b]	6	4
Simon's Rock faculty and staff	4	2
	168	100

[a]Lovejoy's College Guide, *Porter Sargent, Newsweek, Saturday Review,* newspaper articles.
[b]Including two who saw Mrs. Hall on the "Today" show in 1970.
Source: Director of Admissions.

EXHIBIT 6: ***Financial aid granted 1970/71–1973/74***

Academic year	*Number of students*	*Amount of grants and scholarships*
1970–71	24	$53,000
1971–72	16	50,000
1972–73	35	89,000
1973–74	37	98,000

Source: Director of Admissions.

EXHIBIT 7: ***Reasons for coming to Simon's Rock, among forty-four 1973 Class I students***

	Very important (%)	*Somewhat important (%)*	*Total (%)*
I was too limited in my academic choices at my previous school.	80	2	82
This college offers special educational programs.	77	16	93
I was not learning enough at my previous school.	70	18	88
This college has a very good academic reputation.	57	36	93
I didn't have enough personal freedom at my previous school.	57	27	84
I was attracted to Simon's Rock because of the early BA program.	48	30	78
There seem to be very few rules concerning campus life.	30	45	75
I wanted to live away from home.	18	50	68
I was offered financial assistance.	14	18	32
Someone who had been here before advised me to come here.	11	32	43
There seems to be an absence of structure in the academic program.	9	41	50
My parents wanted me to come here.	5	27	32
My teacher advised me.	5	20	25
My guidance counselor advised me.	4	23	27
This college has low tuition.	2	4	6
I wanted to live at home.	2	7	9
I could not get a job.	2	0	2

Source: Director of Admissions.

universities in the country. For those who could not take one of these tests, the Differential Aptitude Test was administered on campus at the time of the interview.

RECRUITING PROBLEMS

Simon's Rock wished to draw its students from the tenth grade, a course that presented a number of problems. There was, inevitably uncertainty about the size of the potential market for experimental colleges. One possible clue to its size was given by Clark Kerr, an educator, in the book *Less Time–More Options,* in which he recommended that the number of high school students given advanced standing in college should be increased by a factor of ten, from fifty thousand to half a million.

But, according to Peter Alford, associate director of admissions, there were only three other U.S. colleges seeking tenth grade students: U.S. International University in San Diego, with probably less that two hundred middle-adolescent students; La Guardia Middle College in New York, which also accepted ninth grade students; and Shimer College, Illinois. Perhaps as many as one third of Shimer's freshman class, believed to be around one hundred, had completed only the tenth grade.

Colleges were much more open to accepting qualified eleventh grade students, and Mr. Alford felt that "almost all" colleges and universities in the country would accept such students. It was not known how many actively recruited them, however.

Recruiting problems arose with three groups —prospective students, their parents, and their teachers and guidance counselors. Because the idea was so novel, few students were aware of the existence of early colleges. And of those who were aware, most did not even consider applying.

Parents of prospective students also knew little about Simon's Rock. Many who did know faced substantial financial obstacles in sending their children. A parent whose child was in tenth grade in high school could count on two more years of free public education. But if the child wanted to go to Simon's Rock the parent would have to pay his expenses. Tuition, fees, and room and board for a resident student were $4,500 in 1973/74 and this figure did not include travel, clothes, entertainment, and the like.[3] On the other hand a parent whose child was in prep school was already paying for his child's education. For him Simon's Rock presented no extra financial burden. In any event administrators at Simon's Rock felt that most of their students were relatively well-to-do.

Simon's Rock was not well known among teachers, guidance counselors, or principals, and students who might benefit from knowing about Simon's Rock could not rely on them for information. But high school faculty and staff were sympathetic. Prep schools saw Simon's Rock as a competitor. As a result Simon's Rock recruiters were not always cordially received at prep schools. Nevertheless in spite of such obstacles, and because of the financial considerations cited above, some 50 to 60 percent of the students at Simon's Rock had transferred from prep school.

RECRUITING METHODS

The student recruitment program conducted by Simon's Rock employed many standard techniques for recruiting college students. The 1973/74 catalog, for example, was attractively designed and contained twenty-three pages of bleed photographs; and the student handbook containing campus regulations and other information for students was decorated with student drawings, woodcuts, and lithographs. (A list of all recruiting techniques used by Simon's Rock is found in Exhibit 8).

EXHIBITS 8: ***Techniques used in student recruiting in recent years***

To reach counselors
- Meetings—national and regional (follow up with those interested)
- High school visits
- Catalog and other mailings (developed mail list)
- Summer visits
- 9th grade school visits (new)
- Area counselor visits (this year)
- More phoning (this year)
- 2–3 phase visit (Chicago); counselor has time to alert students
- College bound
- "Team" visits to cities

To reach teachers
- C Form writers get special letter
- 10th grade teachers in high schools get letters
- Science brochure to biology and physics teachers
- Teacher groups (where are lists?); need faculty help
- Student help to identify interested teachers

To reach parents
- Ads (*New York Times–Monitor*); idea: AMA or other?
- Visits with families: "open houses" with slides and discussion
- Postcards
- Motel "open hours" when visiting a city (not too successful)

To reach students directly
- New poster for high school bulletin boards (postcard to return to us for more information)
- Letter to high school newspapers; exchange of papers
- Ads in high school paper (one pilot project)
- Follow-up of MASC
- Follow up New Hampshire students from St. Paul's Summer School
- Our students (faculty contacts); how can we do more?
- Idea: People around country sending names of worthy 10th and 11th grade students—network of mothers, grandmothers?

- Sending 50 SR Reviews to certain schools (male secondary schools?)
- Brochure and pamphlets—literature now more student-oriented

Follow-up:

- Tickle system (new)—send 4 mailings
  - Step 1. Why wait
    - Postcard
    - Fact Sheet
  - Step 2. Automatically send:
    - Student Speaks
    - Alternatives
    - House of Education
  - Step 3. When postcard received
    - No. 1 letter
    - Preliminary Application Form
    - Catalog
    - Parents' list
  - Step 4. No. 2 letter
    - All necessary forms
    - Checklist
    - PSC when requested
- Phone (increased)
- Student (faculty vacation telephone calls)
- After acceptance, several letters; system now good
- Need more before acceptance—systematic phoning, "more info"; will try this year.
- Idea: telephone marathon

Source: List prepared by Mr. Alford.

The school had an active program of off-campus recruiting. The associate director of admissions visited over forty-five secondary schools in 1970/71 and over sixty-five in 1971/72.

While on these trips admissions representatives visited about three schools a day. Typically the first call lasted from 9 to 10:30 a.m., the second from 11 to 12:30 p.m. (through lunch) and the last from 1 to 2:30 p.m., the latest a school visit could go. The representative would meet with at least one guidance counselor and would also try to see librarians and teachers, particularly of tenth graders. "The brighter kids are often in the library, and that's where the college counselling books are too," explained one member of the admissions staff. "However in calling on these people we must be careful not to undercut the guidance counselor. The problem with the guidance people is that they spend most of their time counselling eleventh and twelfth graders. Few tenth graders have much reason to see them, so naturally they don't know many tenth graders."

Students also participated in recruiting, because administrators felt that students were the best source of new students.

Before 1972, recruiting trips had been confined to Boston, New York, Cleveland, Chicago, Long Island, and New Jersey, but beginning in 1972/73 college personnel began to travel more widely. One trip, for example, was made with College Bound, a group of college admissions officers travelling together to meet guidance counselors and students. This trip covered Richmond, Norfolk, Charlotte, Atlanta, Orlando, Tampa, and Ft. Lauderdale. Mr. Alford estimated that he and his staff spent between seventeen and eighteen weeks on the road during the 1972/73 recruiting period and visited perhaps one hundred and eighty schools. By the beginning of the 1973 academic year, however, two new people had been added to the admissions staff. He commented, "We have to visit the schools, of course. But sheer number of weeks on the road isn't all that important. Preparation for the visits and thorough follow-up of inquiries and the results of Student Search mailings are crucial."

Receipt of a grant from the Carnegie Foundation enabled Simon's Rock to hire Elza Hewat, a former student, as an admissions assistant. Miss Hewat made ninety-one school visits in the winter and spring of 1973 and wrote a report on her activities from which the following excerpts are taken:

> My visits to [ninety-one schools] were conventional recruiting visits. I spoke with guidance counselors and with any students who came to the meetings. I also spoke with several parents of prospective applicants at their homes. Whenever possible I organized trips with a student from Simon's Rock and we visited his or her high school [together.]
>
> The name Simon's Rock generally did not mean very much to [students.] A number of the students who did show up at meetings came because it was

an excuse to miss a class. Altogether I saw about twenty-seven students on my trips. Eight of these [subsequently] came to Simon's Rock for an interview.

Many of the people with whom I talked had never heard of [Simon's Rock.] It is also extremely important that we reach tenth graders and I don't feel that my visits were terribly effective in that area. Guidance counselors are apt to direct their attention to seniors and juniors. Tenth graders are generally neglected and seldom aware that there is such an alternative as an "early college."

I discovered that a number of public schools grouped ninth and tenth grades together and eleventh and twelfth together. This is an ideal situation for Simon's Rock because the 10th grader must make a decision about where to go for the following year. Also there are guidance counselors who deal with them exclusively. Unfortunately I didn't know about these schools ahead of time. We should also experiment with visits to schools ending in ninth grade.

If school visits were scheduled carefully it might be possible to say to a guidance counselor, "I'll call you back in several days when you've had time to get in touch with some students who might be interested in Simon's Rock and we can arrange a second visit.

I found home visits very productive but extremely difficult to arrange. Although I always made it clear to students that I was staying in the area and left a phone number, this didn't seem to be enough. Perhaps phone calls should be made to any students met during the day who seemed worth pursuing and an offer made to visit and talk with parents.

Public schools were the most receptive to Simon's Rock. Private schools tend to see us as a threat. The only schools I felt it was a waste to visit were city schools; to be at all effective, the recruiter should be black.

Good publicity is very important. The recruiter should have some kind of photograph exhibit, something that could stand up on a table at a conference or just sit in the middle of the floor in the office of a guidance counselor. A Simon's Rock poster should go out to schools weeks in advance rather than at last minute.

I think Simon's Rock students should be used in recruiting as much as possible. It's unusual for students to make school visits but guidance counselors are glad to have an opportunity to talk with someone who is presently enrolled and can give them the real inside story.

The school participated in several College Night programs and was represented at a dozen regional and national meetings of guidance counselors. In 1971/72 the school arranged several visits to the families of students then attending Simon's Rock, who opened their houses to friends and neighbors interested in learning more about the college. Direct mail contact was maintained with over one thousand secondary schools, and any teacher who had written a recommendation for a Simon's Rock student received a brief letter on his progress each year. This letter was mailed in March when student counselling was at its height.

The school also participated in the Student Search program, administered by the College Board. Through Student Search Simon's Rock could purchase the names of high school sophomores taking either the Preliminary Scholastic Aptitude Test or the Scholastic Aptitude Test. Most students taking these exams completed a Student Descriptive Questionnaire, which consisted of a series of questions on personal and academic facts. Students' names were included in the Search only if they asked to have the information reported to interested colleges. The information available to Simon's Rock depended on whether it bought the spring or summer Search, but it could order names by any grouping of the characteristics listed in Exhibit 9.

Simon's Rock had used Student Search twice in 1972/73. It purchased from the spring search 3,162 names of tenth graders who had taken the PSAT in the fall 1972 and who had high PSAT scores. (Because there were more than 3,162 students above the cut-off score Simon's Rock purchased a random selection of names.) These names were delivered in May 1973. An admissions packet was sent to each, consisting of an offset letter inviting the student to request more information, a brochure on Simon's Rock and a

EXHIBIT 9: ***Availability of data on student characteristics***

Student characteristics	*Available in:* *Spring search*	*Summer search*
Sex	×	×
Place of residence (state and/or zip code)	×	×
Zip code	×	×
Whether designated college to receive ATP scores		×
Whether designated college as first or second choice	×	
High school attended (public or private)		×
Class in school	×	×
High school rank		×
High school grades	×	×
SAT scores	×	×
Ethnic background		×
Estimated financial contribution from parents		×
Intended college major	×	×
Intended level of education		×

prepaid postal reply card. The costs were approximately as follows:

Names	$100 fee plus 7 cents a name
Envelopes	$ 60
Offset letter	$ 90
Brochure	$210
Post card	$240
Postage	$240

The mailing drew some three hundred and sixty post card replies. These in turn produced twenty to thirty Preliminary Applications and, Mr. Alford guessed, "two or three or four" new students.

The second purchase was a special search. For a flat fee of $1,500 another 2,984 names were received on July 29th, 1973. Because the names were already printed on gummed labels the admissions staff was able to post its mailing the same day. This mailing, which cost approximately the same as one in May, asked interested students not to request information but to return a Preliminary Application. Some sixty applications were returned, which produced seven students for the new academic year.

ADVERTISING AND PUBLICITY

Media advertising has been used sparingly and generally without success. Because of the unusual nature of Simon's Rock long copy was needed. But larger space meant less money available for a number of ads, hence most ads were run only once. The media used were typically the national edition of the *Christian Science Monitor* and the "News in Review" section of the *Sunday New York Times*. These were chosen because they both carried a good deal of educational advertising, and because publicity on Simon's Rock placed in them had produced a good response.

Publicity had generated a large number of inquiries. "Every time we get an article or some press coverage," said Dr. Whitlock, "we see an increase in inquiries." When Mrs. Hall had appeared on the N.B.C. *Today Show,* her appearance generated some thirteen hundred responses and gave Simon's Rock a good number of new students. "It saved us from perdition," said one staff member. Similar favorable results were generated by publicity appearing in the *Christian Science Monitor* and the *Saturday Review—Education Edition*. A story appearing in *Newsweek* in April 1972 was syndicated in one hundred and two daily newspapers, and generated about three hundred and fifty inquiries. John Porter, director of public relations, said: "Getting publicity should be easy for Simon's Rock because it is unique and makes good copy. It's newsworthy. Most schools have to *do* something, say start a new program, to get the attention of reporters and editors. At the same time education isn't as newsworthy as it was during the sixties." Mr. Porter felt that some $5,000 a year would be needed to maintain close contact with major national media.

NOTES

1. A secondary school educates students from ages twelve to seventeen. A public, tuition-free secondary school is a high school. A private secondary school is assumed to prepare its students for college, hence it is a preparatory or prep school, or recently an independent school.
2. The Four-School Study Committee, *16–20: The Liberal Education of an Age Group,* (New York: College Entrance Examination Board, 1970), p. 10.
3. In 1972/73 total income for Simon's Rock was $1,040,000, of which $950,000 came from tuition, fees, and room and board. The principal expenses were administration $206,000; faculty salaries and other instructional expenses, $370,000; food, $161,000; and plant operation and maintenance, $141,000.

ALASKA NATIVE ARTS AND CRAFTS COOPERATIVE, INC.

The artistry of Alaska Natives grew out of a spontaneous urge that embraced many motives, none of which were monetary. The pre-European Alaskan native indulged his creative prowess in embellishments of his person, in recording the details of his unique and colorful culture, and in the symbolic expression of his religion. It did not occur to these people to create such beauty to be sold. The marketing of native crafts before the advent of the white man simply did not exist, as the native had no conception of payment for his art.

Because of the obvious and unavoidable impact of modern society on the traditional native culture, the need of at least a minimal cash flow has become vital to the basic survival of these people. A man must have money for his snow machine or outboard motor in order to engage in subsistence hunting and fishing and money for oil to heat his home. Many rural natives who move to Alaska's urban communities lack the education and skills to adapt to a new life-style. There is infrequent employment for those who seek to live in the isolated areas of their heritage; consequently, they have discovered that an important source of income is the sale of artistic creations and handcrafted items.

The survival of the Alaska Native Arts and Crafts Cooperative, the organization established over 40 years ago to market the creative expression of the aboriginal population of Alaska, has been threatened by an operating deficit. Such important issues as the preservation of a magnificent but imperiled art form versus the uplifting of a destitute and forgotten race are at stake in the formulation of the future of the Alaska firm.

BACKGROUND OF ALASKAN NATIVES

Throughout northwest Alaska and parts of Canada reside a large aboriginal population, which includes numerous tribes of Indians, Eskimos, and Aleuts, referred to vernacularly as natives. These people have for generations endured some of the world's harshest climatic condi-

---

This case was prepared by Professor G. Hayden Green of the University of Alaska, Anchorage, and Walter Greene, University of North Dakota, as a basis for class discussion rather than to illustrate either effective or ineffective handling of an administration situation.

tions. Many native inhabitants of the North still retain a relatively traditional subsistence life-style with hunting and fishing being the mainstay of their livelihood. The Bureau of Indian Affairs (BIA), federal and state agencies, and native leaders have since the turn of the century tried to reduce their dependence on seasonality and volatility of caribou migrations, salmon runs, mammal harvesting, and the public welfare system. This has proven to be no easy task.

Many of the northern villages are hundreds of miles from each other and as much as 800 miles from Anchorage, the state's major population center. The harbors are often frozen eight to nine months out of the year; and only the larger communities receive commercial air transportation, which is sporadic at best. The general level of education in many villages does not exceed that of grammar school, and housing conditions are some of the worst in the United States. Most of the smaller communities and even some of the larger communities do not have public sewers or water systems. These living conditions are compounded by winter temperatures of 50 to 60 °F below zero, and the sun shines only three to six months out of the year. Yet the Alaskan native holds fast to a life-style that has been traditional since man first crossed the land bridge from Asia.

BACKGROUND OF NATIVE ARTS AND CRAFTS

One of the areas upon which concerned groups have placed much hope for shifting total dependence on subsistence living to a partial cash economy has been the development of the arts and crafts trade. These arts and crafts include ivory carving, basketry, skin sewing, dolls, and other traditional items. These products are not to be confused with curios and mass-produced knick-knacks from Japan and Korea which are marketed as cheap imitations, but are works of art, with an individuality of creativity and time-consuming detail which is reflected in their costliness as well as their quality.

HISTORY OF ARTS AND CRAFTS MARKETING

In the past, the purchasing of native crafts was done in a very casual manner. The common means of selling work was through the local store manager who would give, if not cash, food and trade goods in return or through the local BIA teacher, bush pilot, local missionaries, and finally, the seasonal tourist and professional trader-buyer. Consequently, this marketing pattern was unsatisfactory for the craft people. Even today, professional traders seldom visit a particular village more frequently than once a month.

In 1939 a clearing house for native arts and crafts was formed under the sponsorship of the Bureau of Indian Affairs. The intent of the clearing house was to establish a marketing mechanism and maintain a central inventory of native arts and crafts. Juneau, the state capital, located in the southwestern part of Alaska and approximately 800 to 1,000 miles south of some of these villages, was selected as the headquarters. It was chosen mainly for its port, which was on the regular run of the *North Star,* a ship that was the major source of transport in Alaska in those years. Articles were sent to Juneau on consignment, warehoused, and later marketed in retail and military stores throughout Alaska. This was an earnest attempt to resolve the natives' plight, but, as a whole, the program proved ineffective.

In 1956, the BIA reorganized the original clearing house and established a private, nonprofit cooperative, the Alaska Native Arts and Crafts Cooperative. The payment and marketing policy of the new organization remained the same as that of the original establishment. ANAC was not truly serving in a marketing capacity, although this was to be one of its more vital functions when the organization was initiated. Instead, it continued to serve as a sort of clearing house for the crafts.

The managers of ANAC were not well grounded in exactly what marketing is, as funds were not used for advertising or promotional activities. Indeed, when business became poor and funds short, the books show that expenditures for advertising and travel were cut. Although ANAC was another step forward in straightening out the crafts–cash system, it was far from being a successful organization.

OPERATING HISTORY

In the first year of operation in 1936, ANAC's sales were $29,000. In 1938, the financial figure showed sales at $30,000. For the fiscal year 1939, a value of native arts and crafts rose to $98,000 and thereafter enjoyed a phenomenal rise until the mid-1940s. In part this was due to contracts with the U.S. Antarctic Expedition made in 1939 and 1940 and a number of contracts with the U.S. Army for the sewing of fur garments.

Annual reports give the peak value of native arts and crafts as $485,641 during the fiscal year 1945. Immediately thereafter there was a dramatic drop in the reported value of sales to a low of $101,133.43 in fiscal year 1946. This was attributed to the decline of military personnel in Alaska from a high of 152,000 to a low of only 19,000 in 1946.

During the mid-1950s and 1960s ANAC sales declined, inventories increased, and profits declined accordingly, a trend that continued through the 70's (see Table 1).

THE CONTROVERSY

During this more-than-40-year period, Alaska was rampant with different groups who advocated multiple approaches to marketing the arts and crafts of the native population. Their divergent views compounded an already complex situation. Most of them were quite vociferous about their viewpoints. This field of battle had an inhibiting effect on any spirit of conciliation and rapport. Understandably, little real communication has been established among these groups, as their primary concerns were their respective "causes."

There was one faction whose overriding aim was the preservation of native arts at all costs. These people felt that the real value of native art lay in the creation of superior objects by a few talented individuals. They esteemed these objects of art as potential museum pieces and deplored the intemperate production of pieces of lesser quality as a corruptive force within the creative community. The proponents of this viewpoint turned a deaf ear to the social injustice group, who propounded that the ultimate issue here was the economic betterment of the native groups and that the preservation of the art as an issue was "low man on the totem pole." This group supported the community instituting a regular production-line facility for turning out commercialized versions of native crafts for the tourist trade.

There existed another element, composed of a large percentage of politically active natives whose only concern seemed to be that whatever the program instituted, it should be completely administered by natives. It is no mystery that these people frequently came into direct conflict with the group that advocated the hiring of qualified outside administrative leadership as the most efficient way of getting things done.

The question of whether or not the native people even wanted an organization for marketing their goods looms ominously in the background. The answer to this question has not always been in the obvious positive vein that is expected. Some of the leading craftsmen themselves have expressed doubt in this regard.

THE NEW GENERAL MANAGER

This, then, was the situation when Henry Tiffany III was drafted by the board of directors of ANAC to serve as general manager of the firm and to implement some organizational changes to make it more responsive to the needs of Alaskan natives. Henry Tiffany came to Alaska from New York when he was in his early 20s and experienced success in construction and real estate investments. Through repeated association, due to the mobility demanded of him by his enterprises, he became sensitive to the social and environ-

TABLE 1: *Alaska Native Arts and Crafts Association, Inc. (wholesale)*

	Total net sales	*Cost of sales*	*Gross profit*	*Operating and selling expenses*	*Net operating profit (loss)*	*Total other income expense*	*Net profit (loss)*
Representative year 1970s	$133,800.59	$89,346.07	$44,454.00	$58,943.63	($14,489.11)	($7,029.71)	($21,517.42)
Representative year 1960s	130,395.23	84,015.70	46,379.53	52,268.95	(5,889.42)	(7,960.71)	(13,850.13)
Representative year 1950s	181,799.49	129,669.73	52,129.76	46,696.66	5,433.10	272.87	5,705.97

mental difficulties unique to the Alaskan natives. This concern, as well as a natural appreciation of fine crafts and a desire to see the art form preserved, led him to accept the position as general manager of ANAC. In accepting this post he stipulated that ANAC would sever its connection with the Bureau of Indian Affairs, a condition with which the federal agency concurred.

EXPANSION OF ANAC

After three months of research in the development of a long-range organizational plan, the directors met with the new general manager, who presented to them the following proposal: ANAC would open and operate a retail outlet in Anchorage across the street from Alaska's largest hotel. The new retail outlet would include a show room for direct sales to the public, and approximately half of the 2,000-square-feet store was set aside for craft demonstrations by the artists for the public.

At that time it was also decided that the policy of ANAC would be to encourage the creation of arts and crafts which aspired to the quality sought after by museums and exclusive art stores, and it would discourage the poorer quality of work or mass production of existing designs. Tiffany also proposed that ANAC would become involved in the training of its members and sponsoring of conferences plus promotion to the public in order to advance Alaskan crafts to acceptance as an art form.

With the approval of the board of directors, Henry Tiffany embarked on the program of expansion; and, in the ensuing months, he developed a cooperative relationship with over 120 villages statewide; and the buyer network was established in 12 of those villages. He moved the Juneau retail operation from the back of an old building to the Juneau retail center near the ferry system and the tourist trade. To accommodate the wholesale business, a loan was obtained for a 4,000-square-foot warehouse erected near the Anchorage Municipal Airport, at which time the wholesale operation was moved from Juneau to the new facilities.

The new general manager introduced the mechanics for a rebate system to reward craftsmen for superior work whereby the buyers used a quadruplicate invoice upon which the buyer's and craftsman's names were recorded plus the item purchased. Where products sold for a higher price due to superior craftsmanship, the craftsman received a quality rebate. A system for providing craft supplies through the native stores was also introduced by Mr. Tiffany. In essence, ANAC was to provide a supply of craft materials to each village store on consignment in each village that contained an ANAC buyer. This required $300 to $500 to supply the minimum requirements of each village.

The final and most critical element of the new program was the establishment of cash buyers in each of the craft-producing villages. The success of the rebate system and the craft supplies all hinged on having a good buyers' network. To establish such a network, it was proposed that an ANAC representative would visit each village to study the needs of the craftsman, establish a working relationship with the local governing council, study the community's social and economic base, and interview candidates who were interested in serving as an ANAC buyer. The selection and existence of a buyer was completely voluntary and was determined by the local community leaders. It was agreed that most buyers would receive somewhere between 10 and 20% of the value of the items purchased. The buyer was left with cash ranging from between $200 and $1,500.

In addition to the expansion program, Tiffany undertook a personal campaign to educate the public in native arts and crafts—his goal ultimately being the preservation of the arts and the halting of imports and poor-quality craftsmanship.

DEFICITS INCREASE AT ACCELERATED RATE

After several months of operation, with deficits amassing and considerable creditor pressure ensuing, Henry Tiffany wrote a memo to the ANAC board of directors, shown in Exhibit 1.

EXHIBIT 1: ***Memorandum from Henry Tiffany***

During our expansionary period, operating deficits have continued to mount at an accelerated rate (see Tables A and B). A major contributing force in this state of affairs in the buyer system. The system is operating at minimal efficiency, for multiple reasons. Many native buyers entered the program handicapped by both educational and cultural inadequacies. Many did not understand the recordkeeping system; consequently, they are often unable to account for funds either by their presence or absence. Quality is often overlooked in the subjective viewpoint of the buyers, who are not capable of discerning the very best work from those pieces of less worth. Also, as a result of their cultural heritage, nepotism often sets in, which further adds to the problem of second-best material being occasionally purchased for top dollars.

Another contributing factor to the monetary deficits is that retail sales in the Anchorage store are not meeting sales objectives and projections. Although the Anchorage retail outlet is in a high-foot-traffic district of Anchorage and located across from the state's largest hotel, its sales are disappointing. The problem is caused in part

TABLE A: ***Alaska Native Arts and Crafts, current financial statement retail operation***

Assets				
Current assets				
Cash		$ 3,341.89		
Credit cards and layaways		525.68		
Accounts receivable	$ 3,816.21			
Less res. B/D	(1,166.58)	3,002.74		
Inventories (see Schedule A)				
Arts and crafts, Juneau		27,449.80		
Craft supplies, Juneau		1,332.75		
Arts and crafts, Anchorage		32,310.55		
General supplies		2,500.00		
Collection		26,195.80		
Total inventories	$89,788.90			
Total current assets			$ 96,306.10	
Other assets				
Prepaid expense		$ 2,319.85		
Clearing account[a]		4,994.68		
Fixed assets		18,531.57		
Deposits		50.00		
Investments		30,000.00		
Total other assets			$ 55,896.10	
Total assets				$152,202.20
Liabilities and capital				
Current liabilities		$114,539.49		
Long-term liabilities		195,346.75		
Total liabilities			$309,886.24	
Membership fees		$ 926.00		
Retained earnings		(93,591.73)		
Loss from operation		(65,018.31)		
See schedule C				
Fees and retained earnings (deficit)			$(157,684.04)	
Total liabilities and capital				$152,202.50

Schedule C, Income vs. Expense (Income Statement)		
	Juneau to date	Anchorage to date
Sales, arts and crafts	$57,105.32	$91,840.56
Sales, craft supplies	2,319.22	
Repair income	20.60	
Miscellaneous income	75.00	1,502.88
Returns and allowance	(193.58)	(450.00)
Sales discounts[a]	(2,428.60)	(1,621.00)
Sales commission	(344.66)	(20.00)
Postage	–	68.00
Net sales	$56,553.30	$91,320.42
Inventory cost	(40,108.88)	(64,676.45)
Gross profit	$16,444.42	$26,643.97
Expenses	48,264.60	59,842.10
Net loss	$(31,820.18)	$(33,198.13)

[a]Includes credit card discounts.

TABLE B: ***Alaska Native Arts and Crafts, current balance sheet wholesale operation***

Assets				
Current assets				
Cash		$ 936.12		
Buyers fund		1,170.60		
Receivables				
Co-op (intercompany)		38,453.72		
Accounts receivable	$32,612.27			
Less res. B/D	(2,760.00)	29,852.27		
Other receivables		3,806.17		
Inventories (see Schedule A)				
Arts and crafts		11,334.23		
Craft supplies		16,120.64		
General supplies		4,325.43		
Total inventories	$31,780.30			
Total currest assets			$105,999.18	
Other assets				
Prepaid expenses		$ 4,669.77		
Clearing account		8,001.10		
Fixed assets		213,234.18		
Deposits		17,766.40		
Total other assets			$243,671.35	
Total assets				$349,670.53

Liabilities and capital				
Current liabilities		$153,817.86		
Long-term liabilities		344.669.29		
Total liabilities			$498,487.15	
Capital stock		$ 600.00		
Paid in capital		48,828.00		
Preferred stock		572.00		
Retained earnings	(127,304.84)			
Loss from operation	(71,511.78)	(198,826.62)		
Total capital and retained earnings			(148,816.62)	
Total liabilities and capital				$349,670.53

Schedule E, Income vs. Expenses (Statement of Income)

	To date
Sales	
Wholesale	$112,334.84
Intercompany (Co-op)	82,193.98
Craft supplies	20,415.33
Retail	54.11
Catalogs	697.50
Repair income	78.00
Miscellaneous income	3,596.87
Postage, out	1,575.76
Gross sales	$220,946.39
Less:	
Returns	$ 14.00
Discounts	129.26
Sales commissions	3,391.22
Net sales	3,534.48
Net sales	$217,411.91
Cost of goods sold	$152,442.65
Catalog expenses	1,225.88
Postage, freight in	622.30
Breakage, etc.	339.00
	$154,629.83
Gross profit	$ 62,782.08
Expenses	134,293.86
Net operating loss	$(71,511.78)

by the fact that the store has poor window visibility and gives the impression of being more of a museum than a retail business. Consequently, I recommend that we move the store to a different section of Anchorage's downtown area—one more closely associated with the native community.

Figuring largely in the failure of the expansion program coming to fruition is the evolution of a conflict arising from the very system which it doomed. The structure of ANAC is such that a large volume of trade is essential to support the overhead incurred by the new warehouse and the two retail outlets. It has become apparent that high-quality artwork is not available to meet the sales volume needed to support such a system. Consequently, and contrary to the ANAC marketing philosophy, inferior work would have to be purchased to infuse the operation with the cash flow necessary to its survival. I recommend that we begin to nullify the policy of expansion and initiate the mechanics of contracting ANAC's exploratory tentacles of growth into a more compact and refined body of endeavor, the aims of which are more consistent with our original goals.

In an attempt to reverse the increasing deficit position, we should sell the Juneau retail store and move the merchandise in the wholesale warehouse to the Anchorage retail establishment and sell the warehouse. The warehouse should bring a price of $185,000, which will pay off the mortgage on it. A new buyer system must also be instituted.

The financial losses incurred by the firm are of a critical nature and immediate steps must be instituted to reverse the trend. However, we should not be discouraged, as ANAC is a very successful enterprise. In the early years of the formation of ANAC our artists made, at best, a nominal wage. Today, a few artists earn a wage comparable to high-paying white-collar jobs in Anchorage, Alaska. A couple of artists have gained such national prominence that they have almost outgrown ANAC and are being courted by patrons of museums and establishments which exhibit the finest examples of American art.

THE THREAT OF RUMOR TO THE NONPROFIT ORGANIZATION

CHARLES S. MADDEN

THE CASE OF THE MARCH OF DIMES: WHEN THE RUMOR IS FALSE

Alexander James could not recall having been faced with such a problem in his three years as executive director of the local March of Dimes affiliate. As he sat preparing a recommendation to his board of directors, he reviewed the sequence of events that had led his organization from being one of the most respected local charities with contributions of over $600,000 a year, to its present state of controversy with contributions running only about one-third of normal.

James recalled that he had been making arrangements with a group of fraternity people at the local university for a ''dance-a-thon'' when a call came in from his chairman of fund raising, Alice Dobbs. Miss Dobbs asked if she could meet with him to discuss a rather serious charge that had been made by one of their traditionally most generous contributors. James recalled that he laughed when she first told him of the rumor that March of Dimes funds were being used to pay for abortions. Miss Dobbs further explained that she had received a number of phone calls from past donors canceling their pledges while refusing to give a reason for their actions. She felt that it all might be related. His immediate reaction had been to ignore it, but after talking with two other March of Dimes board members, he began to realize the seriousness of the situation.

In the early days of the March of Dimes organization, the purpose of the charity had been to raise monies to fund research that would lead to a cure for polio. It had been something of a ''grass-roots'' volunteer movement that had involved

Prepared by Charles S. Madden, Assistant Professor of Marketing, Texas A&M University.

many hundreds of thousands of door-to-door fund raisers. Upon the successful development of a polio preventative vaccine, the organization went through a temporary identity crisis, resulting in the rededication of the organization to the prevention and treatment of birth defects. Shortly after embarking on the development of goals and methods to be used by this new March of Dimes organization, the question of genetic counseling was raised. In genetic counseling, couples with a family history of conditions leading to a high risk of birth defects are advised concerning their family planning options. From time to time, a couple being advised of a very high risk of birth defects has chosen to have an abortion in those states accepting such a situation as grounds for abortion. More frequently, counseling is done prior to pregnancy with no abortion involved. The March of Dimes' primary thrust is not in that area, however, and rarely is directly involved with such a result of genetic counseling. Clearly, March of Dimes has never funded abortions.

James recalled having been quizzed about any potential link between March of Dimes funds and abortions when speaking before a women's service organization several months ago. He had thought it rather strange at the time, but realized later that because of a very substantial number of Roman Catholics in the local community and a resulting active "Right to Life" antiabortion group, that any potential relationship between a public charity and a pro-abortion position would routinely be scrutinized very thoroughly. He felt that his explanation, differentiating genetic counseling from the mistaken pro-abortion position, had been more than adequate at the time. Thus, when this rumor surfaced, he made every effort to track down its source. After dozens of phone calls, which led in circles, he finally decided that the original source of the rumor was no longer important. Strangely, it seemed that the very act of tracing the rumor had a tendency to confirm it. He had almost decided to ignore the rumor when he was contacted by a local television talk show host, who invited him to appear with the president of the local "Right to Life" group to debate the merits of the March of Dimes' recent "pro-abortion" position.

James had a sinking feeling that he had lost control of the situation as he called Edna Winter, the Right to Life president. Mrs. Winter explained that she had been unaware of the March of Dimes' pro-abortion stance prior to having been contacted by the television station, but seemed eager to have such a forum. James tried to convince Mrs. Winter that the March of Dimes had no position at all on abortion, but she seemed unconvinced. Her final statement led James to believe that she might press for an appearance to condemn the March of Dimes with or without him. By this time, James was having trouble keeping two of his key directors from resigning from the board, not because they believed the rumor, but because they felt their position in the community was being jeopardized because of adverse publicity.

It seemed that the real position of the March of Dimes had become immaterial. The only thing that seemed to matter was the rumor. In several years of attempting to generate a positive public relations program, Alexander James found it ironic that this was the first time he could recall being invited to appear on television to talk about the March of Dimes.

An inadvertent by-product of the controversy was revealed by an annual telephone survey conducted by a marketing research class at the local University. Of the sample of 1400, 48% of the respondents volunteered the March of Dimes in unaided recall as a health-related nonprofit organization when asked to name several that came to mind. In the three previous surveys, the March of Dimes had never done better than 28%. What bothered him, however, was that in questions concerning financial support and willingness to volunteer for such organizations, the March of Dimes slipped from 16% to 11% in willingness to give and from 9% to 3% in proneness to volunteer. When James saw those figures, he realized that the rumor had already taken its toll.

Thus, as James prepared to address an emergency meeting of the board of directors, he felt that the situation had become a no-win game. If he appeared on television to deny the rumor, he risked legitimizing the rumor because all of the advance promotions for the program would mention aspects of the rumor without disclosing the March of Dimes' true position on the matter. If, on the other hand, he did not appear on television, he risked innuendo and misinformation, leading the public to believe that the rumor was really true. In addition to that, he felt the rumor had the capability of destroying the local organization if allowed to continue. Although he had not yet heard from the national organization, he was already concerned that the rumor would spread to jeopardize the program in other cities.

THE CASE OF THE WADE COUNTY REHABILITATION CENTER: WHEN THE RUMOR IS TRUE

For the past eight years the Wade County Rehabilitation Center had been associated as a local affiliate of the Easter Seal Society of America. During that period of time, the relationship between the WCRC and the state and national Easter Seal organizations had been mutually beneficial. The local organization enjoyed widespread support in a city of 85,000 and the surrounding area of another 35,000. The state Easter Seal Society provided periodic advice and support services to the local affiliate, especially with regard to fund-raising activities.

The only problems that had emerged in recent years were in the area of fund-raising. The Rehab Center (as it was commonly called) had conducted a fund-raising activity the previous year, on the suggestion of the national organization. The event was called the "basketball shoot-out" and involved having students in grades 4 through 12 participate in the enlistment of pledges from friends based on the number of basketball goals they could shoot in a three-minute period. It had been very successful in its first year, raising $20,132 with 256 students participating. The success of the event attracted the attention of the state Easter Seal affiliate organization, who demanded half of all contributions collected outside Wade County in outlying schools. The board of the Rehab Center was very disappointed by this policy, as they had done all of the work to promote the fund-raiser in the outlying schools. Other confrontations between the state organization and the local Rehab Center had occurred over the last three years. At other times the working relationship between the Rehab Center and the state Easter Seal Society had been congenial, with some ideas offered by the state organization being used by the local center.

A recent conflict of goals between the Rehab Center and the national Easter Seal organization had resulted from a national telethon. The Easter Seal telethon was being held at a time just prior to the beginning of a major capital fund-raising drive to raise $1 million for a new Rehab Center facility. It was felt by the center's board of directors that local participation in the telethon would diffuse interest in the building program. It was obvious that even though the local Easter Seal affiliate had not carried the telethon on the local station, other stations in surrounding communities would be broadcasting the telethon into the center's principal city. Thus, although there was no local effort, there was a chance that potential donors would make the association between the telethon and the building-fund drive. The cost of participation in the telethon ultimately settled the question in favor of not taking part in the event.

Whenever such conflicts arose between the Rehab Center and the state or national Easter Seal Society, there was always some talk about discontinuation of the affiliation with the society. Jim Drake, the executive director, discouraged such talk because he felt the support of research and other common activities made the society worthwhile to member affiliates. As a licensed physical therapist, Drake felt some professional obligation to keep his local organization affiliated with a state and national organization. He pointed out to the board whenever conflict arose between the center and the society, differences were always in the area of fund raising and were never in more substantive areas. The board agreed that the commitment of the Easter Seal Society to the ideal of rehabilitating crippled children was consistent with their own purposes. That single commonality of purpose kept the center from seriously questioning the leadership of the society.

Jim Drake felt that this traditional acceptance of leadership from the society may be jeopardized as he opened a publicity package from the national society containing a new fund-raising promotion. The "Vote For Your Favorite Bartender" campaign surprised him, as his previous experience with the Easter Seal Society had never included any promotion as controversial as this. It was obvious to Drake that, in the local area, the "bartender" promotion would lose the Rehab Center more friends than it would acquire for them. A significant part of the local community objected to the consumption of alcohol on moral grounds and would find an association between the traditional connotations of "Easter Seal" and an alcohol-related promotion very personally offensive.

Donations made for the Easter Seal Society were to be made in the form of "votes" for a particular bartender. The bartender receiving the greatest number of votes would be named the "favorite" bartender in the area/state/nation. A popular brand of whiskey was sponsoring the contest, with a picture of their product prominently displayed on advertisements promoting the event.

When the idea of the "bartender contest" was presented to the fund-raising committee of the Rehab Center, it was rejected by a vote of 7 to 0. The word about the promotion leaked to the rest of the Rehab Center board of directors from the fund-raising committee rather quickly. There was a proposal at the following monthly meeting that a letter be drafted to the national Easter Seals Society protesting the "bartender" promotion as being in poor taste. The proposal died for lack of a second, but there was a general feeling of relief that the promotion was not to be used locally.

All might have gone well after that except that the Easter Seal Society in another nearby city had decided to run the promotion, using many television spots that were broadcast into the Wade County area. Soon after the beginning of the promotion a trickle of phone calls were received asking whether the Rehab Center was running the promotion locally. A firm denial seemed to satisfy all inquiries. A small group of five (out of 26) Rehab Center board members drafted a letter (shown in Exhibit 1) to the state and national Easter Seal Society.

Although the letter was never mailed to Easter Seal officials because the full board refused to approve its being sent (vote 10 to 12, with 4 members absent). Jim Drake made a last-minute plea for the Rehab Center board to take a more diplomatic stand on the question. He felt that the organization could dissent from the position of the state and national organizations without embarrassing them.

EXHIBIT 1: ***Letter to the Executive Director, Easter Seal Society of America***

Dear Mr. Director:

The undersigned board members of the Wade County Rehabilitation Center, a local affiliate of your organization, must strenuously object to the forthcoming fund raising project, "Elect Your Favorite Bartender."

While some of us feel it is degrading for the Easter Seal Society to provide a platform for the alcohol industry to peddle its products, that is not the primary thrust of our objection. Consider the following ways in which alcoholic beverage use and abuse affect the problems we are dedicated to fighting:

1. A substantial number of disabling and lethal cases of child abuse are related to alcohol each year.
2. In the history of our own small rehabilitation unit, several hundred cases of alcohol-related strokes, heart attacks, and other disabling ailments can be identified.
3. Each year approximately one half of the fatal and disabling automobile accidents in this country are alcohol related. We get far too many of the victims of this tragic statistic in our center each year.

Perhaps if we were less concerned with fund raising and more concerned with people, we could take a stand against alcohol abuse and have fewer people to rehabilitate. It has been facetiously suggested that if we worked out a financially attractive deal with the drug dealers I suppose we would "elect our favorite pusher." Where do we draw the line?

Perhaps this seems something of an overreaction to this promotion, but we are deeply disturbed by this course of action and trust you will reconsider the Society's involvement in such a project.

Thank you for your thoughtful consideration.

Sincerely,

Robert Smithson
Wanda Meeker
Harvey Pickett
Lloyd Davis
Charles Everett

There was still some fear on the board that people in the local area would associate their efforts with the "bartender promotion." Some objected for reasons associated with the tie-in of Easter Seal with alcohol. Others felt that associating any product, alcoholic or otherwise, with the Easter Seal Society was improperly using the name of the society. After such feelings were aired at a luncheon meeting of the board, Jim Drake hired a local marketing research firm to conduct a telephone interview in a sample of the community testing the following questions:

1. Do people perceive a difference between the Wade County Rehabilitation Center and the Easter Seal Society?
2. Do people relate what they see and hear about the Easter Seal Society in other locations to the Wade County Rehabilitation Center?
3. If they disagreed with a policy or action of a national charity, would they withhold money from the local affiliate of that organization?
4. Would people find an association between a health-related nonprofit organization and the alcoholic beverage industry offensive?
5. If the answer to question 4 is yes, would it affect their giving to such an organization?

A summary answering each question accompanied by a research report was received two weeks later. The summary is presented in Exhibit 2.

Drake felt that the image of the Rehab Center should be insulated from changes in the Easter Seal Society's image after this recent controversy. He felt that the Rehab Center must establish a clear strategy for its public relations functions rather than just continue to "fight fires." Thus, as he prepared to report back to the board on the current problem, he looked for ways to improve the image of the Rehab Center while not limiting his response only to the "bartender promotion."

EXHIBIT 2: ***Results of telephone interviews of 700 households in Wade County***

---

1. Do people perceive a difference between the Wade County Rehabilitation Center and the Easter Seal Society?

   While only 23% volunteered the WCRC as one of the local charities that come to mind (unaided recall), over 75% identified it in a list of real and bogus organizations as a local charity. Only 9% of those responding could volunteer an affiliation between the WCRC and the Easter Seal Society, only 16% said that there was, 29% said that there probably was not, and 55% were either unsure or did not know.

2. Do people relate what they see and hear about the Easter Seal Society in other locations to the Wade County Rehabilitation Center?

   Of the 16% saying that there was a local Easter Seal affiliate, almost all agreed that all affiliates of that society used the same themes and goals. Of the 9% who connected the WCRC to Easter Seals, almost all (94%) felt that the WCRC probably acted autonomously from other affiliates.

3. If they disagreed with a policy or action of a national charity, would they withhold money from the local affiliate of that organization?

   36% yes
   19% no
   45% undecided or would decide on a case-by-case basis

4. Would people find an association between a health-related nonprofit organization and the alcoholic beverage industry offensive?

   59% yes
   13% no
   18% undecided or would decide on a case-by-case basis

   This question was further analyzed by respondents' use of alcohol.

Drink alcoholic beverages	62%
Do not drink alcoholic beverages	36%
Refused to say	2%

Would people find an association . . . offensive?

	Yes	*No*	*Undecided*	
Drink	31%	11%	20%	62%
Do not drink	28%	2%	6%	36%
	59%	13%	26%	

Opinions of those who refused to say if they drank are not included in this table, thus adding only to 98%.

5. If the answer to question 4 was yes, would it affect their giving to such an organization?

   Of the 59% who said yes:

   91% (of that number) would affect giving
   6% (of that number) would not affect giving
   3% (of that number) undecided

KENT STATE UNIVERSITY: COPING WITH AN IMAGE CRISIS

"Kent State University was perceived by the respondents as having a friendly and attractive campus with an active social life and considerable freedom to 'do your own thing.' . . . It is still viewed as a school which has had campus unrest. Although students generally claimed unrest was unimportant in their college choice decision, it still showed up as the most negative component of attitude."

This was the conclusion of a study done by Kent State University marketing professors Albert Heinlein and Robert Krampf. Krampf and Heinlein obtained 200 responses from a sample of 1,000 college freshmen who sent their ACT scores to Kent State during the 1975–1976 academic year, two years prior to the 1977 Kent State campus protests concerning the construction of a gymnasium near the site of the May 1970 shootings.

Dr. Bruce Allen, special assistant to the president at Kent State, was reviewing the Heinlein/Krampf study and other data in preparation for a special student recruiting campaign. The date was July 1, 1978, and Dr. Allen, in conjunction with KSU's advertising/public relations agency, had been allocated approximately $100,000 to implement a program to avoid a 30 to 40% decline in the 1978 freshmen class. The situation was critical, as shown in Table 1. These figures were especially distressing when considered in the context of a 1,000-person decline in student enrollment the prior year. The university was already in serious financial difficulties and another bad year could result in retrenchment and a severe campus morale problem.

BACKGROUND

In preparation for the emergency student recruiting campaign, Dr. Allen and the ad agency reviewed the history of Kent State's image problems:

- Prior to May 4, 1970, Kent State was a relatively unknown regional university in a rural area located 15 miles from Akron and 60 miles from Cleveland.
- On May 4, 1970, 78 Ohio national guardsmen fired 54 rounds of ammunition into a group of

Prepared by Dr. Bruce H. Allen, Associate Professor of Marketing, De Paul University.

TABLE 1: ***Statistics on new undergraduate admissions***

Reporting date	Cumulative total new undergraduate student admissions For 1977	For 1978	Change 1977–1978
March	2454	1434	−1021 (−42%)
May	3263	2088	−1145 (−36%)
June	3905	2515	−1390 (−36%)

Vietnam war protesters on the KSU campus who were demonstrating against the policies of the Nixon administration. Four students were killed and nine were wounded. Following the shootings, there were numerous commissions, committees, and court actions reviewing and investigating the courses of the tragedy.

- As a consequence of the unfavorable publicity surrounding the shootings, Kent State's enrollment growth trend was ended in 1971. Total enrollment declined until 1975, when it again approached the level of the early 1970s. (see Table 2). The impact of the image difficulties was clearly manifest in the 28% decline in the 1971 freshmen class (see Tables 3 and 4).
- In response to this image problem, Kent State established a strong public affairs and development division, which coordinated 1973, 1974, 1975, and 1976 radio/TV/print/advertising/public relations campaigns (see Exhibit 1).
- Kent State University enrollment in the fall of 1975 and 1976 reached levels approaching the peak numbers in 1969 and 1970.
- In 1976, the KSU board of trustees voted to construct a gymnasium annex adjoining the present fieldhouse structure located near the site where national guardsmen pursued student protesters and the shootings occurred. Construction was to begin in 1977.
- In late 1976 and 1977, KSU student leaders, some faculty, and other former antiwar leaders voiced anger and protest over the location of the gym annex. They accused the KSU board of administration of a "cover-up" attempt at "burying" the KSU shootings incident and its symbolism in an effort to camouflage the guilty parties. The media publicized the story.
- In spring 1977, students and other sympathizers set up a "tent city" on the proposed construction site. The university president did not remove them and subsequently resigned. The media publicized the story.
- In summer 1977, students left for vacation and a fence was built around the construction site. Protesting students, clergy, and outside sympathizers climbed the fence, were arrested, and taken to jail. The media heavily publicized the story.
- In summer 1977, the university ran an advertising campaign to counter negative publicity. The interim president served as spokesperson (see Exhibits 2 and 3).
- Fall 1977 brought a 1,000-student enrollment decline (see Exhibit 4) and a massive October antigym demonstration on the Kent State cam-

TABLE 2: ***Full-time equivalent enrollment (combined fall and summer enrollment eligible for state subsidy)***

Year	*FTE*[a]	*Fall headcount*
1960	9,984	9,974
1961	10,937	10,510
1962	11,770	11,061
1963	13,294	11,949
1964	15,342	13,425
1965	14,809	14,833
1966	18,217	17,223
1967	19,038	18,528
1968	20,792	19,996
1969	21,930	20,747
1970	22,332	20,950
1971	21,774	20,271
1972	21,079	19,773
1973	19,607	18,534
1974	19,309	18,360
1975	20,109	20,060

[a]Full-time equivalent students.

Source: Ohio Basic Data Series.

TABLE 3: ***Fall headcount enrollments,*[a] *1969–1977***

Rank	*1969*	*1970*	*1971*	*1972*	*1973*	*1974*	*1975*	*1976*	*1977*
Freshmen	7,429	7,488	5,372	5,362	4,958	5,305	6,030	6,147	5,503
Sophomore	3,665	3,613	4,119	3,550	3,196	3,216	3,380	3,470	3,309
Junior	3,289	3,573	3,713	3,679	3,264	3,132	3,250	3,164	3,145
Senior	3,605	3,519	3,777	3,776	3,436	3,155	3,375	3,270	3,106
Special undergrad	144	181	253	251	270	279	363	367	317
Total undergrad	18,132	18,374	17,234	16,618	15,124	15,087	16,398	16,418	15,380
Master's	1,943	2,016	2,048	2,002	2,102	2,142	2,321	2,415	2,444
Doctoral	512	613	703	681	778	768	744	746	804
Special grad	323	354	438	430	472	459	597	795	725
Total grad	2,778	2,983	3,189	3,113	3,352	3,369	3,662	3,956	3,973
No rank	3	13	371	24	83	2	0	0	0
Grand total	20,913	21,370	20,794	19,755	18,559	18,458	20,060	20,374	19,353

[a]Official 15th-day enrollment figures.

Source: Registrar's Report.

TABLE 4: ***Percentage change headcount enrollment,*[a] *1969–1977 (fall quarter)***

	1970	*1971*	*1972*	*1973*	*1974*	*1975*	*1976*	*1977*	*Change 1969–1977*
Freshmen	+0.8	−28.3	−0.2	−7.5	+7.0	+13.7	+1.9	−10.5	−25.9
Sophomore	−1.4	+14.0	−13.8	−10.0	+0.6	+5.1	+2.7	−4.6	−9.7
Junior	+8.6	+3.9	−0.9	−11.3	−4.0	+3.8	−2.7	−0.6	−4.4
Senior	−2.4	+7.3	0	−9.0	−8.2	+7.0	−3.1	−5.0	−13.8
Special undergrad	+25.7	+39.8	−0.8	+7.6	+3.3	+30.1	+1.1	−13.6	+120.1
Total undergrad	+1.3	−6.2	−3.6	−9.0	−0.2	+8.7	+0.1	−6.3	−15.2
Master's	+3.8	+1.6	−2.2	+5.0	+1.9	+8.4	+4.0	+1.2	+25.8
Doctoral	+19.7	+14.7	−3.1	+14.2	−1.3	−3.1	+0.3	+7.8	+57.0
Special grad	+9.6	+23.7	−1.8	+9.8	−2.8	+30.1	+33.2	−8.8	+124.5
Total grad	+7.4	+6.9	−2.4	+7.7	+0.5	+8.7	+8.0	+0.4	+43.0
Grand total	+2.2	−2.7	−5.0	−6.1	−0.5	+8.7	+1.6	−5.0	−7.5

[a]Official 15th-day enrollment figures.

Source: Registrar's Report.

pus. A rally was held on the campus, with a large group of students and former antiwar activists in attendance. Following the rally, groups of protesters began to tear down the fence, the County Sheriff's troups used tear gas and force to restrain them, and a number of persons were arrested. The media were out in force to cover the story.

EXHIBIT 1: *Ad in May and June issues of* **Time** *and* **Newsweek**

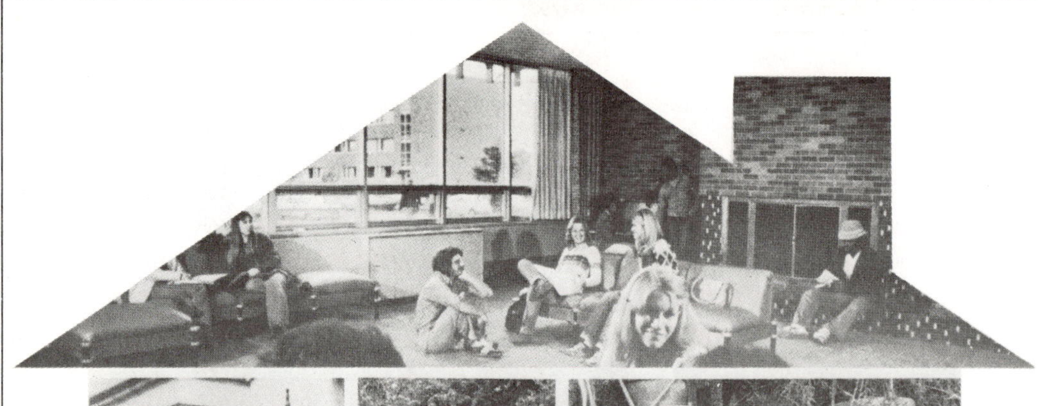

Learning is Something You Live With ... at Kent State

Can you trap learning within the covers of a book? Hem it in by the walls of a classroom? Measure it by a clock?

At Kent State, we believe learning is something you live with . . . We believe an idea becomes an experience and then a commitment.

An idea from a biology class last week can come alive when you walk through Riveredge Park; your experience in the student-run Ambulance Service will help management class ideas make sense. We believe doing can be learning, just as learning is doing.

Kent State is a community for learning, an easy drive from anywhere in northeastern Ohio.

Because it is so convenient, fully 25 per cent of our 20,000 Kent Campus students choose to live at home and commute. The living styles of our students are as varied as the 167 ways to learn a living offered at Kent State.

On campus, students live in traditional residence halls, apartments, and in special living-learning communities where they share their experiences while majoring in architecture, music, foreign languages, peaceful change, and honors studies.

Kent State University Supports Equal Opportunity in Education and Employment

Students living off campus in fraternity and sorority and other private housing are linked to campus by a modern, "no-fare" bus system.

Discover the Kent State you need to know—the 1.2 million volume open stack library, our expanded research facilities, the experimental theatres, Blossom Center, major college sports and nature conservancy centers.

Kent State University is a major Ohio research institution with special interests ranging from America's first novel to liquid crystals, from water pollution control to computer-assisted instruction, from its laboratory school to its Gilbert and Sullivan program.

Kent is all you need from a university and more . . .

Kent State University

a Living/ Learning Center for Northeast Ohio

FOR INFORMATION, Call 1-216-672-2001

EXHIBIT 2: ***Television ad campaign***

EXHIBIT 3: ***KSU president's advertising***

Message Analysis

While a 60-decond message contains only about 150 words, it is entirely possible to convey many pieces of information both directly and subliminally. This was true in the construction of the message used in this campaign.

A dissection of the message would reveal many elements—not all of which would be consciously perceived by the viewers any more than attitudes formed by the broadcast of news about the protests were consciously perceived. Among those elements were these:

Message: Actual script	*Analysis*
Visual: a message of importance to all Ohioans.	An authority-enhancing device aimed at increasing the credibility of the message (i.e., this is not a routine message or commercial).
If you've been watching the TV news lately, you might think the only thing that goes on at Kent State is demonstrating.	A straightforward admission of fact—with a wry twist—aimed at increasing viewership, comprehension, and credibility. Too often, by failing to state the obvious negative, such messages reduce rather than increase believability.
In fact, the business of Kent State is teaching and learning, looking for the solutions to pressing human problems, helping people to find career opportunities, and serving the citizens of Ohio.	Use of word *business* is intentional to underscore positive connotations of the word fiscally and in terms of management. Subliminally, this challenges assumptions that the management of Kent State encourages anarchy, etc. The listing of goals might have been news to many viewers. The visuals enhanced these concepts with science research, medical training, and other strongly supported and accepted programs.
That's what Kent State is really all about. When fall term begins on September 12, some 19,000 students will come to the Kent campus and another 8,000 to	"What it's really all about" underscores for the viewer to overlay this impression over previous mental images and to accept the new images as

the seven regional campuses.	more accurate. "When fall term begins" by its very utterance denies any concerns that the university might not or should not reopen. The date of September 12 is a hidden advertisement to potential students and an advisory to existing students since the quarter began two weeks early this year. "Some 19,000 students"—aimed at subliminally impressing the fact the demonstrations involved only a small portion of the student body. "The seven regional campuses"—underscoring another piece of news to many viewers—that Kent is a regional educational system.
And we expect several thousand more for our continuing education programs.	Intended to further broaden the image of the university as serving more than young people. . . .
They will have a common purpose—to study in more than 160 career fields.	Underscores the broad curriculum at Kent. "To study" again subliminally the impression of nonstop protest because these people have study as "a common purpose."
We have a job to do at Kent State. . . .	"Job"—not "goal," not "mission," not "objective," but plain, Anglo-Saxon "job." It is clear that we mean business, that we're not scatterbrained or ivory tower fakirs.
For our students and for all of the citizens of Ohio . . .	Again, broaden the base beyond those we serve directly to all of those watching. . . .
And that is to help people by providing them the best in educational opportunities.	"Helping people" and "providing opportunities" are the key terms.
That's our job and we're doing it.	A bit pugnacious but intentionally so. Again, we're hardheaded about what we're supposed to be doing. This is softened somewhat by the visual of beautiful, peaceful campus—another subliminal message.
Visual: For information, call, etc.	Intended to pick up any individuals who were inspired to action by the message.

EXHIBIT 4

Source: The Daily Kent Stater.

Following the October arrests, the activism calmed but the image of Kent State had been reimplanted in the minds of the northeastern Ohio citizenry as a troubled, radical, unsafe, and unstable campus. The new president had reorganized his administration, four or six vice-presidents had left, and the public relations director had resigned.

Realizing the severe negative fiscal impact another precipitous decline in enrollment would have on the campus, in July 1977, the President assigned Bruce Allen, a KSU marketing professor with expertise in college and university marketing to undertake a special assignment. In conjunction with the Dix and Eaton Public Relations/Advertising Agency, the task was to do what was possible by September to increase enrollment for fall 1978 and to begin recruiting students for fall 1979 (see Exhibit 5). Dr. Allen and the agency realized that a program had to be designed and implemented very quickly.

THE SUMMER 1978 INITIATIVES

In planning the action initiatives to be taken over the summer of 1978, the planning group of Dr. Allen, Dr. Robert McCoy (executive assistant to the president), and the ad agency separated their task into two phases. Phase I was to be focused on an intensive campaign to achieve the maximum enrollment for fall registration in early September. Phase II was the carrying forward of phase I to begin the student recruiting program for the fall quarter of 1979.

The initial step was to initiate a public media communications campaign to reach two basic markets. One market was recent high school graduates who might be undecided about attending college and could be ''last-minute'' full-time student enrollees at Kent State. The other market consisted of older adult part-time students who typically made college attendance decisions near the time of registration. Through research on reasons why students chose to attend Kent State (see Table 5) and on the current study body's permanent residential locations it was determined that the northeastern Ohio corridor encompassing the metropolitan areas of Cleveland, Akron, Canton, and Youngstown, would be targeted through advertising and public relations. This composite market area comprised a population of almost 3 million people.

The planning group also realized that strong

EXHIBIT 5: ***Newspaper ad***

Ad agency retained to 'market' KSU

Kent State University has hired Dix & Eaton Inc., Cleveland-based advertising and public relations firm, to help direct the university's marketing efforts.

Agency officials met last week with representatives of most of the university's departments—from security guards to graduate schools—to discuss the upcoming marketing effort.

KSU has been trying to overcome the negative image created by the student disturbances on campus and the killing and wounding of students eight years ago. But Henry Eaton, president of the agency, said remaking KSU's image is only a part of the problem.

''This is a very real marketing problem,'' said Eaton, noting that the university faces a declining ''market'' of potential students while at the same time facing competition for students from nearby Cleveland State University and state schools in Youngstown and Akron.

''Even if May 4th never happened, the university still would be faced with a critical marketing problem,'' said John R. Wirtz, a Dix & Eaton account executive and a 1974 graduate of the KSU School of Journalism. Wirtz will be on the agency team that will work with university officials to develop the new program.

The agency will be working with Bruce Allen, assistant professor of marketing at the university. The agency already has met with several students and faculty members to get their reactions and comments about the proposed new campaign.

Wirtz said he even had offers of help from a KSU graduate now working for another Cleveland public relations firm.

Although work has just begun on the efforts, the agency said the university is contemplating a short-term media campaign to run in time for the start of fall classes.

Source: The Cleveland Plain Dealer, July 23, 1978.

TABLE 5: ***Criteria used in the college selection process based on responses from Kent State University*** [a]

Criteria [b]	*Number of responses*	*Percent of persons responding*	*Percent of total responses*
Location	54	74.0	19.2
Course of study	37	50.7	13.2
Academic reputation	36	49.3	12.8
Cost	32	43.8	11.4
Size	22	30.1	7.8
Social life	17	23.3	6.0
Appealing surroundings	15	20.5	5.3
Friends/relatives attend	15	20.5	5.3
Physical facilities	15	20.5	5.3
Other	14	19.2	5.0
Faculty/student association	6	8.2	2.1
Activities	5	6.8	1.8
Athletics (intercollegiate)	4	5.5	1.4
Financial aid	3	4.1	1.1
Admission requirements	2	2.7	0.7
Athletics (intramural)	1	1.4	0.4
Parents' approval	1	1.4	0.4
Recommendations of high school counselor	1	1.4	0.4
Recruiting effort	1	1.4	0.4
Total	281		100.0

[a]Based on 73 respondents.

[b]Criteria and number of responses were obtained from analysis of open-ended question concerning college selection criteria.

Source: Robert Cook, Kent State University DBA dissertation, 1977.

competition existed within northeastern Ohio and the remainder of the state for resident students (Ohio State, Bowling Green, Miami University, and others) as well as for commuter students (University of Akron, Cleveland State, Youngstown State, and Case Western Reserve). Community colleges and other four-year private colleges were also competing for high school graduates and adult students. To make matters more serious, Kent State was ranked behind many of its competitive institutions as a first choice of prospective students taking the ACT exam (see Table 6).

The planning group set a goal of having an intensive advertising campaign reaching northeastern Ohio implemented by early August to run for five weeks until registration in early September. Following an analysis of media coverage and costs in light of budget limitations ($100,000 for the entire year), the ad agency recommended a campaign combining radio and print media. Television was ruled out because of the relatively high cost per message and the necessity of covering numerous media markets while targeting on market segments by age and socioeconomic characteristics.

The next step was to arrive at a campaign theme or positioning. The ad agency's first suggestion was rejected. They recommended the use of an upbeat rock-and-roll jingle used for 20 to 30 seconds of a radio ad, with the other 30 seconds

TABLE 6: *Within-state institutional preferences listed according to the number of times selected choice 1, 1977–1978*

College code	*Institution*	*Location*	*First choice*	*Second choice*	*Third choice*
3312	Ohio State University, The	Columbus	10,038	6,931	5,262
3240	Bowling Green State University	Bowling Green	4,621	4,620	3,698
3294	Miami University	Oxford	4,061	3,779	3,159
3340	University of Cincinnati	Cincinnati	3,798	2,943	2,462
3338	University of Akron	Akron	3,044	1,778	1,401
3368	Youngstown State University	Youngstown	2,115	857	710
3314	Ohio University	Athens	2,019	2,595	2,360
3284	Kent State University	Kent	1,926	2,591	1,988
3344	University of Toledo	Toledo	1,559	1,373	1,181
3270	Cleveland State University	Cleveland	1,510	1,340	1,001
3295	Wright State University	Dayton	1,328	1,088	883
3342	University of Dayton	Dayton	741	1,058	1,064
3265	Cuyahoga Community College—Western	Parma	641	378	279
3244	Case Western Reserve University	Cleveland	632	629	629
3310	Ohio Northern University	Ada	492	585	623
3277	Lakeland Community College	Mentor	491	250	194
3261	Columbus Technical Institute	Columbus	482	492	373
3332	Sinclair Community College	Dayton	452	397	349
3236	Baldwin Wallace College	Berea	363	458	411
3242	Capital University	Columbus	358	602	552
	All other in-state institutions		12,584	12,998	12,138
	Total		53,255	47,742	40,717

Source: The American College Testing Service.

conveying a direct action-oriented suggestion for the listeners to enroll at Kent State. Given the high degree of publicity that the university had been experiencing, the administration rejected the idea for fear that the public would see this as a "slick Madison Avenue" desperation attempt by a school in crisis to "drag in additional bodies."

An emergency meeting of the planning group was called to address this problem. Dr. Allen suggested the application of basic marketing principles which state that consumers will purchase a product that is perceived as being different and superior in its ability to meet their needs. The ad agency and the Kent State Communications Department went into a brainstorming session and arrived at the following potential themes for the campaign:

- We are different and we'll show you the difference is better
- Your future is our business
- Plan for tomorrow at KSU
- Have your tomorrow at KSU
- KSU road to everywhere
- Find yourself
- A ticket to where you want to go
- Passport to the future
- Progression to passport
- A different direction
- Kent can

- Kent State is growing great
- The time, the place, the people (your future)
- Because we're different, we're better
- Kent State makes a difference . . .
- . . . Makes all the difference
- It can make a difference for you

The "Kent State Makes a Difference" theme was selected unanimously by the planning group and KSU administration. It was then decided to use satisfied customers—present students, alumni, and parents—to convey the "Kent State Difference" to the public of northeastern Ohio. It was also determined that a variety of spokespersons—by age, ethnicity, program major, and perceived benefits—would be chosen for the campaign. The same spokesperson was to be featured per week, or biweekly, in newspapers and on radio in each major market. Each person would be interviewed concerning their Kent State experiences and excerpts of the interviews would be used in the ads. Newspaper ads would be placed in the entertainment section of the Thursday, Friday, or Saturday edition; radio spots would run during morning and evening "drive" time and late-evening time slots. The advertising campaign was planned to run from August until early September to stimulate fall registrations, and from October through December to influence persons taking the ACT and SAT exams to send their scores to Kent

EXHIBIT 6

Kent State made the difference for Carol Morgan.

Carol Morgan is married, the mother of three children, a full-time junior high school art teacher, and a graduate of Kent State University. She is currently working on a Master of Fine Arts degree at KSU. In her own words, here's how she put the Kent State difference to work for her:

"I think Kent State is a fantastic place. It has one of the top art programs in the entire United States and I really believe it was the best possible place I could have come to school.

"I was out of high school for 10 years before starting college, never had any formal art training, and was scared to death. But the professors I had in my first few courses really helped me. They took a lot of extra time with me, whenever I needed it—and that's something I've never forgotten. It gave me the encouragement I needed to go on.

"I don't think age has anything to do with going to college if you're willing to take the time to learn what you need to know. I'm really pleased with the University and I hope my children will come here. For me, Kent State definitely made the difference."

Put the Kent State difference to work for you. Registration is August 30 to September 18. For more information call us collect at 216/672-2001.

State. Overall, the campaign was budgeted at \$60,000 of the available \$100,000 budget. Exhibits 6 through 10 provide examples of the advertising.

Other phase I enrollment/image initiatives taken involved:

- Formation of the Institutional Advancement Steering Committee to inform the campus what action was being taken to cope with the image and enrollment problems
- Telephone contact with every current student who had not preregistered and applicants who had not completed their admissions process, to determine their status and assist them in registration
- Publication of a back-to-school summer newspaper describing the exciting events planned for the coming academic year
- An in-depth study of why new freshmen visiting the campus for summer orientation chose to attend Kent State
- Other individual public relations activities

PHASE I RESULTS

Following implementation of the first stage of the advertising campaign and other enrollment initiatives, the fall 1978 statistics were compared with those of the previous year (Table 7).

The Kent State administration was very pleased with the progress made between July 1 and October 1978, documented in Table 8.

PHASE II STRATEGY

In late November, the KSU administration wondered whether phase II of the current advertising program should be continued past December

EXHIBIT 7: ***Script for Carol Morgan ad***

KSU Spot 3

Testimonial: Carol Morgan
Ancr. 1: Lee Taylor — *Running time: 60 seconds*
Ancr. 2: Jan Zima — *Mono. 7½ ips*

Music up and under

C.M.: "I'm Carol Morgan, married and the mother of three children. I'm a full-time art teacher in a junior high school, starting my master's work. . . .

"I was, actually, 28 when I started school, and . . . I checked around and it was the best school in the area that I could possibly come to."

L.T.: "Kent State makes a difference."

C.M.: "(And) it did make a difference. I started in a field that was new to me and I was fortunate. . . . I had profs who were willing to take their time to help me and I've never forgotten that. I'm really . . . really pleased with the university. I hope my children will come here."

L.T.: "Kent State makes *all* the difference."

J.Z.: "Put the Kent State difference to work for you. Applications are being accepted now, and registration is August 30 through September 18.

"To get in touch, call us collect at 672-2001. That's 672-2001 . . . and do it today."

L.T.: "Kent State makes all the difference."

C.M.: "It did make the difference for me . . . a great deal."

Music up and out.

EXHIBIT 8

Kent State made the difference for Paul Warfield

Paul Warfield won't have any trouble making the transition from an All-Pro player in the National Football League to a member of the Hall of Fame in Canton, Ohio. It's only a matter of time.

A greater challenge for Warfield—as well as other former athletes—is making the successful transition from one career to another.

In his own words, here's how Kent State University helped Warfield prepare to move from the playing field to broadcasting.

"While I attended Kent State University during the off-season for three years, I was especially impressed by the quality of instruction in the telecommunications program.

"I feel very proud that I was able to go to Kent State. The University's academic program, whether in telecommunications or whatever, is excellent. Depending on what students want, they can find it at Kent State. There are strong academic programs, social life, fraternities and sororities, intercollegiate athletics. It is all at Kent State University.

"Kent State does make a difference."

When you register for pre-college tests—either ACT or SAT—make sure Kent State gets your test results. We'll do the rest. For more information, call the Admissions Office collect at (216) 672-2001.

Kent State
makes a difference

EXHIBIT 9: ***Script for Paul Warfield ad***

KSU spot 6

Testimonial: Paul Warfield
Air: 10/22–10/29
Running time: 60 seconds

Music up and under

Ancr. 1: Paul Warfield talks about Kent State University.

P.W.: Well, I feel very proud that I was able to go here to school and rightfully so, because here in Northeastern Ohio, in television work, there are a lot of Kent State alumni who are doing quite well. There are many others who are working not only on camera but behind camera in Cleveland. . . .

Ancr. 2: Kent State makes a difference.

P.W.: The academic program here, regardless of whether it is in Telecommunications or whatever, is excellent. Depending on what a student wants. I think he can find it here at Kent State. You know, he can find certainly social life, interfraternity life, academics, intercollegiate athletics . . . it is all here at Kent State University. . . .

Ancr. 2: Kent State makes all the difference.

Ancr. 1: Put the Kent State difference to work for you. When taking the ACT or SAT, make sure Kent State gets your test results. To get in touch, call us collect at 672-2001 . . . that's 672-2001.

Ancr. 2: Kent State makes all the difference.

P.W.: It does make a difference.

Music up and out.

1978. An expenditure of $20,000 per month on advertising was a controversial issue among members of the campus community, especially faculty. Faculty and student groups were questioning whether the image problem had naturally subsided with the passage of time, a tranquil campus situation, and lack of media attention. Some academic deans whose budgets had been cut actually believed that the advertising had little or no impact on the enrollment situation and argued that public approval of the new administration's "no nonsense" approach was the cause for the increase in student interest toward KSU. An additional factor affecting the president's decision was that the October 1978 ACT test scores had been received, reflecting a 78% increase over the same

EXHIBIT 10: ***Media buys for Paul Warfield spot 6***

Radio station		*Gross*	*Net*	
WGAR	12 spots at $54 =	$648.00	$ 550.80	
WWWE	12 spots at 66 =	792.00	673.20	
WABQ	15 spots at 12 =	180.00	153.00	
WAKR	10 spots at 47 =	470.00	399.50	
WKNT	24 spots at 8 =	192.00	192.00	(net only)
WKBN-AM	12 spots at 22 =	264.00	264.00	(net only)
WDOK	12 spots at 56 =	624.00	530.40	
		$3,170.00	$2,762.90	

(exhibit continues)

EXHIBIT 10: *continued*

Newspaper		
Plain Dealer (1½)	3 col. × $10 =	$543.90
Beacon Journal (2⅛)	3 col. × 10 =	367.50
Record Courier (1⅜)	4 col. × 10 =	120.40
Canton Repository (1½)	3 col. × 7 =	152.88
Vindicator (1⅝)	3 col. × 7 =	137.55
Reporter (1¾)	3 col. × 7 =	84.00
Call & Post (1⅝)	3 col. × 7 =	73.50
Hub (1⁹/₁₆)	5 col. × 10 =	84.37
Parma Post	3 col. × 7 =	132.30
South Euclid	3 col. × 7 =	107.10
Shaker	3 col. × 7 =	132.30
Garfield	3 col. × 7 =	111.30
Chagrin/Solon	3 col. × 7 =	68.25
Metro Student News (1¾)	3 col. × 7 =	176.40
		$2,291.75

TABLE 7: *Comparison of enrollment, 1977–1978*

	Headcount: number enrolled		*Headcount: decrease/ increase*	*Percent decrease/ increase*
	1977	*1978*		
Undergraduate students				
Freshmen	5,503	4,499	−1,004	−18.2
Sophomores	3,309	3,090	− 219	− 6.6
Juniors	3,145	2,979	− 166	− 5.3
Seniors	3,106	3,067	− 39	− 1.3
Special	317	379	+ 62	+19.6
Total	15,380	14,014	−1,366	− 8.8
Graduate students	3,973	4,317	+ 344	+ 8.7
Overall enrollment	19,353	18,331	−1,022	− 5.3

TABLE 8: *New undergraduate student admissions*

Reporting date	*Cumulative for fall 1977*	*Cumulative for fall 1978*	*1977–1978 change: Number of admissions*	*1977–1978 change: Percent*
March	2,454	1,434	−1,020	−42
May	3,263	2,088	−1,145	−36
June	3,905	2,515	−1,390	−36
September	5,384	4,008	−1,376	−26
Fall (October) registrations	5,503	4,499	−1,004	−18

period in 1977 and even a 14% increase over 1976 (prior to the gym controversy) (Table 9).

A decision had to be made by December 15 as to media buys and budgeting for January through September 1979. The administrative officers wondered what statistics might be available, or could be collected, to determine the impact to date of phases I and II. They were also concerned as to the impact on enrollment if the advertising program were inadequately funded over the next eight months of the 1979 recruiting season.

TABLE 9: ***ACT score reports sent to Kent State for the classes of 1977–1979***[a]

Testing date	1977	1978	1979	Change 1978–1979 Number	Change 1978–1979 Percent
Oct.	1,824	1,166	2,071	+905	+78
Nov./Dec.	3,461	2,573	—	—	—
Feb.	1,923	1,501	—	—	—
Apr.	1,703	1,053	—	—	—
June	1,607	1,406	—	—	—

[a]—, not available at the date of the case.

V: ATTRACTING RESOURCES

Most organizations in the nonprofit area attempt to attract resources to carry out projects and attain objectives. Organizations attempt to attract people, funds, and forms of support such as votes. Attracting resources is achieved through the proper implementation of the marketing mix. Frequently, selling memberships, recruiting volunteers, or audience attraction can be a big marketing objective of the nonprofit organization. Donor marketing and fund raising is the life blood of many social service organizations.

The first article is "Marketing's Application to Fund Raising," by William A. Mindak and H. Malcolm Bybee. The article examines how effective marketing concepts and tools are when applied to a nonbusiness enterprise. The authors try to determine the answer to this question through the application of marketing techniques to a charitable fund drive for the March of Dimes. They find that careful marketing analysis and planning produced the first net increase in donations the fund had experienced in 12 years.

The next article is "Church Public Relations: A Check-off List" by Ben Ramsey. This article is designed as both a guide and as an evaluation check-off list for the journalist or public relations professional who wants to utilize his or her "talents" in the service of a neighborhood church unit. It is best applied to churches with congregations of 1,000 to 2,000, but it can be useful for smaller units. It is largely based on six works on church public relations (listed in the Bibliography) and on the author's work with Presbyterian public relations units overseas and in Pennsylvania.

The next article is "Direct-Mail Political Fund Raising" by Brian A. Haggerty. According to the author, planning and activating a direct-mail political fund-raising campaign calls for specialized techniques. The article explains some of the tactics, techniques, and axioms of political fund raising.

"Put Your Money on Ice—How a Slogan Sparked a Fund Raising Campaign" by William R. Horne explains how the Canadian Ministry of Labor slashed through the province, leaving behind a host of condemned ice arenas. A community of 7,000 people raised the money to build a $1.5 million replacement rink. The article provides an excellent example of effective fund raising with limited resources.

"The Baptists Want You!" by William Martin examines how the Baptist General Convention of Texas developed an extensive marketing program to increase the membership in their church. This program included consumer research to help determine the creative strategy for the advertising campaign, a marketing budget of more than $1.5 million dollars, and coordination of the efforts of 4,200 Baptist churches, their ministers, and members.

"Implementing the Marketing Process" by Ernest R. Leach examines promotional, delivery, and evaluation techniques for applying the discipline of marketing to higher education.

Cases in this section include "Common Cause," "Second Street Gallery," and "The Milwaukee Blood Center."

Marketing's Application to Fund Raising

WILLIAM A. MINDAK

H. MALCOLM BYBEE

In a recent issue of the *Journal of Marketing,* Professor Kotler and Levy maintained that marketing is a societal activity which goes considerably beyond the selling of toothpaste, soap, and steel [1]. They suggested that the basic concepts of product development, pricing, distribution, and communication also apply to nonbusiness organizations interested in services, persons, and ideas. Further, they challenged marketing people to expand their thinking and to apply their skills to an increasing range of social activity rather than to a narrowly defined business activity.

This article is in part a response to that challenge. It discusses a specific case study which applied marketing concepts to a March of Dimes fund raising campaign. The concepts utilized in the study include many of those suggested by Kotler and Levy, plus some additional systematic factors (which are often peculiar to the marketing of ideas and causes). In addition, the article provides some specific examples of communication factors.

THE CASE STUDY

This particular case concerns a March of Dimes fund raising drive held in Travis Country, Texas, in January, 1970. Despite limited funds and facilities, or perhaps *because* of these limits, the authors had an opportunity to experiment with marketing concepts in an area not traditionally considered a business enterprise.

Anyone who has worked with charitable or volunteer organizations probably is well aware that very few of these organizations have a formally established plan. If they do have a "handbook," it is usually filled with anecdotes, success stories, or invocations to positive thinking. This was not the case for the March of Dimes Foundation, which has pioneered many solicitation techniques that are widely copied by other associations and agencies. However, the perspective of the handbook seemed curiously dated as if one were inspecting the organizational chart of a sales-oriented company back in the 1950s rather than a marketing-oriented company of the 1970s. Despite these difficulties, the authors attempted to translate the Foundation's handbook into a meaningful marketing plan, utilizing recent contributions from systems analyses as well as flow diagrams.

MARKETING ANALYSIS

The first handicap the authors encountered in conducting the marketing analysis was the lack of primary research data about the "heavy giver," his demographic characteristics, the location and size of this particular market, and his basic motivations for giving or not giving. In view of the fact that since its inception in 1934 through 1960 the National Foundation had raised $618.5 million, and that in 1967 it was the fourth largest public health agency in terms of contributions (some $22 million), one would expect a wealth of primary marketing data. However, the policy of the National Foundation of the March of Dimes has been to spend money on medical research rather than on consumer or marketing research. A review of past Chapter records data, in addition to exploratory investigations in the local community, did indicate the following problems:

1. *An apathetic and uninformed public who still considered the major aim of the organization to be the prevention of polio.*

Reprinted with permission from *Journal of Marketing,* July 1971, pp. 13–18; published by the American Marketing Association.

With the advent of the Salk (1955) and later the Sabin (1962) vaccine, an effective prevention for polio was achieved. Although the National Foundation had announced interests in other related diseases, particularly birth defects, as early as 1958, relatively few people had changed their "image" of the March of Dimes.

A preliminary telephone survey conducted in Travis County indicated that only *17.5%* of the respondents volunteered birth defects for the March of Dimes on the unaided recall basis. When aided, only another 13.4% made the association. Thus, 30.9% of those surveyed realized that the March of Dimes was becoming concerned with birth defects.

Therefore, although the product had been redefined, the Travis County public was not aware of this "redefinition."

2. *Decreasing interest in the organization and a subsequent decline in involvement by volunteers.*

This was attributed to a general deemphasis in the importance of birth and child-rearing by women, with subsequent lessened interest in the birth process, and increasing competition from other "causes" needing volunteers.

3. *Declining returns from each campaign in Travis County.*

4. *Lack of primary marketing research data on the composition of donors and the location of prime market segments for the current year or for the previous year.*

5. *Evidence that nationally prepared campaign materials did not apply to the local situation.*

There was a feeling that the national campaign was too organization-centered and not benefit-centered. The use of such themes as "250,000 defective babies are born each year with birth defects" was not personally involving, and the shock effect of a single poster child with missing and disfigured limbs seemed too negative and too removed to be effective.

In addition to the problems, a market analysis indicated several potential opportunities:

1. *A long public association of the March of Dimes Organization with the area of public health.*

   A nationwide opinion survey conducted by the American Institute of Public Opinion found that 83% of the population in the U.S. could identify the March of Dimes.
2. *Recent breakthroughs in the area of birth-defect prevention and detection coupled with a high number of people exposed to the problem.*
3. *The organization and structure of the March of Dimes, with a nucleus of dedicated individuals.*
4. *Receptivity at the local level to experiment with new marketing and communication techniques.*

APPLICATION OF MARKETING TECHNIQUES

Once a marketing plan had been instituted and the problems and opportunities analyzed, various marketing techniques were applied using Kotler and Levy's classification.

Target Group Definition—Market Segmentation. In general, the National Foundation's fund raising strategy was to view its potential market as basically undifferentiated. Although the standard March of Dimes fund drive had attempted to contact business and industry, and conducted a mother's march, and had instituted teenage and school programs, the concept of locating the "heavy donor" or "user" was not used nationally or locally. Thus, very little market segmentation information was available.

However, in the marketing of consumer products, the "heavy-user" concept has been widely accepted as a truism. Several authors have indicated disproportionate consumption skews for several product lines. For instance, fewer than 4% of the male population make 90% of the car rentals; 8% take 98% of the air trips in a year; and 26% of the population used 81% of the instant coffee [2]. What about fund raising? Common sense would indicate that the market for the March of Dimes and birth defects is also segmented, and this was validated by research conducted during the study. The prime market for the March of Dimes was felt to consist of parents. Past research had ascertained that 48.5% of the population could be placed into this category [3]. More realistically, however, it was estimated that only 31.4% (young married, no children; young married, youngest child under six; and young married, youngest child six and over) would comprise the prime target for the campaign.

Another indication that the market could be segmented was provided by an analysis of contributions from the direct-mail campaign. It indicated that five of the 24 census tracts in the Travis County area (containing 19.8% of the population) had made 41.3% of the contributions.

Therefore, the key to a successful March of Dimes campaign appeared to be isolating the "heavy user" rather than marketing to an undifferentiated population.

The Search for a Differential Advantage. Despite more than 10 years of promotion efforts, the "top-of-mind awareness" to the March of Dimes and birth defects was relatively low as shown by the initial telephone survey. It was felt that a thematic perception test would aid in determining which type of appeal would best differentiate the March of Dimes "new" birth defects' image from both the established image of polio as well as from the other charitable causes. This strategy utilized many current and past March of Dimes' slogans and a number of newly created themes. A trivariant analysis [4] test was then conducted on the various thematic appeals.

Twenty-four themes in three specific categories were rated on the three factors of *distinctiveness* (or exclusiveness), *interest* (rather than desirability), and *believability*. The first category of themes included the ones used by the March of Dimes during the last five years:

- Keep our future bright by fighting birth defects today.
- Give for a brighter tomorrow.
- Help make a child whole again.
- Shut the door on birth defects.
- Fight the great destroyer, birth defects.
- Give to the March of Dimes.
- Join the fight against birth defects.
- Where there's help, there's hope.
- Prevent birth defects.

The second category contained locally created themes that were largely centered around the emotional fear technique:

- Your next baby could be born with a birth defect.
- 500,000 unborn babies die each year from birth defects.
- Dying children can be helped.
- Birth-defect babies can't be sent back to the factory.
- Help tomorrow's birth-defect child live.
- Protect your family's health.
- God made you whole. Give to help those He didn't.

The third category also contained locally created themes, but their appeals were more rational:

- 700 children are born each day with a birth defect.
- A birth-defect baby is born every other minute in the U.S.
- Birth defects are: cleft palate, club foot, open spine—curable.
- The March of Dimes has given you: Polio Vaccine, German Measles Vaccine, 110 birth-defects' counseling centers.
- Your gift to the March of Dimes is like money in the bank.
- You owe it to your children to contribute to the March of Dimes.
- Insure your family's health by giving to the March of Dimes.

In trivariant analysis a representative sample rates various themes randomly on three factors. The mean scores for the themes are calculated on each of the factors, and are then plotted on a two-dimensional chart (the mean of the theme on the third factor, believability, is shown in parentheses). Figure 1 charts the results achieved by each of the March of Dimes' themes on the interest and distinctiveness factors, with the believability mean in parentheses. In is conceded that although the test is an efficient means of testing probable effectiveness of factual claims, it seems less applicable to advertising approaches that depend heavily on emotion or upon graphics. Despite these limitations, Figure 1 provides some interesting insights:

1. The majority of the March of Dimes' themes did not score in Quadrant I where the most interesting and most distinctive themes are found.
2. Themes dealing with *positive, active* aspects of giving, the *results of giving,* or a description of what March of Dimes had done with contributions in the past did well in creating interest, in being distinctive, and in being believable.
3. Some of the emotional appeals showed potential in being interesting, but they would need to be altered in order to achieve higher levels of distinctiveness and believability.

In any event, data were available and used to

FIGURE 1: ***Trivariant analysis of possible themes***

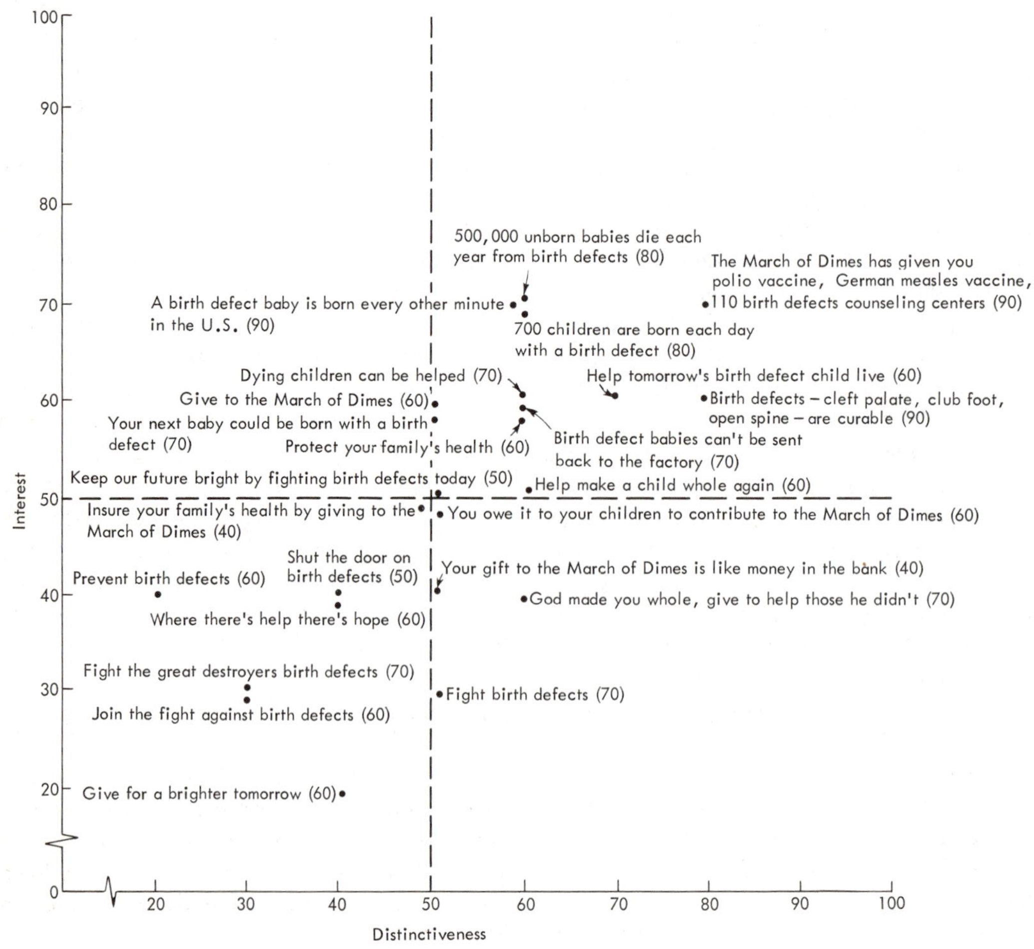

create strategies for finding a differential advantage.

Multiple Marketing Tools. One of the keys to the success of the March of Dimes' campaign was the "mothers' march," a day set aside for personal solicitations in the prospects' homes. Informal interviews with teams of marchers indicated a basic insecurity on the part of the soliciting mother concerning her behavior when confronting a potential donor at the door. Since these women were the key "salesmen," informational and motivational meetings were held. In addition, a detailed fact sheet was designed to explain the method of requesting funds and the use of prepared materials. Also, a brochure was designed to leave at the door in case the prospect was not at home.

Localized publicity materials which related to the other aspects of the promotional mix were prepared for both the print media, with its characteristic of permanence and exposure, and the broadcast news media, with its potential broad impact and visualization. The latter media had not been used with much effectiveness in the past.

Marketing Audit—Continuous Marketing Feedback. Some of the research or feedback techniques used during the campaign such as "top-of-mind awareness" of March of Dimes, pretesting of appeals, and analysis of returns have already been described. The most critical tests concerned the evaluation of the overall impact of the campaign in meeting its objectives.

One of the objectives of the advertising campaign was to increase the association of birth defects with the March of Dimes. A precampaign audit yielded a 30.9% combined aided and unaided recall for the March of Dimes and birth defects. A second audit conducted a week after the direct-mail campaign showed that the figure had risen to 45.3% (a 50% increase). A third audit, conducted a week after the mothers' march, yielded a recall figure of 61.2% (a 100% increase from the pretest). DAGMAR criteria would indicate that the advertising had been effective in achieving penetration.

With respect to "sales," total income realized for the 1970 campaign increased by 33% over the previous year, but the increased expenses of "tailor-making" a direct-mail program, of preparing radio and T.V. announcements, and of providing handouts for mothers increased expenses by 14% over the previous year. Nevertheless, it was the first time in 12 years that contributions *had* increased.

Based on these results, the major recommendation for next year's campaign was to move even more strongly toward the "heavy-user concept" in direct-mail advertising. The mass campaign suggested by the National Foundation consisting of impersonal "occupant-addressed" pieces did not take advantage of what marketers know about family life cycles and market segments. As many as half of the census tracts in the Travis County area could have been eliminated without substantially reducing net returns.

The same concentration could apply to the business and industry mailing. Although the number of direct-mail pieces sent to this sector was tripled, response actually decreased. This was attributed to the fact that a mass of letters was sent, rather than consecutive, selective mailings with personalized follow-up.

Much doubt was cast on the efficacy of publicity in motivating and stimulating response in the form of donations. The National Organization's primary emphasis in its communication program is to prepare news-release material containing appeals designed to elicit cash donations to the March of Dimes. It appears that this approach does not generate adequate donations and, in fact, may jeopardize the placement of other communications into the media dealing with the need for volunteers, meetings, and so forth.

CONCLUSIONS AND IMPLICATIONS

The results of the Travis County "test market" clearly suggest that marketing techniques and philosophy can be applied to ideas and social causes. It also seems clear that they could have national application for a foundation such as the March of Dimes.

Associations and their causes, like products, experience a life cycle. Patton suggests that a product will go through graduated intervals of development, beginning with an introduction stage which is followed by stages of growth, maturity, and decline.

> As volume rises and the market becomes increasingly saturated marketing steps to the center of the stage. Generally speaking at this point all competitive products are reliable and there is less and less to choose between them. Improvements in the product tend to be small with selling features or style changes dominant [5].

The charity "market" has become increasingly competitive. Individual fund raising campaigns, exclusive of the United Fund campaign, are again on the upsurge across the country. Health organizations, which at first attempted to integrate with the United Fund approach, are now conducting their own campaigns. Furthermore, some members of the United Fund are even conducting individual campaigns to supplement their United Fund receipts.

The increasing competition plus the problems already mentioned indicate that the National Foundation of the March of Dimes can be placed in the late stages of the "charity" life cycle, characterized by declining growth and campaign receipts. Even its advantage of being a pioneer in solicitation techniques seems to be dissipated by the competition for the volunteers needed in other organizations.

The question, therefore, is how long can basic market research be viewed as an unnecessary, unwanted expense by an organization such as the March of Dimes.

Research information could be translated into selective promotion, in contrast to the "mass" techniques used in the past. Computer data from the Internal Revenue Service are already available containing information on incomes, number of dependents, and taxes paid for each of the 35,000 postal Zip Code areas. These data, plus a regression and correlation analysis of March of Dimes' data from individual chapter records, could identify the means to efficiently reach the "heavy giver."

The need to apply other marketing management concepts is equally obvious. These concepts include redefining the "product" in a meaningful way, developing new marketing tools for the volunteer, and arranging national test markets to test different types and levels of promotional appeals.

Perhaps readers who have been exposed to the frequently high-pressure techniques of charity organizations and professional fund-raisers with their "disease-of-the-month-club" solicitations might be "appalled" by the prospect of these organizations becoming marketing-minded. At the same time, the dedicated professionals and volunteers associated with these organizations might be "appalled" by the prospect of applying business and marketing techniques to a nonbusiness area.

Both groups might profit from reviewing Kotler and Levy's definition of what marketing really means: sensitively serving and satisfying human needs [1, p.15]. Such a definition of marketing challenges organizations which specialize in the marketing of causes and ideas to ask themselves if they are truly consumer-centered and not simply self-serving. It challenges their understanding of the principle that selling follows rather than precedes the organization's drive to collect funds. It also challenges the marketing man himself to understand that he will have to fit his concepts and techniques to the special goals and objectives of the individual organizations. It is hoped that this case study helps in contributing to the satisfactory acceptance of these challenges.

REFERENCES

[1] Philip Kotler and Sidney Levy, "Broadening the Concept of Marketing," *Journal of Marketing*, Vol. 33 (January, 1969), pp. 10–15.

[2] Carl H. Sandage and Vernon Fryburger, *Advertising Theory and Practice* (Homewood, Ill.: Richard D. Irwin, Inc., 1967), p. 199; Philip Kotler, *Marketing Management* (Englewood Cliffs, N.J.: Prentice-Hall, Inc., 1967), p. 51; Daniel Yankelovich, "New Criteria for Market Segmentation," in

Marketing Management and Administrative Action, Steuart H. Britt and Harper W. Boyd, Jr., eds. (New York: McGraw-Hill Book Co., 1968), p. 189.

[3] John B. Lansing and Leslie Kish, "Family Life Cycle as an Independent Variable," in *Marketing Management and Administrative Action,* Steuart H. Britt and Harper W. Boyd, Jr., eds. (New York: McGraw-Hill Book Co., 1968), p. 213.

[4] Dik Warren Twedt, "New 3-Way Measure of Ad Effectiveness," *Printer's Ink* (September 6, 1957), pp. 22–23. See also Dik Warren Twedt, "How to Plan New Products, Improve Old Ones and Create Better Advertising," *Journal of Marketing*. Vol. 33 (January, 1969), pp. 53–57.

[5] Arch Patton, "Top Management's Stake in the Product Life Cycle," in *Marketing Management and Administrative Action,* Steuart H. Britt and Harper W. Boyd, Jr., eds. (New York: McGraw-Hill Book Co., 1968), p. 324.

Church Public Relations: A Check-off List

BEN RAMSEY

Only a small fraction of public relations practioners are directly involved with national or regional church PR Offices. However, well over half are at least nominally attached to a church or synagog. And, in most cases, these parish-level religious units need all the professional consultation and aid they can get. Their attempts at photography, publications, publicity and long-range PR planning are often painfully amateurish, especially in the light of the professionals listed on their rolls.

This article is designed as both a guide and as an evaluation check-off list for the journalist or public relations professional who wants to utilize his "talents" in the service of a neighborhood church unit. It is best applied to churches with congregations of one to two thousand, but it can be useful to smaller units. It is largely based on seven works on Church PR (listed in the Bibliography) and on the author's work with Presbyterian PR units overseas and in Pennsylvania.

ESTABLISHING THE CHURCH PR TEAM

The first step in revitalizing a parish operation is normally the selection and training of the key personnel (called the "Communication Committee" in my home church). It is comprised of laymen with interests and abilities in writing, art, photography, theatre, etc. It should include ideally:

The *Director of PR,* who will coordinate all activities and staff training efforts. He will work under general guidelines layed down by the senior clergyman and will keep the clergy advised on major plans and projects.

The *News Editor,* who will primarily:

1. Edit, polish and distribute news releases.
2. Establish good relationships with local city editors, church editors, and other media news

Reprinted with permission from *Public Relations Quarterly,* Winter 1977, pp. 17–21.

directors (finding out what they want and when they want it).

3. Assign "reporters" to specific areas such as church education, sports, social events, scouting, music, drama, evangelism, etc.

The *Newsletter Editor,* who works with the clergy, secretaries and reporters to publish the weekly, bi-weekly or monthly publication. If it is a bi-weekly or monthly, it will often involve photography, artwork and offset printing. (A recent New Zealand study noted that members found their newsletter or bulletin the most important single line of communication to their church as a whole.)

The *Art Director,* who assists with everything from the lettering of posters to cartoons for the newsletter.

The *Photographers,* who are generally responsible for recording events of significance. Their output might be used on bulletin boards, in photo releases or in the newsletter. Ideally, several can form a pool, each with his or her specialty (large group shots, color work, action or candid shots, or even film work for TV releases).

The *Bulletin Board Editor,* who may supervise the data and graphics for up to five major boards (concerning everything from sports or general news clippings to official notices or "Letters from Scattered Brethren").

DETERMINING THE GENERAL THRUST

Once the staff is recruited, organized and coached, the next order of business is a general discussion of aims and goals. The basic question concerns the image the church wants to project—to its own in-group members and to the rest of the community out-group. Normally the message is rather simple: "Christianity works!" (It makes people happier, better and more useful. It gives life a point, a purpose and a direction in a time of global confusion and anxiety.)

THE APPLICATION OF THE CHECK-OFF LIST

Once the team swings into action, a check-off list can serve to direct its efforts and to evaluate the results. The questions which follow are not meant to constitute an exhaustive list; they are only meant to suggest the vast range of possible PR activities.

1. The physical plant
   a. Does the appearance of the grounds, buildings and parking lot tend to enhance the desired image?
   b. Is the building properly lighted at night (outside, inside behind the stain-glass windows, etc.)?
   c. If the church is situated near a busy highway or major intersection, is this fact being taken advantage of? Is a display sign properly established, edited and kept up to date with provocative messages? Is it lighted at night?
   d. Are church bells or carillions utilized to remind the community of the existence of the church?
   e. Are signs posted on main roads leading to the church, pointing the way? (Note: Baked enamel signs are usually available at nation headquarters, but a permit may be needed from the local Street Department.)
2. Media and publicity work
   a. Have local professional church editors and other media people been contacted (when they are not likely to be busy) to learn their needs and interests? Are "thank you" notes sent when good news coverage is achieved?
   b. Are all church members periodically reminded (perhaps via a sermon) that church PR is everybody's business? Are they aware of channels and procedures for submitting news?
   c. Are ideas for major features (for church monthlies or Sunday editions of the local papers) farmed out from time to time by the Director of PR or the News Editor?

d. Has a basic publicity brochure been prepared for distribution to new members and prospective members? These would summarize the church's purposes, services, staff, facilities, benefits, etc.
e. Are a series of bulletin boards kept up to date, attractive and newsworthy? Is a clearly designated editor in charge, and do the members know this? Are the boards in high-traffic areas, and are they well lighted?
f. Is the newsletter editor being supplied with a steady flow of items from the designated "reporters" and others? Is the layout reasonably professional? Is the newsletter being mailed at the cheapest postal rate? Is it being sent to absent members (away at college, in the armed service, shut-ins, etc.)? Is a copy sent to local Church Editors? Are copies exchanged with other local churches? (This can lead to a number of new ideas.)
g. When interesting people drop by (like missionaries back from India) are arrangements made for possible radio or TV interviews?
h. Is the church part of a regional plan for the occasional broadcasting of services on radio or TV?
i. Are special events dramatized for possible photo or TV coverage? (For example, a routine ground-breaking ceremony might be enlivened by the use of a team of oxen pulling an ancient plow.)
j. Is an appropriate ad announcing services placed on the newspaper's church page each Saturday?

3. Miscellaneous
   a. Are the church staff members (including janitors) trained to answer the phone effectively? Is the phone listing in the yellow pages attractive and up to date?
   b. Are ushers and other "greeters" trained with PR in mind?
   c. Have cooperative efforts with other local churches been considered to fund advertising (billboards, bumper stickers, signs in buses, radio and TV spots, etc.)?

      (Consider this possibility: a sign in a bus facing a passenger twice each day for many weeks: "Worried, tense, discouraged? Does life seem pointless? Perhaps you suffer from acute, chronic Christlessness, RX: Take a local church seriously.)
   d. Does the PR Committee have a list of members who are in key positions in local clubs and organizations (so they can get up and make announcements or appeals)?
   e. Is there an annual critique of the overall PR effort, and is it coordinated with periodic surveys and audience analysis efforts?
   f. Do the members of the PR Committee occasionally read books on journalism or PR work? Do they attempt to interview experts in the field or even take PR courses at local colleges?

In short, the church is an institution with a product to sell and an image to maintain. There is nothing wrong with its effort to be well organized and professional. Its adversaries are hardly amateurs. As St. Augustine phrased it about 1600 years ago: "Truth must not go unarmed into the arena."

However, church budgets are generally tight and getting tighter. Most churches simply cannot afford to hire professional PR firms. Their only chance for excellence lies in the voluntary, part-time help of PR professionals who also happen to be churchmen. Remember the parable of the servant who did not utilize his God-given "talents."

BIBLIOGRAPHY

Craig, Floyd, *Christian Communicator's Handbook* (Broadman Press: Nashville, 1969).

Jackson, B.F., ed., *Television-Radio-Film for Churchmen* (Abingdon Press: Nashville, 1969).

Jackson, B.F., ed. *Communication—Learning for Churchmen* (Abingdon Press: Nashville, 1969).

Jackson, B.F., ed, *Communication—Learning for Churchmen* (Abingdon Press, Nashville, 1968).

Stoody, Ralph, *A Handbook of Church Public Relations* (Abingdon Press: Nashville, 1959).

Wolseley, Roland, *Interpreting the Church Through Press and Radio* (Muhlenberg Press: Philadelphia, 1951).

Direct-Mail Political Fund Raising

BRIAN A. HAGGERTY

Fund raising, wrote John Price Jones, noted practitioner of the art, "is public relations. . . . As a matter of fact, fund raising is one of the most highly developed types of public relations. It takes better public relations to get a man to give a dollar than it does to convince him to spend a dollar."

Although Mr. Jones referred specifically to raising funds for philanthropic causes, his identification of fund raising with public relations holds true for direct-mail political fund raising, which has become a highly developed enterprise in the last 10 to 15 years.

The literature dealing with philanthropic fund raising is quite extensive. There also exists a substantial body of literature on direct-mail marketing. But the number of easily accessible articles and books on direct-mail and political fund raising, which combines elements of traditional forms of fund raising and elements of direct-mail marketing in a new synthesis, is comparatively limited. A major reason for that lack of information may be that widespread use of direct-mail appeals to raise funds for political candidates and causes is a relatively recent phenomenon.

Sen. Barry Goldwater was the first major political candidate to conduct a successful large-scale campaign to solicit political contributions through direct mail. In the 1964 Presidential campaign, Goldwater Republicans mailed more than 15 million fund-raising appeals and raised $5.8 million, at a cost slightly in excess of $1 million. Sen. Goldwater received 380,000 responses with contributions under $100 each, disproving the long-held rule that direct mail could not be counted on to raise large sums for political campaigns.

The Senator's notable success soon was surpassed by other candidates. In the 1968 Presidential primary campaign, Gov. George Wallace attracted an estimated 750,000 small (under $100) contributors through direct-mail appeals, and raised more than $5 million—76 percent of the income for his campaign.

In the 1972 Presidential campaign, George McGovern elevated direct-mail political fund raising to a high art. McGovern forces used direct mail to raise more than $15 million at a cost of about $4.5 million. Sen. McGovern's opponent, Richard Nixon, raised some $9 million in response to mailings of 30 million fund-raising appeals.

And, prior to the 1976 Presidential campaign, Gov. Wallace's campaign committee raised approximately $12 million through direct mail.

Reprinted with permission from *Public Relations Journal,* March 1979, pp. 10–12.

BROAD POLITICAL USE

Presidential candidates are not the only beneficiaries of direct-mail political fund raising. Richard Viguerie, often called the master of direct mail political fund raising, recently outlined plans to raise more than $35 million for use in up to 50 major political races in 1978. That figure, said Mr. Viguerie, will double the $17 million he and his associates were able to put into the 1976 elections.

What accounts for the rapid rise and the popularity of direct-mail political fund raising? George Gorton, a San Diego based direct-mail specialist whose clients have included the Republican National Committee, Gerald Ford and San Diego Mayor Peter Wilson, suggests two advantages direct mail has over other methods of raising political funds. First, says Mr. Gorton, direct mail draws contributions from the "true believers," people who give though there is nothing in it for them, no promise of access to the candidate. Second, funds received in response to direct-mail appeals free candidates from "the power of big money." A candidate who can rely on a large number of small contributors does not run the risk of becoming obligated to a few large contributors.

Richard Viguerie sees an additional advantage in direct mail for conservative fund raisers. According to Mr. Viguerie, "It's just a fact of life that most of the commercial media in the country are dominated by the people who are left of center—except for one form of mass communications: direct mail."

Direct mail, then, according to Mr. Viguerie, gives conservatives "a method of communicating with their supporters out there that bypasses radio, television and newspapers."

Direct-mail political fund raising also shares a number of advantages with direct-mail marketing in general:

1. It allows users to target their appeals, to make specific appeals to specific groups of persons.
2. It is flexible. Direct mail allows users to single out persons who are to receive the appeal and to address the appeal to as many or as few persons as desired. It offers users a variety of forms and lengths of message and choice of timing of the message.
3. Direct-mail appeals give potential contributors the complete and actual means to take action.

Finally, some provisions of the Federal Election Campaign Act Amendments of 1974 serve to increase the advantages of raising funds through direct-mail appeals. The contribution limits enacted by those amendments make it necessary for candidates to undertake broadly based fund drives in search of more small contributors. And only such fund drives will enable Presidential candidates to qualify for matching public funds. Direct mail is a proven means of establishing a political campaign on a broad base of small contributors, and an effective means for candidates in Presidential campaigns to meet fund-raising requirements to obtain matching funds.

TACTICS, TECHNIQUES AND AXIOMS

Although the literature on direct-mail political fund raising is relatively limited, a close reading of that literature—as well as conversation and communication by mail with a number of direct-mail users and consultants—suggests a variety of tactics, techniques and axioms commonly recommended by practitioners. Some of the most provocative recommendations are those concerning the content and style of fund-raising letters and reply cards. For example:

- Make the letter as personal as possible. Write to one person; do not use phrases such as "many of you," and so on. Ask prospective contributors to write a check to the candidate rather than to a campaign organization. Prospective contributors are more likely to give to a person than to a campaign committee.
- Use "you" rather than "I"—prospective contributors are more interested in what they will derive from their contribution than in what a candidate has done.

- Say what you want to say, but do not use excess wordage. Above all, do not suggest you know something about prospective contributors you have no right to know. George Gorton recalls a fund-raising letter he prepared, in the early stages of his career, on behalf of the Republican National Committee. Since it had been a year of economic slowdown, the letter concluded by suggesting, "We know many of you may not be able to contribute as much as in previous years." Sen. William Brock, over whose signature the letter had been sent, received scores of irate letters demanding to know how he could possibly have any information about the financial condition of those to whom the letters had been mailed.
- Do not feel bound by rules of good grammar. Be conversational. Write as you speak. The important thing is to grab and hold the reader. Thus, run-on sentences, unorthodox paragraphing, and so on may be used.
- Assume the reader is in favor of your candidate or cause, or at least not opposed. Do not waste time defending your position.
- Be directive. Tell the prospective contributor what to do—to sit down, write a check for a specified amount, put it in the envelope provided, and so on.
- Make the letters interesting to read and to look at. Use generously such devices as subheads, indentations, underlining, capitalization of paragraphs, handwritten interjections, spot art, and postscripts.
- Use testimonial letters from office holders and prominent persons. They are powerful.
- Involve the reader. Include issue polls, surveys, ballots with computer-assigned numbers, and so on. Use reply cards to give potential contributors an opportunity to voice their opinions, even if only by checking a Yes or No box regarding their intentions to contribute. Give the reader a sense of participation.
- Make strong appeals. Former Democratic National Committee Treasurer Robert Strauss observed, "It doesn't make any difference whether it's ban the bomb, or bomb the bastards, people contribute in response to emotional appeals." A 1976 letter sent out by the Democratic National Committee over Mr. Strauss' signature indicated that he follows his own advice. The letter read in part: As if the problems he left behind were not enough, we are still paying the price for Richard Nixon. His recent so-called "private" trip to China was yet another intolerable affront we have been forced to put up with. We can be glad that the time will soon be at hand to end the outrages and the mismanagement of two successive Republican administrations. And *end them we will* with a smashing Democratic victory in November!

There is room, however, for rational appeal as well. One of the most successful direct-mail appeals for political contributions was George McGovern's tightly reasoned eight-page letter in January, 1971, announcing his decision to run for the Presidency. The letter was sent to 300,000 persons and raised some $300,000 on an investment of $30,000. Since Mr. McGovern was the choice of fewer than 10 percent of Democrats responding to national polls at that time, the results of that fund-raising effort were remarkable.

IMPORTANCE OF LISTS

Practitioners of direct mail in the political arena generally agree with direct-mail users in other fields that the mailing list is the most important element in a successful direct-mail campaign. And like direct-mail specialists in other fields, they recommend that mailing lists be fresh, well-maintained and accurate.

Moreover, they find that use of computers to maintain mailing lists helps eliminate duplication, which is costly in terms of economics and public relations. Computers also can amass statistical information about potential contributors, thus making it possible to appeal to specific audiences based on age, educational and income levels, and so on.

Finally, like their counterparts in the field of marketing, direct-mail political consultants maintain that mailing lists—in fact, all the elements of a direct-mail package—should be tested before being used.

Measures of success vary according to the type of mailing. According to George Gorton, a two percent return on a prospect mailing—one conducted to build a list of potential contributors—is acceptable. A three percent return is good; four percent is very good. "When we get a five percent or six percent return," he says, "we are ecstatic!"

Measures of success change, Mr. Gorton points out, as the number of mailings to the same people increases. The best list, he claims, is made up of the names of "those who gave to the cause last week." The second best list is made up of those who contributed two weeks ago, and so on.

Mailings to proven contributors should be expected to yield a higher rate of return and a higher average contribution than an initial mailing to prospective contributors. Mr. Gorton points enthusiastically to a mailing he did on behalf of California gubernatorial candidate Pete Wilson. The letter, sent to proven contributors and asking for $100 contributions, produced a 25 percent return! A good average gift, says Mr. Gorton, is $15.

Richard Viguerie agrees with Mr. Gorton—in fact, he goes even further. "When you're first building a list," he says, "it costs $1.20 to raise a dollar."

Mr. Viguerie points with satisfaction to the fact that a prospect mailing of two million letters on behalf of George Wallace in September, 1974, broke even. That mailing, he says, also provided Gov. Wallace with a core list of supporters to whom he can return in the future with appeals for funds.

Like George Gorton, Mr. Viguerie feels that mailings to proven contributors require higher measures of success. Among recent Viguerie company mailings he considers successful was a 231,000-letter mailing on behalf of North Carolina Sen. Jesse Helms, costing $71,000 and grossing over $174,000. According to Mr. Viguerie, that mailing received a 5.3 percent response with a $14.03 average gift. Sen. Helms netted $103,000. The cost to raise each dollar in the campaign was 41 cents!

SLEEPING GIANT WITH PROBLEMS

Richard Viguerie has called direct mail for political fund raising a "sleeping giant," pointing out that there is "a tremendous amount of pioneering work yet to be done." But despite his enthusiastic outlook, there are indications that direct-mail political fund raising may not achieve the promise he sees in it.

Some direct-mail political fund raisers, for example, feel the mailing lists are wearing out. There are just so many people who will respond to such appeals, they say. And the number of those whose names may be added through propsecting is relatively limited.

If the saturation point has not yet been reached, they claim, the proliferation of political fund-raising groups, all of which use the same or similar lists, will soon bring it about. At that point, prospective contributors will simply turn off to the numerous appeals they receive, and the source of funds will dry up.

Moreover, increased postage and other costs since George McGovern's notable success in 1972 also raise a question about the future of direct mail. Rising costs, combined with recently enacted spending limits on political fund raising in Federal election campaigns, may serve to blunt the effectiveness of direct mail, or even to reduce its use drastically in the candidate's repertory of fund-raising approaches.

Finally, legislation seeking to protect individual privacy by restricting the sale and rental of mailing lists is a distinct possibility. In addition, according to George Gorton, there is the possibility of legislation directed against an unethical practice he attributes to some direct-mail consultants—that of establishing front organizations to launch direct-mail campaigns that utilimately reap enormous financial benefits for the consultants.

Abuses, or alleged abuses, by some fund raisers and mailing list brokers may well kill the goose that laid the golden egg.

Put Your Money on Ice–How a Slogan Sparked a Fund Raising Campaign

WILLIAM R. HORNE

The Ministry of Labor slashed through the province leaving behind a host of condemned arenas. Could a community of seven thousand people raise the money to build a $1.5 million replacement? This was the challenge given to Gravenhurst, Ontario.

For a town in the north to lose its major winter indoor recreation facility is an emergency situation. In July 1976 the municipal council organized three committees to oversee the construction of a new building. The building committee would decide what would be built, the site committee where, and the fundraising committee how.

From discussion with users of the old facility and an examination of neighbouring communities, it became apparent that the new arena should have an ice surface of 190 feet × 85 feet with a seven month season and seating for eight hundred fifty. A snack bar, heated viewing area, six dressing rooms and ample storage space were also required.

The committee began by looking at prefabricated steel structures costing about $500,000. A growing need for an auditorium/gymnasium with capacity for four hundred began to also loom large. This structure would cost about $200,000.

The site committee had chosen an abandoned pit owned by Canadian National Railways as the location of the building. The six and a half acres were close to the center of town and provided ample space for parking and the future addition of a swimming pool. The two level site also allowed for a distinctive building design.

Initial plans called for a trade of the CNR pit for six acres of town owned land, but eventually an extremely generous CNR accepted a cash offer of $12,500. Sale of the old arena site netted about this amount. Outstanding debentures on repairs to the forty year old structure absorbed the remainder.

In October the prefab idea was dropped by the building committee and an architect was hired. His model was ready in February. The price tag for the arena and community room including financing and services was $1.5 million.

During the fall the town treasurer applied for federal-provincial grants under the Neighborhood Improvement Plan. The upper levels of govern-

Reprinted with permission from *Public Relations Quarterly,* Fall 1971, pp. 21–22.

ment paying 75% provided the municipality raised the remaining 25%. In addition the provincial lottery would contribute a grant based on a ratio between local contributions and provincial money.

It was determined that a minimum of $150,000 would have to come from local fundraising efforts. From a community with an urban population of four thousand and a surrounding rural area with three thousand it would be a lot to ask for.

The fundraising committee decided that they needed three essential things; wide awareness of and participation in the campaign, a quick growth of funds to show support of the project, and a special hook to get groups and individuals involved to the fullest extent.

The campaign began July 22, 1976 with an effort to get as many residents as possible involved. The three area newspapers were asked to run a regular feature called "Put Your Money On Ice". This column reported on the activities taking place and inspired many groups and individuals to do innovative things.

Ladies made everything from candy to quilts. Men roller skated to other towns. Groups held auctions, suppers and dances. Buttons were sold at fall fairs. The cash returns were low but the involvement was high.

The realization that 1977 was the 100th anniversary of the incorporation of the Village of Gravenhurst provided the hook which got the service clubs into the project in a big way. The building became the Centennial Centre, "the most significant structure in our second century". The future of the community's youth was emphasized.

In September the Legion, Lions, Rotary and Kinsmen pledged a total of $70,000 to be given over a three year period. Instead of the usual "thermometer", a billboard showing a skater circling a rink was set up in the town square. With the pledges the fundraising committee had the early success it needed to keep the smaller groups active. By year's end the skater had reached the halfway point on the "ice" surface, $75,000.

Progress stalled at this point because there was still no drawing or model of the actual structure. Residents had been giving towards a building which had become many things to many people. Without some concrete facts their dreams could become a fundraising nightmare.

The major residential campaign had its own hook and had been planned for many months. The architect's model arrived on February 16 and the "Gold Brick" drive began March 4.

A wall would be built in the arena made of special bricks. Each brick would have an inlaid wood panel attached to it to be inscribed with the donor's name. To buy a brick required a minimum donation of one hundred dollars which had to be given by only one individual or family. A one year payment plan was offered.

Many people volunteered to canvas their neighbourhood for this project. A committee was set up to select and train the ones who would do the job. Advance publicity appeared in all three newspapers and brochures were prepared for the canvassers.

In a two week blitz two hundred fifteen bricks were sold. During the next three weeks the total rose to five hundred thirty six. Some individuals donated as much as one thousand dollars for a brick. Two minor hockey teams brought home provincial championships and enthusiasm was high. At the end of March the "skater" passed $130,000.

Local businessmen had taken part in the campaign via various schemes, the most popular being the donation of a portion of sales for a given period. When the largest industry in the town arranged for its union employees to donate four hours work to the fund and agreed to match the contribution, the result was a cheque for $7,871. The fund went over its goal in mid-May.

Thirty-three advertising boards were available in the new building. Two thirds of these were sold at $500 each before a formal campaign began. Planned events for the summer continued with $180,000 reached by the first anniversary of the campaign. No plans were made to stop collecting.

Many communities with similar needs for fundraising began to call on the town of Gravenhurst to ask how they had managed such a success story.

The fundraising chairman spoke of the publicity, early success from the service clubs, and a well organized gold brick campaign. The building committee chairman mentioned the proven need for the facility and the concern for the children. The mayor praised the generosity and community spirit of his citizens.

When the town council announced the calling of tenders for the building in May 1977 a crowd of over one hundred people stood and applauded loudly. Soon they will be able to stand before a remarkable building and say, "I put my money on ice."

The Baptists Want You!

WILLIAM MARTIN

God, as is His custom, has once again confounded the wise. After listening to a generation of theologians speak bravely of His death, the Almighty has established Himself as the odds-on choice for Comeback of the Decade. Conservative churches are growing, evangelical Christianity has been declared mainstream American religion, and a Southern Baptist Sunday school teacher has become Leader of the Free World. And now, as if that were not enough, the Baptist General Convention of Texas is about to launch a media blitz designed to share the good news of God's love with every man, woman, and child in the state an average of forty times apiece during a four-week period in February and March. The $1.5 million campaign, to be called Good News Texas, will feature commercials for Christ on television and radio, ads in newspapers and other print media, booster spots on billboards, pins on lapels, and an extensive personal visitation program to be run by the local churches. It is going to be pure Baptist. Well, almost pure. To help them do it right, the Baptists have hired one of the largest and most successful advertising firms in the country, the Bloom Advertising Agency of Dallas. Neither Sam nor Bob Bloom has roots in the Christian branch of the Judeo-Christian tradition.

I have mixed feelings about all this. Some of my best friends are Baptists, always have been. Still, I have never been able to shake completely the conviction that Baptists are the Aggies of religion. That in itself is not enough to damn them, but it does sort of set them apart. Part of my problem with Baptists stems from the fact that I grew up in the Church of Christ (Romans 16:16). As you may know, Church of Christ people believe the circle of the saved is rather small, and not many of them would care to sound too certain about their place in it. Baptists, on the other hand, never seem to tire of telling how sure they are they are saved and how good this blessed assurance feels. I thought their "once saved, always saved" doctrine of salvation was unsound—too easy; cheap grace; why, that would mean you could do anything you wanted

Reprinted with permission from *Texas Monthly*, February 1977, pp. 83–87, 149–157. The Appendix to this article was added by the editors.

to—but at least they had some doctrine, which was more than you could say for the Methodists, and at least we all agreed that nothing could send you to Hell faster than kissing the Pope's toe. No, the main problem wasn't doctrine. It was style. No matter what I believed, I could no more have been a Baptist when I was growing up than I could spend every Thursday night at the bowling alley or wear a seafoam-green leisure suit today.

For one thing, Baptists were so *organized* about inviting people to church. Once I was in the barbershop getting my weekly haircut when Mr. Joy Tilley, who was a big Baptist—I think it says something that the counterpart of "staunch Presbyterian," "devout Catholic," and "pillar in the Methodist Church" is "big Baptist"—stuck his head in and invited the barber to come and sit in his pew at a revival then in progress. That astonished me. We had a few elderly members who sort of had squatter's rights to pews they had occupied for years, but we would never have dreamed of assigning somebody a particular pew and then sending them out to drum up people to pack it.

The contrast carried over to the revivals themselves. The mark of a successful Church of Christ revivalist was his ability to drive the nail of terror into slumbering souls. Though some Baptist revivalists made use of hellfire and brimstone, I always felt that the mark of a successful Baptist preacher was his ability to make you laugh and feel good. That didn't seem much like religion to me.

This difference was further reflected in the Sunday schools, where we gave our classes sensible, functional names—"Preschool," "Elementary," "Junior High," and "Young People"—and encouraged attendance by quoting scriptures, especially Hebrews 10:25 ("Forsake not the assembling of yourselves together"), and threatening slackers with hellfire. Baptists called their classes things like "Sunbeams" and "Pioneers" and "Aviators" and drew crowds by having the youth minister bounce over the church bus from a trampoline.

I used to marvel at what they would do to appeal to young people. Our high school assembly programs fell into two primary categories: magicians, myna birds, and trick-shot artists sent out from the Southern School Assemblies organization and—this was before Ms. O'Hair took God out of the schools—preachers holding revivals over at the Baptist church. They would juggle and tell a few jokes and then talk to us earnestly about taking care of our bodies, which are temples of the Holy Spirit (I Corinthians 6:19). Once a revival team from Baylor entertained us with several hymns and gospel tunes arranged for trumpet trio. Then the leader, a young man with the unforgettable name of Horace Oliver Bilderback, placed a trombone mouthpiece in his trumpet and played "Let the Lower Lights Be Burning," while one of his fellow clerics moved an imaginery trombone slide out in front. That, to me, was the pure essence of the Southern Baptist Church.

At times, to be sure, I envied my Baptist friends and made some effort to be one of them. I went to the Baptist Vacation Bible School several years and made bookends and potholders and whatnot shelves, and did right well at a Bible game called Sword Drill—"Attention! Draw swords! (No thumbs over the edges, now.) John 3:16! Charge!"—and I thought it was keen that their pastor, Brother Rose, illustrated his devotional lessons with magic tricks and showed us slides of his trip to the Holy Land. Once, I joined the Royal Ambassadors (and got elected Ambassador-in-Chief) just to have a chance to go to the summer encampment at Alta Frio, but I lost my nerve before the bus left and stayed home. Later, I longed to go on hayrides and swimming parties with the Training Union and even wished I could go into San Antonio and hear Angel Martinez preach in a white suit. But it was just no use. I was like a lonely traveler watching a group of Shriners cutting up in a hotel lobby; it might be fun for a day or two to wear a fez and ride a little motor scooter down Main Street, but you wouldn't want to go home and still have to be one.

Before all the Baptists walk out on me, I have a confession to make. About four or five years ago, I became sort of a Baptist myself. After spending the better part of the sixties studying religion at Harvard, I grew a bit weak on matters of doctrine and decided I would do more harm than good by sticking with the Church of Christ. When I came back to Texas, I cast around a bit and finally wound up at a church that I suppose could be described as liberal and ecumenical, though even now I find it difficult to identify myself as a theological liberal, so strongly was I taught to believe that few states of being are more pernicious. Still, at least half the people in this church grew up as Baptists, a good handful of them are former Baptist preachers, and even though the Union Baptist Association of Houston threw them out for accepting members from other denominations without rebaptizing them, they still persist in calling themselves Baptists. I have had some trouble with it. I am embarrassed when they look at me in amazement because I have never heard of Lottie Moon, and I get a little squirmy when they sing "Do Lord" at the annual retreat up in the woods, and I admit it doesn't make a dime's worth of difference to me whether Baylor wins or loses a football game. Still, we don't have revivals and if we did we wouldn't have trumpets or trombones or jugglers, and nobody checks to see why you haven't been coming to Sunday school and, as far as I can tell, nobody much cares about the details of your belief, so long as you are kind and try to help folk when they need it. It doesn't have anything like the zip of a straight-out evangelical church, but ex-Fundamentalists are some of the best people you'll find anywhere, so I expect I'll keep my letter in a while longer. Besides, if Good News Texas works, we may all be Baptists by summer.

Baptists, of course, have always been aggressive. They sought "A Million More in Fifty-four" and they have sponsored Billy Graham Crusades and hold "Win Clinics" to instruct people in the techniques of personal evangelism. But this is bigger, better, grander than anything they have ever done before.

My immersion in the project came in Dallas at a regional meeting of the Baptist General Convention of Texas (BGCT). The Good News Texas portion of the program was co-chaired by Drs. L. L. Morriss and Lloyd Elder. Morriss, with his smooth gray hair, metal glasses, and high-quality fall woolens, could easily pass for a corporation executive. His speech and manner befit his appearance—one senses he does little by accident. Lloyd Elder's obvious intelligence, warmth, and gentle wit are engaging, but his slightly more rumpled look and apparent unconcern for slickness make it easier to believe he is a seminary professor or church executive.

Morriss declared he was as excited as "an auctioneer at an auction of used furniture," a metaphor I thought fell somewhat short of the mark. He was excited, he said, about what God had done for Texas in the past and about what He is doing now. He introduced Elder, who was also excited. Good News Texas, Elder said, would have three major targets. (1) the 4.7 million Texans—one third of the state's population—who do not belong to any Christian group, persons "who are completely uninvolved in the things of Christ," (2) inactive and apathetic church members, including 700,000 Baptists, and (3) the active membership of local Baptist churches. He summarized what the Bloom Agency had done so far and sketched out the main lines the media campaign would follow. Then he reminded the assembly that Good News Texas "is not a goodwill campaign for the convention. It is not church advertising. It is going with the best product we have, and that is the gospel of Jesus Christ."

Elder then called on Dr. Jimmy Allen, the pastor of San Antonio's First Baptist Church. Allen is a big man who wears his graying hair rather long for a Baptist preacher and gives off an unmistakable impression of high energy. Working from a few notes scribbled on the back of an envelope, he spoke of "the rhythm in the way God moves in His world, in the tide, in our heartbeat, in the very energy levels of our lives." "There are times," he said, "when God moves in great force and power in our lives, and then there are times of wandering in the wilderness when we begin to appreciate the fact that we cannot live in ecstasy all the time.

There must be a hunger before there is filling. There must be thirst before there can be a slaking of thirst. I am convinced we are at the edge of a spiritual awakening in our nation and that some of us are in places where we can already sense the tide of God comining in.''

Allen noted that *Newsweek* had carried Charles Colson's testimonial, that the *Fort Worth Star-Telegram* had printed an editorial that told how to be saved, and that CBS had interviewed members of his church for an hour-long documentary on the meaning of salvation. He went on for about twenty minutes, talking about how much we needed revival and how much he hoped God might choose Baptists to be part of the central apparatus by which He moved. Then, in a hushed voice that visibly moved the audience with its intensity, he concluded: ''I find myself saying, 'God, could this be the time? Lord, could you be ready now? Is it something that will take our breath away?' I find myself saying, 'O Lord, let it be good news, not just for Texas, not just for Texas Baptists, but for a nation and a world that desperately needs to find out that, indeed, there is good news.' ''

Later that afternoon, I sat down with Morriss, Elder, and BGCT executive director Dr. James Landes. Though he was quick to note he is a chemical engineer by training, Dr. Landes' beneficent countenance and rather sermonic manner make it clear he has been around a lot of preachers.

''The rationale of Good News Texas,'' Landes said, ''is the commandment 'Go ye into all the world.' I have seen the heartbreaking conditions so many people are experiencing throughout this state. I had no alternative but to study how to spread the message that there are people in the world who *care,* who are interested in persons just because they are human beings, regardless of race or color or creed, and that the reason these people care is because they believe God *is,* and Christ *is,* and the Scriptures are a mirror of Christ's mind. I realized also that many of our leaders were reaching out for some undergirding arm that could strengthen and help them in their ministry in the local church. So, as I thought and prayed and did a bit of meditating in between fly fishing on the riverbanks of Colorado, I said, 'Lord, if this great big denomination with two million people and forty-two hundred churches and missions will make up its mind to do one thing across a period of a couple of years, there is no telling what good could come of that.' And I thought if we could just plant a seed, maybe it could grow, maybe it could bless a whole state and the nation. I shared that dream with my associates here on the administrative staff and they asked me to share it with the executive board. I came away somewhat shocked but deeply gratified, because men who do not normally react enthusiastically to another evangelistic thrust got to their feet and said, 'This sounds different, get with it!' ''

As we talked, Landes and his colleagues echoed what Jimmy Allen had said about the soon-coming revival. Exciting things are happening among our laymen, they said. Signs of awakening are blowing across our nation. But if revival was coming with or without their help, as they seemed to be saying, why didn't Baptists take their $1.5 million and spend it some other way? ''Somebody has to be the agent,'' Landes replied. ''God always works through an Abraham, a Moses, an Isaac, a Joseph, a John the Baptist. He doesn't work without working through people. If Texas Baptists have the favorable image the research for this project shows we have, then we've got a *responsibility* commensurate with it. If God wants to use us, we have a responsibility to be available.''

I brought up something that had struck me from the moment I saw the first piece of promotional literature about Good News Texas. The logo for the campaign is the Christian fish symbol, with the state of Texas stuffed inside it like Jonah. To accommodate both Amarillo and Laredo, the fish is drawn a bit fat, so that it looks something like a football with a tail or perhaps a Gospel Blimp. Several years ago a mild satire, widely circulated in evangelical circles, described the misadventures of a Christian group that hired a blimp to broadcast sermons and drop leaflets on the hapless community below. Though it attracted great attention, the townspeople were irritated and offended, and the initial spirit and purpose of the enterprise were lost and perverted. I was curious about whether these men had considered the possibility that Good News Texas might be a Baptist version of the Gospel Blimp.

Elder was aware of the perils. "If we just saturated the media with the gospel message," he said, "and expected something to happen automatically, that would be the Gospel Blimp approach. Just pay your money and send up the blimp. But we are making a real effort to keep that from happening. We are trying to equip ministers and lay people in the local churches to be *witnesses,* so that they don't just let the blimp fly over, but can knock on doors and present the gospel to people as caring, sharing neighbors."

Jimmy Allen had said Baptists would need to remember that "when God comes to town, He doesn't always stay in our house. He moves where He chooses to move and leaps over all kinds of barriers." How would they feel if the Methodists or Presbyterians or Church of Christ picked up some new members on Baptist nickels? The prospect did not seem to dismay them. They were, in fact, informing other denominations in the state about their plans so that if the awakening comes, they can also be ready for it. There is, of course, some confidence that their 4,200 outlets will give Baptists a healthy share of whatever market develops.

This ecumenical talk emboldened me to raise a point I regarded as of at least mild interest. Why had they chosen the Bloom Agency? Granted, it was recognzied as one of the best agencies in the country and its Dallas location provided the advantage of close and frequent contact, but was there no sense of incongruity in hiring a Jewish-owned agency to conceive and produce an evangelistic campaign for Southern Baptists? Apparently not. The Baptists chose their agency the same way Procter and Gamble or Exxon might, with a steering committee of seventeen people and a much larger consultation group from across the state that heard presentations by a number of respected firms.

"Bob Bloom is a good salesman," said James Landes. " 'When he was through,' I heard a Baptist preacher from East Texas say, 'I don't need to hear anybody else. The man knows where he is going.' When that group voted, they did so with a great feeling of confidence in the ability and desire of the Bloom Agency to help us do what we wanted to do. It was almost unanimous. It was an overwhelming decision." Landes admitted to some early personal reservations but insisted things had worked out "more beautifully and fantastically than we had expected." Then he suggested I check out the backgrounds of the men at the agency with primary responsibility for the account.

The Bloom Agency occupies several floors of the Zale Building, which sits alongside Stemmons Freeway like a giant homemaker's misplaced toaster. Instead of the customary rooms and hallways, the agency uses "action offices," work spaces defined by movable partitions about five and a half feet high, which can be shaped to fit needs that change with each new client or campaign. Flexible white hoses bring electrical and telephonic nourishment to each of the modules, so that one can tote up the number of offices currently in use by counting the accordion-pleated umbilici. The occupants of these spaces decorate them as if they are planning to stay for years, so I presume one has a fair chance of hanging onto one's own partitions, but I was told reshuffling is not uncommon.

The furnishings run heavily to chrome, glass, and plastic, with plenty of plants and bright colors. Most of the offices are densely decorated in pop-artifactual chic, with tapestries and macrame hangings and inspirational posters framed in Lucite and fire-alarm boxes and street signs and—everywhere—reminders and remnants of past campaigns. Shelves in the reception area hold symbols of the agency's various clients: Bekins, Southwest Airlines, Owens Sausage, Amalie

Motor Oil, Rainbo Bread, Lubriderm Cream, Whataburger, and a score of others. I looked in vain for a New Testament or a Broadman Hymnal, but I guess the display had not yet been brought that far up to date.

Bob Bloom showed me around and talked about the Baptist account. "We are in the consumer advertising business," he explained. "Our job is to communicate with the general public and get a response from them. That is what we do best. We try to generate retail purchases, to get people to buy motor oil, or a home, or seats on an airplane. We have never been involved in anything like this before, but the thing that stimulated us was the feeling that the BGCT could give us what we want in a partnership role, a sharing of responsibilities as opposed simply to doing what we tell them. They know how to listen, how to guide, how to tell us when we are off base, and they know how to stroke, so we are pleased to have the association from that standpoint. I was impressed that they could not only accept but embrace aspects of our craft that we have difficulty getting business people, including some Harvard MBAs, to accept."

How did he account for this? "I'm not really sure," Bloom said. "I guess they are just smart. I had expected a sharp drop-off in intelligence between the leaders of the organization and the men in lower positions. In a business organization like a bank, for example, once you get past the president and a few directors to some of the department heads, you find some terrible prejudices about certain things, a lack of understanding about advertising and research, and an unwillingness to bend. I expected that with the Baptists, but frankly, I found a lot of sharp men at all levels. And they are very flexible. When we got out with the pastors, I expected to confront some prejudice, both from my being Jewish and in their willingness to marry our craft with their pulpit responsibilities. I just didn't find any of that. I found a high degree of comprehension when we went through the various alternatives with them. I kind of expected someone to get up and make an appeal to 'throw all that stuff away and just give people the simple gospel.' It didn't happen. They had smart, agile minds and they really embraced what we were trying to do. If I could get forty rabbis together to do that, I would be terribly surprised. They are also very sincere about the undertaking. It is great to have a client who believes in what he is doing, as opposed to someone who is just grinding out a product."

Did he have any misgivings about mounting a campaign whose basic premise he, as a Jew, did not believe? "I never felt any real sensitivity on that issue, except in regard to the terminology, which was very alien to me. Once I became confident they were willing to accept me as a spokesman for the agency and as a craftsman with some expertise, I became very comfortable with it. My role has been much the same as with any client. I feel I am particularly good at organizational work and strategic thinking. I am not concerned with the technological aspects of a motor oil—what it will or won't do for an engine—and I can't comment on the religious aspects of this project. What I am interested in is how we can communicate the selling points to the customer."

Bob introduced me to his father, Sam Bloom, the agency's founder, who professed an interest in the project that went beyond craftsmanship. He was concerned "about both the standards and ethics which appear to be declining in politics and business." The Baptists, he thought, were on the right track on these matters. Their willingness to lay $1.5 million on the line to bolster the ethics and morality of the state was a courageous act and he was "terribly enthused" to have a part in it.

I visited with most of the key personnel working on the account in the agency's new think tank, a tiered and carpeted room with no furniture except for ashtrays and huge pillows covered in plain, madras, batik, and Marimekko. A tray on one of the lower tiers held coffee, Styrofoam cups, little packets of Cremora, Imperial Sugar, Sweet 'n' Low, and a box of those red-and-white plastic sticks that are too skinny to stir anything. On the assumption, I presume, that ideas generated in the room would be too dramatic to jot down on 3 × 5 cards with a ball-point pen, jumbo pads of paper and Magic Markers lay within easy reach. While a person in Faded Glory jeans with stars on the pockets went out to get Frescas and Tabs and Cokes for the non-coffee drinkers, we took our positions, shifted around a bit to look properly relaxed, and began to talk.

Dick Yob, research director for the project, explained that "the days of doing what we *think* will work are becoming extinct because of the amount of money that is involved. We have to go out and find what really does communicate. Our approach has been to come at this like we would any package goods account, since that is basically what we know how to do." The first step had been to see what problems were bothering Texans these days. To accomplish this, Yob hired the Dallas marketing research firm of Louis, Bowles and Grove, Inc., to show a list of problems to approximately 300 Dallas and Austin citizens—divided evenly between active Baptists, inactive Christians, and non-Christians—and ask which most accurately mirrored their own feelings and which were the problems they heard other people discuss. On both counts, all three groups ranked hypocrisy as the number one problem, by agreeing with such statements as "It's getting harder to trust anybody or anything" and "People are not what they pretend to be. They say one thing and do another."

Survey participants were then offered three possible solutions: (1) reading the Bible, (2) joining a group of active Christians, and (3) entering into a personal relationship with Jesus Christ and following his teachings. All three groups agreed that of the three answers, Christ was the best—though only 27 percent of the inactive Christians and 14 percent of the non-Christians actually felt it was an appropriate solution for them. More than two-thirds of the non-Christians chose none of the three options. In short, despite evidence of considerable spiritual and emotional malaise among backslidden and secular Texans, the field appeared to be something less than white unto harvest. Still, the Baptists and the agency agreed that a personal relation with Jesus was the most commercial of the products they had to offer. The next step was to decide how to package it for wholesale distribution.

At this point, the burden shifted to Bill Hill, the agency's creative director. He did not find the yoke an easy one. What could they say that would communicate effectively to all three target groups? And what vehicle would they use to say it: testimonial? dramatizations? slice of life vignettes? cartoons? jingles? During our first conversation, Hill had a discernible case of advertiser's anxiety. "We are trying to avoid clichés. The men working with us from BGCT are theologians. When they say 'Christ died for you,' there is a lifetime of knowledge behind it and all sorts of subtleties ripple out of it, but to the people they have singled out as the primary audience—non-Christians—that is a cliché and it may be a turnoff. We want to save the Jesus message to the very end of the TV spots, so we can get people nodding and saying, 'Yes, that is a problem. Yes, I would like to have a solution to that problem.' Then, at the end, we want to say, 'That solution is available to you through Jesus Christ.' We are trying to say, in the simplest form possible, that 'something that happened two thousand years ago is a real force that is relevant to your own individual problems right here and right now. If you are really concerned about your own problems and about what is going on in the world, and you have tried everything else, what have you got to lose?' We are not really trying to say *how* Christ is the answer, but simply *that* he is. We may go into *how* a little more in the other media." The problem of doing justice to the gospel in a brief commercial is tough, Hill admitted: "I keep writing forty-two-second commercials because I just can't boil it all down into thirty seconds. In a thirty-second spot, about all we can say is, 'This aspirin contains more pain relievers than all the others combined.' "

Guy Marble outlined the key public relations

aspects of the campaign. His main task would be to bombard local churches throughout the state with newsletters, articles, speeches, posters, lapel buttons, and other communiqués to allow them to take full advantage of the media campaign when it hit their area. The agency people and Baptists both agreed that the word would be barren, like seed on stony ground, unless the local churches were ready not only to urge personal evangelism, but also to accept and nurture those who might be converted. As Jim Goodnight, who has overall responsibility for the account, put it, "We are going to give people the opportunity to respond, but when a guy walks in the back door of a Baptist church some Sunday morning to find what he has been looking for—what happens then will be up to the members of that church. If they are not ready for people who may not share any of their values, then it won't work. If they are ready to accept people 'just as I am,' I believe there will be a tremendous awakening of visible growth in both numbers and spirit." Another promotion task will be to make sure the local churches understand the strategy that will govern the campaign. "When we buy time for these commercials," Goodnight explained, "we are not going to be buying the Sunday Morning Revival Hour. We are going to be buying *Mary Hartmann, Mary Hartmann* and *All in the Family* and *Sonny and Cher*. You can anticipate the kinds of reactions thousands and thousands of Texas Baptists are going to have—'What are we doing supporting that kind of program?' Of course, our purpose is not to support the program. It's where we have to go to reach the people we want to reach."

Despite the frequent comparison of selling the gospel to selling aspirin or motor oil, it seemed clear these men were taking the matter more seriously than that. I recalled what Dr. Landes had said about checking their backgrounds, so I asked each of them to characterize his religious position. The agency didn't exactly turn out to be a collection of Madison Avenue cynics. Dick Yob is a graduate of Catholic University at Marquette, sends his oldest son to parochial school, and is active in the Church. Bill Hill is the son of a Baptist preacher in Amarillo but became so disillusioned with evangelical Christianity by the time he reached high school that for several years he dabbled in Zen, studied Rosicrucian literature, and considered going to live with the Dalai Lama in Tibet. Instead, he got married and became an Episcopalian. For the past seven years, he has participated in Bible class taught by conservative Biblicist Mal Couch, a graduate of fundamentalist Dallas Theological Seminary who specializes in the interpretation of Biblical prophecy. Public relations advisor Guy Marble describes himself as "a lasped Methodist," but his colleague Frank Demarest is a member of the Northwest Bible Church in Dallas (also aligned with the Dallas Theological Seminary) and admits he stands a bit to the right of Southern Baptists in his theology. Jim Goodnight grew up in the Park Cities Baptist Church in Dallas but switched to the Church of Christ after he married the granddaughter of G. H. P. Showalter, a Church of Christ patriarch and former editor of one of its most conservative papers, the *Firm Foundation*. Though he locates himself in "the liberal, ecumenical wing of the Church of Christ" (a figure of speech like "virile impotence"), he is still active in the Preston Crest congregation in Dallas and has taught classes in C. S. Lewis' *Mere Christianity,* hardly a radical treatise.

These men, it turns out, are not the only Christians in the Bloom Agency. "You would be amazed," Goodnight said, "at the number of people within the agency who wanted to work on this account. Not only have a number of these closet Christians surfaced, but about twenty-five of us now meet each Wednesday at noon to pray and share our concerns and testimonials." "It's really neat," Demarest said. "All our working lives we have had this separation between our Christian faith and what we do on our jobs. For me, this is the first time to bring the two together."

"There is a terrible intensity among the people on the team," Hill said. "This is not just another piece of package goods. This is something that is going to affect people's lives. I really feel what I am doing. I keep thinking, 'We are going to save Texas!' and that gets to be a bit of a hang-up and causes a mental block." Another problem, Goodnight observed, is that "each of us gets his own theology and beliefs, his own personal slant woven into it. One of the hardest things to do in any advertising is to wash yourself out of it and consider only the people you are trying to write for and what their needs are."

"With most products." Yob pointed out, "you are selling to people who are already users. It is a matter of getting them to switch brands or buy more of your product. But in this campaign, non-users are the number one target."

That afternoon I attended a meeting between members of the Bloom team and key staff members at the Baptist Building. Mainly, they were catching each other up on how things were going in their sections of the ball park. Jim Goodnight read the strategy statement that had emerged from their research. "What we are trying to do," he said, "is communicate to people that the frustrations they experience with the hypocrisy and lack of integrity in today's world is the result of misplaced priorities, and that the solution is to place their trust in Jesus Christ who will never fail them, rather than on the imperfect things of the world." The Baptists liked that a lot.

Demarest, Marble, and Mary Colias Carter reviewed PR plans. A steady stream of articles would appear in the *Baptist Standard* to "soften up the terrain," and a piece would appear in the next issue of the *Helper,* BGCT's women's magazine. Pastors would be supplied with information they could use to raise money for the program. Every church would receive materials explaining the nature and scope of the project. Marble reported that he and his associates had done "much agonizing posterwise," but promised the first in a series of posters would be ready in "six weeks max."

They also talked a bit about honorary chairmen. Billy Graham had agreed to serve as national honorary chairman, but both the Baptists and the Bloom representatives wanted to make sure the campaign did not become a Graham affair. "We are not going to be able to use him much in a public way," Marble said. "If he is flying from coast to coast, we may be able to get him to stop off at DFW airport for a press conference and say how great Good News Texas is. We can do little things like that without much financial or time commitment, but that will be about the extent of it. Right now, we just want to get half a day with him at his place in North Carolina to produce several short items that could be used to stir up enthusiasm in the local churches." In addition to Graham, two state chairmen would be chosen—people who could generate prestige and interest in Jesus just by their association with the campaign. After all, one Baptist executive observed, "Public relations is the name of the game."

Over the next several weeks, Bill Hill and his associates developed four proto-commercials in "animatic" form—a series of still drawings with voice-overs rather than the live action or true animation that would be used in the final product. Each of the four took a different slant and would be tested to see which, if any, might appeal most to the Texas contingent of a lost and dying world. If none clicked, it would be, quite literally, back to the drawing board. If one seemed clearly better than the others, it would become the model for the actual spots to be used in the campaign. On three successive evenings in early October, representatives of Louis, Bowles and Grove showed the spots to "focus groups" drawn from the three target populations. Active Baptists met the first night in three churches scattered around Dallas.

I am not supposed to identify either the church or the people I observed, so I won't, but I promise you it was a real Baptist church, with a poster thermometer in the foyer that showed how the fund drive was going.

Judy Briggs, a market researcher for Louis, Bowles and Grove, told the group they were to give their reactions to some commercials being prepared for television. She did not say they were Baptist commercials or mention Good News

Texas. She then showed the commercials on a videotape machine and asked the group to fill out a questionnaire after they viewed each one.

The first commercial, identified as "Promises," offered shots of politicians, automobile dealers, and various businessmen making familiar promises—"You've got my word on it.' "It's a sure thing," "You can depend on it." It ended with a note to the effect that Jesus is the only one whose promises can be trusted and "Isn't it time we listened?" The positive responses to "Promises" indicated the Christians held a disillusioned view of humanity: "Everybody is trying to put something over on us." "People will let you down, but if you trust in God, He won't let you down." "You have to put your faith in the Lord and not in other people." I got the message, but I felt sad, and the stark ceiling light illumined other, almost forgotten rooms in my soul, rooms not furnished with warm and reassuring memories, rooms abandoned because the heat had been shut off and the broken panes let in too much damp and cold.

The next example showed a man arising to the sound of a strident alarm and struggling to meet the day as he listened to the depressing litany of the morning news. Then a voice-over announcer asked. "Wouldn't it be a change to wake up one morning without anxiety over what the day might bring? To know that whatever the world throws at you, you'll make it? If that kind of change would be welcome, then get with the one person who can do the changing—Jesus Christ. For a change." This, too, seemed to confirm the experience of the group: "We can't depend on the news being good," they said, "but if we have Jesus Christ with us, it makes no difference. You have to have Him because what problems can you face without Christ?"

The third effort did not lend itself so easily to clichéd response. In this one, a black man told of how he had been a revolutionary, seeking social change by whatever means seemed expedient. But not long ago, he said, he had run across another revolutionary and it had changed his life completely. He can change yours, too, the man promised. Then he said, "My name is Eldridge Cleaver. I'm Living Proof."

Bill Hill had told me one of the commercials would be a testimonial, and I would not have been surprised to have seen Charles Colson or Johnny Cash telling about what God had wrought in their lives. I try to keep up with the box scores on notable conversions, but I had somehow missed the news that the icy soul of Eldridge Cleaver had been warmed with fire from above. I was impressed that Texas Baptists would consider pumping hundreds of thousands of dollars into publicizing the testimony of a man who might still be regarded with skepticism and caution by some of the new white brothers. And I was especially curious about how the members of this largely working-class church might react.

I studied the lone black member of the group, a man about 45. Was he an Uncle Tom who would fear that the sight and sound of this panther in lamb's clothing might stir resentment left over from the sixties and jeopardize his perhaps lately won and still tenuous place in a predominantly white congregation? Would he say of Cleaver, as Peter had said of Christ, "I never knew him"? No, he wouldn't. "This is very beautiful," he said. "It comes from a controversial person a lot of us can identify with. We know Eldridge Cleaver was searching for something he could not find in the world, but only in Jesus Christ. I had much the same problems in my life at one time. It was very hard for me to accept certain things, but now I am able to face these things and accept them." That is not exactly revolution, but it isn't "white folks always been nice to me" either.

A middle-aged woman who had taken much longer than anyone else to fill out her questionnaire spoke next. I sensed she was about to vent a little of the racist spleen we often associate with working-class fundamentalists. "This was also my favorite," she said. "It shows that Christ is a Man for all men. He is not a white man's savior or a black man's savior or a Jew's savior. He is for everyone. I think every minority feels pressures and I think there are times in everybody's life when they feel like they are a minority, even though nobody else may look upon them that way. When you are low man on the totem pole in your office and everybody says, 'You do this' and 'You do that,' and it seems like you do everything for everybody, then you can identify with the feeling of being a little bit left out."

The final commercial depicted a child learning to ice skate with the loving help of a parent-figure in a unisex outfit like the Olympic speed skaters wear. The narrator told how important it is to have someone you can depend on when the going gets a bit hazardous and concluded with the slogan, "Learn to live with Jesus Christ." I liked it best of the four. Its symbolism was aesthetically appealing and I like the way it avoided both the negative connotations about human nature (though I am not especially sanguine about the natural goodness of our kind) and the spurious overgeneralization implicit in any case based on a single testimony. The nine focus groups agreed more strongly than on any other point that "Ice Rink" was clearly the poorest of the four commercials. "It was boring," they said. "It just beat around the bush and didn't really say anything." "I can't ice skate, so I don't identify with that one at all." "A waste of film." I decided not to become a consultant on mass evangelism.

Ms. Briggs asked who they thought might sponsor commercials like these. Oh, the Catholics or SMU or maybe the Dallas Council of Churches. Not one named the Baptists. Baptists have W. A. Criswell; they don't need Eldridge Cleaver.

The meetings with the Baptist groups were designed to see if any of the commercials were likely to run into the kind of opposition that might make funding or other forms of cooperation difficult. But the real test, everyone agreed, would be with those who described themselves as nominal or inactive Christians and those who openly acknowledged they were not religious in any conventional sense. A pool of such people had been obtained by distributing questionnaires in Dallas office buildings; groups representing both sexes and a broad range of ages had been selected from this pool. In keeping with the piety of the groups, we met at a neutral site, the Marriott Inn. Curtiss Grove, a partner in Louis, Bowles and Grove, was moderator for the evening. As we waited for people to assemble, he lamented having to pass up a cocktail party down the hall.

The group looked pretty representative of backsliders I have known: a workingman in his thirties; an overweight balding man who talked knowledgeably about the video equipment; a tall, thin older man who wore a tie with a leisure suit and looked as though he smoked a lot and was perhaps familiar with the taste of liquor; a woman who was pretty in the way that Southwest Airlines stewardesses are pretty, and a thin, serious man who appeared to be with her; a young woman about twenty who wore blue eye shadow and orthodontic braces; a neat woman in her thirties who looked like she was probably in charge of several people where she worked and had a reputation for getting things done on time; one of those ubiquitous, interchangeable young men with a moustache and styled hair and a preference for shiny shirts with sailboats or jockeys on them; a foxy brunette in a suede jacket and lots of bracelets and rings and dark fingernail polish who seemed a poor conversion prospect; and several others I knew then I wouldn't be able to remember. For the most part, they represented a bit higher socioeconomic status than the Baptists I had visited the night before.

Grove is good at his job and easily elicited comments from the group. Interestingly, their reactions were not remarkably different from those of the active Baptists, except that none of them rated the Cleaver commercial highest and four of the twelve designated it their least favorite. (As it turned out, this response was something of an anomaly; the other two groups meeting at the same time felt strongly that the Cleaver spot was the best.) When asked what the commercial sought to accomplish, one man guessed it was trying to stir up pity for Cleaver. Another thought it too controversial even for minority-group people and felt its appeal would be limited to revolutionaries or people "with awful problems."

Each of the other spots got three or four votes as the best of the lot, but what one felt was pungent, another would judge pedantic. The 28-year-old in the shiny shirt said he didn't think any was much better than the others, since they were all about God and the church. A young man about nineteen seemed rather bemused by the whole business, as though he thought his sainted mother had somehow arranged to get him invited to a subtle soul-winning campaign, maybe even paid his way. But all things considered, I think this group uttered more pious clichés than the dedicated Baptists. Since they did not know they had been chosen because of their shared lukewarmness, they seemed to feel some need to let their colleagues know they were believers. In spite of what may have been a bit of overcompensation, however, I sensed almost none of the assurance I had seen and heard the night before. Several people got sad looks on their faces and lit up cigarettes. I believe they were pretty serious about it all. I had agreed not to ask any questions and I may have misread their reaction, but I had not expected what I sensed and it seemed unmistakable. I wouldn't be surprised to learn that the older man in the leisure suit had started going back to church with his wife.

As before, almost no one perceived the commercials as Baptist in origin. The President's Council on Physical Fitness, the Cerebral Palsy Association, an ice rink, the Department of Health, Education, and Welfare, Channel 39, and Sominex all seemed as likely as the Southern Baptists to sponsor such spots.

On the third night, self-designated unbelievers viewed the spots. This was the crucial test, the people at whom the main thrust of the campaign was aimed, but their preferences turned out to differ little from their more pious predecessors. Neither "Morning News" nor "Promises" struck a responsive chord. One man who at first thought "Morning News" was touting CBS news was irriated when it proved to have a religious theme. Another picked up the religious slant earlier but just thought, "Here we go again." A woman complained that "it doesn't tell me what to do with my problems, except give them to someone else. A little information about how Jesus is going to handle my problems would be helpful."

"Promises" caused even stronger negative reactions—one woman characterized it as "hateful" and said, "It made me want to lock myself in a room and shoot anybody that makes promises"—and "Ice Rink" once again came in as the unanimous last choice. One woman described it as "childish the way they wanted you to put yourself in Jesus' hands with no mention of adult choices." Another took issue with the whole ice-skating metaphor; she didn't feel at all like an ice skater, but rather "a yo-yo, every day I feel like a yo-yo." A man about thirty said he felt a better metaphor would be someone playing poker, or perhaps even solitaire. I doubt seriously the Southern Baptists will pick up on that.

Once again the Cleaver commercial was picked as the best—unanimously by one caucus. A man who freely called himself an agnostic said, "I know what Cleaver's life has been, and if this guy says he can pull it out with Christ, well, I may think there is something to it." He admitted to some doubts whether Cleaver might just be trying to escape a prison sentence by publicly embracing religion, but rejected them: "I have not agreed with Cleaver in the past, but I have respected his integrity." Others did question Cleaver's sincerity, but what carried the day was the feeling that "it gave me a choice. It told me what his opinion was, but it didn't say, 'You take my opinion, buddy, because it is good for you too.' "

The success of the Cleaver spot naturally raised the question of whose testimonials people could accept. The subject shouldn't be an ordinary person, someone from the viewer's own neighborhood ("I would figure someone was just trying to get on television and get some publicity"); it certainly shouldn't be Richard Nixon or Patty Hearst ("It is still too close. With Cleaver you can almost feel the guy has paid his debt and now has a whole new slant on life"). The ideal person, one man thought, would be a noncriminal figure who still had room for notable repentance—the two names mentioned were Billy Graham and Earl Scheib, the $29.95 auto paint job man.

Interestingly, the non-Christians had no difficulty accepting the idea that Southern Baptists might be behind the commercials. The use of testimonials seemed "more Baptist" than any of the other approaches, even though Eldridge Cleaver seemed like an unlikely star. One woman suggested that if Baptists were indeed the sponsors, they would do well to hide the fact, since "many people are turned off by their extremist actions."

If the consultants were looking for useful criticism, the non-Christians gave them plenty of that, but if they were looking for some signs that Good News Texas was going to send unbelievers flocking to church, the meeting provided little basis for hope. One man quickly deduced that his group contained no practicing Christians and said, "I think people like us tend to rely on ourselves rather than look outside for some kind of placebo. I don't care whether people believe in Jesus or Muhammad or Darrell Royal; just because they believe it and get out and preach it doesn't mean it's true. I just don't buy the idea that you can blindly put your faith and trust in any person, including Jesus."

The bad news for Good News Texas was that the non-Christians didn't like the whole idea of religious commercials. "I am turned off by commercials of this sort," said one. "It cheapens religion to sell it like toothpaste." "There is nothing in these commercials that appeals to me in any way or makes me feel I should investigate Christianity," another said. "They make it sound like Jesus is going to open up a used-car lot." But one man who also had a negative reaction to selling Jesus on TV conceded that "television is such a powerful communications medium that if they use it right, it can help. There are some people whose only way of touching anything outside their home is television."

It is Bloom's job, then, to see that TV is used right. The hope that any single commercial might provide Baptists with an offer lost Texans could not refuse seemed pretty well dashed. Still, the reponse to news that the sins of the apostle of Black Power had been washed away had proven sufficiently promising to convince Bloom and the BGCT that testimonials were the route to take. At the state convention in San Antonio two weeks later, L. L. Morriss proclaimed that the theme of Good News Texas would be "Living Proof" and would concentrate on "presenting the testimony of people who have experienced the saving grace of our Lord." Dr. Landes announced that Baylor football coach Grant Teaff and actress Jeannette Clift George had agreed to serve as honoary co-chairmen and played a tape from Billy Graham, who said the world was hungry for good news and he was pleased to have a part in the boldest evangelistic venture in the history of Texas Baptists.

By the first of December, some of the top converts in the country had been lined up to add their testimony to Cleaver's. There had been minor problems. Some Christian entertainers had been discouraged from participating by their agents, who feared it might hurt their image with the public. Others had been screened out when their faith was adjudged not yet solid enough to guarantee against an embarrassing relapse during the campaign; no one, for example, would want to take a chance on Jerry Lee Lewis if he were suddenly to go into one of his periodic conversion phases. The final list included country singers Jeannie C. Riley and Connie Smith, Mexican musician Paulino Bernal, Consul-General of Honduras Rosargentina Pinel-Cordova, Houston Oiler Billy "White Shoes" Johnson, and Allan Mayer of Oscar Mayer and Company. A couple of big ones had gotten away. For some reason, Charles Colson had backed out and had to be replaced by Dean Jones, and a former Hell's Angel who conducts a bike ministry on the West Coast didn't leave a forwarding address when he set out on his latest missionary journey. But all the others were ready to go and film crews were heading for Nashville and L.A. to record their stories. We'll see the results soon.

As I wait, I am aware of poignant feelings, I have watched and listened as good, sincere, intelligent men and women groped for a way of making that which stands at the center of their lives plausible and attractive to those who live outside the sacred canopy. Perhaps it will work. I think I could accept that in good grace. I generally feel pretty comfortable around people who take their religion seriously, especially if it is one of the leading brands. But I confess I do not believe historians will remember 1977 as the year the Great Awakening came to Texas. I expect Baptist churches may be stirred up considerably and some wayward Christians may return home like the prodigal. These are the groups that have always responded best to the call of revival. The main work of evangelism in American history—with, it should be noted, some exceptions—has been to keep believers plugged into their systems. That in itself is a significant accomplishment and may well justify the cost and effort involved. Of course, here and there a real scoundrel or a true skeptic may be turned around and set on the Glory Road, but I expect Good News Texas will come and go without making a great deal of difference in the lives of the 4,700,000 sinners at whom it is primarily aimed. That will no doubt discourage a lot of folks, but maybe it shouldn't. After all, even though He knew how to use a bit of dash and sparkle to draw a crowd, Jesus never got anything like a majority, and if the Word of God is anything to go by, He never expected to (Matthew 7:13–14).

APPENDIX: Dignity in Church Advertising [1916]*

O. C. HARN

The church has discovered in advertising, a new force which it believes it can use in furthering its work. There is danger that, in its enthusiasm over its discovery, mistakes may be made. . . .

Dignity is an attribute which should be possessed by all advertising which advertises dignified things. Some advertising men believe that dignity is a handicap to forceful, resultful publicity; but that is because they do not know what dignity is. They confound it with dryness, dullness—old-fogyness.

This is a wrong conception. A dignified man may be the most intensely interesting man in your circle. He may be the best business-getter. He may be the man above all others to whom to look to get things done.

Contrast the dignified methods of . . . advertising success with this sickly attempt found in a collection of church advertisements.

"Don't be a lemon! Tie on to the happy Sunday-nighters."

Or this: A paper wrapper was folded about a piece of pasteboard to imitate chewing gum and the label was printed thus:

Chew this over!	Dr. White's Compound for human ills	The Flavor lasts

This, if you will believe it, was used to advertise the service a church has to offer for the benefit of men!

But, you say, flippant and even vulgar preachers seem to have success in getting serious results. Why will not advertising work similarly?

I would say first that, as it is the exception in the commercial world for trivial advertising to bring the results desired, so is it the exception in the pulpit. . . .

A final caution, do not get the idea that dignity precludes warmth, earnestness, appeal to the emotions, startling effects, and force (or punch, if you like the overworked word—I don't).

The great orator knows well how to use all these means of moving his audience—knows it better than does the clown.

*Excerpt from *Advertising and Selling,* November 1916, p. 15. O. C. Harn was Advertising Manager, National Lead Co., at the time this article was written.

Implementing the Marketing Process

ERNEST R. LEACH

Public educators, occupied since the sixties with increasing enrollments, have given little attention to marketing. Yet, as college enrollments begin to stabilize or decline, it is easy to become entrapped in a negative mentality which focuses on reduction in force policies, budget deficits, and program reductions. The discipline of marketing, applied to higher education, offers a positive alternative which has the potential for increasing enrollments, reducing attrition, and making college services more responsive to the needs of consumers.

"MARKETING" LOADED

Many college staff members view the term "marketing" as being loaded with negative connotations of hucksterism, fast-pitch artists, and slick brochures. Those who have embraced the marketing concept as appropriate for higher education too often do so within the context of the more traditional "product philosophy." This approach assumes that the present product is what the student needs, and the marketing function is to aggressively promote that product. Yet others, often in the same institution, believe it is unethical to "sell" education. This "selling of the school" implies that if a person "buys" the product there will be a guaranteed job or other tangible reward.

In contrast to the traditional "product philosophy," the "marketing process" includes assessment of community and individual needs, the development of promotional and delivery strategies that are responsive to those needs, and evaluation techniques for measuring the effectiveness of those strategies.

INITIATING THE PROCESS

Prince George's Community College, located in the Maryland suburbs of Washington, D.C., serves a county population of more than 700,000. The present enrollment of 19,000 includes 13,700 credit and 5,300 community services students, or approximately 9,000 full-time-equivalent students.

At the conclusion of the advance registration for spring, 1977, there were indicators that the College might not meet budgeted enrollment projections. Both the previous summer sessions and fall enrollments had been somewhat below projections. In the words of the director of institutional research, "The enrollment was increasing at a decreasing rate."

In December, 1976, an ad hoc group of approximately 20 persons representing areas of the College that have responsibility for contacting prospective students was convened to examine college-wide outreach efforts. The brainstorming ideas suggested by this group were organized according to priorities and shared with the administration. A task force on marketing strategies was set up, to be chaired by the dean of student affairs. It included representation from: arts and sciences, technical and career education, and evening and community education faculty; student affairs, community information, college publications, and the student governance board.

As a result, a four-stage—service, promotion, delivery and evaluation—"marketing process" was developed. The way in which it has been implemented at Prince George's Community College may help to guide other colleges.

Reprinted with permission from *Community and Junior College Journal,* December–January 1977–1978, pp. 20–24; published by the American Association of Community and Junior Colleges, Washington, D.C.

SERVICE STAGE

The service stage involves the identification of what services and/or programs are provided for whom. The discovery and description of "market segments" resulted in the identification of new "target markets" and the assessment of unique needs of these subpopulations of potential students.

An examination of service needs revealed that, although Prince George's Community College serves about 34 percent of all college-bound high school graduates in its county, the previous year's service index of 1.63 percent of residents enrolled in credit courses was below that of the community colleges in adjacent counties. The 1970 census data indicated that the median number of school years completed for males 25 years and older is 12.6 for Prince George's County and 15.0 for a neighboring county. The task force observed that more intensive efforts were needed to acquaint Prince George's citizens with postsecondary opportunities.

A review of recent student profiles suggested a demand for learning and support services that are responsive to the needs for a student population that is increasingly older, part-time, minority, and female. These "new students," together with the more traditional sources, were identified in four categories of potential "target markets" based on type of contact with the College rather than population demographics (see Table 1):

- Prince George's Community College students
- Prospective customers
- Community adults
- Junior and senior high school students

PROMOTION STAGE

Promotion is often considered to be synonymous with marketing when in fact it is only one stage of the marketing process. Attention was directed toward providing students with information adequate to make informed choices about educational programs and with expected consumer outcomes for completion of those programs. There was no "hard sell."

A variety of marketing strategies were suggested. Some required only minor modifications in current operating procedures, while others needed thorough review and involved commitment of additional College resources.

Responsibility for each strategy was assigned together with a completion date and identification of additional funds that were needed for implementation. These strategies were in addition to the regular on-going promotional activities such as visits to high schools, paid advertising, news releases, radio announcements, and brochures.

DELIVERY STAGE

Delivery is the key to an effective marketing process that is dependent upon repeat business and customer satisfaction. The best promotional efforts may be ineffective unless colleges can deliver learning and support services that students want at times and locations that are convenient to them. Alexander Astin has observed that it may be more cost effective to invest resources to prevent students from dropping out than to commit those same resources to vigorous recruiting.

Although there is little agreement as to what constitutes true attrition in an era when "stopping in" and "stopping out" have become an acceptable educational behavior, two specific indices were used to describe the attrition experience at Prince George's Community College.

First, the attrition index most clearly affecting credit hours is the number of students not returning from the previous term. This "between-term" attrition for fall-spring has been approximately 34 percent for the past five years. Spring-fall attrition has been approximately 47 percent during the same five year period. In actual numbers, this has represented approximately 5,400 students not returning spring-fall and 4,100 not returning fall-spring.

TABLE 1: ***Marketing strategies***

Target market	*Strategy*	*Type*	*Strategy*
P.G.C.C. students	Promote credit courses with community service students	Learning	Revise course syllabi to include expected instructional outcomes
	Centralize all College mailing lists		Develop internship programs for arts and sciences students
Prospective customers	Staff College information booths with student assistants		Offer concurrent enrollment in developmental programs
	Prepare outdoor directory signs for all college buildings		Develop courses in study skills and career planning
	Develop communication skills workshop for registration and admissions personnel		Develop a pilot academic skills improvement course for able learners
	Install special telephones for registration information		Develop a communications skills center (summer and weekend program)
Community adults	Promote College programs with senior citizens		Expand tutorial services to support classroom learning
	Inform county residents of daily and weekend events on campus		Develop alternative instructional modes for more courses
	Contact all city mayors in the county		Increase number of programs available in learning labs
	Establish information centers in shopping malls and libraries		Develop programmed self-directed registration packet
	Send letters and brochures to all churches and civic associations	Support	Develop improved faculty advisement manual
	Prepare general information posters for libraries, banks, and businesses		Schedule advisement seminars for faculty
	Prepare combined class schedule for mailing to all county residents		Identify undecided students
	Staff information booth at county fair		Implement on-line registration
Junior and senior high school students	Host college/career fair for high school students on campus		Offer diagnostic tests for study skills
	Schedule divisional and departmental articulation meetings with county school faculty		Develop self-accessing slide/tape on study skills
	Send letters to 3,000 graduating seniors		Implement third week warning letter for non-attenders
	Host luncheon for all county school principals		Implement career development center
			Implement on-line CVIS (computer vocational information service) program
		Outreach	Expand credit offerings in summer sessions
			Expand day and evening credit courses at Goddard Space Center, county administration building, Andrews Air Force Base, and county high schools
			Increase counseling and advising support at Andrews Air Force Base

Second, from the perspective of the students, "within-term" attrition represents a more serious problem. This index, as used here, includes all unsuccessfully completed courses within an academic semester. This has been described by the director of institutional research as the "non pass" or "inefficiency rate." The "inefficiency rate" at Prince George's Community College represents approximately 27 percent of all courses attempted and has been a constant ratio during the past five years.

EVALUATION STAGE

From a marketing perspective, these two attrition indices provided a potent catalyst for re-examination of programs of study, courses to be offered, the way in which offerings are packaged and presented to students, including time and place, and the types of learning support systems available to students. Many of the delivery strategies which follow were aimed at reducing unwarranted attrition.

Although evaluation is discussed as a separate stage in the marketing process, it was considered as an integral part of each of the other stages. It was essential to identify changing service needs, access to institutional research studies, census data, and manpower information.

Assessment components which were designed for promotional strategies included surveying by telephone to measure the effectiveness of home-mailed brochures, crosschecking the names of shopping mall and library contacts with actual enrollees, tabulating the number of telephone responses to brochures, and administering questionnaires asking enrollees how they learned about the College.

The lack of sophisticated measurement tools for assessing the effectiveness of learning and support services contributed to the difficulty of evaluating program delivery strategies. Moreover, the confounding influence of several delivery strategies on the same learning outcome made direct cause and effect relationships difficult to measure.

As noted earlier, however, some gross indices such as "between-term" and "within-term" attrition may provide an indication of the effectiveness of delivery systems. Student satisfaction, course and program completions, schedule changes, and job placements are additional indicators that may be useful in the assessment of program effectiveness.

How successful has the "marketing process" been at Prince George's Community College? While the fall semester, 1977, enrollment in community colleges is projected to increase only 2 percent nationally, and enrollment has grown minimally at adjacent community colleges, Prince George's has experienced an increase of 15 percent in student headcount and 12 percent in credit hours. While these statistics lend credibility to the promotional strategies, it is too early to determine the impact of delivery strategies on student attrition.

CONCEPTUAL FRAMEWORK

Evaluation of the marketing strategies has begun and will continue through March 30, 1979. This will allow for assessment of the impact of these proposals through two fall and two spring semesters. It is anticipated that the feedback from this on-going evaluation process will be useful in modifying some of these strategies, suggesting new strategies, and discontinuing those strategies that are not effective.

The "marketing process" presents a conceptual framework for assessing student needs, for developing promotional and delivery strategies that are responsive to those needs, and for evaluating the effectiveness of those strategies. The action proposals were suggested by task force members and others representing all areas of the College. Although a given person or persons were identified as responsible for each strategy, the successful implementation of these proposals has required the support of the entire community.

By design, the terminology "marketing process" has been used rather than "marketing effort" or "marketing project." The strategies that were developed for immediate implementation still need careful review by the constituencies, areas, divisions, and departments of the College. It is hoped that these proposals will generate ideas for new strategies that will make the College more responsive to the needs of its present and potential service clientele.

BIBLIOGRAPHY

Astin, Alexander W. *Preventing Students From Dropping Out.* San Francisco: Jossey-Bass, 1975.

Cope, Robert and Hannah, William. *Revolving College Doors: The Causes and Consequences of Dropping Out, Stopping Out and Transferring.* New York: John Wiley and Sons, 1975.

Drucker, Peter. *Management: Tasks, Responsibilities and Practices.* New York: Harper and Row, 1974.

Larkin, Paul. "Enrollment Report Characteristics of Degree-Credit Students." Prince George's Community College Office of Institutional Research, Report No. 76-14, October 8, 1976.

Larkin, Paul. "How Many Students Are We Losing?" Prince George's Community College Office of Institutional Research, Report No. 77-11, March 14, 1977.

Larkin, Paul. "Student Profile, Fall 1972 and Fall 1973." Prince George's Community College Office of Institutional Research, Report No. 60, October 1973.

Maryland State Board for Community Colleges. "Statewide Master Plan for Community Colleges in Maryland—Fiscal Years 1978–1987." May 1977.

Vavrek, Michael, "Marketing: It's OK—We're OK." *Adult Leadership* (December 1975), 101–102, 118.

COMMON CAUSE

Time to End the Flim-Flam

One of the most moving lines in the Declaration of Independence appears at the very end of that document. In support of the Declaration, the signers say, ". . . we mutually pledge to each other our lives, our fortunes, and our sacred honor." Down the years, many Americans have followed them in that pledge. We have had our full share of rascals and cynics in American history, but we have also had our share of those who gave their lives, literally and figuratively, to make this nation a model for all mankind. They believed the words of the Declaration. They not only pledged but gave their lives, their fortunes, and their sacred honor. All to what end? To create government with a "For Sale" sign on it?

Perhaps at a less critical time in our history we could tolerate rascality in high places. But not now. Our country is in deep trouble. We cannot tolerate the dominance of courthouse politics, the shady deal and the crass payoff. It is time for the citizen to stand up and say "Enough!" It is time to end the flim-flam and put our political institutions into working order. It can be done.[1]

In July 1972, Roger Craver, Director of Development for Common Cause, was considering new avenues for increasing the membership of the two-year-old organization. Mr. Craver felt that the "bread and butter" membership renewals, consisting mainly of better-educated, higher-income, generally middle-class whites, was saturated.

Since he was sure that further extensive mailings to this group would not generate the added members that Common Cause needed, he had explored the possibilities of appealing to other major segments in American life, including disadvantaged groups, retired people, blue-collar laborers, civil service workers, military personnel, youth groups, and academics.

After some hesitation, Mr. Craver decided that youth groups offered the most feasible segment from which to generate new members; however, despite the fact that he and his colleagues at Common Cause had developed considerable experience and expertise in understanding the needs of their current constituency, he felt somewhat at a loss as to what appeals and methods would most effectively attract young people to Common Cause.

THE BEGINNING OF COMMON CAUSE

When John Gardner, now Chairman of Common Cause, was Secretary of Health, Education and Welfare (HEW), he became convinced that the only way to revitalize governmental institutions was through an active citizenry. Common Cause, organized by Gardner in 1970 to work within the system for the benefit of the average person, was meant by its founders to become "the citizens' lobby." Common Cause exemplified the hard-hitting, relentless, and successful citizen action that was sweeping the United States in the early 1970s. According to the Common Cause people, they proved that the average person could "fight city hall . . . and win." They did it, they maintained, by combining widespread citizen concern with the professional lobbying techniques previously used by special interest groups, business, and labor. As John Gardner stated their purpose: "We deal with the basic issue that underlies all others—whether citizens will have access to their own government and whether we can call our government to account."

Mr. Gardner was a well-respected "establishment" man; before he became Secretary of HEW, he was President of the Carnegie Corporation. Since he was deeply involved in many aspects of American society, he was able to enlist the aid of several nationally known individuals as board members, including Mayors John Lindsay (New York) and Carl Stokes (Cleveland), Leonard Woodcock (President of the United Auto Workers), the Rev. Jesse Jackson (civil rights leader), Betty Furness (consumer protection consultant), and Andrew Heiskell (chairman of Time, Inc.).

Washington skeptics, having seen the birth and death of many citizens' organizations, predicted that Common Cause would be an unmitigated disaster. Accordingly, Mr. Gardner thought that a first year's membership goal of 100,000 was optimistic. However, mail poured in at the rate of 1,000 letters per day, and this goal was surpassed in only 23 weeks. At the first anniversary, Common Cause had 200,000 members. This compared with the 155,000 members of the better known League of Women Voters.

ORGANIZATION

Common Cause had only a small staff of trained lobbyists and public relations experts. Volunteers provided the driving force of the organization at both the national and local levels. At any given time in the Washington headquarters, it was not unusual to see a wide variety of people digging through the mounds of mail and computer printouts that threatened to inundate everything and everyone. There was a constant sense of urgent excitement coupled with the more mundane realization that some "staffer' was always dispersing change to pay a volunteer's bus fare. Because of its volunteer nature, Common Cause had internal communications and staff turnover problems. On-the-job training was minimal and work assignments were casually based on personal preferences. The walls virtually bristled with memos, posters, slogans, and instructions. Visitors often commented that moving through the offices was more like swimming than walking. Effectiveness of the local chapters varied a great deal from state to state and from locality to locality. All local chapters were staffed exclusively by volunteers. Chapter activity was conducted in "bursts"; when an issue caught on there was feverish activity frequently followed by extensive periods of lull.

AGENDA

Common Cause was a nonpartisan organization, but as a lobby it did take a firm stand on issues. To determine the priorities of the members, the first newsletter contained a list of 15 proposed areas of action; the letter encouraged members to indicate which of these issues they felt should be pursued by the organization. Because of the difficulties encountered in gauging the opinions of the rapidly growing membership, a similar "referendum" was held in June 1971 (Exhibit 1 lists the results of that second questionnaire). The choice of questions for the referendum had been developed from a set of goals established by the board of governors. In addition to the more formal channels, many members expressed their feelings through letters they sent to the national headquarters in Washington or by local meetings. However, local autonomy in issue selection was not allowed. Common Cause's governing board, composed of 60 persons elected by the membership at large and 20 persons elected by the board, made the decisions as to which issues would be joined, as well as how and when.

EXHIBIT 1: ***Selection of issues by members, July 1971***

Issue	*Percent of respondents who favor*
Overhaul and revitalize government	94.5
Protect and enhance the environment	89.5
Improve criminal justice system	89.4
Withdraw all U.S. forces from Indochina	85.4
Help eliminate poverty	79.7
Fight sex and race discrimination	74.6
Make government accountable	53.3
Tax reform	20.9
Arms control	6.5

Source: Common Cause records.

The agenda issues that were to be the major areas of concentration were quite broad. The new organzation needed, however, to establish quickly a record of success. To do this, Common Cause mounted extensive campaigns for the 18-year-old vote and against the Supersonic Transport (SST) aircraft. Both congressional votes in 1972 went as Common Cause had lobbied, and those "instant victories" were used to attract additional members and jell the present ones into a cohesive unit.

In reviewing the requirements for successful lobbying, Mr. Gardner developed these conclusions:

> The first requirement for effective citizen action is stamina. Arthur Vanderbilt said court reform is no sport for the shortwinded. The same is true of citizen action. The special-interest lobbies never let up. The second requirement is an informed public. The special interests flourish in the dark. Officials begin to respect citizen action when they discover that citizens are watching and the media are reporting what the citizens see. The third requirement is focused action. The gravest weakness of many high-minded citizens is random indignation. They just pick a few targets and moblize strength, numbers, and money in order to have an impact. The fourth requirement is the creation of inside–outside alliances. An effective citizen group doesn't sit outside Congress, or any government body, lobbing mortar shells over the walls. There are ready allies inside for any foward-looking movement, and they have to be found. The fifth requirement is a professional cutting edge. It's a peculiar quirk of high-minded people to believe that only the wicked need good lawyers. Citizens must be prepared to match professional skill and knowledge with their opponents.[2]

INTO ACTION, 1972

By the beginning of 1972, Common Cause had accomplished its short-term objective of keeping alive and was now ready to turn to the longer-term issues of the war in Indochina, campaign finance monitoring and reform, congressional reform (i.e., the end of the seniority system and the end of closed hearings), and equal rights for women.

Common Cause slated its major activity in 1972 toward the monitoring of campaign spending. It had sued both political parties to restrain them from violating the law which prohibited individual contributions of more than $5,000 to a political candidate. It lobbied, sued, and prodded; finally, Congress passed a new campaign-spending law which took effect on April 7, 1972. Armed with this law, Common Cause investigated over 200 candidates for possible violations. TRW, Inc. was also sued for violating a law that prohibited campaign gifts by government contractors. All of those actions were resolved in favor of Common Cause. However, as Fred Wertheimer, who directed the campaign-monitoring project, explained, the new law did not change the enforcement mechanism: "It didn't change the fact that government officials had to go to court to prosecute offenders and never did."

Common Cause favored financing the nation's elections with public subsidies and tax credits instead of large private contributions. According to Wertheimer: "We live in a corrupted political system: It allows people who want preference from the government to provide financial aid to precisely those people who are asking for a favorable political decision. The new law helps deal with this problem. It is comprehensive in its requirement of disclosure and we want to get compliance with it; we want to force candidates to make their financial resources clear."

The major legal battle, however, was with the Committee to Re-elect the President (CRP); the CRP was a privately organized group working for Richard Nixon's reelection. Common Cause sued this group to make public a list of those who contributed to Mr. Nixon's campaign before April 7, 1972, the effective date of the new campaign-financing disclosure law. While technically the CRP would not have to give out this information, there were many pieces of evidence that indicated that there were irregularities in the committee's methods.

Taking legal action was only one of Common Cause's three methods of operation, and it was generally considered to be a means of last resort. Most of Common Cause's efforts went into lobbying through either the professional staff in Washington or a groundswell of public sentiment as expressed in letters and phone calls from citizens to their representatives in Congress. The professional lobbying effort was concentrated in Washington, where it performed in much the same fashion as any other lobby. Members of Congress were bombarded with information in support of Common Cause's issues and the message that it represented over 200,000 citizens.

The professional staff was generally credited by the press nationwide and by the inner sanctums of the Washington power structure as doing an excellent job on the missions it had undertaken (see Exhibit 2), but the only way that Common Cause could effect change was through the force of an active membership. To harness the power of that membership, Common Cause developed an intricate system known as the Washington Connection.

EXHIBIT 2: ***Press comments about Common Cause***

It's heartening to see a calm, unfrantic movement here working to improve American politics, not to destroy or freeze it. Beside our daily dose of bad news, the momentum Common Cause is gaining is good news indeed.

Flora Lewis
Washington Post

The aim of Mr. Gardner's effort is not to found a new party or win a particular campaign. His hope is to freshen the springs of political life, to recruit new talent for both parties and at every level of government, to concentrate attention on the issues that are genuinely significant, to sponsor needed reforms. It is a bold and ambitious undertaking which Mr. Gardner and his colleagues are attempting. Self-government lives by that kind of boldness and ambition.

The New York Times

Democracy just doesn't flourish in the half-light. The public has a right to know exactly how its public servants are performing and how its interests are being served. Americans realizing democracy's great shortchanging through secrecy can be grateful that Common Cause's strong shoulder will be placed against bolted government doors.

Palm Beach (Fla.) *Post*

So you're skeptical about making fundamental changes in the system from within. So now you don't know where to turn. Tell you what. Take a look at Common Cause, the 200,000-member "citizens' lobby." . . . It was Common Cause that forced the Nixon Campaign committee to disclose where its money came from all during 1971 and up to March 9, 1972. . . . It was Common Cause that forced TRW, Inc., a $200,000,000 a year defense contractor, to dissolve a political fund collected from its employees. The message was not lost on other corporations. It was Common Cause that fed hundreds of newspapers and TV and radio stations all the details about how much money candidates for President, Congress, and the Senate were collecting, and more important, just where it was coming from. And that's just a start.

The National Observer

The country has a pressing need for restructuring its political and economic institutions and for a healthier new set of priorities. Common Cause can play an important role in this task.

Sacramento (Calif.) *Bee*

Source: Common Cause records.

THE WASHINGTON CONNECTION

The Washington Connection was primarily a telephone-based activist hot line. The country was broken down by states and the states by congressional district. At the Washington office of Common Cause there were two functions—staff and line. The network staff was composed of two managers (who helped with procedures and problems) and four area supervisors (each of whom was responsible for the network activities in at least 10 states). The line function was headed by a state team leader who was the knowledgeable person about that state. Specific responsibilities were: know all Common Cause issues and national actions; know the Common Cause membership in the state; know local populations, industries, and communities; know current state issues; know local media personnel; and develop and maintain good working relations with the members of the state volunteer team which the leader headed. The members of the state volunteer team performed the other line functions. They were more generally known as district liaison volunteers, and they were the primary contact (by telephone) between Common Cause headquarters and members in a congressional district. These teams were the link in the lobbying program, and success was directly related to how much stimulus and enthusiam could be passed from Washington to the states and how much information could be passed back to Washington.

On a day-to-day basis, the Washington Connection was used to establish a Common Cause organization in each congressional district (see Exhibit 3 for membership information). What was, in effect, established was a telephone net that allowed each member to be contacted during an "alert." Rapid communication during an "alert" was the basis of all the planning. An "alert" situation was defined as one in which the national office decided that immediate member action (rallies, letters, and phone calls to legislative representatives leading to media publicity) was needed to implement a Common Cause project or support an issue. The considerable outflowing of public opinion that was generated during an alert was an important lobbying tool used by the professional staff at the congressional level.

DISTINCTIVE ATTRIBUTES

In defining the difference between Common Cause and the previous, more traditional reform movements, Mr. Gardner said:

> I think the old-style good-government movement had two failings. First, they imagined that we

EXHIBIT 3: ***Membership by state, July 1972***

State	*Number of members*	*State*	*Number of members*
Alabama	530	Montana	532
Alaska	339	Nebraska	713
Arizona	2,040	Nevada	341
Arkansas	513	New Hampshire	1,294
California	38,539	New Jersey	9,751
Colorado	3,593	New Mexico	1,095
Connecticut	6,194	New York	33,823
Delaware	745	North Carolina	2,731
District of Columbia	4,765	North Dakota	334
Florida	5,351	Ohio	7,941
Georgia	1,737	Oklahoma	810
Hawaii	728	Oregon	3,091
Idaho	313	Pennsylvania	11,316
Illinois	10,254	Rhode Island	1,164
Indiana	2,542	South Carolina	478
Iowa	1,884	South Dakota	295
Kansas	1,572	Tennessee	1,447
Kentucky	1,192	Texas	5,607
Louisiana	653	Utah	647
Maine	849	Vermont	1,075
Maryland	8,058	Virginia	5,708
Massachusetts	12,120	Washington	4,433
Michigan	6,466	West Virginia	509
Minnesota	4,876	Wisconsin	3,686
Mississippi	204	Wyoming	230
Missouri	3,415	Total	218,523

Source: Common Cause records.

might achieve a kind of static perfection of governmental processes and then we could all relax and be happy under a good government. They didn't understand that somebody always has too much power and somebody always has too little, and that if you drive the bad guys out of power, the good guys who replace them will soon get accustomed to power and grow to love it and may eventually abuse it. So the struggle never ends. The other failing of the old good-government movements was that they felt themselves to be above politics. But politics is the only forum in which we can resolve our differences. As long as equally worthy people have incompatible goals, somebody has to mediate—unless you want things decided by the whim of a dictator or unless you want to shoot it out. The politicians are our mediators. We have to rehabilitate the whole notion of politics as the kind of free market in which we resolve conflicting purposes. It's always untidy. It will always be grubbier than we might want it to be. But we can't afford to scorn it. . . . There are some extraordinarily good, resilient, effective people in politics. At the other extreme are the crooks and the exploiters. And in the middle are a lot of unheroic types who will respond to pressures, good or bad. Citizen action tries to work with the good guys, immoblize the crooks, and stiffen the spines of the unheroic.[3]

MEMBERSHIP BUILDING

The officers of Common Cause were convinced that a strong, active, growing membership was essential to lobbying success. The larger the membership, they reasoned, the more public pressure Common Cause could control and the more money it would have to support its activities. Additionally, an increased membership would provide a wider base of support and thereby dispel the elite image that some detractors tried to associate with Common Cause. Consequently, a great deal of effort went into recruiting membership, exemplified by the fact that about one-third of all revenues received went into obtaining new members (see Exhibit 4 for a breakdown of the 1972 budget).

Roger Craver's main job as Director of Development was to ensure the continued growth of Common Cause. Mr. Craver, who had an extensive background in public relations, direct-mail advertising, and college and university fund-raising projects, began by evaluating the results of past campaigns as well as determining the current economic resources of the organization.

The total 1972 budget for all activities was projected at $3.4 million (see Exhibits 5 and 6 for 1971 operating statements). This was split into three funds: the Program Fund, the Readiness Alert Fund, and the New Membership Revolving Fund. The Program Fund was financed entirely from the $15 renewal payments of members. This supported the regular legislative-lobbying program, field operations, the newsletter and other publications, and the headquarter's administrative expense. Total 1972 expenditures were projected to be $2.2 million.

The Readiness Alert Fund was financed by contributions in excess of the $15 dues. The 1972 average revenue per member was expected to be about $17.50, therefore, an average of $2.50 per member, or $500,000, was available for this fund. These funds were used to operate the 1972 Campaign Monitoring Project, for lobbying of delegates at the two national political conventions, and for the Peace Action Center. Money in the Readiness Alert Fund could be designated by the governing board for special projects that could not be funded from the regular Program Fund.

The New Membership Revolving Fund financed membership-building efforts. The $15

EXHIBIT 4: ***1972 budget of $3,463,000***

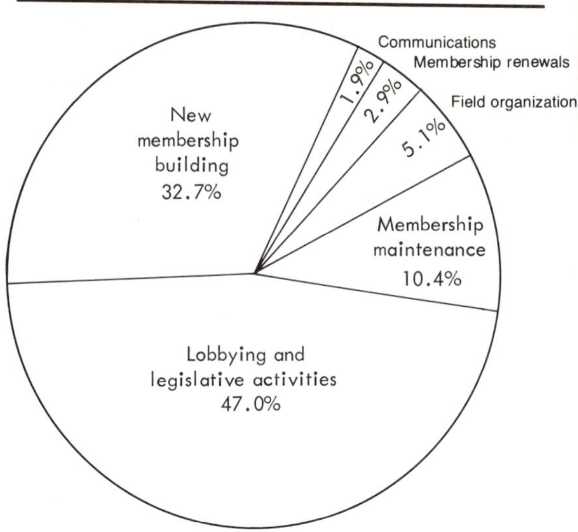

[a]Percentages of lobbying and legislative activities funds:

Campaign financing and campaign monitoring	22.6
Open up the system and congressional reform	29.2
State issues and state reform	15.9
End the war	14.9
Equal rights and state ratification	5.9
Other legislative issues	11.5
Clean water	
D.C. home rule	
Busing	
Welfare reform	
Consumer protection	
No-fault insurance	
Child care	
Gun control	
Miscellaneous	
Total	100.0

Source: Common Cause records.

EXHIBIT 5: ***Statement of revenue and expenditures and changes in fund balance, year ended December 31, 1971***

Revenue	
Memberships	$3,522,544
Contributions	664,851
Grant from Stern Fund	43,000
Other	23,281
	$4,253,676
Expenditures	
Salaries	$ 884,627
Payroll taxes and employee benefits	85,082
Postage and mailing	683,179
Printing and publications	611,856
Membership mailing lists and advertising	495,653
Consultant fees and expenses	416,056
Computer processing	334,401
Telephone and telegraph	172,010
Office rent	109,786
Staff travel	92,228
Furniture, equipment, and leasehold improvements	68,403
Special projects	55,835
Office supplies and expenses	47,907
Stern Fund project	36,976
Other	90,951
	$4,184,950
Excess of revenue over expenditures	$ 68,726
Fund balance beginning of period	249,388
Fund balance end of period	$ 318,114

Source: Common Cause records.

EXHIBIT 6: ***Statement of assets, liabilities, and fund balance, December 31, 1971***

Assets	
Cash	$206,356
Certificates of deposit	200,000
Prepaid expenses	60,167
Total assets	$466,523
Liabilities and fund balance	
Liabilities	
Accounts payable	$109,145
Other	39,264
Total liabilities	$148,409
Fund balance	318,114
Commitments	
Total liabilities and fund balance	$466,523

TABLE 1: ***Membership renewal rates***

Period	*Renewal rate (%)*
Initial membership	—
First renewal	61
Second renewal	76
Third renewal[a]	85[b]

[a] Projected.
[b] This meant that for every 100 initial memberships, only 39 would still belong to Common Cause after three years.

dues from *new* members were plowed back into this fund. Mr. Craver thought that it cost $10.25 to obtain a new member. On the other hand, it cost an average of $0.99 to renew a membership; a maximum of four renewal notices would be sent (costing in total $1.40), while some members renewed their membership automatically.

Table 1 shows the membership renewal rates.

In establishing the 1972 membership goal, Mr. Craver felt that a total membership of 200,000 was necessary to finance the current level of activities; however, as Mr. Craver said: "Our goal is to get as many as possible."

METHODS OF MEMBERSHIP RECRUITING

In the past, membership drives had been somewhat limited. Free publicity, newspaper stories, brochures, and some direct mailings had resulted in the initial flood of 200,000 members. However, since 1970, Common Cause had really only been able to hold a steady position. Roger Craver was quite worried about future propsects. He said: "Lots of us here are worried about the future; we will have to do something or else we will slowly wilt on the vine."

Consequently, during June 1972, Mr. Craver had placed a full-page advertisement in the Sunday edition of each of the following newspapers: *New York Times, Washington Post, San Francisco Chronicle, Christian Science Monitor,* and *National Observer*. He felt that these papers were circulated in areas that offered the most potential; however, to judge by the returned coupons, total ad expenses exceeded total direct memberships by $10,000. Paid newspaper ads did not seem to be effective in attracting additional members. Other alternatives that he had under consideration were public service announcements on radio and television; aside from the production costs, these were free, but they were most often aired only during low-audience-rating times. In addition, there were several restrictions on content that led Mr. Craver to feel that this means of advertisement was of little use to Common Cause. As a result, membership procurement relied mostly on direct mail. Mr. Craver maintained that this was the only consistently effective way of gaining new members.

Historically, January, February, and September had been the best months to use direct mail. Mr. Craver had conducted an extensive test to measure the responses to each of eight different membership ad packets. The most successful one was a 6 inch × 9 inch envelope (eventually sent to one million people) with the outside caption:

For Sale: The United States Government

All Bids Will Be Handled in Secrecy.
Details Are Sealed in This Envelope.

Inside was a four-page letter from John Gardner which was a hardhitting injunction against the evils in government. This mailing generated 113,000 new members. The 6 inch × 9 inch envelope, however, was expensive; Craver was pleased to discover that a small and cheaper package, sent to five million people, produced comparable results. He estimated that Common Cause's present middle-class, well-educated, and high-income white market was potentially 16 million people, representing over 20 million households. Total package costs (lists, labor, printing, and postage) were $153,744 per million in quantities exceeding one million. Subscription and membership lists were purchased from other groups and organizations which often had many of the same people; one major disadvantage of these was the annoyance caused current membership by duplicate mailings. The list purge, or "cleaning" process at Common Cause was expensive, but Mr. Craver was not entirely certain as to the magnitude of the problem, except to say that it was noticeable at a rate above 5% duplication.

ALTERNATIVE MARKETS

Roger Craver felt that the youth of America had changed greatly during the early 1970s. He detected what he thought to be a shift away from the "radical approach" to one that could be described as "working within the system." If this were true, he felt, young people would find Common Cause to be an organization "tuned in" to their needs. After all, he reasoned, Common Cause's credo was one of gradual changes in government which would return more power to the people.

However, Mr. Craver foresaw several potential problems if he pursued the youth market. First, he was concerned that substantial influx of young people into Common Cause might conceivably antagonize large segments of the existing membership, especially the older, less active members. He felt that some campus activity could be characterized as "shirt-pocket agenda"—that is, highly volatile but not necessarily long-lived. If this happened, Common Cause headquarters would probably lose control of the membership, which would result in the disintegration of the organization. As it was, Common Cause was relatively homogeneous, and Mr. Craver did not want to develop internal factions and conflicts. Mr. Craver was also afraid that the good name and lobbying effectiveness of Common Cause would be ruined if a few kids staged a hippie demonstration in the name of Common Cause.

Second, there was a matter of economics. He felt that the regular $15 membership fee might be too high for young people, but it cost $7 a year to service a member with newsletters, administrative overheads, and so on. This meant that direct mail, newspapers, and other expensive means of attracting members could not be used to attract youth. This left volunteer person-to-person selling as the only other alternative he saw, but Common Cause had no contacts or representatives on the thousands of high school and college campuses across the nation.

On the other hand, the youth market offered great potential. Mr. Craver estimated that appropriate potential members might number as high as nine million in college and 18 million in high school. Youth also represented activism. Common Cause would increasingly need to rely on its members taking action on the issues. Volunteers were always in short supply to perform the telephone, administrative, and research tasks. If Common Cause were to expand its scope of activities into state and local reform, a greatly increased number of volunteers would be needed. There was also the good chance that a person who joined Common Cause as a youth might be an active, dues-paying member for years. Mr. Craver felt very strongly about this point, but he could not guess as to how many would remain for how long. Thus he did not know what short-term deficit spending might mean in long-term members.

Therefore, Mr. Craver felt that it was best to run some sort of market test that could be controlled in such a way that if he was not successful, he could terminate it without having created a great deal of confusion and anxiety among the current members. Mr. Craver decided to talk to approximately 15 college representatives and a number of political science and civics teachers at the high school level. He wanted, at the same time, to test a new membership price of $7.50. If it costs $7.00 a year just to service a new member with newsletters and the like, that only left $0.50 for acquiring new members. A prime consideration was the development of a low-cost method for attracting youth. Mr. Craver felt that direct mail was prohibitive and that media space and time was too expensive, which left it up to point-to-point, people-to-people contact, point-of-purchase, and other methods, which frankly had proved unsuccessful in the past, although to a different audience.

NOTES AND REFERENCES

[1] John W. Gardner, *In Common Cause,* W. W. Norton & Co., New York, 1972, p. 43.

[2] Elizabeth Drew, "Conversation with a Citizen," *The New Yorker,* July 23, 1973, pp. 35–55 (reproduced by permission).

[3] Elizabeth Drew, "Conversation with a Citizen," *The New Yorker,* pp. 35–55, July 23, 1973.

SECOND STREET GALLERY

At the first regular meeting that Lindsay Nolting, newly elected president, chaired, and which coincided with the Second Street Gallery's first anniversary, the directors reviewed the gallery's progress to date from its founding on February 11, 1973.

THE ART GALLERY IN SOCIETY—A SYNOPSIS

The art museums and galleries were caught in the 1960s in the problems of contemporary society. Having slumbered in historical contexts for decades, the museums were now seen as irrelevant and obsolete. Financial sources dried up, costs outstripped income, and the possibility of collapse became immediate rather than remote. In the panic, many museums and galleries reassessed their roles in society. New galleries were founded on principles far different from those of their more famous, now expiring ancestors.

Dr. Eric Larrabee, Provost of Arts and Humanities at New York State University at Buffalo, identified five stages in the history of art galleries:

16th century	Stage 1: The Wunderkammer—a cabinet of curiosities for private enjoyment
17th century	Stage 2: Expanded versions of private collections for the public
18th–19th centuries	Stage 3: The great museum (e.g., Metropolitan), "temples" devoted to the worship of the fine arts
1940	Stage 4: The universities of the common man—state universities in the United States in the 1940s
1965	Stage 5: The new, relevant, community-oriented, "with-it" art gallery—in tune with an egalitarian society

There are many, including the directors of the Second Street Gallery, who saw the problems of the contemporary gallery as incentives to a healthy change. They held that "art should be kicking and screaming in the middle of contemporary society, rather than literally and figuratively transferred out of reach and out of touch." A prospective gallery had to know with great precision what kind of gallery it wanted to be, what constituents it needed to attract, and whom it hoped to benefit. Marketing was a critical factor to its success.

ESTABLISHMENT OF THE SECOND STREET GALLERY

Eleven resident artists, brought together by the vision and energy of Eugene Markowski, 41, associate professor of art at the University of Virginia, opened the Second Street Gallery in February 1973. Markowski had been thinking about such a gallery since 1971. The arrival of several newcomers from art circles in other cities was the catalyst for the gallery's foundation. Five months of cooperative planning preceded the opening; the gallery was to function both as an outlet for the exhibition of the artists' works and an opportunity for the area residents to view and buy quality works of modern art.

Discussions of basic organizational questions were necessarily addressed by the original group: How does one form an organization? What types of organizations are possible? Which are better for the founders' purposes? What are realistic revenue expectations? The original members, whose

This case was prepared by Robert D. Hamilton III and John V. O. Kennard under the supervision of Professor Leslie E. Grayson of the University of Virginia.

backgrounds were nonorganizational, had some difficulty focusing on these questions.

They looked at the population size, per capita income, education, occupational stratification, the results of earlier area galleries, and intangibles such as the community's cultural environment. A recognized risk was the fact that the Charlottesville–Albemarle, Virginia, area was a traditional, conservative, and slow-paced environment of 80,000 people. The region was a proven marketplace for antique dealers, purveyors of horse prints, and family portrait articles, but little attempt had been made to sell or show modern art prior to 1973. But, Charlottesville was a growing community. The University of Virginia was located there, as well as a new community college. The trend seemed to be away from a small-town conservative mold into a more exciting university–town community.

As a result of their deliberations, the Second Street Gallery founders concluded that projected sales of art alone would never cover expenses. It was also decided that not all work exhibited would be for sale. Consequently, the decision was made that the gallery would have to "go out" to the community with innovative programs, lectures, and experiments. Their first year's exhibition and lecture schedule is given in Exhibit 1. Establishing the gallery as a nonprofit organization would make contributions tax deductible, usually a good selling point. The founders hoped that the community efforts would attract gifts and donations of both cash and services to help offset the estimated $9,000 annual operating costs.

A location was found in downtown Charlottesville with convenient parking nearby. The exhibition rooms were on the second floor of a local stockbroker's building. Five spacious rooms displayed a variety of contemporary works, well exhibited with natural and spot lighting. A sixth room, used as an office, also displayed art books sold at a discount and small artifacts.

Early in the development of the gallery, managerial assistance came from several sources. John V. O. Kennard, a student in the Graduate School of Business Administration (GSBA) at the University of Virginia and husband of one of the founders, was the business manager for the first six months of the gallery's existence. Opportunity

EXHIBIT 1: ***Exhibition and lecture schedules for the 1973–74 season***

Exhibitions

Sunday Sept. 30–Thursday Oct. 25
Peter Fink Photographs
Sunday Oct. 28–Thursday Nov. 22
Henry Stindt One-man Show
also Prisoner Art Exhibition
Sunday Nov. 25–Thursday Dec. 20
Lindsay Nolting One-woman Show
Sunday Jan. 6–Thursday Jan. 31
Priscilla Rappolt One-woman Show
Sunday Feb. 3–Thursday Feb. 28
George Roland One-man Show
Sunday Mar. 3–Thursday Mar. 28
Paul Martick One-man Show
Sunday Mar. 31–Thursday Apr. 25
Annual Artists Juried Show
Sunday Apr. 28–Thursday May 16
Collectors Show

Lectures

Sunday Oct. 14
"Leonardo da Vinci" by Frederick Hartt
Sunday Oct. 21
"Photojournalism" with Murray Weiss and Jim Carpenter
Sunday Nov. 4
"Erotic Art Panel Discussion" with Eugene Markowski and others
Sunday Dec. 9
"Chinese Glass" by Zachary Taylor
Sunday Jan. 20
"Electronic Music" by Donald MacInnis
Sunday Feb. 20
"Printmaking" by George Roland
Sunday Mar. 10
"Stained Glass" by Paul Martick
Sunday May 12
"Georgian Architecture" by Pauline King

All lectures are planned for 3:00 p.m.

Consultants, Inc. (OCI), a nonprofit service organization of the GSBA, kept the financial records so that donors were assured that the books were professionally kept. Another GSBA student, Robert D. Hamilton, decided to write his term paper for the Management of Nonprofit Organizations seminar on the gallery.

ATTRACTING FINANCIAL SUPPORT

Since it was obvious that the member artists could not finance the gallery themselves, community support had to be attracted. Museums and galleries in large cities were having difficulties raising funds, and obviously the problems would be compounded in a small community. In its appeal to the 500 potential donors for funding, the Second Street Gallery sent a flyer (Exhibit 2) which stressed participating in a community venture as the motivation for giving. These names were culled from members of a country club, concert and theater lists, and "outstanding" members of the community, selected for their interest in previous civic enterprises.

The Second Street Gallery members set about attainment of financial backing through the following do's and don'ts:

1. Select the most skillful salesperson (or the least unskillful) and send him or her out to canvas prospective donors. Leave the less "outgoing" behind to do the construction and redecorating work. This was a natural, self-selection process.
2. Maximize "in-kind" contributions from businesspersons. Whereas many business-people balk at cash gifts, they somewhat more readily part with their inventories, especially since they can count their contributions at retail instead of at cost.
3. Gather a few "outsiders" to lend professional support to the cause by word of mouth. A reassuring word from a prominent community member to a prospective donor will ease the donor's anxiety about giving.
4. Never be bashful about explaining the direct benefits to a donor (i.e., public display of name in gallery). Five classifications of potential contributors were identified (see the section on marketing).

Exhibit 2: ***Flyer***

The Second Street Gallery, a regional artists' cooperative, is a nonprofit association of the area's leading painters, sculptors, printmakers, and photographers. The cooperative has been formed to acquaint people in central Virginia with emerging expressions of contemporary art and culture. The artists will present their works regularly to the public in a permanent gallery supported by those who wish to foster excellence in and understanding of contemporary art. While all works of art are for sale, it is the educational and innovative aspects of the cooperative and the artists' commitment to enriching their community that make the Second Street Gallery unique in central Virginia.

Knowing of your interest in art, we ask your assistance. We are eager to open the Second Street Gallery as soon as operating expenses can be met. The members of the cooperative have already made financial commitments to secure a permanent exhibition space. Now contributions are needed to begin operations and to assure the cooperative's success. If you wish to contribute to the Second Street Gallery for the encouragement of excellence in contemporary art, please send your gift to

The Second Street Gallery
P.O. Box 1095
Charlottesville, Va. 22902

George Roland
President

The Second Street Gallery is located in Charlottesville at 116 Second Street, N.E.

The Second Street Gallery was particularly successful in raising "in-kind" contributions. Over $5,000 in carpeting was installed by Charlottesville's two leading rug firms. The same quality was also evident in most other examples, which included lighting, wiring, glass, air conditioners, furniture, plants, and refreshments, which were served at the monthly openings of exhibitions. The impact of these "in-kind" contributions in raising both the quality and size of the original investment was significant, as can be seen through the first quarterly receipts and disbursement schedule (Exhibit 3). It was estimated that original investment came to $10,000; $6,213 was "in-kind" and the remainder from artists and contributors.

SECURING COMMITTED ARTIST MEMBERS

Idealistically, a cooperative gallery sounded wonderful. Reality, however, raised its usual problems shortly after conception of the project.

EXHIBIT 3: ***First quarterly statement of cash receipts and disbursements, January 15–April 15, 1973***

Value of contributions "in-kind"		$6,213.00
Cash receipts		
Patrons, contributors, and members		$2,090.00
Artists' dues		1,550.00
Sale of art[a]		109.52
Sale of art books		37.85
Total		$3,787.37
Cash disbursements for expenses		
Printing	$172.50	
Advertising	11.70	
Office supplies	125.86	
Insurance	257.00	
License fees	30.50	
Rent	505.40	
Renovation and remodeling	905.00	
Salaries and wages	266.00	
Sales taxes	8.13	
Telephone	82.94	
Postage	234.97	
Total		$2,600.02
Purchase of equipment (assets)		$ 340.58
Cash in bank, April 15, 1973		$ 846.77

[a]Not including sale of 13 works from printmaker's show.

Minimal standards of participation and commitment evolved, and the work load was spread out as evenly as possible. Since the directors all had full-time jobs elsewhere, evidence of commitment to the gallery was not always obvious. Putting together a show once a month, roughly, was tedious and time consuming. An informal and somewhat amorphous nucleus centered around Messrs. Markowski, Martick, Roland, and Mrs. Kennard, and it provided a locus for decision making in which new directors became involved as they joined. The original group of artist members came from different geographical areas, generally had a high level of formal art education and training, and as a group provided the public with a variety of art forms. Exhibit 4 is a synopsis of an article describing the artists' styles and interests. A summary of their education is included in Exhibit 5.

EXHIBIT 4: ***Article "Artists' Cooperative Offers Variety," by Ruth Latter***

Gene Markowski, an associate professor of art at [*sic*], who is the catalyst responsible for founding the gallery, has on view a series of his highly distinctive, geometrized and perforated paintings and prints. Markowski has been carefully developing his unique style over a period of several years.

In all of his decoratively structured compositions, delicately shaded or superimposed color areas are balanced with endless rows of tiny punctures. He is certainly one of the most innovative artists in the area.

No less intriguing are the splendidly vibrating color harmonies of George Roland, a new art instructor at UVa. A single redundant biomorphic design weaves in and out of a rainbow of sensuous colors in Roland's acrylic paintings and silk screen prints. His brilliantly decorative works are the most eye-catching in the exhibit.

Perhaps, the most original artist in the group is Henry Stindt, an instructor at both the Virginia Art Institute and the UVa School of Continuing Education. A versatile artist, at home in many media, Stindt has on view a meandering assemblage of hinged two-by-fours and a nautical sculpture of wood and grid-patterned rope.

A more than competent weaver and sculptor, Linda Kinnard [*sic*] has a heavily looped and colorful woven hanging on view, as well as a rigid assemblage of metal drainpipes of varying lengths.

Unfortunately, once you have seen the works of these four artists, you have seen it all.

Paul Martick, a new art instructor at UVa, is an eclectic who combines haphazard brushwork with leaping black lines and arrows. One unusual painting on view resembles fireworks exploding in a flower garden. . . .

One hopes that future exhibitions at the Second Street Gallery will live up to the promises of its founding members. These include offering the community "the best art produced in the Charlottesville area" and "the most experimental art ever seen in the Charlottesville area." Whether these experimental efforts will include such innovations of the last few years as Body Art, Multi Media Environments, Photo Realism and Verist Sculpture remains to be seen.

Nevertheless, we in the community wish them well. A gallery such as this was long overdue.

Source: The Daily Progress.

EXHIBIT 5: ***Second Street Gallery Directors***

Moe Brooker, painter

B.F.A., Pennsylvania Academy of Fine Arts; M.F.A., Temple University. Assistant Professor of Art at the University of Virginia since 1973.

Michael Christopherson, sculptor

B.F.A., University of Wisconsin; M.F.A., Washington University. Assistant Professor of Art at the University of Virginia since 1973.

Letty Roegge Frazier, painter

Studied with Hal McIntosh, Bob Harmon, and Ellett Twery. Has won awards in regional shows since 1964. Affiliated with galleries in Lynchburg and Roanoke, Virginia.

Eugene Markowski, painter

B.F.A., Washington University School of Fine Art; M.F.A., University of Pennsylvania School of Fine Art. Assistant Professor of Art at the University of Pennsylvania, Associate Professor of Art at the University of Virginia since 1970.

Paul Martick, painter

Educated at Tufts University and Boston Museum School. Associate Professor of Art at the University of Virginia since 1971.

Lindsay Nolting, painter

Atelier de la rue du Dome, Academie Julian, Paris, France; Art Students' League, New York City, studied with Stamos and Glasier. Affiliated with two artists' cooperatives before Second Street Gallery: Marche d'Art Contemporain, Paris, and the Abingdon Square Painters, New York City.

Priscilla Rappolt, painter

B.F.A., art education, Richmond polytechnic Institute; M.F.A., painting, Virginia Commonwealth University. Also studied at the Boston Museum School and at the Art Students' League, New York City.

George Roland, painter, printmaker

B.F.A., with honors, Virginia Commonwealth University; M.F.A., painting and printmaking, University of Wisconsin. Associate Professor of Art at the University of Virginia since 1971.

Henry Stindt, painter and sculptor, conceptualizer

B.A., Pennsylvania State University; M.F.A., Pratt Institute, Brooklyn, New York. Also studied at the Slade School of Art, University of London.

From the time the gallery opened until the middle of May, four members, all students at the university, left. Two found the professional expectations and the general quality and quantity of work too demanding. Two others withdrew after a relatively acrimonious discussion. It was their contention that they were getting neither attention nor exhibition space commensurate with their talents. From this low point of only seven member artists remaining, new talent gradually brought membership up to nine. Five of these were affiliated with the university.

During the first Annual Area Artist Juried Show, the work of an artist from nearby Lynchburg was reviewed and accepted by a majority of the members. Shortly after that Linda Kennard resigned from the gallery when her husband accepted a job in New York after his graduation. Two faculty members who had recently joined the Art Department at the University of Virginia (one from Philadelphia and the other from Wisconsin) were asked to join as artist members.

On the average, two applications per month were received by the gallery from those seeking admittance as a full member and/or seeking to show work on consignment. Samples of each artist's work were evaluated and voted on by all members. Although a unanimous vote was not a prerequisite, a large majority was required.

Overall, the centrifugal force of the individualism of the nine artists resulted in varying degrees of seriousness and cooperation from one meeting to the next. The guarantees of tenacity of purpose and good faith were, as could be expected, frail and delicate. Other forces, however, were successful in keeping the organization coherent. Early favorable publicity was found to bring the group together and stir enthusiasm; a complimentary local preopening press could be an exciting reward for the work hours put in. The artists participated in two radio and one local television programs. These media encounters helped produce feelings of group solidarity and, by focusing the attention of the town on their efforts, made failure something that was to be avoided at all costs.

Artist members expressed numerous group and personal objectives for the gallery. It was viewed as a "service to the community"; "An opportunity to show—to see what the reaction of the public is"; "a chance to get some kind of an art sector going in Charlottesville." From the artists' point of view, during the last decade a three-tier market in modern American art has developed. For collectors of "prestigious" modern American art, "life these days seems to be one profit-making thrill after another," as prices skyrocket. "Prestigious" artists are now pressing to obtain royalties on the resale profits on their work. Some artists are already under contracts which entitle them to about 15% of the profit on any resale. Of course, the vast majority of artists are still poor; they are the lower part of the three-tier market. The poor artists are satisfied if they have enough money to pay for their studio, canvas, and paint.

MARKETING (OR RAISING FUNDS)

Five classifications of contributors were identified according to the size of the donation.

- Artist's dues ($200)
- Patron ($200)
- Contributor ($50)
- Regular Member ($15)
- Student Member ($5)

The present and projected membership profile, together with the estimated operating expenses, are shown in Exhibit 6.

A contribution entitled the member to attend the openings of shows of member artists and lectures that were given on an average of twice per month. Attendance varied from 2 to 20 people per day. Total annual attendance was estimated at 2,500, which included a number of repeaters. For the 11 exhibitions, the average number of visitors was between 200 and 300. Lectures were generally less well attended.

In an effort to increase the number of contributors, pamphlets describing the gallery and soliciting gifts were placed in the lobbies of movie theaters and motels. In the fall of 1973 a mailing list of approximately 1,400 people was compiled from nine different organizations (Exhibit 7). A prominent local woman added her name as chairperson of a membership drive. A sample of the request for contributions is shown in Exhibit 8.

The gallery appealed to the city council for support, even if it meant only a token contribution. In this appeal, as in subsequent appeals, the joint notions of "usefulness" and "stability" had to be gotten across. Although the group's organizational, financial, and marketing efforts of the first year had met with some success, the directors wondered what decisions could or should be made

EXHIBIT 6: ***Estimated annual operating expenses and membership status***

Rent	$3,000
Wages (attendant)	3,500
Printing and postage (15 openings at $60)	900
Advertising	50
Telephone	300
Insurance	
Annual premium	157
Special collectors show	150
Office supplies	200
Costs of exhibitions (15 at $40)	600
Utilities	120
Maintenance and refurbishing	300
Total	$9,277

		At present	
Sources of revenue	*Projected*	*Number*	*Amount*
Patrons (10 estimated)	$2,000	4	$ 800
Contributors (10 estimated)	750	4	200
Artists' dues (8 estimated)	1,600	8	1,550
Regular members (300 at $15)	4,500	50	750
Student members (100 at $5)	500	60	300
Total	$9,350		$3,600

EXHIBIT 7: ***Sources of names for mailing list***

1. Friends of the Library
2. Virginia Center for Creative Arts
3. English-Speaking Union
4. Wednesday Music Club
5. Albemarle Art Association
6. Virginia Museum, Local Chapter
7. Orange Garden Club
8. Downtown Charlottesville, Inc.
9. New University of Virginia faculty, September 1973
10. Suggestions from Second Street Gallery members
11. People who have expressed an interest

EXHIBIT 8: ***The Second Street Gallery***

The 2nd Street Gallery opened its doors on February 11, 1973. The founders, artists, businessmen, teachers and friends, wished to provide an exhibition space for paintings, sculpture, photography, graphics and a place to hold lectures and programs of interest to all who appreciate and enjoy the arts. The quality of the work and potential interest and value of the exhibition for the community are the central considerations in presenting programs. In order to be free to offer variety and flexibility in the kinds of exhibitions presented, the Gallery must free itself of the necessity of selling works of art to survive. While many works are for sale, and the Gallery is glad to sell what it can, it is central to our philosophy that saleability not determine whether something is shown.

Funds for operating the Gallery come from gifts, annual memberships, and sales of art work and books. The Gallery is not a part of, or supported by, any institution or organization. Its sole support and continuance depend on the citizens of the Charlottesville-Albemarle area. The Gallery has received tremendous support from merchants, who have contributed both materials and money to its establishment. The Gallery's artists each contribute $200.00 annually to its support; they hang all the shows, arrange for lectures, provide refreshments at openings and do all cleaning, mailing, etc., without salary. Our lecturers, many of whom are noted scholars in their fields, have freely donated their time to the Gallery and the community, for which we are very grateful.

The family memberships are the financial backbone of the Gallery. Memberships are $15.00 per year for families and $5.00 per year for students. In addition to the satisfaction of supporting this worthwhile effort, members receive the following benefits: free admission to all lectures, invitations to the Sunday afternoon previews of exhibitions, where refreshments will be served, and the artist will be on hand to talk with guests, discounts on Abrams art books and discounts on classes at the Gallery.

The 2nd Street Gallery, in addition to showing the work of individuals has already provided a number of other shows of interest to the community. The Collector's Show, for example, consisted of works of art from local collections. It contained works never before shown in the area, from the Orient and the West, from the third to the twentieth centuries. We hope to repeat this popular show next year with a new group of works.

Our opening show this year will be an exhibition of the work of Peter Fink, an internationally known photographer, represented in the permanent collections of the Bibliotheque Nationale in Paris, the Metropolitan Museum of Art, the Museum of Modern Art and the Chicago Art Institute among others.

While the Gallery is open to everyone, it is our hope that more and more of our neighbors will join us by becoming members, which will help ease the financial burdens and allow us to expand our offerings. The Gallery has applied to the Federal Government for tax-exempt status as a non-profit educational organization. We wish to thank all who have supported us before this status has been obtained.

A list of our exhibitions and lectures for this season appear on the reverse side.

To become a member, just fill out the form and mail it to the Gallery.

Mrs. William E. Craddock, Membership Chairman
George Roland, President
Eugene Markowski, Vice President
Paul Martick, Treasurer
Lindsay Nolting, Secretary
Gallery phone: 977-7284

Artists who would like to become members in the Gallery are cordially invited to apply by writing or phoning the Gallery. We are always glad to greet new talent, regardless of the artist's style or age.

about setting future objectives and plans and how these plans might be financed. Once the gallery reached its first anniversary, the members' thoughts turned from survival to establishing a firm base. This required all the working members to get together and develop a budget for the coming year, which was easier said than done. While the members had a much better idea as to what they wanted the gallery to be and do than they had had a year earlier, the setting down of those ideas in budget form still posed a problem.

THE MILWAUKEE BLOOD CENTER

The Milwaukee Blood Center (MBC) was established in 1946 by the Junior League to meet the emerging needs for blood in the Milwaukee area. The MBC has experienced substantial growth and is now a major regional blood center. The Milwaukee Blood Center is a member of two blood banking trade associations: the American Association of Blood Banks and the Council of Community Blood Centers. MBC is affiliated with the Medical College of Wisconsin. For a discussion of the current state of blood donation in the United States see the Appendix.

In 1976, the Milwaukee Blood Center moved to a new location at the western edge of the downtown area and adjacent to Marquette University. Within several blocks of their location there are five hospitals which MBC serves. The first floor of the building was renovated for use in blood collection. Free parking is provided behind the building for donors. The MBC also makes exten-

This case was prepared by Professor Patrick E. Murphy, Marquette University, and Ron Franzmeier, Zigman-Joseph-Skeen, as a basis for class discussion rather than to illustrate either effective or ineffective handling of an administrative situation. Reprinted with permission from Marquette University.

sive use of the five mobile units for drawing blood at business and organization sites. Furthermore, three satellite stations are utilized in suburban and neighboring city locations.

CURRENT SITUATION

In fiscal 1979, volunteer donors in southeastern Wisconsin gave 91,500 units of blood to support patients' needs in the 33 hospitals that the Milwaukee Blood Center served. As Exhibit 1 shows, donations have increased steadily during the decade of the 1970s and the 1979 total was 5,500 over the previous year.

However, local demand for blood *exceeded* local donations by 3,100 units, which had to be obtained from other blood centers. The major objective of donor recruitment programs is to make this region self-sufficient.

Eighty percent of the blood collected in the region was given by members of 900 donor clubs sponsored by business, schools, churches, and other civic, labor, and community groups in southeastern Wisconsin. The other 20% was drawn from individuals at MBC's central location in Milwaukee and parttime satellite stations located within the six-county area that the center serves.

These donors made it possible for the Milwaukee Blood Center to keep pace with the increasing demand for blood products in the region. Patients in the 33 hospitals served by the center required 5,400 more units of whole blood and packed red blood cells than were needed in 1978. The MBC also experienced a dramatic increase in the need for blood components.

The increased need for blood and blood components is related in part to the growing number of open heart, hip replacement, and kidney transplant operations being performed. Regular transfusions of blood platelets are demanded by a growing number of patients undergoing chemotherapy for cancer.

A MARKETING APPROACH

Administrators at MBC felt that the amount of blood collected from donor clubs was reaching a steady-state position. In fact, a few mobile drives had to be canceled because of layoffs or slow-

EXHIBIT 1: ***Number of volunteer blood donations, 1970–1979***[a]

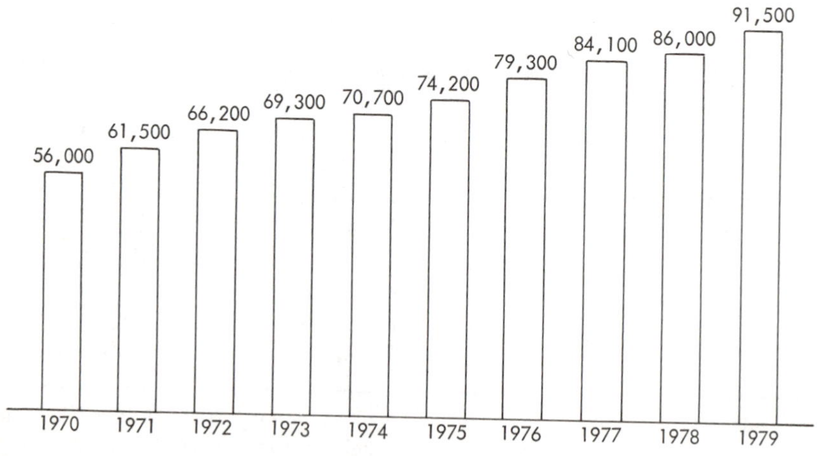

[a] During fiscal year 1979, 60,000 donors provided the 91,500 units of blood collected in the region. As demand continues to increase, the Blood Center must recruit more donors to avoid having to ask for more donations each year from the same people.

downs at local industries. Also, the demographic projections for the southeastern Wisconsin area indicate that the area will not grow in population. Therefore, the administration felt that a program aimed at the individual donor was needed. To facilitate this process the Milwaukee Blood Center sought the services of a local marketing consulting firm.

With the assistance of the consultant, the administrators were able to relate the marketing-mix elements to the process of blood donation. The product/service that they are offering is the unique satisfaction which the donor receives from the act of contributing a pint of his/her blood. This satisfaction cannot be derived from writing a check or volunteering time. The price not only represents the real cost of physical discomfort of the donor, inconvenience, and time lost that could be spent in other ways, but also the psychological cost of fear of the total experience. The place or distribution element is directly related to the center's location or availability of mobile units or satellite stations. Finally, promotion entails the personal selling effort engaged in by the donor recruiters and the mass-media efforts. The Milwaukee Blood Center employs four full-time donor recruiters who call on industry and other donor clubs.

The mass-media promotion used by the Milwaukee Blood Center took the form of Public Service Announcements. These announcements are free, but often aired late at night or at times when few people are watching or listening. Also, publicity is utilized by the Blood Center when they are experiencing a large shortage of donations. The problem with this type of promotion is that the Blood Center has no real control over the frequency with which their message reaches the target audience. Therefore, the Blood Center has relied heavily on other means of reaching prospective donors, such as printed brochures, direct-mail materials, and telephone solicitation.

MARKETING RESEARCH

The consultant and administration agreed that before a marketing program could be developed for the MBC, marketing reserach was necessary. Specifically, they needed to know more about their market area's donation patterns and certain attitudes of thought leaders and donors toward the Blood Center.

One part of the marketing research encompassed a study of the present geographic market area. It includes six counties which comprise the southeastern region of Wisconsin. These counties are: Milwaukee, Waukesha, Ozaukee, Washington, Racine, and Kenosha. Exhibit 2 shows the population and donation profile of this area for fiscal 1979. One important figure in this table is the percentage of population which actually donates. It is only 3% for the Blood Center area, while the national figure is between 5 and 6%. In the county-by-county breakdown, Racine and Kenosha residents are not donating at a percentage equal to their population proportion.

A second phase of the initial marketing research effort entailed a "thought leader" study. Approximately 10 governmental and mass-media leaders in Racine, Kenosha, and Waukesha were interviewed regarding their perception of attitudes that people in their area had toward the Blood Center. Thought leaders in Milwaukee were not surveyed because the Blood Center administrators had frequent contact with them. One consistent finding was that they felt there was some reluctance of people in these cities to donate to the "Milwaukee" Blood Center. Most citizens did not realize that the Blood Center served the entire southeastern Wisconsin region.

Research was also conducted with first-time donors. One hundred first-time donors were surveyed via telephone. They were prompted to donate by the 1979 Winter Blood Telethon which was carried by a local television station. These donors were asked why they had never donated before. Their responses are shown in Exhibit 3. The most frequently mentioned reason was—no one ever asked me to donate. Some of the more obvious reasons, such as "too busy" and "afraid to give," were designated by a much smaller percentage of the donors.

Another survey was conducted at the downtown

EXHIBIT 2

Market—Donor Statistics

Region's population	1,710,000
Donors	55,000 (3.2%)
Donations needed	102,000 (6%)

Population and Donation Profile of Counties Served by Milwaukee Blood Center

County	*Population*	*Percent of MBC region population*	*Units drawn in county*	*Percent of total units drawn in MBC region*
Milwaukee	982,000	57.4	56,000	61
Waukesha	276,000	16.1	15,800	17
Ozaukee	68,000	4.0	4,200	5
Washington	80,000	4.7	4,000	4
Racine	178,000	10.4	6,600	7
Kenosha	126,000	7.4	4,000	4
Other	—	—	1,400	2
Approximate region total	1,710,000	100	92,000	100

EXHIBIT 3: ***Reasons why people have not donated blood before***

	Was a reason (%)	*Was not a reason (%)*	*No answer; don't know (%)*
You thought you had a medical condition which kept you from giving.	16	83	1
You thought giving blood was painful.	29	70	1
You never knew your blood was needed.	30	70	0
You were afraid of giving blood.	30	70	0
You didn't know where to go to give blood.	31	69	0
The location of the MBC was inconvenient.	22	77	1
No one ever asked you to donate before.	62	37	1
You were too busy to give blood.	37	61	2

Milwaukee drawing station. Donors were asked to fill out a short questionnaire while they were being served refreshments after donating; 462 donors responded over a two-week period. One of the major findings of this survey was that nearly one-third of the respondents (32.4%) indicated that they would be likely to donate more often if there was a drawing station located more conveniently to their home.

CONCLUSION

When the consultant presented these research findings to the administration of MBC, they indicated that the consultant should develop a comprehensive marketing strategy (plan) based on these results. The administrators urged the consultants to be innovative and not to be concerned about organizational resistance to change. The only limiting factors that the administration placed on the marketing plan was that they could not afford paid television advertising. Major mass-media resources for the Milwaukee area are shown in Exhibit 4. The Milwaukee Blood Center's Board of Directors is scheduled to meet in three weeks and the administrator wants to present the comprehensive marketing program to them at that time.

APPENDIX: Current Status of Blood Donation in the United States

The blood collection system in America is going through some major changes, which may not be fully understood by the public.

Credits for Donating. There used to be a national system of credits for blood donors (hence the concept of blood "banking"). If you gave a pint of blood, a credit was given to you, your family, or whomever you designated to be the recipient of that credit. If you or your family needed a blood transfusion, you could draw on those credits and did not have to worry about replacing the blood. Those who had no credits for previous donations were assessed a penalty charge, called a nonreplacement fee, unless they were able to find someone who would donate to replace the blood used.

This system of credits proved very costly to maintain and involved the transfer of paper credits rather than blood. It also seemed to place an unfair burden on the elderly and others who did not have friends or family members able to replace the

EXHIBIT 4: ***Major mass-media resources in Milwaukee area***

Newspaper

	Name	*Circulation*	*Frequency*	*Cost per column inch*
Milwaukee	*Journal*	329,000	Daily	$13.58
	Sentinal	165,205	Daily	7.84
	Post	262,000	Weekly (suburban)	3.92
Kenosha	*Kenosha News*	31,620	Daily	4.84
	Kenosha Labor Press	21,500	Weekly	3.92
Racine	*Labor News*	16,000	Weekly	3.05
	Journal Times	40,000	Daily	4.75
Waukesha	*Freeman*	26,000	Daily	3.86

Radio

	Name	*Format*	*Average cost (per 30-second spot)*
Milwaukee	WTMJ	Mid road	$67.50
	WOKY	AM rock	35.00
	WZUU	FM rock	27.00
	WBCS	Country/western	22.00
Kenosha	WLIP	Mid road	7.75
	WJZQ	FM rock	6.35
Racine	WRJN	Mid road	7.50
	WRKR	AM rock	11.00
	WWEG	Country/western	10.00

blood used. For these reasons, nearly 80% of the blood centers in the country have dropped the system of credits and no longer charge a nonreplacement fee. Blood is simply made available to all who need it and the only charge made is for the costs of the collecting and processing it (and this is covered by most insurance programs).

Paid Donors. It was very common practice at one time for donors to be paid for the blood they gave. Research has determined that the incidence of infectious hepatitis in blood from donors who have been paid is far greater than that in blood which comes from volunteer donors. As a result, most communities no longer pay donors or offer them any reward of monetary value.

Regional Blood Centers. At one time, many small communities had their own blood program—usually organized by the local hospital and industry leaders. Physicians have conducted research into how to use blood efficiently, and about how to separate it into various components. Today, a patient is rarely given whole blood. They receive only those components that are required.

Testing, processing, and separating blood into its components required specialized staff and equipment which would be very costly to duplicate in every community. As a result, the country's blood collection system is being regionalized. Blood is being collected in small communities, but it is transported to regional blood centers, where it is processed. The blood is stored at these centers, with the quantities and types of blood needed being returned to the small towns so that their supply is always adequate.

As a result of this regulation, many of the small-town blood programs are now a part of regional programs. They are subject to new regulations and have suffered a loss of local identity.

Fewer Restrictions on Donors. Research has greatly improved our understanding of how disease is and is not transmitted through blood transfusions. As a result, many people who once were rejected as blood donors because of some childhood disease can now donate. At one time, the average rejection rate was 12% (i.e., 12% of the people who came in to donate were rejected as donors on the basis of their medical history). Today, only 5% of those who come in are turned away because of past illnesses.

Donors between the ages of 17 and 65 who are in good health are eligible to donate. In special circumstances individuals older or younger than those ages may be donors. A person may donate once every 10 weeks (five times per year). However, individuals who donate in the United States usually do so less than once a year.

VI: ADOPTING MARKETING

The adoption of marketing to further organizations, persons, plans, causes, and ideas is the focus of this section. Marketing is viewed as a pervasive activity that can be adopted in a variety of situations to develop exchange between two parties. Marketing is useful in furthering the objectives of social units that desire something in an exchange relationship.

The first article in Part VI is ''Social Marketing: An Approach to Planned Social Change'' by Philip Kotler and Gerald Zaltman. Can marketing concepts and techniques be effectively applied to the promotion of social objectives, such as brotherhood, safe driving, and family planning? The applicability of marketing concepts to such social problems is examined in this article. The authors show how social causes can be advanced more successfully through applying principles of marketing analysis, planning, and control to problems of social change. See Karen F. A. Fox and Philip Kotler, ''The Marketing of Social Causes: The First Ten Years,'' *Journal of Marketing,* Fall 1980, pp. 24–33, for an update of this article.

The second article is ''Marketing Down the Road: The Role of Marketing Analysis in Transportation Planning,'' by Daniel J. Brown, Philip B. Schary, and Boris W. Becker. Public involvement is becoming important in public planning. People feel better about the governmental agencies that serve them, but both procedural and substantive problems have arisen. Public inputs have limited usefulness, are not representative, and create conflicts. They suggest that marketing analysis may have promise in alleviating these problems.

The final selection is ''A Concept Sector within the Economy'' by Seymour H. Fine. This paper explores a sector of the economy constituted of those institutions sponsoring ideas and social issues—concepts—in contrast to organizations selling goods and services. The concept sector cuts across traditional boundaries of sector distinction because its members include profit-making, nonprofit public organizations, as well as the hybrid ''quasis.'' It is characterized by the criterion that its ''product mix'' consists of abstract concepts unrelated to conventional products.

Cases in this section include ''Tulsa Philharmonic,'' ''Community Health Plan,'' and ''The Undercroft Montessori School.''

Social Marketing: An Approach to Planned Social Change

PHILIP KOTLER

GERALD ZALTMAN

In 1952, G. D. Wiebe raised the question "Why can't you sell brotherhood like you sell soap?"[1] This statement implies that sellers of commodities such as soap are generally effective, while "sellers" of social causes are generally ineffective. Wiebe examined four social campaigns to determine what conditions or characteristics accounted for their relative success or lack of success. He found that the more the conditions of the social campaign resembled those of a product campaign, the more successful the social campaign. However, because many social campaigns are conducted under quite un-market-like circumstances, Wiebe also noted clear limitations in the practice of social marketing.

A different view is implied in Joe McGinniss's best-selling book *The Selling of the President 1968*.[2] Its theme seems to be "You can sell a presidential candidate like you sell soap." Once Nixon gave the word: "We're going to build this whole campaign around television . . . you fellows just tell me what you want me to do and I'll do it," the advertising men, public relations men, copywriters, makeup artist, photographers, and others joined together to create the image and the aura that would make this man America's favorite "brand."

These and other cases suggest that the art of selling cigarettes, soap, or steel may have some bearing on the art of selling social causes. People like McGinniss—and before him John K. Galbraith and Vance Packard—believe everything and anything can be sold by Madison Avenue, while people like Wiebe feel this is exaggerated. To the extent that Madison Avenue has this power, some persons would be heartened because of the many good causes in need of an effective social marketing technology, and others would despair over the spectre of mass manipulation.

Unfortunately there are few careful discussions of the power and limitations of social marketing. It is the authors' view that social marketing is a promising framework for planning and implementing social change. At the same time, it is poorly understood and often viewed suspiciously by many behavioral scientists. The application of commercial ideas and methods to promote social goals will be seen by many as another example of business's lack of taste and self-restraint. Yet the application of the logic of marketing to social goals is a natural development and on the whole a promising one. The idea will not disappear by ignoring it or railing against it.

This article discusses the meaning, power, and limitations of social marketing as an approach to planned social change. First, this will require delineating the generic nature of marketing phenomena and some recent conceptual developments in the marketing field. This will be followed by a definition of social marketing and an examination of the conditions under which it may be carried out effectively. The instruments of social marketing are defined, followed by a systems view of the application of marketing logic to social objectives.

Reprinted with permission from *Journal of Marketing*, July 1971, pp. 3–12; published by the American Marketing Association.

WHAT IS MARKETING?

The following statement testifies that there is no universal agreement on what marketing is.

> It has been described by one person or another as a business activity; as a group of related business activities; as a trade phenomenon; as a frame of mind; as a coordinative, integrative function in policy making; as a sense of business purpose; as an economic process; as a structure of institutions; as the process of exchanging or transferring ownership of products; as a process of concentration, equalization, and dispersion; as the creation of time, place and possession utilities; as a process of demand and supply adjustment; and many other things.[3]

In spite of the confusing jumble of definitions, the core idea of marketing lies in *the exchange process. Marketing does not occur unless there are two or more parties, each with something to exchange, and both able to carry out communications and distribution*. Typically the subject of marketing is the exchange of goods or services for other goods or services or for money. Belshaw, in an excellent study of marketing exchange and its evolution from traditional to modern markets, shows the exchange process in marketing to be a fundamental aspect of both primitive and advanced social life.[4]

Given that the core idea of marketing lies in exchange processes, another concept can be postulated, that of marketing management, which can be defined as:

> Marketing management is the analysis, planning, implementation, and control of programs designed to bring about desired exchanges with target audiences for the purpose of personal or mutual gain. It relies heavily on the adaptation and coordination of product, price, promotion, and place for achieving effective response.[5]

Thus marketing management occurs when people become conscious of an opportunity to gain from a more careful planning of their exchange relations. Although planned social change is not often viewed from the client's point of view, it involves very much an exchange relationship between client and change agent.[6]

The practice of marketing management as applied to products and services has become increasingly sophisticated. The responsibility of launching new products on a national basis involving the investment and risk of millions of dollars and the uncertainties of consumer and competitor responses, has led to an increased reliance on formal research and planning throughout the product development and introduction cycle. Marketing management examines the wants, attitudes, and behavior of potential customers which could aid in designing a desired product and in merchandising, promoting, and distributing it successfully. Management goes through a formal process of strategy determination, tactical programming, regional and national implementation, performance measurement, and feedback control.

There has been a shift from a sales to a marketing orientation in recent years. A sales orientation considers the job as one of finding customers for existing products and convincing them to buy these products. This sales concept is implicit in *The Selling of the President 1968,* since one is actually not developing a new "product" for the job, but rather trying to sell a given one with a suggestion that it is somewhat "new and improved." The marketing concept, on the other hand, calls for most of the effort to be spent on discovering the wants of a target audience and then creating the goods and services to satisfy them. This view seems privately and socially more acceptable. In private terms, the seller recognizes that it is easier to create products and services for existing wants than to try to alter wants and attitudes toward existing products. In social terms, it is held that this marketing philosophy restores consumer sovereignty in the determination of the society's product mix and the use of national resources.

In practice, since at any time there are both products in existence and new products being born, most marketing efforts are a mixture of selling and marketing; that is, a change strategy and a response strategy. In both cases, marketing management is becoming a sophisticated action technology that draws heavily on the behavioral sciences for clues to solving problems of communication and persuasion related to influencing the acceptability of commercial products and services. In the hands of its best practitioners, marketing management is applied behavioral science.

SOCIAL MARKETING

An increasing number of nonbusiness institutions have begun to examine marketing logic as a means to furthering their institutional goals and products. Marketing men have advised churches on how to increase membership, charities on how to raise money, and art museums and symphonies on how to attract more patrons. In the social sphere, the Advertising Council of America has conducted campaigns for social objectives, including "Smokey the Bear," "Keep America Beautiful." "Join the Peace Corps," "Buy Bonds," and "Go to College." In fact, social advertising has become an established phenomenon on the American scene. Sandage says:

> True, (advertising's) communication function has been confined largely to informing and persuading people in respect to products and services. On the other hand, it can be made equally available to those who wish to inform and persuade people in respect to a city bond issue, cleaning up community crime, the "logic" of atheism, the needs for better educational facilities, the abusive tactics of given law and enforcement officers, or any other sentiment held by any individual who wishes to present such sentiment to the public.[7]

Social advertising has become such a feature of American society that it is no longer a question of whether to use it, but how to use it. It has been very successful in some cases and conspicuously unsuccessful in others. At fault to a large extent is the tendency of social campaigners to assign advertising the primary, if not the exclusive, role in accomplishing their social objectives. This ignores the marketing truism that a given marketing objective requires the coordination of the promotional mix with the goods and services mix and with the distribution mix. Social marketing is a much larger idea than social advertising and even social communication. To emphasize this, the authors define social marketing in the following way:

> Social marketing is the design, implementation, and control of programs calculated to influence the acceptability of social ideas and involving considerations of product planning, pricing, communication, distribution, and marketing research.

Thus, it is the explicit use of marketing skills to help translate present social action efforts into more effectively designed and communicated programs that elicit desired audience response. In other words, marketing techniques are the bridging mechanisms between the simple possession of knowledge and the socially useful implementation of what knowledge allows.

THE REQUISITE CONDITIONS FOR EFFECTIVE SOCIAL MARKETING

Some clues concerning the difference between social advertising and social marketing are contained in early papers by Lazarsfeld and Merton and by Wiebe which attempt to explain the limitations of social advertising.[8]

Lazarsfeld and Merton's Analysis. Lazarsfeld and Merton took exception with the view of many people that mass media can easily be used to control people's minds: "It is our tentative judgment that the social role played by the very existence of the mass media has been commonly overestimated."[9] They believed that the effectiveness of mass media for propaganda purposes depended on three conditions, one or more of which is lacking in most propaganda situations. The first conditon is real or psychological *monopolization* by the media; that is, a condition marked by the absence of counter-propaganda. This characterizes the totalitarian state and accounts for the greater effectiveness of these regimes in molding public opinion through mass media. It is found occasionally in free societies under special circumstances, such as a wartime effort. For example, Kate Smith's effectiveness in selling war bonds over the radio during World War II was partially due to the marathon nature of the event and the fact that everyone believed in the cause; i.e., there was no counter-propaganda. However, most campaigns in a free society in peace time compete with so many other causes and everyday distractions that the monopoly condition is lacking, and this condition reduces the effectiveness of such campaigns.

Lazarsfeld and Merton said the second condition required for effective mass propaganda is *canalization,* the presence of an existing attitudinal base for the feelings that the social communicators are striving to shape. They asserted that typical commercial advertising is effective because the task is not one of instilling basic new attitudes or creating significantly new behavior patterns, but rather canalizing existing attitudes and behavior in one direction or another. Thus, the seller of toothpaste does not have to socialize persons into new dental care habits, but rather into which brand of a familiar and desired product to purchase. If the preexisting attitudes are present, then promotional campaigns are more effective, since canalization is always an easier task than social reconditioning.

The authors accept this idea but would add that many business marketing situations also involve the task of reshaping basic attitudes rather than canalizing existing ones. For example, consider business efforts to influence farmers to change time-honored farming practices, doctors to try out new drugs, and males to dress with more fashion and flair. Canalization is always easier, but the authors would like to emphasize that business marketers, like social marketers, often try to diffuse fundamentally new products and services which require major attitudinal reorientations.

Lazarsfeld and Merton call the third condition *supplementation* by which they mean the effort to follow up mass communication campaigns with programs of face-to-face contacts. In trying to explain the success of the rightist Father Coughlin movement in the thirties, Lazarsfeld and Merton observe:

> This combination of a central supply of propaganda (Coughlin's addresses on a nationwide network), the coordinated distribution of newspapers and pamphlets and locally organized face-to-face discussions among relatively small groups —this complex of reciprocal reinforcement by mass media and personal relations proved spectacularly successful.[10]

This approach is standard in many closed societies and organizations and suggests another key difference between social advertising and social marketing. Whereas a social advertising approach contrives only the event of mass media communication and leaves the response to natural social processes, social marketing arranges for a stepdown communication process. The message is passed on and discussed in more familiar surroundings to increase its memorability, penetration, and action consequences. Thus supplementation, monopolization, and canalization are critical factors influencing the effectiveness of any social marketing effort.

Wiebe's Analysis. An additional contribution was made by Wiebe in his attempt to understand the differential effectiveness of four social campaigns.[11] He explained the relative effectiveness of these campaigns in terms of the audience member's experience with regard to five factors:

1. *The force:* The intensity of the person's motivation toward the goal as a combination of his predisposition prior to the message and the stimulation of the message.
2. *The direction:* Knowledge of how or where the person might go to consummate his motivation.
3. *The mechanism:* The existence of an agency that enables the person to translate his motivation into action.
4. *Adequacy and compatibility:* The ability and effectiveness of the agency in performing its task.

5. *Distance:* The audience member's estimate of the energy and cost required to consummate the motivation in relation to the reward.

To show how these factors operate, Wiebe first analyzed the Kate Smith compaign to sell bonds during World War II. This campaign was eminently successful, according to Wiebe, because of the presence of force (patriotism), direction (buy bonds), mechanism (banks, post offices, telephone orders), adequacy and compatibility (so many centers to purchase the bonds), and distance (ease of purchase). In fact, extra telephone lines were installed on the night of the campaign at 134 CBS stations to take orders during her appeal. The effort to buy bonds

> was literally reduced to the distance between the listener and his telephone. Psychological distance was also minimized. The listener remained in his own home. There were no new people to meet, no unfamiliar procedures, no forms to fill out, no explanation, no waiting. . . .[12]

In the case of a campaign to recruit Civil Defense volunteers, many of the same factors were present except that the social mechanism was not prepared to handle the large volume of response, and this reduced the campaign's success. Teachers, manuals, equipment, and registration and administration procedures were *inadequate,* and many responding citizens were turned away and disappointed after they were led to believe that their services were urgently needed.

The third campaign, a documentary on juvenile delinquency, did not meet with maximum success because of the *absence of a mechanism*. Instead of being directed to an existing agency, people were urged to form neighborhood councils themselves. This certainly takes far more effort than simply picking up the phone to buy a war bond, or "stopping in" to register at the nearest Civil Defense unit.

The fourth campaign revolved around the goal of the Kefauver committee hearings to arouse citizens to "set their house in order." This campaign met with a notable lack of success, however, because citizens were not *directed* to an appropriate mechanism despite the fact that one existed in principle in the political party organizations. Political party organizations apparently left much to be desired in terms of availability and compatibility. The skepticism prevalent at the time concerning the chances of anything beneficial happening as a result of the hearings was ample evidence that considerable psychological distance existed between the audience and the mechanisms for action.

The Social Marketing Approach. The Lazarsfeld and Merton conditions and the Wiebe factors provide a useful background for viewing the conceptual framework used by marketing strategists. Marketers view the marketing problem as one of developing the right *product* backed by the right *promotion* and put in the right *place* at the right *price*. These key variables in the marketing mix have been named the four P's by McCarthy.[13] The authors shall examine each of these variables, designated control variables, in terms of some well-known social issues.

Product. In business marketing, sellers study the needs and wants of target buyers and attempt to design products and services that meet their desires. If well-designed and affordable, these products will be purchased. In social marketing, sellers also have to study the target audiences and design appropriate products. They must "package" the social idea in a manner which their target audiences find desirable and are willing to purchase. This corresponds to Wiebe's idea of a mechanism.

Product design is typically more challenging in the social area than it is in the business area. Consider the problem of marketing "safer driving." The social objective is to create safer driving habits and attitudes in the population. There is no one product that can accomplish this. Various products have to be designed that will make partial contributions to the social objective. A public education media campaign providing tips on safe driving is one such product; the offering of "defensive driving courses" is another, the creation of insurance policies which reduce premiums for safer drivers is still another product. In general, the social marketer remains aware of the *core product* (safer driving) and tries to create various tangible products and services which are "buyable" and which advance the social objective.

Identical reasoning is required by those who market *altruistic causes* (e.g., charity giving, blood donation), *personal health causes* (e.g., nonsmoking, better nutrition), and *social betterment causes* (e.g., civil rights, improved housing, better environment). In each case, the social marketer must define the change sought, which may be a change in values, beliefs, affects, behavior, or some mixture. He must meaningfully segment the target markets. He must design social products for each market which are "buyable," and which instrumentally serve the social cause. In some social causes, the most difficult problem will be to innovate appropriate products; in other cases it will be to motivate purchase.

Promotion. The marketing man's second control variable is promotion. It is the communication persuasion strategy and tactics that will make the product familiar, acceptable, and even desirable to the audience. Wiebe's counterpart to promotion is "force." The social campaign strategist will tend to think of this as mass media communication, but promotion is actually a much larger idea. To the marketing man, promotion includes the following major activities:

Advertising: Any paid form of nonpersonal presentation and promotion of products, services, or ideas by an identified sponsor.

Personal selling: Any paid form of personal presentation and promotion of products, service, or ideas by an identified sponsor.

Publicity: Any unpaid form of nonpersonal presentation and promotion of products, services, or ideas where the sponsor is unidentified.

Sales promotion: Miscellaneous paid forms (special programs, incentives, materials, and events) designed to stimulate audience interest and acceptance of a product.

Each of these promotional tools involves complex issues in strategy and tactics. With respect to advertising, the marketer has to determine the size of the total advertising budget, the choice of appeals, the development of attention-getting copy, the selection of effective and efficient media, the scheduling of the advertising inputs, and the measurement of overall and segment-level results. With respect to personal selling, the marketer must determine the size of the total sales force, the development of sales territory boundaries and assignments, the development of personal presentation strategies, the degree and type of salesforce motivation and supervision, and the evaluation of salesforce effectiveness. Publicity necessitates arranging for significant news about the product to appear in various media. Sales promotion calls for developing special display, premiums, programs, and events that might be useful in stimulating interest or action.

Each of these activities is a specialty in which the experts have achieved sophisticated levels of knowledge and techniques. This is especially apparent when one examines social campaigns developed by amateurs where the appeals and copy seem very naive. Even behavioral science consultants to social campaign organizations often fail to make a maximum contribution because of their inability or reluctance to view the issue in broad marketing terms instead of in strictly social or ethical terms.

Recently Nathaniel Martin criticized the Indian government for failing to handle family planning as a marketing problem.

> Selling birth control is as much a marketing job as selling any other consumer product. And where no manufacturer would contemplate developing and introducing a new product without a thorough understanding of the variables of the market, planners in the highest circles of Indian government have blithely gone ahead without understanding that marketing principles must determine the character of any campaign of voluntary control. The Indians have done only the poorest research. They have mismanaged distribution of contraceptive devices.

> They have ignored the importance of "customer service." They have proceeded with grossly inadequate undertrained staffs; they have been blind to the importance of promotion and advertising.[14]

This is not to deny that the Indian government has undertaken some innovative promotional approaches. Referral fees are paid to salesmen, barbers, and others who bring in consenting males for sterilization. The consenting male is given a transistor radio or a small payment to cover his costs of being absent from work. Women have been offered gifts for consenting to use intrauterine contraceptive devices. But Martin feels that the total program lacks the qualities of an organized, well-planned, and continuous marketing effort.[15]

An example of careful promotional planning for a social objective is found in the American Cancer Society efforts to raise money for cancer research. In their brochure directed to local units, they attempt to educate the volunteer and professional chapters on the handling of newspapers, pictures, company publications, radio and television, movies, special events, and controversial arguments. For example, in terms of special events:

> Dramatic special events attract attention to the American Cancer Society. They bring color, excitement, and glamour to the program. Well planned, they will get excellent coverage in newspapers, on radio and TV, and in newsreels. . . . A Lights-on-Drive, a one-afternoon or one-night House-to-House program have such dramatic appeal that they stir excitement and enthusiasm . . . keep in mind the value of bursts of sound such as fire sirens sounding, loud-speaker trucks, fife and drum corps. . . . A most useful special event is the ringing of church bells to add a solemn, dedicated note to the launching of a drive or education project. This should be organized on a Division or community basis, and the church bell ringing may be the signal to begin a House-to-House canvass. Rehearsals of bell ringing, community leaders tugging at ropes, offer good picture possibilities.[16]

Some readers might be critical of this approach to a worthwhile social objective, but two things should be mentioned. The first is that this should not be identified as the *marketing approach to social objectives*. Many persons mistakenly assume that marketing means hard selling. This is only a particular style of marketing, and it has its critics both inside and outside the profession. There are many firms that market their products with taste and sensitivity; examples include Xerox, Container Corporation, and Hallmark. It is important to recognize that this is not nonmarketing but rather a style of marketing that was chosen in the belief of its greater effectiveness in accomplishing the goals of the organization.

Second, the issue is not whether a particular approach suits one's personal taste, but whether it works. If a "hard" marketing style raises substantially more money for cancer research than a "soft" marketing style, it must be respected by those who think cancer research is more important than personal aesthetics.

Place. The third element of the marketing approach to social campaigns calls for providing adequate and compatible distribution and response channels. Motivated persons should know where the product can be obtained. Place is equivalent to two of Wiebe's five conditions for an effective mass communication campaign (direction, and adequacy and compatibility). The poor results of many social campaigns can be attributed in part to their failure to suggest clear action outlets for those motivated to acquire the product. The current campaign to interest people in the pollution problem may suffer from this defect. It is succeeding in making everyone not only aware of environmental pollution but also fearful of it. People want to do something about it. But for the most part they cannot act because there is not a clear product to "buy" (such as a petition to sign, an election in which to choose an antipollution candidate, or a pending piece of national legislation). Nor does the average person have a clear picture of the alternative channels of action for expressing his interest in the issue. There are so many ad hoc organizations working without coordination and at times with cross-purpose, that the average person is likely to "tune out" from further messages because of personal frustration. Saturation campaigns unaccompanied by the provision of adequate response channels may result in "interest overkill."

The importance of place has been recognized in several campaigns. The most notable example is the Kate Smith bond-selling campaign and its imaginative establishment of telephone order channels during the broadcast. Strategists of anti-cigarette campaigns have recognized the need for action channels by setting up smoker's clinics in many large cities. They could even go further and provide telephone advice and even social calls if the economics would justify these additional channels. An advertising agency is planning a campaign called "Pick Your Issue" in which several different social issues would be individually featured. The point would be made that because the busy citizen does not have time to become involved in all issues, this should not be an excuse to remain uninvolved in any issues. The good citizen should "pick an issue." Each issue advertisement will contain information on the organizations active in that area and inform the citizen about where to write for further information.

Thus, place means arranging for accessible outlets which permit the translation of motivations into actions. Planning in this area entails selecting or developing appropriate outlets, deciding on their number, average size, and locations, and giving them proper motivation to perform their part of the job.

Price. The final control variable that must be planned is price. Price represents the costs that the buyer must accept in order to obtain the product. It resembles Wiebe's concept of distance and incorporates some aspects of adequacy and compatibility. Price includes money costs, opportunity costs, energy costs, and psychic costs. Thus, the cost to persons asked to appear for immunization shots includes any possible money charge, any opportunities foregone, the expenditure of energy, and the psychological concerns aroused by inoculation. The cost of giving up smoking is largely psychological, since there is actually a financial saving in breaking the habit. The cost of using seat belts is the charge for buying them, the effort to lock and unlock them, and the psychological cost of not being completely sure one is better off in an accident wearing them or not wearing them.

The functioning of this concept can also be illustrated in terms of an interesting phenomenon in health care services where many poor patients prefer to patronize unlicensed practitioners and pay a fee instead of going to the free hospital. In Caracas, Venezuela, for example, although there is a free hospital for the indigent, many of them patronize private clinics which cost them 20 bolivares for consultation. Why? Because while there is no charge at the free hospital, there is a substantial cost to the patient in terms of energy and psychological abuse. When a patient arrives at the hospital, he has to wait to see a social worker first. When he is finally interviewed, the social worker asks many questions about his income to determine whether he is really indigent. Then he sees a number of other hospital staff members for various tests, and again is asked about his income. Finally, he sees the doctor who might discover that he really needs to see a specialist who will not be available for several weeks. Throughout the experience, the person is made to feel inferior and a nuisance. Therefore, it is not surprising that he wishes to avoid these energy and psychological costs even if it means paying for the services.

But even monetary charges may play a useful role in leading the poor back to free hospital services. In private correspondence, a social psychologist suggested:

> It is a surprising discovery that even free medical care presents a marketing problem. Maybe we should apply dissonance theory and introduce such medical care at a high price to make it look more desirable. Then let us apply a cents-off special introductory offer to make the service attractive.

The marketing man's approach to pricing the social product is based on the assumption that members of a target audience perform a cost-benefit analysis when considering the investment of money, time, or energy in the issue. They somehow process the major benefits and compare them to the major costs, and the strength of their motivation to act is directly related to the magnitude of the excess benefit. This type of conceptualization of behavior is found not only in the economist's model of economic man, but also in behavioristic theory with its emphasis on rewards and costs, in Gestalt theory with its emphasis on positive and negative valences, and in management theory with its emphasis on incentives and constraints. The marketer's approach to selling a social product is to consider how the rewards for buying the product can be increased relative to the costs, or the costs reduced relative to the rewards, or trying to find a mix of product, promotion, place, and price that will simultaneously increase the rewards and reduce the costs. The main point is that social marketing requires that careful thought be given to the manner in which manageable, desirable, gratifying, and convenient solutions to a perceived need or problem are presented to its potential buyers.

THE SOCIAL MARKETING PLANNING PROCESS

The "four P's" of marketing management are integrated in an administrative process framework in Figure 1. Continuous information is called from the *environment* by the *change agency*. *Plans and messages* are created and sent through *channels to audiences,* and the results are monitored by the *change agency*.

The change agency operates a research unit and a planning unit. The research unit collects several types of information. It monitors the environment—economic, political, technological, cultural, and competitive influences—for important developments affecting its social policies and objectives. For example, a family planning agency would monitor economic-demographic developments (income and population trends), political developments (liberalization of birth control information), technological developments (new birth control techniques and devices), cultural developments (attitudinal changes toward birth control), and competitive developments (actions of similar and competing groups). The research unit also collects information on the past effectiveness of various programs as well as information on audience attitudes, desires, and behavior.

The change agent's planning unit formulates short- and long-range social marketing plans on the basis of this information. For example, the family planning organization carefully considers the role of different products, promotions, places, and prices. It would identify the major channels of communication and distribution, such as mass or specialized media, paid agents, and volunteer groups. It would differentiate the programs intended for its primary target market (large and low-income families), secondary target market (other childbearing families), tertiary target market (sources of funds and additional volunteer efforts), and miscellaneous target markets (politicians and church groups). Finally, it would continuously gather effectiveness measures on these programs for recycling its planning.

This approach represents an application of business marketing principles to the problem of marketing social change. It is already manifest in some of the larger social change agencies. For example, consider the work of the National Safety Council. Its staff includes an advertising manager, a sales promotion management, an Advertising Council of America coordinator, a research director, and a program director. One of its products is a defensive driving course. Figure 2 shows the various channels through which this course is marketed along with the promotional tools it uses. The National Safety Council reaches potential prospects through business firms, service organizations, schools, and the police and court system. For the 1970s, the National Safety Council has adopted

> a four point marketing program. . . . One of the first objectives is to increase the sales effectiveness of our existing 150 state and local safety council cooperating agencies. . . . The second part of the

FIGURE 1: ***Social marketing planning system***

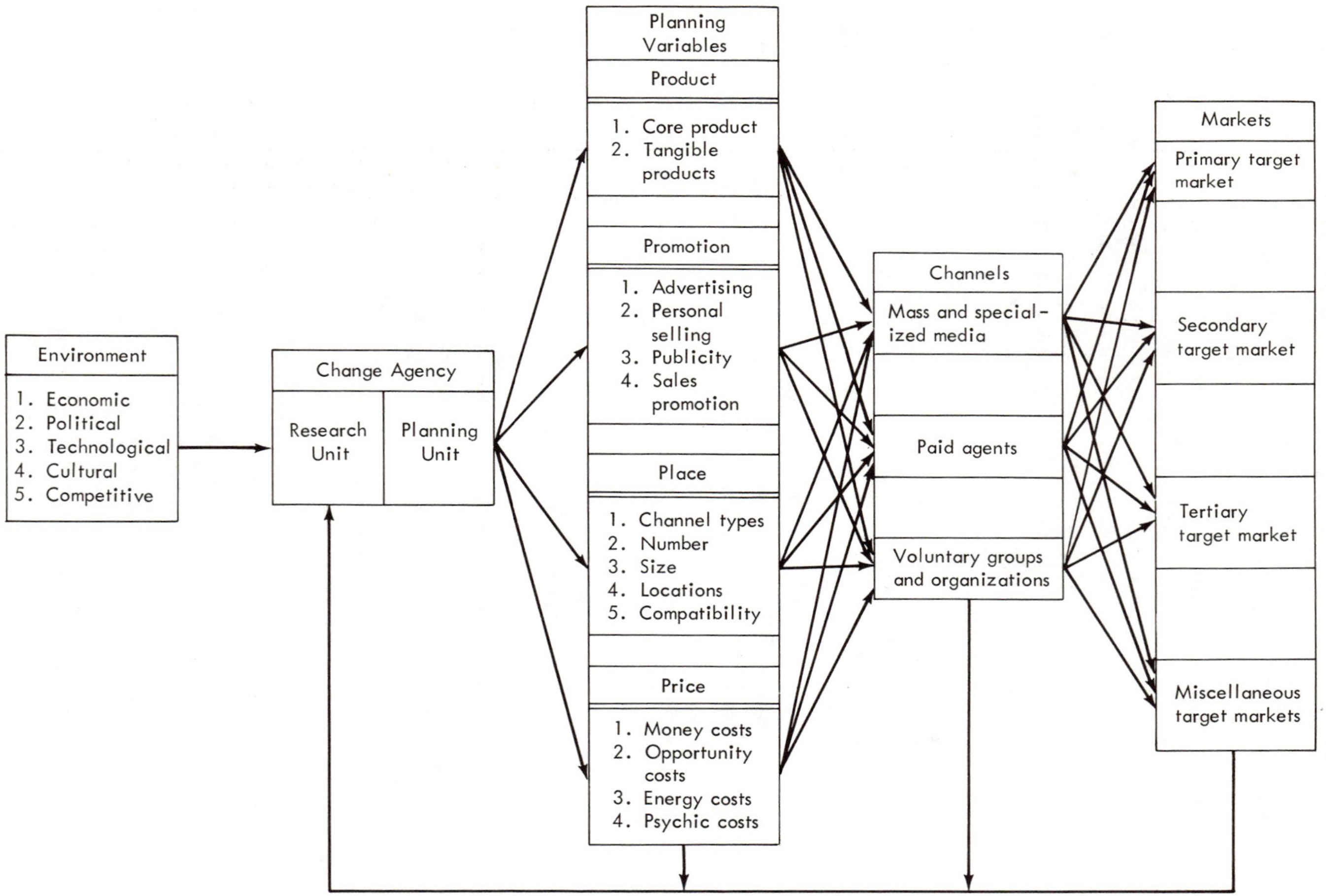

Environment

1. Economic
2. Political
3. Technological
4. Cultural
5. Competitive

Change Agency

Research Unit

Planning Unit

Planning Variables

Product

1. Core product
2. Tangible products

Promotion

1. Advertising
2. Personal selling
3. Publicity
4. Sales promotion

Place

1. Channel types
2. Number
3. Size
4. Locations
5. Compatibility

Price

1. Money costs
2. Opportunity costs
3. Energy costs
4. Psychic costs

Channels

Mass and special-ized media

Paid agents

Voluntary groups and organizations

Markets

Primary target market

Secondary target market

Tertiary target market

Miscellaneous target markets

FIGURE 2: ***Marketing channels and tools: defensive driving course***

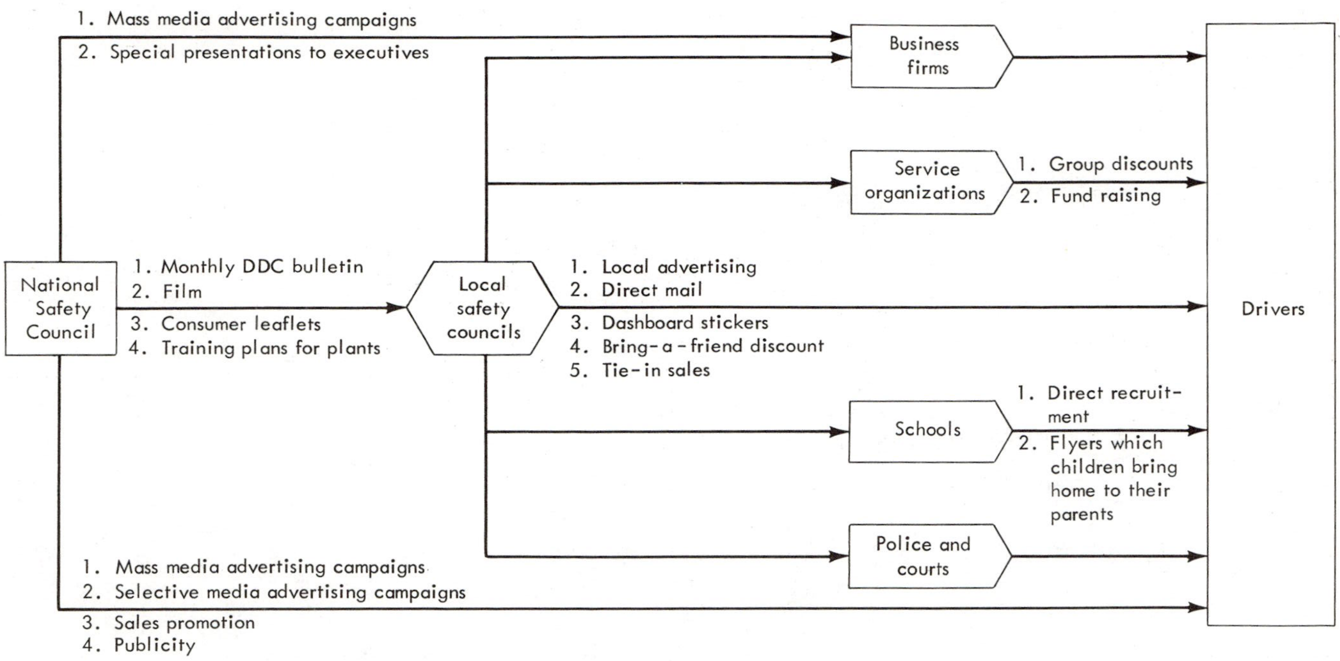

> program is to create 500 new training agencies in communities not now served by safety councils. . . . A third part of the marketing program will be aimed at selling big industry on adopting DDC as a training course for all employees or selected categories of employees in plant-run training programs. . . . The fourth part of the marketing plan deals with a nationwide promotional effort built around a series of community special-emphasis campaigns running from February 1 through Memorial Day each year of the decade.[17]

This example illustrates the possibilities of the marketing approach for furthering social causes. The National Safety Council and several other social agencies have graduated from occasional campaign organizations to full-time marketing organizations which go through cycles of information gathering, planning, product development, measuring, and reprogramming.

Social Implications of Social Marketing. The authors believe that specific social causes could benefit from marketing thinking and planning. Problems of pollution control, mass transit, private education, drug abuse, and public medicine are in need of innovative solutions and approaches for gaining public attention and support. Marketing men by their training are finely attuned to market needs, product development, pricing and channel issues, and mass communication and promotion techniques, all of which are critical in the social area.

At the same time, social marketing is sufficiently distinct from business marketing to require fresh thinking and new approaches. Social marketing typically has to deal with the market's core beliefs and values, whereas business marketing often deals with superficial preferences and opinions. Social marketing must search harder for meaningful *quid pro quos* to gain acceptance or adoption of its products. Social marketing has to work with channel systems that are less well-defined and less pecuniarily motivated. Only through applying marketing concepts and tools to a large number of cases will the powers and limits of the social marketing approach be learned.

In addition, there is the definite possibility that the overt marketing of social objectives will be resented and resisted. There will be charges that it is "manipulative," and consequently contributes to bringing the society closer to Orwell's 1984. There will be charges that even if not manipulative, social marketing will increase the amount of "promotional noise" in the society, which is found distasteful both because it emphasizes "trivial differences" and because it is "noise." Finally, social marketing will be accused of increasing the costs of promoting social causes beyond the point of a net gain either to the specific cause or the society as a whole. In the charities industry, professional marketing increases the absolute cost of raising money, but it usually succeeds in raising more money after these costs are taken into account. However, when one considers the entire picture, it is possible that the total amount donated to charities may not increase by the same amount as the professional marketing costs.

The authors are concerned with these possible dysfunctional consequences, and they must obviously be subtracted from the potential benefits that social marketing might produce. Since social marketing is just emerging, those concerned are encouraged to monitor it closely in the same dispassionate spirit that business marketers have so ably analyzed and documented the many manifestations of business marketing practice over the years.

SUMMARY

This article considered the applicability of marketing concepts to the problem of promoting social causes. Social marketing was defined as the design, implementation, and control of programs calculated to influence the acceptability of social ideas and involving considerations of product planning, pricing, communication, distribution, and marketing research.

Too often social advertising rather than social marketing is practiced by social campaigners.

Lazarsfeld and Merton attributed the failure of many social advertising campaigns to the frequent absence of conditions of monopolization, canalization, and supplementation in the social arena. Wiebe, in his examination of four campaigns, concluded that a campaign's effectiveness depended on the presence of adequate force, direction, an adequate and compatible social mechanism, and distance. To the marketer, the sudcess of the campaign depends on the proper development of product, promotion, place, and price considerations. These concepts were defined and were shown to have applicability to social causes. The social marketing process calls for marketing research and the subsequent development of a well-conceived product and appeals moving through mass and specialized communication media and through paid agents and voluntary groups to reach targeted audiences. The marketing style may be hard or soft, depending on which is deemed most effective in accomplishing the social objectives.

A marketing planning approach does not guarantee that the social objectives will be achieved, or that the costs will be acceptable. Yet social marketing appears to represent a bridging mechanism which links the behavioral scientist's knowledge of human behavior with the socially useful implementation of what that knowledge allows. It offers a useful framework for effective social planning at a time when social issues have become more relevant and critical.

NOTES

1. G. D. Wiebe, "Merchandising Commodities and Citizenship on Television," *Public Opinion Quarterly,* Vol. 15 (Winter, 1951–52), pp. 679–691, at p. 679.
2. Joe McGinniss, *The Selling of the President 1968* (New York: Trident Press, 1969).
3. Marketing Staff of the Ohio State University, "A Statement of Marketing Philosophy," JOURNAL OF MARKETING, Vol. 29 (January, 1965), p. 43.
4. Cyril S. Belshaw, *Traditional Exchange and Modern Markets* (Englewood Cliffs, N.J.: Prentice-Hall, Inc., 1965).
5. Philip Kotler, *Marketing Management: Analysis, Planning and Control,* Second Edition (Englewood Cliffs, N.J.: Prentice-Hall, 1972).
6. Arthur H. Niehoff, *A Casebook of Social Change* (Chicago: Aldine, 1966); Warren G. Bennis, Kenneth D. Benne and Robert Chin, *The Planning of Change* (New York: Holt, Rinehart & Winston, 1969).
7. C. H. Sandage, "Using Advertising to Implement the Concept of Freedom of Speech," in *The Role of Advertising,* C.H. Sandage and V. Fryburger, eds. (Homewood, Ill.: Richard D. Irwin, Inc., 1960), pp. 222–223.
8. Paul F. Lazarsfeld and Robert K. Merton, "Mass Communication, Popular Taste, and Organized Social Action," in *Mass Communications,* William Schramm, ed (Urbana, Ill.: University of Illinois Press, 1949), pp. 459–480, and same reference as footnote 1.
9. Lazarsfeld and Merton, same reference as footnote 8, p. 462.
10. Lazarsfeld and Merton, same reference as footnote 8.
11. Same reference as footnote 1.
12. Same reference as footnote 1, p. 633.
13. E. Jerome McCarthy, *Basic Marketing: A Managerial Approach,* Third Edition (Homewood, Ill.: Richard D. Irwin, Inc., 1968), pp. 31–33.
14. Nathanial A. Martin, "The Outlandish Idea: How Marketing Man Would Save India," *Marketing/ Communications,* Vol. 297 (March, 1968), pp. 54–60.
15. For two analyses of the marketing issues and opportunities in the family planning issue, see Julian L. Simon, "A Huge Marketing Research Task—Birth Control," *Journal of Marketing Research,* Vol. 5 (February, 1968), pp. 21–27; and Glen L. Urban, "Ideas on a Decision-Information System for Family Planning," *Industrial Management Review,* Vol. 10 (Spring, 1969), pp. 45–61.
16. *Public Information Guide* (New York: American Cancer Society, Inc., 1965), p. 12.
17. Chris Imhoff, "DDC's Decisive Decade," *Traffic Safety Magazine,* Vol. 69 (December, 1969), pp. 20 and 36.

Marketing Down the Road: The Role of Marketing Analysis in Transportation Planning

DANIEL J. BROWN

PHILIP B. SCHARY

BORIS W. BECKER

In recent years, transportation planners have been required to incorporate broadly based public input into the transportation planning process [13, 18]. This requirement has created difficulties, both in completing particular projects and in developing acceptable participation procedures.

Since there are important parallels between the relationship of public planners to the public and the relationship of marketers to their markets, a number of marketing scholars have investigated the role of marketing research in public policy [4, 12, 19]. This paper goes beyond previously published reports in addressing the role of marketing research in an increasingly important aspect of public planning. It will focus on three topics that are central to the application of marketing concepts to this problem, and each will constitute a major subdivision of the paper. First is the experience with public inputs in transportation planning. Second is a comparison of the task of marketing managers in the private sector with the job of their public planner counterparts. Third is a marketing strategy for planners to employ in incorporating public involvement into the planning process. The overall purpose of the paper is to identify how marketing can make public inputs more effective.

THE PROBLEM OF PUBLIC INVOLVEMENT

Before they were required to incorporate broad public inputs, transportation planners were free to exercise personal judgment, based on available data combined with their own understanding and convictions about specific aspects of their plan. Before the decision, public inputs were confined to the advice of local governments and agencies about scope and general direction. After the decision, the same agencies provided the scrutiny of formal review and approval. The planner served as expert, approaching specific problems with a set of alternative solutions, serving the public without direct consultation.

As the work of planners became more visible through the implementation of their plans, conflicts arose between planners and public. Some citizens perceived planners to be antagonistic toward public desires. Freeways, in particular, became a battleground as the cost-benefit ratios of additional construction turned negative in the public eye [11]. That planners were appointed technicians rather than elected officials did not help; opponents often viewed them as partisan to business interests or entirely incompetent [16].

In an effort to make projects more attuned to public desires, Congress forced government agencies to include public inputs in planning almost all transportation projects which involve Federal funds, virtually all transportation projects. Voluntary public meetings and citizens' advisory groups became the most common vehicles for eliciting this input. Such groups have played the role of mediator between the public-at-large and the planning agency.

The public, acting through these intermediary institutions, has manifested enough power to force

Reprinted with permission from *Proceedings of the American Marketing Association Educators' Conference,* 1978, pp. 359–362; published by the American Marketing Association.

planners to modify their plans or even to stop projects entirely [2, 11, 15, 16]. In concept, the role of these new institutions was to give a voice to the public. Their intervention, however, has created new problems: (1) public inputs have become predominantly negative and, therefore, not very useful, (2) these inputs are not representative of the entire populations, and (3) these inputs incite conflict not only between the public and the planner but also among various partisan groups within the community.

The first problem is that voluntary public meetings or citizens' advisory groups demonstrate what the public does not want. They rarely identify preferred options that can then be used to meet the transportation needs of the public. Participation has demonstrated, on the part of the public, both a lack of technical knowledge and a lack of long range vision, particularly in the context of unfamiliar technological environments.

A second problem is that "public" inputs do not necessarily represent the public as a whole. While the public consists of multiple clusters of individuals holding pluralistic points of view, only a few of the most vocal and partisan actually become involved in public meetings or advisory boards [2, 8, 11, 14]. Evidence indicates that participation is self-selecting and biased in favor of certain interests and against others [1]. Groups such as the elderly who have a vital stake in the outcome, are seldom heard at all.

Third, the public forum for participation becomes an arena for conflict among different groups, each espousing its own cause [17]. Often the result of this conflict is either a nullification of the input or a paralysis of the entire planning process [11].

The degree of conflict and the amount of externality created by the project are closely related. If you proposed a freeway through my neighborhood so that you can drive to work, I may not accept willingly the degradation of my environment for your convenience. If my advocacy is successful, I may force you to choose a different route or abandon the idea altogether.

Thus, the old problem has given way to new problems and, to date, no approach has been devised to solve them. For the transportation planner, the question is whether or not marketing, which deals with similar problems, can help. For the professional marketer the question is to apply the most effective combination of marketing concepts and methodology.

PUBLIC INPUTS IN MARKETING MANAGEMENT TERMS

The magnitude of the problems explored in the last section is sufficient to compel an evaluation of public inputs in marketing management terms. The discussion that follows will employ a view of the public participation arena suggested by Figure 1.

Even though one is concerned with private goods purchased by individual customers and the other is concerned with public goods purchased collectively by society, there are several parallel elements between marketing and planning.

1. Both are responsible for providing "products" to a consuming public that decides whether or not the products are acceptable. The transportation product task involves not only the mechanical aspects of making the product available, but also the more important determination of the configuration of the system to be offered. For the transportation planner, the system might include road beds, transit services or bicycle paths. These are shown in Figure 1 as alternatives 1, . . . , *n*.

Both are concerned with product attribute preferences on the part of customers. In order to design products which incorporate appropriate characteristics or features, the planner must be able to identify preference structures. Successful systems must possess those characteristics which customers deem to be both important and attractive.

Marketing in the public sector means more than "selling" the public on existing or conceived systems as some would assume [9, 10]. Even in the private sector, marketing is ineffective in getting customers to purchase products which are not attractive on their own merits [6].

2. Although planners sometimes prefer to deal with a "consensus" of the public as a whole [11,

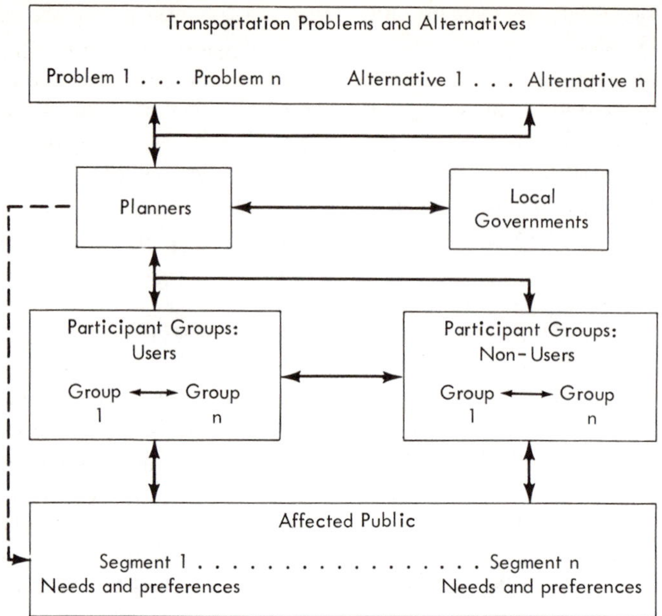

FIGURE 1: ***Public inputs from a marketing perspective***

17], segmentation is as necessary in transportation planning as it is in marketing management. Both face segmented markets, different groups of customers with unique and specialized needs which are expressed through product choices. The mass transit market, for example, has been characterized as consisting of five consumer segments: managerial/professional, clerical occupations, inner city residents, the elderly, and suburban housewives [9].

It is important to note, however, that segmentation has three unique aspects in the context of transportation planning. All are shown diagrammatically in Figure 1. First, the planner should use segmentation at both the market and participant level. Failure to match participant segments with their corresponding market segments and failure to make sure that all market segments are represented will insure an unrepresentative set of inputs. Second, "horizontal" conflict is relatively unknown in private sector marketing. Third, nonuser segments, which often can be ignored in the case of private sector marketing, are extremely important in the case of a public transportation system. For many projects, the nonusers must pay a financial subsidy on behalf of the users. In other projects, nonusers must bear nonpecuniary externalities, such as higher noise levels (as in the case of air traffic) or in pollution. As the effect of these externalities becomes larger and larger, the voice of the nonuser is heard through the public input process.

3. Both operate in environments where customers are free to choose among alternate products. In transportation this might reflect model preferences such as taking the bus or driving a car. On the other hand, planners have a monopoly over the transportation system as a whole, so they are able to manage all options available to the public. The only major check on this power is the resistance of the public itself.

The market operates differently in the world of transportation planning in other ways as well. First, there are extensive time lags between commitment and use. Consumers can vote with their patronage only after the public has paid for the system with taxes or indebtedness. Second, resources may be immobile. Transportation systems of questionable conception cannot be transferred to other uses. Those justified on nonmarket grounds, such as the Bay Area Rapid Transit (BART), may become financial liabilities requiring public subsidies [20]. Marketing may thus be even more important in the public sector than it is in the private sector!

4. The mechanism for public inputs is more formal and inflexible than in the case of the private decision maker. In the private sector, failure to take public input into account may merely mean marketing failure. A similar omission in transportation planning also becomes a violation of the law.

WHAT CAN MARKETING CONTRIBUTE?

The premise of this discussion is that the concepts embodied in modern marketing have a unique and positive contribution to make in providing public inputs for transportation planning. The framework for specifying potential contributions is the "marketing concept," which declares a consumer orientation the principal means of satisfying organizational goals. However, along with lacking a true consumer orientation, transportation planning often fails to formulate any specific operational goals [7, 9].

Transportation planning in the public sector does not ordinarily have objectives as clearly defined as those of profit-seeking firms in the private sector. The marketing concept suggests a surrogate measure: system utilization. Simple use of the system is a necessary, but not sufficient, condition for success. In the face of adequate utilization, success is determined by the actual external costs imposed upon nonusers, relative to their willingness to absorb such costs. Given a standard of utilization and expressed constraints, marketing strategy can be used to help achieve the target goal.

A fundamental characteristic of a consumer orientation is the use of marketing research to provide useful information about the needs and preferences of consumers. Not only are preferences important, but also the strengths of such preferences must be measured.

If some attribute of the system is considered undesirable, it may be possible to combine that negative characteristic with some positive characteristic from another part of the system in order to create a "bundle of attributes" which is desirable in light of the needs of other segments. The use of trade-off techniques such as conjoint analysis hold promise in this area. At the minimum, this approach might result in "sweetening the pot" for those who might otherwise oppose the system.

A second advantage of a consumer orientation is that planners become sensitive to different demands of a factionalized public consisting of users and affected nonusers. The use of marketing research to segment the market will provide information about different needs, such as motivations for travel, specific physical requirement and differing attitudes toward the use of public facilities. Marketing research can also identify how many people have what sorts of needs and what the characteristics of these people are.

Such information about different segments is necessary to insure that public participation is representative at the level of the voluntary public meeting or citizens' advisory council. Representatives of all segments might be solicited to participate in formal input procedures, or a direct communication link between underrepresented segments and planners might be established through marketing research survey techniques using representative random samples. Such a channel of communication is shown by the broken line at the left of Figure 1, that bypasses and supplements the ordinary participation process. A more radical suggestion would be to replace the voluntary meetings and citizens' advisory groups entirely with representative survey information.

At a pragmatic level, it is important to provide consumer advocacy where it can shape the direction of the system in order to achieve higher levels of utilization. At a more abstract level, representation is associated with the working of the democratic process and could increase public confidence that planning and spending done in their name is truly affected by them.

Under current conditions, much of the public input which reaches the planner cannot be expected to represent the public interest. Those who select themselves to serve on advisory boards or to appear at public meetings provide inputs which should not be taken at face value. Yet, without efforts to determine the desires of the public, the planner has no basis for evaluating what is said at meetings or to argue contrary positions.

The third advantage of a consumer orientation can be seen in a potential for conflict resolution among different user groups and between user groups and nonuser groups. The discipline of marketing has no expertise in the case of intractable conflict, such as a zero-sum game. Fortunately, true zero-sum situations are rare in transportation planning. One can often increase the payoff of the game through compromise and comprehensive planning that looks beyond a single transportation project. Bargainable situations then arise, leading to a system which, in total, may improve the position of several, perhaps even all, of the segments involved. Marketing research can define the preference functions and trade-offs that would be acceptable to different segments. Some pioneering work has been done in this direction by the New York State Department of Transportation [3, 5]. Using this information planners could define bargaining positions and then attempt to negotiate between groups.

DISCUSSION

We began this discussion by examining the process by which public input has become a part of transportation planning. Then we looked at the role of marketing analysis in making public input more effective. The primary contributions are three-fold: first, application of the marketing concept—a public orientation to meet organizational goals; second, segmentation as a means of understanding the public and the participation process; third, utilization of marketing research as a channel of communication with both user and nonuser groups.

Although we have discussed public input in the context of transportation planning, the application of the discussion is much broader. Inclusion of public inputs is becoming popular in other areas of government planning, for example electrical power and mental health facilities. In some cases, it has even spread into the sphere of governmentally regulated monopolies, such as television cable service. Over time, more and more governmental agencies and private companies can expect to become involved. Optimistically, a marketing perspective can help newcomers to the public participation arena avoid some of the problems transportation planners have encountered.

BIBLIOGRAPHY

[1] Brown, Daniel J. and Philip B. Schary. "Consumer Participants in Transportation Planning: The Elderly, the Poor, and Special Interests," in William D. Perreault, ed., *Advances in Consumer Research,* 4 (1977), 138–141.

[2] Cupps, D. Stephen. "Emerging Problems of Citizen Participation," *Public Administration Review,* 37 (September/October 1977), 478–487.

[3] Donnelly, E. P., S. M. Howe, and J. A. DesChamps. "Trade-Off Analysis: Theory and Applications to Transportation Policy Planning," *High Speed Ground Transportation Journal,* 11 (Spring 1977), 93–110.

[4] Dyer, Robert F. and Terence A. Shimp. "Enhancing the Role of Marketing Research in Public Policy Decision Making," *Journal of Marketing,* 41 (January 1977), 63–67.

[5] Eberts, Patricia M. and K.-W. Peter Koeppel, "The Trade-Off Model: Empirical and Structural Findings," *Preliminary Research Report No. 123,* Albany, NY: State Department of Transportation Planning Research Unit, 1977.

[6] Hartley, Robert F. *Marketing Mistakes,* Columbus, Ohio: Grid, Inc., 1976.

[7] Houston, Franklin S. and Richard E. Homans. ''Public Agency Marketing: Pitfalls and Problems,'' *MSU Business Topics*, 25 (Summer 1977), 36–40.

[8] Jackson, John S. III and William L. Shade. ''Citizen Participation, Democratic Representation and Survey Research,'' *Urban Affairs Quarterly*, 9 (September 1973) 57–89.

[9] Kangan, Norman and William A. Staples. ''Selling Urban Transit,'' *Business Horizons*, 18 (February 1975), 57–66.

[10] Murin, William J. ''Urban Transportation Planning, Politics and Policy Making,'' *Public Administration Review*, 37 (January/February 1977), 89–97.

[11] Park, Ki Suh. ''Achieving Positive Community Participation in the Freeway Planning Process,'' *Highway Research Record*, 380 (1972), 14–21.

[12] Ritchie, J. R. Brent and Roger J. LaBreque. ''Marketing Research and Public Policy: A Functional Perspective,'' *Journal of Marketing*, 39 (July 1975), 12–19.

[13] Schary, Philip B., Daniel J. Brown and Boris W. Becker. ''Consumers as Participants in Transportation Planning,'' *Transportation*, 6 (July 1977), 135–148.

[14] Shermer, Julie Hetrick. ''Interest Group Impact Assessment in Transportation Planning,'' *Traffic Quarterly*, 29 (January 1975), 29–49.

[15] Sloan, Allan K. *Citizen Participation in Transportation Planning: The Boston Experience*. Cambridge, MA: Ballinger Publishing Co., 1974.

[16] Taebel, Delbert A. ''Citizens Groups, Public Policy, and Urban Transportation,'' *Traffice Quarterly*, 27 (October 1973), 503–515.

[17] Travis, Kenneth M. and Stanley C. Plog. ''Community Involvement in Transportation Planning: A New Approach,'' *Highway Research Record*, 380 (1972), 8–13.

[18] U.S. Department of Transportation. *Effective Citizen Participation in Transportation Planning*, (Washington, D.C.: U.S. Department of Transportation, 1976).

[19] Wilkie, William L. and David M. Gardner. ''The Role of Marketing Research in Public Policy Decision Making,'' *Journal of Marketing*, 38 (January 1974), 38–47.

[20] Zwerling, Stephen. *Mass Transit and the Politics of Technology: A Study of BART and the San Francisco Bay Area*. New York: Praeger, 1974.

A Concept Sector within the Economy

SEYMOUR H. FINE

This paper explores a sector of the economy believed to be at the threshold of a fascinating emergence. The sector is constituted of those institutions sponsoring ideas and social issues—concepts—in contrast to organizations purveying goods and services. As yet unnamed, one could assign to it an appellation such as the idea industry or more eloquently, the concept sector. The concept sector cuts across traditional boundaries of sector distinction because its members include profit-making, nonprofit public organizations, as well as the hybrid ''quasis.'' It is characterized by

Prepared by Professor Seymour H. Fine and presented at the Joint Conference of the American Marketing Association and the European Society for Opinion and Marketing Research, Paris, France, March 31, 1981.

the criterion that its "product mix" consists of abstract concepts unrelated to conventional products.

To test the hypothetical presence of the concept sector, a survey was conducted among institutions sponsoring a broad spectrum of ideas and social issues. The aim of the survey was to learn about the processes by which concepts were being disseminated, and to examine those processes from a marketing viewpoint.

Results of the study demonstrate that concepts are indeed being marketed but in an ad hoc manner, and not too effectively. Moreover, practitioners seem reluctant to associate themselves with the marketing rubric. One concludes that marketers face an interesting challenge in the marketing of marketing to this fascinating and relatively untapped sector of the economy.

INTRODUCTION

Traditionally, the marketing discipline has been associated with exchange transactions involving goods and services. Within the past decade, attention has increasingly been paid to the marketing of another class of product offerings, quite apart from tangible goods or rendered services. That category subsumes a wide assortment of such ideas and social issues as support the police, suicide prevention, capital punishment, and others listed in Table 1. Concepts are conceived, initiated, sponsored, advocated, promulgated, dis-

TABLE 1: ***Some current ideas and social issues***

55-mph speed limit	Exporting	Military recruiting	Religion
200-mile fishing limits	Fair housing	Minimum wage	Safety
911-emergency number	Family planning	Motorcycle helmets, use	Save Chrysler
Abortion rights	Fashion trend	Museums	Save the whales
Affirmative action	Fire prevention	Nature conservation	Scouting
Alcoholism control	Fluoridation	New York City	Seat belt use
Banking innovation	Foreign aid	Nuclear energy	Shoplifting
Birth defects	Forest fire prevention	Nudism	Smokending
Blood	Foster parenthood	Nutrition	Social security
Blue laws	Franchising	Obesity prevention	Social welfare
Buy American goods	Fraternal organizations	One-dollar coin	Solar energy
Cancer research	Free enterprise	Outdoor living	Space program
Capital punishment	Freedom of the press	Peace	Subsidies, government
Care packages	Fund raising	Peace corps	Suicide hot line
Carpooling	Gay rights	Pet adoption	Tax reform
Child abuse	Gun control	Physical fitness	Tax shelters
Child adoption	Handicapped, employ the	Poetry	Tourism
Consumer cooperatives	Health maintenance organizations	Police, support of	Trade associations
Credit purchasing	Health, value of	Politics	Two-dollar bill
Crime prevention	Legalized gambling	Pollution control	UNICEF
Divorce	Literacy	Population control	Union label, buy
Draft registration	Littering prevention	Prayers in schools	United Way
Drilling, offshore	Mainstreaming	Prison reform	Urban planning
Drinking age	Manpower programs	Product safety	VD hotline
Drunk driving	Marriage	Productivity in industry	Vegetarianism
Education, continuing	Mass transportation	PTA	Veterans' rights
Energy conservation	Mental Health	Recycling wastes	Vivisection
Equal Rights Amendment	Metric system	Redlining	Voter registration
Euthanasia		Reforestation	Wife abuse prevention

seminated, and adopted by methods that resemble the marketing process. When that process involves concepts it has been termed *social marketing*.

Yet it must be noted that the expression social marketing has also been applied to those aspects of business dealing with public policy and social responsibility; social marketing has thus become something of a catch-all phrase. Accordingly, some attempt will be made here to capture the context of this paper by also using the terms "idea marketing" and "concept marketing."

An important aim of this paper is to highlight the need that advocates of social causes have for applying marketing principles in their work. If adopting a marketing orientation in the dissemination of societally beneficial ideas will facilitate the spread of those ideas, the purpose of this paper will have been well served.

THE CONCEPT SECTOR

Managers in the concept sector design social products, and perform the entire gamut of marketing functions. Whether they realize it or not they are businesspeople; they are merchants. But to delimit the scope of this paper, only originators—"producers" of concepts—will be discussed. (They shall also be referred to as sponsors or initiators of ideas.) "Middlemen" operating between the producer and consumer are discussed elsewhere (Fine, 1981, Chap. 7). These intermediaries include the mass media, opinion leaders, and pressure groups of various types.

Concept producers seem close to the realization that marketing philosophies and methodologies are applicable to the social products they sponsor. Some have known it for years. But to most others, it is a revelation and one may expect that those newly initiated will embark upon exciting ventures.

In reality the concept sector is ancient. What is new is its formulation as a businesslike activity through the application of marketing thought. Ideas are nonmaterial products that have been bought and sold in both open and closed marketplaces since time immemorial. From Plato's notions about the nature of a perfect republic to Marx's thoughts about an ultimate classless society, the merchandising of concepts has been ever present.

Government, A Special Case. Politics is a special but important case of idea marketing, with the politician marketing the idea, "Vote for me!" Perhaps one of the oldest members of the idea sector, only recently has the politician been studied formally from a marketing viewpoint (Rothschild, 1978). Once they have successfully sold the "Vote for me" idea, politicians produce and market a host of other concepts, in aspiration of yet additional objectives:

> More news emanates from officials than from any other source. . . . Bureaucratic need accounts for the volume of details on the inner workings of government published in the American press. Officials engaging in intragovernmental politicking to achieve the policy outcomes they desire exploit the press tactically (Sigal, 1973, p. 336).

Legislative and regulative agencies themselves make an important contribution to the idea sector. For example, advocacy of one side in an issue is given tremendous impetus when it attains legal status. A current case in point in the United States is the issue of "mainstreaming" disabled youngsters in public schools—including them in regular classes—in contrast to educating them in special facilities. United States Public Law 504, against discrimination, and specifically, Public Law 94142, give parents the legal right to insist that public schools mainstream all children having such disabilities as muscular dystrophy, retardation, hearing impairment, and so forth, in the belief that mainstreaming provides the least restrictive environment. In many cases compliance has necessitated large expenditures by school systems for equipment, structural modifications in buildings, and special staff. Most people would not concern themselves with the idea that handicapped children should be schooled in the same classes as normal children. But after enactment of mainstreaming laws, society was confronted with the reality of the idea, and people soon caught on to its democratic implications.

Because politics is a discipline in its own right and discussed in a large literature, this paper only touches upon the subject peripherally. Let it suffice here to give merely some idea of the magnitude of promotion of ideas by government: In all, public and nonprofit expenditures on advertising in the United States are approximated at $2 billion annually (Rosenberg, 1977, p. 80). Only 23 organizations, corporate and otherwise, had larger ad budgets in 1979 than the U.S. government. This poses a question about government domination of the concept sector:

> the growing advertising budgets of federal government agencies do indicate the increasing need to promote ideas. But this growth may represent social harm, in terms of government monopolizing the marketing of ideas . . . (which) could have a very dangerous, dampening effect on the free marketplace of ideas (Novelli, 1980).

The author believes that the concept sector is sufficiently broad to mediate that possibility. In a democracy, ideas are infused and spread by so many sponsors, one hopes that although government might be the most prominent, it is not the most controlling or overruling advocate influencing the concept market.

Nor can the idea marketer afford to underestimate the importance of involving bureaucrats in the planning of programs. Calling government a "neglected cluster of professionals," Wharton (1977) raises the question:

> The politicians are the persons who must adopt, finance, advocate, and defend the policies, programs, and projects recommended by scientific and technical professionals. Have we neglected the politicians' critical role? (p. 17).

Most governments engage in the marketing of social products. For example, it is commonplace to see huge posters in (primarily) socialist countries portraying political leaders in the effort to enhance the nationalist image. There too, are posted photos of outstanding conscientious factory workers in campaigns designed to stress productivity in industry for the good of the state. These programs also disseminate the state's economic achievements, emphasizing levels of production of critical materials, such as uranium. For another noteworthy example, the Chinese government, with the flip of a switch, broadcasts to a billion people the admonition that family size should be limited to one child. In fact, in many parts of the world one almost perceives more evidence of the marketing of social, economic, and cultural items than tangibles.

Business Firms. Although the majority of idea initiators are public and nonprofit institutions, a study to be described below indicated that about 25% are commercial firms sponsoring concepts quite apart from ideas that underlie their conventional goods or services. The present work considers beyond its scope those ideas about products per se (the "sizzle behind the streak"), and instead focuses only on intangibles when they are themselves taken as products. Some commercial establishments do espouse ideas that although profit-inspired, are product-independent and thus qualify for inclusion here. If Christian Dior designs a princess-style knee-length gown, a new product is launched, but in the process the general idea of knee-length dresses is advanced. Similarly, Resorts International, Inc., could promote either its casino (a service) in Atlantic City or the idea of legalized gambling. Oil companies, in what appeared as a strategy of the demarketing of their tangible product, sought to attain image enhancement by advertising the idea of fuel conservation. Indeed, all such "institutional" ads fall within the idea rubric, because by definition they directly promote no products or services, but only the good name of the firm—an idea (Sethi, 1979).

Until recently, business firms in the United States were constrained from voicing their opinions on issues. For decades, "commercial speech" was not entitled to the same First Amendment protection as "political" speech. But these restrictions are undergoing liberalization:

> From the marketplace of goods and services, corporations of late have begun to push into the mar-

> ketplace of ideas and are demanding the same rights as everyone else.
>
> Last year they scored a major victory when the United States Supreme Court ruled that companies could campaign for or against state referendums (Graham, 1979, p. A8).

Trade associations, as spokesmen for individual firms within any given industry, constitute a significant portion of the concept sector. To the (large) extent that they promote use of the tangible products merchandised by their constituent member firms, they are beyond the scope of this paper. But some trade associations are sources of ideas only indirectly related to product promotion. Many have community affairs and/or public affairs departments. Thus the United States Brewers Association maintains an Alcohol Programs Division fostering responsible use of alcoholic beverages.

What about the employees of an organization supplying ideas and issues? Should they be possessed of a higher level of altruism than their counterparts in commercial enterprises? Because these institutions market idealogically and sociologically oriented products, does it follow that the work requires of their personnel a value system differing from that of employees in firms purveying goods and services? Is it safe to assume that by the very nature of the work, one is likely to observe a greater degree of charity on the part of individuals engaged in the concept sector? It would seem these questions demand positive answers, yet there does not appear to be much evidence one way or the other.

HOW DO THEY MARKET?

One may expect that business organizations apply their experience in commercial marketing to the sponsorship of ideas and issues as well. But what about public and nonprofit institutions? In general, how much do idea merchants know about their craft? How, in the first place, do they feel about marketing? How do they *do* marketing? In order to learn about the nature of marketing as practiced by concept-sector institutions, the author conducted a study to ferret out answers to such questions. The project took the form of an exploratory survey of a variety of organizations whose principal commonality is their mission to sponsor an impalpable or social product.

The Study Design. A compendium of social products (see Table 1) evolved out of several focus group discussions attended by a team of market research students. From this list, items were then allocated to team members who were charged with the task of seeking out institutions sponsoring the specified concepts.

The *sample* was a "convenience" sample of such organizations. They were selected informally; no systematic methods nor randomization were employed to select respondents, except that team members attempted to include both local and national institutions in the study. Every effort was made to administer the questionnaires by personal interview. In cases where they were mailed, follow-up phone calls were made to those institutions not responding within a few weeks. Out of 475 institutions contacted, 222 questionnaires were returned of which 197 were suitable for analysis—a usable return rate of 41.5% Others were either returned by post offices as undeliverable or improperly or incompletely filled out. A few institutions were excluded when it became clear from the responses that they promoted not ideas, but goods or services.

Survey instrument design was guided generally by the knowledge–attitude–practice (KAP) model familiar to social marketers. One seeks information about what respondents know, feel, and are doing about a particular topic. That model has been applied widely in nutrition and birth control studies and is a useful research guide for many social cause projects. In addition to questions asking for descriptive characteristics about the institution, respondents were asked if they had "considered their sponsored idea as a 'product' to be marketed" (never, rarely, sometimes, frequently, or constantly). Another question asked whether the institution has "a marketing department or equivalent." Respondents' perceptions were sought relating to organizational goals, terms associated with marketing, familiarty with and use of marketing concepts, and experience with various promotional methods and media.

Results of the Study. Frequency analysis results are given in Table 2 in separate columns for 49 business firms (25% of the sample), 89 nonprofits (45%), and 59 government agencies (30%). More than half (112) of the institutions surveyed had been established over 20 years and had budgets in excess of $1 million. Most of the

TABLE 2: ***Frequencies on selected variables in the institutional study***

Characteristic	*Business firms (n = 49)*	*Nonprofit organizations (n = 89)*	*Public agencies (n = 59)*
Age of the institution			
Less than 6 years	15	15	6
6–20 years	6	22	21
Over 20 years	28	52	32
Annual budget (000s)			
Less than 100	6	26	8
100–1000	11	28	15
Over 1000	32	35	36
Number of employees			
Less than 20	15	43	17
20–100	7	29	12
Over 100	27	17	30
Considered idea as a product			
Rarely, never	6	13	9
Sometimes, frequently	9	27	17
Constantly	34	49	33
Marketing department or equivalent			
Yes	40	57	35
No	9	32	24
Organizational goals			
Resources	21	18	25
Survival	7	9	2
Clients	17	14	11
Education	4	48	20
Knowledge of marketing, average	7.06	5.88	6.03
Attitude toward marketing			
Advertising	21	3	5
Propaganda	0	0	0
Public opinion	4	6	2
Persuasion	8	10	8
Public interest	2	15	16
Puffery	0	1	0
Education	8	47	25
Public relations	1	2	2
Other	5	5	1

institutions (84%) in the study were main facilities; only 31 out of 197 were branch offices. They served a fairly evenly distributed representation of national, regional, state, and local jurisdictions. The business firms and public agencies in the sample were generally larger than the nonprofits in terms of number of employees.

In all of the three classes of institutions a majority reported they "constantly" considered their designated concepts as products to be marketed. On the other hand, responses to the "marketing department or equivalent" question varied significantly according to type of institution, with the private sector predominantly positive and the others negative. Related to that result was the finding that business firms had larger marketing staffs and indicated more knowledge of marketing concepts than did their public and nonprofit counterparts. Yet in actual utilization and effectiveness of promotional methods, very little difference seemed apparent between the institutional types.

One question was intended to capture respondents' perceptions about the primary goal of the organization. The responses were placed into four categories: (1) acquisition of, and return on resources, (2) survival, (3) increase and satisfaction of clientele, and (4) educating the public with existing and new concepts (products). Not surprisingly, goals of private-sector firms emphasize resources. However, a majority of nonprofit (54%) see their principal objective as public education, something true of only 8% of the private firms. With public agencies, on the other hand, a large number (42%) mirror business firms' concern with resources, as against the goal of education (22%).

If stated objectives are indicative of organizational policy, it appears that public and nonprofit institutions share a pattern of disdain for their clients. In fact, even business firms place client satisfaction second to resource conservation as a main objective. That less than 20% of public and nonprofit institutions and only 33% of the firms consider their principal goal to be satisfying customers is one of the sadder findings of this study. It highlights the need for a marketing approach to concept dissemination. But the objective of survival fared worst, making the poorest showing with public and nonprofit organizations, and ranking second-to-last with private firms as well. It appears that *the concept sector is a society of the here and now!*

Attitude toward marketing. The survey item listing a series of "terms one might associate with marketing" asked respondents to select the one believed "to be most descriptive of your marketing process." Given popular myths about marketers forcing unwanted goods down the throats of unsuspecting consumers, it is astonishing that not one organization selected propaganda as a term associated with marketing, and only one in the entire sample of 197 selected puffery. (Yet it would be naive to overlook a social-desirability bias in these responses.) Education ranked first among public and nonprofit institutions but only moderately with business firms. Conversely, advertising was significantly first choice with the private sector but unpopular with publics and nonprofits as "terms associated with marketing." The latter group also associates "public interest" with the marketing connotation and all institutions seem aware that marketing is a form of persuasion.

Knowledge about formal marketing concepts was measured by listing nine concepts, including consumer orientation, segmentation, positioning, and so on, with provision for "other" and asking whether each is familiar to, and used by the organization. For each case, a composite score was calculated as the number of concepts acknowledged as being familiar. Thus each respondent could receive a score from 1 to 10. Private-sector firms with an average score of 7.08 proved most knowledgable about marketing, followed by government agencies (6.03), and finally the nonprofits, scoring 5.88.

The most unfamiliar concept of all is the key marketing model, the four Ps—product, price, promotion, and place. To be sure, many individuals might be quite familiar with these marketing-mix elements without being aware of the "four Ps" appellation. Nonetheless, the fact that ignorance of that expression pervaded all three sectors is an indictment against marketers themselves. *One may suggest that marketing needs marketing!* Significantly, all sectors also agree in reporting they "always use" consumer orientation, a finding in direct contradiction to the poor showing earlier of client satisfaction as an organizational goal. This raises some question as to the candor with which attitudinal and opinion-based information was obtained—what social researchers call response bias.

Some Observations about the Survey. The survey drew written comments from approximately one respondent in four. Many expressed acceptance, delight, and surprise at the prospect of a systematic study of idea sponsors. What came through in these comments was genuine interest in, and a need and desire to learn more about concept marketing:

> Completing this form was very useful to me—the process, it helped me to focus on actually what we're seeing, promoting. That is something I've had little time to consider (a local chapter of Parents Anonymous).

> This is a very interesting concept (idea marketing). I would be interested in results of the study, as well as knowing whether the project will be extended to include the developing of a marketing plan for an agency such as ours (a state division of civil rights).

A score or more respondents said that they had retained photocopies of their questionnaires for the purpose of discussing the project with team members after mailing back their originals.

A most significant finding to emerge from the study is that institutions sponsoring ideas and social issues certainly do engage in marketing practices, but for the most part, in an ad hoc manner. Many seem unaware of, or are reluctant to admit that they are promoting a "product." This was clear from some of the reasons given for a response of "No" to the question, "Do you have a marketing department or equivalent?" In each of the cases cited below, after denying the presence of a marketing department or equivalent, respondents indicated effective use of advertising media, and some also admitted that several staffers were involved with marketing. One can only conclude from such inconsistency that these responses reveal considerable confusion about marketing:

> PR is handled by our executive director (an organization sponsoring prevention of wife abuse).

> Congress does not provide funds for marketing in its VD control appropriations (the education specialist of a federal public health agency, who then reported engaging in extensive media activity).

> Would publicity qualify for equivalent of marketing? (director of public relations of an institution promoting the idea of responsible pet ownership).

> We have never thought of ourselves as marketing a product. We have people who are assigned ERA as their "item" (an administrator of a regional League of Women Voters).

> Don't understand the term (marketing); we do lobbying, letter writing to appropriate government and commercial concerns (a group crusading for the rights of the left-handed).

> We do not promote literacy; it is a fact of life. If people want to be helped they come in. Word of mouth and referrals are our best means of promotion (a reading improvement association).

> Not applicable (a National Guard recruiting officer!).

> Marketing fluoridation is not a function of government—promotion and public awareness is (an official of a public health service).

> We disseminate information without the marketing connotation. Besides, demand is too great to justify marketing (a national center for the prevention of child abuse).

> We are a weekly newspaper; we do sell ads but not ideas (a gay rights organization).

A prominent institution promoting the United Nations asserts that it "constantly" considers arms control as a "product to be marketed" and engages in multimedia campaigns, yet it emphatically denies it has a "marketing department or equivalent'' because ''each program develops its own strategy for its own audience.'' And the same situation apparently prevails with a national retail organization fighting shoplifting, a dental association espousing fluoridation, and the national headquarters of a major political party in its campaign to stimulate voter registration. After 75 years in existence a national group ''never thought of suicide prevention as a marketable product.'' ''Promoting (motorcycle) helmet use is everyone's job'' states a national commission on highway safety as a reason for its diffidence to marketing.

Beyond the questionnaires, a number of mail and phone communications between respondents and team members revealed the same tenor of narrow and confused perceptions about marketing. Typical was the following remark in a letter from the public information officer of a federal agency:

> We do not market anything. We do advocate firearms security, good citizenship, and responsible ownership of guns, and we have sponsored programs endorsing these concepts.

Unbelievably, some private-sector firms suffer from similar confusion. A multibranch savings and loan association widely advertises the idea of interest-bearing checking accounts, but ''does no marketing because we have no person with that expertise.''

Implications. A line in the *Arabian Nights* admonishes: ''He who knows and knows not he knows, he is asleep; awake him.'' A sizable segment of institutions espousing social causes admit to their marketing role only after being awakened to that reality. It is ironic that although they themselves are promoters of concepts, they have been slow to adopt the *marketing concept*. On the other hand, there is evidence that a few members of the idea sector are increasingly assuming consumer orientation and engaging in strategic marketing planning both for their own benefit as well as that of society.

Admonishing concept sponsors to employ solid social science research in planning for concept dissemination, Mendelsohn (1973) argues that:

> Most evidence on the failures on information campaigns actually tells us more about flaws in the communicator—the originator of messages—than it does about shortcomings either in the content or in the audience (p. 51).

The challenge ahead is to respond to that mandate as marketers inevitably become involved in the concept sector.

Shortcomings of the Study. Recognizing one's blind spots is an integral part of research evaluation. For one thing, the concept of social marketing should have been explained more thoroughly at the beginning. Furthermore, if the questions relating to the various media had preceded the ''marketing department or equivalent'' item, the concept of idea-marketing might have been clearer. Perhaps the most serious blind spot was the researchers' inability to anticipate the large number of de facto marketing activities in which institutions engage, but under names other than marketing. These include education, publicity, arranging for guest speakers, publishing brochures, and so on. An executive of an organization concerned with child abuse wrote: ''When you change marketing to public education, the questionnaire becomes applicable.'' The presence of technical marketing terms bothered a few respondents: ''Dear Seymour, You were doing fine until question 19 and then your academic prejudice took over,'' commented an advocate of mainstreaming children.

DISCUSSION

This paper has postulated the existence and potential importance of a concept sector in the economy. Its members are individuals and institutions initiating ideas and social issues. They were examined in a survey whose results attest to the need for formalization of the sector's structure as well as a need to market marketing to its members.

The major issue in the emergence of a concept

sector is what sociologist Max Weber described as the routinization of charisma—the exercise of influence. It has been a part of human character as far back in time from which written records are available and presumably before that. A principal purpose in this paper was to convince readers involved with idea marketing that it is a viable discipline. Attempts to structure and systemize that discipline should mediate the creeping, ad hoc, anecdotal nature of concept dissemination and give structure and course to the process.

The Road Ahead. Among the tasks remaining, an important one is to treat in detail, and with candor, the ethical dilemma posed by concept marketing. Is intervention into idea dissemination justified by the ''societally beneficial'' expression employed in this paper? Who is to define that term? Is it the interventionist or the consumer who knows better which ideas are best for the individual? Do we need a Consumers Union for concepts? These questions comprise an important issue that must be assigned for further research.

This paper is timely. It is difficult to imagine a period in history when restrictions on the spread of ideas have been so relaxed, at least in the United States. Government, church, and family are as liberal as they have been at virtually any other time. Many ideas and issues considered blasphemous only a few decades ago are freely and openly exchanged in the marketplace. One witnesses a freer proliferation of concepts as minority groups, women, and children are becoming emancipated from their former inferior roles. Moreover, as illiteracy rates rise, the number and concern of participants in idea transmission increases. New communication technology facilitates the spread of ideas—good as well as bad—across vast regions on a scale unprecedented in history. So it is time for a free trade in ideas to itself be discussed more freely.

What seems clear is that the concept sector adds to the economy a dimension of caring about mental and social needs of the consuming populace. Marketing scholars and practitioners may look with pride at the acceptance of their discipline as a problem-solving forum. It is about time:

> Although recent years have seen an encouraging trend toward addressing important social issues with marketing tools, marketing research has concentrated in the past on the ''cold sores'' of society and ignored the ''cancers.'' Few of the impressive analytical powers of marketing researchers have been applied to solving important social problems (Rogers and Leonard-Barton, 1978, p. 496).

The present paper, by drawing attention to many real-world problems from a marketing orientation, should encourage other researchers to become aware of the power of marketing technology as a tool in dealing with the roots of some of these issues.

As the concept sector materializes, one anticipates that marketers will engage in exciting joint ventures with social scientists and policymakers in such fields as ecology, social services, law, international development, education, and urban planning, to mention but a few.

REFERENCES

Fine, Seymour H. *The Marketing of Ideas and Social Issues,* New York: Praeger, forthcoming, May 1981.

Graham, Bradley. ''Business Is Fighting for Its Right to Speak,'' *The* (Bergen) *Record,* April 2, 1979, p. A8.

Mendelsohn, Harold. ''Some Reasons Why Information Campaign Can Succeed,'' *Public Opinion Quarterly,* Vol. 37, 1973, pp. 50–61.

Novelli, William D. Personal communication, 1980.

Rogers, E. M., and Dorothy Leonard-Barton. ''Testing Social Theories in Marketing Settings,'' *American Behavioral Scientist,* Vol. 21, 1978, pp. 479–500.

Rosenberg, Larry J. *Marketing,* Englewood Cliffs, N.J.: Prentice-Hall, 1977.

Rothschild, Michael L. ''Political Advertising: A Neglected Policy Issue in Marketing,'' *Journal of Marketing Research,* Vol. 15, 1978, pp. 58–71.

Sethi, S. Prakash. "Institutional/Image Advertising and Idea/Issue Advertising as Marketing Tools: Some Public Policy Issues," *Journal of Marketing,* Vol. 43, 1979, pp. 68–78.

Sigal, Leon V. "Bureaucratic Objectives and Tactical Use of the Press," *Public Administration Review,* Vol. 33, 1973, pp. 336–345.

Wharton, Clifford R., Jr. "The Role of the Professional in Feeding Mankind: The Political Dimension," *War on Hunger,* January 1977.

TULSA PHILHARMONIC

The city of Tulsa traces its origins to 1836 when a band of Creek Indians called the Lochapokas chose a settlement site along a bend of the Arkansas River. *Tulsey,* which was later changed to Tulsa, began as the center of governmental and religious functions for the Creek Nation. But its history took a drastic change when on April 15, 1897, oil was first discovered north of the city. Another discovery was made four years later just west of the city and the richest small oil field in the world came in 1905 with the nearby Glenn Pool discovery.

Within two years 500 wells were pumping black crude and Tulsa had become the oil capital of the world. The Glenn Pool discovery brought oil men named Getty, Sinclair, Skelly, and Phillips. It also brought thousands of workers and the bedroom community of Tulsa had grown in population to 7,298 by the statehood year of 1907.

Among the newcomers moving to Tulsa during the early years of the oil booms were persons interested in developing good musical performances and assuring the availability of good theater and opera. A small group of musicians played overtures and *entr'acte* music in the Little Theater. Starlight Concerts sponsored by the University of Tulsa were held each summer in Skelly Stadium on the university campus. An orchestra called the Civic Symphony was formed.

But the orchestra moved to Oklahoma City during the Great Depression of the 1930s, returning occasionally to Tulsa to play winter concerts. Nearly two decades passed and the determination to have a permanent orchestra in Tulsa grew. The belief that a full-time symphony orchestra is a civic as well as cultural asset prompted the Chamber of Commerce to appoint a committee to determine ways and means of accomplishing this goal. In 1948, the Tulsa Philharmonic Society was formed. The society had the responsibility for the development, well-being, management, and support of the Tulsa Philharmonic Orchestra. On November 1, 1948, the orchestra held the opening concert of its first season with H. Arthur Brown, formerly of El Paso, as conductor.

GROWTH OF THE TULSA PHILHARMONIC

Brown served as conductor until 1957 when he left Tulsa to become conductor of the Los Angeles Symphony and the Hollywood Bowl Orchestra.

This case was prepared by Professor Louis E. Boone of the University of Central Florida as a basis for classroom discussion and not to illustrate either effective or ineffective handling of an administrative situation.

The late Vladimir Goldschmann succeeded him and continued with the orchestra for four years. The 1961–1962 season saw Franco Autori take command of the musical direction of the orchestra. Skitch Henderson served as director until his resignation in 1974, at which time Thomas Lewis was named music director and conductor. Concerts were held in the 2,727-seat Tulsa Municipal Theater. Table 1 shows the annual season ticket sales and number of concerts for the years 1954–1975.

Specific programs were selected by the conductor and aimed primarily at a classical music audience. As Table 1 indicates, there appears to be a 1,700-person base of classical support. Fluctuations in season ticket sales are affected by such variables as the reputation of the conductor, program content, and guest appearances. For instance, the increased attendance in 1966 was attributed to a guest appearance by Van Cliburn.

TABLE 1: ***Season ticket sales and number of concerts by TPO, by year***

Year	*Season ticket sales*	*Number of concerts*
1954	1,738	12
1955	1,649	12
1956	2,096	10
1957	1,742	10
1958	[a]	1
1959	2,557	10
1960	2,166	10
1961	2,434	10
1962	2,451	10
1963	2,394	10
1964	2,204	10
1965	2,163	10
1966	2,330	10
1967	2,133	10
1968	1,974	10
1969	1,769	10
1970	1,693	10
1971	2,737[b]	10
1972	2,737[b]	10
1973	1,794	10
1974	1,893	10
[illegible]5	1,969	10

[illegible]n tickets offered in 1958.

The Tulsa Philharmonic Orchestra (TPO) also devoted some of its efforts to the young people in the Tulsa area. Each spring it presented a Lollipop Concert to introduce young children to the arts. Ten Young People's Concerts were conducted annually for fifth- and sixth-grade students in both the public and private schools. An additional 60 in-school concerts were performed by various TPO ensembles.

The arrival of Skitch Henderson in 1971 resulted in sell-outs for his first two years. His attempts to mix classical and pop music coupled with heavy advertisements as classical concerts resulted in disaster the third year. The classical audience was upset at concerts that were advertised as classical yet containing pop music; those who preferred popular music were unhappy with the classical arrangements. Season ticket sales for 1973 dropped 34% below those of the previous year.

A NEW BUSINESS MANAGER JOINS THE TPO

In 1975, Ken Hertz joined the staff as assistant business manager. Hertz, 26, received his undergraduate degree in music from the State University of New York and had previously served as manager of the Cape Cod Symphony. At SUNY, he had taken an elective course in principles of marketing.

Hertz was one of the growing ranks of persons who recognized that business expertise was a crucial—although often nonexistent—requirement for a successful philarmonic orchestra. Table 2 shows the 1975 budget for the TPO. Hertz felt that by 1977, the budget would approximate $500,000. Cash flows were a continuous problem since season ticket renewals were made in January and February, but cash was not received until September.

Second, there was the question of what target

TABLE 2: ***1975 budget of the TPO***

Receipts		*Disbursements*
Sales	$ 58,000	
Contributions	100,000	
Endowment	60,000	
Other	74,000	
Total	$292,000	$292,000

audience the TPO was attempting to satisfy. One faction in the TPO simply felt that "good" music should be the objective; the right audience would appear. Others felt strongly that musical education should be an important role. Still others felt that a blend of pop and classical music would allow the TPO to serve the community best.

Another question concerned whether Monday night was the most appropriate week night for TPO performances. The society had already decided to move into the new $15 million Tulsa Performing Arts Center when it was completed in early 1977. The new center would have a seating capacity of 2,364, almost 300 less than the Municipal Theater. The reduced capacity and increased rental fees would further affect revenues and expenses. Hertz wondered what effect a price increase would have on attendance. He was also studying a new report from the Ford Foundation.

THE FORD FOUNDATION STUDY[1]

In 1974, the Ford Foundation sponsored a study of the audience for four performing arts—ballet, opera, symphony, and theater—in 12 cities. Three cities were chosen from each of the four geographic regions of the country: New York, Philadelphia, and Boston (East); Washington, Atlanta, and Houston (South); Chicago, Cincinnati, and Minneapolis (Midwest); and Los Angeles, San Francisco, and Seattle (West).

The study had three objectives:

1. To measure the size and the characteristics of the audience for the four performing arts; to answer the questions: How many people attend what? How often? Under what circumstances?
2. To measure the attitudes and motivations of attenders and prospective attenders; to answer the questions: What satisfactions do people want from a performance? What satisfactions do they believe the performing arts provide?
3. To identify opportunities for the performing arts, to assess what might be done by performing arts organizations or by others to attract more people to attend performances, and to induce those who now attend occasionally to attend more frequently.

The sample size was 6,000: 500 persons in each city contacted by telephone after being selected by a random procedure from telephone directories. Once the interviews were completed, the sample was weighted to conform to the sex, age, and education distribution of the population of the 12 cities as reported by the 1970 Census.

Findings of the Ford Foundation Study. Tables 3 to 8 summarize key findings of the Ford Foundation audience study.

THE TULSA STUDY

Hertz recognized a number of questions concerning the TPO that needed answers if he was to be successful in increasing attendance, providing maximum audience satisfaction, and increasing revenues. In considering the current season ticket holders, he sought out methods for increasing the number of times they actually attended each sea-

TABLE 3: ***Percentage of respondents attending a live professional symphony concert in the past year***

Method	*Percent exposed during past year*
On television	30
On radio	28
On records/tape	25
Live amateur	6
Live professional	10
Any form	51

Source: Ford Foundation Study, p. 6.

TABLE 4: ***Exposure to live professional performances of the four arts***

Among those who attended	*Percent who also attended:* Theater	*Opera*	*Symphony*	*Ballet*	*Percent attending no other arts*
Symphony	45	27	—	27	36
Theater	—	13	31	19	63
Opera	50	—	75	25	25
Ballet	60	20	60	—	20

Source: Ford Foundation Study, p. 11.

TABLE 5: ***Exposure to live professional symphony during past year by age***

Age	*Total percent exposed*
Under 20	13
20–29	11
30–39	10
40–49	9
50 and over	7

Source: Ford Foundation Study, p. 17.

TABLE 6: ***Income composition of audiences of live professional symphony during past year***

Income	*Total percent exposed*
Up to $7,500	12
$7,500 to $15,000	37
$15,000 to $25,000	34
$25,000 and over	19

Source: Ford Foundation Study, p. 13.

TABLE 7: ***Educational composition of audience of live professional symphony during past year***

Education	*Percent*
Some high school	21
High school graduate	18
Some college	24
College graduate	37

Source: Ford Foundation Study, p. 14.

TABLE 8: ***Total percent exposed to live professional symphony last year, by occupation***

Occupation	*Percent*
Executive–managerial	14
Professional	18
Teaching	27
Student	15
Homemaker	7
White collar	11
Blue collar	4
Retired	7

Source: Ford Foundation Study, p. 13.

son. He wondered if potential audiences could be converted into ticket purchasers if he changed such variables as time, concert location, concert night, ticket prices, parking and transportation, guest artists, different types of music, advertising, and image.

After reading the Ford Foundation report, he wondered whether the national characteristics truly reflected the Tulsa audience. What types of people actually attended the concerts, and why? Where did they obtain information about the concerts?

He simultaneously recognized a danger of alienating present concertgoers if he made the wrong decisions in his attempts to increase attendance. The TPO could not be "all things to all people" and any changes must take into consideration the reactions of the core market of season ticket holders.

Hertz decided to contact a local university professor and discuss the need for a profile of current concertgoers and a determination of the best methods of satisfying present and potential market targets.

Development of Hypotheses. The TPO needed greater attendance at its concerts, but lacked pertinent information to stimulate attendance increases. The research focused on eight hypotheses:

1. The typical Tulsa concertgoer is demographically similar to concertgoers in other cities.
2. The image of the TPO curtails the desire of people to attend.
3. More people will attend concerts if a greater variety of music is performed.
4. Concert time and night do not meet consumer desires.
5. Attendance will increase if information pertaining to concerts (subject, date, and time) is widely publicized.
6. Current promotional activities do not reach the market target.
7. People who attend the TPO also attend other cultural events in Tulsa (i.e., opera, ballet, theater).
8. Newspaper advertising will better reach the market target.

Methodology. Two separate surveys were conducted to test the hypotheses. One survey focused on persons who attend TPO concerts and a second study was designed to obtain information from potential concertgoers. The universe for the first survey was defined as all individuals living within the Tulsa SMSA who hold season tickets; the universe for the second survey was defined as the entire population within the city of Tulsa.

A systematic sample of 331 persons holding season tickets was selected from a list of subscribers. A questionnaire was then mailed to each household (see Appendix A). The expected response rate was high because of the interest of season ticket holders in the future of the TPO.

For the survey of the general public, a stratified probability sample of 236 residence telephones was selected. All residence telephones in Tulsa were divided according to telephone exchange (i.e., geographical area), and the number of numbers selected for the sample in each area corresponded to the size of that area in relation to the other exchanges. For those exchanges with more than one telephone prefix, the number of calls to be made within that exchange was divided equally between each prefix. The four-digit numbers required to complete each telephone number were chosen at random from a table of random pairs.

Telephone interviews were utilized to obtain information from the general public. The questionnaire used was divided into two parts: one for persons who were aware of the existence of the TPO and one for those who were not. The telephone questionnaire is shown in Appendix B.

Findings. The results of the two surveys are shown on the two questionnaires in Appendixes A and B.

NOTE

1. The information in this section is based upon *The Finances of the Performing Arts, Vol. II. A Survey of the Characteristics and Attitudes of Audiences for Theatre, Opera, Symphony and Ballet in 12 U.S. Cities,* Ford Foundation, 1974.

QUESTIONS

1. Compare the findings with the hypotheses established for the survey. In what ways are Tulsa residents similar to concertgoers in other cities? What are the major differences?
2. Should Hertz use these findings to develop a marketing strategy for TPO?
3. What steps would you recommend that he take in developing plans for the future?

APPENDIX A: Mail Survey of Season Ticket Holders and Responses to Each Question

EXHIBIT 1: ***Cover letter for mail questionnaires***

Dear Tulsa Philharmonic Subscriber:

We need your help! You can help us by completing the enclosed questionnaire.

Your answers will provide us with some much needed information regarding the interests and characteristics of current Tulsa Philharmonic subscribers. This information will help the Tulsa Philharmonic better serve you and other subscribers.

I am currently a marketing student at the University in

charge of coordinating thirty-five students working on this project. We need your help in order for this study to be successful. Your help will make a major contribution to our education.

Since this is a statistical study, you represent many subscribers. Won't you please answer the questions and return them to me *within the next few days* in the stamped envelope provided.

We are counting on your help.

Thank you very much,

Diane J. Jackson

EXHIBIT 2: ***Mail questionnaire***

Please check the appropriate answer

1a. How many times did you attend Tulsa Philharmonic concerts last season?

- 15.5% None of the concerts
- 9.8% 1–4 concerts
- 41.8% 5–9 concerts
- 33.0% Every concert

1b. If 4 or less concerts attended, please indicate the principal reasons why.

- 9.3% Conflicts with other activities
- 2.6% Inadequate parking facilities
- 4.1% Location of concerts
- 2.6% Inconvenient night and time
- 0.5% Transportation
- 2.1% Didn't enjoy the music
- ______ Others (please specify) ____________

2. Which night of the week is most convenient for you to attend the concerts?

75.8 Mon   13.9 Tues   9.8 Wed   7.7 Thurs   10.3 Fri   6.7 Sat   2.6 Sun

3. What concert starting time would be most convenient for you?

1.0 7:00 p.m.   14.9 7:30   73.2 8:00   8.2 8:30   2.6 No response

4. Do you think the current ticket price is:

6.3 Too high   3.7 Too low   87.3 Just right   2.7 No response

5. Where have you seen/heard advertisements for the Tulsa Philharmonic?

- 63.4 Newspaper
- 39.2 Radio
- 64.9 Mail brochure
- 24.7 Television
- 11.3 Magazines
- 13.9 None/Do not remember

6. What radio station do you listen to most often?

- 31.4 KWEN
- 32.5 KRAV
- 3.6 KAKC
- 9.3 KVOO
- 3.1 KELI
- 38.1 KRMG
- 4.1 KXXO
- 13.4 KWGS
- 10.3 Other/None

Most frequent time of listening?

- 45.9 7:00 a.m.–12 noon
- 16.0 12 noon–4:00 p.m.
- 24.7 4:00 p.m.–6:00 p.m.
- 43.3 After 6:00 p.m.

7. Which type(s) of music would you prefer to hear at the Tulsa Philharmonic?

- 5.7 Jazz
- 93.3 Classical
- 38.1 Modern classical
- 0.0 Country/western
- 0.0 Rock
- 8.2 Popular
- ____ Other (please specify) ____________________

8. In your opinion, is the Tulsa Philharmonic:

- 42.8 Good family entertainment
- 41.8 Good for an evening with friends
- 78.9 Cultural experience
- ____ Other (please specify)____________________

9. Please check events attended in the last year.

- 7.7 Ballet
- 6.2 Opera
- 19.6 Theater
- 4.1 Ballet and opera
- 3.6 Ballet and theater
- 17.0 Opera and theater
- 27.8 All three
- 11.3 None
- 2.6 No response

Although it is not necessary to identify yourself in any way, would you please answer the following questions for statistical tabulation purposes only.

10. A. Age:

- 1.5 18–24
- 6.7 25–34
- 24.2 35–49
- 39.2 50–64
- 27.3 65+
- 1.0 No response

B. Head of household education:

- 0.5 Some high school
- 5.7 High school graduate
- 23.7 Some college
- 68.0 College graduate
- 2.1 No response

C. Family income:

- 5.2 Under $7,500
- 7.7 $7,500–$10,000
- 14.4 $10,000–$15,000
- 23.7 $15,000–$25,000
- 20.6 $25,000–$50,000
- 17.0 $50,000+
- 11.3 No response

D. Occupation of household head:

- 5.7 Teaching
- 21.3 Professional
- 1.0 Student
- 13.3 Executive/managerial
- 8.6 White collar
- 23.6 Homemaker
- 12.7 Retired
- 1.3 Blue collar
- 4.0 Other

Thank you very much for your cooperation.

APPENDIX B: Telephone Survey of Tulsa Residents and Responses to Each Question

EXHIBIT 1: ***Telephone survey for general public***

Hello. This is ______________ from the Marketing Department at the University of Tulsa. We are interested in your opinion of the Tulsa Philharmonic Orchestra, and would like to ask you a few questions. This is in no way a solicitation of business, and will take only a small amount of your time.

1. Did you know that Tulsa has a philharmonic orchestra?

   80% Yes   20% No

   (check one of the following if respondent volunteers additional information)

   12.7% Have heard of it, but know little about it.
   3.5 Am quite familiar with the orchestra.
   3.5 Attend the concerts.
   0.0 Am a season ticket holder.
   0.0 Have never heard of it.
   0.0 Not familiar with it.
   ____ Other ______________

If the respondent answers "yes" to question 1

2. Have you ever attended a Tulsa Philharmonic concert(s)?

   (Don't ask if answered above)   39.3 Yes   60.7 No

   If yes: Approximately how many concerts did you attend last season?

   1.7 All   20.8 1–4
   17.9 5–9   59.5 None

3. Would you attend more concerts if they were more widely publicized?

   46.2 Yes   53.8 No

3a. If yes, what would be the best way to inform you about the concerts?

   21.4 Newspaper   4.6 Brochure
   22.5 Radio   ____ Other
   23.7 Television   ____ No opinion
   .6 Magazine

3b. What radio stations do you listen to most often?

   8.7 KWEN   7.5 KELI
   4.6 KRAV   11.6 KRMG
   12.1 KAKC   6.9 KXXO
   8.1 KVOO   8.1 None

What is the most frequent time of listening?

21.4 7:00 a.m.–12 noon

6.4 12 noon–4:00 p.m.

11.6 4:00 p.m.–6:00 p.m.

23.1 After 6:00 p.m.

4. Which type(s) of music would you prefer to hear at the Tulsa Harmonic?

19.1 Jazz

50.3 Classical

22.0 Modern classical

20.8 Country/Western

15.6 Rock

22.5 Popular

_____ Other

5. In your opinion, is the Tulsa Philharmonic:

38.7 Good family entertainment

41.6 Good for an evening with friends

52.0 Cultural experience

_____ Other (please specify) ____________________

6. Have you attended the ballet, opera, or theater in the last year?

9.2 Ballet

2.9 Opera

11.6 Theater

2.3 Ballet and opera

1.2 Ballet and theater

0.0 Opera and theater

4.0 All three

65.9 None

2.9 No response

7. Would you be interested in attending concerts in the future?

63.0 Yes

37.0 No

If yes: a. Which night of the week is most convenient for you to attend the concerts?

9.2 Sun 19.1 Mon 16.2 Tues 12.7 Wed 12.1 Thurs 32.9 Fri 38.7 Sat

b. What concert starting time would be most convenient for you? (Give choices)

7.5 7:00 p.m. 21.47 7:30 32.9 8:00 1.7 8:30 36.4 No response

c. What do you think is a reasonable ticket price per concert?

4.0 Less than $2.00 21.4 2–3.99 23.1 4–6.00 4.0 Above $6.00

Although it is not necessary to identify yourself in any way, would you please answer the following questions for statistical tabulations purposes only?

8. A. Age:

19.7 18–24 28.9 25–34 24.9 35–49 19.1 50–64 2.9 65+ 4.7 No response

Thank you very much for your cooperation.

If the respondent answers "no" to question 1

2. In your opinion, do you think it is desirable for Tulsa to have a philharmonic orchestra?

 90.7 Yes 9.3 No

3. What is your favorite type of music?

 9.3 Jazz
 20.9 Classical
 9.3 Modern classical
 37.2 Country/western
 25.6 Rock
 25.6 Popular
 ____ Other (please specify)

4. Have you attended the ballet, opera, or theater in the last year?

 7.0 Ballet
 2.3 Opera
 0.0 Theater
 2.3 Ballet and theater
 88.4 None

5. Would you attend more concerts if they were more widely publicized?

 37.2 Yes 62.8 No

If yes: a. What would be the best way to inform you about concerts?

 14.0 Newspaper
 11.6 Radio
 20.9 Television
 2.3 Magazine
 4.7 Brochure
 ____ Other
 ____ No opinion

b. What radio station do you listen to most often?

 4.7 KWEN
 4.7 KRAV
 11.6 KAKC
 7.0 KVOO
 7.0 KRMG
 0.0 KXXO
 29.3 Other/None

What is the most frequent time of listening?

 20.9 7:00 a.m.–12 noon
 2.3 12 noon–4:00 p.m.
 9.3 4:00 p.m.–6:00 p.m.
 9.3 6:00 p.m.–7:00 a.m.

Although it is not necessary to identify yourself in any way, would you please answer the following questions for statistical tabulation purposes only?

6. Age:

 27.9 18–24 16.3 25–34 18.6 35–49 18.6 50–64 16.3 65+ 2.3 No response

7. In your opinion, are symphony concerts:

 32.6 Good family entertainment

 18.6 Good for an evening with friends

 20.9 Cultural experience

 _____ Other (please specify) ________________________________

Thank you very much for your cooperation.

COMMUNITY HEALTH PLAN

The Community Health Plan, Inc., known as CHP is Rhode Island's first nonprofit health maintenance organization (HMO), established in June 1971.

With the support and assistance of local organized labor leadership, CHP became the first viable alternative to sometimes costly and piecemeal medical coverage and services. For the first time in Rhode Island, families were offered the opportunity to obtain total family care at a reasonable cost under one roof.

THE BASIC HMO MODEL

The term HMO has been used to designate a variety of health care delivery systems. But the most commonly accepted definition is that of "a medical care delivery system which accepts responsibility for the organization, financing and delivery of health care services for a defined population." The HMO is characterized by the combination of a financing mechanism—prepayment—with a particular mode of delivery—group practice—by means of a managerial-administrative organization responsible for insuring the availability of health services for a subscriber population.

The principles of operation of HMOs may be divided into six primary characteristics:

1. *Responsibility for organizing and delivering health services:* The HMO is not merely a financing mechanism but is concerned with obtaining, through contracts with providers, an assured source of supply of health services for its members.
2. *Prepayment:* Costs of the organization are met through fixed periodic payments from subscribers. Many plans, however, supplement the prepayment income with co-payments charged at the time treatment is incurred (e.g., a $2.00 charge for an office call).
3. *Group practice:* Physicians are organized into multispecialty groups of sufficient size to maintain facilities which are capable of providing comprehensive, continuous care. In the early stages, a developing HMO may include only primary-care physicians in the group and

This case was prepared by Professor David Loudon and Professor Albert Della Bitta, both of the University of Rhode Island, as a basis for class discussion rather than to illustrate either effective or ineffective handling of an administrative situation.

depend on referrals to outside specialists for those services beyond their capabilities.

4. *Comprehensive benefits:* Although "comprehensiveness" varies, most plans offer a complete range of medical services, including some forms of preventive care.
5. *Compensation of physicians:* The physicians are usually compensated through the "capitation" principle (the payment of an amount of money equal to a fixed per capita sum for each subscriber multiplied by the number of subscribers enrolled). In addition, most physician groups participate in any savings generated through effective management of the plan.
6. *Voluntary enrollment:* Most HMOs enroll through a dual-choice mechanism under which employees may choose between an indemnity plan or the HMO.

Group practice prepayment was initiated in this country in a small clinic in Elk City, Oklahoma, in 1932, and first implemented on a large scale by the Kaiser Foundation Health Plan on the West Coast. Since then, plans have been organized by diverse groups: for example, consumers at Puget Sound, physicians at Ross-Loos, a medical school at the Harvard Community Health Plan, and an insurance company at Columbia, Maryland—and in equally diverse forms. In 1970, approximately 75 HMOs provided health care for over eight million people nationally. The data derived from those participants indicate that HMOs have been able to supply health care for substantially less dollar outlay than has the predominant fee-for-service system.

COMMUNITY HEALTH PLAN

CHP embraces all the concepts that make up the HMO definition—prepayment, group practice, and the organizational responsibility for insuring the availability of health services for the defined service population.

The prepaid premium covers all benefits outlined in the CHP contract and precludes any additional expense to the subscriber except for items excluded under that contract. By and large, it can be said that all routine medical expenses are covered by the prepayment mechanism, as are most unexpected major medical eventualities: surgery, hospitalization, specialty consultations required by CHP physicians, and so on.

Although CHP has been widely respected in its two years of service to the Rhode Island community, the same problems experienced by other HMOs have also presented themselves in this setting. Group practice remains a fairly new and innovative concept about which some individuals remain skeptical, given long-standing relationships with private physicians. The newness of the organization also presented questions, at first, concerning its stability as compared to older, more established methods of health care delivery and insurance.

CHP started with 1,200 members (subscribers and their families), although the opening enrollment was forecasted at 6,000. Currently, the organization has 12,000 subscribers who have been offered the CHP plan on a dual choice basis through their particular group setting—usually at their place of employment. CHP's marketing team is responsible for tapping the available group resources and arranging for dual choice to be offered to those groups.

Because of insufficient enrollment CHP has found it necessary to secure large loans from the Prudential Insurance Company. The organization is now nearing its operational break-even point estimated at 16,000 members. However, at that point CHP will not be retiring its debt or setting money aside for expansion or replacement of capital equipment.

CHP has also had problems administratively. The fourth director of the organization is Mr. Philip Nelson, who was recently brought in by Prudential in an effort to strengthen the organization and ensure its success. As CHP enters its third year of operation, Nelson is looking forward to refining the organization's existing services and operations. He hopes to expand the organization to include new markets, additional medical capabilities, and larger more numerous treatment facilities.

One of Mr. Nelson's first tasks as director was to evaluate the marketing facets of CHP. In order to familiarize himself with the proposed marketing thrust of the organization, Mr. Nelson requested a copy of the association's 1973 marketing plan, which had been prepared by Mr. Ralph Wilbur, director of marketing. Prior to receiving the plan Mr. Nelson was reviewing CHP's past marketing strategies and decisional inputs. He expected that this review would suggest directions for future marketing activities.

Product. A principal marketing advantage of prepaid group practice programs over traditional health insurance is their comprehensive benefit package. In addition, they have the potential to deliver broader benefits for less than the cost of similar benefits under a fee-for-service plan.

In designing a HMO benefit package, a primary consideration is given to mandatory elements, those which are essential to provide flexibility for the medical group treating patients. Any additions to this package must take into account the attractiveness of benefits to potential subscribers, the cost effectiveness of such benefits, and the nature and price of competitive benefit packages in the community. Although most programs include copayments and deductibles, CHP has none (except for a house-call provision). The CHP benefit package is described in a brochure distributed to prospective members. A copy of part of this brochure is shown in Exhibit 1.

Promotion. A substantial part of the work of a HMO is involved with promotion. For example, the community must be educated about prepaid group practice; management and union leadership must be sold on the idea of dual choice for the firm's employees; individuals must be enrolled in the program.

The marketing department at CHP consists of four employees. Mr. Wilbur is the director, with previous experience in marketing but not in the health field. The three other personnel had no previous experience in marketing prior to joining CHP. These four individuals act as marketing representatives for CHP, calling on employees and employers in an effort to sell the concept of prepaid group practice.

Prospective subscribers appear to respond best to three sales themes: (1) comprehensive services are delivered at one place, (2) services are completely prepaid, and (3) very high quality medical care is obtained.

In addition to personal selling efforts, CHP has utilized newspaper advertising twice. Physicians are bound by professional codes of conduct which consider it unethical to solicit patients directly or indirectly. Thus any promotion must be handled delicately so that no charges of unethical conduct arise. In addition, HMOs have been subjected to charges of socialized medicine and on occasion have suffered from the stigma associated with these charges. For these reasons, prepaid group practice programs generally have been very conservative in advertising and promoting. Some groups do not aggressively seek out new business but rely upon their reputations to attract new group accounts. However, for new prepaid programs in their infancy there is pressure to meet enrollment quotas and educate the citizenry; thus promotion is sometimes more aggressive.

In November 1972, CHP ran a newspaper advertisement (Exhibit 2). As a result, the Rhode Island Medical Society lodged a complaint against CHP over its merchandising tactics.

Pricing. A 1964 study compared out-of-pocket costs in a prepaid group practice with two traditional health insurance plans. It was found that the premium of the prepaid program covered 76% of costs of physician services, prescription drugs, and hospitalization while the other programs covered 55% and 59% of these costs. Thus price can be a significant marketing advantage in terms of out-of-pocket costs associated with prepaid programs.

Although copayments are a feature of most prepaid plans, CHP has only one. A reason for the use of copayments is that they allow prepaid pre-

EXHIBIT 1: ***Medical, surgical and hospital services***

In the community health center	Visits to doctor's office	No charge
Diagnosis and treatment — specialists' care — continued care of chronic conditions — eye examinations — pediatric checkups for children — physical checkups — no limit on number of visits	Laboratory tests—x-ray—physical therapy	No charge
	Casts and dressings	No charge
	Injections—allergy injections	No charge
In the hospital		
Unlimited days at no charge for semi-private care when arranged by CHP physician	Services of physicians and surgeons and other health personnel, including operations	No charge
	Room and board — general nursing — use of operating room — anesthesia	No charge
Private room fully paid when medically needed	X-ray and laboratory examinations — x-ray therapy	No charge
	Dressings — casts — blood transfusions if blood is replaced	No charge
Ambulance service		Provided without charge if authorized by CHP personnel
In your home	House calls by CHP physicians	$5 for first visit for each acute illness; no charge after first visit for the same illness; house calls will be made at the judgment of a CHP physician
Maternity care	Full physician's services, including pre-natal care	No charge
	Hospital care — full hospital care is provided to a member after 180 days continuous family membership in CHP — or when continued combined membership in an alternate plan and CHP totals 180 days of family coverage	No charge

EXHIBIT 2: ***CHP newspaper advertisement***

ATTENTION FEDERAL AND STATE EMPLOYEES
AND OTHER EMPLOYEE GROUPS
WITH THE CHP
PLAN YOU RECEIVE
TOTAL FAMILY
HEALTH CARE

Yes, emergency medical care and advice is available to you 24 hours a day, 365 days a year, under the Comprehensive Health Care Plan provided by CHP.

There is no other plan to match CHP. Besides providing full in-hospital coverage for a semiprivate room, other hospital service charges, and all surgical and medical charges, the plan has many unique features not generally offered by other plans, such as:

• Full coverage for all visits to your CHP physician or other specialists to whom you may be referred by your CHP doctor—whether for treatment, advice, diagnosis, or just a check-up.

• Full coverage for all visits to CHP pediatricians at the CHP family health care center, including well baby care, inoculations, and immunizations.

• Complete maternity care, including prenatal, delivery, and postnatal care by your CHP obstetrician, at no charge to you.

• Eye examinations and prescriptions for glasses from your CHP vision center.

November 15–30 is open enrollment period for federal and state employees and their families. (It's always open enrollment for other groups of employees.)

Whether you live in Rhode Island or southeastern Massachusetts, you owe it to yourself and your family to take advantage of this once-a-year opportunity to join CHP for complete personal and family care. Obtain CHP literature and application forms from your payroll clerk or by calling CHP. Visit the new Health Care Center—plenty of free parking.

OPEN HOUSE

TODAY 1 to 4 p.m.

TOMORROW EVENING 7 to 9 p.m.

COMMUNITY HEALTH PLAN
North Providence, R. I.

A nonprofit organization

---

minums to be set more competitively. Many programs include small charges for office visits ($1 to $3). With such an approach Nelson believes that CHP could reduce its price below its major competitor, which presently writes about 85% of the health insurance in the state.

CHP's primary competitor offers a low-option benefit package which fits the needs of a particular group of employees in the state: namely, low-pay, low-fringe-benefit industries such as jewelry and textiles. The competitor's plan pays only 60% of health care expenses but costs substantially less than CHP's only plan, a high-option benefit package.

Another variable influenced by competition concerns the number of price steps. The major competitor and CHP both have two price steps: one rate for a single person and another rate for families (regardless of size). However, Mr. Nelson has considered adding another price step so that the rates would be categorized three ways: for one person, two, and three or more. The result if implemented should be to skew CHP's membership more to one- and two-person enrollees since their rates would be lower than at present. However, large families would have a greater incentive to subscribe to the competitor's plan because their rate would increase with CHP. Although Mr. Nelson was considering such a move, he was unsure what ramifications this might have on employer's acceptance, membership size, CHP's break-even point, or competitive reaction.

Location. CHP is located adjacent to a medium-size hospital in North Providence, one of the most heavily populated areas of the state. It is convenient to the main traffic arteries in the northern part of the state.

Mr. Nelson estimates that CHP will exhaust the capacity of the present facility when it reaches 16,000 enrollees, and thus thought must be given to expanded facilities and their location.

One of the current barriers to greater enrollment is the distance some members may have to travel in order to reach the facility for care. Studies of other HMO programs indicate that distances of 10 or more miles from the facility significantly retards membership and utilization of the facility by existing members. However, because CHP presently lacks precise knowledge on the geographic distribution of its membership, Nelson is uncertain of the extent to which this should be a problem at CHP.

If CHP were to open additional locations, there are a number of areas in the state to which it might expand. Exhibit 3 presents state population data. Two appealing locations to Nelson are Warwick and South Kingstown. Warwick's population has expanded very rapidly. The city offers a central location in the state and it features the state's two major regional shopping centers. The other area considered would be near the state university, which is located in South Kingstown and has a student and employee population of over 15,000. In fact, preliminary negotiations had been undertaken in the past between CHP and the university concerning the possibility of CHP's assuming a major role in the student health service.

EXHIBIT 3: ***Rhode Island population figures by counties, cities, and towns***

	Population	
	1960 (Census)	*1970 (Census)*
Bristol county	37,146	45,937
Barrington	13,826	17,554
Bristol	14,570	17,860
Warren	8,750	10,523
Kent County	112,619	142,382
Coventry	15,432	22,947
East Greenwich	6,100	9,577
WARWICK	68,504	83,694
West Greenwich	1,169	1,841
West Warwick	21,414	24,323
Newport County	81,405	94,228
Jamestown	2,267	2,911
Little Compton	1,702	2,385
Middletown[a]	12,675	29,621
NEWPORT[a]	47,049	34,231
Portsmouth	8,251	12,521
Tiverton	9,461	12,559
Providence County	568,778	581,470
Burrilville	9,119	10,087
CENTRAL FALLS	19,858	18,716
CRANSTON	66,766	74,287
Cumberland	18,792	26,605
EAST PROVIDENCE	41,955	48,207
Foster	2,097	2,626
Glocester	3,397	5,160
Johnston	17,160	22,037
Lincoln	13,551	16,182
North Providence	18,220	24,337
North Smithfield	7,632	9,349
PAWTUCKET	81,001	76,984
PROVIDENCE	207,498	179,116
Scituate	5,210	7,489
Smithfield	9,442	13,468
WOONSOCKET	47,080	46,820
Washington County	59,540	85,706
Charlestown	1,966	2,863
Exeter	2,298	3,245
Hopkinton	4,174	5,392
Narragansett	3,444	7,138
New Shoreham	486	489
North Kingstown[a]	18,977	29,793
Richmond	1,986	2,625
South Kingstown	11,942	16,913
Westerly	14,267	17,248
State totals	858,488	949,723

Note: Names of cities are shown in capital letters.
[a]Areas with extensive Navy facilities and housing. In Newport 10,218 shipboard naval personnel were counted in the city in 1960, but none in 1970.

A short period after Nelson had received these aspects of CHP's marketing situation, Mr. Wilbur submitted the proposed marketing plan for 1973. The plan is presented in Exhibit 4. Mr. Nelson looked forward to learning from the report what marketing directions were planned for CHP during the coming year.

EXHIBIT 4: ***1973 marketing program for Community Health Plan***

Preface

The following recommended marketing program is based on the premise that the prepaid, group practice health care concept offered by the Rhode Island Community Health Plan is a highly marketable program. This is not to say that it is absolutely perfect and that *no* improvements could be made in the plan. Slight improvements may be made.

We face certain problems . . . some of which come under the category of demographics. Our market is unlimited by age. Every employed individual and adult family member with or without children is a prospective enrollee. However, at our present stage of growth and development, with one Health Care Center located in North Providence, CHP is somewhat limited geographically. While we are located almost in the heart of the Providence metropolitan area and the extension of Route 295 will place us in close proximity to a major expressway, our present facility is still far removed from southern areas of the state, both on the east and west sides of Narragansett Bay. Obviously, the answer is the future establishment of a family health care facility somewhere south of Warwick, which is the fastest-growing city in the state. With this as a future goal, we still have the advantage of being located in an area with the greatest mass concentration of population in Rhode

Island. Even a modest share of enrollees out of the potential in our present location could flood the CHP center.

Based on a successful marketing program, the initial CHP planning grant projected an enrollment of 17,500 persons by June 1973, and 20,000 by June 1974. If these enrollments are attained, it leads to immediate consideration of a larger facility in the metropolitan area and/or a second facility in southern Rhode Island, plus expansion of the medical staff. We call your attention to goals and objectives later in this presentation.

A problem we will always face under our present concept is the disruption of previously established doctor–patient relationships. This is a particularly difficult problem with a segment of the female population. We see no simple solution to this problem. The Marketing Department's job will be to "sell" the CHP concept, the high degree of competence, experience, and professionalism and ongoing availability and accessibility of our staff physicians, as well as the importance of containment of the cost of health care.

In presenting a marketing "game plan," it is necessary to discuss some basic marketing techniques:

1. It is absolutely essential that the general public be totally aware of and familiarized with the existence of the product or service (Community Health Plan). We have made great strides in this direction during the past two months. However, *much* remains to be done. To use a very hackneyed expression, CHP must become a "household word."
2. After CHP is known to the mass public, we must educate the people to accept the CHP concept of prepaid, group practice health care . . . the total health care . . . the preventive health care available under the plan.
3. Finally, we must break down old associations, market the acceptability of the CHP plan, and *motivate* the individual to enroll. Once he is enrolled, we must provide the highest quality of health care, thereby creating satisfied customers, each of whom in a sense becomes a member of our Marketing Department, spreading the word of his satisfaction and the CHP concept. Once we have acquisition, we must have a very concentrated effort in retention . . . and this objective must permeate the entire CHP staff in their dealings with our membership. This is an extremely important area of the CHP marketing program . . . the constant liaison with the employer contacts and union representatives. It is through them that we gain the entre to the employee groups and the growth of our membership. This requires constant telephone and personal contact, *especially personal contact,* with visual presentations and/or visits to the CHP Family Health Care Center. Through good advertising and public relations, we hope to gain total public awareness of the CHP plan and the entrée to management and unions.

How do we accomplish these objectives? Without high public mass media exposure, success will be slow in coming. It is essential that we establish a firm advertising and public relations budget. This can be formulated by setting an enrollment goal and a cost of acquisition for each individual enrollee. During the Blue Cross–Blue Shield open enrollment period in October 1972, we have learned that their cost of acquisition was $5.00 per enrollee.[a] Figuring our cost of acquisition at $2.50 and now projecting a total membership of *25,000* by December 31, 1973, or an increase of approximately 1,000 per month, we arrive at an advertising and public relations budget of $30,000 for 1973. We propose to spend this money in the following manner:

Advertising and Public Relations Budget

1. Outdoor Advertising: A "roving," painted, high-quality 14 x 48 foot billboard. Such an illuminated billboard would be moved and the copy changed every two months or six times in a year with the board facing north on Route 95 on the downtown Providence area, south on the expressway, at the intersection of Route 146 and other choice locations. It is estimated (in fact, guaranteed) that such a board delivers 18,250,000 impressions a year.
   Total cost, including production for year — $7,800.00
2. *Providence Sunday Journal,* Business and Industry Section: 600-line ad once a month for 12 months. Directed toward employers and unions. Total estimated impressions: 4,800,000 a year.
   Total cost, including production for a year — $5,400.00
3. Balance of advertising would be spread over television, radio, and other daily and weekly newspapers at selected times during the year. (Heavy

concentration during November as they are federal and state reopening enrollment periods, etc.)

Total cost, including production for year `	$10,000.00
4. Public relations budget for year	$ 2,000.00
5. Printing (new brochure, newsletter, including photography, etc.	$ 4,400,00
6. Mimeograph machine (used)	$ 400.00
Total 1973 advertising and public relations budget	$30,000.00

Other Activities

1. It is the Marketing Department's opinion that a new CHP general-purpose brochure is needed. Generally, the brochure would be more colorful with more graphic art work to attract the eye and the reader's attention. We are securing estimates of the cost of printing.
2. Also under way is the preparation of a CHP Newsletter to be mailed to the entire membership three or four times a year. This can be an invaluable tool in the education and retention of our membership.
3. What can we get free? In the months of November and December 9172, CHP was highly successful in gaining a large amount of free public service and news coverage in all the media. This increased our public image and visibility enormously. Because we are a nonprofit organization, we are in a better position to secure such coverage than a commercial, profit-making organization. Every effort will be made to secure free public exposure in all the mass media.

System for Follow-up of New and Old Marketing Group Leads

In order to guard against the possibility that any Marketing Representative might neglect the proper follow-up with a particular group at a future date, each representative should maintain a "tickler file" divided by months. At our weekly marketing meeting, we shall continue to discuss the prospective groups with which each representative is in contact so that there is no unnecessary duplication. I do not feel it would be advantageous to establish any geographical territories to be assigned to our representatives since all of us have hundreds of contacts all over the state and established entrées with business and industry. However, we should all be aware of each other's activities in order to preclude the possibility that two of us would be pounding on different doors in the same plant at the same time.

OUR GOAL:

25,000
MEMBERS
by
December 31, 1973

---

[a]Blue Cross–Blue Shield spends in excess of $250,000 per year in advertising and public relations. They spent $40,000 during the open enrollment period to attract about 8,000 new members (total individuals).

QUESTIONS FOR DISCUSSION

1. As Mr. Nelson, what would be your reaction to Wilbur's proposed marketing program?
2. How might the plan be improved?
3. What are the unique features of this organization which influence marketing decisions?
4. What recommendations would you make regarding CHP's marketing strategy?

THE UNDERCROFT MONTESSORI SCHOOL

GENERAL BACKGROUND INFORMATION

The following case deals with the marketing of a social service. The principal decision makers in the case are concerned parents who have volunteered to manage the affairs of a private school of modest size located in a residential area of the city of Tulsa. Management of the school has been conservative, concentrating upon enhancing the overall quality of the existing program. Enrollment at the school has been at near full capacity levels for the past five years and the present board of trustees is considering the possibilities of expansion. There is some uncertainty among the members about which direction expansion should proceed, if at all, and little agreement has been reached.

THE UNDERCROFT MONTESSORI SCHOOL PROGRAM: OBJECTIVES AND STRATEGY

Administration of the School. Business management of the school is currently conducted by a board of trustees composed of 15 members. Board members are elected for three year terms by the school corporation, which consists of all the parents of children enrolled. The members are assigned to one of six standing committees which are responsible for planning financial, educational, facilities, volunteers and hospitality, public relations and scholarship activities. There is also an executive committee consisting of the president, vice president, assistant vice president, treasurer, and secretary. The purpose of the latter committee is to coordinate planning decisions between the six standing committees and to execute routine transactions related to the business activities of the school.

Objectives. There are two primary institutional objectives of which the board is most concerned as a body. These are educational quality and financial viability. The following objective statement is an excerpt from the *General Information and School Policy* manual provided for parents:

> The Undercroft Montessori School is dedicated to the Montessori philosophy and method of education through the senses. A child attending Undercroft will be exposed to a method which should facilitate the growth of inner discipline and later complex reasoning through the free choice and organized use of didactic materials within an atmosphere conducive to these ends.

Specific educational objectives related to the child's developmental process in the general areas of motor, sensory, and language (symbols) are embodied in the comprehensive directress training program which are not at issue in this case. In addition, detailed professional and staff objectives are defined in *Staff Manual for Undercroft Montessori School*.

The second primary objective is to ensure the routine financial integrity of the school. That is, a major goal of the board is to establish and maintain an adequate flow of funds to compensate staff, provide and maintain educational materials and facilities, and provide scholarships. The major source of funds has been internal through tuition payments. Although modest surpluses have been recognized as desirable, breaking even in any given year has been considered satisfactory. Exhibit 1 is a summary of financial performance over the past several years of school operation.

This case was prepared by the authors at The University of Tulsa as a basis for class discussion rather than to illustrate either effective or ineffective handling of an administrative situation. Presented at a Southern Case Research Association Workshop, New Orleans, Louisiana, November 1978.

EXHIBIT 1: ***The Undercroft Montessori School, Inc.***

Comparative Income Statement 1974–1978

	Period July 1 through June 30				
	1978	*1977*	*1976*	*1975*	*1974*
Revenue from operations and contributions					
Interview fees	$ 590	$ 560	$ 460	$ 560	$ 490
Tuition	62,172	62,020	62,148	53,768	51,181
Interest	1,057	1,225	913	534	67
Contributions	2,121	1,395	1,255	2,340	500
Total revenue and contributions	$65,940	$65,200	$64,776	$57,202	$52,238
Operating expenses and overhead					
Salaries	$44,945	$39,679	$42,649	$38,591	$33,356
Payroll taxes	3,228	3,148	3,289	3,159	3,964
Insurance, health	2,914	2,373	1,871	1,384	872
Office supplies	1,646	1,789	1,402	1,268	924
Office telephone	420	400	466	562	369
Teacher training	193	608	38	582	441
Travel expenses				1,194	497
Classroom supplies	1,142	1,500	1,183	1,677	1,541
Classroom snacks	294	158	236	236	181
Classroom expendables	202	1,268	949	158	45
Building, custodial	1,835	1,571	1,275	1,406	849
Building, maintenance	497	701	498	829	2,722
Building, supplies	422	437	428	166	341
Building, utilities	1,124	1,083	953	767	717
Building, security	737	827			
Insurance, property	906	655	435	410	1,048
Grounds, maintenance	49	431		15	
Grounds, landscaping	475	405	445	740	562
Grounds, lighting	265	209	204	187	
Interest, mortgage	324	378	421	425	504
Interest, land contract	774	778	783	786	790
Dues and subscriptions	478	801	399	525	461
Advertising	435	394	238	204	149
Depreciation	2,835	2,788	2,571	2,185	1,415
Miscellaneous	658	1,346	1,793	1,766	2,041
Total expenses and overhead	$66,598	$63,727	$62,526	$59,222	$53,588
Net income	$ (658)	$ 1,473	$ 2,250	$(2,020)	$(1,350)

Strategy. Educational quality is partly provided through affiliation with the American Montessori Society and a system for internal staff development and review. The AMS provides a current file of certified directresses, regional workshops, and observers to review and evaluate school programs. Promotion of the school to stimulate enrollment has been largely through word of mouth. Some advertising has also been employed in local Tulsa newspapers at a modest level. These are usually planned to coincide with the annual fall open house, for interested parents.

Allocation of funds for advertising has been a somewhat controversial issue among members of the board. The argument against advertising has centered around previous enrollment, which has been near full-capacity levels for the past several years. Some members have asked the question: Why advertise when classes are full? The question has been unresolved.

THE JANUARY MEETING OF THE EXECUTIVE COMMITTEE

An executive committee meeting was held at the beginning of the year to review the current financial situation and long-term plans for the program. The school had an opening for an assistant directress and, during the process of hiring, it was learned that salaries had increased substantially due to rising demand for qualified Montessori staff. A recent report by the treasurer indicated that a deficit was incurred during operations in 1977–1978. Tuition had been increased at the beginning of the previous year from $625 to $675 for the half-day program and from $1150 to $1250 in the all-day program. However, a number of routine expenses had increased significantly beyond expectations. Although a tuition increase in the 1979 budget seems indicated, several members of the Board have expressed concern about the possible adverse effects upon current prospective new parents.

The Growth Issue. During the meeting it became apparent that aspirations held by members of the committee for future school development varied considerably. The focus of the debate centered largely upon direction of growth. Three alternatives were perceived feasible: (1) vertical expansion to include a program for older children, (2) horizontal expansion in the form of enhancement to the existing program, or (3) deferment of proposed program changes until financial stability was permanently assured. Tables 1 through 9 provide demographic and other data provided to the board members.

The present ratio of children to directress was considered nearly ideal and any form of expansion or enhancement would require additional facilities, equipment, and staff.

Another topic of discussion arose among board members about the relative merits of a full-time professional school administrator. His or her role in the organization would be similar to that of a principal in a regular public elementary school.

Nancy Martin. Nancy Martin has served one full school year as president of the school corporation and chairperson of the board of trustees. Before assuming her present position, she was responsible for the activities of the hospitality and arrangement committee. Despite the fact that the unanimous opinion of the board is that she has done an outstanding job, Nancy is not entirely satisfied with her accomplishments as president. At the beginning of the meeting, Nancy expressed her opinion that the school has a number of significant strengths such as private facilities, reputation in the community, and an exceptional head directress. However, in Nancy's view, there are crucial weaknesses as well. Among these are considerable uncertainty about enrollment from semester to semester. Nancy candidly admitted having experienced considerable anxiety about the

TABLE 1: ***National preprimary school enrollment of children 3–5 years old, 1965–1976***

Year	*Total 3–5 population (thousands)*	*Number 3–5 enrollment (thousands)*	*Number as percent of total*
1965	12,549	3,407	27.1
1968	11,905	3,928	33.0
1969	11,424	3,949	34.6
1970	10,949	4,104	37.5
1971	10,610	4,148	39.1
1972	10,166	4,231	41.6
1973	10,344	4,234	40.9
1974	10,393	4,699	45.2
1975	10,186	4,958	48.7
1976	9,726	4,790	49.2

Source: U.S. Bureau of the Census, Current Population Reports.

TABLE 2: ***Estimated national enrollment (thousands) in independent nursery schools and kindergartens compared to total enrollment at all levels, 1978–1985***

	Year								
Level	*1975*	*1978*	*1979*	*1980*	*1981*	*1982*	*1983*	*1984*	*1985*
Public	489	464	474	497	526	559	593	626	657
Nonpublic	1,531	1,594	1,714	1,869	2,043	2,229	2,421	2,609	2,779
Total enrollment all levels									
Public	54,163	53,436	52,862	52,353	52,056	51,855	51,895	52,125	52,485
Nonpublic	9,181	9,348	9,478	9,636	9,808	9,975	10,132	10,258	10,369

Source: U.S. Department of Health, Education and Welfare; National Center for Education Statistics, "Preprimary Enrollment, 1975."

TABLE 3: ***Projected allocation of total population (thousands) by county in Tulsa standard metropolitan statistical area, 1976–2000***

	Year					
County	*1976*	*1980*	*1985*	*1990*	*1995*	*2000*
Creek	50.6	53.2	58.8	66.2	74.8	84.0
Mayes	27.9	30.1	34.7	41.2	49.2	58.2
Osage	32.6	32.0	33.6	36.8	41.3	45.7
Rogers	34.3	38.3	45.6	54.9	66.0	78.2
Tulsa	422.8	441.4	471.3	503.8	533.1	564.1
Wagoner	27.4	31.0	37.8	46.5	57.2	69.0
Tulsa SMSA	595.6	626.0	681.8	779.4	821.6	899.2

Source: "Population and Employment: Methods, Procedures, and Projections," Economic Planning Group, Tulsa Metropolitan Area Planning Group and Metropolitan Tulsa Chamber of Commerce, January 1978.

TABLE 4: ***Projected allocation of total population (thousands) by age group in Tulsa standard metropolitan statistical area, 1978–2000***

	Year					
Age range	*1978*	*1980*	*1985*	*1990*	*1995*	*2000*
0–4	46.4	46.7	53.9	57.8	60.4	63.8
5–9	50.1	50.9	54.1	63.4	68.7	71.8
10–14	54.4	53.2	56.2	60.9	71.1	76.8
Total all ages	610.8	626.1	681.9	749.4	821.7	899.5

Source: "Detailed Demographic Projections: Tulsa SMSA (1980–2000)," Economic Developent Planning Group, Tulsa Metropolitan Area Planning Commission and Metropolitan Tulsa Chamber of Commerce, March 1978.

TABLE 5: ***Forecast of school enrollment (thousands) in Tulsa standard metropolitan statistical area, 1975–2000***

	Year					
Level	*1975*	*1980*	*1985*	*1990*	*1995*	*2000*
Nursery	2.9	2.9	3.4	3.8	4.1	4.4
Kindergarten	8.7	9.0	9.6	11.3	12.3	12.9
Elementary	87.5	85.8	91.1	102.9	116.5	124.8
Total all levels, including high school	160.0	160.8	146.0	180.8	200.9	220.6

Source: "Detailed Demographic Projections: Tulsa SMSA (1980–2000)," Economic Development Planning Group, Tulsa Metropolitan Area Planning Commission and Metropolitan Tulsa Chamber of Commerce.

TABLE 6: ***Preprimary enrollment and population of children 3–5 years old by family income and occupation of head of household, October 1975***

	Total 3–5-year-old population (thousands)	*enrollment (thousands)*
Family income		
Less than $3000	607	246
$3000–$4999	947	470
$5000–$7499	1,350	556
$7500 or over	6,627	3,449
Total in four income groups	9,531	4,621
Occupation		
White collar	3,455	2,030
Manual/services	4,473	1,922
Farm	286	92
Unemployed	1,626	703
Total in four occupation groups	9,840	4,797

Source: Standard Education Almanac, 1977–78, Marquis Academic Media.

possibility of being unable to open the school in the fall of 1977 due to slow preenrollment during the previous spring. A sufficient number of parents eventually reserved positions, but Nancy recalled a few anxious moments. The school presently does not have sufficient cash reserves to support essential operations without outside contributions if enrollment should fall below about 65 students. Nancy said that she is aware of the general interest of many board members and parents for vertical expansion of the school's program, but frankly she does not agree that this objective is realistic in view of the more or less continuous tight financial situation and other more immediate administrative difficulties. In Nancy's words: "How can we even think about expansion when we barely have enough money to meet our day-to-day expenses? Before we consider expanding, which would necessarily mean an additional classroom, staff, and materials, I would rather hire a professional school administrator first and quit trying to run the school by committees."

Don Keele. Don Keele has the greatest longevity on the board of any active member having served approximately five years both as president and treasurer of the corporation. Don agreed with

TABLE 7: ***Preprimary enrollment of children 3–5 years old by metropolitan status and age, October 1975***

	Population and enrollment (thousands)			
Age group	*Total 3–5 population*	*Metropolitan central enrollment*	*Metropolitan other enrollment*	*Nonmetropolitan enrollment*
3 years	3,177	260	1,158	1,028
4 years	3,499	451	1,304	1,146
5 years	3,509	810	1,368	1,128
Total 3–5 years	10,185	1,521	3,830	3,302

Source: Standard Education Almanac, 1977–78, Marquis Academic Media.

TABLE 8: ***Tabulation of private nonsectarian and parochial schools in Tulsa County[a] with academic offerings, 1977***

	Nonsectarian	*Parochial*	*Total schools*
Preschool and kindergarten	12	8	20
Elementary K–6	4	17	21
Total schools	16	25	41

[a]Schools listed do not include trade, professional, or remedial schools.

Source: Tulsa Telephone Directory, 1977.

TABLE 9: ***Competitive Tulsa institutions offering early childhood development programs, August 1978***

	Ages/grades	*Previous enrollment*	*Approximate number of teachers*	*Tuition per semester*
	Representative Nonsectarian private schools			
Undercroft Montessori 3745 S. Hudson	2½–6 years Prekindergarten to kindergarten Half-day and all-day sessions	90	6	\$338 (½ day), \$625 (all day)
Montessori Child Development School 4803 South Lewis	2½–6 years Prekindergarten to kindergarten Half-day sessions	40	2	\$350 (½ day)

Betty Rowland Nursery School and Kindergarten 2505 E. Skelly Drive	3–5 years Prekindergarten to kindergarten Half-day sessions	42	2	$338 (½ day)
Helen's Private Kindergarten 3416 E. 33rd Street	2½–5 years Kindergarten to kindergarten Half-day and all-day sessions	38	4	$284 (½ day), $518 (all day)
Anne Simpson's New School for Elementary Education 230 E. 18 Street	Prekindergarten through grade 6	31 pre- and kindergarten (100–120 in grades 1–6)	2 (6 for grades 1–6)	$264 (½ day), $340 (all day)
Representative Parochial Private Schools				
Holland Hall 5666 E. 81 Street	Prekindergarten through grade 12	60 pre- and kindergarten (800 in grades 1–12)	20	$875 (½ day), $1,295 (all day)
Villa Teresa Kindergarten and Preschool 1861 E. 15 Street	Prekindergarten through kindergarten	N.A.	4	$360 (all day)
Southpark Christian School 10811 East 41st Street	Prekindergarten through grade 4 Half-days and all day	40	3	$225 (½ day) $473 (all day)
New Haven Methodist Pre-school 5603 South New Haven	Prekindergarten Half days	135	7	$225
Representative Day Care Centers with Partial Academic Offering				
LaPetite Day Care and Preschool 6287 East 38th Street (3 locations)	Ages 2–6 years Hourly, half-day, all day	100	11	$332 (½ day), $585 (all day)
National Child Care Center 11633 East 31st Street (4 locations)	1½–12 years Hourly, half-day,	100	10	$448 (½ day), $644 (all day)
Southside Child Care 5544 South Peoria	Infant through kindergarten All day	45	4	$750 (all day)

Approximate number of private preschool and kindergarten institutions (nonsectarian and parochial) with academic offerings	20
Approximate number of day care institutions with partial academic offerings	40
Approximate number of parochial preschools	8

Nancy in terms of the present strengths of the school organization and program, but said that he does not agree with her problem priorities. Don believes strongly that the curriculum should expand to include 7- through 12-year-olds. That is, the program should be comprehensive from the traditional preschool through the equivalent of a sixth grade. Don admitted that there would be problems involved in securing additional qualified staff (two directresses and assistants) and classrooms (two) plus routine accreditation requirements with the state. But the return would be considerable. In Don's opinion, a comprehensive program would be very worthwhile from the parent's point of view in that it would relieve the planning problem of where to continue the child's education after kindergarten. Don acknowledged that funding the expansion would be the most difficult task and pointed out that fund-raising efforts in the past had met with modest success at best. These had been directed toward parents of children both currently and previously enrolled, and had been in the form of garage sales, carnivals, and direct solicitations.

Betty Kaylor. Betty Kaylor, chairperson of the education committee, was not entirely in agreement with the president or treasurer in terms of problems and goals. Betty argued that staffing instability and lack of physical space, in her opinion, are the two most pressing issues confronting the board. Betty pointed out that, since April 1974, ten directresses and/or assistants had retired or resigned for various reasons. Continuity from one class to the next had been difficult to maintain and Betty acknowledged the fact that the school had been almost totally dependent upon the head directress. She had been invaluable in smoothing the transition periods and minimizing any overall reduction in classroom effectiveness.

Betty was also concerned with lack of adequate indoor space to develop motor skills during inclement weather. The school had a very attractive outdoor playground area and a fair complement of equipment adjacent to the classrooms. But in Betty's opinion, this alternative was not as convenient for a planned and supervised set of activities compatible with the recommended Montessorian methodology. In short, Betty believed that another classroom was needed that would serve as a gymnasium and also relieve some of the congestion in the art room. The latter was also housing the musical instruments and instruction.

Richard Carroll. At the close of the meeting, Nancy expressed her appreciation to the members of the committee for their contributions, but said that she was disappointed that a decision could not be reached on fall tuitions and the growth question. Don said that the tuition decision must be rendered soon in order to complete the 1979 budget and report to the parents. In Don's opinion the tuition and growth issues were related in some way, but a firm informational base did not presently exist to guide decision making. Nancy agreed with Don, and admitted that she probably could not decide how to vote if motions were made on either issue that evening. She said that the arguments had been appealing, but not entirely persuasive. Clearly, more information was needed before decisions of such crucial importance could be reached. Don moved that a special committee be appointed to study the economic aspects of a tuition increase and the broader growth issue, and make recommendations to the executive committee at the next meeting in February. Don's motion carried and a new member, Richard Carroll, was appointed chairman.

Richard had been serving in the capacity of assistant treasurer since the beginning of the previous fall term. He had recently completed graduate study in business at the University of Tulsa and was employed as a market analyst by a local petroleum firm. For the next several weeks after the meeting, Richard investigated school files and references at the public library. Summary tables from his investigation are presented in Appendix B. After reviewing the data, Richard was uncertain as to what conclusions should be drawn. Richard believed that the committee expectations of the results of his study were high and that considerable weight would be placed upon his personal recommendations. He also recognized that the opportunity costs of any decision taken by the board would be very large and, therefore, he must choose his recommended course carefully.

HISTORICAL INFORMATION

Brief History of the Montessori Method

Early history of the movement. The Montessori method of early childhood education was developed by a remarkable Italian woman physician, who was also a mathematician, anthropologist, lecturer, and writer. Maria Montessori (1870–1952) held the distinction of being the first woman in Italian history to graduate from a school of medicine, receiving double honors in medicine and surgery.[1] After her internship, she was appointed assistant doctor at the psychiatric clinic at the University of Rome, where she specialized in childhood diseases and mental disorders. Many retarded children at that time were committed to asylums with the adult insane and denied educational benefits. Through her experiences and research at the clinic, Dr. Montessori became convinced that childhood mental disorders could often be traced to educational as well as medical problems. Her writings on the subject gained the attention of the state administrators, and in 1898 she was appointed director of the state orthophrenic school for retarded children. While supervising the other teachers at the institution, Dr. Montessori was able to test many of her theories in her classes. It was at the institution that the framework for her unique teaching method was developed.

Results of the method with retarded children were gratifying, and it became obvious to Dr. Montessori that many of the methodological elements could be generalized and applied to the task of educating normal children. An opportunity to extend the new method occurred in 1907. A Roman building association offered Dr. Montessori facilities to organize a child day care center in a slum area of the city for the purpose of reducing a vandalism problem. The opportunity to work with normal children was appealing, and the first "Casa dei Bambini" (Children's House) was opened with 60 students ranging in age from 3 to 6 years old. Results were immediately successful and five additional houses were opened by the end of the following year.

Montessori in the United States. Recognition of the merits of the method spread rapidly throughout Europe and eventually became institutionalized in some countries. The first American "Children's House" was opened in Tarrytown, New York, in 1912 and soon thereafter a number of public schools, as well as private schools, from coast to coast claimed adoption of Montessori ideas and concepts.[2] In 1960 the American Montessori Society was formed. There are currently about 1,800 affiliated Montessori schools in the United States, and new ones are opening at the rate of 75 per year.[3]

The Montessori Method: Learning How to Learn. The basic Montessorian thesis commonly shared is that the child carries within the unseen potentialities of the person that she or he will eventually become. Development of these potentialities begins at a very early age, during which time the child's mental set is particularly absorbent. The period from 2½ to 6 years is believed to be of crucial importance. The method recognizes and employs the normal physiological development of the motor, sensory, and intellect capabilities. Carefully designed didactic materials and an observer/counselor called a directress are included in the method. Children are believed to be the best teachers, however, and emphasis is placed upon self-actualization.

The ultimate objectives of the early childhood phase are to develop self-confidence, discipline, and preparedness to deal with an expanding environment. During this phase, the child in a meaningful sense learns how to learn. The directress assumes a supporting role by providing a comprehensive but controlled environment, enhanced by alternative sets of physical, intellectual, emotional, and social stimuli. But the child is largely free to explore or pursue things of personal interest and learns by observing, comparing, classifying, and reasoning. That is, the child is allowed to encounter freely, in a natural way, environmental phenomena. Learning occurs by discovery and positive reward enjoyed through accomplishment.[4]

History of the Undercroft Montessori School: Fifteen Years "Under the Croft." In February 1963, a group of interested Tulsa mothers formed a study group to discuss the Montessori approach to learning. The study group aroused further interest and led to the formation of the Tulsa Montessori Educational Association. This association sponsored a series of lectures by Miss Lena Wichramaratne of Sri Lanka, a close associate of Dr. Maria Montessori and a teacher-trainer of the Association Montessori Internationale.

The lectures stimulated enough interest among parents to establish Tulsa's first Montessori school. A directress was obtained and space was located in the basement of the Trinity Episcopal Church in downtown Tulsa. In honor of its original location under the croft of the church, the school was named Undercroft Montessori School. In 1966, the school was able to move to its present location at 3745 South Hudson Avenue. Expanded facilities permitted expansion of the staff, curriculum, and enrollment. At present, the staff includes two fully certified Montessori directresses, a specialized arts and crafts teacher, a music teacher, and two assistants. Children are offered a full range of Montessori activities in practical life and sensorial experiences, language, mathematics, science, geography, music, art, crafts, cooking, in-school demonstrations, and field trips.

The Undercroft Montessori School was formed and remains a private, nonsectarian, nonprofit, parent-run corporation working with preschool and kindergarten children between the ages of 2½ and 6 years of age. In 1965, Undercroft affiliated with the American Montessori Society and has continued this affiliation by meeting the high standards of this group.

Undercroft has grown from an opening enrollment of 30 children in September 1964 to an enrollment of approximately 90 children in 1978 (see Exhibit 2). The school now offers the regular half-day program and an all-day program for children 4 years of age and kindergarten age. Classes are currently housed in a 3½ room, single-floor, frame structure which is owned by the school. There is an outstanding mortgage on the land and building of approximately $24,000.

EXHIBIT 2: ***Levels of enrollment at Undercroft Montessori School, 1974–1978***

	September enrollment				
Session	*1978*	*1977*	*1976*	*1975*	*1974*
Morning session	34	36	33	39	49
Afternoon session	30	29	25	31	50
All-day session	26	21	23	16	—
Total enrollment	90	86	82	86	99

REFERENCES

[1] R. C. Orem, "Maria Montessori," *The Encyclopedia of Education* (New York: Macmillan, 1971), pp. 388–393.

[2] Anne E. George, *The Montessori Method: Scientific Pedagogy as Applied to Child Education in the Children's Houses,* 3rd ed. (New York: Stokes, 1912).

[3] R. C. Orem, *Montessori: Her Method and the Movement* (New York: Putnam, 1974), p. 47.

[4] Ibid., pp. 95–124.